# Causal Graphical Models and Their Applications

# Causal Graphical Models and Their Applications

Guest Editors

**Luis Enrique Sucar**
**David Danks**

MDPI

Basel • Beijing • Wuhan • Barcelona • Belgrade • Novi Sad • Cluj • Manchester

*Guest Editors*
Luis Enrique Sucar
Computer Science Department
National Institute of Astrophysics, Optics and Electronics
Puebla
Mexico

David Danks
Department of Philosophy
University of Virginia
Charlottesville, VA
USA

*Editorial Office*
MDPI AG
Grosspeteranlage 5
4052 Basel, Switzerland

This is a reprint of the Special Issue, published open access by the journal *Entropy* (ISSN 1099-4300), freely accessible at: https://www.mdpi.com/journal/entropy/special_issues/BSPSAJX3SL.

For citation purposes, cite each article independently as indicated on the article page online and as indicated below:

Lastname, A.A.; Lastname, B.B. Article Title. *Journal Name* **Year**, *Volume Number*, Page Range.

**ISBN 978-3-7258-7929-8 (Hbk)**
**ISBN 978-3-7258-7930-4 (PDF)**
**https://doi.org/10.3390/books978-3-7258-7930-4**

# Contents

# About the Editors

**Luis Enrique Sucar**

Luis Enrique Sucar holds a Ph.D. in Computing from Imperial College, London (1992); an M.Sc. in Electrical Engineering from Stanford University, USA (1982); and a B.Sc. in Electronics and Communications Engineering from ITESM, Mexico (1980). He has been a researcher at the Electrical Research Institute and a professor at ITESM, Monterrey, and is currently Senior Research Scientist at the National Institute for Astrophysics, Optics and Electronics, Puebla, Mexico. He has been an invited professor at the University of British Columbia, Canada; Imperial College, London; INRIA, France; CREATE-NET, Italy; and the Institute for Astrophysics of Canarias, Spain. He has more than 400 publications and has supervised more than 100 Ph.D. and M.Sc. theses. Dr. Sucar received the National Science Prize from the Mexican President; he is a Member Emeritus of the National Research System, a Life Senior Member of IEEE, and a member of the Mexican Science Academy. He is associate editor of the journals *Pattern Recognition, Computational Intelligence* and *Frontiers in Rehabilitation* and has served as president of the Mexican AI Society and the Mexican Academy of Computing. His main research interests are in probabilistic graphical models, causal reasoning and their applications in robotics, computer vision, astrophysics and biomedicine.

**David Danks**

David Danks earned a Ph.D. in Philosophy from the University of California, San Diego, in 2001 and an A.B. in Philosophy from Princeton University in 1996. He is currently a Polk JSF Distinguished University Professor of Philosophy, AI, and Data Science at the University of Virginia. He was previously a faculty member at the University of California, San Diego and Carnegie Mellon University, as well as a research scientist at the Florida Institute for Human & Machine Cognition. He has more than 125 publications, including multiple research books, and received research funding from a range of sponsors. He has received a James S. McDonnell Foundation Scholar Award, as well as an Andrew Carnegie Fellowship. He has served on multiple advisory boards, including as an inaugural member of the National AI Advisory Committee (USA). His main research interests are in causal modeling, computational cognitive science, and AI ethics and policy.

entropy

ditorial

# ;ausal Graphical Models and Their Applications

uis Enrique Sucar [1,*] and David Danks [2]

[1] Instituto Nacional de Astrofísica, Óptica y Electrónica (INAOE), Santa María Tonantzintla, Puebla 72840, Mexico
[2] Department of Philosophy, School of Data Science, University of Virginia, Charlottesville, VA 22904, USA; danks@virginia.edu
* Correspondence: esucar@inaoep.mx

## 1. Introduction

The study of causality [1] examines the relations and regularities found in a given environment that are stronger than merely probabilistic (or associative) relations [2], in the sense that a causal relation allows for evaluating a change in the consequence given a change in the cause. Causation is crucial not only for predictive accuracy, but also for control, explanation, and intervention [3]. Causality is central to much of the scientific enterprise and even everyday life, and there has been increasing interest in recent decades in causal modeling, inference, and reasoning. This research has historically fallen into two different traditions, causal graphical models [4,5] and potential outcomes [6,7]. The former provides excellent interpretability and characterization of structural properties, while the latter focuses more on parameter estimation and quantitative causal modeling. These two approaches are equally powerful in terms of causal representation and inference [8] and subsume other approaches [9], but highlight different information and methods [10]. This Special Issue focuses on cutting-edge research with causal graphical models.

Causal models provide a deeper understanding of a domain by identifying the direct and indirect causes of certain events, in contrast with associative models, including most neural/deep network approaches. These representations enable us to perform types of reasoning that are not possible, at least in a direct way, with associative models [11]: (i) *interventions*, where we want to find the effects of an external agent or event forcing a variable to a specific value (in contrast with merely observing that variable's value), and (ii) *counterfactuals*, where we want to reason about what would have happened if certain information had been different from what actually happened. Both types of causal reasoning are closely connected with explanations, since an effect can be explained by its causes, regardless of the correlations it may have with other variables.

Causality usually cannot be directly observed, and so a long-standing goal of causality researchers has been causal discovery [12–14]: inferring the underlying causal model (or information about it) from observational data. Perhaps surprisingly, multiple causal discovery methods have been developed and successfully applied in different fields, such as biology, medicine, and economics, among others. Although we usually cannot directly infer causation from one observed correlation, causal discovery methods demonstrate that patterns of associations can be highly informative about causation.

This Special Issue presents recent advances in causal reasoning and causal discovery based on causal graphical models, including novel applications in different domains. It includes contributions from theory to applications in the following aspects:

**Theory:** A higher algebraic K-theory of causality is developed by studying the classifying spaces of observationally equivalent causal models; a *mutation sampler* (a rational process

 https://doi.org/10.3390/10.3390/e28040405

model of human causal reasoning that yields normatively correct inferences when sufficient cognitive resources are available but introduces systematic errors when they are not) is used to predict the existence of conditions in which Markov violations should disappear entirely.
**Causal reasoning:** Identification of causal outcomes is achieved when the available probabilities are more general, such as noisy observations or coarse-grained specification of the variables' values; there are improvements in the identification of causal effects when some of the variables are functionally determined by their parents in the graphical model.
**Causal discovery:** An approach for dealing with insufficient data is developed that combines expert knowledge as a hard constraint and the structural prior gained via data learning as a soft constraint.
**Applications:** A novel technique based on causal models for business process management is devised; a framework that applies causal inference to canonical single-stage principal–agent problems in multi-agent contexts is developed; and a review of causal-based legal language processing is conducted.

Next we provide a brief summary of each article in this Special Issue.

## 2. Overview of Published Articles

Bejos et al. [15] apply causal graphical models to incentive design in a multi-agent context, which are central to economics and multi-agent systems. They introduce Causal Incentive Design (CID), a framework that applies causal inference to canonical single-stage principal–agent problems. Within CID, the operating rules of a principal–agent problem are formalized using an additive-noise causal graphical model. Incentives are modeled as interventions on a function space variable, which correspond to policy interventions in the principle–follower causal relation. This approach establishes a causal decision-making pipeline that enables commitment to a high-performing incentive in a single-shot game, supported by regret guarantees.

Friend et al. [16] investigate identification of causal quantities when the probabilities available for inference are those of the outcomes of more generic schemes than the usual joint probability distribution for the causal model's variables, such as noisy observation procedures, or only coarse-grained specification of the variables' values. Using process theories, they formulate graphical causal models as second-order processes that respond to such data collection instruments. Their main finding is that in the case of Markovian models, as long as the available instruments satisfy marginal informational completeness, the probabilities they produce suffice for identification of interventional quantities, just as those produced by perfect passive observations do.

The mutation sampler is a rational process model of human causal reasoning that yields normatively correct inferences when sufficient cognitive resources are available but introduces systematic errors when they are not. Rehder [17] uses the mutation sampler to predict the existence of conditions in which Markov violations should disappear entirely. Asking subjects to reason about a novel causal structure with nothing but generative causal relations (a cause makes its effect more likely) resulted in Markov violations in the usual positive direction. But simply describing one of four causal relations as inhibitory (the cause makes its effect less likely) resulted in the elimination of those violations. Theoretical model fitting confirmed how this novel result is predicted by the mutation sampler.

Causal discovery involves searching intractably large spaces; however, decomposing the search space into classes of observationally equivalent causal models can make it tractable. Mahadevan [18] studies the topological structure underlying causal equivalence to develop a categorical formulation of a transformational characterization of Bayesian networks. It characterizes Pearl's structural causal models (SCMs) in terms of Cartesian cPROPs, where the morphisms that define the endogenous variables are purely determin-

https://doi.org/10.3390/10.3390/e2804040

istic. A higher algebraic K-theory of causality is developed by studying the classifying spaces of observationally equivalent causal cPROP models, constructing their simplicial realization through the nerve functor. A real-world domain modeling genetic mutations in cancer is used to illustrate the framework.

In the face of insufficient data, the accuracy and efficiency of causal discovery is greatly reduced, resulting in a false perception of causality. To solve this problem, Dang [19] et al. propose the use of expert knowledge as a hard constraint and the structural prior gained via data learning as a soft constraint. They develop a fitness-rate-rank-based multiarmed bandit (FRRMAB) hyper-heuristic that integrates soft and hard constraints into the learning process. For linear structural equation models, soft constraints are obtained via partial correlation analysis. The experimental results on different networks show that the proposed method has higher scalability and accuracy.

Chen and Darwiche [20] study the identification of causal effects, motivated by two improvements to identifiability that can be attained if one knows that some variables in a causal graph are functionally determined by their parents. First, an unidentifiable causal effect may become identifiable when certain variables are functional. Secondly, certain functional variables can be excluded from observation without affecting the identifiability of a causal effect, which may significantly reduce the number of needed variables in observational data. Their treatment of functional dependencies in this context mandates a formal, systematic, and general treatment of positivity assumptions, which are prevalent in the literature on causal effect identifiability and interact with functional dependencies, comprising another contribution of the presented work.

Conventional methods for process monitoring often fail to capture the causal relationships that drive outcomes, making it hard to distinguish causal anomalies from mere correlations in activity flows. Montoya [21] et al. introduce (CaProM), an innovative technique based on causality techniques, applied during the planning phase in business process environments. The technique combines two causal perspectives: anomaly attribution and distribution change attribution. It was validated with a industry dataset from the banking sector, comprising 562 activity flow plans. The study monitored causal structures during the planning and execution stages, allowing the identification of the main factor behind a major deviation from planned values.

Recent advances in legal language processing have highlighted limitations in correlation-based artificial intelligence approaches, prompting exploration of Causal Artificial Intelligence (AI) techniques for improved legal reasoning. Tritto [22] et al. examine the challenges, limitations, and potential impact of Causal AI in legal language processing compared to traditional correlation-based methods. Their findings reveal that while Causal AI frameworks demonstrate superior capability in capturing legal reasoning compared to correlation-based methods, significant challenges remain in handling legal uncertainty, computational scalability, and potential algorithmic bias. The scarcity of comprehensive real-world implementations and overemphasis on transformer architectures without causal reasoning capabilities represent critical gaps in current research. Future development requires balanced integration of AI innovation with law's narrative functions, particularly focusing on scalable architectures for maintaining causal coherence while preserving interpretability in legal analysis.

**Author Contributions:** Writing—original draft preparation, L.E.S.; writing—review and editing, L.E.S. and D.D. All authors have read and agreed to the published version of the manuscript.

**Funding:** This research received no external funding.

**Conflicts of Interest:** The authors declare no conflicts of interest.

https://doi.org/10.3390/10.3390/e28040405

## References


1. Beebee, H.; Hitchcock, C.; Menzies, P. (Eds.) *The Oxford Handbook of Causation*; Oxford University Press: Oxford, UK, 2012.
2. Pearl, J. *Causality*; Cambridge University Press: Cambridge, UK , 2009.
3. Hausman, D.M. *Causal Asymmetries*; Cambridge University Press: Cambridge, UK , 1998.
4. Pearl, J. *Probabilistic Reasoning in Intelligent Systems: Networks of Plausible Inference*; Morgan Kaufmann: San Francisco, CA, USA 1988.
5. Spirtes, P.; Glymour, C.; Scheines, R. *Causation, Prediction, and Search*; MIT Press: Cambridge, MA, USA, 2000.
6. Rubin, D.B. Causal Inference Using Potential Outcomes: Design, Modeling, Decisions. *J. Am. Stat. Assoc.* **2005**, *100*, 322–33 [CrossRef]
7. Rubin, D.B. Direct and indirect causal effects via potential outcomes. *Scand. J. Stat.* **2004**, *31*, 161–170. [CrossRef]
8. Richardson, T.S.; Robins, J.M. Single World Intervention Graphs (SWIGs): A Unification of the Counterfactual and Graphica Approaches to Causality. *Cent. Stat. Soc. Sci. Univ. Wash. Work. Pap.* **2013**, *128*, 2013.
9. Richardson, T.S.; Robins, J.M. Potential outcome and decision theoretic foundations for statistical causality. *J. Causal Inferenc* **2023**, *11*, 20220012. [CrossRef]
10. Imbens, G.W. Potential outcome and directed acyclic graph approaches to causality: Relevance for empirical practice in economic *J. Econ. Lit.* **2020**, *58*, 1129–1179. [CrossRef]
11. Sloman, S.A. *Causal Models: How People Think About the World and Its Alternatives*; Oxford University Press: Oxford, UK, 2009.
12. Sucar, L.E. *Causal Discovery: Foundations, Algorithms and Applications*; Springer Nature: Cham , Switzerland, 2026.
13. Vowels, M.J.; Camgoz, N.C.; Bowden, R. D'ya Like DAGs? A Survey on Structure Learning and Causal Discovery. *ACM Compu Surv.* **2022**, *55*, 1–36. [CrossRef]
14. Glymour, C.; Zhang, K.; Spirtes, P. Review of causal discovery methods based on graphical models. *Front. Genet.* **2019**, *10*, 52 [CrossRef] [PubMed]
15. Bejos, S.; Morales, E.F.; Sucar, L.E.; de Cote, E.M. Single-Stage Causal Incentive Design via Optimal Interventions. *Entropy* **202** *28*, 4. [CrossRef] [PubMed]
16. Friend, I.; Kissinger, A.; Spekkens, R.W.; Wolfe, E. Compositional Causal Identification from Imperfect or Disturbing Observation *Entropy* **2025**, *27*, 732. [CrossRef] [PubMed]
17. Rehder, B. A Magic Act in Causal Reasoning: Making Markov Violations Disappear. *Entropy* **2025**, *27*, 548. [CrossRef] [PubMed
18. Mahadevan, S. Higher Algebraic K-Theory of Causality. *Entropy* **2025**, *27*, 531. [CrossRef] [PubMed]
19. Dang, Y.; Gao, X.; Wang, Z. A Novel Hyper-Heuristic Algorithm with Soft and Hard Constraints for Causal Discovery Using Linear Structural Equation Model. *Entropy* **2025**, *27*, 38. [CrossRef] [PubMed]
20. Chen, Y.; Darwiche, A. Identifying Causal Effects Under Functional Dependencies. *Entropy* **2024**, *26*, 1061. [CrossRef] [PubMed
21. Montoya, F.; Astudillo, H.; Díaz, D.; Berríos, E. Causal Learning: Monitoring Business Processes Based on Causal Structure *Entropy* **2024**, *26*, 867. [CrossRef] [PubMed]
22. Tritto, P.P.; Ponce, H. Causal Artificial Intelligence in Legal Language Processing: A Systematic Review. *Entropy* **2025**, *27*, 35 [CrossRef] [PubMed]


### Short Biography of Authors

**Luis Enrique Sucar** is Senior Research Scientist at the National Institute for Astrophysics, Optic and Electronics, Puebla, Mexico. He received the National Science Prize from the Mexican Presiden is Member Emeritus of the National Research System, and Life Senior Member of IEEE. His mai research interests are in probabilistic graphical models, causal discovery and their applications i robotics, astrophysics and biomedicine. He received a Ph.D. in Computing from Imperial Colleg London, and a M.Sc. in Electrical Engineering from Stanford University.

https://doi.org/10.3390/10.3390/e2804040

**David Danks** is the Polk JSF Distinguished University Professor of Philosophy, AI, & Data Science at the University of Virginia. His research interests include the ethical, psychological, and policy issues around AI, novel causal discovery methods, and computational cognitive models. He was the recipient of a James S. McDonnell Foundation Scholar Award, as well as an Andrew Carnegie Fellowship. He received a Ph.D. in Philosophy from University of California, San Diego, and an A.B. in Philosophy from Princeton University.



https://doi.org/10.3390/10.3390/e28040405

entropy

MDPI

Article

# Single-Stage Causal Incentive Design via Optimal Intervention

**Sebastián Bejos [1,*], Eduardo F. Morales [1], Luis Enrique Sucar [1] and Enrique Munoz de Cote [2]**

[1] Computer Science Department, National Institute of Astrophysics, Optics and Electronics, Puebla 72840, Mexico; emorales@inaoep.mx (E.F.M.); esucar@inaoep.mx (L.E.S.)

[2] Mutable Tactics, London CB2 9PJ, UK; enrique@mutabletactics.ai

* Correspondence: sebastian.bejos@inaoep.mx

**Abstract**

We introduce Causal Incentive Design (CID), a framework that applies causal inference to canonical single-stage principal–agent problems (PAPs) characterized by bilateral private information. Within CID, the operating rules of PAPs are formalized using an additive-noise causal graphical model (CGM). Incentives are modeled as interventions on a function space variable, $\Gamma$, which correspond to policy interventions in the principal–follower causal relation. The causal inference target estimand $V(\Gamma)$ is defined as the expected value of the principal's utility variable under a specified policy intervention in the post-intervention distribution. In the context of additive-Gaussian independent noise, the estimand $V(\Gamma)$ decomposes into a two-layer expectation: (i) an inner Gaussian smoothing of the principal's utility regression; and (ii) an outer averaging over the conditional probability of the follower's action given the incentive policy. A Gauss–Hermite quadrature method is employed to efficiently estimate the first layer, while a policy-local kernel reweighting approach is used for the second. For offline selection of a single incentive policy, a Functional Causal Bayesian Optimization (FCBO) algorithm is introduced. This algorithm models the objective functional $\gamma \mapsto V(\gamma)$ using a functional Gaussian process surrogate defined on a Reproducing Kernel Hilbert Space (RKHS) domain and utilizes an Upper Confidence Bound (UCB) acquisition functional. Consequently, the policy value $V(\gamma)$ becomes an interventional query that can be answered using offline observational data under standard identifiability assumptions. High-probability cumulative-regret bounds are established in terms of differential information gain for the proposed FBO algorithm. Collectively, these elements constitute the central contributions of the CID framework, which integrates causal inference through identification and estimation with policy search in principal–agent problems under private information. This approach establishes a causal decision-making pipeline that enables commitment to a high-performing incentive in a single-shot game, supported by regret guarantees. Provided that the data used for estimation is sufficient, the resulting offline pipeline is appropriate for scenarios where adaptive deployment is impractical or costly. Beyond the methodological contribution, this work introduces a novel application of causal graphical models and causal reasoning to incentive design and principal–agent problems, which are central to economics and multi-agent systems.

**Keywords:** causal inference; applications of causal graphical models; incentive design; principal–agent problems; hierarchical Stackelberg games; Bayesian optimization; Gaussian process; information gain; differential entropy; regret analysis

## 1. Introduction

In an incentive design (ID) problem, a central institution alters the behavior of self-interested agents to improve overall performance by implementing an incentive function that adjusts their individual payoffs. The central institution, typically represented as a principal agent, may aim to drive the system's performance towards a more desirable behavior, such as maximizing revenue or social welfare within the multi-agent system. This work concentrates on the single-stage canonical principal–agent problem (PAP), in which an incentive designer agent (the principal) commits to an incentive function that influences the behavior of a single follower. The interaction is a one-shot hierarchical inverse Stackelberg game, in which the principal first announces an incentive function; the follower then responds optimally based on that commitment, and the outcomes are realized without any subsequent adaptation or additional rounds. We maintain the assumption of private information for both players; specifically, the principal is unaware of the follower's utility function and vice versa.

The single-stage PAP is the canonical problem in incentive design (ID) because it includes the core structural features in a one-shot setting: the principal commits once to an incentive, the follower best-responds, and outcomes are realized; information asymmetry and incomplete knowledge persist; and strategic reasoning is driven by ex ante beliefs about utilities or types. While there is no intertemporal adaptation or belief updating between rounds, the principal–agent (leader–follower) tension remains fundamental: one party creates incentives in the face of uncertainty, while the other optimizes behavior in response to that commitment. These features remain structurally invariant when extending the single-period formulation to multiple followers and multiple principals. With private information on both sides, the design task still entails bilateral inference at design time—reasoning about the other party's unknown objectives—which is the core difficulty that scales to richer multi-agent settings. Thus, the single-stage formulation preserves the irreducible skeleton of ID problems and the central epistemic and incentive-alignment challenges that govern their multi-agent variants [1].

Consider a lender as the principal and a borrower as the follower. The lender must choose, once, a contract rule—an incentive function that maps borrower attributes or application information to loan terms (e.g., interest rate, credit limit, collateral, or a repayment rebate). The borrower then decides whether to accept the contract and, if funded, how much effort to exert toward repayment. Both sides hold private information (e.g., the borrower's risk and effort costs, and the lender's risk appetite and cost structure). The outcome—acceptance, repayment, or default, and the lender's realized payoff—occurs once; there is no opportunity to update terms after observing behavior. This one-shot contract choice is exactly a single-stage PAP: the lender designs the incentive rule under uncertainty; the borrower best-responds; the realized payoff reflects both the selection induced by the rule and the behavioral response it elicits.

We treat the principal's single-stage choice as the endpoint of a finite-horizon sequential optimization carried out before deployment. The principal starts from historical observations of the system—past incentive rules, the follower's responses, and realized payoffs—and uses them to estimate the principal's expected utility under any candidate incentive function. A data-efficient search procedure (Bayesian optimization over a space of incentive functions) iteratively proposes candidate incentives, updates beliefs about expected utility using the accumulated evidence, and records the most promising options. After a fixed number of iterations, the principal selects one incentive function—the estimated best—to implement in the single-stage game. This procedure makes no restrictive assumptions about the players' utility forms and respects the private-information

https://doi.org/10.3390/e28010004

setting; it is simply a principled way to use prior observations to select a high-value one-shot incentive.

### 1.1. Approach and Contributions

Even in the single-stage canonical principal–agent problem (PAP), it is difficult to predict how a committed incentive will affect the follower's behavior under bilateral private information. We address this challenge by integrating causal inference with incentive design: we represent the single-stage PAP as a causal graphical model (CGM) in which the incentive function is treated as an intervention on the function space variable $\Gamma$, and we target the principal's utility variable $J_L$ under that policy, $V(\gamma) \equiv \mathbb{E}[J_L \mid \mathrm{do}(\Gamma = \gamma)]$. This causal target is identified via the $g$-formula, enabling estimation of policy values from observational data without requiring controlled experiments. We then cast policy selection as a black-box sequential offline optimization over a function space of incentives, using Bayesian optimization to efficiently search among costly evaluations of $V(\gamma)$ before committing to a single policy in the one-shot game.

In the proposed framework, the leader's policy $\Gamma$ acts as a functional intervention, the follower's action is an explicit mediator, and the leader's payoff $J_L$ is the outcome node. The policy value $V(\gamma) = \mathbb{E}[J_L \mid do(\Gamma = \gamma)]$ constitutes an interventional and counterfactual query on this causal graphical model, which can be identified and estimated from observational data (offline logs) under the assumptions of positivity and additive noise. Accordingly, this work advances causal reasoning with graphical models and introduces a novel application domain in incentive design and principal–agent models, thereby complementing established applications in biology, medicine, and economics.

We formalize the single-stage canonical PAP (one principal and one follower) as an additive-noise CGM with endogenous variables $\{\Gamma, \Omega_L, \Omega_F, J_F, J_L\}$ that capture the inverse-Stackelberg semantics $\Omega_L = \gamma(\Omega_F) + U_L$, where incentives are interventions $\mathrm{do}(\Gamma = \gamma)$. From this model, we derive a non-parametric identification of $V(\gamma)$ by marginalizing over $\Omega_L$ and $\Omega_F$. In the additive-Gaussian setting, the estimand becomes a nested expectation with two interpretable components: an inner expectation (a Gaussian smoothing of the outcome regression $\mu_L(\Omega_L, \Omega_F, \Gamma)$) and an outer expectation over the mediator law $p(\Omega_F \mid \Gamma = \gamma)$ induced by the incentive. Practically, we compute the inner term by Gauss–Hermite quadrature and approximate the outer term by policy-local kernel reweighting in policy space; a linear credit-market example (affine pricing rule) illustrates a closed-form specialization.

We optimize $\gamma \mapsto V(\gamma)$ over an admissible set $\Gamma$ modeled as a Reproducing Kernel Hilbert Space (RKHS) $\mathcal{H}_k$. A functional Gaussian process (GP) surrogate on $\mathcal{H}_k$—with a functional RBF kernel driven by RKHS distances between incentive functions—provides posterior mean and uncertainty over policy values. A functional GP-UCB acquisition functional trades off exploration and exploitation to propose the next incentive to evaluate, building a data set $\{(\gamma^t, \widehat{V}(\gamma^t))\}_{t=1}^{T}$ from which we select the best $\gamma^+$ to deploy in the single-stage game. We provide high-probability cumulative-regret bounds for this Stackelberg Functional Causal Bayesian Optimization (FCBO) procedure in terms of *differential information gain*, with guarantees for both finite policy sets and infinite (non-parametric) RKHS domains.

Our pipeline builds on established ingredients: causal identification via the g-formula and policy interventions [2,3], RKHS/GP surrogates for Bayesian optimization [4–6], and GP-UCB-style exploration with information-gain regret analysis [7,8]. We have four new key contributions: (i) a PAP-specific CGM that treats incentives as functional interventions and makes the follower action an explicit mediator of policy value; (ii) a two-layer identification and estimation recipe for single-stage PAPs, using Gaussian inner smoothing

https://doi.org/10.3390/e2801000

with policy-local outer reweighting; (iii) a functional GP surrogate on an RKHS of incentive rules with a policy-space RBF and support-aware acquisition; and (iv) regret bounds stated in terms of differential information gain for the Stackelberg functional setting with a uniform sub-Gaussian envelope for estimator noise. Figure 1 sketches the full CID pipeline (identification and estimation of $V(\gamma)$ and FCBO policy search) and Figure 2 depicts one FCBO iteration; shaded boxes on Figures 1 and 2 mark components introduced in this paper. Our contributions can be summarized as follows:

- **CID for single-stage PAPs.** We establish a generic CGM for the single-stage canonical PAP in which incentives are formalized as functional interventions, yielding a principled causal estimand for policy value $V(\gamma) = \mathbb{E}[J_L \mid \mathrm{do}(\Gamma = \gamma)]$ identified from observational data via the $g$-formula.
- **Semi-parametric estimation strategy.** We develop a practical, modular estimator for $V(\gamma)$ under additive Gaussian noise: (a) learn the principal's action mechanism and outcome regression; (b) compute the inner Gaussian expectation by Gauss–Hermite quadrature; and (c) approximate the induced mediator law with policy-local kernel weights. A linear credit-market pricing example provides a closed form that clarifies the roles of policy parameters and the induced borrowing response.
- **Functional Bayesian optimization for incentives.** We propose the *Stackelberg FCBO* algorithm: a functional GP surrogate on $\mathcal{H}_k$ with a functional GP-UCB acquisition functional to sequentially (offline) optimize over incentive functions when policy evaluations are expensive and noisy.
- **Theoretical guarantees.** We prove high-probability cumulative-regret bounds that scale with $\sqrt{T\,\beta_T\,\mathcal{I}_T}$, where $\mathcal{I}_T$ is the information gain and $\beta_T$ is the exploration schedule. We extend the analysis from finite admissible sets to infinite RKHS domains via covering arguments and uniform approximation—quantifying the data-efficiency and reliability of the offline design that precedes the one-shot deployment.

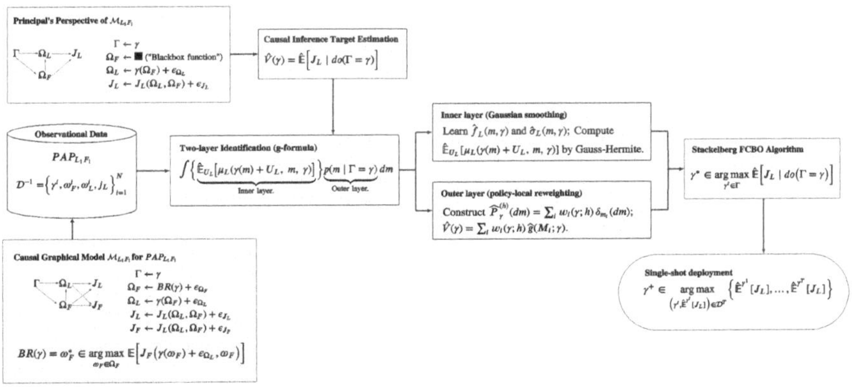


**Figure 1.** Overview of the CID pipeline. Identification yields a two-layer estimand; the estimator feeds a functional GP surrogate and a support-aware GP-UCB search to select a single policy offline. Shaded boxes indicate contributions introduced in this paper.

https://doi.org/10.3390/e28010004

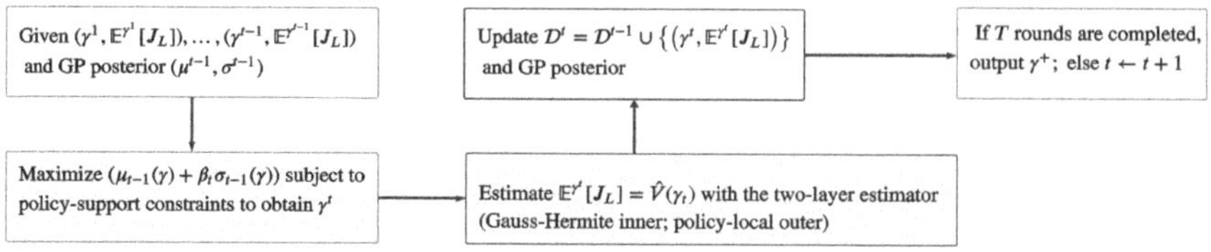


**Figure 2.** One iteration of Stackelberg FCBO algorithm. Novel elements are highlighted with shaded boxes: support-aware GP-UCB selection and the nested estimator used for off-policy evaluation.

### 1.2. Related Work

Incentive design (ID) has long been studied in economics and control through the lens of principal–agent theory [9,10]. Within this tradition, the single-stage (one-shot) PAP is a canonical formulation of contracting under asymmetric information: the principal commits to a contract, the agent best-responds, and outcomes are realized once. Classical approaches model uncertainty with priors over types and often assume a known mapping from actions to outcomes, yielding foundational results in adverse selection and moral hazard [1,9]. Control-theoretic treatments similarly emphasize leader–follower structure but typically rely on parametric models of dynamics and payoffs (e.g., early closed-loop Stackelberg formulations and multi-level control [10], and modern bilevel optimization theory and hardness results [11]).

More recently, the machine learning literature has approached ID through online learning paradigms—such as multi-armed bandits, reinforcement learning, and Bayesian optimization [5,12]—where the principal adapts incentives across rounds while observing partial feedback. This work has produced algorithms for repeated principal–agent settings, combinatorial bandits for dynamic preferences [13,14], meta-gradient methods for adaptive mechanism design [12,15], and BO-based procedures that steer multi-agent systems toward desirable equilibria [16]. While powerful, these approaches are inherently multi-stage and often treat the environment as a black box, emphasizing empirical adaptation rather than explicit reasoning about how a committed incentive causes behavioral change in a one-shot deployment. Beyond incentive design, robustness studies in multilayer transportation networks similarly demonstrate that inter-layer coupling critically governs aggregate performance—see the bilayer railway–aviation analysis with discrete cross-layer assignment [17].

A parallel line of research integrates causal reasoning into sequential decision-making [18–21]. Causal bandits, counterfactual policy evaluation, and causal reinforcement learning utilize graphical models to structure exploration and target the effects of interventions [22,23]. In Causal Bayesian Optimization (CBO) [24], the optimization routine exploits known causal structure among inputs to identify high-value interventions more efficiently. These methods, however, typically consider atomic (variable-level) interventions and multi-round interactions. In contrast, our focus is on a one-shot commitment problem: the principal must select a single incentive function before deployment and cannot adapt it afterward.

Our work connects these strands by introducing a causal, offline design pipeline tailored to the single-stage PAP. We represent the principal–agent interaction with a causal graphical model (CGM) and interpret incentives as functional (conditional) interventions and policies as interventions on the node that embodies the principal's rule. This yields a policy value target for the principal (the expected utility under the post-intervention distribution) that can be identified from observational data via the g-formula and estimated without requiring online experimentation. To efficiently search over a space of incentive functions before deployment, we adopt a Functional Bayesian Optimization pro-

https://doi.org/10.3390/e280100(

cedure [6,25]: a functional Gaussian process surrogate on an RKHS of admissible incentives, coupled with a UCB-type acquisition functional, guides a small number of costly offline evaluations of policy value. Taken together, the proposed approach complements classical single-stage contract theory by supplying a causal identification–estimation pathway for policy value under private information. Finally, our analysis provides high-probability regret guarantees in terms of differential information gain, quantifying how efficiently the offline procedure learns the principal's objective over the function space.

Our emphasis is on the *theoretical underpinnings* of single-stage causal incentive design, specifically, (i) identification of policy value under functional interventions; (ii) a two-layer estimation approach with policy-local support diagnostics; and (iii) support-aware Functional Bayesian Optimization with regret control under a uniform sub-Gaussian envelope. To maintain focus and adhere to space constraints, we reserve numerical simulations and applied case studies for subsequent work that will use the present framework as a baseline to explore design choices, including policy classes, kernel metrics, and bandwidth selection across various domains.

### 1.3. Outline

The rest of the paper is organized as follows. The preliminary background, Section 2, first reviews the bilevel viewpoint of hierarchical Stackelberg games and inverse Stackelberg formulations. We then formalize the single-stage principal–agent problem (SS-PAP) and specify the information model with bilateral private information. The background closes with the essentials of causal graphical models (CGMs) and the notions of hard and functional (policy) interventions used later for identification and estimation. We introduce our Causal Incentive Design (CID) framework for canonical SS-PAPs in Section 3. We present an additive-noise Gaussian CGM for the canonical single-stage PAP and its assumptions, define the principal's policy value target estimand $V(\gamma) = \mathbb{E}[J_L \mid \mathrm{do}(\Gamma = \gamma)]$, and provide a semi-parametric identification formula for $V(\gamma)$ via the g-formula. We then describe a practical offline estimation pipeline for the identification formula in general and provide an illustrative credit-market example with an affine pricing rule that demonstrates a closed-form specialization of the estimand. Section 4 details the *Stackelberg FCBO* procedure for offline policy selection. We model the objective $\gamma \mapsto V(\gamma)$ with a functional Gaussian-process surrogate over an RKHS of admissible incentives and employ a functional GP-UCB acquisition functional. We then present the Stackelberg FCBO algorithm and provide high-probability cumulative-regret bounds in terms of differential information gain. Section 5 reflects on the implications of CID for single-shot incentive design and outlines directions for empirical validation and broader multi-agent extensions.

## 2. Preliminary Background

The background is organized into three components: (i) the Stackelberg and inverse Stackelberg perspectives for incentive design (Section 2.1); (ii) the single-stage principal–agent problem (PAP) setting and the information model for the single-stage PAP with bilateral private information (Section 2.2); and (iii) the fundamentals of causal graphical models (CGMs), hard interventions, and functional (policy) interventions, which serve as the foundation for interpreting incentives as policies (Section 2.3).

### 2.1. Incentive Design as Inverse Stackelberg Games

Games characterized by a hierarchical decision-making structure, where one or more players, called the leaders, declare their strategy first and impose this strategy upon the other players, called the followers, are referred to as Stackelberg games. If leaders declare their strategy as a mapping from the followers' decision space into their own decision space,

https://doi.org/10.3390/e28010004

we refer to this as inverse Stackelberg games. The essence of a Stackelberg game can be described considering the basic single-leader single-follower single-stage game as follows. Let us denote by $\omega_L \in \mathbf{\Omega}_L \subseteq \mathbb{R}^{n_L}$ and $\omega_F \in \mathbf{\Omega}_F \subseteq \mathbb{R}^{n_F}$ the leader and follower decision variables, respectively. The leader chooses an action or decision from its decision space $\mathbf{\Omega}_L$, and the follower, informed of the leader's choice, subsequently chooses an action from its decision space $\mathbf{\Omega}_F$. Each player aims to maximize its utility functions $J_L$: $\mathbf{\Omega}_L \times \mathbf{\Omega}_F \to \mathbb{R}$ and $J_F$: $\mathbf{\Omega}_L \times \mathbf{\Omega}_F \to \mathbb{R}$, both functions of the decision spaces $\mathbf{\Omega}_L$ and $\mathbf{\Omega}_F$.

Since the leader acts first and announces his decision $\omega_L$, which is subsequently made known to the follower, the follower's action becomes a function of the leader's action $\omega_F = r_F(\omega_L)$. The function $r_F$: $\mathbf{\Omega}_L \to \mathbf{\Omega}_F$ is called the reaction function of the follower (as it indicates how the follower will react to the leader's decision). Knowing $\omega_L$, the follower chooses $\omega_F^*$, with

$$\omega_F^* \in \arg\max_{\omega_F \in \Omega_F} J_F(\omega_L, \omega_F) = J_F(\omega_L, r_F(\omega_L)).$$

Taking into account the aforementioned, before the leader announces his decision $\omega_L$, he will realize how the follower will react and hence based on this knowledge, the leader will choose and subsequently announce the leader's optimal decision $\omega_L^* \in \mathbf{\Omega}_L$, with

$$\omega_L^* \in \arg\max_{\omega_L \in \mathbf{\Omega}_L} J_L(\omega_L, r_F(\omega_L)).$$

In contrast to the original Stackelberg game discussed above, in the inverse Stackelberg game, the leader acts first by deciding and announcing an incentive function $\gamma$ to the follower, instead of $\omega_L$. This incentive function is a mapping of the follower's decision space to the leader's decision space, i.e., $\gamma$: $\mathbf{\Omega}_F \to \mathbf{\Omega}_L$, so the leader's decision now follows directly from the follower's decision. Note that the Stackelberg game is a special case of the inverse Stackelberg game where the incentive function maps to a constant, that is, the case in which $\gamma$: $\mathbf{\Omega}_F \to \{\omega_L\}$. In addition, the incentive function approach allows the leader to first determine a particular desired point $(\omega_L^d, \omega_F^d)$ that he intends to achieve. A natural choice for this $(\omega_L^d, \omega_F^d)$ would be a global optimum of the leader $(\omega_L^*, \omega_F^*) \in \arg\max_{\omega_L \in \mathbf{\Omega}_L, \omega_F \in \mathbf{\Omega}_F} J_L(\omega_L, \omega_F)$. Given the desired point, the problem can be formulated as follows:

$$\begin{aligned} \text{Find:} \quad & \gamma \in \Gamma, && (1) \\ \text{s.t.} \quad & (\omega_L^d, \omega_F^d) \in \arg\max_{\omega_F \in \mathbf{\Omega}_F} J_F(\gamma(\omega_F), \omega_F), && (2) \end{aligned}$$

where $\Gamma = \{\gamma\colon \mathbf{\Omega}_F \to \mathbf{\Omega}_L\}$ is the admissible set of incentive functions $\gamma$ from which the leader can choose. Even this static inverse Stackelberg problem with a single leader and a single follower is hard to solve analytically because of the function composition, the fact that there could be more than one best answer and the fact that the follower response might not be unique. We can say for sure that this inverse Stackelberg game is at least strongly NP-hard, as it can be posted as the following program:

$$\begin{aligned} (\omega_L^d, \omega_F^d) \in & \arg\max_{\omega_L \in \mathbf{\Omega}_L, \omega_F \in \mathbf{\Omega}_F} J_L(\gamma(\omega_F), \omega_F), && (3) \\ \text{s.t.} \quad \omega_F^d \in & \arg\max_{\omega_F \in \mathbf{\Omega}_F} J_F(\gamma(\omega_F), \omega_F). && (4) \end{aligned}$$

https://doi.org/10.3390/e28010004

Taking $\omega_L$ as a free variable for $\gamma(\omega_F)$, this is equivalent to a bilevel optimization problem formulation shown in Equation (5) next, which is proven to be strongly NP-hard even when the objective functions are linear [11].

$$\begin{aligned}\max_{\mathbf{x}_U \in \mathbf{X}_U, \mathbf{x}_L \in \mathbf{X}_L} \quad & F(\mathbf{x}_U, \mathbf{x}_L), \\ \text{s.t. } & \mathbf{x_L} \in \arg\max\Big\{ f(\mathbf{x}_U, \mathbf{x}_L) \mid g_i(\mathbf{x}_U, \mathbf{x}_L) \leq 0, i \in \mathbf{I} \Big\}, \\ & G_j(\mathbf{x}_U, \mathbf{x}_L) \leq 0, j \in \mathbf{J},\end{aligned} \tag{5}$$

where $\mathbf{X}_U$, $\mathbf{X}_L$ denote the decision space of the upper and lower levels, respectively, $F$: $\mathbf{X}_U \times \mathbf{X}_L \to \mathbb{R}$ is the upper-level objective function, $f$: $\mathbf{X}_U \times \mathbf{X}_L \to \mathbb{R}$ is the lower-level objective function, and the functions $g_i$: $\mathbf{X}_U \times \mathbf{X_L} \to \mathbb{R}$, $G_i$: $\mathbf{X}_U \times \mathbf{X}_L \to \mathbb{R}$ represents the lower-level and upper-level constraints respectively, for $i \in \mathbf{I} \subseteq \mathbb{N}$, $j \in \mathbf{J} \subseteq \mathbb{N}$. This nested two-level optimization task structure requires that only optimal solutions of the lower-level task are acceptable as feasible solutions of the upper-level task.

### 2.2. The Single-Stage Principal–Agent Problem

In practice, the leader and follower agents base their decisions on a set of information that is readily accessible to them. Incentive design (ID), also known as contract theory, investigates inverse Stackelberg games under a variety of information models available to the leader and the follower agent and the information asymmetries between them. In this domain, the inverse Stackelberg game is called the principal–agent problem, with the leader as the principal and the follower as the agent. The way this information set is conceived and theoretically described is a major factor in how the fields of economics, control theory, and machine learning approach the principal–agent problem.

In this research, we focus on the single-stage principal–agent problem (SS-PAP), which is a hierarchical inverse Stackelberg game with a specific information model played between a single principal (leader) and a single follower. This single-stage game problem is as follows: First, the principal decides or selects an incentive function $\gamma$ from a predetermined set of functions $\Gamma = \{\gamma\colon \mathbf{\Omega}_F \to \mathbf{\Omega}_L\}$, and announces $\gamma$ to the follower, without knowledge of the follower's utility. Then, with knowledge of this incentive function $\gamma$, the follower agent selects an action $\omega_F{}^* \in \mathbf{\Omega}_F$ that maximizes his utility $J_F(\gamma(\omega_F), \omega_F)$. We do not impose restrictive assumptions on the functional form of utilities. Regarding the information model, we assume that both the principal and the follower agent possess private information, i.e., the utility function of the follower is unknown to the principal and vice versa. The outcome or result in this single-stage principal–agent problem are the utilities $J_F(\omega_F^*), \omega_F^*)$ and $J_L(\omega_F^*), \omega_F^*)$ after the principal decides the incentive function $\gamma$. Our focus is on the principal's perspective of the problem, where the principal wants to select the incentive function $\gamma$ that maximizes its utility $J_L$.

We assume that the principal solves this problem as a sequential optimization problem with finite horizon $T$, using previously observed historical data, given as $N$ observations $\mathcal{D}^{-1} = \{(\gamma^i, \omega_F^i, \omega_L^i, J_L^i)\}_{i=1}^N$ of the system. That is, using $\mathcal{D}^{-1} = \{(\gamma^i, \omega_F^i, \omega_L^i, J_L^i)\}_{i=1}^N$, to estimate $\mathbb{E}[J_L^t]$ given that an incentive function $\gamma^t \in \Gamma$ is applied, for rounds $T$, the principal decides on the best $\gamma^* \in \Gamma$ to implement in the SS-PAP. In other words, the principal (as the decision-maker), at each stage $t \in [T]$, is responsible for the development of a policy $\pi^t$: $\mathcal{D}^{t-1} \to \gamma^t$, where $\mathcal{D}^{t-1} = \{(\gamma^1, \mathbb{E}[J_L^1]), \ldots, (\gamma^{t-1}, \mathbb{E}[J_L^{t-1}])\}$; and when the accumulated history data set $\mathcal{D}^T$ is complete, the principal decides the incentive function $\gamma^+$ such that

$$\gamma^+ \in \operatorname*{arg\,max}_{(\gamma^t, \mathbb{E}[J_L^t]) \in \mathcal{D}^T} \Big\{ \mathbb{E}[J_L^1], \ldots, \mathbb{E}[J_L^T] \Big\}. \tag{6}$$

https://doi.org/10.3390/e28010004

Therefore, we deal with a sequential optimization problem, and we take a Bayesian approach to the optimization of the functional objective of the principal. Appendix C provides details about Bayesian optimization (BO), which specializes in sequentially optimizing objectives with the above-mentioned characteristics, relying on a statistical model of the objective function whose beliefs guide the algorithm in making the most fruitful decisions.

### 2.3. Causal Graphical Models and Causal Inference

This research proposes solving the single-stage principal agent problem (SS-PAP) as defined in the previous subsection by incorporating causal reasoning. In this section, we provide the essential concepts of causal inference required to understand the Causal Incentive Design (CID) framework proposed in Section 3 to solve SS-PAP.

A causal graphical model (CGM) consists of a directed acyclic graph (DAG) $\mathcal{G}$, which is called the causal structure, together with a four-tuple $\langle \boldsymbol{U}, \boldsymbol{V}, \boldsymbol{F}, p(\boldsymbol{U})\rangle$ where

- $\boldsymbol{U}$ is a set $\{U_i\}_{i\in[p]}$ of exogenous (unobserved) variables, which are determined by factors external to the model;
- $\boldsymbol{V}$ is a set $\{V_i\}_{i\in[p]}$, with $p \in \mathbb{N}$, of endogenous (observed) variables.
- $\boldsymbol{F} = \{f_{V_1}, \ldots, f_{V_p}\}$ is a set of functions known as structural equations, such that $V_i = f_{V_i}(\boldsymbol{pa}(v_i), u_i)$, for each $V_i \in \boldsymbol{V}$, with $\boldsymbol{pa}(V_i) \subset \boldsymbol{V}$ denoting the parents of $V_i$;
- $p(\boldsymbol{U})$ is a set of probability distributions $\{p(U_i)\}_{i\in[p]}$ for each $U_i$, where $U_i$ is a random disturbance distributed according to $p(U_i)$, independently of all other $U_j$ with $i \neq j$.

The set of vertices in the causal structure $\mathcal{G}$ corresponds to a set of random variables $\boldsymbol{V} = \{V_1, \ldots, V_p\}$ and each edge of the set of edges $\boldsymbol{E}$ represents a direct functional relationship between the corresponding variables, expressed by saying that $V_i$ is the direct cause of $V_j$ for an edge $(V_i, V_j) \in \boldsymbol{E}$. So, the graph $\mathcal{G}$ encodes the causal relationship between the variables in $\boldsymbol{V}$. We assume that the system $\boldsymbol{V}$ is causally sufficient, and therefore there are no variables in $\boldsymbol{V}$ that are common direct causes of at least two observed variables that are unmeasured. Let $\mathcal{G}$ be the causal structure of a CGM, i.e., a directed acyclic graph (DAG) with variables $\boldsymbol{V}$. The statistical model associated to $\mathcal{G}$ consists of all distributions that factorize as

$$p(\boldsymbol{V}) = \prod_{V\in\boldsymbol{V}} p(V \mid \boldsymbol{pa}_{\mathcal{G}}(V)), \tag{7}$$

where $\boldsymbol{pa}_{\mathcal{G}}(V)$ denotes the parents of $V$ in $\mathcal{G}$.

The notation $do(X = x)$ indicates an idealized experiment or intervention in which the values of $X$ are set to $x$, for some $X \in \boldsymbol{X} \subseteq \boldsymbol{V}$. Hard interventions is the term used to describe this category of interventions. A fundamental problem in Causal Inference is to identify $p(y|do(X = x))$ from observational data. In practice, experimental data are not always accessible due to the fact that randomized controlled experiments might be impractical, costly, or even unethical. Within the causal system $\boldsymbol{V}$, we distinguish three different types of variables: no manipulative variables $\boldsymbol{C}$, treatment variables $\boldsymbol{X}$ that can be set to specific values, i.e., intervene them, and a target variable $Y$ that represents the outcome of interest. For a fully observed causal system $\boldsymbol{V}$ with a causal structure DAG $\mathcal{G}$, the post-intervention distribution can be identified through the *g-formula*, also known as the truncated formula. We follow the standard g-formula identification [26]:

$$p(\boldsymbol{V} \setminus X \mid do(X = x)) = \prod_{V\in\boldsymbol{V}\setminus X} p(V \mid \boldsymbol{pa}(V))\Big|_{X=x}. \tag{8}$$

So, a CGM induces joint observational and interventional probability distributions given in Equations (7) and (18). Pearl (see [26]) formalized the concept of causal effect of $X$ on $Y$ after manipulating $X$, that is, doing $X = x$ for some $x \in \mathcal{R}(X)$, where $\mathcal{R}(\cdot)$ denotes

https://doi.org/10.3390/e280100(

the range of a random variable, as the expected value of the distribution $p(Y|do(X=x))$, i.e., the distribution of $Y$ after operation $do(X=x)$, denoted as $\mathbb{E}_{p(Y|do(X=x))}[Y]$ or $\mathbb{E}[Y \mid do(X=x)]$. Like any ordinary probability distribution, $p(\cdot \mid do(X=x))$ obeys the same rules of conditioning and marginalization. So, we can specify expectations in the conventional manner, as shown in Equation (9).

$$\mathbb{E}[Y \mid do(X=x)] = \int_{\mathcal{R}(Y)} y\, p(y \mid do(X=x))dy \tag{9}$$

The traditional hard interventions discussed above are unconditional actions that simply force a variable $X$ to adopt a designated value $x$. Functional interventions refer to a broader category of interventions in which a variable $X$ is manipulated to respond in a predetermined manner to a set of other observable variables $\mathbf{Z} \subseteq \boldsymbol{Pa}(X)$ in the causal system through a functional relationship $X = g(\mathbf{z})$. Specifically, a functional intervention can be considered as a substitution of the structural equation $f_X \in \boldsymbol{F}$, of the intervened variable $X$, with a deterministic function of some parents in the CGM. In other words, by a functional intervention, we substitute the structural equation $X = f_X(\mathbf{pa(x)}, \mathbf{u_x})$ with a function $X = g(\mathbf{z})$ for some $\mathbf{Z} \subseteq \boldsymbol{Pa}(X)$ in the causal model. It is important to note that hard interventions are the specific instance of functional interventions in which the structural equation $f_X$ is substituted by a constant function $g$.

Pearl first explored functional interventions under the name of conditional actions in [2]. More recently, Correa and Bareinboim in [3] introduced a new set of inference rules that extends the do-calculus for hard interventions in [2] to derive claims about functional interventions. Following these, let $p(y \mid do(X = g(\mathbf{z})))$ stand for the post-intervention distribution of $Y$ established under the policy $X = g(\mathbf{z})$. To compute the post-intervention distribution $p(y \mid do(X = g(\mathbf{z})))$ for the functional intervention $do(X = g(\mathbf{z}))$, we condition on $\mathbf{Z}$ and write

$$\begin{aligned}
&p(y \mid do(X = g(\mathbf{z}))) \\
&= \int_{\mathcal{R}(\mathbf{Z})} p(y \mid do(X = g(\mathbf{z})), \mathbf{z}) p(\mathbf{z} \mid do(X = g(\mathbf{z}))) \\
&= \int_{\mathcal{R}(\mathbf{Z})} p(y \mid do(X = g(\mathbf{z})), \mathbf{z}) p(\mathbf{z}) \\
&= \mathbb{E}[p(y \mid do(X = g(\mathbf{z})), \mathbf{z})] \text{ with } x = g(\mathbf{z}),
\end{aligned} \tag{10}$$

where the equality $p(\mathbf{z} \mid do(X = g(\mathbf{z}))) = p(\mathbf{z})$ comes from the fact that $\mathbf{Z}$ cannot be a descendant of $X$, and therefore any intervention in $X$ has no effect on the distribution of $\mathbf{Z}$. Thus, the causal effect of a functional intervention $X = g(\mathbf{Z})$ can be computed from the expression $p(y \mid do(X = x), \mathbf{z})$ by substituting $x$ for $g(\mathbf{z})$ and taking the expectation over $\mathbf{Z}$.

## 3. Causal Incentive Design for Single-Stage Canonical PAPs

In this section, we develop the proposed Causal Incentive Design (CID) framework by showing how causal inference can be incorporated into the principal–agent problem described in Section 2.2 to solve it. First in Section 3.1, we propose the general additive-noise Gaussian CGM $\mathcal{M}_{L_1F_1}$ that represents the dynamics of the single-stage canonical principal–agent problem $PAP_{L_1F_1}$ and describe its key semantic aspects and underlying assumptions. This $PAP_{L_1F_1}$ is the canonical version in which the principal–agent problem is analyzed with a single principal controlling a unique decision variable $\omega_L \in \boldsymbol{\Omega}_L$ and a single follower agent with a unique decision variable $\omega_F \in \boldsymbol{\Omega}_F$. The core concepts of CID can be elucidated through the examination of the canonical principal–agent problem $PAP_{L1F1}$ and the CGM $\mathcal{M}_{L_1F_1}$ that represents it.

https://doi.org/10.3390/e28010004

The CID for the single-stage PAP is developed in three parts: (i) specification of the additive-noise CGM for the single-stage PAP and definition of the policy-value target $V(\gamma) = \mathbb{E}[J_L \mid do(\Gamma = \gamma)]$ (Section 3.1); (ii) derivation of a semi-parametric identification for $V(\gamma)$ via the g-formula, demonstrating its decomposition into an inner Gaussian smoothing and an outer expectation over the follower's action (Section 3.2); and (iii) presentation of a two-layer estimator (Section 3.3), which first computes the inner Gaussian expectation (Section 3.3.3), and then approximates the outer expectation using policy-local kernel reweighting with accompanying diagnostics (Section 3.3.4).

### 3.1. A Causal Graphical Model for the Single-Stage Canonical Principal–Agent Problem

We consider the single-stage canonical principal–agent problem $PAP_{L_1F_1}$ as a causal system with endogenous observable random variables $\mathbf{V} = \{\Gamma, \Omega_L, \Omega_F, J_F, J_L\}$, where $\Gamma$ is the admissible set of incentive functions with range $\mathcal{R}_\Gamma = \Gamma$. The variables $\Omega_L, \Omega_F$ represent the decision variables of the principal and the follower, respectively, with ranges $\mathcal{R}_{\Omega_L} = \mathbf{\Omega}_L$ and $\mathcal{R}_{\Omega_F} = \mathbf{\Omega}_F$, where $\mathbf{\Omega}_L, \mathbf{\Omega}_F$ are the decision spaces of the principal and the follower, respectively. The variables $J_F, J_L$ represent the values of the utility functions of the follower and the principal, respectively.

**Definition 1.** *The CGM $\mathcal{M}_{L_1F_1}$ for $PAP_{L_1F_1}$ has endogenous variables set $\mathbf{V}$, exogenous variables set $\boldsymbol{U}$, and structural equations set $\mathbf{F}$ given as follows:*

$$\mathbf{V} = \{\Gamma, \Omega_L, \Omega_F, J_F, J_L\}, \quad \boldsymbol{U} = \{U_{\Omega_L}, U_{\Omega_F}, U_{J_F}, U_{J_L}\}, \quad \mathbf{F} = \{f_\Gamma, f_{\Omega_L}, f_{\Omega_F}, f_{J_F}, f_{J_L}\}, \text{ with}$$

$$\Gamma := \gamma \tag{11}$$
$$\Omega_F := f_{\Omega_F}(\gamma, \epsilon_{\Omega_F}) = BR(\gamma) + \epsilon_{\Omega_F} \tag{12}$$
$$\Omega_L := f_{\Omega_L}(\gamma, \Omega_F, \epsilon_{\Omega_L}) = \gamma(\Omega_F) + \epsilon_{\Omega_L} \tag{13}$$
$$J_F := f_{J_F}(\Omega_L, \Omega_F, \epsilon_{J_F}) = J_F(\Omega_L, \Omega_F) + \epsilon_{J_F} \tag{14}$$
$$J_L := f_{J_L}(\Omega_L, \Omega_F, \epsilon_{J_L}) = J_L(\Omega_L, \Omega_F) + \epsilon_{J_L} \tag{15}$$

*where $\epsilon_{\Omega_F} \in \mathcal{R}_{U_{\Omega_F}}, \epsilon_{\Omega_L} \in \mathcal{R}_{U_{\Omega_L}}, \epsilon_{\Omega_{J_F}} \in \mathcal{R}_{U_{J_F}}, \epsilon_{\Omega_{J_L}} \in \mathcal{R}_{U_{J_L}}$; with $p(U_i) = \mathcal{N}(0, \sigma_i^2)$ for all $U_i \in \boldsymbol{U}$ and $p(\mathbf{U})$ is jointly independent. The function $\gamma : \mathcal{R}_{\Omega_F} \to \mathcal{R}_{\Omega_L} \in \Gamma$ is an incentive function, decided by the principal from the function space $\Gamma$. The functional $BR(\gamma)$ is the best response functional for the follower agent given $\gamma$. The functions $J_F(\omega_L, \omega_F)$, $J_L(\omega_L, \omega_F)$ are the utility functions of the follower and the leader, respectively, in the $PAP_{L1F1}$.*

#### Assumptions Underlying the CGMs for Single-Stage Canonical PAPs

The CGM $\mathcal{M}_{L_1F_1}$ is an additive-noise Gaussian, Structural Causal Model (SCM); not inherently linear, as we do not assume that the structural equations $f_{V_i}(\boldsymbol{pa}(v_i), u_i)$, for each $V_i \in \boldsymbol{V}$, hold a specific functional form. We assume that the set of endogenous variables $\mathbf{V} = \{\Gamma, \Omega_L, \Omega_F, J_F, J_L\}$ in the CGM—namely, the incentives variable $\Gamma$, the principal's decision variable $\Omega_L$, the follower's decision variable $\Omega_F$, and their respective utilities $J_L$ and $J_F$—is causally sufficient. That is, there are no latent common causes outside this set that jointly influence any two of these variables.

The causal structure $\mathcal{G}_{L_1F_1}$ of $\mathcal{M}_{L_1F_1}$, has directed edges from $\Gamma$ to $\{\Omega_L, \Omega_F\}$, from $\Omega_L$ to $\{J_F, J_L\}$, and from $\Omega_F$ to $\{\Omega_L, J_F, J_L\}$. The variable $\Gamma$ does not depend on an exogenous random variable or any other variable in the causal system; it is a deterministic root variable whose value is decided and fixed by the principal choice of $\gamma \in \Gamma$. Thus, $\gamma$ acts as a fixed input to the causal system, selected by the principal agent.

https://doi.org/10.3390/e2801000

The best response functional $BR(\gamma)$ in the structural Equation (13), is the mapping from the principal's chosen incentive function $\gamma$ to the action $\omega_F^*$ that maximizes the follower's utility. That is,

$$BR(\gamma) = \omega_F^* \in \underset{\omega_F \in \Omega_F}{\arg\max}\, \mathbb{E}\Big[J_F\big(\gamma(\omega_F) + \epsilon_{\Omega_L}, \omega_F\big)\Big]. \tag{16}$$

This formulation reveals how the follower's decision responds to the incentive function chosen by the principal. The structural Equation (14), $\Omega_L := f_{\Omega_L}(\gamma, \Omega_F, \epsilon_{\Omega_L}) = \gamma(\Omega_F) + \epsilon_{\Omega_L}$, is central to represent the inverse Stackelberg game semantics. It expresses that after the principal proposes the incentive function $\gamma$, the principal's action $\Omega_L$ is given as a function $\gamma(\omega_F)$ of the follower's action $\omega_F$. This composition in the directed acyclic triangle $\Gamma \to \Omega_F$, $\Omega_F \to \Omega_L$, $\Gamma \to \Omega_L$, with the structural Equations (13) and (14), and it highlights how the principal's concrete action $\Omega_L$ responds to the follower's action, influenced by the incentive function $\gamma$ selected by the principal. The utility variables $J_L$ and $J_F$ are defined as functions of $(\Omega_L, \Omega_F)$, consistent with conventional formulations of principal–agent problems.

The generative causal model $\mathcal{M}_{L_1F_1}$ must be examined from two perspectives: the principal's and the follower's. From the principal's view, the follower's utility $J_F$ is an unobservable or hidden variable. So, for the principal, the set of hidden variables is $\mathbf{H}_L = \{J_F\}$, while the set of observable variables is $\mathbf{O}_L = \{\Gamma, \Omega_L, \Omega_F, J_L\}$, with $\mathbf{H}_L \cup \mathbf{O}_L = \mathbf{V}$. On the other hand, from the follower's view, $\mathbf{H}_F = \{J_L\}$ and $\mathbf{O}_F = \{\Gamma, \Omega_L, \Omega_F, J_F\}$, with $\mathbf{H}_F \cup \mathbf{O}_F = \mathbf{V}$. These separated perspectives are just marginalizations of the same generative SCM $\mathcal{M}_{L_1F_1}$, but maintain consistency with the information model in $PAP_{L_1,F_1}$.

It is also important to establish that, with respect to the information model in $PAP_{L_1,F_1}$, the principal views the follower mechanism $f_{\Omega_F}(\gamma, U_{\Omega_F})$ as a black box. In other words, the principal does not know the function $BR(\gamma)$ that the follower uses to decide $\omega_F$, but only observes the decision $\omega_F$. This work centers on the principal's perspective, and for the remainder, we will concentrate exclusively on this view of the causal model $\mathcal{M}_{L_1F_1}$, assuming $\mathbf{V} = \mathbf{O}_L \cup \mathbf{H}_L$ and treating $f_{\Omega_F}(\gamma, U_{\Omega_F})$ as a black box.

### 3.2. A Non-Parametric Identification for the Causal Inference Target

In the Causal Incentive Design (CID) framework, with respect to the single-stage $PAP_{L_1F_1}$, the principal's objective is to determine an incentive function $\gamma^*$ such that its utility $J_L$ is maximized, utilizing prior observations of the system in question. To accomplish this, the principal should first be able to estimate the expected value of their utility $J_L$, in the particular scenario where the incentive function $\gamma$ is applied, ideally utilizing only observational data.

In the context of causal inference, this requires determining whether the expected value of the utility of the principal $\mathbb{E}[J_L]$ in the post-intervention distribution $p(J_L \mid do(\Gamma = \gamma))$ is identifiable. In other words, determine whether

$$\mathbb{E}_{p\left(J_L \mid do(\Gamma=\gamma)\right)}[J_L] \quad \text{or equivalently,} \quad \mathbb{E}\big[J_L \mid do(\Gamma = \gamma)\big], \tag{17}$$

can be estimated using exclusively observational data from variables $(\Gamma, \Omega_L, \Omega_F, J_L)$, i.e., a data set $\mathcal{D} = \{\gamma^i, \omega_F^i, \omega_L^i, j_L^i\}_{i=1}^N$ of $N \in \mathbb{N}$ observations of the system. We also employ the simpler notation $\mathbb{E}^\gamma[J_L]$ to denote $\mathbb{E}\big[J_L \mid do(\Gamma = \gamma)\big]$. Recall that the variable $J_F$ is a hidden variable from the principal's perspective; so the principal has no knowledge or information about this variable.

https://doi.org/10.3390/e28010004

Identification via the g-Formula

We first use the g-formula over the principal's perspective to construct a non–parametric identification for the causal inference target $\mathbb{E}[J_L \mid do(\Gamma = \gamma)]$, which is then adequate to become a semi-parametric target estimand by considering the Gaussian additive independent errors on the CGM $\mathcal{M}_{L_1F_1}$. The g-formula over the principal's perspective for the intervention $do(\Gamma = \gamma)$ is given by

$$p(\mathbf{O}_L \setminus \Gamma \mid do(\Gamma = \gamma)) = \prod_{O_L \in \mathbf{O}_L \setminus \Gamma} p(O_L \mid \mathrm{pa}(O_L))\Big|_{\Gamma = \gamma}. \tag{18}$$

That is, we obtain the post-intervention distribution $p(\mathbf{O}_L \setminus \Gamma \mid do(\Gamma = \gamma)) = p(\omega_F, \omega_L, j_L \mid do(\Gamma = \gamma))$, removing all factors from the pre-intervention distribution $p(\mathbf{O}_L)$ corresponding to the intervened variable and substituting $\Gamma = \gamma$ into the remaining factors. So, the post-interventional distribution $p(\omega_F, \omega_L, j_L \mid do(\Gamma = \gamma))$ is factorized as shown in Equation (19). Then, we can estimate the target post-intervention distribution $p(j_L \mid do(\Gamma = \gamma))$ by marginalizing the variables $\omega_F$ and $\omega_L$ on the factorization for $p(\omega_F, \omega_L, j_L \mid do(\Gamma = \gamma))$, as shown in Equation (20).

$$p(\omega_F, \omega_L, j_L \mid do(\Gamma = \gamma)) = p(\omega_F \mid \Gamma = \gamma)\; p(\omega_L \mid \omega_F, \Gamma = \gamma)\; p(j_L \mid \omega_L, \omega_F, \Gamma = \gamma) \tag{19}$$

$$p(j_L \mid do(\Gamma = \gamma)) = \iint p(j_L \mid \omega_L, \omega_F, \Gamma = \gamma)\; p(\omega_L \mid \omega_F, \Gamma = \gamma)\; p(\omega_F \mid \Gamma = \gamma)\, d\omega_L\, d\omega_F. \tag{20}$$

The target functional value $V(\gamma) = \mathbb{E}[J_L \mid do(\Gamma = \gamma)]$ under the incentive function (policy) $\gamma$ is the expectation of $J_L$ in the post-intervention world, that is,

$$V(\gamma) = \mathbb{E}^{\gamma}[J_L] = \int j_L\, p(j_L \mid do(\Gamma = \gamma))\, dj_L. \tag{21}$$

Therefore, substituting the factorization form (Equation (20)) of the post-intervention distribution $p(j_L \mid do(\Gamma = \gamma))$, we obtain the following:

$$V(\gamma) = \int j \Big\{ \iint p(j \mid \omega_L, \omega_F, \Gamma = \gamma)\, p(\omega_L \mid \omega_F, \Gamma = \gamma)\, p(\omega_F \mid \Gamma = \gamma)\, d\omega_L\, d\omega_F \Big\} dj. \tag{22}$$

$$= \iint \Big\{ \int j\, p(j \mid \omega_L, \omega_F, \Gamma = \gamma)\, dj \Big\}\, p(\omega_L \mid \omega_F, \Gamma = \gamma)\, p(\omega_F \mid \Gamma = \gamma)\, d\omega_L\, d\omega_F, \tag{23}$$

where the exchange of integrals is allowed by the Tonelli/Fubini Theorem. Observe that the inner integral is the following conditional mean:

$$\int j\, p(j \mid \omega_L, \omega_F, \Gamma = \gamma)\, dj = \mathbb{E}[Y \mid \Omega_L = \omega_L, \Omega_F = \omega_F, \Gamma = \gamma] \tag{24}$$

Let us denote $\mu_L(\omega_L, \omega_F, \gamma) := \mathbb{E}[Y \mid \Omega_L = \omega_L, \Omega_F = \omega_F, \Gamma = \gamma]$. Thus, we have

$$V(\gamma) = \iint \mu_L(\omega_L, \omega_F, \gamma)\; p(\omega_L \mid \omega_F, \Gamma = \gamma)\; p(\omega_F \mid \Gamma = \gamma)\, d\omega_L\, d\omega_F \tag{25}$$

$$= \int \Big\{ \int \mu_L(\omega_L, \omega_F, \gamma)\; p(\omega_L \mid \omega_F, \Gamma = \gamma)\, d\omega_L \Big\}\; p(\omega_F \mid \Gamma = \gamma)\, d\omega_F. \tag{26}$$

https://doi.org/10.3390/e2801000

From structural Equation (14), $\Omega_L := f_{\Omega_L}(\gamma, \Omega_F, \epsilon_{\Omega_L}) = \gamma(\Omega_F) + \epsilon_{\Omega_L}$, if $U_{\Omega_L}$ has density $f_{U_{\Omega_L}}$, then for a fixed $\omega_F$, we have $p(\omega_L \mid \omega_F, \Gamma = \gamma) = f_{U_L}(\omega_L - \gamma(\omega_F))$. Hence, the inner integral of Equation (26) becomes

$$\int \mu_L(\omega_L, \omega_F, \gamma)\, f_{U_L}(\omega_L - \gamma(\omega_F))\, d\omega_L. \tag{27}$$

Which, by the change of variable $r = \omega_L - \gamma(\omega_F)$, $d\omega_L = d(r + \gamma(\omega_F))$, becomes

$$\int \mu_L(\gamma(\omega_F) + t, \omega_F, \gamma)\, f_{U_{\Omega_L}}(r)\, d(r + \gamma(\omega_F)) = \mathbb{E}_{U_{\Omega_L}}\left[\mu_L(\gamma(\omega_F) + U_{\Omega_L}, \omega_F, \gamma)\right], \tag{28}$$

since $r = \omega_L - \gamma(\omega_F) = \epsilon_{\Omega_L} \sim p(U_{\Omega_L})$, as $\Omega_L = \gamma(\omega_F) + U_{\Omega_L}$ with $U_{\Omega_L} \perp \Omega_F$. Therefore, Equation (26) can be expressed as

$$\begin{aligned} V(\gamma) &= \int \left\{ \int \mu_L(\omega_L, \omega_F, \gamma)\, p(\omega_L \mid \omega_F, \Gamma = \gamma)\, d\omega_L \right\} p(\omega_F \mid \Gamma = \gamma)\, d\omega_F \\ &= \int \left\{ \mathbb{E}_{U_{\Omega_L}}\left[\mu_L(\gamma(\omega_F) + U_{\Omega_L}, \omega_F, \gamma)\right] \right\} p(\omega_F \mid \Gamma = \gamma)\, d\omega_F. \end{aligned} \tag{29}$$

The outer integral of Equation (29) corresponds to averaging over the follower's action distribution $p(\Omega_F \mid \Gamma = \gamma)$ induced by the policy $\gamma$. Recall that from the principal's perspective, the follower mechanism $\Omega_F = f_{\Omega_F}(\gamma, U_{\Omega_F})$ is unknown and is treated as a black-box mechanism.

### 3.3. Estimations on the Semi-Parametric Identification Formula

We now demonstrate how to estimate $V(\gamma)$; first through a working example in the context of the credit market, and subsequently, we describe how the estimation can be conducted in general under additive, independent, mean-zero Gaussian noise, without committing to a particular parametric form for the structural functions. In this section, for simplicity and clarity on the estimation task, we rename two of the causal system variables. Here, we use $M := \Omega_F$ to denote the follower's action and refer to it as the mediator, because it acts as a *mediator* on the causal path from a fixed incentive policy $\gamma \in \Gamma$ to the principal's utility $J_L$. We refer here to the principal's utility as the *outcome* of the system, and we denote it here as $Y := J_L$ for convenience.

Before going into the details for the estimation on the linear parametrized PAP example and the general case estimation; we provide an introduction of the general components to learn on the identified estimand:

$$V(\gamma) = \mathbb{E}[Y \mid do(\Gamma = \gamma)] \tag{30}$$

$$= \int \{ \underbrace{\mathbb{E}_{U_L}[\mu_L(\gamma(m) + U_L,\ m,\ \gamma)]}_{\text{Inner expectation for the outcome model.}} \} \underbrace{p(m \mid \Gamma = \gamma)}_{\text{Black-box mediator conditional.}} dm, \tag{31}$$

where $\mu_L(\omega_L, m, \gamma) = \mathbb{E}[Y \mid \Omega_L = \omega_L,\ M = m,\ \Gamma = \gamma]$, and $\Omega_L = \gamma(M) + U_L$ holds. The two main components are inner expectation for the outcome model and the outer black-box mediator conditional, as shown in Equation (31).

For the first, we unpack the nested structure by first estimating the action mechanism $\Omega_L = f_{\Omega_L}(\gamma, M, U_L) = \widehat{f}_L(\gamma, M) + \widehat{\sigma}_L(\gamma, M)\, U_L$ by learning $\widehat{f}_L(\gamma, M)$ and $\widehat{\sigma}_L(\gamma, M)$ from the data; i.e., regress $\Omega_L$ on $(M, \Gamma)$ for the mean $\widehat{f}_L$ and regress squared residuals on $(M, \Gamma)$ to obtain $\widehat{\sigma}^2_L$. With these, we learn the conditional outcome mean $\mu_L(\omega_L, m, \gamma) = \mathbb{E}[Y \mid \Omega_L = \omega_L,\ M = m,\ \Gamma = \gamma]$ as regression problem with features $(\Omega_L, M, \Gamma)$ and outcome $Y$. Then, the inner expectation for the outcome model (see Equation (31)) may be computed by Gauss–Hermite quadrature or Monte Carlo using common random numbers across $m$ to reduce variance.

The second main component is the post-intervention mediator law (what the follower does under the policy $\gamma$); the black-box mediator conditional $p(m \mid \Gamma = \gamma)$. We approximate $p(m \mid \Gamma = \gamma)$ near the target policy by a policy-local reweighting of the observation, selecting a policy-space metric $d_{\mathcal{G}}$ and kernel $K$ with bandwidth $h$. Thus, the outer expectation over the mediator law under a fixed $\gamma$ is computed by policy-local kernel weights. Therefore, in general, the inner layer (first component) is a Gaussian smoothing of the outcome regression around the mean principal's action (in linear models, the variance drops out and we recover the closed form; in general, we keep a small quadrature); and the outer layer (second component) is a weighted average over observed mediators. The kernel with bandwidth provides a principled way to compute those weights with global regularization as we show in the following sections.

Since empirical performance is determined by domain-specific design choices, such as policy parameterization, kernel selection on policy space, bandwidth $h$, and support criteria, we defer numerical examples and simulations to future work that will focus on applied instantiations of the present framework. We concentrate on formal properties that hold independent of the chosen application.

#### 3.3.1. The Estimation of a Linear Parametrized Instance

Consider a financial institution that is required to establish a transparent pricing plan before evaluating a potential borrower's response. The bank (the principal) announces an affine policy, which includes a fixed fee and an interest "slope" that is dependent on the size of the loan. The bank, thereafter, observes how much the business (the follower) actually borrows. This is an instance of a canonical $PAP_{L_1F_1}$, which we can parameterize as the following linear Gaussian Structural Causal Models (SCM).

$$\Gamma := \gamma_{(\alpha,\beta)}(m) = \alpha m + \beta, \tag{32}$$

$$M := \mu_M(\alpha,\beta) + U_M, \quad U_M \sim \mathcal{N}(0,\sigma_M^2), \tag{33}$$

$$\Omega_L := \alpha M + \beta + U_{\Omega_L}, \quad U_{\Omega_L} \sim \mathcal{N}(0,\sigma_L^2), \tag{34}$$

$$Y := b + r\,\Omega_L + q\,M + U_Y, \quad U_Y \sim \mathcal{N}(0,\sigma_Y^2), \tag{35}$$

with $U_M, U_{\Omega_L}, U_Y$ mutually independent and independent of $\Gamma$. We model the bank's pricing rule as an affine policy $\gamma_{(\alpha,\beta)}(m) = \alpha m + \beta$, with $\alpha \geq 0$, $\beta \geq 0$; so, we have an affine pricing as the incentive functions family. As we have assumed from the principal's perspective, the follower's mechanism and utility remain hidden from the principal. So, the function $\mu_M(\alpha,\beta)$ is an unknown function for the principal. In this context, we can see $\Omega_F$ as the realized cash inflow from the borrower, i.e., the bank collections follow the mechanism $\Omega_L = \gamma(M) + U_L = \alpha M + \beta + U_L$; the interest or the cash inflow $M$ plus the fee actually received at the single stage, possibly noisy. The principal utility is consider linear given as $Y = b + r\,\Omega_L + q\,M + U_Y$, where $b$ represents the baseline overheads, $r$ is the realization factor that converts collections into value (often $r \approx 1$ if a dollar collected is a dollar of revenue before costs; r < 1 if haircuts rules apply), and $q$ is the marginal value of the loan size $M$. It is typically negative if it aggregates funding cost, expected credit loss, and capital operating costs per unit of balance.

$$\begin{aligned} \underbrace{J_L}_{\textit{Profit}} &= \underbrace{r\Omega_L}_{\textit{Collections}} + \underbrace{q\,M}_{\textit{Funding and risk cost per unit}} + \underbrace{b}_{\textit{Fixed margin}} \\ &= r\,(\alpha M + \beta) + q\,M + b. \end{aligned}$$

https://doi.org/10.3390/e28010004

In short, profit is given as the collections minus (negative $q$) the funding cost per size. This aligns with the canonical $PAP_{L_1F_1}$, where the utility of the principal depends on the decisions of the leader $\Omega_L$ and the follower $\Omega_F$.

Given this outcome model, the conditional mean $\mu_L(\omega_L, m, \gamma)$ used inside the g-formula identification in Equation (29) is

$$\begin{aligned}\mu_L(\omega_L, m, \gamma) &= \mathbb{E}[Y \mid \Omega_L = \omega_L,\, M = m,\, \Gamma = \gamma] \\ &= b + r\,\omega_L + q\,m,\end{aligned}$$

since $\mathbb{E}[U_Y \mid \Omega_L, M, \Gamma] = 0$. Then, we reduce $\mathbb{E}_{U_{\Omega_L}}\big[\mu_L(\gamma(m) + U_{\Omega_L},\, m,\, \gamma)\big]$, the inner expectation over the principal's action noise $U_{\Omega_L}$ in the identification formula, using $\Omega_L = \gamma(m) + U_{\Omega_L}$ and $\mathbb{E}[U_{\Omega_L} \mid M = m, \Gamma = \gamma] = 0$. If we fix $m$, the inner term becomes

$$\begin{aligned}\mathbb{E}_{U_{\Omega_L}}\big[\mu_L(\gamma(m) + U_{\Omega_L},\, m,\, \gamma)\big] &= \mathbb{E}\big[\, b + r(\gamma(m) + U_{\Omega_L}) + q\,m\,\big] \\ &= b + r\,\gamma(m) + q\,m. \end{aligned} \tag{36}$$

Because $\mu_L$ is linear on $\omega_L$ and $U_{\Omega_L}$ is mean-zero (conditional on $m$), the action-noise variance do not affect the mean; only the mean of $\Omega_L$ matters at this step. We reduce the outer integral by plugging the reduced inner term (36) into the outer integral in (29), and take the (outer) expectation with respect to the mediator law $p(m \mid \Gamma = \gamma)$:

$$\begin{aligned}V(\gamma) &= \int (b + r\,\gamma(m) + q\,m)\; p(m \mid \Gamma = \gamma)\, dm \\ &= b \;+\; r\,\mathbb{E}\big[\gamma(M) \mid \Gamma = \gamma\big] \;+\; q\,\mathbb{E}[M \mid \Gamma = \gamma].\end{aligned}$$

Now, substituting the affine policy $\gamma_{(\alpha,\beta)}(m) = \alpha m + \beta$:

$$\begin{aligned}\mathbb{E}\big[\gamma(M) \mid \Gamma = (\alpha, \beta)\big] &= \mathbb{E}[\alpha M + \beta \mid \Gamma = (\alpha, \beta)] \\ &= \alpha\,\mu_M(\alpha, \beta) + \beta,\end{aligned}$$

with $\mu_M(\alpha, \beta) := \mathbb{E}[M \mid \Gamma = (\alpha, \beta)]$. Hence,

$$\begin{aligned}V(\alpha, \beta) &= b + r\big(\alpha\,\mu_M(\alpha, \beta) + \beta\big) + q\,\mu_M(\alpha, \beta) \\ &= b \;+\; r\,\beta \;+\; (r\alpha + q)\,\mu_M(\alpha, \beta)\,. \end{aligned} \tag{37}$$

Therefore, the expression in (37) for $V(\alpha, \beta)$ is the estimand we want to approximate from the data, given as $N$ i.i.d. observations $\{(\alpha_i, \beta_i, M_i, \Omega_{L,i}, Y_i)\}_{i=1}^N$. The formula in (37) depends on (i) the outcome coefficients $(b, r, q)$, and (ii) the black-box mean of the mediator under policy $\mu_M(\alpha, \beta) = \mathbb{E}[M \mid \Gamma = (\alpha, \beta)]$. We estimate them separately in two steps and subsequently input them into the closed form. In a first step, we estimate $(\hat{b}, \hat{r}, \hat{q})$ from a regression of $Y$ on $(\Omega_L, M)$; and in a second step, the estimation of $\hat{\mu}_M(\alpha, \beta)$ is performed through the regression of $M$ with respect to the variables $(\alpha, \beta)$. The closed form estimator is then

$$\hat{V}(\alpha, \beta) = \hat{b} + \hat{r}\beta + (\hat{r}\alpha + \hat{q})\hat{\mu}_M(\alpha, \beta). \tag{38}$$

A natural way to estimate $(\hat{b}, \hat{r}, \hat{q})$ is by weighting observations according to their location in relation to $(\alpha, \beta)$. Then, a weighted least-squares (WLS) fit yields $(\hat{b}, \hat{r}, \hat{q})$ that are tuned to the neighborhood of the target policy $\gamma_{(\alpha,\beta)}$. That is, for a target incentive policy $\gamma_{(\alpha,\beta)}(m) = \alpha m + \beta$, we fit a local linear outcome model $Y \approx b \,+\, r\,\Omega_L \,+\, q\,M \,+\, \varepsilon$, by weighting observations according to their proximity to $\gamma_{(\alpha,\beta)}$ in the policy space.

https://doi.org/10.3390/e28010004

Let $X_i = [1, \Omega_{L,i}, M_i]$ and $y_i = Y_i$ for $i \in [N]$, and arrange the data in the matrix $X \in \mathbb{R}^{n\times 3}$, and the vector $y \in \mathbb{R}^n$. A practical choice for a distance $d\big((\alpha_i, \beta_i), (\alpha, \beta)\big)$ in the policy space is an isotropic distance defined as

$$d\big((\alpha_i, \beta_i), (\alpha, \beta)\big) = \sqrt{(\tilde{\alpha}_i - \tilde{\alpha})^2 + (\tilde{\beta}_i - \tilde{\beta})^2},$$

with standardized coordinates $\tilde{\alpha} = (\alpha - \bar{\alpha})/\widehat{\mathrm{sd}}(\alpha)$ (and analogously for $\beta$).

Let $K(\cdot)$ be a radial kernel (Gaussian or Epanechnikov) and $h > 0$ a scalar bandwidth. We then define the unnormalized weights as follows:

$$\tilde{w}_i(h) = K\bigg(\frac{d\big((\alpha_i, \beta_i), (\alpha, \beta)\big)}{h}\bigg), \qquad w_i(h) = \frac{\tilde{w}_i(h)}{\sum_{j=1}^{n} \tilde{w}_j(h)}, \qquad \sum_i w_i(h) = 1,$$

and $W = \mathrm{diag}\big(w_1(h), \ldots, w_n(h)\big)$. Then, the WLS estimator $\widehat{\theta} = (\hat{b}, \hat{r}, \hat{q})^\top$ is

$$\widehat{\theta} = \begin{bmatrix} \hat{b} \\ \hat{r} \\ \hat{q} \end{bmatrix} = \big(X^\top W X\big)^{-1} X^\top W y.$$

We estimate $\mu_M(\alpha, \beta) = \mathbb{E}[M \mid \Gamma = (\alpha, \beta)]$ for a fixed policy $(\alpha, \beta)$, regressing the realized mediator $M$ on the policy coordinates $(\alpha, \beta)$, using observed tuples $\{(\alpha_i, \beta_i, M_i)\}_{i=1}^N$. We proceed similarly in this regression with the idea of weighting observations according to their proximity to $\gamma_{(\alpha,\beta)}$. Let $\theta_i = (\alpha_i, \beta_i)$ and $\theta = (\alpha, \beta)$ denote observed and target incentive policies. We use the same policy-space isotropic distance and unnormalized weights as in the previous regression.

We can approximate $\mu_M$ by a local plane around $\theta = (\alpha, \beta)$, given as the linear combination $\theta_0 + \theta_1(\alpha_i - \alpha) + \theta_2(\beta_i - \beta)$ of the variables $(\alpha_i - \alpha)$ and $(\beta_i - \beta)$. Thus, using the approximation $M_i \approx \theta_0 + \theta_1(\alpha_i - \alpha) + \theta_2(\beta_i - \beta)$, the WLS problem is given by

$$\min_{\theta_0, \theta_1, \theta_2} \sum_{i=1}^{N} w_i(h) \Big[M_i - \{\theta_0 + \theta_1(\alpha_i - \alpha) + \theta_2(\beta_i - \beta)\}\Big]^2, \tag{39}$$

with the same kernel weights $w_i(h)$. Then, the estimate of the mean at the target is the intercept in this linear model. Therefore, $\hat{\theta}_0$ represents the estimated mean value of the plane at the specific target policy $(\alpha, \beta)$ and $\hat{\mu}_M(\alpha, \beta) = \hat{\theta}_0$. In matrix form, let the local design row be $x_i = [1, \alpha_i - \alpha, \beta_i - \beta]$, arranging in the matrix $X \in \mathbb{R}^{n\times 3}$ the $x_i$, and $W = \mathrm{diag}\big(w_1(h), \ldots, w_n(h)\big)$. A local linear WLS estimator for $\mu_M(\alpha, \beta) = \mathbb{E}[M \mid \Gamma = (\alpha, \beta)]$ is

$$\widehat{\boldsymbol{\theta}} = (X^\top W X)^{-1} X^\top W \boldsymbol{M}, \qquad \widehat{\mu}_M(\alpha, \beta) = \widehat{\theta}_0, \text{ with } \boldsymbol{M} = (M_1, \ldots, M_n)^\top$$

### 3.3.2. The Estimation in the General Gaussian Additive-Noise Case

We model the conditional distribution of the leader's realized action $\Omega_L$ given the mediator $M$ and policy $\gamma$ as the following Gaussian:

$$p(\Omega_L \mid M = m, \Gamma = \gamma) \sim \mathcal{N}\big(f_L(m, \gamma), \sigma_L^2(m, \gamma)\big) \tag{40}$$

We learn non-parametrically the mean map $f_L$: $M \times \mathcal{A} \to \mathbb{R}$ and the variance map $\sigma_L^2$: $M \times \mathcal{A} \to (0, \infty)$ from data $\{(M_i, A_i, \Omega_{L,i})\}_{i=1}^N$ using RKHS regression kernel, i.e., Kernel Ridge Regression (KRR) on $(M, \Gamma)$ [4,27]. Therefore, to learn the mean function $f_L$, we solve the KRR problem, where the goal is to find a function $f$ that minimizes a regularized loss function.

$$\widehat{f}_L(m,\gamma) \in \arg\min_{f\in\mathcal{H}_{MA}} \left(\omega_{Li} - f(m_i,\gamma_i)\right)^2 + \lambda_f \|f\|^2_{\mathcal{H}_{MA}}. \tag{41}$$

The first term measures how well the function fits the training data. The second term is a regularization penalty, which penalizes the complexity of the function as measured by its norm in the RKHS, using the regularization hyperparameter $\lambda_f$ that balances the trade-off. By the representer theorem, the solution of problem (41) can be expressed as a linear combination of kernel functions centered at the training data points $f(\cdot) = \sum_{i\in[N]} \alpha_{fi} k_{MA}(x_i,\cdot)$. In matrix form, $\widehat{f}_L(m,a) = k_{(m,a)}^\top \boldsymbol{\alpha}_f$, where $k_{(m,a)} = \left(k_{MA}(x_1,(m,a)),\ldots,k_{MA}(x_n,(m,a))\right)^\top$; and $\boldsymbol{\alpha}_f = \left(K + \lambda_f I\right)^{-1}\boldsymbol{y}$, where $K \in \mathbb{R}^{N\times N}$ with $K_{ij} = k_{MA}(x_i,x_j)$, $\boldsymbol{y} = (y_1,\ldots,y_N)^\top$.

A product kernel on $(m,a)$ can capture interactions as in our case, where the effect of $m$ on $\Omega_L$ depends on policy $\gamma$. So, we can establish a product kernel on $(m,a)$ as follows:

$$k^{\text{prod}}_{MA}\left((m,a),(m',a')\right) = \underbrace{\exp\left(-\frac{(m-m')^2}{2\,\ell_M^2}\right)}_{k_M(m,m')} \times \underbrace{\exp\left(-\frac{\|a-a'\|^2}{2\,\ell_\Gamma^2}\right)}_{k_\Gamma(a,a')}.$$

Likewise, for the variance function $\sigma_L^2(m,\gamma)$, we compute the residuals $r_i = \omega_{Li} - \widehat{f}_L(m_i,\gamma_i)$; and we can define pseudo-responses $z_i = \log(r_i^2 + \epsilon)$ with small $\epsilon > 0$, for numerical stability. Modeling $\log \sigma_L^2(m,\gamma) = v(m,\gamma)$ in an RKHS, guarantees strict positivity after exponentiation, turns multiplicative scale effects into additive structure, and improves residual behavior under Gaussian assumptions. Therefore, we fit KRR on $(m,\gamma) \to z$ and solve

$$\widehat{v}_L(m,\gamma) \in \arg\min_{v\,\in\mathcal{H}_{MA}} \left(z_i - v(m_i,\gamma_i)\right)^2 \;+\; \lambda_v \,\|v\|^2_{\mathcal{H}_{m\gamma}}. \tag{42}$$

As before, $v(\cdot) = \sum_{i\in[N]} \alpha_{vi} k_{MA}(x_j,\cdot)$ with $\boldsymbol{\alpha}_v = (K + \lambda_v I)^{-1}\boldsymbol{z}$ and $\boldsymbol{z} = (z_1,\ldots,z_n)^\top$. We predict $\widehat{v}(m,a)$ and set $\widehat{\sigma}_L^2(m,a) = \exp\left(\widehat{v}(m,a)\right) > 0$.

Using the above, we can now estimate $\mu_L(\omega,m,a) = \mathbb{E}[Y \mid \Omega_L = \omega, M = m, \Gamma = a]$. We can use a weighted KRR formulation to compute $\widehat{\mu}_L(\omega,m,a)$ with observations $x_i = (\omega_i,m_i,a_i)$, and output $y_i = Y_i$, $i = 1,\ldots,n$. Let $k_X$ be a positive-definite kernel on $x = (\omega,m,a)$ with RKHS $\mathcal{H}_X$. Then, we solve the following weighted regularized least-squares problem:

$$\widehat{\mu}_L(x) \in \arg\min_{\mu\in\mathcal{H}_X} \sum_{i=1}^n w_i(\gamma)\left(y_i - \mu(x_i)\right)^2 \;+\; \lambda_\mu \,\|\mu\|^2_{\mathcal{H}_X}, \tag{43}$$

employing $\mu(\cdot) = \sum_{i\in[N]} \alpha_{\mu i}\, k_X(x_i,\cdot)$, $\boldsymbol{\alpha}_\mu = \left(KW + \lambda I_n\right)^{-1} W\,\boldsymbol{y}$; thus, $\widehat{\mu}_L(x) = k_x^\top \boldsymbol{\alpha}$, where $K_{ij} = k_X(x_i,x_j)$, $K \in \mathbb{R}^{n\times n}$, $W = \operatorname{diag}(w_1(\gamma),\ldots,w_n(\gamma))$, $\boldsymbol{y} = (y_1,\ldots,y_n)^\top$ and $k_x = [k_X(x_1,x),\ldots,k_X(x_n,x)]^\top$. The policy weights $w_i(\gamma) \geq 0$ with $\sum_i w_i(\gamma) = 1$, prioritize fidelity near $\gamma$. More details about these weights are given in Section 3.3.4.

#### 3.3.3. Computing the Inner Gaussian Expectation

So far, we have estimated what appears within the curly brackets before integration, in the identification Formula (29), shown again below for clarity:

$$\begin{aligned} V(\gamma) &= \int \left\{ \int \mu_L(\omega_L,m,\gamma)\; p(\omega_L \mid m,\Gamma=\gamma)\, d\omega_L \right\} p(m \mid \Gamma=\gamma)\, dm \\ &= \int \left\{ \mathbb{E}_{U_{\Omega_L}}\left[\mu_L(\gamma(m) + U_{\Omega_L},m,\gamma)\right] \right\} p(m \mid \Gamma=\gamma)\, dm, \end{aligned}$$

where $\mu_L(\omega_L, m, \gamma) := \mathbb{E}[Y \mid \Omega_L = \omega_L, M = m, \Gamma = \gamma]$. That is, we show before how to estimate $\mu_L(\omega_L, m, \gamma)$ and $p(\omega_L \mid m, \Gamma = \gamma)$ and now we show how to approximate

$$\begin{aligned}\int \mu_L(\omega_L, m, \gamma)\, p(\omega_L \mid m, \Gamma = \gamma)\, d\omega_L &= \mathbb{E}_{U_{\Omega_L}}\left[\mu_L(\gamma(m) + U_{\Omega_L}, m, \gamma)\right] \\ &= \mathbb{E}_{U_{\Omega_L}}\left[\mu_L(\Omega_L,\ m,\ \gamma) \mid M{=}m, \Gamma{=}\gamma\right] \\ &= g_{U_{\Omega_L}}(m; \gamma).\end{aligned}$$

An efficient and natural way to compute the inner Gaussian expectation $\widehat{g}_{U_{\Omega_L}}(m;\gamma)$ is by the Gauss–Hermite (GH) quadrature method. The integral for $g_{U_{\Omega_L}}(m;\gamma)$ can be expressed as

$$g_{U_{\Omega_L}}(m;\gamma) = \int_{-\infty}^{\infty} \mu_L(\omega_L,\ m,\ \gamma)\, \frac{1}{\sqrt{2\pi}\,\sigma_{\Omega_L}} \exp\!\left(-\frac{(\omega_L - \mu_{\Omega_L})^2}{2\sigma^2_{\Omega_L}}\right) d\omega_L,$$

where $\mu_{\Omega_L} := \widehat{f}_L(\gamma, m)$, $\sigma_{\Omega_L} := \sigma_L(\gamma, m) > 0$, which we previously estimate and $p(\Omega_L \mid (M{=}m, \Gamma{=}\gamma)) \sim \mathcal{N}(\mu_{\Omega_L}, \sigma^2_{\Omega_L})$.Writing $\Omega_L = \mu_{\Omega_L} + U_L$ with $U_L \sim \mathcal{N}(0, \sigma^2_{\Omega_L})$, the change of variables $U_L = \sigma_{\Omega_L} Z$, i.e., $Z = U_L/\sigma_{\Omega_L}$, transforms the expectation to the standard-normal scale. No information is lost; it is the same integral expressed in a convenient form for the GH method. Therefore, with a standard normal $Z \sim \mathcal{N}(0,1)$, equivalently, we have

$$g_Z(m;\gamma) = \mathbb{E}_Z\left[\mu_L(\mu_{\Omega_L} + \sigma_{\Omega_L} Z,\ m,\ \gamma)\right] = \int_{-\infty}^{\infty} \mu_L(\mu_{\Omega_L} + \sigma_{\Omega_L} z,\ m,\ \gamma)\, \frac{e^{-z^2/2}}{\sqrt{2\pi}}\, dz. \tag{44}$$

The GH method approximates integrals of the form $\int_{-\infty}^{\infty} e^{-x^2} f(x)\, dx \approx \sum_{m=1}^{M} w_m^{GH} f(x_m^{GH})$, where $\{x_m^{GH}, w_m^{GH}\}_{m=1}^{M}$ are Hermite nodes and weights. To bring the standard-normal expectation (44) to this form, set $z = \sqrt{2}\,x$ ($dz = \sqrt{2}\,dx$), yielding

$$g_Z(m;\gamma) = \frac{1}{\sqrt{\pi}} \int_{-\infty}^{\infty} \underbrace{\mu_L(\mu_{\Omega_L} + \sigma_{\Omega_L}\sqrt{2}\,x,\ m,\ \gamma)}_{f(x^{GH})} \quad \underbrace{e^{-x^2}}_{\text{GH weights } w^{GH}} \quad dx. \tag{45}$$

$$\approx \frac{1}{\sqrt{\pi}} \sum_{m=1}^{M} w_m^{GH}\, \mu_L(\mu_\Omega + \sigma_\Omega \sqrt{2}\, x_j,\ m,\ \gamma), \tag{46}$$

where the computable approximation in (46) for the definite integral in (45) is given by applying a $M$-point rule GH. The sum of all the weights for the GH rule is always $\sum_{m=1}^{M} w_m^{GH} = \int_{-\infty}^{\infty} e^{-x^2}\, dx = \sqrt{\pi}$ and the Golub–Welsch Algorithm is a standard numerical method for computing the nodes and weights of any Gaussian quadrature rule, including the Gauss–Hermite quadrature. Unlike Monte Carlo, GH has no sampling variance; this stability is valuable when comparing many candidate policies $\gamma$. The inner integral is always one-dimensional (action noise), so GH is computationally light, and the nodes $\{x_m^{GH}, w_m^{GH}\}_{m=1}^{M}$ are pre-computable and reusable.

#### 3.3.4. Policy-Local Empirical Measure Construction in the Outer Integral

Finally, the identified value of a fixed policy $\gamma$ can be written as a conditional expectation $\mathbb{E}[g_\gamma(M) \mid \Gamma = \gamma]$, since:

$$\begin{aligned}V(\gamma) &= \int \left\{\mathbb{E}_{U_{\Omega_L}}\left[\mu_L(\gamma(m) + U_{\Omega_L}, m, \gamma)\right]\right\} p(m \mid \Gamma = \gamma)\, dm, \\ &= \int g_{U_{\Omega_L}}(m;\gamma)\, p(m \mid \Gamma = \gamma)\, dm, \\ &= \mathbb{E}[g_\gamma(M) \mid \Gamma = \gamma]\end{aligned}$$

https://doi.org/10.3390/e28010004

So, the task is to estimate the expectation over the mediator distribution under policy $\gamma$. We estimate this by a local kernel smoother in policy space. We observe i.i.d. $\{(m_i, \gamma_i, \dots)\}_{i=1}^{N}$ with realized policies $\gamma_i$ (e.g., $\gamma_i = (\alpha_i, \beta_i)$). Because $\Gamma$ is continuous, the event $\{\Gamma = \gamma\}$ has probability zero; therefore, we approximate the conditional expectation by *localizing* to policies $\gamma_i$ that are close to $\gamma$ and form a policy-local empirical distribution over the observed mediators $\{M_i\}$. For that policy-local empirical distribution, we may define a distance $d(\gamma_i, \gamma)$ in the policy space. Since $\gamma_i, \gamma$ lie in an RKHS $H_k$, we use $d(\gamma_i, \gamma) = \|\gamma_i - \gamma\|_{H_k}$ to reflect the policy geometry. Additionally, we select a non-negative, radial kernel $K(u) \geq 0$ with $u = d/h$ and a bandwidth $h > 0$ as the Gaussian kernel, also known as the Radial Basis Function (RBF) kernel $K(u) = \exp(-u^2/2)$. So, as in the linear parametrized instance before, we define the unnormalized weights:

$$\tilde{w}_i(\gamma; h) = K\Big(\frac{d(\gamma_i, \gamma)}{h}\Big), \qquad w_i(\gamma; h) = \frac{\tilde{w}_i(\gamma; h)}{\sum_{j=1}^{n} \tilde{w}_j(\gamma; h)} \geq 0, \text{ with } \sum_{i \in [N]} w_i = 1, \tag{47}$$

Thus, we approximate $\mathbb{E}[g_\gamma(M) \mid \Gamma = \gamma]$ using a policy-local empirical measure supported on the observed mediators for the conditional $p(m \mid \Gamma = \gamma)$. The policy-local empirical distribution for approximating $p(m \mid \Gamma = \gamma)$ is defined as

$$\widehat{P}_\gamma^{(h)}(dm) = \sum_{i=1}^{n} w_i(\gamma; h)\, \delta_{m_i}(dm), \tag{48}$$

where $\delta_{Mm_i}$ is the unit mass at $m_i$. Intuitively, $\widehat{P}_\gamma^{(h)}$ is the law of $M$ one would obtain by resampling historical mediators with probability proportional to how close their policies $\gamma_i$ are to the target $\gamma$. This approximation for $p(m \mid \Gamma = \gamma)$ turns the outer integral into an interpretable, positivity–respecting kernel average. Integrating the test function $\widehat{g}_{U_{\Omega_L}}(\cdot; \gamma)$ against this measure yields

$$\widehat{V}(\gamma) = \widehat{\mathbb{E}}[g_\gamma(M) \mid \Gamma = \gamma] \tag{49}$$

$$= \int \widehat{g}_{U_{\Omega_L}}(m; \gamma)\, \widehat{P}_\gamma^{(h)}(dm) \tag{50}$$

$$= \sum_{i=1}^{n} w_i(\gamma; h)\, \widehat{g}(M_i; \gamma), \tag{51}$$

which is precisely the outer half of the nested g-computation estimator $\widehat{V}(\gamma)$. The policy-local reweighting in (49)–(51) implicitly requires a *positivity (overlap)* condition: for any target policy $\gamma$, there must be sufficient probability mass of logged policies in a neighborhood of $\gamma$ so that the conditional law $p(M \mid \Gamma = \gamma)$ can be well approximated by the empirical measure $\widehat{\mathbb{P}}_\gamma^{(h)}$. In finite samples, this induces an *empirical support constraint*: $\widehat{V}(\gamma)$, which is reliable only if the weights $w_i(\gamma; h)$ do not degenerate. We quantify local support via the *effective sample size* (ESS):

$$\text{ESS}(\gamma; h) := \frac{\left(\sum_{i=1}^{N} w_i(\gamma; h)\right)^2}{\sum_{i=1}^{N} w_i(\gamma; h)^2}.$$

The ESS is a measure of how many independent samples the weighted sample set is equivalent to. A low ESS indicates high variance and instability in the estimate $\widehat{V}(\gamma)$ because the estimate is dominated by a small number of data points. We also define the *support set*:

$$\mathcal{S}_{\text{support}}(h, \tau, w_{\max}) := \Big\{\gamma \in \Gamma : \text{ESS}(\gamma; h) \geq \tau, \max_i w_i(\gamma; h) \leq w_{\max}\Big\}.$$

https://doi.org/10.3390/e28010004

The support set $\mathcal{S}_{\text{support}}$ defines the region in the policy space $\Gamma$ where the estimate $\widehat{V}(\gamma)$ is considered empirically reliable. Policies $\gamma$ outside this set are not trustworthy due to a lack of data overlap. The $\text{ESS}(\gamma;h) \geq \tau$ condition ensures that the evaluation is based on a sufficiently large effective sample size, preventing the estimate from being dominated by just a few data points. By requiring $\text{ESS}(\gamma;h) \geq \tau$, we enforce a degree of overlap between the target policy $\gamma$ and the logged policies. Higher $\tau$ means we demand better overlap and a more stable estimate, which shrinks the support set $\mathcal{S}_{\text{support}}$. The $\max_i w_i(\gamma;h) \leq w_{\max}$ condition directly guards against extreme importance weights, which are a hallmark of poor overlap or model mismatch in off-policy evaluation. This constraint helps bound the influence of rare, yet highly weighted, events. Policies $\gamma$ that require assigning an enormous weight to any single data point are excluded from the support set. Lower $w_{\max}$ means we tolerate less weight variance and demand better weight balance, which also shrinks the support set $\mathcal{S}_{\text{support}}$. The effective sample size (ESS) serves as a proxy for uncertainty in the outer expectation. A small ESS suggests high estimator variance and low information, which necessitates a trust-region restriction in policy space. Conversely, a large ESS indicates data-supported proposals and reduced uncertainty.

## 4. A Functional Bayesian Optimization Algorithm for Single-Stage Canonical PAPs

Functional Bayesian Optimization (FBO) is the version of Bayesian Optimization (BO) (see Appendix C) in which the domain $\mathbf{D}$ of the objective function to maximize $f_{obj}$: $\mathbf{D} \to \mathbb{R}$ is a space of functions. We leverage the sequential optimization process of Bayesian optimization and the use of the Gaussian Process Upper Confidence Bound (GP-UCB) acquisition function (see Appendix C.2) to solve the single-stage canonical $PAP_{L_1F_1}$. Specifically, we propose an FBO algorithm to sequentially solve the following optimization problem.

$$\gamma^* \in \arg\max_{\gamma^t \in \Gamma} \mathbb{E}\Big[J_L \mid do(\Gamma = \gamma^t)\Big]. \tag{52}$$

This is an objective functional, since its domain is a space of incentive functions $\Gamma$. We employ a GP-UCB acquisition functional (see Appendix C.2 and Section 4.2) in the proposed FBO algorithm as the strategy to guide the selection of the best next incentive function evaluation $\gamma^t$ in the sequential optimization of Equation (52). Additionally, we use a GP-UCB acquisition functional to establish upper bounds on the cumulative regret $R^T$ for sequentially optimizing the objective functional in Equation (52) with horizon $T$ when the FBO algorithm described in the following subsections is employed.

In order to describe the proposed FBO algorithm to solve Equation (52), we begin by establishing a functional Gaussian process as a surrogate function model for the objective functional in Section 4.1. For this, we set up a functional space for the incentive functions space $\Gamma$, which allows the definition of a Gaussian process kernel over this space of functions in Section 4.1.1, and in light of this, we show how to compute the posterior distribution for this functional Gaussian process in Section 4.1.2. Later, the GP-UCB acquisition functional for functional search is described in Section 4.2. Having these elements available, we present, in Section 4.3, Algorithm 1 to solve Equation (52). This algorithm is referred to as the Stackelberg Functional Causal Bayesian Optimization (FCBO) algorithm for $PAP_{L1F1}$. In Section 4.4, we show cumulative-regret bounds results in terms of differential information gain for the Stackelberg FCBO algorithm.

https://doi.org/10.3390/e2801000

**Algorithm 1:** Stackelberg FCBO for single-stage $PAP_{L1F1}$

**Input** : $\mathcal{D}^{-1} = \{(\gamma^i, \omega_F^i, \omega_L^i, J_L^i)\}_{i=1}^N$; the $\mathcal{H}_k$ specification; the horizon $T$; the functional GP kernel $K$ on $\Gamma \subset \mathcal{H}_k$; the exploration schedule $\{\beta_t\}_{t=1}^T$; and the CGM $\mathcal{M}_{L1F1}$ for a $PAP_{L1F1}$ from the principal's perspective.

**Output:** $\mathcal{D}^T = \{(\gamma^t, \mathbb{E}^{\gamma^t}[J_L^t])\}_{t \in [T]}$, with $\gamma^t \in \mathcal{H}_k^d$ or $\gamma^t \in \mathcal{H}_k$

.<br>
Initialize functional GP $\mathcal{GP}(\mu^0(\gamma), K^0(\gamma, \gamma'))$ ;<br>
**for** $t = 1, \ldots, T$ **do**<br>
    Select $\gamma^t \in \arg\max_{\gamma \in \mathcal{H}_k} \mu^t(\gamma) + \beta^t \sigma^t(\gamma)$ (see Section 4.2);<br>
    Estimate $\mathbb{E}^{\gamma^t}[J_L]$ as $\widehat{V}(\gamma^t) = \widehat{\mathbb{E}}\left[J_L \mid do(\Gamma = \gamma^t)\right]$ (see Section 3.3);<br>
    Set $\mathcal{D}^t \leftarrow \mathcal{D}^{t-1} \cup \{(\gamma^t, \mathbb{E}^{\gamma^t}[J_L^t])\}$;<br>
    Update functional GP $\mathcal{GP}(\mu^t(\gamma), K^t(\gamma, \gamma'); \mathcal{D}^t)$ (see Equation (55));<br>
**end**<br>
**return** $\mathcal{D}^T = \{(\gamma^t, \mathbb{E}^{\gamma^t}[J_L^t])\}_{t \in [T]}$;

### 4.1. Functional Gaussian Process Surrogate Model

We employ a Reproducing Kernel Hilbert Space (RKHS) as a space of functions for the domain of the objective functional $\mathbb{E}^{\gamma^t}[J_L]$: $\Gamma \rightarrow \mathbb{R}$ in Equation (52). Taking $\Gamma$ as $\mathcal{H}_k$, that is, $\mathbb{E}^{\gamma^t}[J_L]$: $\mathcal{H}_k \rightarrow \mathbb{R}$, where $\mathcal{H}_k$ is an RKHS with reproducing kernel $k$: $\mathbf{X} \times \mathbf{X} \rightarrow \mathbb{R}$ and $\mathbf{X} \subseteq \mathbb{R}$ (see Appendix B), allows us to directly define a Gaussian process kernel over functions in $\mathcal{H}_k$ (see Section 4.1.1). In each round $t$, an incentive function $\gamma^t \in \mathcal{H}_k$ is selected by means of a GP-UCB acquisition functional (see Section 4.2) and a noisy evaluation $\mathbb{E}^{\gamma^t}[J_L]$ is returned.

We use a Gaussian process (GP) as a surrogate model for the objective functional $\mathbb{E}^{\gamma^t}[J_L]$: $\mathcal{H}_k \rightarrow \mathbb{R}$. We assume specifically that the input function space is an RKHS $\mathcal{H}_k$, which allows us to define a GP kernel over functions in a RKHS function space in Section 4.1.1. Therefore, the GP we use for this objective functional with domain $\mathcal{H}_k$ is given as a stochastic process $F_\gamma = \{f(\gamma) \mid \gamma \in \mathcal{H}_k\}$, in which every finite collection of random variables $f(\gamma)$ has a multivariate normal distribution. So, we use this GP $F_\gamma = \{f(\gamma) \mid \gamma \in \mathcal{H}_k\}$, with $F_\gamma \sim \mathcal{GP}(\mu(\gamma), K(\gamma, \gamma'))$ as a surrogate model for $\mathbb{E}^{\gamma^t}[J_L]$. Next, based on [6], we formulate a GP kernel $K(\gamma, \gamma') = cov[f(\gamma), f(\gamma')]$ with $\gamma, \gamma' \in \mathcal{H}_k$. See [4] for GP fundamentals and [6,25] for functional BO surrogates.

#### 4.1.1. Functional Gaussian Process Kernel

Based on the RKHS $\mathcal{H}_k$ kernel $k$, the GP kernel $K(\gamma, \gamma') = cov[f(\gamma), f(\gamma')]$ can be constructed. We focus here on the construction of a functional version of the standard Radial Basis Function (RBF) kernel, which we assume in the regret analysis of this functional Bayesian framework.

The functional RBF can be stated as in Equation (53), where $\|\cdot\|_{\mathcal{H}_k}$ is the norm in the RKHS $\mathcal{H}_k$, so $\|\gamma, \gamma'\|_{\mathcal{H}_k}^2$ is the squared distance between the functions $\gamma, \gamma' \in \mathcal{H}_k$, which can be calculated as the internal product $\langle \gamma - \gamma', \gamma - \gamma' \rangle_{\mathcal{H}_k}$ in the RKHS $\mathcal{H}_k$.

$$K(\gamma, \gamma') = \exp\Big(-\frac{\|\gamma, \gamma'\|_{\mathcal{H}_k}^2}{2\sigma^2}\Big). \tag{53}$$

Thus, the squared distance $\|\gamma, \gamma'\|_{\mathcal{H}_k}^2$ in a functional RBF between two incentive functions $\gamma$ and $\gamma'$ is given by Equation (54), with $v_i, v_j, \xi_i, \xi_j \in \mathbb{R}$, $n, m \in \mathbb{N}$, $x_i, x_j, x_i', x_j' \in \mathbf{X}$.

https://doi.org/10.3390/e28010004

$$\langle \gamma - \gamma', \gamma - \gamma' \rangle_{\mathcal{H}_k} = \sum_{i \in [n]} \sum_{j \in [n]} v_i v_j k(x_i, x_j) - 2 \sum_{i \in [n]} \sum_{j \in [m]} v_i \xi_j k(x_i, x'_j) + \sum_{i \in [m]} \sum_{j \in [m]} \xi_i \xi_j k(x'_i, x'_j). \quad (54)$$

We reserve lower-case $k(x, x')$ for the reproducing kernel of the input RKHS $\mathcal{H}_k$ over $X$, and upper-case $K(\gamma, \gamma')$ for the Gaussian-process kernel over incentive functions $\Gamma = \mathcal{H}_k$. Thus, $k$ appears only inside $\| \cdot \|_{\mathcal{H}_k}$ and expansions like Equation (54), while $K$ and its posterior $K^t$ govern GP means, covariances, and Gram matrices.

#### 4.1.2. Functional Gaussian Process Posterior Distribution

After building the functional RBF kernel primarily by finding out how to measure the distance between the elements $\gamma$ of the function space $\mathcal{H}_k$, the posterior distribution of the functional GP $F_\gamma \sim \mathcal{GP}(\mu(\cdot), K(\cdot, \cdot))$ may be updated in a way very similar to a scalar GP. The posterior distribution is again a GP $F_\gamma \sim \mathcal{GP}(\mu(\cdot), K(\cdot, \cdot))$, with functional mean $\mu^t(\cdot)$ and covariance kernel $K^t(\cdot, \cdot)$ given as follows:

$$\begin{aligned} \mu^t(\gamma) =& \mathbf{k}^t(\gamma)^\top (G^t + \sigma^2 I)^{-1} \mathbf{y}^t, \\ K^t(\gamma, \gamma') =& K(\gamma, \gamma') - \mathbf{k}^t(\gamma)^\top (G^t + \sigma^2 I)^{-1} \mathbf{k}^t(\gamma'), \end{aligned} \quad (55)$$

where $\mathbf{k}^t(\gamma) = [K(\gamma, \gamma^1), K(\gamma, \gamma^2), \ldots, K(\gamma, \gamma^t)]^\top$, $G^t$ is the $t \times t$ Gram matrix with entries $G_t[i, j] = K(\gamma_i, \gamma_j)$, for $i, j \in [t]$ (see Appendix B), and $\mathbf{y}^t = [y^1, \ldots, y^t]^\top$ is the vector of estimations $y^1 = \mathbb{E}^{\gamma^1}[J_L], \ldots, y^t = \mathbb{E}^{\gamma^t}[J_L]$.

### 4.2. *Upper Confidence Bound Acquisition Functional*

The functional version of the GP-UCB acquisition function (see Appendix C.2, Equation (A20)) is given in Equation (56):

$$\alpha_{\text{fGP-UCB}}(\gamma; \mathcal{D}, \beta^t) = \mu^t(\gamma) + \beta^t \sigma^t(\gamma), \quad (56)$$

where $\sigma^t(\gamma) = \sqrt{K^t(\gamma, \gamma)}$ (see Equation (55)). This acquisition functional can be interpreted as the strategy to choose an incentive function as follows:

$$\gamma^{t+1} = \arg\max_{\gamma \in \mathcal{H}_k} \mu^t(\gamma) + \beta^t \sigma^t(\gamma), \quad (57)$$

which if we remove the second term $\beta^t \sigma^t(\gamma)$ and optimize just for $\mu^t(\gamma)$, i.e., maximizing the expected reward based on the posterior distribution so far, this rule would be too greedy too soon and would lead to getting stuck in shallow local optima. Instead, the full objective $\mu^t(\gamma) + \beta^t \sigma^t(\gamma)$ in Equation (57) prefers both incentive functions $\gamma$ where $f(\gamma)$ is uncertain, that is, with large $\sigma^t(\gamma)$, and where we expect to achieve high rewards, i.e., with large $\mu^t(\gamma)$. Thus, it implicitly deals with the trade-off between exploration and exploitation. An interpretation of this intervention rule is that it greedily selects the intervention functions $\gamma$ such that $f(\gamma)$ should be a reasonable upper bound on $f(\gamma^*)$, where $\gamma^*$ is the optimal incentive function (see Appendix C.2; this follows the GP-UCB principle [7]). The UCB term $\beta_t^{1/2} \sigma^{t-1}(\gamma)$ promotes policies with high expected information gain about the functional value. As shown in the regret analysis in Section 4.4, this connects the functional acquisition directly to *mutual-information* control. Our analysis offers theoretical guidance for acquisition, specifically through trust-region methods using ESS and weight caps. Empirical tuning and benchmarking are intentionally deferred to a companion, application-driven study.



https://doi.org/10.3390/e28010004

### 4.3. The Stackelberg FCBO Algorithm for Single-Stage Canonical PAPs

We present a Functional Causal Bayesian Optimization (FCBO) algorithm for the single-stage $PAP_{L1F1}$ by integrating all components of Sections 4.1 and 4.2. We refer to this algorithm, shown in Algorithm 1, as the Stackelberg FCBO algorithm for the single-stage $PAP_{L1F1}$. Recall that Algorithm 1 addresses the optimization problem of Equation (52).

Algorithm 1 gets as input a data set of past observations of the system, $\mathcal{D}^{-1} = \{(\gamma^i, \omega_F^i, \omega_L^i, J_L^i)\}_{i=1}^N$; the specification of the incentive function space given as an RKHS $\mathcal{H}_k$, where $\gamma^t \in \mathcal{H}_k^d$ (finite function space) or $\gamma^t \in \mathcal{H}_k$ (infinite function space); the number of rounds $T$ contemplated in the sequential optimization; the kernel $K$ of the functional GP; the exploration schedule $\{\beta_t\}_{t=1}^T$; and the CGM $\mathcal{M}_{L1F1}$ for a $PAP_{L1F1}$ from the principal's perspective. The functional space $\mathcal{H}_k$ can be specified by stating the reproducing kernel $k$ of the RKHS $\mathcal{H}_k$ (see Appendix B). In addition, the functional GP kernel $K$ over $\Gamma \subset \mathcal{H}_k$ must be specified (by default, we can use the functional RBF kernel of Equation (53)). In Algorithm 1, we use a time-indexed exploration coefficient $\beta^t$ to match the high-probability guarantees in Section 4.4. For these results, we instantiate

$$\beta^t = 2\log\left(\frac{t^2\pi^2|\Gamma|}{6\,\delta}\right),$$

so, the acquisition is $\mu^t(\gamma) + \beta^t\sigma^t(\gamma)$. In practice, one may instead tune a constant confidence level $\rho$ and set $\beta = \Phi^{-1}(\rho)$ (where $\Phi^{-1}$ is the quantile function, i.e., the inverse cumulative distribution function (CDF); see Appendix C.2). This is equivalent to using a constant exploration coefficient $\beta^t \equiv \beta$. Our regret bounds in Section 4.4 hold whenever the run uses the exploration schedule $\{\beta^t\}_{t=1}^T$ as $\beta^t = 2\log(\frac{t^2\pi^2|\Gamma|}{6\delta})$ or any schedule that dominates it pointwise. We can set the exploration schedule in this way for default in Algorithm 1.

The $\mathcal{M}_{L1F1}$ from the principal's perspective have the induced DAG, from the set of observable variables $\mathbf{O}_L = \{\Gamma, \Omega_L, \Omega_F, J_L\}$, with arrows $\Gamma \to \Omega_L$, $\Gamma \to \Omega_F$, $\Omega_F \to \Omega_L$, $\Omega_L \to J_L$ and $\Omega_F \to J_L$, as causal structure. Additionally, the follower utility $J_F$ is an unobservable or hidden variable, and the follower mechanism $f_{\Omega_F}(\gamma, U_{\Omega_F})$ is a black box function. Algorithm 1 returns the accumulated history data set $\mathcal{D}^T$ after $T$ rounds in the sequential optimization:

$$\mathcal{D}^T = \left\{(\gamma^1, \mathbb{E}^{\gamma^1}[J_L]), \ldots, (\gamma^T, \mathbb{E}^{\gamma^T}[J_L])\right\}. \tag{58}$$

Modeling $f(\gamma)$ as a sample from $F_\gamma = \{f(\gamma) \mid \gamma \in \mathcal{H}_k\}$ with $F_\gamma \sim \mathcal{GP}(\mu(\gamma), K(\gamma, \gamma'))$, as a surrogate model for the objective functional $\mathbb{E}^{\gamma^t}[J_L]$: $\mathcal{H}_k \to \mathbb{R}$ (see Section 4.1). We completely specified this GP by its mean functional $\mu(\gamma) = \mathbb{E}[f(\gamma)]$ and kernel functional $K(\gamma, \gamma') = \mathbb{E}\big[(f(\gamma) - \mu(\gamma))(f(\gamma') - \mu(\gamma'))\big]$. We assume, without loss of generality (see [4]), a GP with mean function zero, i.e., $\mu \equiv 0$, as prior distribution over $F_\gamma$. So, we initialize the functional GP in line 2 with $\mu^0(\gamma)$ as the zero function and $K^0(\gamma, \gamma')$ as the functional RBF in Equation (53), to begin the inductive process of Algorithm 1.

From Line 3 to Line 8, the sequential optimization is performed, going through $T$ rounds. The decision on the incentive function $\gamma^t$ is made employing the GP-UCB acquisition functional (see Section 4.2) as a policy $\pi^t$: $\mathcal{D}^{t-1} \to \gamma^t$. The expected value of $J_L$ on the post-intervention distribution $p(J_L \mid do(\Gamma = \gamma^t))$ is estimated by computing $\widehat{V}(\gamma^t) = \widehat{\mathbb{E}}\Big[J_L \mid do(\Gamma = \gamma^t)\Big]$, using the techniques developed in Section 3.3. The estimation of $\mathbb{E}^{\gamma^t}[J_L]$, is the approach by which Algorithm 1 gets information about the objective functional of Equation (52) to guide the search for $\gamma^*$. To complete a round $t$ in the sequential optimization process outlined in Algorithm 1, first the data set $\mathcal{D}^t$ is updated

https://doi.org/10.3390/e28010004

in Line 6 by adding the new observation pair $(\gamma^t, \mathbb{E}^{\gamma^t}[J_L])$. Then, in Line 7, the surrogate functional, i.e., the functional GP $\mathcal{GP}$, for the objective functional of the optimization problem in Equation (52), is updated using $\mathcal{D}^t$. Figure 2 complements Algorithm 1 with a flow-chart of one FCBO round. The support-aware GP-UCB step and the two-layer estimator are highlighted as novel elements.

Once the $T$ rounds are completed, Algorithm 1 returns $\mathcal{D}^T$. Observe that, despite the fact that the algorithm returns the cumulative history data set in Equation (58), it implicitly addresses the optimization problem of Equation (52), since the following holds for large $T$:

$$\gamma^* \approx \gamma^+ \in \underset{(\gamma^t, \mathbb{E}^{\gamma^t}[J_L]) \in \mathcal{D}^T}{\arg\max} \left\{ \mathbb{E}^{\gamma^1}[J_L], \ldots, \mathbb{E}^{\gamma^T}[J_L] \right\}. \tag{59}$$

That is, due to the convergence result in Section 4.4 for Algorithm 1, we maintain the best incentive function $\gamma^+$ from $(\gamma^+, \mathbb{E}^{\gamma^+}[J_L]) \in \mathcal{D}^T$ to solve Equation (52), as $\gamma^+$ approximates the optimum $\gamma^*$ of the functional optimization problem in Equation (52). Furthermore, we can bound the expected cumulative regret $\mathbb{E}[R^T_{\mathcal{D}T}]$ using Algorithm 1 to address the singe stage canonical $PAP_{L1F1}$. This result is presented in the following subsection.

### 4.4. Information-Theoretic Regret Bounds on the Stackelberg FCBO Algorithm

The cumulative-regret bounds for Algorithm 1 are derived by adapting the regret bounds results in terms of differential information gain (see Section 4.4.1) from [7] to our problem setting. In our setting, each observation $y_t = \widehat{V}(\gamma_t)$ aggregates information about an interventional query $V(\gamma_t)$ on the underlying CGM. The resulting regret bounds therefore quantify how quickly an information-guided sequence of interventions $do(\Gamma = \gamma_t)$ converges, in policy value, to the best available intervention in the considered class. First, in Section 4.4.2, we deal with the setting in which the set of admissible incentive functions $\Gamma$ is finite. Specifically, we assume that $\Gamma$ is represented as the finite RKHS $\mathcal{H}^d_k$ provided in Appendix B, so $|\Gamma| = d \in \mathbb{N}$. Then, we show how to extend the results for the finite case from Section 4.4.2 to the general case where $\Gamma$ is an infinite RKHS $\mathcal{H}_k$ in Section 4.4.3.

Recall from Section 4.1 that the objective functional in Equation (52) is viewed as a sample path $f$ of the functional GP $F_\gamma = \{f(\gamma) \mid \gamma \in \mathcal{H}_k\}$ with $F_\gamma \sim \mathcal{GP}(\mu(\gamma), K(\gamma, \gamma'))$. Algorithm 1 uses a centered GP $\mathcal{GP}(\mu \equiv 0, K(\gamma, \gamma'))$ as a prior distribution $\mathcal{GP}(\mu^0(\gamma), K^0(\gamma, \gamma'))$ over $F_\gamma$. So, we are assuming a priori that the objective functional in Equation (52) is a sample path $f$ from a centered GP $\mathcal{GP}(\mu \equiv 0, K(\gamma, \gamma'))$. The initialization of the functional GP in Algorithm 1 also specified $K^0(\gamma, \gamma')$ as the functional RBF in Equation (53). However, following the analysis in [7], we do not assume a specific functional kernel.

At round $t$, the observation is $y_t = \widehat{V}(\gamma_t)$ with estimation error $\varepsilon_t: = y_t - V(\gamma_t)$. We assume that $\{\varepsilon_t\}_{t \geq 1}$ forms a conditionally *sub-Gaussian martingale-difference* sequence with respect to the algorithm's filtration $\{\mathcal{F}_t\}$, i.e., $\mathbb{E}[\varepsilon_t \mid \mathcal{F}_{t-1}] = 0$ and $\mathbb{E}[\exp(\lambda \varepsilon_t) \mid \mathcal{F}_{t-1}] \leq \exp(\lambda^2 R^2/2)$ for all $\lambda \in \mathbb{R}$ and some envelope $R > 0$ (cf. kernelized bandit analyses with conditionally sub-Gaussian noise [8]). The variance may depend on $\gamma_t$ (heteroskedasticity). For the analysis, we further assume a uniform bound $\mathrm{Var}(\varepsilon_t \mid \mathcal{F}_{t-1}) \leq \sigma^2_*$ on the support set where the Stackelberg FCBO algorithm proposes candidates. Under this *uniform envelope*, the standard GP-UCB high-probability confidence sets and regret bounds apply, with $\sigma^2_*$ entering the information-gain and $\beta_t$ expressions (Section 4.4.1).

#### 4.4.1. Differential Information Gain

A primary concern in the regret analysis of Algorithm 1 is to measure the efficiency with which $\tau$ noisy observations $\mathcal{D}^\tau = \{(\gamma^1, \mathbb{E}^{\gamma^1}[J_L]), \ldots, (\gamma^\tau, \mathbb{E}^{\gamma^\tau}[J_L])\}$, and acquire

https://doi.org/10.3390/e2801000

knowledge about the objective functional $\mathbb{E}\left[J_L \mid do(\Gamma = \gamma^t)\right]$ in Equation (52). This learning process becomes apparent through the improvement of the GP surrogate model $\mathcal{GP}(\mu(\gamma), K(\gamma, \gamma'))$ for $\mathbb{E}\left[J_L \mid do(\Gamma = \gamma^t)\right]$, after the observation process in which the Algorithm 1 decides on $\gamma_t$, by the GP-UCB acquisition functional policy $\pi^t$: $\mathcal{D}^{t-1} \to \gamma^t$, and then, after the follower response $\omega_F$, computes $\widehat{V}(\gamma^t) = \widehat{\mathbb{E}}\left[J_L \mid do(\Gamma = \gamma^t)\right]$ to obtain the observed pair $\left(\gamma^t, \mathbb{E}^{\gamma^t}[J_L]\right)$. The informativeness of this observation process, as a function of the number of observations $\tau$, provides a way to bound the ability to learn about the objective functional $\mathbb{E}\left[J_L \mid do(\Gamma = \gamma^t)\right]$.

Here, we use the notation $\hat{\mathbb{E}}^{\gamma^t}[J_L] = \mathbb{E}^{\gamma^t}[J_L] + \epsilon^t$, to explicitly distinguish between the assumed noisy observations $\hat{\mathbb{E}}^{\gamma^t}[J_L]$ and exact observations $\mathbb{E}^{\gamma^t}[J_L]$ on the objective functional $\mathbb{E}\left[J_L \mid do(\Gamma = \gamma^t)\right]$. The information capacity of an arbitrary set of sampling points $\Gamma^\tau = \{\gamma^1, \ldots, \gamma^\tau\} \subset \Gamma$ regarding the objective functional $\mathbb{E}\left[J_L \mid do(\Gamma = \gamma^t)\right]$ can be measured by the mutual information $I^\tau$, also known as information gain, between $\mathbf{f}^\tau = \{\mathbb{E}^{\gamma^1}[J_L], \ldots, \mathbb{E}^{\gamma^\tau}[J_L^\tau]\}$ and the noisy observations $\mathbf{y}^\tau = \{\hat{\mathbb{E}}^{\gamma^1}[J_L], \ldots, \hat{\mathbb{E}}^{\gamma^\tau}[J_L]\}$ at these points. That is, measuring the reduction in uncertainty over $\mathbb{E}\left[J_L \mid do(\Gamma = \gamma^t)\right]$ resulting from the disclosure of $\mathbf{y}^\tau$, which is calculated as in Equation (60).

$$\begin{aligned} I^\tau(\mathbf{f}^\tau; \mathbf{y}^\tau) &= H(\mathbf{f}^\tau) - H(\mathbf{f}^\tau \mid \mathbf{y}^\tau) \\ &= H(\mathbf{y}^\tau) - H(\mathbf{y}^\tau \mid \mathbf{f}^\tau) = I^\tau(\mathbf{y}^\tau; \mathbf{f}^\tau), \end{aligned} \tag{60}$$

as mutual information is symmetric, and where $H(\mathbf{f}^\tau)$ denotes the differential entropy of $\mathbf{f}^\tau$ and $H(\mathbf{y}^\tau \mid \mathbf{f}^\tau)$ denotes the conditional differential entropy of $\mathbf{y}^\tau$ given $\mathbf{f}^\tau$. The differential entropy of a set of multivariate Gaussian distributed random variables is calculated as $H(X_1, \ldots, X_n) = H(\mathcal{N}_n(\boldsymbol{\mu}, K)) = \frac{1}{2}\log[(2\pi e)^n |K|]$, where $|K|$ denotes the determinant of the covariance matrix $K$ (see [28]). Thus, we can write its covariance as $K^\tau + \sigma^2 I$, that is, separating the additive noise into a diagonal matrix $\sigma^2 I$, where $K^\tau = \left[K(\hat{\mathbb{E}}^\gamma[J_L], \hat{\mathbb{E}}^{\gamma'}[J_L]\right.$ for every $\hat{\mathbb{E}}^\gamma[J_L], \hat{\mathbb{E}}^{\gamma'}[J_L] \in \mathbf{y}^\tau$. Then, we can compute $H(\mathbf{y}^\tau)$ as follows:

$$H(\mathbf{y}^\tau) = \frac{1}{2}\log[(2\pi e)^\tau |K^\tau + \sigma^2 I|]. \tag{61}$$

To compute $H(\mathbf{y}^\tau \mid \mathbf{f}^\tau)$, observe that given $\mathbf{f}^\tau$, the only randomness left is the noise, which has covariance $\sigma^2 I$, so

$$H(\mathbf{y}^\tau \mid \mathbf{f}^\tau) = \frac{1}{2}\log[(2\pi e)^\tau |\sigma^2 I|] = \frac{1}{2}\log[(2\pi e)^\tau \sigma^{2\tau}]. \tag{62}$$

Putting all together, the information gain $I^\tau(\mathbf{f}^\tau; \mathbf{y}^\tau)$ is given by $\frac{1}{2}\log\left[|I + K^\tau \sigma^{-2}|\right]$ as shown next in Equation (63):

$$\begin{aligned} I^\tau(\mathbf{f}^\tau; \mathbf{y}^\tau) &= H(\mathbf{y}^\tau) - H(\mathbf{y}^\tau \mid \mathbf{f}^\tau) \\ &= \frac{1}{2}\log[(2\pi e)^\tau |K^\tau + \sigma^2 I|] - \frac{1}{2}\log[(2\pi e)^\tau |\sigma^2 I|] \\ &= \frac{1}{2}\log\left[\frac{|K^\tau + \sigma^2 I|}{|\sigma^2 I|}\right] = \frac{1}{2}\log\left[|I + K^\tau \sigma^{-2}|\right] \end{aligned} \tag{63}$$

$$I(\mathbf{f}_t; \mathbf{y}_t) = H(\mathbf{y}_t) - H(\mathbf{y}_t \mid \mathbf{f}_t) = \frac{1}{2}\log\left|\mathbf{I} + \sigma^{-2}\mathbf{K}_t\right|$$

In our setting, we define the maximum information gain $\mathcal{I}^T$ after $T$ rounds as

$$\mathcal{I}^T = \frac{1}{2}\log\left|\mathbf{I} + \Sigma_T^{-1}\mathbf{G}^T\right|, \qquad \Sigma_T := \mathrm{diag}(\sigma_1^2, \ldots, \sigma_T^2), \tag{64}$$

https://doi.org/10.3390/e28010004

where $\mathbf{I}$ is the identity matrix and $\mathbf{G}^T$ is the covariance matrix. For notational simplicity in the stated bounds we adopt the conservative specialization $\Sigma_T \preceq \sigma_*^2 \mathbf{I}$, which yields $I_T \leq \frac{1}{2} \log |\mathbf{I} + \sigma_*^{-2} G_T|$ and recovers the expressions in our regret constants.

After presenting the concept of mutual information on differential entropy to assess the informativeness with respect to the objective functional $\mathbb{E}[J_L \mid do(\Gamma = \gamma^t)]$ of a noisy set of observations $\mathbf{y}^\tau = \{\hat{\mathbb{E}}^{\gamma^1}[J_L], \ldots, \hat{\mathbb{E}}^{\gamma^\tau}[J_L]\}$ at a certain set of sampling points $\Gamma^\tau = \{\gamma^1, \ldots, \gamma^\tau\} \subset \Gamma$. We are now able to present the regret analysis for Algorithm 1 in terms of information gain $\mathcal{I}^\tau(\mathbf{f}^\tau; \mathbf{y}^\tau)$.

4.4.2. Regret Bound for a Finite Incentive Function Space

The cumulative regret in a sequential optimization process is the loss in reward resulting from the inability to predict the points that maximize the objective function, in advance. For Algorithm 1, this is the error between the decided incentive functions $\gamma^1, \ldots, \gamma^T$ and those that maximize the objective functional $\mathbb{E}[J_L \mid do(\Gamma = \gamma)]$. That is, letting $\gamma^* \in \arg\max_{\gamma^t \in \Gamma} f(\gamma)$, with $f(\gamma) = \mathbb{E}[J_L \mid do(\Gamma = \gamma^t)]$, for a incentive function choice $\gamma^t$ in round $t$, we incur instantaneous regret $r^t = f(\gamma^*) - f(\gamma^t)$, and the cumulative regret $R_T$ is defined as $R^T = \sum_{t=1}^T r^t$.

Theorem 1 establishes a probabilistic bound for the cumulative regret of Algorithm 1, ensuring its convergence and efficiency with high probability. Considering a confidence bound $\delta \in (0, 1)$, the result of Theorem 1 is that the cumulative regret $R^T$ of Algorithm 1 is bound by the square root of a linear expression of the information gain $\mathcal{I}^T(\mathbf{f}^T; \mathbf{y}^T)$, with probability of at least $1 - \delta$. Recall from previous Section 4.4.1 that information gain $\mathcal{I}^T(\mathbf{f}^T; \mathbf{y}^T)$ is a measure of the reduction in uncertainty over the objective functional, resulting from the disclosure of observations $\mathbf{y}^T = \{\hat{\mathbb{E}}^{\gamma^1}[J_L], \ldots, \hat{\mathbb{E}}^{\gamma^T}[J_L]\}$, generated by the decision of the incentive function, i.e., sampling points, $\Gamma^\tau = \{\gamma^1, \ldots, \gamma^\tau\} \subset \Gamma$. The linear expression for the information gain in the specified upper bound includes the low coefficients $\beta^T$ and $C_1$. The coefficient $\beta^t$ is the exploration coefficient in the acquisition functional (see Section 4.2) on the strategy to choose the next incentive function in Equation (57), which for the purpose of the bound we use $\beta^t = 2\log(\frac{t^2\pi^2|\Gamma|}{6\delta})$, for all $t \in [T]$. This choice reconciles the exploration coefficient used in Algorithm 1 with the regret analysis: any implementation that uses $\beta^t$ above (or a pointwise larger schedule) satisfies the bound of Theorem 1. For the auxiliary coefficient $C_1$, we use $C_1 = \frac{4\sigma^2}{\log(1+\sigma^{-2})}$. Theorem 1 given below assumes the finite functional space $\mathcal{H}_k^d$, which was established in the Appendix B, as the finite set of allowed incentive functions, i.e., $\Gamma = \mathcal{H}_k^d$ so $|\Gamma| = d$ for some $d \in \mathbb{N}$. Recall from Section 4.1 that the objective functional in Equation (52) is viewed as a sample path $f$ of the functional GP $F_\gamma = \{f(\gamma) \mid \gamma \in \mathcal{H}_k\}$ with $F_\gamma \sim \mathcal{GP}(\mu(\gamma), K(\gamma, \gamma'))$. Assume further that the observation errors $\{\varepsilon_t\}$ are conditionally $R$-sub-Gaussian and form a martingale-difference sequence with a uniform variance envelope $\mathrm{Var}(\varepsilon_t \mid \mathcal{F}_{t-1}) \leq \sigma_*^2$ over the proposal support.

**Theorem 1.** *Let $\delta \in (0,1)$ and assume that $\Gamma$ is finite, with $\Gamma = \mathcal{H}_k^d$ for some $d \in \mathbb{N}$. Running Algorithm 1 using $\beta^t = 2\log(\frac{t^2\pi^2|\Gamma|}{6\delta})$ for a sample path $f(\gamma) = \mathbb{E}[J_L \mid do(\Gamma = \gamma)]$ of a functional GP $F_\gamma = \{f(\gamma) \mid \gamma \in \mathcal{H}_k^d\} \sim \mathcal{GP}(\mu(\gamma), K(\gamma, \gamma'))$ with mean function $\mu^t(\gamma^t) = 0$ and covariance function $K^t(\gamma, \gamma')$, we get a cumulative-regret bound of $\mathcal{O}^* \sqrt{T\mathcal{I}^\tau(\mathbf{f}^\tau; \mathbf{y}^\tau) \log |\Gamma|}$ with high probability. Specifically,*

$$\Pr\left\{ R_{DT}^T \leq \sqrt{C_1 T \beta^T \mathcal{I}^T(\mathbf{f}^T; \mathbf{y}^T)} \right\} \geq 1 - \delta,$$

*for all $T \geq 1$, where $C_1 = \frac{4\sigma^2}{\log(1+\sigma^{-2})}$.*

https://doi.org/10.3390/e28010004

The proof of Theorem 1 is provided in Appendix A by demonstrating a series of partial results given as Propositions A1–A4.

4.4.3. Regret Bound on an Infinite Incentive Function Space

The regret bound of Theorem 1 is established under the assumption that the set of admissible incentive functions $\Gamma$ is finite, specifically $\Gamma = \mathcal{H}_k^d$. In practice, however, the Stackelberg FCBO algorithm can operate over a continuous, potentially infinite-dimensional admissible set of incentive functions $\Gamma \subset \mathcal{H}_k$, where $H_k$ is a bounded RKHS. In this subsection, we extend the cumulative-regret analysis of the Stackelberg FCBO algorithm to an infinite admissible space of incentive functions $\Gamma \subset \mathcal{H}_k$ where $\mathcal{H}_k$ is a bounded separable RKHS. This corresponds to the setting where incentive functions $\gamma^t \in \Gamma = \mathcal{H}_k$ are sampled and optimized over a non-parametric space of continuous functions. In accordance with the infinite domain analysis in [7], we assume that the functional $f(\gamma)$, with $f(\gamma) = \mathbb{E}[J_L \mid do(\Gamma = \gamma)]$ is Lipschitz continuous and is a member of the RKHS that is induced by the functional kernel.

Applying the regret bounds of Theorem 1 to a finite subset of $H_k$ obtained by discretizing $H_k$ does not ensure that the regret bound is applicable to the original continuous infinite domain $H_k$. The issue is that the objective functional $f\colon H_k \to \mathbb{R}$, even if continuous, may not be well approximated on all of the function space $H_k$ by its restriction to a finite set, and this would only control regret over the discretized surrogate problem, not the full functional optimization problem:

$$\gamma^* \in \arg\max_{\gamma^t \in \Gamma \subset \mathcal{H}_k} \mathbb{E}\Big[J_L \mid do(\Gamma = \gamma^t)\Big].$$

Furthermore, regret is accumulated over the true sequence of evaluations, which may lie outside any fixed discretization. So, to rigorously lift the regret guarantees from a finite discretization to the full RKHS domain $H_k$, we require uniform approximation of both (i) the infinite set of admissible incentive functions and (ii) the objective functional $f\colon H_k \to \mathbb{R}$ itself. Therefore, the key step is to approximate the infinite-dimensional domain $H_k$ and the functional $f(\gamma)$ in a way that allows the application of the previously developed finite-set regret analysis from Theorem 1.

In order to overcome this, we approximate the infinite function space by constructing a finite-dimensional subspace by means of two applications of the Stone–Weierstrass theorem (see Appendix D). In the first application, the objective functional $f\colon \Gamma \to \mathbb{R}$, with $\Gamma \subset \mathcal{H}_k$ compact, is uniformly approximated on $\Gamma$ by finite linear combinations of kernel sections $K(\cdot, \gamma_i)$ associated with a carefully chosen finite set of basis incentive functions $\{\gamma_1, \ldots, \gamma_d\} \subset \mathcal{H}_k$. As a consequence, for every $\varepsilon_1 > 0$, there exists such a finite set and coefficients $\alpha_1, \ldots, \alpha_d \in \mathbb{R}$ satisfying

$$\sup_{\gamma \in \Gamma} \left| f(\gamma) - \sum_{i=1}^{d} \alpha_i K(\gamma_i, \gamma) \right| < \varepsilon_1,$$

and the set $\{\gamma_i\}_{i=1}^d \subset \Gamma$ then acts as a basis of reference incentive functions, and the approximant $\sum_{i=1}^d \alpha_i K(\gamma_i, \gamma)$ providing a finite-dimensional parametric model for $f$. Details of this construction are given in Appendix D, where an explanation of two formal methods for selecting such basis incentive functions (one based on minimal $\varepsilon$-covers and one based on spectral decomposition of the kernel operator) is also provided in Appendix D.2.

https://doi.org/10.3390/e28010004

From the first application of the Stone–Weierstrass theorem, we obtained a finite set of basis incentive functions $\{\gamma_1, \ldots, \gamma_d\} \subset \mathcal{H}_k$ and coefficients $\{\alpha_i\}$ such that $f(\gamma)$ is uniformly approximated, to within an error $\varepsilon_1 > 0$, by

$$\sum_{i=1}^{d} \alpha_i K(\gamma_i, \gamma).$$

In the second application, each basis function $\gamma_i$ is itself uniformly approximated on the compact input domain $\Omega_F$, the input space of the follower's decision variable, by a polynomial $p_i^{(n)}$ of degree at most $n$, so that the entire approximation to $f$ is parameterized by finitely many coefficients. That is, we now apply the Stone–Weierstrass theorem a second time, but this time to each basis function $\gamma_i$ individually, treating it as a continuous scalar-valued function on the compact domain $\Omega_F$. Let $\mathcal{P}_n$ denote the algebra of real polynomials on $\Omega_F$ of degree at most $n$. The Stone–Weierstrass theorem on $\Omega_F$, compact in the Euclidean topology, ensures that $\mathcal{P}_n$ is uniformly dense in $C(\Omega_F, \mathbb{R})$. Therefore, for any $\varepsilon_2 > 0$ and for each $i \in \{1, \ldots, d\}$, there exists a polynomial $p_i^{(n)} \in \mathcal{P}_n$ such that

$$\sup_{x \in \Omega_F} \left| \gamma_i(x) - p_i^{(n)}(x) \right| < \varepsilon_2.$$

Therefore, each $\gamma_i$ can be replaced by a polynomial $p_i^{(n)}$ of degree $\leq n$ with uniform approximation error $\varepsilon_2$ on $\Omega_F$. So, the resulting functional approximation becomes

$$f(\gamma) \approx \sum_{i=1}^{d} \alpha_i K(p_i^{(n)}, \gamma),$$

where $K$ is evaluated between the polynomial surrogate $p_i^{(n)}$ and the input $\gamma$.

Replacing each $\gamma_i$ with $p_i^{(n)}$ parameterises the basis incentive functions by their polynomial coefficients. So, the full parameterisation of the approximant to $f$ now consists of (1) the $d$ coefficients $\{\alpha_i\}$ from the first approximation step, and (2) the coefficients of the $d$ polynomials $\{p_i^{(n)}\}$, each with finitely many coefficients determined by its degree $n$. This yields a finite-dimensional cross-parameter space:

$$\Theta_{d,n} = \left\{ \left( \alpha_1, \ldots, \alpha_d, \mathrm{coeffs}(p_1^{(n)}), \ldots, \mathrm{coeffs}(p_d^{(n)}) \right) \right\}$$

that fully describes the approximant to $f$. Hence, the second Stone–Weierstrass application replaces infinite-dimensional basis functions $\gamma_i \in \mathcal{H}_k$ with finite-dimensional polynomial surrogates $p_i^{(n)}$, thus turning the problem of learning $f$ over $\Gamma$ into an optimization over the finite-dimensional parameter set $\Theta_{d,n}$.

This two-step reduction maps the original optimization problem over the infinite-dimensional domain $\Gamma \subset \mathcal{H}_k$ to an optimization over a finite-dimensional parameter space, while controlling the approximation error. The uniform error $\varepsilon_2$ in approximating each $\gamma_i$ propagates to the approximation of $f$ in a way controlled by the Lipschitz constant of $f$ with respect to $\gamma$, ensuring that the total error from both applications remains bounded when $d$ and $n$ are chosen large enough. So, by Lipschitz continuity of $f$ on $\Gamma$ with respect to $\|\cdot\|_{\mathcal{H}_k}$, with constant $L > 0$, this perturbation changes the output of $f$ by at most $L\,\varepsilon_2$. Consequently, the regret bound in the infinite-dimensional case satisfies

$$R_{\mathrm{inf}}^{T} \leq R_{\mathrm{finit}}^{T} + T(\varepsilon_1 + L\,\varepsilon_2),$$

where $R_T^{\mathrm{finit}}$ is the cumulative-regret bound from the finite-basis case. By choosing the basis size $d$ and polynomial degree $n$ large enough, both $\varepsilon_1$ and $\varepsilon_2$ can be made arbitrarily

https://doi.org/10.3390/e2801000

small, so that the additive term $T(\varepsilon_1 + L\,\varepsilon_2)$ remains negligible compared to the leading $\sqrt{T}$-scale term in $R_T^{\text{inf}}$. See Theorem 2 below for explicit assumptions and a sublinear cumulative-regret guarantee in the infinite-domain setting.

This reduction method explicitly connects the choice of basis to the covering number $N(\Gamma, \|\cdot\|_{\mathcal{H}_k}, \varepsilon)$, which determines the discretization size $|\Gamma_\varepsilon|$, where $\Gamma_\varepsilon = \{\gamma_1, \ldots, \gamma_d\}$ and

$$N(\Gamma, \|\cdot\|_{\mathcal{H}_k}, \varepsilon) = \min\Big\{|\Gamma_\varepsilon| \colon \Gamma_\varepsilon \subset \Gamma \text{ is an } \varepsilon\text{-cover of } \Gamma, \text{ for } \|\cdot\|_{\mathcal{H}_k}\Big\}.$$

In the finite function space regret analysis of Theorem 1 (See Equation (A4)), the confidence parameter has the form $\beta^T = 2\log(\frac{\pi^2 T^2}{6\delta}|\Gamma|)$, which leads to following:

$$\beta^T = 2\log\left(\frac{\pi^2 T^2}{6\delta} N\Big(\Gamma, \|\cdot\|_{\mathcal{H}_k}, \varepsilon\Big)\right) \leq 2\log\left(\frac{\pi^2 T^2}{6\delta}|\Gamma_\varepsilon|\right); \tag{65}$$

as in practice, the set may come from a near-minimal cover so $d = |\Gamma_\varepsilon| \geq N(\Gamma, \|\cdot\|_{\mathcal{H}_k}, \varepsilon)$, i.e., the selected set forms a valid but not necessarily minimal $\varepsilon$-cover; typically bounded by a small factor (often at most logarithmic in $N$ for standard greedy covering procedures on compact metric spaces (See Appendix D.2). This relationship in Equation (65) shows that $\beta^T$ grows logarithmically with $T$ but also depends logarithmically on the covering number of $\Gamma$, so reducing $d$ toward the minimal covering number directly leads to a smaller $\beta_T$ and, therefore, a tighter regret bound. Nevertheless, even for a valid, but not necessarily minimal, $\varepsilon$-cover, $|\Gamma_\varepsilon|$ is constant for a fixed $\varepsilon$, so $\beta_T \in \mathcal{O}(\log T)$.

Considering all the elements mentioned above and following the same reasoning as in the proof of Theorem 1 (See Appendix A), the regret analysis for $R^T_{finit}$ can be extended to the infinite-dimensional domain $\Gamma \subset H_k$ using a discretization argument as follows. We first construct an $\epsilon_T$-cover $\Gamma_{\epsilon_T} \subset \Gamma$ in the $\mathcal{H}_k$ norm, with size $|\Gamma_{\epsilon_T}| = d_{\epsilon_T}$, so that every $\gamma \in \Gamma$ is within $\epsilon_T$ of some $\tilde{\gamma} \in \Gamma_{\epsilon_T}$. A union bound over all $\gamma \in \Gamma_{\epsilon_T}$ and all $t \leq T$ yields, with probability at least $1-\delta$, a uniform confidence interval of the form

$$|f(\gamma) - \mu^{t-1}(\gamma)| \leq \sqrt{\beta^T}\sigma^{t-1}(\gamma) + L\epsilon_T,$$

where $\beta^T = 2\log(\frac{T^2\pi^2}{6\delta}d_{\epsilon_T})$ and $L$ is the Lipschitz constant of $f$ in the $\mathcal{H}_k$ norm, $\|\cdot\|_{\mathcal{H}_k}$.

Applying this bound to both the optimal $\gamma^*$ and the chosen $\gamma^t$ in the round $t$ shows that the instantaneous regret satisfies $r^t = f(\gamma^*) - f(\gamma^t) \leq 2\sqrt{\beta^T}\sigma^{t-1}(\gamma^t) + 2L\epsilon_T$ (Proposition A2). Summing over $t = 1, \ldots, T$ and using Cauchy–Schwarz together with the information gain bound $\sum_{t=1}^T \sigma^2_{t-1}(\gamma_t) \leq C_1 I^\tau(\mathbf{f}^\tau; \mathbf{y}^\tau)$ (Proposition A3), we obtain

$$R^T_{\text{inf}} = \sum_{t=1}^T \Big[f(\gamma^*) - f(\gamma^t)\Big] \leq 2\sqrt{C_1 T\beta^T \mathcal{I}^T(\mathbf{f}^T; \mathbf{y}^T)} + 2TL\epsilon_T. \tag{66}$$

Choosing $\epsilon_T = \frac{1}{T}$ makes the additive term $2TL\epsilon_T$ a constant, which can be upper-bounded by $\frac{\pi^2}{6}$, using $\sum_{t=1}^\infty \frac{1}{t^2} = \frac{\pi^2}{6}$. The final result is the high-probability bound.

$$R^T_{\text{inf}} \leq \sqrt{C_1 T\beta^T \mathcal{I}^T(\mathbf{f}^T; \mathbf{y}^T)} + \frac{\pi^2}{6}. \tag{67}$$

**Theorem 2.** *Let $\Gamma \subset \mathcal{H}_k$ be compact in $\|\cdot\|_{\mathcal{H}_k}$, and let $K\colon \Gamma \times \Gamma \to \mathbb{R}$ be bounded and continuous. Suppose observations follow $y^t = f(\gamma^t) + \varepsilon^t$ with $\sigma$-sub-Gaussian noise $\varepsilon^t$, and $f\colon \Gamma \to \mathbb{R}$ is a sample path of the centered functional GP* GP$(0, K)$ *and is L-Lipschitz with respect to* $\|\cdot$

https://doi.org/10.3390/e28010004

$\|_{\mathcal{H}_k}$. *For analysis, fix any discretization schedule* $\{\varepsilon^t\}_{t=1}^T$ *and an* $\varepsilon^t$*-cover* $\Gamma_{\varepsilon^t} \subset \Gamma$ *with size* $N(\Gamma, \|\cdot\|_{\mathcal{H}_k}, \varepsilon^t)$. *Run Algorithm 1 with GP-UCB and the exploration schedule*

$$\beta^t = 2\log\left(\frac{\pi^2 t^2 N(\Gamma, \|\cdot\|_{\mathcal{H}_k}, \varepsilon^t)}{6\delta}\right), \qquad \delta \in (0,1).$$

*Let* $\mathcal{I}_T$ *denote the (maximum) information gain after T rounds. Then, with probability at least* $1-\delta$,

$$R_{inf}^T \leq \sqrt{C_1 T \beta^t \mathcal{I}_T} + 2L\sum_{t=1}^T \varepsilon^t, \qquad C_1 = 4\sigma^2 \log(1+\sigma^{-2}).$$

*In particular, if* $\sum_{t=1}^{\infty} \varepsilon^t < \infty$ *(e.g.,* $\varepsilon^t = c/t^2$*), then* $R_{inf}^T = \tilde{O}(\sqrt{T\mathcal{I}_T})$ *is sublinear; if moreover* $\mathcal{I}_T = o(T)$, *then* $R_{inf}^T = o(T)$.

**Proof.** Combine the finite-$|\Gamma|$ GP-UCB bound with a union bound over the $\varepsilon^t$-covers $\Gamma_{\varepsilon^t}$ to obtain uniform confidence bands on $\Gamma_{\varepsilon^t}$, which yields

$$\beta^t = 2\log(\pi^2 t^2 N(\Gamma, \|\cdot\|_{\mathcal{H}_k}, \varepsilon^t)/(6\delta)).$$

Lipschitz continuity lifts these bands from $\Gamma_{\varepsilon^t}$ to all $\Gamma$, adding $2L\varepsilon^t$ to per-round regret; summing over $t$ produces the stated bound. The two-step uniform-approximation argument (via discretization) recovers $R_{\text{inf}}^T \leq R_{\text{finit}}^T + T(\varepsilon_1 + L\varepsilon_2)$, absorbed by $\sum_t \varepsilon^t$ when the schedule is summable. □

Therefore, schedule $\beta^t$ mirrors the finite-set case with $|\Gamma|$ replaced by the covering number, and the bound extends Theorem 1 by adding a discretization penalty $2L\sum_t \varepsilon^t$. Contemplating the following assumptions for the infinite-domain analysis: (i) $f \sim \text{GP}(0, K)$ on $\Gamma$ with $K$ bounded and continuous. (ii) $f$ is $L$-Lipschitz in $\|\cdot\|_{\mathcal{H}_k}$ on $\Gamma$. (iii) Noise $\varepsilon^t$ is $\sigma$-sub-Gaussian and Algorithm 1 uses $\beta^t$ as above. (iv) $\Gamma \subset \mathcal{H}_k$ is compact and covers $\Gamma_{\varepsilon^t}$ exist with size $N(\Gamma, \|\cdot\|_{\mathcal{H}_k}, \varepsilon^t)$. (v) The information gain $\mathcal{I}_T$ is finite.

#### 4.4.4. Practical Implications of the Regret Bounds

The regret bounds for Stackelberg FCBO turn our theory into concrete guarantees for one-shot incentive design. They quantify, with high probability, how far the principal's expected utility under the selected incentive can be from that of the best admissible incentive, before deployment. This matters in practice because the single-stage PAP requires a single commitment—there is no opportunity to "learn on the fly."

The bounds certify a maximum difference in actual versus expected performance at the time of decision-making, offering an up-front measure of acceptable risk for using an incentive in important decisions (such as setting credit terms, granting subsidies, or allocating resources). Because the bound scales with differential information gain—that is, the knowledge added by each experiment—each offline evaluation reflects its informational value. This allows practitioners to prioritize experiments that reduce uncertainty the most, rather than running large, costly test batteries.

The bounds yield practical stopping rules. For example, stop when the acquisition-driven Upper Confidence Bound (a statistical estimate indicating the highest likely value) on the best candidate falls below a target gap (such as a minimum acceptable return on investment, ROI, or a maximum loss threshold). It also helps determine how many offline evaluations are needed to reach a desired near-optimality level, meaning how close the chosen candidate is to the optimal option.

In summary, the regret bounds provide actionable guarantees for offline policy selection: they quantify residual risk, guide the allocation of evaluation effort, and ensure



https://doi.org/10.3390/e28010004

that the final one-shot incentive is provably close to optimal under the given causal model and data.

*4.5. On Extending CID to Multi-Follower Single-Stage Principal–Agent Problems*

This subsection addresses the extension of the CID framework for single-stage principal–agent problems (SS–PAPs) to account for multiple followers. We illustrate this extension by presenting two contrasting CGMs for the base case of a PAP consisting of one principal and two followers. We use the notation $\mathcal{M}_{L_v^m F_u^n}$, where the superscripts $m$, $n$ represent the number of principal agents and follower agents in the CGM, respectively (we omit the superscript when it is equal to one, as in the canonical CGM $\mathcal{M}_{L_1F_1}$), and the subscripts $v$, $u$ the number of variables controlled by the principals, followers, respectively. To show how causal inference on canonical SS–PAPs can be extended to multi-follower SS–PAPs, we employ two representative models: the CGM $\mathcal{M}_{L_2F_1^2}$ with individualized incentives and independent follower utility functions, and the CGM $\mathcal{M}_{L_1F_1^2}$ with universal incentives and joint utility functions. For these CGMs, the endogenous variables are incentive function space variable $\Gamma$; follower actions $\Omega_F^1, \Omega_F^2$; principal action $\Omega_{L_1}, \Omega_{L_2}$ (individualized) or action $\Omega_L$ (universal); utilities variables $J_F^1$, $J_F^2$, $J_L$. We assume as before that the exogenous variables are mutually independent, mean-zero; and Gaussian when needed for analytic smoothing: $U_{A^1}, U_{A^2}$ (follower action noises), $U_{L_1}, U_{L_2}$ or $U_L$ (leader-action noises) and $U_{J_F^1}, U_{J_F^2}, U_{J_L}$ (utility noises). In this subsection, for clarity in the notation, we sometimes use $a^1$, $a^2$ or $a^i$, $a^{-i}$ for the followers actions $\omega_F^1$ and $\omega_F^2$, and $\mathcal{A}_1$, $\mathcal{A}_2$ for $\Omega_F^1$, $\Omega_F^2$. As has been consistently acknowledged in this research, we assume the principal's perceptive; i.e., the principal does not have knowledge about the followers utilities nor their best-response maps.

4.5.1. CGMs with Individualized Incentives and Independent Follower Utilities

In $\mathcal{M}_{L_2F_1^2}$, the principal has two decision variables $\Omega_{L_1}$ and $\Omega_{L_1}$, i.e., it must decides on two distinct incentive functions $\gamma_1 \in \Gamma$ and $\gamma_2 \in \Gamma$, one for each follower. This type of CGM for SS–PAPs with multiple followers allows the selection of distinct incentives for different followers, which is useful in multi-agent systems where it is important to break symmetries between followers. Furthermore, in the $\mathcal{M}_{L_2F_1^2}$ CGM, the utility function of each follower does not depend on the decisions of the other followers, i.e., there is no interference between the follower utilities: $J_F^i$ depends only on its own channel (though principal utility $J_L$ may couple channels). $\Gamma_1 \to \Omega_F^1$ and $\Gamma_2 \to \Omega_F^2$ via best responses (68), as shown in the structural equations **F** given below:

$$\Omega_F^1 = \mathrm{BR}_1(\Gamma_1, U_{A^1}), \qquad \Omega_F^2 = \mathrm{BR}_2(\Gamma_2, U_{A^2}), \tag{68}$$

$$\Omega_{L_1} = \Gamma_1(\Omega_F^1) + U_{L_1}, \qquad \Omega_{L_2} = \Gamma_2(\Omega_F^2) + U_{L_2}, \tag{69}$$

$$J_F^1 = g_F^1(\Omega_{L_1}, \Omega_F^1) + U_{J_F^1}, \qquad J_F^2 = g_F^2(\Omega_{L_2}, \Omega_F^2) + U_{J_F^2}, \tag{70}$$

$$J_L = g_L(\Omega_{L_1}, \Omega_{L_2}, \Omega_F^1, \Omega_F^2) + U_{J_L}. \qquad \Gamma_1 = \gamma_1;\ \Gamma_2 = \gamma_2 \tag{71}$$

Therefore, choosing policies $\Gamma_1{=}\gamma_1, \Gamma_2{=}\gamma_2$, the principal wants to estimate the causal estimand $V(\gamma_1, \gamma_2) = \mathbb{E}[J_L \mid \mathrm{do}(\Gamma_1{=}\gamma_1, \Gamma_2{=}\gamma_2)]$ and targets incentive policies $\gamma_1^*$ and $\gamma_2^*$ such that

$$\gamma_1^*, \gamma_2^* \in \underset{\gamma_1 \in \Gamma_1, \gamma_2 \in \Gamma_2}{\arg\max}\ \mathbb{E}\Big[J_L \mid do(\Gamma_1 = \gamma_1, \Gamma_2 = \gamma_2)\Big]. \tag{72}$$

https://doi.org/10.3390/e28010004

Using the $g$-formula, the identification formula for $V(\gamma_1, \gamma_2)$ admits the familiar nested expectation form:

$$V(\gamma_1, \gamma_2) = \iint \underbrace{\mathbb{E}_{U_{L_1}, U_{L_2}}\Big[g_L\big(\gamma_1(a^1) + U_{L_1},\ \gamma_2(a^2) + U_{L_2},\ a^1,\ a^2\big)\Big]}_{\text{inner expectation (Gaussian smoothing)}} \tag{73}$$

$$\times\ p(a^1 \mid \Gamma_1 = \gamma_1)\ p(a^2 \mid \Gamma_2 = \gamma_2)\ da^1\, da^2, \tag{74}$$

4.5.2. CGMs with Universal Incentive and Joint Follower Utilities

In contrast, in $\mathcal{M}_{L_1 F_1^2}$, incentives are said to be universal, that is, the incentive function $\gamma$ is applied equally to all followers, and here the utility function of each follower depends on the decisions of the other followers. The structural equations $\mathbf{F}$ for $\mathcal{M}_{L_1 F_1^2}$ are given in Equations (76)–(79).

$$\Gamma = \gamma \tag{75}$$

$$(\Omega_F^1, \Omega_F^2) = \Phi(\Gamma, U_{A^1}, U_{A^2}) \quad \text{(Joint best-response equilibrium map)}, \tag{76}$$

$$\Omega_L = \Gamma(\Omega_F^1, \Omega_F^2) + U_L, \tag{77}$$

$$J_F^i = g_F^i(\Omega_L, \Omega_F^1, \Omega_F^2) + U_{J_F^i}, \quad i \in \{1, 2\}, \tag{78}$$

$$J_L = g_L(\Omega_L, \Omega_F^1, \Omega_F^2) + U_{J_L}. \tag{79}$$

The direct causal relations from arrows $\Gamma \to (\Omega_F^1, \Omega_F^2)$ are via the joint best-response equilibrium map $\Phi$; as shown in the structural Equation (76). One can write $\Omega_F^1 = \mathrm{BR}_1(\Gamma_1, U_{A^1})$, $\Omega_F^2 = \mathrm{BR}_2(\Gamma_2, U_{A^2})$, and define $\Phi$ as the fixed-point solver. That is, each follower $i$ has payoff $J_F^i(a^i, a^{-i}; \gamma)$ with the best-response correspondence:

$$\mathrm{BR}_i(\gamma, a^{-i}) \ \in\ \arg\max_{a^i \in A_i} u_i(a^i, a^{-i}; \gamma), \qquad i \in \{1, 2\},$$

and the joint best-response correspondence is

$$\mathcal{B}_\gamma(a^1, a^2) \ = \ \mathrm{BR}_1(\gamma, a^2) \times \mathrm{BR}_2(\gamma, a^1) \ \subseteq\ \mathcal{A}_1 \times \mathcal{A}_2,$$

for compact action sets $\mathcal{A}_i \subset \mathbb{R}^{d_i}$. So, $\mathcal{B}_\gamma(a^1, a^2)$ takes an action profile $(a^1, a^2)$ as input and returns the set of all possible joint actions where each player is best responding to the input action of the other player. A Nash equilibrium under $\gamma$ is then any fixed point $(a^{1\star}, a^{2\star}) \in \mathcal{B}_\gamma(a^{1\star}, a^{2\star})$, as $a^{1\star} \in \mathrm{BR}_1(\gamma, a^{2\star})$, i.e., follower 1's action is a best response to follower 2's action; and $a^{2\star} \in \mathrm{BR}_1(\gamma, a^{1\star})$, i.e., follower 2's action is a best response to follower 1's action. However, in scenarios where the followers game presents multiple Nash Equilibria (NE), the conventional method of defining NE as a fixed point fails to provide clarity on the actual outcome that players will select, resulting in a model that lacks predictive capability. Therefore, it is important to consider some additional assumptions for this joint best-response equilibrium map $\Phi$, such as the existence of the equilibrium and the specification of an equilibrium selection rule, where the goal is to move from the Nash equilibrium correspondence (a set of possible outcomes) to a unique joint action law (a single predicted outcome).

Under $\mathcal{M}_{L_1 F_1^2}$ the principal wants to estimate the causal estimand $V(\gamma) = \mathbb{E}[J_L \mid \mathrm{do}(\Gamma = \gamma]$ and targets the incentive function $\gamma^*$ such that:

$$\gamma^* \in \arg\max_{\gamma \in \Gamma} \mathbb{E}\Big[J_L \mid do(\Gamma = \gamma)\Big]. \tag{80}$$

https://doi.org/10.3390/e2801000

By the $g$-formula, the identification for $V(\gamma)$ also admits the nested expectation form:

$$V(\gamma) = \iint \underbrace{\mathbb{E}_{U_L}\Big[g_L\big(\gamma(a^1,a^2)+U_L,\, a^1,\, a^2\big)\Big]}_{\text{inner expectation (Gaussian smoothing)}} \; p(a^1,a^2 \mid \Gamma{=}\gamma)\; da^1\, da^2. \tag{81}$$

In the identification formula for $V(\gamma)$, we can observe the importance of having a joint best-response equilibrium map $\Phi$ with an equilibrium selection rule. In multiple equilibria cases, $p(a^1, a^2 \mid \Gamma = \gamma)$ becomes non-unique, ambiguous, and very hard to estimate from data; so it is important to impose or learn an equilibrium selection rule that makes the joint action law unique or as unambiguous as possible.

## 5. Discussion

This work formalizes the Causal Incentive Design (CID) framework for the canonical single-stage principal–agent problem (SS–PAP) by treating incentives as interventions in a causal graphical model (CGM). The causal target $V(\gamma) = \mathbb{E}[J_L \mid do(\Gamma = \gamma)]$ is the expected value of the principal's utility variable $J_L$ under a specified policy intervention $\Gamma = \gamma$ in the post-intervention distribution $p(J_L \mid do(\Gamma = \gamma))$. The construction of an estimand by the identification of $V(\gamma)$ is via the g-formula, and the selection of a single deployment incentive policy is through a Functional Bayesian Optimization algorithm. The process pipeline on CID for SS–PAPs is explicitly offline: historical data records from the system are mapped into estimates of $V(\gamma)$, which are then optimized *prior* to a one-shot commitment. This connection between causal identification and sample-efficient search yields high-probability regret guarantees for the offline selection step.

A central contribution is the anatomy of the estimand $V(\gamma)$ as a nested expectation with two interpretable layers: (i) an inner Gaussian smoothing of the outcome regression around the principal's induced action, and (ii) an outer averaging with respect to the follower's induced action law $p(M \mid \Gamma = \gamma)$; which extends to multi-follower setting. The inner layer admits quadrature-based evaluation (e.g., Gauss–Hermite), while the outer layer is handled by a policy-local reweighting scheme that respects positivity and interpretability. In the affine credit-market specialization (Section 3.3.1), this decomposition collapses to a closed form, clarifying how pricing slope and fees interact with induced borrowing behavior.

The CID framework demonstrate a recent advance in causal reasoning grounded in causal graphical models (CGMs): policies are formalized as functional interventions on a policy node, policy value is represented as an interventional or counterfactual query, and identification and estimation are performed directly on the CGM using observational logs. Additionally, the single-stage principal–agent model examined here introduces a novel application domain for CGMs in incentive design, complementing established applications in biology, medicine, and economics, and facilitating further exploration of multi-agent scenarios.

The remainder of the Discussion is structured as follows. Section 5.1 revisits the Stackelberg FCBO procedure and interprets the information–gain regret bounds as causal decision guarantees for one-shot policy selection in single-stage PAPs. Section 5.2 reviews the primary modeling, identification, and learning assumptions of the CID framework, including the CGM structure, positivity/overlap, the additive-noise model, and the uniform sub-Gaussian noise envelope used in the regret analysis. Section 5.3 discusses the practical scope of the current single-stage, offline analysis, emphasizing limitations related to policy-local support, potential model misspecification such as heavy-tailed noise or unmodeled confounding, and robustness considerations, as well as the importance of effective-sample-size diagnostics. Section 5.4 analyzes the computational demands of the CID pipeline

https://doi.org/10.3390/e28010004

and the FCBO algorithm, specifying how time and memory requirements scale with the number of logged units, the number of policy evaluations, and GP updates, and indicating regimes in which value estimation or surrogate modeling is the dominant computational cost. Section 5.5 describes extensions of the CID framework and nested estimand beyond the single-follower case, considering individualized versus joint incentives and the impact of interactions among multiple followers on the CGM, identification, and the design of learning algorithms.

### *5.1. Offline Functional BO and Causal Decision Guarantees*

The Stackelberg FCBO algorithm models $\gamma \mapsto V(\gamma)$ as a black-box functional objective on a Reproducing Kernel Hilbert Space (RKHS) and uses a functional GP surrogate with a GP-UCB-style acquisition functional. The resulting cumulative-regret bounds for the Stackelberg FCBO algorithm scale with $\sqrt{T\,\beta^t\,\mathcal{I}_T}$, where $\mathcal{I}_T$ is an information gain term. This offers concrete guidance on evaluation budgets (sampling costs), stopping rules (such as UCB gaps), and the exploration schedule prior to the one-shot deployment; i.e., determining when enough data have been collected to make a final decision.

In contrast to online-learning methods such as bandits and reinforcement learning over actions, CID for SS–PAPs is distinctly one-shot and offline, utilizing intrinsic causal structure in PAPs and causal reasoning to assess policies without the need for deployment. In relation to causal BO methods, we argue that interventions $do(\Gamma = \gamma)$ in the function-valued random variable $\Gamma$, which involve functional (conditional) interventions $do(\Omega_L = \gamma(\omega_L))$, since

$$\mathbb{E}\Big[J_L \mid do(\Gamma = \gamma)\Big] \approx \mathbb{E}\Big[J_L \mid do(\Gamma = \gamma), do\big(\Omega_L = \gamma(\omega_L)\big)\Big],$$

are the right abstraction for causal reasoning about incentive functions in PAPs. In $\mathcal{M}_{L_1F_1}$, the node $\Gamma$ explicitly represents the incentive policy and is connected to both $\Omega_L$ and $\Omega_F$. These connections $\Gamma \to \Omega_L$ and $\Gamma \to \Omega_F$, together with $\Omega_F \to \Omega_L$, $\Omega_L \to J_L$, and $\Omega_F \to J_L$, constitute the minimal policy-aware motif that captures how incentives $\gamma \in \Gamma$ shape the leader's realized decision $\Omega_L$ and the follower's decision $\Omega_F$, to produce the principal's utility variable $J_L$ in the system. In structural terms, the leader's action is generated by the policy applied to the follower context, $\Omega_L = \gamma(\Omega_F)$, while the adoption of a policy also reshapes the distribution of follower variables through $\Gamma \to \Omega_F$.

This inverse Stackelberg-aware approach makes the hierarchical semantics explicit: the dependence between principal and follower decisions is encoded both by $\Omega_F \to \Omega_L$ (the policy takes follower context as input) and through behavior modifications driven by incentive policies $\Gamma \to \Omega_L$ and $\Gamma \to \Omega_F$ (the policy governs how actions are produced and how follower behavior is distributed under intervention). Moreover, the follower decision $\Omega_F$ acts as a mediator $M$ in the causal path from $\Gamma$ to $J_L$ in the principal's perspective of $\mathcal{M}_{L_1F_1}$, in agreement with the intrinsic semantics of PAPs.

The CID framework for SS–PAPs illustrates the fundamental difference between considering the causal relations between the input variables ($\Gamma$, $\Omega_F$ in SS–PAPs ) and not considering them in an optimization problem. This variation is the central motivation in the causal decision-making framework of Causal Bayesian Optimization (CBO) [24] over classical Bayesian optimization. In this sense, the CID framework for SS–PAPs exhibits PAPs, inverse Stackelberg games, and bilevel optimization problems, as a fundamental family of problems that elucidates this important distinctness (between BO and CBO), given that the hierarchical semantics of an inverse Stackelberg game rely on the causal relationships $\Gamma \to \Omega_L$, $\Gamma \to \Omega_F$ and $\Omega_F \to \Omega_L$. Disregarding the causal relationships between these three variables $\Gamma$, $\Omega_F$, and $\Omega_L$ merely distorts the semantics of the functional optimization problem that solves a PAP.

https://doi.org/10.3390/e28010004

### 5.2. Assumptions

The identification and estimation of CID are based and rely on the following assumptions: (i) *Consistency*: the recorded outcome equals the counterfactual under the realized policy. (ii) *Causal sufficiency*: for variables $\{\Gamma, \Omega_L, \Omega_F, J_L, J_F\}$ in the generative CGM $\mathcal{M}_{L_1F_1}$; (iii) *Black-box follower's best-response*: we work over the principal's perspective where the observed variables are $\{\Gamma, \Omega_F, \Omega_L, J_L\}$ and the follower's best-response is considered a black-box function. (iv) *Positivity (overlap)*: in a policy-local sense, we assume that there exists a neighborhood $\mathcal{N}_\rho(\gamma)$ such that $p(\Omega_F \mid \Gamma \in \mathcal{N}_\rho(\gamma)) > 0$ wherever the estimator needs support to approximate $p(\Omega_F \mid \Gamma = \gamma)$. (v) *Policy compliance*: The action implemented by the principal is consistent with the distribution of $\Omega_L = \gamma(\Omega_F) + U_L$ in practical deployment, as it is presupposed. Otherwise, if this alignment is not achieved, the action $do(\Gamma = \gamma)$ and the behavior observed in practice will differ significantly. (vi) *Additive, zero-mean Gaussian noise SCM*: featuring mutually independent exogenous terms; in the leader's action, in particular, allowing inner Gaussian smoothing on the identification formula. We also assume i.i.d. logged units and no interference across units, i.e., the Stable Unit Treatment Value Assumption (SUTVA). Violations or weak forms of these conditions, such as latent confounding, measurement error, or insufficient policy-local overlap, can bias $V(\gamma)$ and compromise the calibration of uncertainty. (vii) *Noise envelope for regret analysis:* While the outer estimator is heteroskedastic across $\gamma$, we assume a uniform sub-Gaussian envelope on $\varepsilon_t = \widehat{V}(\gamma_t) - V(\gamma_t)$ over the proposal support. This implies a diagonal noise model in Section 4.4.1 with $\Sigma_T \preceq \sigma_*^2 \mathbf{I}$, under which the stated GP-UCB bounds hold (see [8,29]).

### 5.3. Scope and Limitations

The present CID analysis is *single-stage and offline*: it commits once to a policy and cannot adapt after deployment. Dynamics (carry-over effects), learning-by-doing, and path-dependent constraints are beyond the scope of this paper. The follower mechanism is treated as a black box (we observe $\Omega_F, \Omega_L, J_L$, but not the follower utilities); this pushes strategic dependence into the observed mediator law and increases sensitivity to support gaps in $\Omega_F$ near the target policy $\gamma$. So, in the absence of extensive historical policy support, the sensitivity in the outer layer increases. The additive Gaussian assumption simplifies the inner layer but may under-represent heavy tails or heteroskedasticity; when noise departs from Gaussian, it can lead to inaccuracies in inner smoothing and variance estimates.

For diagnostics and protection against weak overlap: (i) Monitor weight distributions, to look for outlier weights pointing to weak overlap and high variance. (ii) Monitor the effective sample size (ESS), which measures the effective number of independent samples you have after applying the weights.

$$\mathrm{ESS}(\gamma; h) := \frac{\left(\sum_{i=1}^{N} w_i(\gamma; h)\right)^2}{\sum_{i=1}^{N} w_i(\gamma; h)^2}.$$

A low ESS relative to the total sample size ($N$) indicates that a few heavily weighted units dominate the estimation, signaling a high variance problem. (iii) Monitor sensitivity to the policy-space bandwidth, by re-running the evaluation using different values for this bandwidth parameter $h$. If the value of the new policy changes significantly when you slightly adjust the bandwidth, the estimate is unstable and highly dependent on a tuning parameter, which reduces confidence in the result. (iv) Reduce overfitting bias in the outer layer employing sample-splitting, cross-fitting, and orthogonalization.

In practice, Algorithm 1 can constrain candidate policies to a trust region $\mathcal{S}_{\text{support}}$ (see Section 3.3.4 for the definition of $\mathcal{S}_{\text{support}}$), adapt the bandwidth $h$ to balance bias–variance and/or inflate posterior uncertainty as $\gamma$ approaches the boundary of $\mathcal{S}_{\text{support}}$. Crucially,

https://doi.org/10.3390/e28010004

kernel reweighting does not create support: if $\gamma$ is far from the historical policies, $\widehat{\mathbb{P}}_{\gamma}^{(h)}$ collapses, and $\widehat{V}(\gamma)$ becomes high-variance (and possibly biased). Therefore, the practical search space of Algorithm 1 is data-dependent and effectively limited to neighborhoods of previously observed policies. Because the outer estimator relies on policy-local overlap, we can incorporate a policy-support score $s(\gamma) := \mathrm{ESS}(\gamma; h)/N$ into the selection. Concretely, we can either constrain GP-UCB to $\gamma \in \mathcal{S}_{\mathrm{support}}(h, \tau, w_{\max})$ (hard trust region) or use a soft penalty $\widetilde{A}_t(\gamma) = A_t(\gamma) \cdot \varphi(s(\gamma))$, where $A_t(\gamma)$ is the acquisition function, with $\varphi(s) \downarrow 0$ as $s \downarrow 0$, i.e., this penalty function must approach zero as the policy-support score $s(\gamma)$ approaches zero. Conversely, when $s(\gamma)$ is high (close to 1), $\varphi(s)$ should be close to 1 to minimally impact the acquisition function $A_t(\gamma)$. This prevents proposals in regions where $p(M \mid \Gamma = \gamma)$ cannot be estimated from logs and makes the practical search space explicit and data-dependent.

### 5.4. Time–Space Complexity over a Full FBO Run

Estimating $V(\gamma)$ once via the semi-parametric identification formula (assuming additive, zero-mean Gaussian noise) costs $\mathcal{O}\big(N\,(P + C_\gamma + Q_{\mathrm{eff}}\,C_\mu)\big)$, under policy-local reweighting over $N$ recorded tuples, and where $P$ is the policy-space representation size, $C_\gamma$ is the cost to compute $\gamma(\Omega_F)$ once, $Q_{\mathrm{eff}}$ is the inner integration budget (e.g., Gauss–Hermite nodes or MC points), and $C_\mu$ is the cost to evaluate the fitted outcome regression once. Across a BO horizon of $T$ iterations (one evaluation per step), the total cost to produce these off-line evaluations is $\mathcal{O}\big(T\,N\,(P + C_\gamma + Q_{\mathrm{eff}}\,C_\mu)\big)$. With local reweighting over only the top $L \ll N$ nearest policies, this becomes $\mathcal{O}\big(T\,(P \log N + L\,(P + C_\gamma + Q_{\mathrm{eff}}\,C_\mu))\big)$. The one-time training of the outcome model contributes an upfront $C^{\mu}_{\mathrm{train}}$ that is then amortized. The memory requirement for the estimator is $\mathcal{O}(N)$ (or $\mathcal{O}(L)$ when local weighting is applied), in addition to $\mathcal{O}(N\,P)$ if the policy embeddings are stored in cache. The quadrature nodes are $\mathcal{O}(Q_{\mathrm{eff}})$ and can be considered negligible.

The implementation of an exact functional Gaussian Process surrogate with incremental updates throughout the execution adds $\mathcal{O}\big((1 + B)\,T^3 + (1{+}B)\,T^2\,P\big)$ for Cholesky updates and acquisition scoring of $B$ candidates per iteration. Since, across the full horizon $T$, kernel updates are $\sum_{t=1}^{T} \mathcal{O}(N_t P) = \mathcal{O}(T^2 P)$; Cholesky factorizations are $\sum_{t=1}^{T} \mathcal{O}(N_t^2) = \mathcal{O}(T^3)$; and total UCB functional acquisition scoring work (each needs mean and variance) $\sum_{t=1}^{T} \mathcal{O}\big(B\,(N_t P + N_t^2)\big) = \mathcal{O}\big(B\,(T^2 P + T^3)\big)$, where $N_t$ is the number of observed policy evaluations at iteration $t$ (so $N_t = t$). Merging the estimation cost and exact GP updates plus functional acquisition work cost, the total end-to-end time is

$$\text{Total time} \approx C^{\mu}_{\mathrm{train}} + \underbrace{\mathcal{O}\big(T\,N\,(P + C_\gamma + Q_{\mathrm{eff}} C_\mu)\big)}_{\text{For all } \widehat{V}(\gamma) \text{ evaluations}} + \underbrace{\mathcal{O}\big((1 + B)\,T^3 + (1 + B)\,T^2 P\big)}_{\text{For the exact functional GP}}.$$

Replace $N$ by $L$ and add $T\,P \log N$ under local weighting. Comparing the estimation cost $T\,N\,(P + C_\gamma + Q_{\mathrm{eff}}\,C_\mu)$ of $V(\gamma)$ with the dominant cubic GP term $(1{+}B)\,T^3$, we can establish that GP dominates when

$$T \gg \sqrt{N\,(P + C_\gamma + Q_{\mathrm{eff}} C_\mu)/(1{+}B)},$$

while the estimation cost of $V(\gamma)$ dominates below that scale. In terms of space, the exact GP stores dense Gram/Cholesky factors of size $T \times T$, i.e., $\mathcal{O}(T^2)$.

### 5.5. Toward Multi-Follower Settings

We outline a multi-follower generalization of CID that preserves the CGM semantics of the canonical case. Let followers be indexed by $i \in [n]$ with contexts $\Omega_F^{(i)}$, and let the leader's (possibly vector-valued) action be $\Omega_L$. The policy node $\Gamma$ represents the incentive rule(s) chosen by the principal and, in the policy-augmented CGM, carries arrows $\Gamma \to \Omega_L$ and $\Gamma \to \Omega_F^{(i)}$ for all $i$. As in the single-follower case, contexts feed into the leader's realized action via $\Omega_F^{(i)} \to \Omega_L$, but now the post-intervention law involves the joint mediator $M = (\Omega_F^{(1)}, \ldots, \Omega_F^{(n)})$, since both $\Omega_L$ and $\{\Omega_F^{(i)}\}$ affect the principal's payoff $J_L$. Two instructive extensions clarify how identification and learning must adapt beyond the canonical case: (i) the regime IIIU: individualized incentives with conditionally independent follower utilities (factorized mediator law), and (ii) the regime UIJU: universal incentives with joint follower utilities (coupled actions via a joint best-response map).

In the IIIU regime, the principal deploys a collection of incentive functions (e.g., one per channel, segment, or product), and the followers' utilities are *conditionally independent* given their own contexts and the relevant part of the policy. Graphically, the mediator law factorizes under interventions as follows:

$$p\Big(M \,\Big|\, do\Big(\{\Gamma^{(i)} = \gamma^{(i)}\}\Big)\Big) = \prod_{i=1}^{n} p\Big(\Omega_F^{(i)} \,\Big|\, do(\Gamma^{(i)} = \gamma^{(i)})\Big). \tag{82}$$

Estimation and optimization inherit a separable structure: outer-layer reweighting and inner smoothing decompose over $i$, enabling parallel computation and straightforward uncertainty aggregation. Surrogate modeling should mirror this factorization (e.g., with parallel GPs, modeling the functional objective as a sum or collection of independent functional GPs or using block-diagonal kernels over policy components, where the overall kernel is constructed by combining separate, independent kernels for each component), and identifiability reduces to policy-local overlap for each channel. This setting suits applications where incentives are personalized or targeted and cross-follower externalities are negligible.

In the UIJU regime, a single policy $\gamma$ applies to all followers whose actions are strategically coupled; so, we use a joint best-response map $A = \Phi(\gamma, M, U_F)$, with exogenous terms $U_F$, where we use $A$ to denote the actions carried out by followers $\{\omega_F^{(1)}, \ldots, \omega_F^{(n)}\}$. The identification requires an *equilibrium-selection* rule to make the post-intervention law; i.e., $p(A \mid M, do(\Gamma = \gamma))$ is well defined through a selection mapping $S\colon\ (\gamma, M) \mapsto A$. Three practical approaches are (i) *Uniqueness*: Assume that $do(\Gamma = \gamma)$ almost surely results in a unique equilibrium outcome $A$. (ii) *Parametric selection*: Encode tie-breaking or stability criteria in $S$ and learn its parameters from observed play. (iii) *Stochastic selection*: Models the choice among equilibria as a stochastic process, where each equilibrium is chosen with a specific probability.

Surrogate modeling for the UIJU regime should reflect cross-follower dependence (e.g., using multi-task GPs with coregionalization and structured kernels over policy components), and outer-layer estimation must use joint reweighting over $M$ (and, if modeled, $A$) rather than product weights. Positivity must hold in a joint sense: support near $\gamma$ is needed for the relevant regions of the $(M, A)$-space, a stricter requirement than in the individualized case.

## 6. Conclusions

This study introduces a principled, offline framework for single-stage incentive design using causal inference, grounded in causal graphical models (CGMs) and information-theoretic analysis. The single-stage principal–agent problem (SS–PAP) is formalized as a CGM, where the principal's incentive rule is modeled as a functional intervention on a policy node $\Gamma$, the follower's action serves as an explicit causal mediator, and the principal's payoff $J_L$ is the outcome. The causal target estimand is defined as the principal's expected utility under an incentive policy intervention, $V(\gamma) = \mathbb{E}[J_L \mid do(\Gamma = \gamma)]$, which quantifies

https://doi.org/10.3390/e28010004

how a committed incentive causally influences the follower's behavior and the principal's payoff under private information.

For the identification of the estimand, a semi-parametric expression for $V(\gamma)$ is derived using the g-formula, which decomposes into an inner Gaussian smoothing over noise and an outer expectation with respect to the post-intervention distribution of the mediator. Building on this structure, a two-layer estimator is proposed for offline logs: the inner layer computes a Gaussian expectation, implemented numerically via Gauss–Hermite quadrature, while the outer layer approximates the interventional mediator law using policy-local kernel reweighting with effective-sample-size and weight-cap diagnostics. This design explicitly addresses the bias–variance trade-off and ensures that off-policy evaluation maintains overlap in policy space.

For policy selection, the value functional $\gamma \mapsto V(\gamma)$ is embedded in a functional Gaussian process surrogate over a Reproducing Kernel Hilbert Space (RKHS) of admissible incentives, and a support-aware GP-UCB search is performed. The resulting regret bounds are characterized in terms of differential information gain, directly connecting the exploration–exploitation trade-off to information-theoretic quantities under a uniform sub-Gaussian envelope for estimator noise. Collectively, these components establish a unified pipeline for causal reasoning and optimal intervention design in single-stage principal–agent settings using only offline observational logs.

The proposed offline approach is particularly suitable in scenarios where adaptive experimentation is infeasible, ethically constrained, or operationally costly. For instance, this applies when contracts, tariffs, or credit terms must be fixed prior to deployment and cannot be iteratively adjusted. Within this regime, the analysis clarifies the conditions under which causal identification is possible, the extent to which extrapolation in policy space is feasible while maintaining overlap, and methods for quantifying uncertainty through effective sample size and information gain.

The CID framework extends beyond the canonical single-follower case. In a multi-follower generalization, the nested form of the estimand is preserved, but a strong dependence emerges based on the interaction of follower utilities. In regimes with individualized incentives and conditionally independent utilities, identification, estimation, and surrogate modeling decompose across followers, enabling parallelization and simpler diagnostics. Conversely, in regimes with universal incentives and jointly coupled utilities, identification depends on equilibrium-selection assumptions, and outer-layer estimation must address joint mediator laws and stricter positivity requirements. These extensions demonstrate both the robustness of the two-layer CID structure and the additional challenges encountered in more complex multi-agent systems.

Overall, the presented CID framework advances the field of causal graphical models and their applications by integrating a CGM-based representation of principal–agent interactions with explicit causal reasoning about policy interventions and information-theoretic guarantees for offline policy search. This framework establishes a foundational link between causal inference and policy search in principal–agent problems, supporting reliable single-stage incentive design in complex systems and providing a basis for future research involving empirical studies, richer policy classes, and more complex multi-follower environments.

*Future Work*

The proposed approach enables the integration of causal reasoning into incentive design, especially for canonical single-stage PAPs. It also reveals opportunities to strengthen robustness in causal inference estimation, improve computational scalability, validate the framework under realistic constraints, and expand to multi-follower and multi-stage PAPs.

https://doi.org/10.3390/e28010004

Future work will address these limitations and explore extensions to make CID dependable at scale and deployable in practice.

Beyond the scope of this work, an important future extension is a robust identification toolkit that tolerates limited policy-local overlap in data logs and mild unmeasured confounding. Specifically, we plan to incorporate partial-identification estimation bounds, i.e., reporting intervals for the causal target estimand $V(\gamma)$ rather than a single point estimation, with techniques based on [30] tailored to policy interventions, or proximal/negative-control strategies when credible proxy variables are available. In addition to targeted sensitivity analyses using weight clipping and bandwidth sweeps with effective sample size diagnostics. By addressing this limitation, the practical utility of CID improves in data regimes where perfect overlap and strict sufficiency are unrealistic.

Other aspects for strengthening robustness involve exploring beyond additive-Gaussian noise and augmenting policy-local reweighting with structural conditional density models to learn the mediator law given an incentive policy $p(M \mid \Gamma)$. Regarding the first, we plan to replace the inner Gaussian smoothing with robust or heavy-tailed quadrature methods, such as Student-t distributions or mixture models, which can better account for outliers and extreme data points. In addition, to explore heteroskedastic noise models and variance-adaptive smoothing, to propagate these refinements into uncertainty quantification. Regarding conditional density models for $p(M \mid \Gamma)$, the plan is to utilize conditional normalizing flows or score-based estimators while preserving the identification logic and benchmarking bias–variance trade-offs. These improvements are essential to reduce bias in heavy-tailed regimes and to maintain calibrated uncertainty when noise scale depends on context.

The forthcoming work will involve the complete extension of CID to multi-follower over the distinct configurations. This will require adaptations to surrogate modeling tailored to specific regimes and adjusting the regret bounds. Many systems are situated between regimes: individualized incentives with conditionally independent follower utilities and universal incentives with joint follower utilities. A pragmatic approach is to adopt clustered dependence: partition followers into groups with strong in-group coupling and weak cross-group effects. The CGM should then mix block-factorized mediator laws with group-level equilibrium selection. For a large amount of followers, exchangeability and mean-field approximations can effectively reduce dimensionality. These techniques summarize follower interactions through aggregate statistics (such as empirical means or occupancy measures), which can be used as input to the system's laws and particularly on the joint best-response map, yielding scalable identification and surrogate models with kernels over aggregates. This implies measuring similarity between two policies based on the similarity of their predicted aggregate statistics, making the optimization process efficient for massive populations.

Beyond the existing framework, a promising direction is constraint-aware CID. The core motivation is that incentive policies deployed in real-world settings (such as credit, pricing, or subsidies) must reliably satisfy constraints, and not just on average. This means mitigating the risk of rare and catastrophic failures. Essential constraints include safety (avoiding dangerous or unintended side effects), budget (ensuring costs remain within defined limits), and fairness (ensuring similar treatment or impact across groups, minimizing disparities in approval rates or resource allocation). The planned efforts on this matter involve implementing three interconnected components in the search process for policy interventions: (i) constrained acquisitions that enforce high-probability feasibility; (ii) risk-sensitive objectives and chance constraints; and (iii) fairness controls. The analysis of this extension must delineate clear Pareto trade-offs, enabling decision-makers to trans-

https://doi.org/10.3390/e28010004

parently assess trade-offs between maximizing utility and satisfying constraints such as safety, fairness, and budget.

A paramount direction is to generalize from the single-stage setting to multi-stage environments, where incentives are applied over time. Specifically, we plan to formalize a dynamic CGM with history-dependent policies $\Pi$, identify the causal target $V(\Pi)$ with a sequential (stage-wise) analogue of our two-layer estimator, and lift the optimization to a Dynamic Functional Causal Bayesian Optimization algorithm that accounts for temporal causal relations and stage-wise uncertainty. This expansion is essential to capture learning-by-doing, carryover effects, and path-dependent constraints—features central to many real-world deployments.

Finally, translating these theoretical gains into robust real-world value is a key long-term goal. This involves curated benchmarks (credit pricing, platform subsidies, and market mechanisms), rigorous baselines (contextual bandits with off-policy evaluation (OPE), policy-gradient RL with OPE, and non-causal BO), and comprehensive reporting of offline policy regret, uncertainty coverage, and constraint satisfaction—with open, reproducible artifacts. Future work will include detailed simulations and case studies to demonstrate (a) calibration of the two-layer estimator under policy dispersion and overlap constraints; (b) separation of outer policy-local reweighting and inner Gaussian smoothing through ablation studies; and (c) performance of end-to-end Functional Causal Bayesian Optimization (FCBO) with support-aware acquisition across representative policy classes.

Additionally, it is essential to monitor run-time and memory usage as policy classes and evaluation budgets expand. The primary bottleneck in Bayesian Optimization (BO) is the Gaussian Process (GP) surrogate model, which often has cubic time complexity over the BO horizon. This can be overcome by replacing costly exact computations with approximations, such as random-feature surrogates chosen in the policy space, and by coordinating multi-fidelity evaluations of $V(\gamma)$. That is, using "cheap samples" that can be sampled quickly at a low computational cost in the inner layer of the identification formula to gain a coarse understanding of the policy's value, and reserve the expensive, high-accuracy estimations (like high-fidelity quadrature for integrating probabilities) for only the most promising policies. This is essential for validating scalability in resource-constrained environments and for enabling larger, more expressive policy classes without sacrificing regret guarantees.

Taken together, these directions aim not only to refine the current methodology but also to broaden CID's theoretical and practical footprint. Specifically, the field must transition from single-stage to multi-stage decision-making; move from brittle point estimates to robust identification; progress from exact, heavy surrogates to scalable multi-fidelity optimization; expand from isolated agents to coupled, constraint-laden systems; and shift from stylized demonstrations to reproducible, high-stakes applications. Advancing along these directions will facilitate the development of reliable, deployable incentive designs grounded in causal reasoning.

**Author Contributions:** Conceptualization, S.B., E.F.M., L.E.S. and E.M.d.C.; methodology, S.B., E.F.M., L.E.S. and E.M.d.C.; formal analysis, S.B., E.F.M. and E.M.d.C.; investigation, S.B., E.F.M., L.E.S. and E.M.d.C.; resources, S.B., E.F.M., L.E.S. and E.M.d.C.; writing—original draft preparation, S.B.; writing—review and editing, S.B., E.F.M., L.E.S. and E.M.d.C.; supervision, E.F.M., L.E.S. and E.M.d.C.; project administration, E.F.M., L.E.S. and E.M.d.C.; funding acquisition, E.F.M., L.E.S. and E.M.d.C. All authors have read and agreed to the published version of the manuscript.

**Funding:** S.B. is supported by Secretaría de Ciencia, Humanidades, Tecnología e Innovación (SECIHTI), Scholarship Number 1562. Instituto Nacional de Astrofísica, Óptica y Electrónica (INAOE).

**Institutional Review Board Statement:** Not applicable.

**Data Availability Statement:** Data are contained within the article.

https://doi.org/10.3390/e2801000

**Conflicts of Interest:** The authors declare no conflicts of interest.

## Abbreviations

The following abbreviations are used in this manuscript:

| | |
|---|---|
| BO | Bayesian Optimization |
| CBO | Causal Bayesian Optimization |
| CID | Causal Incentive Design |
| CGM | Causal Graphical Models |
| FCBO | Functional Causal Bayesian Optimization |
| FBO | Functional Bayesian Optimization |
| GP | Gaussian Process |
| MAS | Multi-Agent System |
| PAP | Principal–Agent Problem |
| RKHS | Reproducing Kernel Hilbert Space |
| SCM | Structural Causal Model |

## Appendix A. Regret Bound Proofs in a Finite Function Space

Details for the proofs of the propositions needed to prove Theorem 1 are presented here next. Proposition A1 provides a high probability bound on the difference $|f(\gamma) - \mu_{t-1}(\gamma)|$, between the true function value $f(\gamma)$ and the posterior mean $\mu_{t-1}(\gamma)$ across the time steps $1, \dots, T$ and the incentive functions $\gamma = \{\gamma^1, \dots, \gamma^T\} \subseteq \Gamma$ in the finite functional decision space $\Gamma$, showing that the posterior mean $\mu_{t-1}(\gamma)$ is a good estimate of the function value $f(\gamma)$, with $\gamma = \{\gamma^1, \dots, \gamma^{t-1}\} \subseteq \Gamma$ up to a confidence width of $\sqrt{\beta^t}\sigma_{t-1}(x)$.

**Proposition A1.** *Let $\Gamma$ be the finite decision set and $\delta \in (0,1)$ be the desired confidence level. Select $\delta$ over the open interval $(0,1)$ and set $\beta^t = 2\log(\frac{\pi^2 t^2}{6\delta}|\Gamma|)$. Then*

$$|f(\gamma) - \mu^{t-1}(\gamma)| \leq \sqrt{\beta^t}\sigma^{t-1}(\gamma) \quad \forall \gamma \in \Gamma, \forall t \geq 1,$$

*holds with probability greater than or equal to $1 - \delta$.*

**Proof.** We show that for appropriately chosen confidence parameters $\{\beta^t\}$ for $t \in [T]$, every such confidence interval is always valid, with high probability. A random variable $X \sim \mathcal{N}(0,1)$ has the upper bound of the tail probability $\Pr(X > c) \leq \frac{1}{2}e^{-\frac{c^2}{2}}$ for $c > 0$ (see [31]), and $\Pr(|X| > c) = 2\Pr(X > c)$ as the standard normal distribution is symmetric. For a fixed $t \geq 1$, conditioned on observations $\mathbf{y}^{t-1} = \{\hat{\mathbb{E}}_{p_{\gamma^1}}[J_L^1], \dots, \hat{\mathbb{E}}_{p_{\gamma^T}}[J_L^{t-1}]\}$, the sequence of incentive functions $\gamma = \{\gamma^1, \dots, \gamma^{t-1}\} \subseteq \Gamma$ are deterministic and the posterior distribution $f(\gamma) \sim \mathcal{N}(\mu^{t-1}(\gamma), {\sigma^{t-1}}^2(\gamma))$ at time $t-1$. We normalize this Gaussian as $Z = \frac{f(\gamma) - \mu^{t-1}(\gamma)}{\sigma^{t-1}(\gamma)} \sim \mathcal{N}(0,1)$ so we can apply the previous tail bound and symmetry property to $Z$. Therefore, we have the following bound, using $X = Z$ and $c = \sqrt{\beta^t}$:

$$\Pr\left\{\left|\frac{f(\gamma) - \mu^{t-1}(\gamma)}{\sigma^{t-1}(\gamma)}\right| > \sqrt{\beta^t}\right\} = \Pr\left\{|f(\gamma) - \mu^{t-1}(\gamma)| > \sqrt{\beta^t}\sigma^{t-1}(\gamma)\right\} \leq e^{-\frac{\beta^t}{2}}. \quad \text{(A1)}$$

As we want the confidence interval to hold for all $\gamma \in \Gamma$ and all time steps $t \in [T]$ in Algorithm 1, we use the union-bound inequality to construct the appropriate parameters $\{\beta^t\}$ for $t \in [T]$. Let $\mathcal{E}$ be the event that at least one confidence interval fails for some $\gamma \in \Gamma$ at some time step $t \in [T]$ in the Algorithm 1, so

https://doi.org/10.3390/e28010004

$$\mathcal{E} = \bigcup_{\gamma\in\Gamma, t\in[T]} |f(\gamma) - \mu_{t-1}(\gamma)| > \sqrt{\beta^t}\sigma^{t-1}(\gamma).$$

Applying the union bound, we know that

$$\begin{aligned}\Pr(\mathcal{E}) =& \Pr\left\{\bigcup_{\gamma\in\Gamma, t\in[T]} |f(\gamma) - \mu_{t-1}(\gamma)| > \sqrt{\beta^t}\sigma^{t-1}(\gamma)\right\} \\ \leq& \sum_{t\in[T]}\sum_{\gamma\in\Gamma} \Pr\left\{|f(\gamma) - \mu_{t-1}(\gamma)| > \sqrt{\beta^t}\sigma^{t-1}(\gamma)\right\}.\end{aligned}$$

By running Algorithm 1 up to $T$ time steps, we have $T|\Gamma|$ possibilities that $\{|f(\gamma) - \mu_{t-1}(\gamma)| > \sqrt{\beta^t}\sigma^{t-1}(\gamma)\}$, and as we want to ensure that $\Pr(\mathcal{E}) \leq \delta$, we can set

$$\Pr\left\{|f(\gamma) - \mu_{t-1}(\gamma)| > \sqrt{\beta^t}\sigma^{t-1}(\gamma)\right\} \leq \frac{\delta}{T|\Gamma|}. \tag{A2}$$

So, combining this with Equation (A1), we can solve equation $e^{-\frac{\beta^t}{2}} = \frac{\delta}{T|\Gamma|}$ for $\beta^t$, getting $\beta^t = 2\log\frac{T|\Gamma|}{\delta}$. Finally, to analyze Algorithm 1 for $T \to \infty$, the identity $\sum_{t=1}^{\infty}\frac{1}{t^2} = \frac{\pi^2}{6}$ is used to design a time-dependent probability budget for each time step and considering the union of infinitely many events. This increases the confidence parameter $\beta_t$ over time, so that the probability of failure decreases suitably quickly, and the probability of failure anywhere and at any time is small. So, we now want

$$\Pr(\mathcal{E}) = \Pr\left\{\bigcup_{t=1}^{\infty}\bigcup_{\gamma\in\Gamma}\left\{\left|f(\gamma) - \mu_{t-1}(\gamma)\right| > \sqrt{\beta^t}\sigma^{t-1}(\gamma)\right\}\right\} \leq \delta.$$

Similar to Equation (A2), but now taking advantage of the identity $\sum_{t=1}^{\infty}\frac{1}{t^2} = \frac{\pi^2}{6}$, we set

$$\Pr\left\{|f(\gamma) - \mu_{t-1}(\gamma)| > \sqrt{\beta^t}\sigma^{t-1}(\gamma)\right\} \leq \frac{\delta}{|\Gamma|}\cdot\frac{6}{\pi^2 t^2}. \tag{A3}$$

Then, by the union bound inequality for this $T \to \infty$ case, we have the following:

$$\begin{aligned}\Pr(\mathcal{E}) \leq& \sum_{t=1}^{\infty}\sum_{\gamma\in\Gamma} \Pr\left\{|f(\gamma) - \mu_{t-1}(\gamma)| > \sqrt{\beta^t}\sigma^{t-1}(\gamma)\right\} \\ \leq& \sum_{\gamma\in\Gamma}\sum_{t=1}^{\infty}\frac{\delta}{|\Gamma|}\cdot\frac{6}{\pi^2 t^2} = \sum_{\gamma\in\Gamma}\frac{\delta}{|\Gamma|}\cdot\frac{6}{\pi^2}\sum_{t=1}^{\infty}\frac{1}{t^2} = \sum_{\gamma\in\Gamma}\frac{\delta}{|\Gamma|} = \delta\end{aligned}$$

So, as above, using the tail bound from Equation (A1), we can solve for $\beta_t$ the equation $e^{-\frac{\beta^t}{2}} = \frac{6\delta}{\pi^2 t^2|\Gamma|}$, from which we obtain that

$$\beta^t = 2\log(\frac{\pi^2 t^2}{6\delta}|\Gamma|) \tag{A4}$$

□

**Proposition A2.** *For a fixed $t \geq 1$. If $|f(\gamma) - \mu^{t-1}(\gamma)| \leq \sqrt{\beta^t}\sigma^{t-1}(\gamma)$ for all $\gamma_1, \ldots, \gamma_{t-1} \in \gamma \subseteq \Gamma$, then the instantaneous regret $r_t = f(\gamma^*) - f(\gamma^t) \leq 2\sqrt{\beta^t}\sigma^{t-1}(\gamma^t)$.*

https://doi.org/10.3390/e28010004

**Proof.** Algorithm 1 selects the incentive function $\gamma^t \in \Gamma$ According to the acquisition functional

$$\gamma^t = \arg\max_{\gamma \in \Gamma} \mu^{t-1}(\gamma) + \beta^t \sigma^{t-1}(\gamma).$$

So, $\forall \gamma \in \Gamma$, $\mu^{t-1}(\gamma) + \beta^t \sigma^{t-1}(\gamma) \leq \mu^{t-1}(\gamma^t) + \beta^t \sigma^{t-1}(\gamma^t)$. In particular, for the unknown optimal incentive function $\gamma^*$, we have that

$$\mu^{t-1}(\gamma^*) + \beta^t \sigma^{t-1}(\gamma^*) \leq \mu^{t-1}(\gamma^t) + \beta^t \sigma^{t-1}(\gamma^t). \tag{A5}$$

By hypothesis, in the particular cases of $\gamma^*$ and $\gamma^t$ we have

$$f(\gamma^*) \leq \mu^{t-1}(\gamma^*) + \sqrt{\beta^t} \sigma^{t-1}(\gamma^*) \tag{A6}$$

$$f(\gamma^t) \geq \mu^{t-1}(\gamma^t) - \sqrt{\beta^t} \sigma^{t-1}(\gamma^t). \tag{A7}$$

Then, using inequalities, we have the following bound for instantaneous regret $r^t$

$$\begin{aligned} r^t &= f(\gamma^*) - f(\gamma^t) \\ &\leq \mu^{t-1}(\gamma^*) + \sqrt{\beta^t} \sigma^{t-1}(\gamma^*) - \left(\mu^{t-1}(\gamma^t) - \sqrt{\beta^t} \sigma^{t-1}(\gamma^t)\right) \\ &\leq \mu^{t-1}(\gamma^t) + \sqrt{\beta^t} \sigma^{t-1}(\gamma^t) - \left(\mu^{t-1}(\gamma^t) - \sqrt{\beta^t} \sigma^{t-1}(\gamma^t)\right) \\ &= 2\sqrt{\beta^t} \sigma^{t-1}(\gamma^t) \end{aligned}$$

□

Proposition A3 shows that the information gain for a selected set of incentive functions can be expressed in terms of the predictive variances and that we can bound this variance in terms of the information gain.

**Proposition A3.** *For any finite sequence of incentive functions* $\gamma^1, \ldots, \gamma^\tau \in \Gamma$

$$\sum_{t=1}^{\tau} (\sigma^t)^2(\gamma^t) \leq \frac{\sigma^2}{\log(1 + \sigma^{-2})} I^\tau(\mathbf{f}^\tau; \mathbf{y}^\tau).$$

**Proof.** Following Section 4.4, $\mathbf{y}^\tau = \{y^1, \ldots, y^\tau\} = \{\hat{\mathbb{E}}_{p_{\gamma^1}}[J_L^1], \ldots, \hat{\mathbb{E}}_{p_{\gamma^\tau}}[J_L^\tau]\}$, where the incentive functions $\gamma^1, \ldots, \gamma^T$ are deterministic conditioned on $\mathbf{y}^{\tau-1}$. From Equation (63), we know that $I^\tau(\mathbf{f}^\tau; \mathbf{y}^\tau) = H(\mathbf{y}^\tau) - H(\mathbf{y}^\tau \mid \mathbf{f}^\tau)$. Using the chain rule for differential entropy, we have the following alternative expressions for $H(\mathbf{y}^\tau)$ in Equation (A8) and $H(\mathbf{y}^\tau \mid \mathbf{f}^\tau)$ in Equation (A9), equivalent to Equation (63).

$$\begin{aligned} H(\mathbf{y}^\tau) &= H(y^1, \ldots, y^\tau) \\ &= \sum_{t=1}^{\tau} H(y^t \mid y^1, \ldots, y^{t-1}) \\ &= \sum_{t=1}^{\tau} \frac{1}{2} \log\left[2\pi e((\sigma^{t-1})^2(\gamma^t) + \sigma^2)\right]. \end{aligned} \tag{A8}$$

$$H(\mathbf{y}^\tau \mid \mathbf{f}^\tau) = \sum_{t=1}^{\tau} H(\epsilon^t) = \sum_{t=1}^{\tau} \frac{1}{2} \log\left[(2\pi e)\sigma^2\right], \tag{A9}$$

since given $\mathbf{f}^\tau$, the only randomness left is noise, as $y^t = \hat{\mathbb{E}}_{p_{\gamma^t}}[J_L^t] = f(\gamma^t) + \epsilon^t$, with $\epsilon^t \sim \mathcal{N}(0, \sigma^2)$. So, using Equations (A8) and (A9), now we can express the information gain for the selected incentive functions as follows:

$$
\begin{aligned}
I^{\tau}(\mathbf{f}^{\tau};\mathbf{y}^{\tau}) &= H(\mathbf{y}^{\tau}) - H(\mathbf{y}^{\tau} \mid \mathbf{f}^{\tau}) \\
&= \sum_{t=1}^{\tau} \frac{1}{2}\log\left[2\pi e((\sigma^{t-1})^2(\gamma^t)+\sigma^2)\right] - \sum_{t=1}^{\tau}\frac{1}{2}\log\left[(2\pi e)\sigma^2\right] \\
&= \frac{1}{2}\sum_{t=1}^{\tau}\log\left[\frac{(\sigma^{t-1})^2(\gamma^t)+\sigma^2}{\sigma^2}\right] = \frac{1}{2}\sum_{t=1}^{\tau}\log\left[1+\frac{(\sigma^{t-1})^2(\gamma^t)}{\sigma^2}\right]
\end{aligned}
\tag{A10}
$$

Observe that in Equation (A10), we have expressed the information gain for a selected set of incentive functions exclusively in terms of predictive variances. Now, we use the elementary inequality for all $z \in [0,1]$, $z \leq \frac{1}{\log(1+z^{-1})}\log(1+z)$, and definite $z^t = \frac{\sigma^{t-1^2}(\gamma^t)}{\sigma^2}$ so that $\sigma^{t-1^2}(\gamma^t) = \sigma^2 z^t$, and then we have

$$
z^t \leq \frac{1}{\log(1+(z^t)^{-1})}\log(1+z^t) \leq \frac{1}{\log(1+\sigma^{-2})}\log(1+z^t), \tag{A11}
$$

because $z^t \leq \sigma^{-2}$. Now multiplying both sides of Equation (A11) by $\sigma^2$ ans sum over $t = 1, \ldots, T$ we have

$$
\begin{aligned}
\sum_{t=1}^{T}(\sigma^{t-1})^2(\gamma^t) &\leq \frac{\sigma^2}{\log(1+\sigma^{-2})}\sum_{t=1}^{T}\log(1+z^t) \\
&= \frac{\sigma^2}{\log(1+\sigma^{-2})}\sum_{t=1}^{T}\log\left[1+\frac{(\sigma^{t-1})^2(\gamma^t)}{\sigma^2}\right] \\
&= \frac{\sigma^2}{\log(1+\sigma^{-2})}I^{\tau}(\mathbf{f}^{\tau};\mathbf{y}^{\tau})
\end{aligned}
\tag{A12}
$$

□

**Proposition A4.** *Let $\delta \in (0,1)$ be the desired confidence level and let $\beta^t = 2\log(\frac{\pi^2 t^2}{6\delta}|\Gamma|)$. Then, the following holds with probability at least $1-\delta$:*

$$
\sum_{t=1}^{T}(r^t)^2 \leq \beta^T C_1 I^T(\mathbf{f}^T;\mathbf{y}^T) \quad \forall T \geq 1, \tag{A13}
$$

*where $C_1 = \frac{4\sigma^2}{\log(1+\sigma^{-2})}$.*

**Proof.** From Propositions A1 and A2, we have that $\{(r^t)^2 \leq 4\beta^t(\sigma^{t-1})^2(\gamma^t),\ \forall t \geq 1\}$ with probability at least $1-\delta$, by squaring both sides of expression $r^t \leq 2\sqrt{\beta}\sigma^{t-1}(\gamma^t)$ in Proposition A2. So, as for the monotonic increasing property of $\beta^t$, $\beta^t \leq \beta^T$ for all $t \in [T]$ and the result from Proposition A3, we have

$$
\begin{aligned}
\sum_{t=1}^{T}(r^t)^2 &\leq 4\sum_{t=1}^{T}\beta^t(\sigma^{t-1})^2(\gamma^t) \\
&\leq 4\beta^T\sum_{t=1}^{T}(\sigma^{t-1})^2(\gamma^t) \\
&\leq \beta^T\frac{4\sigma^2}{\log(1+\sigma^{-2})}I^{\tau}(\mathbf{f}^{\tau};\mathbf{y}^{\tau}) \\
&\leq \beta^T C_1 I^{\tau}(\mathbf{f}^{\tau};\mathbf{y}^{\tau})
\end{aligned}
\tag{A14}
$$

□

Finally, Theorem 1 is a consequence of applying the Cauchy–Schwarz inequality $\sum_{t=1}^{T} r^t \leq \sqrt{T\sum_{t=1}^{T}(r^t)^2}$ to the result in Proposition A4 with which we obtain the following bound:

$$R^T = \sum_{t=1}^{T} r^t \leq \sqrt{T\sum_{t=1}^{T}(r^t)^2} = \sqrt{T\beta^T C_1 I^\tau(\mathbf{f}^\tau; \mathbf{y}^\tau)} \tag{A15}$$

## Appendix B. Reproducing Kernel Hilbert Spaces

Before describing the notion of Reproducing Kernel Hilbert Space (RKHS) functional space, we discuss kernel functions. Let $\mathbf{X}$ be a nonempty set and let $\mathbb{R}^{\mathbf{X}}$ be the set of all functions of real value on $\mathbf{X}$. Recall that a Hilbert space $\mathcal{H}$ is a complete vector space, i.e., all Cauchy sequences converge, with an inner product $\langle\cdot,\cdot\rangle_{\mathcal{H}}$ that gives rise to a norm $\|h\|_{\mathcal{H}} = \langle h,h\rangle_{\mathcal{H}}$ for every $h \in \mathcal{H}$. A function $k$: $\mathbf{X}\times\mathbf{X} \to \mathbb{R}$ is called a kernel on $\mathbf{X}$ if there exist a real Hilbert space $\mathcal{H}$ and a map $\Phi$: $\mathbf{X} \to \mathcal{H}$ such that for all $x, x' \in \mathbf{X}$, we have $k(x,x') = \langle\Phi(x),\Phi(x')\rangle$. We call $\Phi$ a feature map and $\mathcal{H}$ a feature space of $k$. Furthermore, we must know that a kernel is positive definite in the sense that for all $n \in \mathbb{N}$, $\omega_1,\ldots,\omega_n \in \mathbb{R}$, and all $x_1,\ldots,x_n \in \mathbb{R}$, we have $\sum_{i\in[n]}\sum_{j\in[n]}\omega_i\omega_j k(x_i,x_j) \geq 0$. The matrix $K = (k(x_j,x_i))_{ij}$ is called the Gram matrix, and the positive definiteness of the kernel $k$ is equivalent to saying that the determinant of $K$ must be non-negative. A functional space RKHS $\mathcal{H}_k$ in $\mathbf{X}$ is a Hilbert space $\mathcal{H} \subset \mathbb{R}^{\mathbf{X}}$ with a kernel function $k$: $\mathbf{X}\times\mathbf{X} \to \mathcal{H}$, which is called the reproducing kernel, where for all $x \in \mathbf{X}$ and all functions $f \in \mathcal{H}$, we have $f(x) = \langle f, k_x\rangle_{\mathcal{H}}$, where $k_x = k(\cdot,x) \in \mathcal{H}$.

In addition to the definition, a more intuitive approach to understand the rationale underlying an RKHS function space can be achieved through the following construction, which involves the formation of a Hilbert function space (an RKHS) from a kernel $k$: $\mathbf{X}\times\mathbf{X} \to \mathbb{R}$. Given $\mathbf{X}$ and a function $k$, consider a feature map $\Phi$: $\mathbf{X} \to \mathbb{R}^{\mathbf{X}}$, defined as $x \mapsto \Phi(x) = k_x = k(x,\cdot)$, known as the reproducing kernel map. That is, the point $x \in \mathcal{X}$ is mapped to a function $k_x$: $\mathbf{X} \to \mathbb{R}$, so $k_x(y) = k(x,y)$ for $y \in \mathbf{X}$. Now, we can construct a vector space by considering the images $\{k_x \mid x \in \mathcal{X}\}$ as a spanning set, i.e., construct a vector space containing all linear combinations of the functions $k(\cdot,x)$. Thus, given a kernel $k(x,x')$, the RKHS of functions $\mathcal{H}_k$ and its inner product are given in Equation (A16) and Equation (A17), respectively.

$$\mathcal{H}_k = \Big\{h(\cdot) = \sum_{i\in[n]}\omega_i k(x_i,\cdot) \mid \omega_i \in \mathbb{R}, n \in \mathbb{N}, x_i \in \mathbf{X}\Big\}, \tag{A16}$$

$$\langle h,g\rangle = \Big\langle \sum_{i\in[n]}\omega_i k(x_i,x), \sum_{j\in[m]}\xi_j k(x_j',x)\Big\rangle = \sum_{i\in[n]}\sum_{j\in[m]}\omega_i\xi_j k(x_i,x_j'), \tag{A17}$$

with $\omega_i, \xi_j \in \mathbb{R}$, $n,m \in \mathbb{N}$, $x_i, x_j \in \mathbf{X}$. From the inner product defined in Equation (A17), we can deduce the reproducing properties: $\langle k(\cdot,x),h\rangle = h(x)$, $\langle k(\cdot,x),k(\cdot,x')\rangle = k(x,x')$ and we can see that $\langle\Phi(x),\Phi(x')\rangle = \langle k(\cdot,x),k(\cdot,x')\rangle = k(x,x')$. Hilbert spaces of scalar-valued functions with reproducing kernels were introduced and studied in [32]. The kernel $k$ in this appendix is the reproducing kernel on $\mathbf{X}$ for $\mathcal{H}_k$. In the main text, the GP over functions $\Gamma \subset \mathcal{H}_k$ uses a distinct kernel $K(\gamma,\gamma')$ (see Section 4.1.1), constructed from $\|\cdot\|_{\mathcal{H}_k}$.

*A Finite Reproducing Kernel Hilbert Space*

Here, we provide the construction of the functional space $\mathcal{H}_k^d$ used for the regret analysis for Algorithm 1 in Theorem 1. The most general construction of a RKHS can be achieved using a positive semidefinite kernel defined on a finite set. Let $X = \{x_1, x_2, \ldots, x_d\}$ be a finite nonempty set. Let $k$: $X \times X \to \mathbb{R}$ be a symmetric and positive semidefinite kernel function, i.e., for any choice of real coefficients $c_1,\ldots,c_d$, we have $\sum_{i=1}^{d}\sum_{j=1}^{d} c_i c_j k(x_i,x_j) \geq 0$.

https://doi.org/10.3390/e28010004

We have a finite RKHS by defining the function space $\mathcal{H}_k^d$ as the span of kernel sections at the finite points $\mathcal{H}_n := \text{span}\{k(\cdot, x_1), k(\cdot, x_2), \ldots, k(\cdot, x_n)\}$. So, every function $f \in \mathcal{H}_k^d$ has the form $f(x) = \sum_{i=1}^n c_i k(x, x_i)$, for some vector of coefficients $\mathbf{c} = (c_1, \ldots, c_d)^\top \in \mathbb{R}^d$. The Gram matrix is defined as $K \in \mathbb{R}^{n \times n}$ by $K_{ij} := k(x_i, x_j)$. Since $k$ is positive semidefinite, the matrix $K$ is symmetric and positive semidefinite. For functions $f, g \in \mathcal{H}_k^d$ defined by

$$f(x) = \sum_{i=1}^{n} c_i k(x, x_i), \quad g(x) = \sum_{i=1}^{n} b_i k(x, x_i), \tag{A18}$$

So, the inner product is given by $\langle f, g \rangle_{\mathcal{H}_k^d} := \mathbf{c}^\top K \mathbf{b}$, and the associated norm is given by $\|f\|_{\mathcal{H}_k^d}^2 = \langle f, f \rangle_{\mathcal{H}_k^d} = \mathbf{c}^\top K \mathbf{c}$. The space $\mathcal{H}_k^d$ satisfies the reproducing property $f(x_j) = \langle f, k(\cdot, x_j) \rangle_{\mathcal{H}_k^d}, \quad \forall j = 1, \ldots, d$, because for any $f \in \mathcal{H}_n$, we have

$$f(x_j) = \sum_{i=1}^{d} c_i k(x_j, x_i) = \langle f, k(\cdot, x_j) \rangle_{\mathcal{H}_k^d}. \tag{A19}$$

The aforementioned construction can be further extended to consider $\mathcal{H}_k^d$ as a finite-dimensional RKHS of a generic kernel, with an infinite and continuous input space $X \subseteq \mathbb{R}^d$. The key idea is to restrict the RKHS to a finite-dimensional subspace by choosing a finite number of basis functions associated with the kernel.

## Appendix C. Bayesian Optimization

Given a real-valued objective function $f_{obj}\colon \mathcal{X} \to \mathbb{R}$ defined over some domain $\mathcal{X}$, Bayesian optimization (BO) takes a probabilistic approach to methodically search for a point $x^* \in \arg\max_{x \in \mathcal{X}} f_{obj}(x)$, that achieves the global maximum value $f_{obj}^*(x) = \max_{x \in \mathcal{X}} f_{obj}(x)$. It is worth highlighting that we do not presume any assumptions about the characteristics of the domain $\mathcal{X}$. In particular, it is not required to be a Euclidean space; it may be a space with a more complex structure, such as a function space, which is the focus of our investigation. In addition, BO differs from traditional optimization, as it does not require $f_{obj}(x)$ to have a known restricted functional form. BO is an instance of the more general framework of sequential optimization where the input is an initial (possibly empty) data set $\mathcal{D} = \{(x, y)\}$ from which we want to design a sequence of experiments to gather information about $f_{obj}(x)$. In each interaction, a policy optimizer selects a point $x^\alpha$ where we make our next observation. Having selected the point $x' = x^\alpha$, we can obtain feedback from the system under study to obtain $f_{obj}(x')$. We append the newly observed information to update the data set, i.e., $\mathcal{D}' = \mathcal{D} \cup \{(x', y')\}$. We repeat until the termination condition is reached. There are different mechanisms by which the decision is made to terminate the sequential optimization process. For our purpose in this research, we assume a stopping criteria by exhausting an experimentation budget, that is, a finite time horizon $T \in \mathbb{N}$. Also, we discard the strong assumption of having an exact observation model and instead adopt an additive Gaussian noise observation model, i.e., the value $f_{obj}(x)$ observed at $x$ modeled as $y = f_{obj}(x) + \epsilon$, where $\epsilon \sim \mathcal{N}(0, \sigma^2)$ represents the measurement error.

What distinguishes BO from the more general sequential optimization framework is that BO relies on Bayesian inference (Bayes' Theorem) to reason about the uncertain quantities of a system of interest in light of our prior knowledge and any available data. This specially includes the objective function $f_{obj}$, which is typically treated as a stochastic process in this context, i.e., a probability distribution over an infinite family of random variables $y = f_{obj}(x) + \epsilon$ in a probability space, indexed by points $x \in \mathcal{X}$.

*Appendix C.1. Gaussian Process Surrogate Model*

We focus on the Gaussian process (GP) representation of the objective function $f_{obj}$. A GP is a stochastic process such that every finite collection of random variables in the stochastic process has a multivariate normal distribution. The distribution of a GP is the joint distribution of all those (infinitely many) random variables, and as such it is a distribution over functions with a continuous domain. Thus, a GP can be used as a prior probability distribution over functions to perform Bayesian inference, i.e., to compute posterior distribution refining our initial beliefs according to the observed data.

We specify a Gaussian process as $\mathcal{GP}(\mu(\cdot), k(\cdot,\cdot))$ with mean function $\mu$ and covariance kernel $k$ that is presumably bounded: $k(x, x') \leq 1$, for all $x \in \mathcal{X}$, without loss of generality. The mean function $\mu(x) = \mathbb{E}(f_{obj} \mid x)$ determines the expected value of our model for $f_{obj}$ at any location $x$, thus serving as a location parameter that represents the central tendency of our stochastic model for $f_{obj}(x)$. On the other hand, the covariance kernel $k(x, x') = cov[f_{obj}, f'_{obj} \mid x, x']$ determines how deviations from the mean are structured in our model for $f_{obj}$, i.e., for its samples $f_{obj}(x) \sim \mathcal{GP}(\mu(x), k(x,\cdot))$, encoding also expected properties for our stochastic model of $f_{obj}$ such as differentiability and smoothness. The squared exponential, also known as the Radial Basis Function (RBF) kernel, and the kernels of the Matérn family of kernels, are two examples of frequently used kernels in the GP framework.

*Appendix C.2. Acquisition Functions*

Every BO method fundamentally has two major components: (i) First, a probabilistic surrogate model to represent the belief over the black-box objective function $f_{obj}$, as the Gaussian processes previously discussed. (ii) Second, an acquisition function (AF), $\alpha$: $\mathcal{X} \to \mathbb{R}$, which establishes a utility value for the candidate evaluation points from the posterior distribution of the probabilistic surrogate model to select the next optimal evaluation point. Specifically, an acquisition function $\alpha$: $\mathcal{X} \to \mathbb{R}$ assigns a score to each point in the domain reflecting our preferences over locations for the next observation.

Even though there is a large collection of acquisition functions, we restrict our attention to the Gaussian Process Upper Confidence Bound (GP-UCB) acquisition function. The Upper Confidence Bound criterion is commonly used to deal with the exploration-exploitation dilemma and to evaluate strategies in Multi-Armed Bandit (MAB) algorithms. The GP-UCB acquisition function is an extension of the UCB criteria on MAB to BO, as BO can be interpreted as an infinite-armed bandit problem. Assume we have gathered an arbitrary data set $\mathcal{D}$, and consider an arbitrary point $x \in \mathcal{X}$. Consider the quantile function associated with the predictive distribution $p(y \mid x, \mathcal{D})$ given by

$$q(\rho; x, \mathcal{D}) = \inf\{y' \mid \Pr(y \leq y' \mid x, \mathcal{D}) \geq \rho\}.$$

This quantile function satisfies the relation $y \leq q(\rho; x, \mathcal{D})$ with probability $\rho \in (0,1)$, so we can interpret $q(\rho; x, \mathcal{D})$ as an Upper Confidence Bound (UCB) on the objective function $y$, i.e., say that the value of $y$ will exceed the bound only with tunable probability $1 - \rho$. As a function of $x$, we can elucidate $q(\rho; x, \mathcal{D})$ as an optimistic estimate of $y$, suggesting that we observe where this Upper Confidence Bound is maximized, resulting in the acquisition function $\alpha_{\text{UCB}}(x; \mathcal{D}, \rho) = q(\rho; x, \mathcal{D})$, where $q$ is the quantile function with confidence $\rho \in (0,1)$. For a Gaussian process, this quantile takes the simple form of Equation (A20):

$$\alpha_{\text{GP-UCB}}(x; \mathcal{D}, \rho) = \mu(x) + \beta\sigma(x), \tag{A20}$$

where $\beta = \Phi^{-1}(\rho)$ depends on the confidence level and can be computed from the inverse Gaussian cumulative distribution function ($\Phi^{-1}$ denotes the quantile function,

https://doi.org/10.3390/e28010004

i.e., the inverse cumulative distribution function (CDF)). Employing low confidence values (e.g., $\rho = 0.8$) diminishes recognition for sites with high uncertainty, hence favoring exploitation substantially. Increasing the confidence parameter (e.g., $\rho = 0.95$ or $\rho = 0.99$) leads to increasingly exploratory behavior. The policy implemented by sequentially maximizing Upper Confidence Bounds is backed by robust theoretical guarantees. Srinivas et al. [7] demonstrated that this policy is guaranteed to effectively maximize the objective at a non-trivial rate for GP models under reasonable assumptions. In the main text, (Sections 4.2 and 4.3), we parameterize the acquisition by a (possibly time-varying) exploration coefficient $\beta^t$. For the regret analysis (Section 4.4), we take $\beta^t = 2\log(\frac{t^2\pi^2|\Gamma|}{6\delta})$, which is equivalent to using a time-varying confidence level $\rho^t = \Phi(\beta^t)$.

## Appendix D. Functional Approximation via the Stone–Weierstrass Theorem

The Stone–Weierstrass theorem provides sufficient conditions for approximating continuous functions on compact spaces using elements from a subalgebra. In its classical real-valued formulation, it characterizes when an algebra of continuous functions is uniformly dense in the full space $C(X, \mathbb{R})$, the Banach space of real-valued continuous functions on a compact Hausdorff space $X$, endowed with the uniform norm (see, for instance, ref. [33]).

Let $(X, d)$ be a compact Hausdorff space and let $C(X, \mathbb{R})$ denote the space of continuous real-valued functions on $X$, equipped with the uniform norm

$$\|g\|_\infty := \sup_{x\in X} |g(x)|.$$

A subset $A \subset C(X, \mathbb{R})$ is called an algebra if it is closed under pointwise addition, scalar multiplication, and pointwise multiplication. We say that $A$ separates points of $X$ if for every pair of distinct points $x, y \in X$, there exists $g \in A$ such that $g(x) \neq g(y)$. This means the algebra is rich enough to distinguish any two points of the domain. We say that $A$ contains the constants if the constant function $\mathbf{1}(x) \equiv 1$ belongs to $A$.

**Theorem A1** (Stone–Weierstrass Theorem). *If $A \subset C(X, \mathbb{R})$ is a subalgebra that separates points of $X$ and contains the constants, then $A$ is dense in $C(X, \mathbb{R})$ with respect to the uniform norm. That is, for every $f \in C(X, \mathbb{R})$ and every $\varepsilon > 0$, there exists $g \in A$ such that*

$$\|f - g\|_\infty < \varepsilon.$$

In our context, $X$ will be either the compact subset $\Gamma \subset \mathcal{H}_k$ of admissible incentive functions, or the compact input domain $\Omega_F$ of a follower's decision variable. The algebra $A$ will be constructed from either (1) the span of kernel sections $K(\cdot, \gamma_0)$ with $\gamma_0 \in \Gamma$ for the approximation of the functional $f\colon \Gamma \to \mathbb{R}$, or (2) the span of kernel sections $k(\cdot, x)$ with $x \in \Omega_F$ or the polynomial algebra $\mathcal{P}_n$ for the approximation of scalar-valued incentive functions $\gamma\colon \Omega_F \to \mathbb{R}$.

The separation property follows from the positive definiteness of the kernels $K$ or $k$, which guarantees that kernel sections distinguish distinct points. The constants are contained in the algebra because constant functions can be obtained (or approximated) from kernel sections or are trivially included in $\mathcal{P}_n$.

Theorem A1 then ensures that any continuous target functional or incentive function can be uniformly approximated by finite linear combinations of functions from these algebras, which is the foundation for the two approximation steps described in the following subsections.

https://doi.org/10.3390/e2801000

*Appendix D.1. Approximation of the Objective Functional*

Let $\mathcal{G} \subset H_k$ be a compact subset of the RKHS of incentive functions, equipped with the topology induced by the RKHS norm $\|\cdot\|_{H_k}$. That is, a sequence $\{\gamma_n\} \subset H_k$ converges to $\gamma \in H_k$ if and only if $\|\gamma_n - \gamma\|_{H_k} \to 0$. We consider the objective functional $f\colon \mathcal{G} \to \mathbb{R}$ defined by

$$f(\gamma) = \mathbb{E}[J_L \mid \mathrm{do}(\Omega_L = \gamma(\omega_F))],$$

which we assume to be continuous with respect to $\|\cdot\|_{H_k}$. The functional kernel $K\colon H_k \times H_k \to \mathbb{R}$ induces a family of evaluation maps of the form $\gamma \mapsto K(\gamma, \gamma_0)$ for fixed $\gamma_0 \in \mathcal{G}$. We define the algebra

$$\mathcal{A}_1 := \mathrm{span}\{K(\cdot, \gamma_0) \mid \gamma_0 \in \mathcal{G}\} \subset C(\mathcal{G}, \mathbb{R}).$$

This algebra separates points, since $K$ is strictly positive definite and for $\gamma_1 \neq \gamma_2$, there exists $\gamma_0$ such that $K(\gamma_1, \gamma_0) \neq K(\gamma_2, \gamma_0)$. Also, constants functions are included in this algebra, since $K(\gamma, \gamma)$ is bounded below by a positive value and adding scaled copies yields constant approximations. Hence, according to the Stone–Weierstrass theorem, $\mathcal{A}_1$ is uniformly dense in $C(\mathcal{G}, \mathbb{R})$, and any continuous objective functional $f$ can be approximated by elements of the algebra $\mathcal{A}_1$. The algebra described above is equivalent to the following algebra

We can rewrite this $\mathcal{A}_1$ in the language that we need for regret bounds. Let $\Gamma \subset \mathcal{H}_k$ be a compact subset of the RKHS of incentive functions, endowed with the norm topology $\|\cdot\|_{\mathcal{H}_k}$. We assume that the objective functional $f\colon \Gamma \to \mathbb{R}$ is continuous, $f \in C(\Gamma)$. We rewrite this algebra $\mathcal{A}_1$ as follows:

$$\mathcal{A}_1 := \mathrm{span}\{K(\cdot, \gamma_0) \mid \gamma_0 \in \Gamma\},$$

where $K\colon \mathcal{H}_k \times \mathcal{H}_k \to \mathbb{R}$ is the functional kernel used in the GP prior. Because $K$ is positive definite, $\mathcal{A}_1$ separates points in $\Gamma$ and contains constant functions, as stated above. By the Stone–Weierstrass theorem, $\mathcal{A}_1$ is dense in $C(\Gamma)$ under the uniform norm.

So, as a consequence, for every $\varepsilon_1 > 0$, there exists a finite set $\{\gamma_1, \ldots, \gamma_d\} \subset \Gamma$ and coefficients $\alpha_1, \ldots, \alpha_d \in \mathbb{R}$ such that

$$\sup_{\gamma \in \Gamma} \left| f(\gamma) - \sum_{i=1}^{d} \alpha_i K(\gamma_i, \gamma) \right| < \varepsilon_1.$$

Therefore, the finite set $\{\gamma_i\}_{i=1}^{d}$ plays the role of a basis of reference incentive functions. Each $\gamma \in \Gamma$ is represented through its coordinates $\big(K(\gamma_1, \gamma), \ldots, K(\gamma_d, \gamma)\big)$ in this basis. The approximant $\sum_{i=1}^{d} \alpha_i K(\gamma_i, \gamma)$ is a finite-dimensional parametric model for $f$, with parameters $\{\alpha_i\}$. Thus, the algebraic density statement of Stone–Weierstrass and the finite-basis parametric view are equivalent; both state that a continuous functional $f$ in $\Gamma$ can be uniformly approximated by an element of the finite-dimensional span of kernel sections $K(\cdot, \gamma_i)$. This is the first step in reducing the infinite-dimensional functional optimization problem to one over a finite parameter space.

*Appendix D.2. Selection Methods of a Finite Set of Basis Incentive Functions*

In practice, the first application of the Stone–Weierstrass theorem requires the construction of a finite set $\{\gamma_1, \ldots, \gamma_d\} \subset \mathcal{H}_k$ such that the algebra they generate, $\mathcal{A}_1 = \mathrm{span}\{K(\cdot, \gamma_i) : i = 1, \ldots, d\}$, separates points and contains the constants, ensuring density in $C(\mathcal{H}_k, \mathbb{R})$ under the uniform norm on compact subsets. Below, we describe two formal approaches for constructing such a set.

https://doi.org/10.3390/e28010004

Method 1: $\varepsilon$-cover-based selection. Let $\Gamma \subset \mathcal{H}_k$ be compact in the RKHS norm $\|\cdot\|_{\mathcal{H}_k}$. For $\varepsilon > 0$, an *$\varepsilon$-cover* of $\Gamma$ with respect to the $\mathcal{H}_k$ norm is a finite subset $\mathcal{G}_\varepsilon \subset \Gamma$ such that for every $\gamma \in \Gamma$, there exists $\tilde{\gamma} \in \mathcal{G}_\varepsilon$ satisfying $\|\gamma - \tilde{\gamma}\|_{\mathcal{H}_k} \leq \varepsilon$. An $\varepsilon$-cover is said to be minimal if it has the smallest possible cardinality among all $\varepsilon$-covers of $\Gamma$. The minimal cardinality is called the *$\varepsilon$-covering number* and is denoted by $N(\Gamma, \|\cdot\|_{\mathcal{H}_k}, \varepsilon)$.

Given $\varepsilon > 0$, a minimal $\varepsilon$-cover can be constructed by iteratively selecting points from $\Gamma$ such that (i) the first point is chosen arbitrarily from $\Gamma$, (ii) each subsequent point is chosen so that it lies at $\mathcal{H}_k$-norm distance strictly greater than $\varepsilon$ from all previously chosen points, and (iii) the process stops once the selected points cover $\Gamma$ in the sense above. This greedy selection achieves a covering whose cardinality is within a factor of optimal for compact metric spaces. *Basis selection.* Once a minimal (or near-minimal) $\varepsilon$-cover $\mathcal{G}_\varepsilon = \{\tilde{\gamma}_1, \ldots, \tilde{\gamma}_d\}$ is obtained, we set $\{\gamma_1, \ldots, \gamma_d\} := \mathcal{G}_\varepsilon$. By properties of continuous positive-definite kernels $K$, the kernel sections $K(\cdot, \gamma_i)$ separate points in $\Gamma$ and constants are contained in $\mathcal{A}_1 = \mathrm{span}\{K(\cdot, \gamma_i)\}$.

By the Stone–Weierstrass theorem, $\mathcal{A}_1$ is then dense in $C(\Gamma, \mathbb{R})$ in the uniform topology (see, for instance, [27]). This method explicitly links the choice of basis to covering numbers $N(\Gamma, \|\cdot\|_{\mathcal{H}_k}, \varepsilon)$, which determines the discretization size $|\mathcal{G}_\varepsilon| = d$, which are also relevant in the analysis of the confidence parameter $\beta_T$ in the regret bounds.

Method 2: Spectral decomposition of the kernel operator. Assume that $K\colon \Gamma \times \Gamma \to \mathbb{R}$ is continuous and positive-definite on a compact $\Gamma$ with associated Mercer decomposition

$$K(\gamma, \gamma') = \sum_{m=1}^{\infty} \lambda_m \, \phi_m(\gamma) \, \phi_m(\gamma'),$$

where $(\lambda_m)_{m \geq 1}$ are positive eigenvalues and $(\phi_m)_{m \geq 1}$ are orthonormal eigenfunctions in $L^2(\Gamma, \mu)$ for some finite Borel measure $\mu$. Select $\gamma_i \in \Gamma$ such that $\gamma_i$ corresponds to the RKHS representative associated with $\phi_i$, and take $d$ large enough so that $\sum_{m>d} \lambda_m$ is below a desired threshold. The kernel sections $K(\cdot, \gamma_i)$ inherit the properties of separation and constant inclusion, and the span of the first $d$ eigenfunctions produces a finite-dimensional approximation space whose richness improves with $d$. For details on Mercer expansions and spectral selection strategies, see [34].

In both methods, the returned finite set $\{\gamma_1, \ldots, \gamma_d\}$ serves as a basis for the algebra $\mathcal{A}_1$, ensuring that the approximation property required by the Stone–Weierstrass theorem holds to within the desired tolerance on compact subsets of $\mathcal{H}_k$.

## References

1. Ratliff, L.J.; Dong, R.; Sekar, S.; Fiez, T. A perspective on incentive design: Challenges and opportunities. *Annu. Rev. Control Robot Auton. Syst.* **2009**, *2*, 305–338.
2. Pearl, J. A probabilistic calculus of actions. In *Uncertainty in Artificial Intelligence*; Morgan Kaufmann: San Mateo, CA, USA, 1994 pp. 454–462.
3. Correa, J.; Bareinboim, E. A Calculus for Stochastic Interventions: Causal Effect Identification and Surrogate Experiments. In Proceedings of the AAAI Conference on Artificial Intelligence, New York, NY, USA, 7–12 February 2020; Volume 34, pp. 10093–10100
4. Williams, C.K.; Rasmussen, C.E. *Gaussian Processes for Machine Learning*; The MIT Press: Cambridge, MA, USA, 2006.
5. Snoek, J.; Larochelle, H.; Adams, R.P. Practical bayesian optimization of machine learning algorithms. *Adv. Neural Inf. Process Syst.* **2012**, *25*.
6. Vien, N.A.; Zimmermann, H.; Toussaint, M. Bayesian Functional Optimization. In Proceedings of the Thirty-Second AAAI Conference on Artificial Intelligence, New Orleans, LA, USA, 2–7 February 2018; pp. 4171–4178.
7. Srinivas, N.; Krause, A.; Kakade, S.M.; Seeger, M.W. Information-theoretic regret bounds for Gaussian process optimization in the bandit setting. *IEEE Trans. Inf. Theory* **2012**, *58*, 3250–3265. [CrossRef]
8. Chowdhury, S.R.; Gopalan, A. On kernelized multi-armed bandits. In Proceedings of the International Conference on Machine Learning, PMLR, Sydney, Australia, 6–11 August 2017; pp. 844–853.
9. Laffont, J.J.; Martimort, D. *The Theory of Incentives: The Principal-Agent Model*; Princeton University Press: Princeton, NJ, USA, 2009

https://doi.org/10.3390/e28010004

Basar, T.; Selbuz, H. Closed-Loop Stackelberg Strategies with Applications in the Optimal Control of Multilevel Systems. *IEEE Trans. Autom. Control* **1979**, *24*, 166–179. [CrossRef]

Dempe, S.; Zemkoho, A. (Eds.) *Bilevel Optimization: Advances and Next Challenges*; Springer International Publishing: Berlin/Heidelberg, Germany, 2020.

Yang, J.; Wang, E.; Trivedi, R.; Zhao, T.; Zha, H. Adaptive Incentive Design with Multi-Agent Meta-Gradient Reinforcement Learning. In Proceedings of the 21st International Conference on Autonomous Agents and Multiagent Systems, Virtual, 9–13 May 2022; pp. 1436–1445.

Ho, C.-J.; Slivkins, A.; Vaughan, J.W. Adaptive Contract Design for Crowdsourcing Markets: Bandit Algorithms for Repeated Principal–Agent Problems. *J. Artif. Intell. Res.* **2016**, *55*, 317–359. [CrossRef]

Fiez, T.; Sekar, S.; Zheng, L.; Ratliff, L.J. Combinatorial Bandits for Incentivizing Agents with Dynamic Preferences. In Proceedings of the 34th Conference on Uncertainty in Artificial Intelligence, Monterey, CA, USA, 6–10 August 2018; pp. 247–257.

Guresti, B.; Vanlioglu, A.; Ure, N.K. IQ-Flow: Mechanism Design for Inducing Cooperative Behavior to Self-Interested Agents in Sequential Social Dilemmas. In Proceedings of the 22nd International Conference on Autonomous Agents and Multiagent Systems, London, UK, 29 May–2 June 2023; pp. 2143–2160.

Mguni, D.; Jennings, J.; Macua, S.V.; Sison, E.; Ceppi, S.; Cote, E.M.D. Coordinating the Crowd: Inducing Desirable Equilibria in Non-Cooperative Systems. In Proceedings of the 18th International Conference on Autonomous Agents and Multiagent Systems, Montreal, QC, Canada, 13–17 May 2019; pp. 386–394.

Jiang, J.; Wu, L.; Yu, J.; Wang, M.; Kong, H.; Zhang, Z.; Wang, J. Robustness of bilayer railway-aviation transportation network considering discrete cross-layer traffic flow assignment. *Transp. Res. Part D Transp. Environ.* **2024**, *127*, 104071. [CrossRef]

Lattimore, F.; Lattimore, T.; Reid, M.D. Causal Bandits: Learning Good Interventions via Causal Inference. *Adv. Neural Inf. Process. Syst.* **2016**, *29*, 1181–1189.

Bareinboim, E.; Forney, A.; Pearl, J. Bandits with Unobserved Confounders: A Causal Approach. *Adv. Neural Inf. Process. Syst.* **2015**, *28*, 1342–1350.

Lee, S.; Bareinboim, E. Structural Causal Bandits: Where to Intervene? *Adv. Neural Inf. Process. Syst.* **2018**, *31*, 6276–6286.

Lee, S.; Bareinboim, E. Structural Causal Bandits with Non-Manipulable Variables. In Proceedings of the Thirty-Third AAAI Conference on Artificial Intelligence, Honolulu, HI, USA, 27 January–1 February 2019; pp. 4164–4172.

Buesing, L.; Weber, T.; Zwols, Y.; Racaniere, S.; Guez, A.; Lespiau, J.B.; Heess, N. Woulda, Coulda, Shoulda: Counterfactually-Guided Policy Search. *arXiv* **2019**, arXiv:1811.06272.

Madumal, P.; Miller, T.; Sonenberg, L.; Vetere, F. Explainable Reinforcement Learning Through a Causal Lens. In Proceedings of the AAAI Conference on Artificial Intelligence, New York, NY, USA, 7–12 February 2020; Volume 34, pp. 2493–2500.

Aglietti, V.; Lu, X.; Paleyes, A.; González, J. Causal Bayesian Optimization. In Proceedings of the 23rd International Conference on Artificial Intelligence and Statistics, Online, 26–28 August 2020; Volume 108, pp. 22–31.

Gultchin, L.; Virginia, A.; Alexis, B.; Silvia, C. Functional Causal Bayesian Optimization. In Proceedings of the Thirty-Ninth Conference on Uncertainty in Artificial Intelligence, Pittsburgh, PA, USA, 31 July–4 August 2023; Volume 216, pp. 756–765.

Pearl, J. *Causality: Models, Reasoning, and Inference*, 2nd ed.; Cambridge University Press: Cambridge, UK, 2009.

Cucker, F.; Smale, S. On the mathematical foundations of learning. *Bull. Am. Math. Soc.* **2002**, *39*, 1–49. [CrossRef]

Thomas, M.T.C.A.J.; Joy, A.T. *Elements of Information Theory*; Wiley-Interscience: New York, NY, USA, 2006.

Goldberg, P.; Williams, C.; Bishop, C. Regression with input-dependent noise: A Gaussian process treatment. *Adv. Neural Inf. Process. Syst.* **1997**, *10*, 493–495.

Bejos, S.; Sucar, L.E.; Morales, E.F. Estimating Bounds on Causal Effects Considering Unmeasured Common Causes. In Proceedings of the International Conference on Probabilistic Graphical Models (PMLR), Nijmegen, The Netherlands, 11–13 September 2024; pp. 498–514.

Zhang, T. *Mathematical Analysis of Machine Learning Algorithms*; Cambridge University Press: Cambridge, UK, 2023.

Aronszajn, N. Theory of reproducing kernels. *Trans. Am. Math. Soc.* **1950**, *68*, 337–404. [CrossRef]

Rudin, W. *Principles of Mathematical Analysis*, 3rd ed.; International Series in Pure and Applied Mathematics; McGraw-Hill: New York, NY, USA, 1976.

Bach, F. On the equivalence between kernel quadrature rules and random feature expansions. *J. Mach. Learn. Res.* **2017**, *18*, 1–38.



https://doi.org/10.3390/e28010004

*entropy*

MDPI

*Article*

# Compositional Causal Identification from Imperfect or Disturbing Observations

**Isaac Friend [1,*], Aleks Kissinger [1], Robert W. Spekkens [2] and Elie Wolfe [2]**

1 Department of Computer Science, University of Oxford, Oxford OX1 3QD, UK; aleks.kissinger@cs.ox.ac.uk
2 Perimeter Institute for Theoretical Physics, 31 Caroline Street North, Waterloo, ON N2L 2Y5, Canada; rspekkens@perimeterinstitute.ca (R.W.S.); ewolfe@perimeterinstitute.ca (E.W.)
* Correspondence: icf22@cantab.ac.uk

**Abstract**

The usual inputs for a causal identification task are a graph representing qualitative causal hypotheses and a joint probability distribution for some of the causal model's variables when they are observed rather than intervened on. Alternatively, the available probabilities sometimes come from a combination of passive observations and controlled experiments. It also makes sense, however, to consider causal identification with data collected via schemes more generic than (perfect) passive observation or perfect controlled experiments. For example, observation procedures may be noisy, may disturb the variables, or may yield only coarse-grained specification of the variables' values. In this work, we investigate identification of causal quantities when the probabilities available for inference are the probabilities of outcomes of these more generic schemes. Using process theories (aka symmetric monoidal categories), we formulate graphical causal models as second-order processes that respond to such data collection instruments. We pose the causal identification problem relative to arbitrary sets of available instruments. Perfect passive observation instruments—those that produce the usual observational probabilities used in causal inference—satisfy an abstract process-theoretic property called *marginal informational completeness*. This property also holds for other (sets of) instruments. The main finding is that in the case of Markovian models, as long as the available instruments satisfy this property, the probabilities they produce suffice for identification of interventional quantities, just as those produced by perfect passive observations do. This finding sharpens the distinction between the Markovianity of a causal model and that of a probability distribution, suggesting a more extensive line of investigation of causal inference within a process-theoretic framework.

**Keywords:** causal identification; process theories; causal Bayesian networks; directed acyclic graphs; acyclic directed mixed graphs; string diagrams

## 1. Introduction

One use of causal graphical models is to formulate and solve problems of *identification of causal effects*—or *causal identification*—in which hypotheses about the existence and direction of causal relationships between variables are used together with observational data to infer the effects of interventions. The interventions with effects to be computed may be either "atomic" interventions, represented with Pearl's "do" operator [1], or more complicated ones involving randomness or dependence on other variables in a model [2]. Similarly, the data available for inference may be simply the joint probabilities of outcomes of what we will call *perfect passive observation*, or may be outcome probabilities associated with various kinds of combinations of perfect passive observation via controlled experiments [3]. In this work, we define graphical causal models in a way that is equivalent to standard ones but is designed to support reasoning about quite general classes of interactions between an agent and a causal data-generating process. This framework allows us to pose and solve new kinds of causal identification problems based on these more general types of probing schemes. We demonstrate the application of such a framework in the case of Markovian models, i.e., those in which every variable can be observed at least in some way. It is well known that for a Markovian causal model associated with a directed acyclic graph, all the model's parameters, and hence essentially all interventional quantities, are identifiable from the graph and the joint distribution of the model's variables under perfect passive observation. Identifiability seems to depend on the existence of a certain factorization of that distribution. We consider probing schemes that may yield only partial information about variables' values and that may also disturb those values. The outcome distributions for these schemes cannot generally be factored in the same way as distributions obtained via perfect passive observations; however, if the probing scheme satisfies certain abstract criteria, then it may serve as well as ordinary perfect passive observations for the purpose of identification in Markovian models.

In a graphical causal model as we define it, each node in a directed graph corresponds to an *intervention locus* where a variable "arrives" and then "leaves", with the possibility for probing or manipulation in between. A generic interaction with a variable at a locus is represented by an *instrument*, examples of which include a perfect passive observation, which reports the value of a variable without changing it, and a *surgical* intervention, which discards the incoming value and sets the outgoing value. With all types of probing schemes represented by the same sort of mathematical entity, we can pose different kinds of causal identification problems by declaring different kinds of interaction to be available as means of gathering data for inference. Thus, we can ask about identification of causal quantities from statistics generated under combinations of passive observation and controlled experiments [4], or more generally under probing schemes that cannot obviously be classified as purely observational or purely experimental. Formulating and solving identification problems using these more generic probing schemes is the main contribution of the present paper.

The mathematical technology used in this paper is that of *process theories*, which are categories for composing input–output processes in sequence and in parallel. These categories arise in logic, computation, physics, and topology [5]. They admit graphical calculi of *string diagrams*, which we use to represent and calculate with processes. The present article builds on an approach to causal inference [6,7] in which the qualitative causal hypotheses in a directed acyclic graph specify a morphism in a *syntactic* process theory; then, a concrete data-generating process conforming to those hypotheses is a functorial interpretation of that morphism in a *semantic* process theory of matrices (the first of these cited works addresses causal identification only with ordinary observational data, i.e., data from perfect passive observations; the second does not discuss identification at all). This article also shares technical infrastructure with [8] and the conference paper [9]. It generalizes a result from [9] (specifically, it generalizes the $\mathbf{Mat}[\mathbb{R}_+]$ case of Proposition 28 of [9] to graphs with arbitrarily many nodes and to instruments that may not be $\circ$-separable), but uses a different technique and is not concerned with the parallel treatment of classical and quantum causal models.

## 2. Process Theories, Bayesian Networks, and Causal Identification

A Bayesian network of the most basic kind consists of a directed acyclic graph and a probability distribution that is Markov-compatible with that graph. For example, a joint distribution $P(ABCDE)$ is Markov-compatible with the graph

$G :=$ 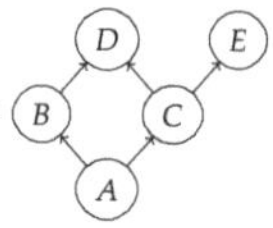 (1)



precisely when

$$P(ABCDE) = P(A)P(B|A)P(C|A)P(D|BC)P(E|C). \quad (2)$$

### 2.1. Process Theories

We represent both the distribution and the factorization implied by the graph using process-theoretic formalism. A *process theory* is a certain kind of category used for representing the parallel and sequential composition of input–output processes (e.g., matrices). It consists of objects, called *system-types* (e.g., integers indicating cardinalities of variables), and morphisms between system-types, called *processes*, with the ordinary composition $\circ$ viewed as sequential composition of processes, and another operation $\otimes$ for composing system-types and processes in parallel.

One of the system-types, say $I$, is a unit for $\otimes$ (i.e., for any system-type $A$, $A \otimes I = A = I \otimes A$) and represents "empty" systems. It appears as the domain of processes "with no input" and as the codomain of processes "with no output". Processes of the form $\rho : I \to A$ are called *states*, and processes of the form $\pi : A \to I$ are called *effects* (the term "effect" comes from quantum theory, where it refers to a physical effect resulting from a measurement [10]). Processes of the form $\lambda : I \to I$ are called *numbers* or *scalars*.

For any system-type $A$, the identity process $id_A : A \to A$ represents "doing nothing" to any given "instance" of that system-type. The interaction of $\circ$, $\otimes$, and identity processes is subject to axioms guaranteeing that those two operations and the identity processes appropriately model sequential and parallel composition of processes. A precise definition of process theory in terms of *symmetric monoidal categories* follows. Further details on symmetric monoidal categories can be found in Mac Lane [11]. The process-theoretic language and diagrams in this paper largely follow the conventions in Coecke and Kissinger [12].

**Definition 1.** *A strict monoidal category $(\mathcal{C}, \otimes, I)$ is a category $\mathcal{C}$ with a functor $\otimes : \mathcal{C} \times \mathcal{C} \to \mathcal{C}$, called the monoidal product, and an object $I \in \mathcal{C}$, called the monoidal unit, such that for objects $A$, $B$, and $C$ and morphisms $f, g$, and $h$,*

- $(A \otimes B) \otimes C = A \otimes (B \otimes C)$
- $(f \otimes g) \otimes h = f \otimes (g \otimes h)$
- $A \otimes I = I \otimes A = A$
- $f \otimes id_I = f = id_I \otimes f$

*with $id_X$ denoting the identity morphism for any object $X$.*

Because $\otimes$ is a functor, if $f, f', g$, and $g'$ are morphisms such that the composites $f' \circ f$ and $g' \circ g$ are defined, then

$$(f' \otimes g') \circ (f \otimes g) = (f' \circ f) \otimes (g' \circ g).$$

In this paper, morphisms are interpreted as processes, objects are interpreted as the input and output systems (more precisely, types of systems) of those processes, and the ordinary composition $\circ$ and monoidal product $\otimes$ are interpreted as operations for composing processes in sequence and in parallel, respectively. Therefore, it is useful for each category to have special morphisms for interchanging the order of systems, as in a circuit model of computation, where the lines representing two registers in a diagram may need to be brought together so that a box representing a gate can be applied to them.

**Definition 2.** *A strict symmetric monoidal category is a strict monoidal category with an isomorphism $\sigma_{A,B} : A \otimes B \to B \otimes A$ for every pair of objects $A, B$ such that for any morphisms $f : A \to A', g : B \to B'$ and any object $C$,*

$$\sigma_{B,A} \circ \sigma_{A,B} = id_{A \otimes B}$$
$$\sigma_{A,I} = id_A$$
$$(g \otimes f) \circ \sigma_{A,B} = \sigma_{A',B'} \circ (f \otimes g)$$
$$(id_B \otimes \sigma_{A,C}) \circ (\sigma_{A,B} \otimes id_C) = \sigma_{A,B \otimes C}.$$

A *process theory* is a strict symmetric monoidal category. Referring to a strict symmetric monoidal category as a process theory connotes a conception of the morphisms in the category as input–output processes; accordingly, to aid thinking and communication, we introduce the additional special terminology of system-types, processes, states, effects, and numbers/scalars for the objects and morphisms in a certain process theory. The isomorphisms $\sigma_{A,B}$ are called *swap maps*.

In this paper, processes are denoted by *string diagrams*, with generic processes depicted as boxes and objects as wires in diagrams read from bottom to top.

$f : A \to B \rightsquigarrow$ 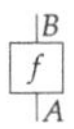

$\rho : I \to A \rightsquigarrow$ 

$\pi : A \to I \rightsquigarrow$ 

Boxes depicting states and effects may have either triangular or rectangular shape. Certain processes are depicted by special icons such as dots, with wires indicating their input and output system-types. The unit system-type $I$ and identity process $I \to I$ are depicted by empty space. Other identity processes $A \to A$ are depicted by extensions of the wires that depict the objects.

$id_A : A \to A \rightsquigarrow$ 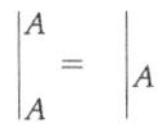

$id_I : I \to I \rightsquigarrow$ 


Sequential composition is indicated by boxes that are plugged together, while parallel composition is indicated by boxes or wires placed side-by-side (examples in the context of causal modeling can be found in Otsuka and Saigo [13]). Crossing wires indicate a swap map. The axioms for process theories ensure that a diagram deformed in such a way that connections are preserved represents the same process as the original.

### 2.2. The Process Theory $\mathbf{Mat}[\mathbb{R}_+]$

All our causal models in this paper will involve a process theory of matrices of non-negative real numbers, within which processes on classical probabilistic systems with finitely many configurations can be modeled. This process theory, called $\mathbf{Mat}[\mathbb{R}_+]$, has as system-types natural numbers, interpreted in this paper as the cardinalities of random variables. Sometimes, when discussing a generic system-type $A$, we want to refer specifically to the cardinality of the random variable associated with $A$; this cardinality is written $|A|$.

The processes $M : m \to n$ are the $n \times m$ matrices with entries that are non-negative real numbers $\{M^i_j \mid 1 \le i \le n, 1 \le j \le m\}$. Sequential composition is matrix multiplication; thus, identity maps are identity matrices.

Parallel composition of processes is given by the tensor product of matrices (aka the Kronecker product). The unit system-type is 1 (for which the identity process is the $1 \times 1$ matrix $[1] : 1 \to 1$); thus, scalars in this process theory are $1 \times 1$ matrices, or equivalently non-negative real numbers.

For each system-type $n$ in $\mathbf{Mat}[\mathbb{R}_+]$, let $d_n : n \to 1$ be the $1 \times n$ matrix (i.e., row vector) consisting of all 1s. This effect, called *discarding*, is depicted below.

$d_A : A \to I \quad \rightsquigarrow$ 

For a fixed system-type $A$ in $\mathbf{Mat}[\mathbb{R}_+]$, the state

is the column vector with 1 in position $i$ and 0s elsewhere, encoding certainty that a system is in the $i$th configuration. We sometimes call this state a "standard basis state". The effect

which we sometimes call a "standard basis effect", is the matrix transpose of this state. For any labeled state (respectively, effect) in $\mathbf{Mat}[\mathbb{R}_+]$, the effect (respectively, state) with the same label is provided by matrix transposition. We also call standard basis states *pure* states.

**Definition 3.** *A process $f : A \to B$ in $\mathbf{Mat}[\mathbb{R}_+]$ is called* normalized *if $d_B \circ f = d_A$, or diagrammatically as shown below.*

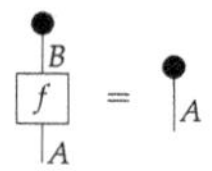 (3)

The normalization condition means that if the output of the process is discarded, then the actual process that took place is irrelevant. We can use Equation (3) to simplify composite processes by letting discard maps "fall through" normalized components.

From the definitions of discarding and normalization, it follows that normalized states in $\mathbf{Mat}[\mathbb{R}_+]$ are column vectors with entries summing to 1 (i.e., probability distributions), while normalized processes are matrices with columns each summing to 1 (i.e., stochastic maps, equivalent to conditional probability distributions with $P(i|j) := M^i_j$).

For a normalized state $\rho$ on system-type $A$, the composite

of $\rho$ with effect $i$ is the probability of a system described by a random variable with $|A|$ values and distribution $\rho$ being found in the $i$th configuration if checked. Effect $i$ can be said to represent the property of being in the $i$th configuration.

The theory $\mathbf{Mat}[\mathbb{R}_+]$ has a *copy* map for each system-type $A$, defined by

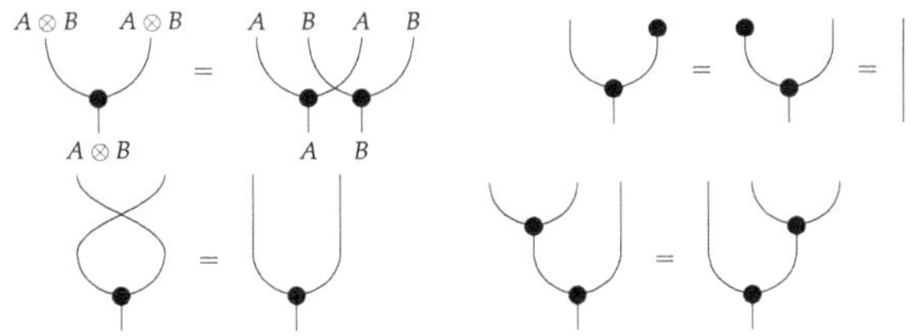


(4)

and the requirement that the copy map for $I$ be $id_I$. In light of the last of the above equations, it makes sense to draw copy maps with arbitrarily many outputs, as shown below.

A copy map with one output is an identity map; a copy map with no outputs is a discard map. Process theories with such families of copy and discard maps [14] are called *copy-discard process theories*. Concretely, the copy map $A \to A \otimes A$ is the matrix that copies pure normalized states; composing it with any of the $|A|$ standard basis states $i : I \to A$ yields $i \otimes i$.

### 2.3. *Bayesian Networks in* $\mathbf{Mat}[\mathbb{R}_+]$

To understand how a graph such as the one in (1) constrains probability distributions (or, in causal inference, causal data-generating processes) but does not determine a single distribution (or data-generating process), it is useful to first associate with each graph a formal string diagram composed of labeled boxes and wires (and black dots), then consider the class of (usually many) processes in $\mathbf{Mat}[\mathbb{R}_+]$ that can result from interpreting the boxes in the formal string diagram as specific matrices. The formal string diagram either depicts a process in a *syntactic* process theory defined by the graph [6], or is itself such a process [9]. We arrive at a specific distribution (or data-generating process) by interpreting the components of the formal diagram as specific normalized processes in $\mathbf{Mat}[\mathbb{R}_+]$. In the causal context, we call the formal string diagram associated with a graph a *syntactic causal structure* and call its interpretations in $\mathbf{Mat}[\mathbb{R}_+]$ *semantic causal structures*. For now, we will not distinguish carefully between a string diagram carrying a (perhaps arbitrary) interpretation in $\mathbf{Mat}[\mathbb{R}_+]$ and one divorced from any interpretation; later, we introduce special notation for this distinction.

To form the abstract string diagram associated with a directed acyclic graph $G$, we first introduce a box $a : X_1 \otimes \ldots \otimes X_n \to A$ for every node $A$ in $G$ with parents $\{X_1, \ldots, X_n\}$. Each node in the graph now has an abstract *system-type label* that can appear on the input or output wires of boxes, and there is one box for each node. We compose these boxes by connecting each output $A$ to an output of the overall diagram as well as to the inputs of each of the boxes associated with children of $A$ in $G$, introducing copy maps where necessary. Calling a normalized state in $\mathbf{Mat}[\mathbb{R}_+]$ Markov with respect to $G$ means that it factorizes according to that diagram for some interpretation of the boxes as normalized processes (i.e., stochastic matrices). For example, a normalized state $\omega : I \to A \otimes B \otimes C \otimes D \otimes E$ is

Markov with respect to the graph $G$ from (1) when it can be decomposed as shown below for some normalized processes $a, b, c, d,$ and $e$.

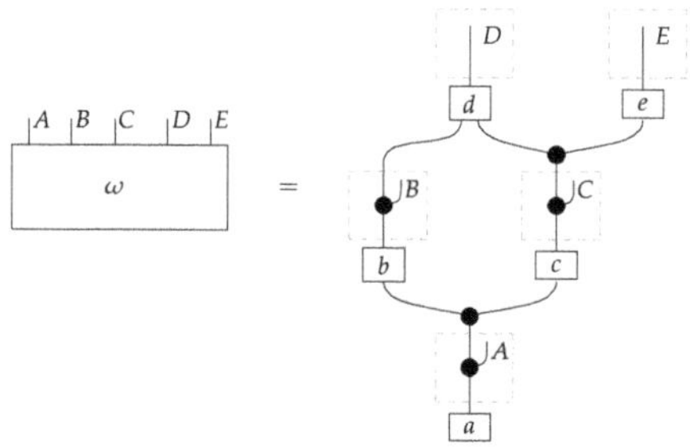


(5)

This diagrammatic condition corresponds precisely to the factorization of $P(ABCDE)$ in (2), where $P(ABCDE)$ is the joint probability distribution provided by the state $\omega$. The diagram on the right-hand side of (5), with the boxes read as the appropriate stochastic matrices, is said to represent the state $\omega$ (i.e., the probability distribution $P(ABCDE)$) as a Bayesian network. Bayesian networks can efficiently represent probability distributions in many computational contexts. A Bayesian network representation allows a state on many variables (output system-types)–which generally requires a number of parameters exponential in the number of variables–to be specified by relatively few conditional probabilities. If each of five variables has cardinality 10, then a generic joint state on the five variables involves $10^5$ numbers. If the state is Markov-compatible with graph $G$ in this example, it can be represented as a Bayesian network as in (5), and this representation involves only 1310 numbers: 10 for matrix $a$, 100 for each of the $10 \times 10$ matrices $b, c,$ and $e$, and 1000 for the $10 \times 100$ matrix $d$.

Inference with Bayesian networks is efficient because updates can be made "locally" and then propagated only to those matrices where they might make a difference. In the current example, assume that a specific distribution Markov-compatible with $G$ is stored as a Bayesian network. To update the distribution on $A, B, D,$ and $E$ using new knowledge that $C$ has taken value $i$, we can compose the state $\omega$ with the effect $i : C \to I$ having 1 in position $i$ and 0s elsewhere (the $i$th standard basis effect for $C$). Any standard basis effect $i$ in $\mathbf{Mat}[\mathbb{R}_+]$ satisfies

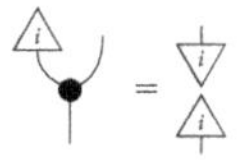

(6)

and the result is the same regardless of which of the two outputs of the copy map is plugged into the effect. Therefore, the updated state up to normalization is as follows.

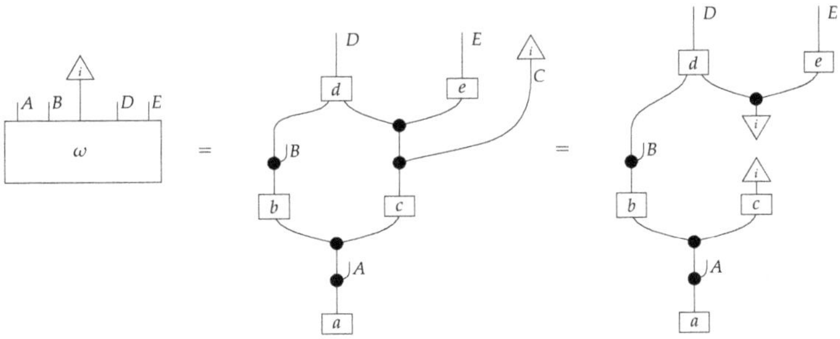


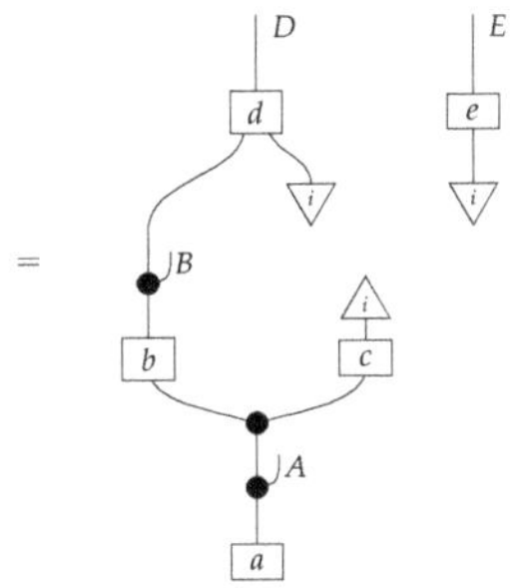


Suppose that we wish to know the new distribution for $E$ alone. Up to normalization, this state is as follows.

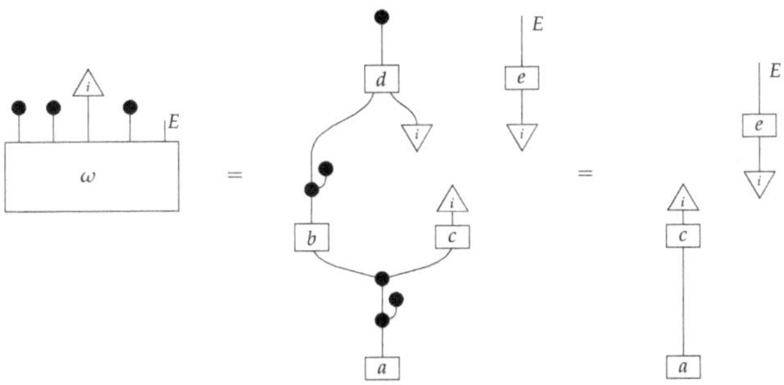


We can see that the normalized state will be some scalar times

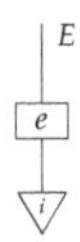


but the latter diagram is already a normalized state (it is a column of the matrix $e$). Therefore, we can obtain the new distribution for $E$ simply by extracting the appropriate column of $e$. If we are only interested in this distribution, then we do not need to update any other part of the joint state.

### *2.4. Interventions and Causal Identification*

For the kind of probabilistic inference just demonstrated, it does not matter why the joint distribution is known to be Markov-compatible with a particular graph, or equivalently, why the state is known to decompose according to a particular string diagram. In causal inference, on the other hand, it is assumed that the reason the state decomposes according to the string diagram is that the data have been generated by actual mechanisms represented by maps such as $a, \ldots, e$. For each of these maps, the inputs and outputs are assumed to depend on those of the other maps in a manner corresponding to the connections in the diagram. Each box is understood to determine (stochastically) the value of its output variable given any value of its input variable, and to do so independently of the operation of the other mechanisms in the network. A concept of *local intervention* is introduced, with which we can imagine overriding the value of the variable associated with a single wire while leaving the rest of the network unchanged. In the running example, an intervention whereby variable $B$ is forcibly set to a chosen value $i$ is represented as follows.

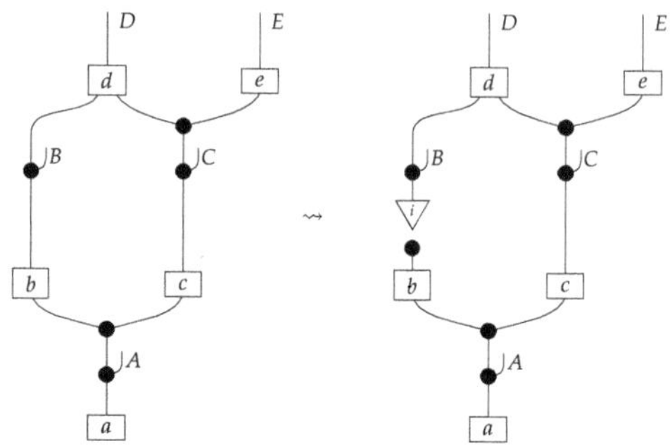


(7)

The output of process $b$ is no longer input to $d$; instead, the state $i$ is input. The intervention, which in Pearl's formalism is implemented by the famous "do" operator, results in a different joint state from $\omega$, called an *interventional distribution*. A Bayesian network understood as responding to interventions in this way is called a *causal Bayesian network*. A *causal identification* problem in the setting of causal Bayesian networks concerns inferring properties of the interventional distribution that a fixed, but initially incompletely known, causal Bayesian network would generate in response to certain hypothetical interventions.Interventions in a causal Bayesian network represent actions that for modeling purposes are considered performable at least "in principle" (where the meaning of "in principle" can vary with the application) in real-world causal scenarios associated with the network.

The inputs for an identification problem involving a causal Bayesian network include assumptions about the "shape" of the network and some of the data generated by the network. Typically, "shape" assumptions are simply given as the directed acyclic graph itself, with nodes labeled by variables; on the other hand, the data are given as a joint state resulting from no intervention, and as such are understood to represent an "observed distribution". If the joint state has an output for every node of the graph, then the causal Bayesian network is called *Markovian*. On the other hand, the joint state may only have outputs corresponding to some but not all of the variables; in other words, some variables may be unobserved or "latent", in which case the causal Bayesian network is called *non-Markovian*.

For example, one could be confronted with an unknown data-generating process satisfying causal assumptions given by the graph $G$ in (1), with the observational distribution $P(BCDE)$ of the form shown below.

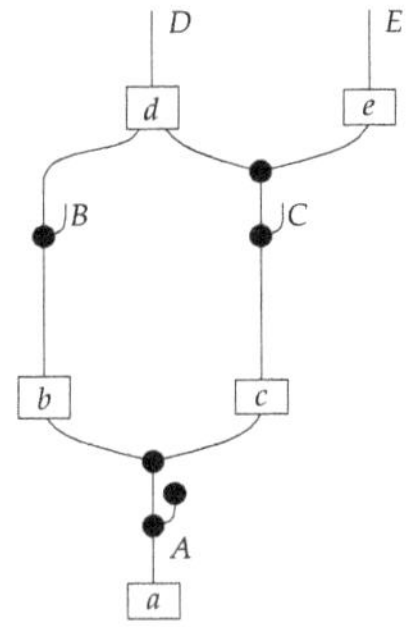


(8)

In this scenario, $A$ is a latent variable; note that the extra copy of $A$ output from the original state in (5) is discarded. One might be interested in the causal influence of $B$ on $D$, meaning the distribution

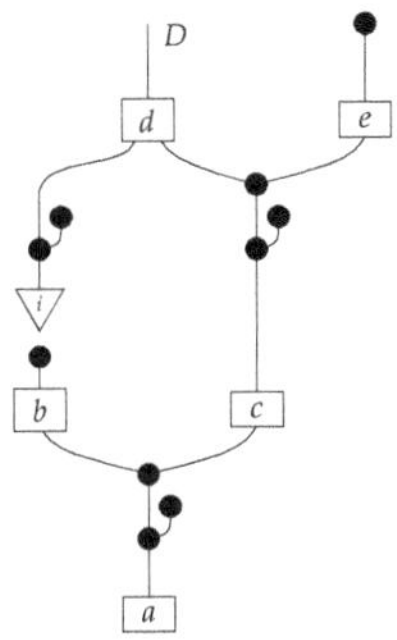


for every standard basis state $i$ on $B$. In Pearl's notation, such a distribution is written as $P(D|do(B = i))$. In general, the requested causal quantity may or may not be computable from the given information. There may be multiple causal Bayesian networks with the same graph that yield the same observational distribution (on a particular subset of the variables) but differ in the interventional distribution that one wants to infer. This is not the case for the current example, where despite the latent confounder $A$ it is still possible to tell whether observed correlations between $B$ and $D$ are due to causal dependence of $D$ on $B$ or to joint dependence on variable $A$. However, if $C$ were also latent, then distinguishing the causal influence of $B$ on $D$ from correlation underwritten by $A$ would be impossible. Various criteria discovered over the years following Pearl's introduction of the "do" operator (criteria summarized in Pearl's book [1]) can indicate whether the causal quantity of interest is computable, or *identifiable*, from a graph and an observational distribution. These criteria have to do with what kinds of paths exist between those vertices in the graph labeled by observed variables and those labeled by latent variables.

Jacobs, Kissinger, and Zanasi [6] cast some of these graphical criteria (and the associated procedures for computing interventional distributions when they are identifiable) in terms of process theories. In their presentation, as in ours here, a graph specifies an abstract string diagram—a formal composition of labeled boxes and black dots—that encodes qualitative hypotheses for a causal scenario. That *syntactic causal structure* constrains numerical parameters such that the concrete data-generating process in any causal model based on that syntactic causal structure is consistent with the qualitative hypotheses encoded in the syntactic causal structure. Thus, the syntactic causal structure plays the same role in this framework as labeled graphs do in other presentations.The values of numerical parameters are specified by a *semantic causal structure*, in which each component of the syntactic causal structure is *interpreted* via a *functor of process theories* as a particular stochastic matrix in **Mat**$[\mathbb{R}_+]$. The entire semantic causal structure is a process in **Mat**$[\mathbb{R}_+]$ that determines (perhaps stochastically) the results of interventions in the causal scenario. Then, in an identification problem, one is given a graph—and consequently the syntactic causal structure—together with limited access to the semantic causal structure, typically in the form of an observational probability distribution. With these inputs, one tries to infer further properties of the semantic causal structure that permit the computation of interventional quantities. (Some authors use the term "causal structure" to refer only to the kinds of patterns of causal dependence typically specified by graphs; here, we use the word "structure" in a more mathematical sense. In general, many semantic causal structures will be consistent with a single syntactic causal structure, i.e., a single syntactic causal structure will have many interpretations. The goal of causal identification is roughly to figure out which of the possible semantic causal structures in fact characterizes a causal scenario assumed to be governed by a certain syntactic causal structure).

**Example 1.** *It is well known that for any Markovian causal model based on a directed acyclic graph, any interventional quantity is identifiable from the graph and the probability distribution that the model generates under passive observation. Although this situation is sometimes described as "no intervention", we de-emphasize this description, as later in this paper we treat passive observation as just one kind of intervention regime). In our terminology, we can state this result for the case of the graph G in* (1) *as follows.*

*When given as an input for causal identification, graph G tells us that the unknown causal model has the form on the right-hand side of* (5)*; that is, it tells us that that diagram is the scenario's syntactic causal structure. Also given is the concrete probability distribution produced by the semantic causal structure. This distribution is encoded in the state $\omega$, or equivalently in the following numbers:*

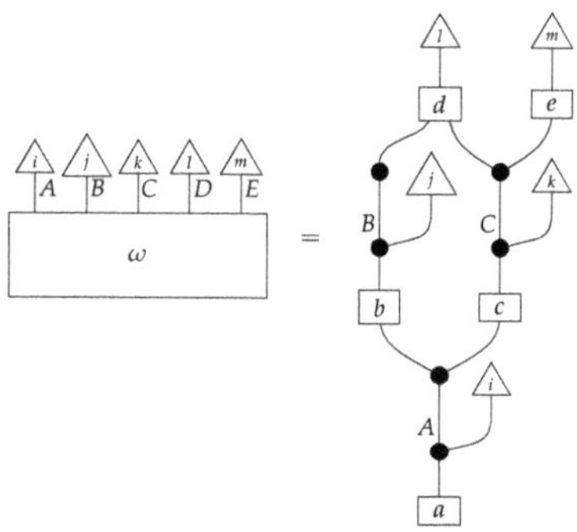


*where the effects $i, j, k, l$, and $m$ run independently over the standard basis effects for the system-types $A, B, C, D$, and $E$ in* ***Mat***$[\mathbb{R}_+]$ *(there are $|A|$ different effects $i$, $|B|$ different effects $j$, etc.). The matrix values (i.e., interpretations) of the boxes are not given; knowing them would allow us to identify arbitrary interventional quantities of the kind exemplified in* (7).

*As it happens, for any given normalized state (i.e., distribution) on $A \otimes B \otimes C \otimes D \otimes E$ in* ***Mat***$[\mathbb{R}_+]$*, there is only one joint interpretation of the boxes $a, b, c, d$, and $e$ in* (5) *that gives rise to this particular state; that is, the values of the boxes (and consequently the response of the model to interventions) are determined by the overall state (observational data).*

According to Pearl [15], noting the identifiability of Markovian models is the beginning of causal analysis in graphical models. We will continue to concentrate on Markovian models, reformulating them to address the question of identifiability if the given probabilities result from noisy and disturbing observations.

## 3. Instruments, Tomography, Combs, and Examples of Causal Inference

Because a set of matrices of non-negative real numbers is closed under sums, every hom-set in **Mat**$[\mathbb{R}_+]$ can be given the structure of a commutative monoid. Moreover, this monoidal structure is compatible with both sequential and parallel composition of processes in the sense that (for instance) composing the zero matrix $m \to n$ (i.e., the additive identity element) in sequence or in parallel with another process yields another zero matrix, and addition is distributive over both sequential and parallel composition. This "enrichment" of the process theory in the category of commutative monoids (see Mac Lane [11] for further details) implies that sums distribute over entire diagrams. Sums can therefore be introduced without parenthetical grouping, as shown below.

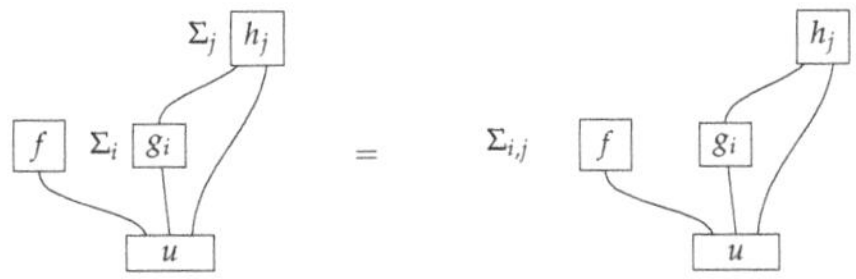

(9)

When composed with a normalized state, the sum of standard basis effects $i$ and $j$ provides the probability of the $i$th configuration plus the probability of the $j$th configuration. This sum can be said to represent the property of being in the $i$th or the $j$th configuration (for $i \neq j$). The sum of all the effects $i$ where the label $i$ runs from 1 to $|A|$ is the discarding map. This map's composition with a normalized state yields the number 1. The sum can be said to represent the property of "being in some configuration", which is satisfied with probability 1 by any system with a normalized state.

Sums in **Mat**$[\mathbb{R}_+]$ allow for the definition of mathematical entities representing quite generic ways in which agents may interact with processes. The concept of *instrument* used here is derived from quantum information science.

**Definition 4.** *A **Mat**$[\mathbb{R}_+]$-valued instrument of type $A \to A'$, where $A$ and $A'$ are system-types in **Mat**$[\mathbb{R}_+]$, is a finite set of maps, each of which has the form $\phi : A \to A'$, and of which the sum is a normalized map. Each map $\phi$ is called a* branch *of the instrument.*

When an agent carries out a procedure represented by an instrument, one of the instrument's branches is implemented and reported to the agent. The probability of a specific branch generally depends on both the branch and the process that the agent is probing with the instrument. An instrument with a single branch represents a procedure that results in the realization of that branch with probability 1.

**Example 2.** *For system-type $A$ in **Mat**$[\mathbb{R}_+]$, the $|A|$ standard basis effects constitute an instrument of type $A \to I$, as the sum of the standard basis effects is a discarding map, which is normalized. Suppose that an agent is confronted with (as many independent preparations as wanted of) an unknown normalized state $\rho : I \to A$ in **Mat**$[\mathbb{R}_+]$. When the agent "applies" the instrument to a single preparation, exactly one of the $|A|$ effects/branches is realized; effect $i$ is realized with probability $i \circ \rho$. By applying the instrument to a large number of preparations of $\rho$, the agent can use the frequencies to estimate the probabilities $i \circ \rho$. These probabilities determine the state $\rho$; indeed, they are the entries in the column vector.*

**Example 3.** *Let $A^{(2)}$ denote the system-type of a binary random variable with values denoted* 1 *and* 2. *(Mathematically, the system-type is the number* 2*, corresponding to the number of values, but we adopt alternative notation to distinguish between the values and the system-type.) Let*

$$\phi = \begin{bmatrix} 0.8 & 0.9 \end{bmatrix} \qquad \phi' = \begin{bmatrix} 0.2 & 0.1 \end{bmatrix}.$$

*Effects $\phi$ and $\phi'$ are the branches of an instrument of type $A^{(2)} \to I$. Suppose that we apply this instrument to an unknown normalized state $\rho : I \to A^{(2)}$) representing the variable's distribution. On a single "trial", if the variable's true value is* 1*, then $\phi$ is realized with probability* 0.8 *and $\phi'$ with probability* 0.2*. If the true value of the variable is* 2*, then $\phi$ is realized with probability* 0.9 *and $\phi'$ with probability* 0.1*. On each trial, the received information is simply which of $\phi$ and $\phi'$ has been realized. This information does not allow us to deduce from the trial which value the variable has taken, as we could in the previous example. Over a large number of trials, we can learn the probabilities $\phi \circ \rho$ and $\phi' \circ \rho$. Knowing the values of the instrument branches allows us to infer the entries in the vector $\rho$ from these probabilities, i.e., to infer the unknown state.*

In the above example, branch $\phi$ has higher likelihood than branch $\phi'$ for either value of the random variable modeled by $\rho$. However, the difference in relative likelihoods suffices for inference of $\rho$. A somewhat more intuitive example is one in which each value of the random variable makes a different instrument branch more likely but not certain, in such a way that the instrument represents a small deviation from the perfect observation in Example 2.

**Example 4.** *Let*

$$\phi = \begin{bmatrix} 0.8 & 0.1 \end{bmatrix} \qquad \phi' = \begin{bmatrix} 0.2 & 0.9 \end{bmatrix}.$$

*If we consider $\phi$ and $\phi'$ fuzzy versions of the predicate "has value* 1*" and "has value* 2*", respectively, then the instrument with branches $\phi$ and $\phi'$ "errs" twenty percent of the time when the true value of the random variable is* 1 *and ten percent of the time when true value is* 2*. If we know that we are using this instrument, we can infer an unknown state (on system-type $A^{(2)}$) exactly in the limit of infinitely many trials. Although this instrument is more informative on a single trial than the instrument in Example 3, the way in which the empirically revealed branch probabilities determine an initially unknown state is mathematically the same in both examples.*

**Example 5.** *A discarding map $d_A$ in $\boldsymbol{Mat}[\mathbb{R}_+]$ is the sole branch of an instrument of type $A \to I$. An agent applying this instrument to an unknown normalized state on system-type $A$ is told on each trial only that the single branch has been realized; the agent learns nothing about the state.*

**Example 6.** *Let $A^{(3)}$ denote the system-type of a ternary random variable with values denoted* 1, 2, *and* 3 *($A^{(3)}$ is convenient notation for the system-type* 3*). Let*

$$\phi = \begin{bmatrix} 1 & 0 & 0.5 \end{bmatrix} \qquad \phi' = \begin{bmatrix} 0 & 1 & 0.5 \end{bmatrix}.$$

*These two effects are the branches of an instrument of type $A^{(3)} \to I$. If we apply this instrument to an unknown normalized state on system-type $A^{(3)}$, then on a trial when we learn that $\phi$ has been realized, we can be certain that the true value of the random variable on that trial was not* 2*. If, on the other hand, we learn that $\phi'$ has been realized, we can be certain that the true value of the random variable was not* 1*. This instrument, however, does not allow us to infer from infinitely many trials the value (i.e., probability distribution) of an arbitrary state. Let the arbitrary state be*

$$\begin{bmatrix} a \\ b \\ c \end{bmatrix}.$$

*The probabilities of $\phi$ and $\phi'$ when the instrument is applied to this state are $a + 0.5c$ and $b + 0.5c$, respectively. If we learn these probabilities from many trials, then we learn two linear equations in three unknowns. We also know the normalization condition $a + b + c = 1$. These three equations do not generally have a unique solution for $a, b,$ and $c$.*

*Now, suppose that we have access to both the instrument $\{\phi, \phi'\}$ and another instrument $\{\pi, \pi'\}$ with*

$$\pi = \begin{bmatrix} 0 & 0 & 1 \end{bmatrix} \qquad\qquad \pi' = \begin{bmatrix} 1 & 1 & 0 \end{bmatrix}.$$

*Although neither instrument by itself suffices to determine arbitrary unknown normalized states, both instruments together do suffice: with the entries in the state called $a$, $b$, and $c$, as above, using the first instrument allows us to estimate $a + 0.5c$ and $b + 0.5c$, while using the second allows us to estimate $c$ and $a + b$. The resulting system of linear equations in $a, b,$ and $c$ has a unique solution.*

The procedure of inferring an unknown state using the probabilities of various instrument branches (that may not be standard basis effects) is called *state tomography*. For an unknown state $\rho$ and a known effect $\pi$ of appropriate type, once the probability $\pi \circ \rho$ is known, it does not matter what instrument (of which $\pi$ is a branch) was used to learn that probability. This irrelevance of the instrument under which an effect was realized extends to the instruments described below, for which the branches are not effects.

An agent's preparation of a normalized state is represented by a one-branch instrument $\{\rho : I \to A\}$. State preparation instruments can be used along with instruments made up of effects to perform *process tomography* on unknown normalized processes in $\mathbf{Mat}[\mathbb{R}_+]$ with generic input and output system-types.

**Example 7.** *Suppose that an agent is confronted with an unknown normalized process $f : A \to B$ in $\mathbf{Mat}[\mathbb{R}_+]$. In addition, suppose that the agent has access to a $|B|$-branch instrument consisting of the standard basis effects for $B$ and that for each standard basis state $i : I \to A$ the agent has access to state preparation instrument $\{ß : I \to A\}$ (that is, the agent can prepare any standard basis state at will). If the agent prepares standard basis state $i$ at the input of $f$, then the result is the state shown below.*

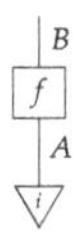


*If the agent now takes the instrument of type $B \to I$ consisting of the standard basis effects $j$ and applies it at the output of $f$, then each branch $j$ is realized with the following probability.*

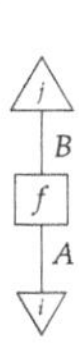

(10)

*The agent can learn these probabilities (for all standard basis effects $j$) by performing the experiment with the fixed state preparation instrument $\{i\}$ for infinitely many trials. By repeating this procedure with the preparation instruments for all standard basis states $i$, the agent can learn the probabilities*

(10) *for all $i$ and $j$. These probabilities are the entries in the matrix $f$; therefore, the agent has now learned the value of $f$.*

As some of these examples of state tomography suggest, other instruments $B \to I$ could be substituted for the instrument consisting of the standard basis effects, and process tomography would remain possible. Process tomography would also remain possible if the standard basis state preparations were replaced by certain other state preparations.

**Example 8.** *Let single-branch state preparation instruments $\{\psi\}$ and $\{\psi'\}$ be defined by*

$$\psi = \begin{bmatrix} 0.5 \\ 0.5 \end{bmatrix} \qquad \psi' = \begin{bmatrix} 0.9 \\ 0.1 \end{bmatrix}.$$

*These instruments together with the two instruments $\{\phi, \phi'\}$ and $\{\pi, \pi'\}$ of type $A^{(3)} \to I$ from Example 6 suffice for tomography of an unknown normalized process $f : A^{(2)} \to A^{(3)}$ in **Mat**$[\mathbb{R}_+]$. By applying each of the four possible combinations consisting of an instrument of type $I \to A^{(2)}$ and an instrument of type $A^{(3)} \to I$, we can learn the following probabilities from infinitely many trials:*

$$\begin{array}{cc} \phi \circ f \circ \psi & \phi \circ f \circ \psi' \\ \phi' \circ f \circ \psi & \phi' \circ f \circ \psi' \\ \pi \circ f \circ \psi & \pi \circ f \circ \psi' \\ \pi' \circ f \circ \psi & \pi' \circ f \circ \psi'. \end{array}$$

*These numbers are not themselves the entries of the matrix $f$, but they allow the entries to be determined. Here, we have essentially performed a controlled experiment on the black-box process $f$, but it is controlled in an unusual sense, as we could not choose the value to feed into $f$, only which of two known distributions the value would be drawn from.*

What matters for the tomography of a process $f : A \to B$ in **Mat**$[\mathbb{R}_+]$ is whether we can prepare enough linearly independent states and whether enough linearly independent effects appear in the instruments of type $B \to I$.

**Definition 5.** *A set of effects $\mathcal{E} = \{\pi : A \to I\}$ in a process theory is called* informationally complete *for system-type $A$ if any state $\rho : I \to A$ is uniquely determined by the set of numbers $\{\pi \circ \rho | \pi \in \mathcal{E}\}$. Similarly, a set of states $\mathcal{S} = \{\rho : I \to A\}$ is called informationally complete for $A$ if any effect $\pi : A \to I$ is uniquely determined by the set of numbers $\{\pi \circ \rho | \pi \in \mathcal{S}\}$.*

**Example 9.** *In **Mat**$[\mathbb{R}_+]$, an informationally complete set of states for system-type $A$ is a set of $|A|$ linearly independent column vectors of length $|A|$, while an informationally complete set of effects for $A$ is the set of transposes of such a set of column vectors. In particular, the set of standard basis states on $A$ is informationally complete, as is the associated set of effects.*

Tomography of arbitrary unknown normalized processes $f : A \to B$ (for fixed $A$ and $B$) in **Mat**$[\mathbb{R}_+]$ is possible if one has access to preparation instruments for all of an informationally complete set of normalized states on $A$ and access to instruments of type $B \to I$ for which union (a set of effects) is informationally complete for $B$.

The following property of **Mat**$[\mathbb{R}_+]$ regulates the tomography of processes with multiple inputs or multiple outputs.

**Proposition 1.** *In the process theory **Mat**$[\mathbb{R}_+]$, any process*

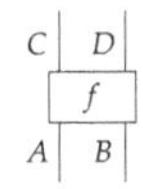

*is determined by numbers*

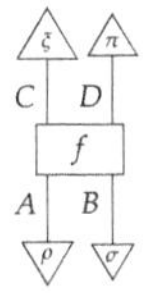

(11)

*where $\rho, \sigma, \xi$, and $\pi$ index any informationally complete sets of states or effects for the appropriate system-types. We call this property tomographic locality.*

**Proof.** The proposition follows from the prior characterization of informationally complete sets together with facts about tensor products in algebra, specifically, that tensor products of basis elements in two vector spaces span the tensor product of the spaces. □

Thus, one way to perform process tomography on an unknown normalized process $f : A \otimes B \to C \otimes D$ in $\mathbf{Mat}[\mathbb{R}_+]$ is to select an informationally complete set of normalized states $\{\rho : I \to A\}$, an informationally complete set of normalized states $\{\sigma : I \to B\}$, an informationally complete set of effects $\{\xi : C \to I\}$, and an informationally complete set of effects $\{\pi : D \to I\}$, then learn the probabilities in (11). In terms of instruments, for every pair of states $\rho$ and $\sigma$, it is necessary to probe $f$ over many "trials". On each trial, prepare the states $\rho$ and $\sigma$ on $f$'s inputs by applying the corresponding state preparation instruments, and measure $f$'s outputs with an instrument $C \to I$ and an instrument $D \to I$ for which the branches are the effects from $\{\xi : C \to I\}$ and $\{\pi : D \to I\}$, respectively. We assume for simplicity that each of the two sets of effects $\{\xi : C \to I\}$ and $\{\pi : D \to I\}$ forms a single instrument; in this case, only one pair of measurement instruments is needed for the process tomography protocol, while many single-branch state preparation instruments are needed. Alternatively, it may be that there are multiple instruments comprising different subsets of, e.g., $\{\xi : C \to I\}$. Then, for each fixed pair $\rho$ and $\sigma$, one would need to vary the measurement instrument $C \to I$). On each trial with states $\rho$ and $\sigma$, an effect $\xi$ and an effect $\pi$ will be realized. As the number of trials with fixed states $\rho$ and $\sigma$ approaches infinity, it becomes possible to estimate exactly the probabilities (11) for the fixed $\rho$ and $\sigma$ and for all $\xi$ and $\pi$. By varying the states $\rho$ and $\sigma$ in this procedure, we can obtain all of the probabilities necessary to determine the value of $f$.

The causal models to be defined in this paper involve second-order processes that take various first-order processes as input and determine the probabilities of outcomes of either "observational" or more "interventional" interactions with systems. Thus, for example, a causal model based on the graph

(12)

will involve a process

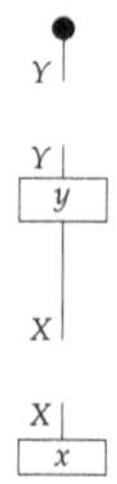


(13)

in $\mathbf{Mat}[\mathbb{R}_+]$, where $x$ and $y$ are normalized. Each variable now corresponds to an input–output pair, depicted as a gap in the wire. This splitting of variables into an input and an output is similar to the situation in a single-world intervention graph [16], where nodes are split in two. The idea of a causal model as a second-order process with an input and an output for each node appears in works [17,18] focused on "quantum causal models".

The gap formed by an input–output pair represents an *intervention locus* where a "system" arrives and then leaves, with an opportunity for interaction in between. The interactions in this case correspond to instruments of types $X \to X$ and $Y \to Y$; that is, when an instrument is applied at a gap, a branch is realized and reported to the agent applying the instrument. The "state" of the system that is fed forward depends on which branch has been realized.

If $f : X \to X$ is a branch of the instrument applied at the $X$ gap and $g : Y \to Y$ is a branch of the instrument applied at the $Y$ gap, then the joint probability of realizing $f$ and $g$ is as follows.

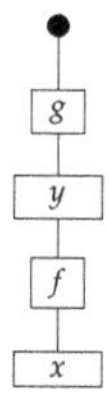


As shown below, the sum of these numbers over all pairs of branches $f$ and $g$ is 1, as the sums of the branches $f$ and of the branches $g$ are normalized maps.

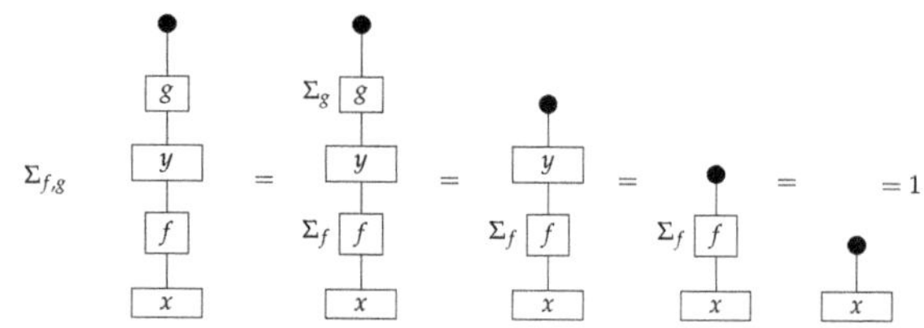

Following the quantum information literature [19], we call second-order processes with gaps *combs*. Each of these combs can still be specified as an ordinary first-order process in $\mathbf{Mat}[\mathbb{R}_+]$. Thus, the comb in (13) is a matrix $X \otimes Y \to X \otimes Y$, and is equivalently depicted as follows.

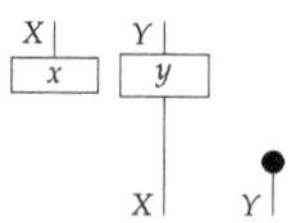


For technicalities regarding translation between the two representations—ensuring, e.g., consistency of calculations of the numbers generated by composition with processes $X \to X$ and $Y \to Y$—see Jacobs, Kissinger, and Zanasi [6]. In this paper, all combs are depicted in the style of (13). It is useful to keep in mind, however, that a comb is ultimately a matrix of numbers (in our setting, a matrix of conditional probabilities governing a causal scenario); for our purposes, causal inference will involve learning these matrix entries by applying instruments.

**Example 10.** *For any system-type A in* $\mathbf{Mat}[\mathbb{R}_+]$*, there is an instrument* $A \to A$ *for which the only branch is* $id_A$*. Applying this instrument at a gap does not extract any information for the agent, and leaves the variable to pass through undisturbed.*

**Example 11.** *For system-type A in* $\mathbf{Mat}[\mathbb{R}_+]$*, the perfect passive observation instrument of type* $A \to A$ *has* $|A|$ *branches forming a set (mathematically, the instrument is the set).*

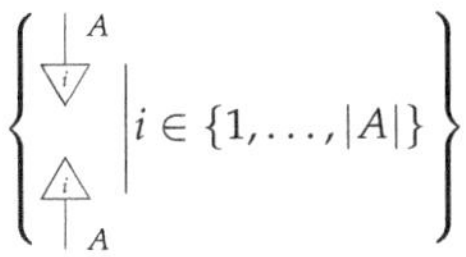

Knowing which branch of a perfect passive observation instrument has been realized means being certain of the value that a random variable has taken and being certain that the variable retains that value after observation.

**Example 12.** *For the comb in* (13)*, for perfect passive observation instruments* $X \to X$ *and* $Y \to Y$ *at the X and Y loci, respectively, the joint branch probabilities are*

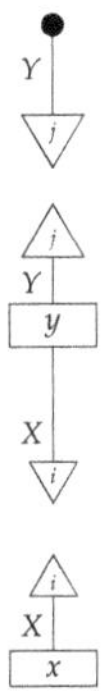

(14)

*where i runs from* 1 *to* $|X|$ *and j from* 1 *to* $|Y|$*. If we apply the instruments for infinitely many trials and record the frequency of each pair of branches* $i \circ i : X \to X$ *and* $j \circ j : Y \to Y$*, we learn a table indexed by i and j in which the entries are the probabilities in* (14)*. These probabilities would typically be written as* $P(X = i, Y = j)$*. They factorize as expected for a causal model conforming to the graph* (12)*—they have the form* $P(X = i)P(Y = j|do(X = i))$*, or equivalently the form shown below.*

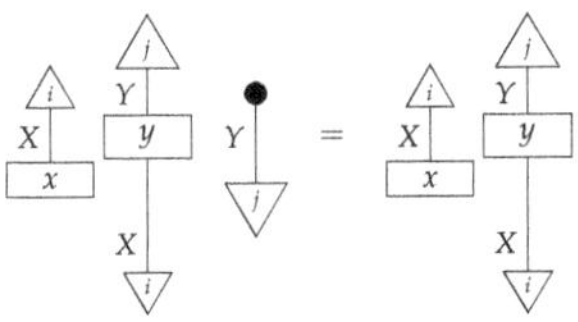

**Example 13.** *Another important example of an instrument of type* $A \to A$ *that can be applied at a gap in a comb is one that discards the incoming system and prepares a fixed normalized state* $\psi$ *for the outgoing system. A single-branch "discard-and-prepare" instrument has the following branch.*

*If $\psi$ is a standard basis state, then this instrument corresponds to what is called an "atomic" or "do" intervention. The state $\psi$ may also be mixed, either because the agent carrying out the intervention procedure cannot fully control which value the variable has after the intervention—and the resulting uncertainty is represented by a specific probability distribution—or because the intervention procedure is designed to randomize the value in a specific way.*

*One example of a causal identification task is to use joint branch probabilities for perfect passive observation instruments in order to infer how perfect passive observations at one locus would turn out if a discard-and-prepare instrument were applied at another locus. Suppose that in the comb* (13), $|X| = |Y| = 2$ *and, initially unbeknownst to us, we have*

$$x = \begin{bmatrix} 0.8 \\ 0.2 \end{bmatrix} \qquad y = \begin{bmatrix} 0.6 & 0.3 \\ 0.4 & 0.7 \end{bmatrix}.$$

*We learn the probabilities* (14) *for all four pairs of values of i and j.*

| | | j | |
|---|---|---|---|
| | | 1 | 2 |
| i | 1 | 0.48 | 0.32 |
| | 2 | 0.06 | 0.14 |

*Now, we would like to infer the probability*

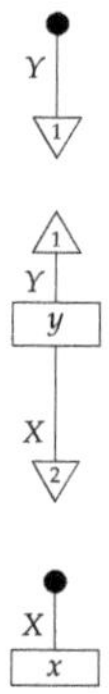

(15)

*i.e., the probability that passive observation at locus Y results in branch 1 if the value leaving X is forcibly set to 2. Because x and the standard basis state $1 : I \to Y$ are normalized, we know that among the three scalars in (15), the top and bottom are each equal to 1 and the desired probability is as follows.*

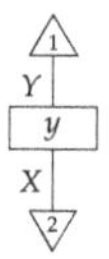

(16)

*The reader, knowing the value of the process y, can see that the desired probability is 0.3; however, from the perspective of the agents confronted with the inference problem, we do not yet know the value of y. We can transform the expression for the desired quantity into an expression with a value that is immediately computable from the known numbers* (14)*. First, we note the following:*

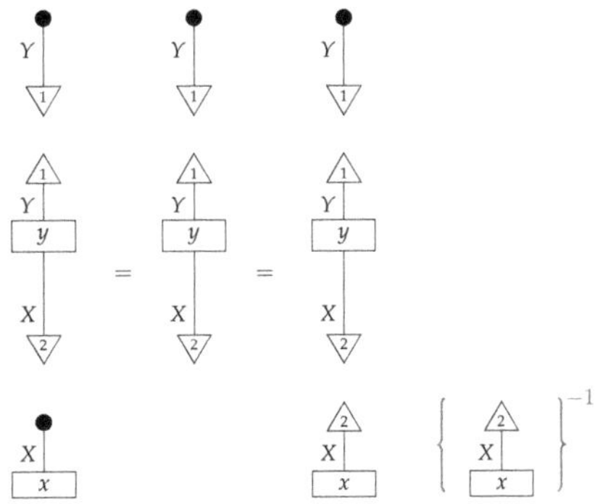

*where the inverse of a scalar is indicated by the scalar inside* $\{-\}^{-1}$. *Next, we rewrite the scalar being inverted in terms of numbers* (14).

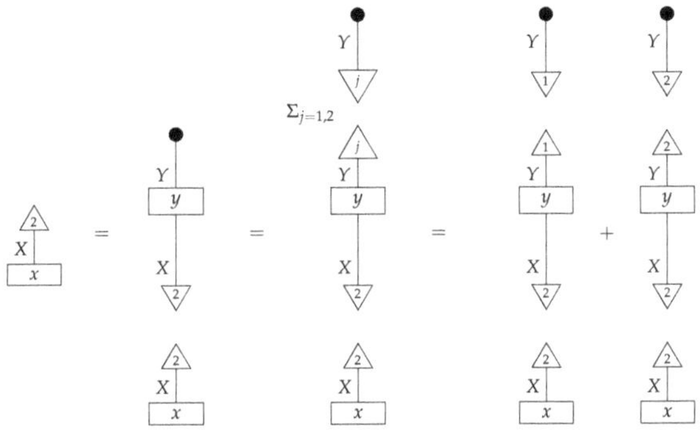

*For the first equality, we have used normalization of both y and a standard basis state; for the second equality, we have used normalization of the sum of the perfect passive observation branches at Y. The equation combining the far left-hand number with the far right-hand number essentially recovers the former from a joint probability distribution by marginalization.*

*We now know that the desired interventional probability is as follows:*

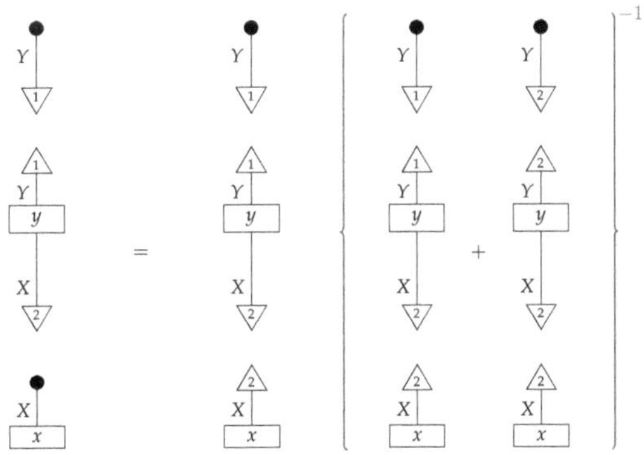

*which we can compute by referring to the table of joint probabilities from perfect passive observations; we obtain* $0.06 \times (0.06 + 0.14)^{-1} = 0.3$, *as the reader expected.*

The last example demonstrates how probabilities from perfect passive observation instruments are in fact what would normally be called observational probabilities. In our example, the "Markov assumption", i.e., the assumption encoded in the graph (12) that the unknown comb has the form in (13), is used in the inference in the sense that the inference procedure does not apply to a two-locus comb of totally unknown shape. Of course, the direction of the edge indicates that the comb has locus $X$ before locus $Y$; just as importantly, though, the Markov assumption rules out (most) combs of the form

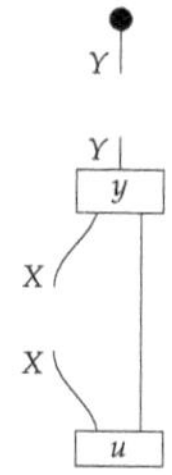


(17)

for which the just-presented inference protocol would not work. Put another way, for generic combs of the form in (17), the probabilities for perfect passive observation instruments at the $X$ and $Y$ loci do not uniquely determine the probabilities for discard-and-prepare instruments at the $X$ locus and perfect passive observation instruments at the $Y$ locus. This is essentially a statement of the well-known fact that observational data do not suffice to distinguish between causal influence of variable $X$ on variable $Y$ and joint influence of a latent confounder on both $X$ and $Y$. To continue emphasizing the language of instruments, let us state explicitly what would suffice to determine the interventional quantity

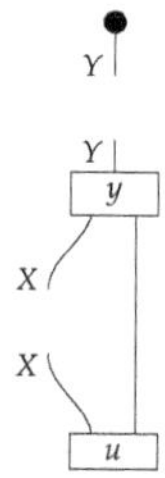


namely, the ability to implement the discard-and-prepare instrument with sole branch

and implement a perfect passive observation instrument at the $Y$ locus, for infinitely many trials.

**Example 14.** *Let the effects $\phi$ and $\phi'$ on system-type $A^{(2)}$ be as in Example 4:*

$$\phi = \begin{bmatrix} 0.8 & 0.1 \end{bmatrix} \qquad \phi' = \begin{bmatrix} 0.2 & 0.9 \end{bmatrix}.$$

*In addition, let*

$$\psi = \begin{bmatrix} 1 \\ 0 \end{bmatrix} \qquad \psi' = \begin{bmatrix} 0 \\ 1 \end{bmatrix}.$$

*Consider the instrument of type $A^{(2)} \to A^{(2)}$ of which the branches are $\psi \circ \phi$ and $\psi' \circ \phi'$. Suppose that an agent applies this instrument to an intervention locus representing a binary variable. On a single trial, if the true value of the variable arriving at the locus is 0, then with probability 0.8, branch $\psi \circ \phi$ is realized and reported to the agent, and value 0 is fed forward; with probability 0.2,* *branch $\psi' \circ \phi'$ is realized and reported and value 1 is fed forward. If the true value of the variable arriving at the locus is 1, then with probability 0.9 branch $\psi' \circ \phi'$ is realized and reported and value 1 is fed forward; with probability 0.1 branch $\psi \circ \phi$ is realized and reported and value 0 fed forward. (The specification of the value that is fed forward in each case is redundant, as it follows from whether the branch that is realized on the trial contains state $\psi$ or state $\psi'$.) The agent knows the values of the branches, and for its own record-keeping can name branch $\psi \circ \phi$ "0" and branch $\psi' \circ \phi'$ "1". Now, on each trial, the instrument reports the correct value of the variable with probability 0.8 if the true value is 0 and with probability 0.9 if the true value is 1. Whichever value is reported is also fed forward; thus, when the instrument misreports the value of the variable, it also changes the value to match the report.*

*Now, suppose that we (taking the place of "the agent") apply this instrument at the X locus in the comb (13) and a perfect passive observation instrument of type $A^{(2)} \to A^{(2)}$ at the Y locus. Again, $|X| = |Y| = 2$. ($A^{(2)}$, X, and Y all denote the same system-type in $\mathbf{Mat}[\mathbb{R}_+]$, but X and Y also denote loci and the associated input and output wires.) The matrix value of the comb, determined by the values of x and y in Example 13, is initially unknown to us, but we do know the comb shape, perhaps from the graph (12). We are going to infer the value of the entire comb, which will allow us to infer the results of any counterfactual combination of instruments at the two loci.*

*The probabilities learned from infinitely many trials are the following.*

| | | Y | |
|---|---|---|---|
| | | i = 1 | i = 2 |
| X | $\psi \circ \phi$ | 0.396 | 0.264 |
| | $\psi' \circ \phi'$ | 0.102 | 0.238 |

*First, we determine the scalars $\phi \circ x$ and $\phi' \circ x$ by rewriting them in terms of probabilities we can look up in the table:*

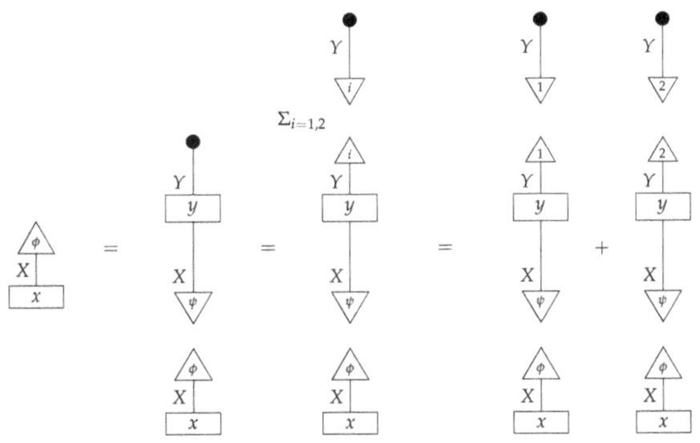

*and*

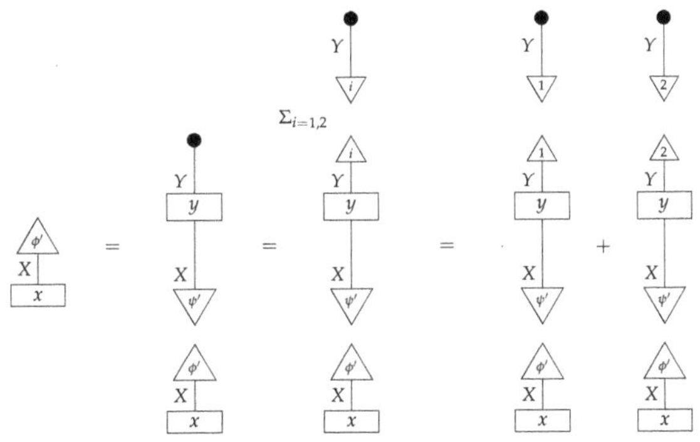

*thus,* $\phi \circ x = 0.396 + 0.264 = 0.66$ *and* $\phi' \circ x = 0.102 + 0.238 = 0.34$. *These numbers allow us to determine the value of* $x$*, as the effects* $\phi$ *and* $\phi'$ *form an informationally complete set. The computation of the matrix entries of* $x$ *from these numbers is essentially a "change of basis" computation, and we omit it.*

*Now, we wish to determine the process* $y$*. Its matrix entries*

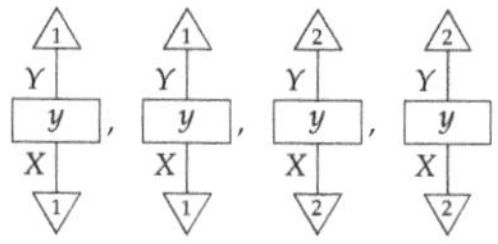

*are also known as*

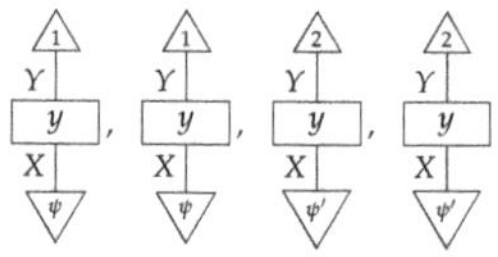

*respectively. We can compute each one using the already known numbers* $\phi \circ x$ *and* $\phi' \circ x$ *and the probabilities in the table. For example,*

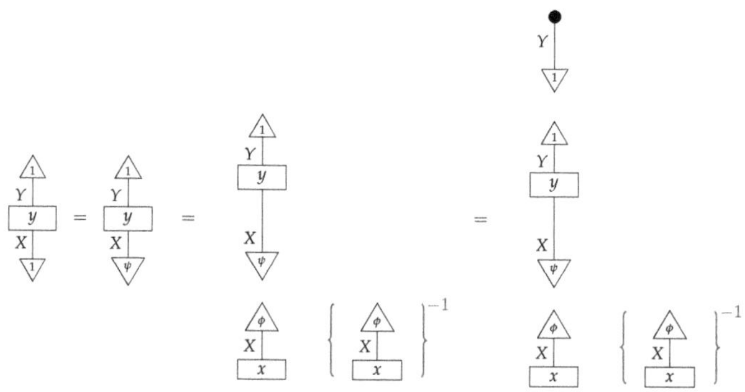

*that is, the* $(1,1)$ *entry of* $y$ *is the* $(\psi \circ \phi, 1)$ *entry of the table of branch probabilities times* $(\phi \circ x)^{-1}$*, or* $0.396/0.66 = 0.6$*, as the reader expects from prior knowledge of the matrix* $y$*. We can compute the other entries of* $y$ *similarly.*

In the next section, we are going to return to the language of syntactic and semantic causal structures to more rigorously reformulate the causal models from Section 2 (which in general include copy maps corresponding to forks in graphs) using combs and instruments, thereby treating the kind of observation implicit in the state-based representation on the same footing as other kinds of probing such as that represented by discard-and-prepare instruments or the instrument $\{\psi \circ \phi, \psi' \circ \phi'\}$ in Example 14. The semantic causal structure involved in a causal model will be a comb in $\mathbf{Mat}[\mathbb{R}_+]$ with an intervention locus for each variable, producing probabilities when instruments are assigned to all the loci. What are normally called "observational data" are then the probabilities generated under one particular instrument assignment, namely, the assignment of a perfect passive observation instrument to every locus.

For example, instead of the state in (5), a causal model based on the graph $G$ in (1) can be represented with a comb $A \otimes B \otimes C \otimes D \otimes E \to A \otimes B \otimes C \otimes D \otimes E$, as shown below.

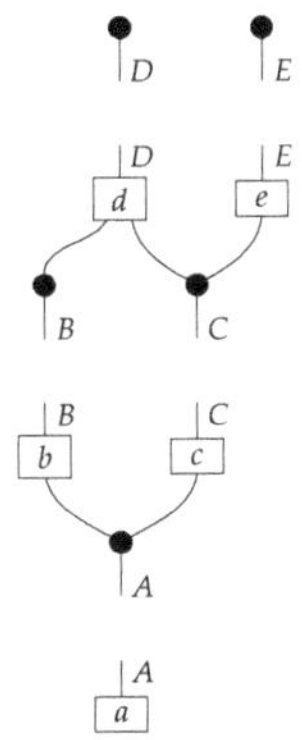

(18)

This comb (18) provides the observational data encoded in the state $\omega$ in (5): the probability of any particular joint outcome for the variables in joint state $\omega$ in (5) is provided by the composite of $\omega$ with the appropriate standard basis effects as shown below.

$$P(A = i, B = j, C = k, D = l, E = m) \; =$$

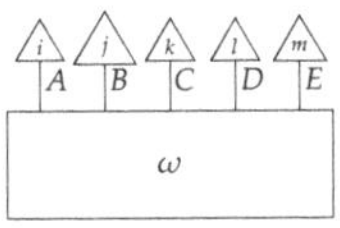

Per Equation (6), the right-hand expression is equal to the joint probability of perfect passive observation branches at all five gaps in the comb:

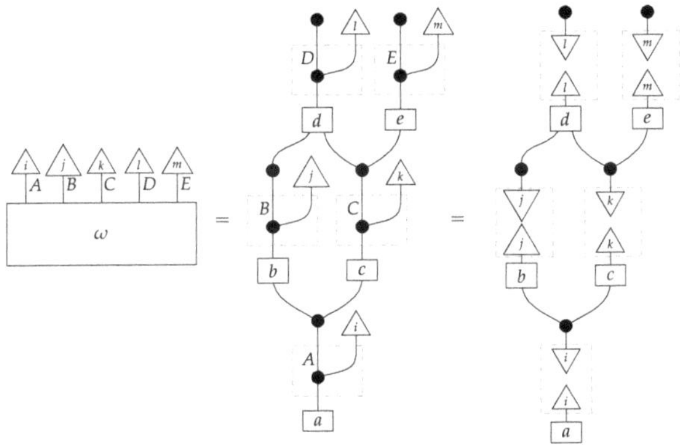

(19)

where the middle expression involves the original Bayesian network representation from (5). This equivalence helps to justify the definition of perfect passive observation instruments. Knowing the probabilities of "values of random variables" encoded in the state $\omega$, i.e., knowing the state, is the same as knowing the outcome probabilities for perfect passive observation instruments.

The comb in (18) assigns probabilities to joint outcomes for any combination of instruments $A \to A$, $B \to B$, $C \to C$, $D \to D$, and $E \to E$ applied at the five gaps. For example, the joint probabilities for a discard-and-prepare instrument preparing standard basis state $i$ at the $B$ gap and perfect passive observation instruments at all other gaps follow.

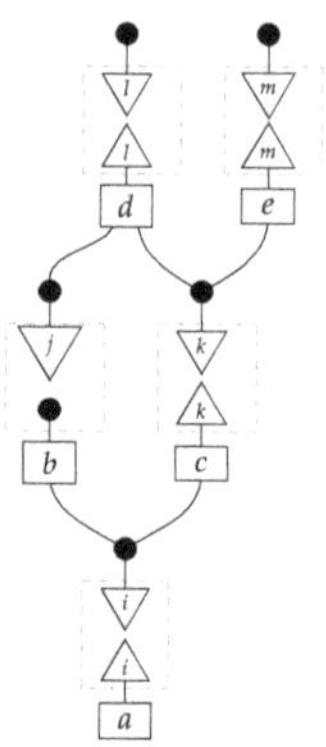


These probabilities are the same as those encoded in the joint state on the right-hand side of (7). In order to obtain the probabilities from (7), we simply compose the joint state with the appropriate standard basis effects. (There is a slight difference in the handling of discard-and-prepare interventions between representations such as (7) and the new comb representations. In the comb representation of the causal Bayesian network in our running example, if the single-branch discard-and-prepare instrument at the $B$ gap prepares a mixed state $\psi$ instead of a standard basis state $i$, then there is no way to model observation of the actual value about which $\psi$ encodes uncertainty. In contrast, in the representation from (7) with $i$ replaced by $\psi$, the copy map on $B$ models perfect passive observation of variable $B$ immediately after the preparation of $\psi$.)

By passing from states (as in (5)) to combs (as in (18)), we treat perfect passive observation as just one among many kinds of instrument that can in principle be applied to probe the process governing a causal scenario. Hence, we can precisely pose new kinds of causal identification problems such as the one solved in Example 14, by declaring that the statistics available for use in the inference are the outcome probabilities associated with instruments other than perfect passive observation. The task is then to use those statistics together with qualitative assumptions encoded in a graph to deduce a property of the data-generating process that implies how the process would respond to other instruments. For simplicity, we focus on identifying the value of the entire comb. In the next section, we will define in full the syntactic process theory associated with an arbitrary directed acyclic graph, explain how to construct the syntactic causal structure from the graph, and define causal models in terms of interpretation functors from the syntactic process theory into $\mathbf{Mat}[\mathbb{R}_+]$.

## 4. Functorial Causal Models

Given a directed acyclic graph $G$, we formulate the syntactic causal structure for $G$-based Markovian causal models as a process in a syntactic process theory constructed as follows. First, we form a *free process theory*, i.e., a free strict symmetric monoidal category $\mathbf{Free}(\Sigma_G)$ over a *signature* $\Sigma_G$ determined by the graph $G$. Here, a process-theoretic signature provides the symbols from which processes in the free process theory may be formed. It consists of a set of system-type symbols $A, B, C, \ldots$ and a set of labeled boxes and other icons, all of which have input and output wires labeled with system-type symbols. For each vertex $X$ in $G$, the signature $\Sigma_G$ has a system-type symbol $X$ and a box labeled $x$ with an output wire labeled $X$ and input wires labeled by the system-type symbols for $X$'s parents in $G$. Also for each vertex $X$, there are (i) an icon

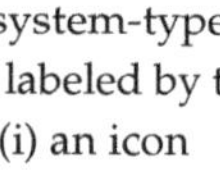


called "copy" with as many outputs as vertex $X$ has children in $G$, and (ii) an icon

called "discard" or $d_X$. If vertex $X$ has no children in $G$, then (i) and (ii) are identical.

The free process theory $\mathbf{Free}(\Sigma_G)$ has the following system-types: a unit system-type $I$, the system-type symbols in $\Sigma_G$, and terms that are formal combinations of those symbols joined by $\otimes$, e.g., $A \otimes I \otimes C \otimes A \otimes A \otimes D$. Its processes include identity maps for all system-types, swap maps for all pairs of system-types, and diagrams that can be formed from those maps and boxes in $\Sigma$ via sequential and parallel composition. Processes are equal if and only if their diagrams are identical up to rearrangements that preserve connections.

To form the syntactic process theory $\mathbf{Syn}(\Sigma_G)$ for $G$-based causal models, we impose equations between processes in $\mathbf{Free}(\Sigma_G)$. "Imposing" equations means constructing a quotient process theory, which is defined as one wherein the system-types are the same as those of the original but wherein the processes are equivalence classes of processes from the original theory. We can treat individual representatives of the equivalence classes as being themselves processes in the quotient process theory, replacing them with other representatives at any point in a calculation. The equations defining $\mathbf{Syn}(\Sigma_G)$ include those in (4), which make the "copy" icon behave as an abstract copy map that interacts with discarding in a way that mirrors the copy–discard interaction in $\mathbf{Mat}[\mathbb{R}_+]$ ($\mathbf{Syn}(\Sigma_G)$ is a copy–discard process theory), and equation

$$d_B \circ f = d_A$$

for every map $f : A \to B$ in $\mathbf{Free}(\Sigma_G)$. The latter condition mirrors the normalization condition in $\mathbf{Mat}[\mathbb{R}_+]$, and we accordingly call the processes in $\mathbf{Syn}(\Sigma_G)$ (which all satisfy it) "normalized".

The syntactic causal structure for graph $G$ is now a process $c_G$ in $\mathbf{Syn}(\Sigma_G)$, constructed as follows. For each vertex $X$, we connect the output wires of the $X$ copy icon to the input wires of the boxes associated with $X$'s children. The resulting diagram has an input and an output wire for each vertex in $G$. We arrange these input–output pairs to form gaps in a comb.

For example, the graph in (1) gives as $c_G$ the process (18) (viewed as a formal diagram, not a matrix in $\mathbf{Mat}[\mathbb{R}_+]$).

A semantic causal structure realizing the qualitative hypotheses in $G$ is the image of $c_G$ under a certain *functor of process theories* $F : \mathbf{Syn}(\Sigma_G) \to \mathbf{Mat}[\mathbb{R}_+]$, called an *interpretation functor*.

**Definition 6.** *For process theories $\mathcal{C}$ and $\mathcal{C}'$ with unit system-types $I$ and $I'$ and families of swap maps $\sigma$ and $\sigma'$, respectively, a functor of process theories $F : \mathcal{C} \to \mathcal{C}'$ is a strict symmetric monoidal functor, i.e., an ordinary functor of categories $\mathcal{C} \to \mathcal{C}'$, such that for system-types $A$ and $B$ in $\mathcal{C}$:*

1. $F(A \otimes B) = F(A) \otimes F(B)$
2. $F(\sigma_{A,B}) = \sigma'_{F(A),F(B)}$
3. $F(I) = I'$.

In order for a functor of process theories $F : \mathbf{Syn}(\Sigma_G) \to \mathbf{Mat}[\mathbb{R}_+]$ to be a legitimate interpretation functor, we require that $F$ send copy and discard maps in $\mathbf{Syn}(\Sigma_G)$ to copy and discard maps in $\mathbf{Mat}[\mathbb{R}_+]$, respectively (this requirement makes $F$ a *copy–discard functor*). Normalization of all processes in $\mathbf{Syn}(\Sigma_G)$ ensures that these processes' images under $F$ are stochastic matrices. In particular, the entire semantic causal structure $F(c_G)$ is a stochastic matrix.

For a DAG $G$, a copy–discard functor $F : \mathbf{Syn}(\Sigma_G) \to \mathbf{Mat}[\mathbb{R}_+]$ is called a *$G$-based causal model*. A $G$-based causal model implicitly includes the syntactic causal structure $c_G$

defined by $G$ along with the semantic causal structure $F(c_G)$. The same term will be used to refer to the semantic causal structure $F(c_G)$.

*4.1. Non-Markovian Models*

A model constructed according to the procedure presented thus far is *Markovian*; each vertex in the graph has a corresponding input–output pair in the syntactic and semantic causal structures, meaning that the model mathematically allows us to consider probing at any node in the network. On the other hand, we may want to consider *non-Markovian* models based on a directed acyclic graph, in which some loci corresponding to vertices are "latent". For a directed acyclic graph $G$ with a list of vertices that are to correspond to latent loci, the prescription for forming the syntactic causal structure is as above, with one additional final step: for each locus that is to be latent, we join the output to the input with an identity map of the appropriate type, thereby closing the gap in the diagram.

In the example with graph (1), if $A$ is to be the sole latent locus, then the syntactic causal structure is as follows.

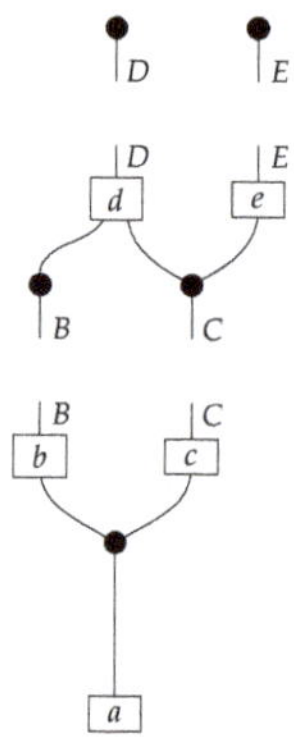


(20)

*4.2. Causal Structures for ADMGs*

More complicated kinds of graphs—featuring, e.g., bidirected edges or directed hyperedges—can represent causal hypotheses for non-Markovian scenarios without specifying all of the latent variables [20,21]. For example, the following Acyclic Directed Mixed Graph (ADMG)

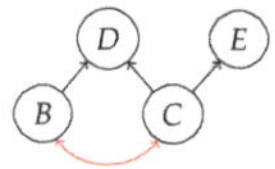


(21)

encodes, in addition to familiar hypotheses represented by black directed edges, the hypothesis (represented by a red bidirected edge) that there may be latent variables which simultaneously influence both $B$ and $C$. Examples of DAGs consistent with these hypotheses are $G$ from (1) with $A$ latent,

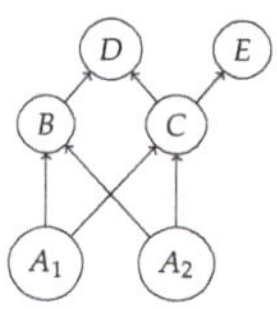


with $A_1$ and $A_2$ latent, and

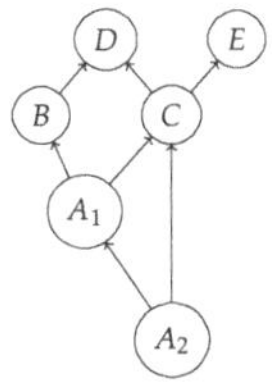


also with $A_1$ and $A_2$ latent.

It is possible to state a recipe for constructing a syntactic causal structure from an ADMG, similar to the way a syntactic causal structure is constructed from a DAG. The difference is that there are now processes (states) corresponding to bidirected edges. For example, the syntactic causal structure for the ADMG in (21) is as follows.

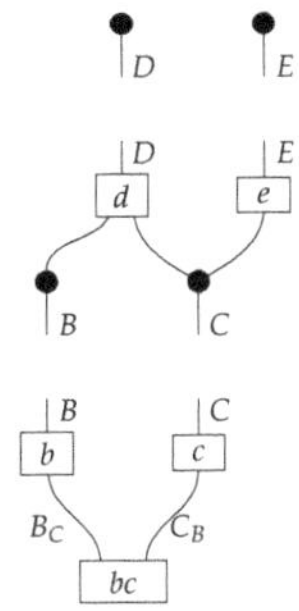


(22)

Again, a causal model based on the graph is provided by a copy–discard functor $F : \mathbf{Syn}(\Sigma_G) \to \mathbf{Mat}[\mathbb{R}_+]$, and $F(c_G)$ is called the semantic causal structure.

We leave a more thorough description of AMDG-based functorial causal models to other work; here, we simply note that the process-theoretic approach with both a syntactic and a semantic process theory allows us to understand very clearly how an ADMG represents "margins" of DAG-based models in the causal context. For example, at the level of syntactic causal structures, "marginalizing" (by plugging in an identity map) locus $A$ in (18), which is based on the DAG in (1), yields (20), which also has the form (22) based on the ADMG (21). Alternatively, marginalizing in a single semantic interpretation of (18) results in a semantic causal structure that can be specified by a semantic interpretation of either (20) or (22).

## 5. Local Intervention Regimes and Identification

We use the term *intervention locus* to refer to an input–output pair in the semantic causal structure as well as to the corresponding input–output pair in the syntactic causal structure. If an instrument of type $X \to X$ is assigned to each locus $X$, then the semantic causal structure assigns probabilities to all possible combinations of branches. From here on, a single label will often stand for a locus (in both the syntactic and semantic causal structures), its input and output system-types in the syntactic causal structure, and its input and output system-types in the semantic causal structure.

**Definition 7.** *A* local intervention regime *assigns an instrument of type $A \to A$ to each locus $A$ in an interventional causal model.*

"Implementing" a local intervention regime for one iteration of a repeated causal scenario represented by a causal model results in the joint realization of a combination of maps at all the loci: at each locus, one branch of the instrument assigned to that locus is realized. The joint probability of this combination of local outcomes is the number resulting from plugging the maps into their loci in the semantic causal structure. The sense in which the causal models just defined are "causal" is that for a given local intervention regime, changing the instrument assigned to a locus (thereby creating a new local intervention regime that agrees with the first at all but one locus) might result in different outcome probabilities for the loci where the instruments are unchanged. In other words, a choice at one locus might "cause" events at other loci.

In a causal identification problem, one is given a graph (indicating a syntactic causal structure) and outcome probabilities from probing the initially unknown semantic causal structure with one or more local intervention regimes. Causal inference consists essentially in using outcome probabilities for some local intervention regimes to infer those for other local intervention regimes. The problem of causal identification is to use outcome probabilities from a limited set of local intervention regimes together with the shape of the syntactic causal structure (or the graph) to infer probabilities of outcome combinations under other local intervention regimes.

In the standard identification setup (e.g., in Pearl [1]), the probabilities available for inference are those that in our framework are generated under local intervention regimes consisting only of perfect passive observation instruments. We will study identification tasks based on data from other kinds of instruments.

The set of local intervention regimes whose outcome statistics are to be used for inference is specified as follows: for each locus $A$, an *accessible set* $\mathcal{I}_A$ of instruments $A \to A$ is given. An *accessible* local intervention regime is then a local intervention regime in which each instrument comes from the accessible set for the locus to which the instrument is assigned. The probabilities available for inference are the probabilities that can be "learned" from accessible local intervention regimes—that is, for each accessible local intervention regime, the joint probability of each combination of branches will be considered known.

The quantity to be identified in a causal identification problem is the image of some map in the syntactic process theory under the interpretation functor $F$. In this paper, we focus for simplicity on identifying the entire semantic causal structure $F(c_G)$.

In full, the causal identification problem studied in this paper is defined by the following in each instance: a causal model consisting of a directed acyclic graph $G$, a set of latent loci and an interpretation functor $F$, and an accessible set $\mathcal{I}_A$ of instruments for each locus $A$. The inputs for the identification task are the graph $G$ and the set of latent loci—which together prescribe how to construct the syntactic causal structure $c_G$—along with the data generated by $F(c_G)$ under each accessible local intervention regime. For each accessible local intervention regime, a table is provided in which every combination of instrument branches realizable at the various loci on a single "trial" is associated with its probability. The collection of tables specifies the set of accessible local intervention regimes, and consequently the accessible sets of instruments. The probabilities in these tables are called *accessible probabilities*. The task is to compute $F(c_G)$. If this task is possible, we say that $F(c_G)$ (or "the model") is *identifiable* from the accessible sets of instruments (and the graph with the list of latent loci).

We assume from here on that all DAG-based models are *strictly positive* in the following sense (it is straightforward to formulate the corresponding assumption for models based on ADMGs and other kinds of decorated graphs): a causal model $F$ based on a DAG $G$ is called strictly positive if, for every process $x$ in $\mathbf{Syn}(\Sigma_G)$ corresponding to a vertex $X$ in $G$, the stochastic matrix $F(x)$ in $\mathbf{Mat}[\mathbb{R}_+]$ has only strictly positive entries. Our strict positivity assumption plays a similar role to that of requirements in the standard causal inference literature that distributions be strictly positive; in both cases, strict positivity guarantees that the conditional probabilities needed for calculations of interventional quantities are defined. Intuitively, if one wants to infer a "do"-conditional probability $P(Y = y|do(X = i))$

from observational data, one needs the possibility $X = i$ to be realized in those data. Our restriction to strictly positive models brings the following fact into our calculations: in $\mathbf{Mat}[\mathbb{R}_+]$, when a matrix $f$ with only strictly positive entries is composed with a state $\rho$, then as long as some entries in $\rho$ are non-zero, the resulting state $f \circ \rho$ has only strictly positive entries. If $f$ and $\rho$ are normalized, then $f \circ \rho$ corresponds to a strictly positive probability distribution.

Our version of the most common kind of identification task involves accessible sets consisting only of perfect passive observation instruments (each accessible set is a singleton). In these cases, we speak of quantities being identifiable "from perfect passive observation".

**Proposition 2.** *Models based on the DAG in* (1) *with A and C latent or based on the ADMG in* (21) *are not identifiable from perfect passive observation.*

**Proof.** As in the discussion of comb shape (17), this is an example illustrating our framework using an established fact from the causal inference literature: in general, (interventional quantities associated with) non-Markovian models are not identifiable from "observational data". □

**Proposition 3.** *Models based on the DAG in* (1) *with only A being latent are identifiable from perfect passive observation.*

Put another way, any semantic interpretation of (20) is discernible from knowledge of the syntactic causal structure and the statistics from a local intervention regime consisting only of perfect passive observation instruments.

From here on, we distinguish boxes in a syntactic process theory from their images in $\mathbf{Mat}[\mathbb{R}_+]$ by indicating the latter in boldface; thus, $\boldsymbol{x}$ indicates the image $F(x)$ of a process $x$ under interpretation functor $F$.

**Proof.** An arbitrary semantic causal structure is

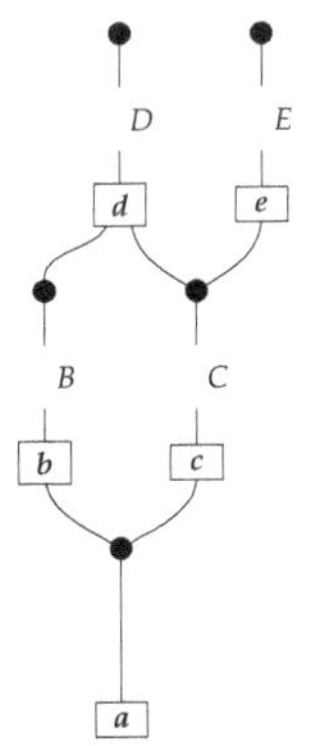


and the accessible probabilities are

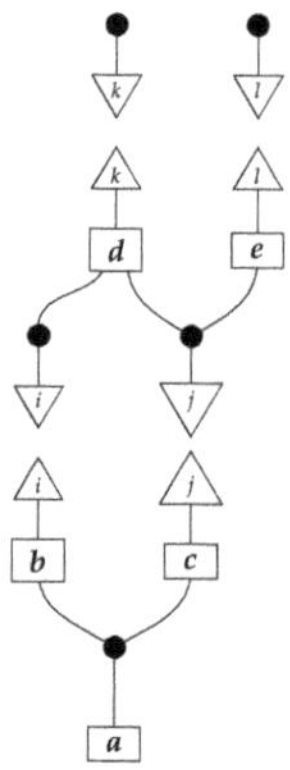

where the indices $i, j, k$, and $l$ take values from 1 to $|B|, |C|, |D|$, and $|E|$, respectively. Identification proceeds in several steps. First, we learn the value of

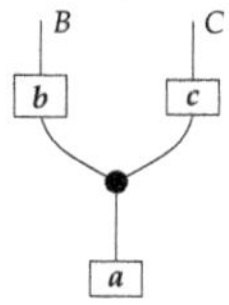

(23)

by computing its matrix entries

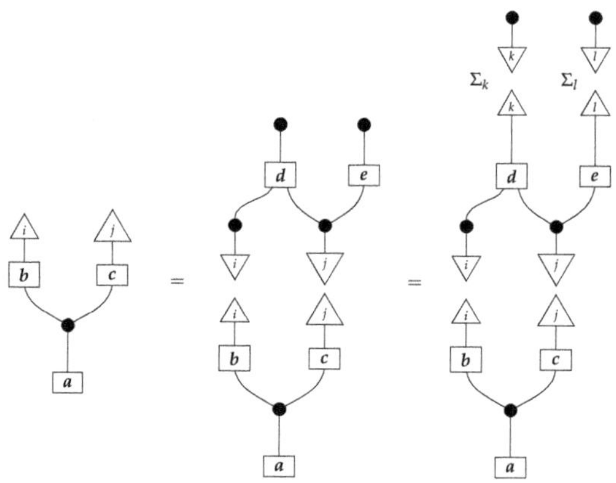

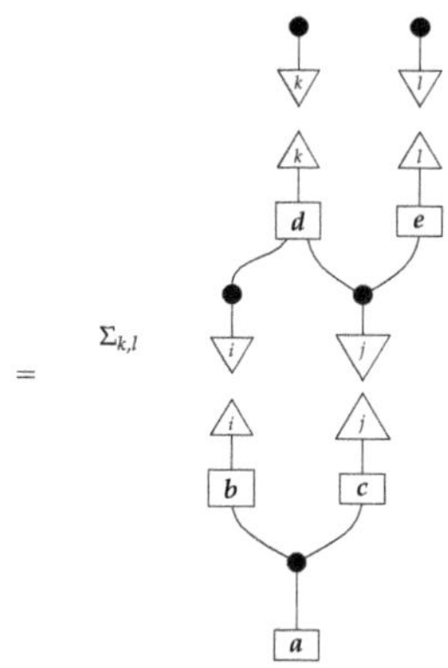

The reason for the first equality is that

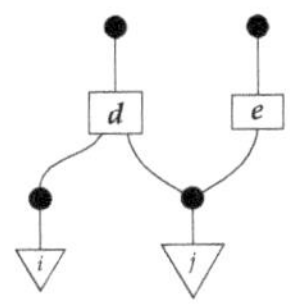

is the scalar 1, since $\boldsymbol{d}$ and $\boldsymbol{e}$ are normalized; the second equality follows from the fact that adding the branches of an instrument (here, a perfect passive observation instrument) results in a normalized map (here, an identity map), which discarding "falls through".

Next, we use the matrix entries of (23) together with the accessible probabilities to compute the process

(24)

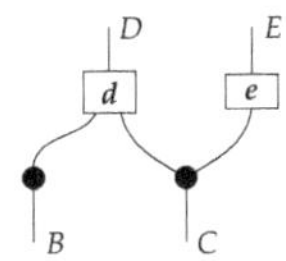


for which the matrix elements are

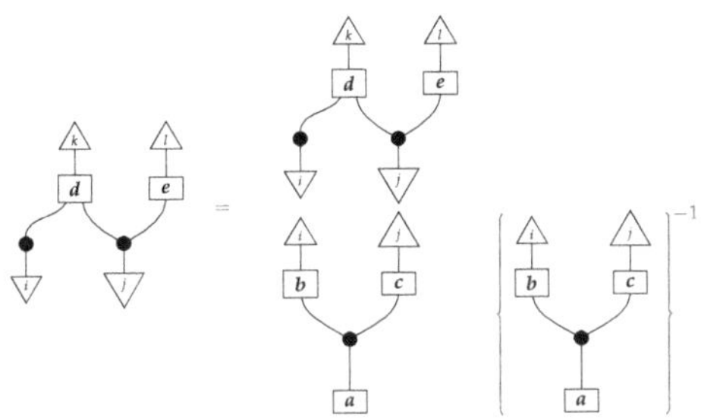

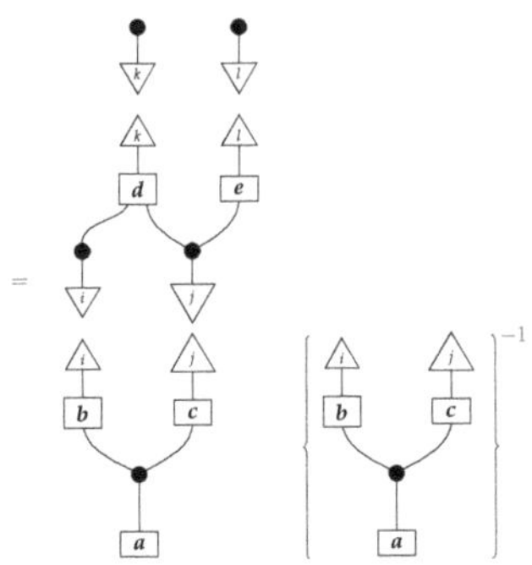

where the right-hand side is in the form of a product of an accessible probability and the inverse of a number already known from the previous step.

We now know the values of processes (23) and (24), which together with the two discard maps make up the semantic causal structure; hence, we know the semantic causal structure. □

This proof has two notable features. First, it was not necessary to compute the value of the image of every box in $\mathbf{Syn}(\Sigma_G)$ on its own. Indeed, doing so is impossible in this example, as the state (23) (equivalently, its matrix entries) does not fix unique values of the matrices $\boldsymbol{a}, \boldsymbol{b}$, and $\boldsymbol{c}$. Second, the accessible instruments were perfect passive observation instruments; thus, we computed matrix entries rather directly from accessible probabilities, in the sense that the accessible probabilities were products of matrix entries of processes in the semantic causal structure. This would not be the case for accessible instruments other than perfect passive observation instruments, but it might still be possible to compute the values of component processes in the semantic causal structure. For example, if we could somehow obtain the numbers

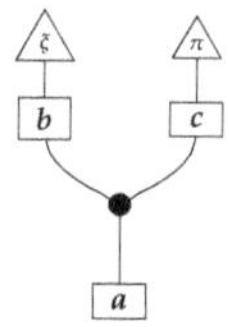


from the accessible probabilities for informationally complete sets of effects $\{\xi\}$ and $\{\sigma\}$, then, even if the effects were not standard basis effects, we would be able to compute the value of the process in (23).

**Proposition 4.** *Markovian models based on DAGs are identifiable from perfect passive observation.*

**Proof.** This is a statement of a well-known fact represented in our framework. It follows from the uniqueness of factorization described in Example 1 together with the equivalence between the matrix entries of a state and the probabilities of perfect passive observation branches, as in (19). □

The proposition for Markovian models defined with combs in this paper follows from Theorem 1 below. For now, we can consider the representation of a DAG-based causal model as a state (for example, in (5)). In causal identification from perfect passive observation, the state (i.e., probability distribution) $\omega$ is provided together with the graph $G$ indicating that the causal mechanisms $a, b, c, d$, and $e$ are arranged as in (5). A special feature of a Markovian model—i.e., one in which each box's output is copied to an output of the overall state, as opposed to being discarded as in (8)—is that the probability distribution is consistent with only one set of values for the five mechanisms. The five factors on the right-hand side of $P(ABCDE) = P(A)P(B|A)P(C|A)P(D|BC)P(E|C)$ of the observational distribution specify the five stochastic matrices in (5). In other words, for a Markovian model, the observed conditional probabilities are also the values of the stable and autonomous mechanisms. This narrative for the state-based representation suggests that it is the Markovianity of a *probability distribution* relative to a DAG that allows for the identification of a Markovian *causal model* based on that DAG. We will show with the comb representation that Markovianity of accessible probability distributions need not be understood as the condition making Markovian models identifiable. If the accessible instruments satisfy a certain abstract condition (met in particular by perfect passive observation instruments and some other instruments in Section 3), then Markovian models are identifiable even though the accessible probability distributions may not be Markovian for the graphs.

**Definition 8.** *A set of maps $\phi : A \to A'$ in $\mathbf{Mat}[\mathbb{R}_+]$ is called* marginally informationally complete *if it satisfies both of the following conditions:*

1. *The set of effects* 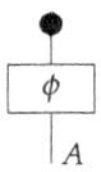 *is informationally complete for A.*
2. *For any normalized state* $\rho : I \to A'$ *with full support, the set of states* 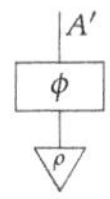 *is informationally complete for* $A'$.

The following proposition follows from Proposition 6 below.

**Proposition 5.** *The set of branches of a perfect passive observation instrument* $A \to A$ *is marginally informationally complete.*

**Definition 9.** *A set of instruments of type* $A \to A'$ *is called marginally informationally complete if the union of the instruments (with each instrument viewed as a set of maps) is a marginally informationally complete set of maps.*

Thus, Proposition 5 states that a perfect passive observation instrument by itself constitutes a marginally informationally complete set of instruments.

The following two examples include assertions of marginal informational completeness of certain singleton sets of instruments, justified by Proposition 6 below.

**Example 15.** *Consider a locus A corresponding to a binary random variable (i.e.,* $|A| = 2$*). Suppose that one is able to probe it with an instrument that reports the true value of the variable arriving at that locus, but that also disturbs the variable such that the value to be fed forward is flipped with probability* 0.1. *The branches of this instrument are the following:*

$$\begin{bmatrix} 0.9 \\ 0.1 \end{bmatrix} \circ \begin{bmatrix} 1 & 0 \end{bmatrix}, \qquad \begin{bmatrix} 0.1 \\ 0.9 \end{bmatrix} \circ \begin{bmatrix} 0 & 1 \end{bmatrix}.$$

*The set containing only this instrument is marginally informationally complete.*

It is not necessary that the disturbance be "symmetric", as in this instrument, nor that the effects be standard basis effects.

**Example 16.** *Let*

$$\phi = \begin{bmatrix} 0.8 & 0.9 \end{bmatrix} \qquad \phi' = \begin{bmatrix} 0.2 & 0.1 \end{bmatrix} \qquad \psi = \begin{bmatrix} 0.5 \\ 0.5 \end{bmatrix} \qquad \psi' = \begin{bmatrix} 0.9 \\ 0.1 \end{bmatrix}.$$

*The instrument with branches* $\psi \circ \phi$ *and* $\psi' \circ \phi'$ *constitutes a single-instrument marginally informationally complete set of instruments of type* $A^{(2)} \to A^{(2)}$ *(recall that we use the notation* $A^{(2)}$ *for the system-type 2, in order to reserve the notation "2" for a value of the random variable). When a locus representing a binary random variable (with values denoted* 1 *and* 2*) is probed with this instrument, if the variable's true value is* 1*, then* $\psi \circ \phi$ *is realized with probability* 0.8 *and* $\psi' \circ \phi'$ *with probability* 0.2. *If the true value of the variable is* 2*, then* $\psi \circ \phi$ *is realized with probability* 0.9 *and* $\psi' \circ \phi'$ *with probability* 0.1. *If branch* $\psi \circ \phi$ *is realized, then the value of the variable fed forward after the probing is totally randomized. If branch* $\psi' \circ \phi'$ *is realized, then the value fed forward is* 1 *with probability* 0.9 *and* 2 *with probability* 0.1.

The instruments in these examples have the property that each branch has the form $\psi \circ \phi$ for an effect $\phi$ and a state $\psi$, i.e., each branch is $\circ$-*separable*. If all instruments in a set consist only of $\circ$-separable branches, then marginal informational completeness of the set of instruments can be checked with the following criterion.

**Proposition 6.** *A set of maps $\psi \circ \phi : A \to A'$ in $\mathbf{Mat}[\mathbb{R}_+]$ composed of states $\psi : I \to A'$ and effects $\phi : A \to I$ is marginally informationally complete if and only if: (i) the set of all effects $\phi$ is informationally complete for $A$, and (ii) the set of all states $\psi$ is informationally complete for $A'$.*

**Proof.** Suppose that we have a set of maps

(25)

in $\mathbf{Mat}[\mathbb{R}_+]$ such that the set of effects $\phi$ is informationally complete for $A$ and the set of states $\psi$ is informationally complete for $A'$.

(i) The set of effects

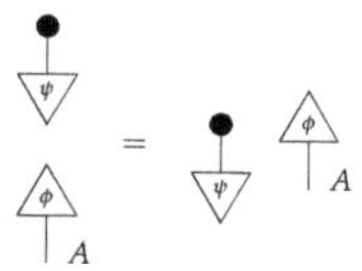

is informationally complete for $A$, as scaling each of a linearly independent set of row vectors results in a linearly independent set.

(ii) For any state $\rho : I \to A'$ with full support, the set of states

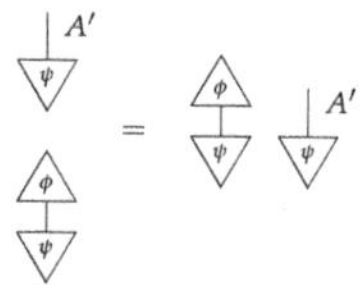

is informationally complete for $A'$ by a similar consideration about preservation of linear independence under scaling.

Conversely, suppose that the set of maps (25) satisfies conditions 1 and 2 in Definition 8. Then, the effects

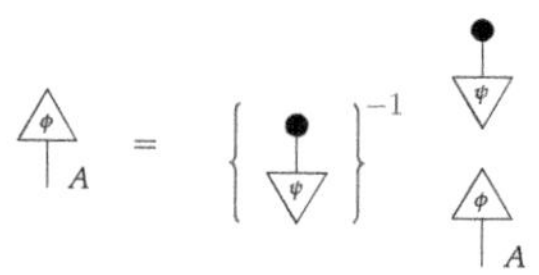

are re-scalings of the effects $d_{A'} \circ \psi \circ \phi$ supposed to form an informationally complete set. To see that the states $\psi$ form an informationally complete set, we can plug a fixed state $\rho : I \to A'$ with full support into each of the maps (25). The resulting states $\psi \circ \phi \circ \rho$ on $A'$ are supposed to form an informationally complete set, and the states

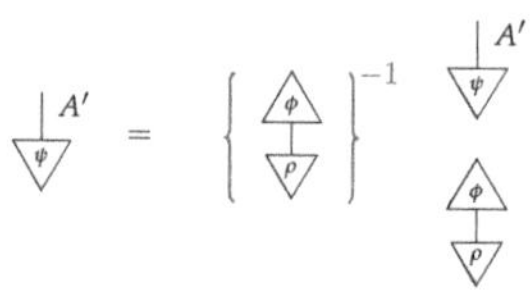

are re-scalings of these states. □

We would also like to deal with instruments for which the branches are not $\circ$-separable. For a given locus, consider a probing procedure for which one of the possible outcomes tells the observer the following: the variable may have had either value 1 or 2 when arriving at the locus, and both possibilities should be assigned equal probability, but with certainty that the value upon leaving the locus is the same as the value upon arriving. The instrument branch corresponding to this outcome is

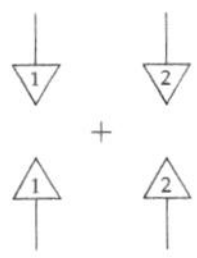


which is non-$\circ$-separable. An instrument with branches that are sums of perfect passive observation branches represents an observation that is "imperfect" or "coarse-grained" but not "disturbing". Loosely speaking, although a $\circ$-separable instrument can represent a procedure for which outcomes carry only incomplete "information" about the values arriving at and leaving the locus, it cannot represent a procedure that results in "shared information" between the incoming and outgoing systems that is inaccessible to the observer. However, procedures of the latter sort, such as coarse-grained non-disturbing observations, are among the first that come to mind when one thinks of generalizing from perfect passive observation. The (classical version of the) identifiability result demonstrated for a three-node graph in [9] covers only $\circ$-separable instruments. The main result of the present paper, in Theorem 1, is that a Markovian model is identifiable whenever the accessible set of instruments at each locus is marginally informationally complete regardless of whether or not all the accessible instruments are $\circ$-separable.

**Theorem 1.** *Markovian models are identifiable whenever the accessible set of instruments at each locus is marginally informationally complete.*

We begin by demonstrating identifiability for the example of three-locus models based on the graph

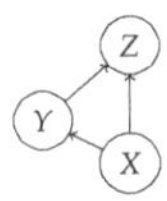


(26)

with the following syntactic causal structure.

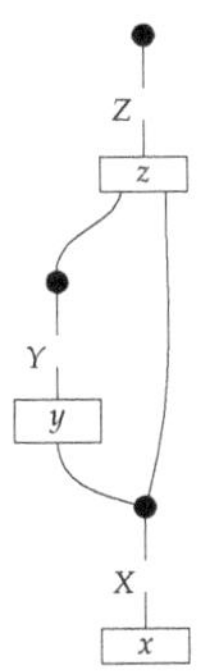


A semantic causal structure has the form shown below.

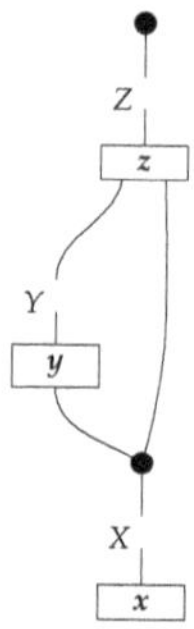


First, $x$ is determined by the probabilities formed by its composition with the informationally complete set of effects $d_X \circ f$, with the maps $f$ forming a marginally informationally complete set. These probabilities are obtained from accessible probabilities via marginalization of the outcomes at $Y$ and $Z$. Here, $g$ and $h$ vary over the branches of single instruments; that is, all the local intervention regimes from which data are collated share the same choices of instruments at $Y$ and $Z$.

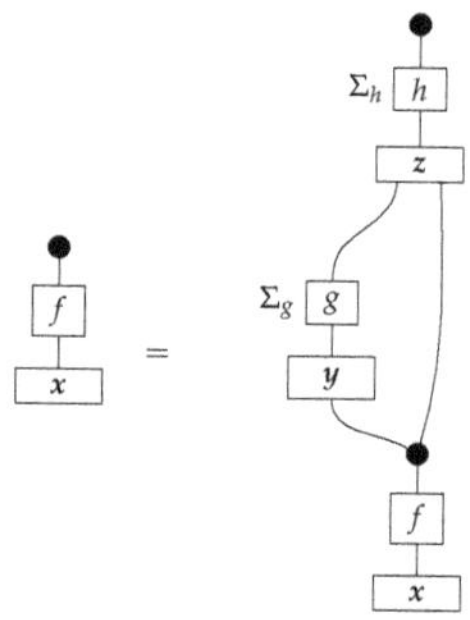

Next, $y$ is determined as follows:

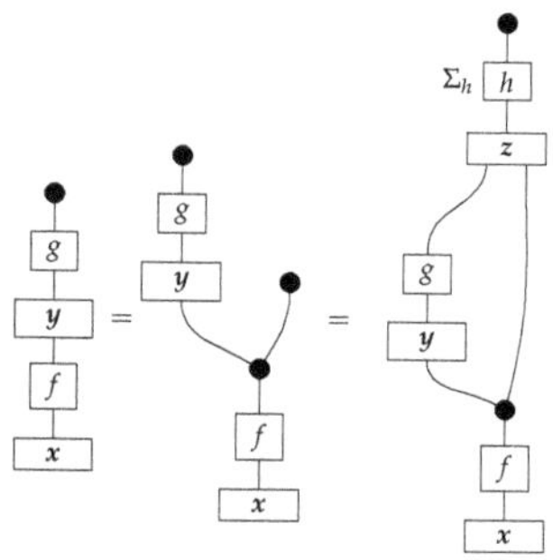

now with both $f$ and $g$ varying over marginally informationally complete sets but with $h$ varying over the branches of only one instrument. The numbers on the left for various $f$ and $g$ determine $y$, because the assumption of marginal informational completeness of the sets $\{f\}$ and $\{g\}$ implies that the set of states $f \circ x$ is informationally complete for $X$ (the input system-type of $y$) and the set of effects $d_Y \circ g$ is informationally complete for $Y$ (the output system-type of $y$).

Now, consider the set of accessible probabilities

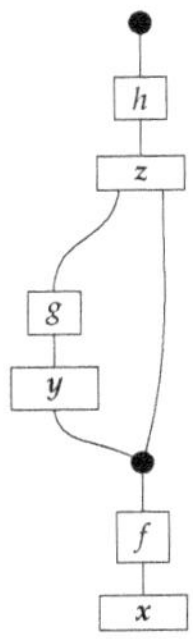


where $f$, $g$, and $h$ vary over marginally informationally complete sets. Marginal informational completeness of $\{h\}$ and $\{f\}$ implies that the set of effects $d_Z \circ h$ and the set of states $f \circ x$ are informationally complete for $Z$ and $X$, respectively. Thus, knowing these probabilities amounts (by tomographic locality) to knowing the value of the process

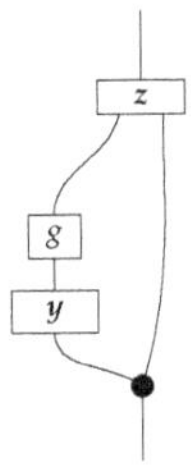


for each $g$. Therefore, for every pure (normalized) state

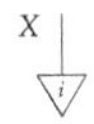


we can compute the quantity

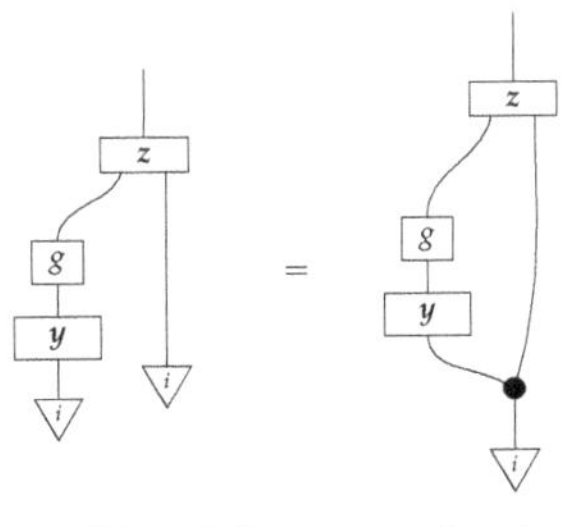


for each $g$. For each $i$, the state $y \circ i$ has full support due to the assumption that the model is strictly positive. Hence, by the assumed marginal informational completeness of $\{g\}$, varying $g$ with fixed $i$ yields an informationally complete set of states $\rho = g \circ y \circ i$. All in all, we now know a set of quantities

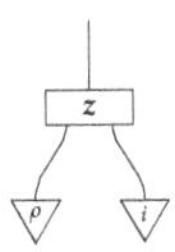


with $\rho$ and $i$ varying independently over informationally complete sets. This set of states determines the process $z$ by tomographic locality.

**Proof of Theorem 1.** If the given graph has $m$ nodes, then the unknown model can be rewritten in a form without explicit common-cause maps:

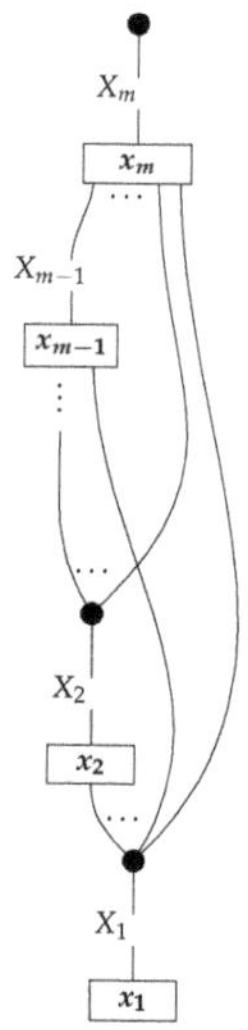


(27)

Here, the processes $\boldsymbol{x}_i$ for $i$ from 1 through $m$ have been linearly ordered in correspondence with a topological ordering of the graph. The topological ordering also dictates the labeling of nodes in the graph and loci in the syntactic and semantic causal structures. The copy map for type $X_i$ and for $i$ between 1 and $m$ has $m - i$ output wires, which connect as inputs to the boxes $\boldsymbol{x}_{m-i}$ through $\boldsymbol{x}_m$. Typically, the topological ordering does not have the property that every vertex is a parent (in the graph) of every vertex subsequent to it (in the ordering); however, there is no loss of generality in adding connections to the diagram of the unknown model. In effect, we declare that we might not make full use of the causal hypotheses encoded in the graph. For example, if node $X_i$ precedes $X_j$ in the topological ordering but there is no edge from $X_i$ to $X_j$ in the graph, then map $x_j$ in the syntactic causal structure has no input $X_i$, and similarly, the map $\boldsymbol{x}_j$ in the original semantic causal structure has no such input. The semantic causal structure remains unchanged if we substitute for $\boldsymbol{x}_j$ a map $\boldsymbol{x}_j \otimes d_{X_i}$ (composed with appropriate swap maps) that does have an input $X_i$. We make this kind of substitution everywhere it is possible, but retain the names of maps from the semantic causal structure for convenience.

The proof of identifiability constructs an iterative identification procedure, proceeding by double induction. Suppose that the value of $\boldsymbol{x}_i : X_1 \otimes \ldots \otimes X_{i-1} \to X_i$ is known for all $i < n$. We show how to compute $\boldsymbol{x}_n$.

For any locus $X_k$, let $\{\phi_k\}_\phi$ be the set of branches appearing in instruments in the accessible set $\mathcal{I}_{X_k}$. Consider the set of processes

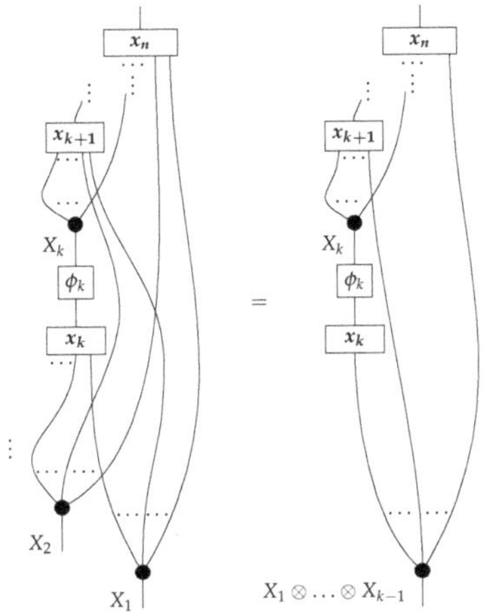


(28)

where, for all loci $X_i$ with $i$ between $k$ and $n-1$ (inclusive), all possible branches $\phi_i$ are plugged in such that the set of processes is indexed by $\phi_k, \ldots, \phi_{n-1}$. The left-hand diagram has inputs $X_1$ through $X_{k-1}$, each followed by a copy map with $n-k+1$ outputs connected to the boxes $\boldsymbol{x_k}$ through $\boldsymbol{x_n}$. The diagram has one output, from $\boldsymbol{x_n}$.

We will show by induction that this set of processes can be computed for every $k$ from 1 through $n$. In the base case, there are no input wires. Each locus from $X_1$ through $X_{n-1}$ is filled with an instrument branch. Each locus after $X_n$ is filled with each of the branches of one accessible instrument and the results are summed so that the discarding map following the final locus $X_m$ "falls through" every component process after $\boldsymbol{x_n}$. For every such combination of branches, the resulting state on $X_n$ is tomographically determined by the results of various instruments at $X_n$; that is, for fixed $\phi_1, \ldots, \phi_{n-1}$, the state

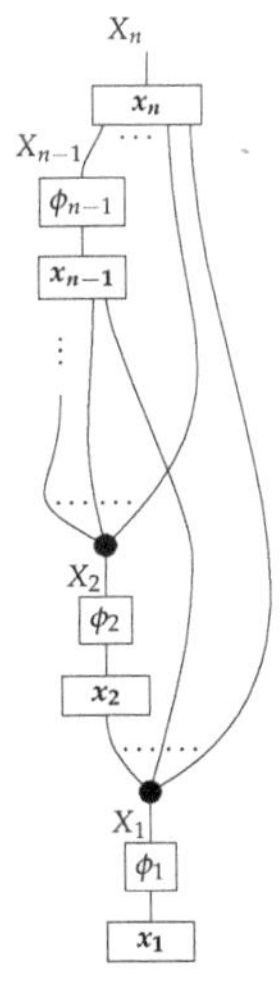


is determined by numbers

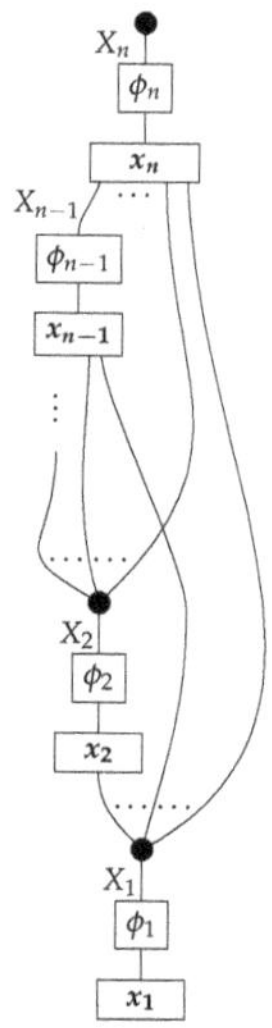

with $\phi_n$ varying, as marginal informational completeness of the set $\{\phi_k\}_\phi$ implies that the set of effects $d_{X_n} \circ \phi_n$ is informationally complete for $X_n$.

Now, suppose the set of processes (28) is known for some fixed $k$. We will show how to compute the set for $k+1$. For each $X_i$ with $i$ between 1 and $k-1$ (inclusive), we introduce the set $\{\epsilon_i\}_\epsilon$ of states on $X_i$ (i.e., column vectors), each having entry 1 in exactly one position and 0s elsewhere. This set is informationally complete for $X_i$ (the set of product states $\{\epsilon_1 \otimes \ldots \otimes \epsilon_{k-1}\}$, where each $\epsilon$ varies independently, is informationally complete for $X_1 \otimes \ldots \otimes X_{k-1}$). Moreover, the states are copied by the copy map for $X_i$. We can plug an arbitrary $\epsilon_i$ into input wire $X_i$ for each $i$ from 1 through $k-1$. The result is shown below.

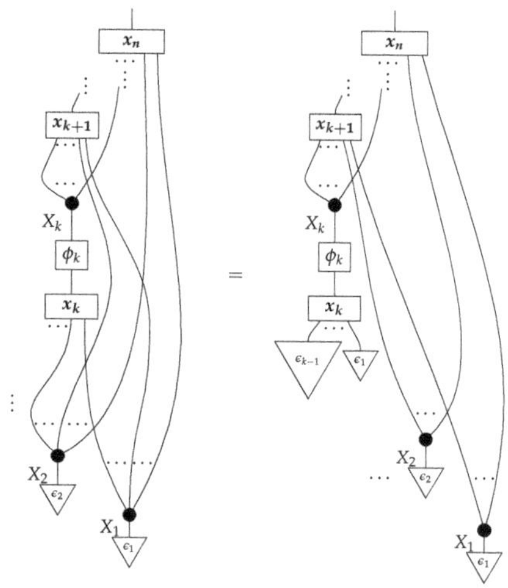

The copy maps on $X_1$ through $X_{k-1}$ in the right-hand diagram each have $n-k$ outputs connected as inputs to boxes $\boldsymbol{x_{k+1}}$ through $\boldsymbol{x_n}$. The states $\epsilon_i$, as used here, have not been realized via local intervention regimes; rather, they are simply known processes for which composites with other known processes can be computed.

The state $\boldsymbol{x_k} \circ (\epsilon_{k-1} \otimes \ldots \otimes \epsilon_1)$ has full support per the standard strict positivity assumption about unknown models. Therefore, the set of states $\phi_k \circ \boldsymbol{x_k} \circ (\epsilon_{k-1} \otimes \ldots \otimes \epsilon_1)$ with $\phi$ varying is informationally complete for $X_k$, meaning that the process

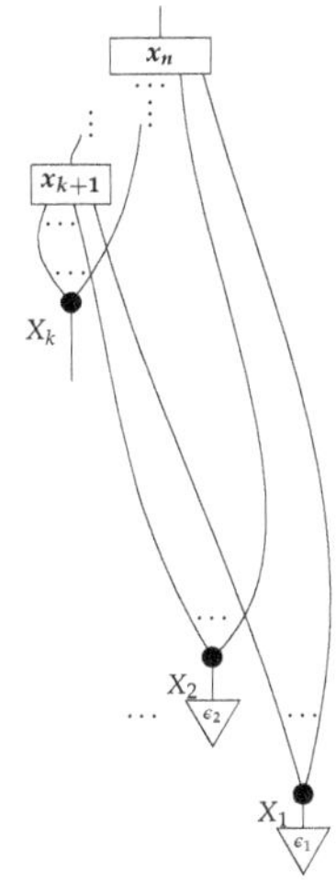

is known. Now, because the states $\epsilon_1$ through $\epsilon_{k-1}$ are arbitrary choices from the relevant sets of vectors, varying them yields knowledge of the following process.

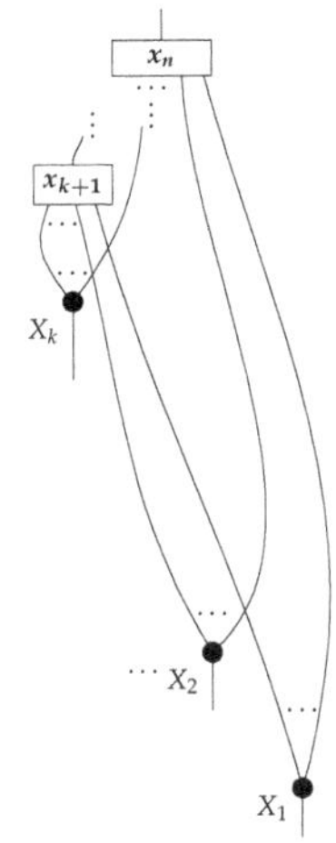

This completes the inner inductive step. Iterating eventually eliminates from the known process all boxes prior to $x_n$ while reducing each copy map's number of outputs to one, making the final known process simply

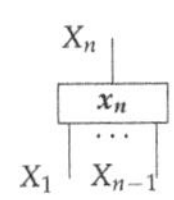

up to reordering of the input wires. Thus, the outer inductive step is completed. □

**Example 17.** *The theorem guarantees that Markovian models based on the two-node graph in (12) with $|X| = |Y| = 2$ are identifiable if the accessible set of instruments at X consists of the single instrument with branches $\psi \circ \phi$ and $\psi' \circ \phi'$ in Example 14 and if the accessible set of instruments at Y consists of the same instrument. By Proposition 6, the accessible sets in this case are marginally informationally complete. The theorem also covers Example 14 itself, in which the instrument used at Y is a perfect passive observation instrument.*

**Example 18.** *For the three-node graph in* (26) *with* $|X| = |Y| = 2$ *and* $|Z| = n$*, where* $n$ *is a positive integer, Markovian models are identifiable if the accessible set of instruments at* $X$ *is the singleton consisting of the instrument in Example 15, the accessible set at* $Y$ *is the singleton consisting of the instrument in Example 16, and the accessible set at* $Z$ *is the singleton consisting of a perfect passive observation instrument* $n \to n$.

## 6. Discussion

In this paper, we have presented a graphical causal modeling framework in which new and quite general kinds of causal identification problems can be posed. We have solved a problem only in the case of Markovian models, illustrating with this simple but important case the kind of reasoning our framework can support and the power of marginally informationally complete sets of instruments. Our main result raises the question of how much of the established theory of causal identification remains intact if we translate it to our framework and let the accessible sets of instruments be arbitrarily marginally informationally complete sets rather than singletons consisting of perfect passive observation instruments. Further investigation need not focus on marginally informationally complete sets of instruments, however; indeed, we can start with a causal model and ask what kinds of local intervention regimes would permit identification of various causal quantities.

Using the formalism in this paper also makes it possible to move beyond local intervention regimes and reason about intervention regimes in which the outcome of an intervention at one locus determines or influences the choice of instrument at another locus. Moreover, as indicated in Section 4.2, it is straightforward to modify the DAG-specific recipes in order to handle causal modeling based on other kinds of graphs that capture different kinds of qualitative hypotheses about the nature of latent variables.

Finally, many of the abstractions used in this paper are derived from quantum information science, and the ideas developed here may in turn be applied to the very active research area of "quantum causal modeling". Initial studies of quantum causal identification with methods similar to those in this paper can be found in [8,9].

**Author Contributions:** Conceptualization, I.F., R.W.S. and E.W.; methodology, I.F. and A.K.; investigation, I.F., A.K., R.W.S. and E.W.; writing—original draft preparation, I.F.; writing—review and editing, I.F., A.K., R.W.S. and E.W. All authors have read and agreed to the published version of the manuscript.

**Funding:** This publication was made possible through the support of the ID# 62312 grant from the John Templeton Foundation as part of the 'The Quantum Information Structure of Spacetime' Project (QISS) (https://www.templeton.org/grant/the-quantum-information-structure-of-spacetime-qiss-second-phase, accessed on 3 June 2025). The opinions expressed in this publication are those of the author(s) and do not necessarily reflect the views of the John Templeton Foundation.

**Data Availability Statement:** No new data were created or analyzed in this study. Data sharing is not applicable to this article.

**Acknowledgments:** I.F. and A.K. thank Jonathan Barrett for collaboration closely related to this work. I.F. is grateful for the hospitality of Perimeter Institute, where part of this work was carried out. Research at the Perimeter Institute is supported in part by the Government of Canada through the Department of Innovation, Science, and Economic Development and by the Province of Ontario through the Ministry of Colleges and Universities.

**Conflicts of Interest:** The authors declare no conflicts of interest.

## eferences


1. Pearl, J. *Causality*, 2nd ed.; Cambridge University Press: Cambridge, UK, 2009. [CrossRef]
2. Correa, J.; Bareinboim, E. A Calculus for Stochastic Interventions: Causal Effect Identification and Surrogate Experiments. *Proc. AAAI Conf. Artif. Intell.* **2020**, *34*, 10093–10100. [CrossRef]
3. Lee, S.; Correa, J.D.; Bareinboim, E. General Identifiability with Arbitrary Surrogate Experiments. In *Proceedings of Machine Learning Research, Proceedings of the 35th Uncertainty in Artificial Intelligence Conference, Tel Aviv, Israel, 22–25 July 2019*; Adams, R.P.; Gogate, V., Eds.; PMLR: Westminster, UK, 2020; Volume 115, pp. 389–398.
4. Colnet, B.; Mayer, I.; Chen, G.; Dieng, A.; Li, R.; Varoquaux, G.; Vert, J.P.; Josse, J.; Yang, S. Causal Inference Methods for Combining Randomized Trials and Observational Studies: A Review. *Stat. Sci.* **2024**, *39*, 165–191. [CrossRef]
5. Baez, J.; Stay, M. Physics, Topology, Logic and Computation: A Rosetta Stone. In *New Structures for Physics*; Coecke, B., Ed.; Springer: Berlin/Heidelberg, Germany, 2011; pp. 95–172. [CrossRef]
6. Jacobs, B.; Kissinger, A.; Zanasi, F. Causal Inference by String Diagram Surgery. In *Foundations of Software Science and Computation Structures, Proceedings of the 22nd International Conference, FOSSACS 2019, Held as Part of the European Joint Conferences on Theory and Practice of Software, ETAPS 2019, Prague, Czech Republic, 6–11 April 2019*; Bojańczyk, M.; Simpson, A., Eds.; Springer: Cham, Switzerland, 2019; pp. 313–329.
7. Lorenz, R.; Tull, S. Causal models in string diagrams. *arXiv* **2023**, arXiv:2304.07638.
8. Friend, I.; Kissinger, A. Identification of causal influences in quantum processes. *Phys. Rev. A* **2024**, *109*, 042214. . [CrossRef]
9. Barrett, J.; Friend, I.; Kissinger, A. Quantum and Classical Markovian Graphical Causal Models and Their Identification. In *Leibniz International Proceedings in Informatics, Proceedings of the 33rd EACSL Annual Conference on Computer Science Logic (CSL 2025), Amsterdam, The Netherlands, 10–14 February 2025*; Endrullis, J., Schmitz, S., Eds.; LIPICS: Dagstuhl, Germany, 2025; Volume 326, pp. 48:1–48:23, ISSN 1868-8969. [CrossRef]
10. Ludwig, G. Ensembles and Effects. In *Foundations of Quantum Mechanics I*; Ludwig, G., Ed.; Springer: Berlin/Heidelberg, Germany, 1983; pp. 41–82. [CrossRef]
11. Mac Lane, S. Monoids. In *Categories for the Working Mathematician*; Mac Lane, S., Ed.; Springer: New York, NY, USA, 1978; pp. 161–190. [CrossRef]
12. Coecke, B.; Kissinger, A. *Picturing Quantum Processes: A First Course in Quantum Theory and Diagrammatic Reasoning*; Cambridge University Press: Cambridge, UK, 2017. [CrossRef]
13. Otsuka, J.; Saigo, H. Process theory of causality: A category-theoretic perspective. *Behaviormetrika* **2024**, *51*, 21–36. [CrossRef]
14. Cho, K.; Jacobs, B. Disintegration and Bayesian inversion via string diagrams. *Math. Struct. Comput. Sci.* **2019**, *29*, 938–971. [CrossRef]
15. Pearl, J. An Introduction to Causal Inference. *Int. J. Biostat.* **2010**, *6*, 7. [CrossRef]
16. Richardson, T.R.; Robins, J.M. *Single World Intervention Graphs (SWIGs): A Unification of the Counterfactual and Graphical Approaches to Causality*; Technical Report 128; Center for Statistics and the Social Sciences, University of Washington: Seattle, WA, USA, 2013.
17. Barrett, J.; Lorenz, R.; Oreshkov, O. Quantum Causal Models. *arXiv* **2019**, arXiv:1906.10726.
18. Costa, F.; Shrapnel, S. Quantum causal modelling. *New J. Phys.* **2016**, *18*, 063032. [CrossRef]
19. Chiribella, G.; D'Ariano, G.M.; Perinotti, P. Quantum Circuit Architecture. *Phys. Rev. Lett.* **2008**, *101*, 060401. [CrossRef] [PubMed]
20. Richardson, T. Markov Properties for Acyclic Directed Mixed Graphs. *Scand. J. Stat.* **2003**, *30*, 145–157. [CrossRef]
21. Evans, R.J. Graphs for Margins of Bayesian Networks. *Scand. J. Stat.* **2016**, *43*, 625–648. [CrossRef]

*entropy*

Article

# A Magic Act in Causal Reasoning: Making Markov Violations Disappear

**Bob Rehder**

Psychology Department, New York University, 6 Washington Place, New York, NY 10012, USA; bob.rehder@nyu.edu

**Abstract:** A desirable property of any theory of causal reasoning is to explain not only why people make causal reasoning errors but also *when* they make them. The *mutation sampler* is a rational process model of human causal reasoning that yields normatively correct inferences when sufficient cognitive resources are available but introduces systematic errors when they are not. The mutation sampler has been shown to account for a number of causal reasoning errors, including *Markov violations*, the phenomenon in which human reasoners treat causally related variables as statistically dependent when they are normatively independent. A Markov violation arises, for example, when an individual reasoning about a causal chain $X \rightarrow Y \rightarrow Z$ treats $X$ as informative about the state of $Z$ even when the state of $Y$ is known. Recently, the mutation sampler was used to predict the existence of previously untested experimental conditions in which the *sign* of Markov violations would switch from positive to negative. Here, it was used to predict the existence of conditions in which Markov violations should *disappear* entirely. In fact, asking subjects to reason about a novel causal structure with nothing but *generative* causal relations (a cause makes its effect more likely) resulted in Markov violations in the usual positive direction. But simply describing one of four causal relations as *inhibitory* (the cause makes its effect less likely) resulted in the elimination of those violations. Theoretical model fitting confirmed how this novel result is predicted by the mutation sampler.

**Keywords:** causal reasoning; causal knowledge; Markov violations; rational process model; causal graphical models

## 1. Introduction

Decades of research have asked: How do people draw causal inferences about the world around them? On the one hand, this research has revealed that people are often subtle and sophisticated causal reasoners: their causal inferences are sensitive to the direction of the causal arrow; they know that an intervention will affect the variable's effects but not its cause; during learning they can control for alternative causes and are able to use temporal information to infer causal direction; and so on. Indeed, when it is available virtually all humans judgments are deeply influenced by causal knowledge [1–6]. Yet research has also shown that people commit systematic errors. So a challenge for theories of human causal reasoning is how to account for human ability to often draw sophisticated inferences while also explaining the common errors we make.

Recently, Davis and Rehder proposed a model called the *mutation sampler*, whose goal is to account for this phenomenon [7]. The mutation sampler is an instance of the species of models known as *rational process models*: models that are characterized by an algorithm for computing a normative answer but whose performance can be gracefully


https://doi.org/10.3390/10.3390/e2706054

degraded when cognitive resources are scarce [8–12]. As a result, the mutation sampler yields predictions that are close-to-optimal (reflecting the normative algorithm) but that also exhibit systematic deviations from optimality (reflecting cognitive resource limitation). In fact, there is now a substantial body of evidence supporting the mutation sampler as a viable model of human causal reasoning [7,13–15].

An important step in the development of any new psychological theory is to identify novel situations for which the theory makes interesting and perhaps surprising predictions. In this article, I will first describe a robust causal reasoning error known as *Markov violations* and discuss how the mutation sampler accounts for such errors in a variety of past experimental conditions. On the basis of the explanation that the mutation sampler provides for Markov violations, I will then identify new experimental conditions for which such errors should, in fact, disappear. I will then present new experimental evidence testing those conditions.

## 2. The Mutation Sampler

Figure 1A presents a typical scenario, in which experimental subjects are asked to draw causal inferences [15]. For example, in the domain of economics, meteorology, or sociology, university undergraduates were first taught novel causal knowledge that formed the *common cause* network shown in the top of the figure ($E_A \leftarrow C \rightarrow E_B$). In the domain of economics, some subjects were told that "Low interest rates cause small trade deficits" ($C \rightarrow E_A$) and also that "Low interest rates cause high retirement savings" ($C \rightarrow E_B$). They also received a short description of the mechanisms responsible for these causal relations. After learning this information, the subjects were asked to draw several causal inferences. For example, the subjects might be presented with an economy that had low interest rates and normal retirement savings and asked to predict whether it had small trade deficits; that is, they were asked to judge $p(E_A = 1|C = 1, E_B = 0)$. The graph in Figure 1A presents subject ratings (on a scale of 0–100) for a number of conditional probability judgments.

The mutation sampler attempts to account for such judgments by assuming that a core component of causal reasoning is *sampling*; specifically, sampling over the states of the causal system being reasoned about. When its variables are binary, a common cause system consists of eight distinct states, as represented by the lattice at the bottom of Figure 1A. According to the mutation sampler, human reasoners draw causal inferences by first sampling over these states using Markov chain Monte Carlo (MCMC) methods; specifically, the Metropolis Hastings rule. As the number of samples grows large, this rule guarantees that the samples will approximate the network's underlying joint distribution; that is, the probability that the system will be in each of its eight possible states. These approximated joint distributions can then be used to compute any causal inference (e.g., a conditional probability) that is needed.

As mentioned, without any additional assumptions the mutation sampler will simply approximate the causal network's normative joint distribution. For example, suppose that we know that in a common cause network the probability of the cause C is represented by parameter $w_c$, that the strength of the two causal relationships is represented by $w_{C,E_A}$ and $w_{C,E_B}$, and that each effect can be caused by unspecified exogenous causes, causes not shown in the network, the strength of which is represented by $w_{E_A}$ and $w_{E_B}$. Also, suppose that the probability of an effect $E_i$ is given by a logistic function $p(E_i = 1|C) = 1/(1 + exp(-(w_{CE_i}C + w_{E_i})))$, where the cause C is coded as 1 when present and $-1$ when absent. Given that the semantics of a common cause network allow us to write its joint distribution as $p(C, E_A, E_B) = p(E_A|C)p(E_B|C)p(C)$, we can then compute the causal network's joint distribution for any parameterization $w_c$, $w_{C,E_A}$, $w_{C,E_B}$, $w_{E_A}$, and $w_{E_B}$. This is the distribution that the mutation sampler's MCMC samples will, when normalized, approximate.

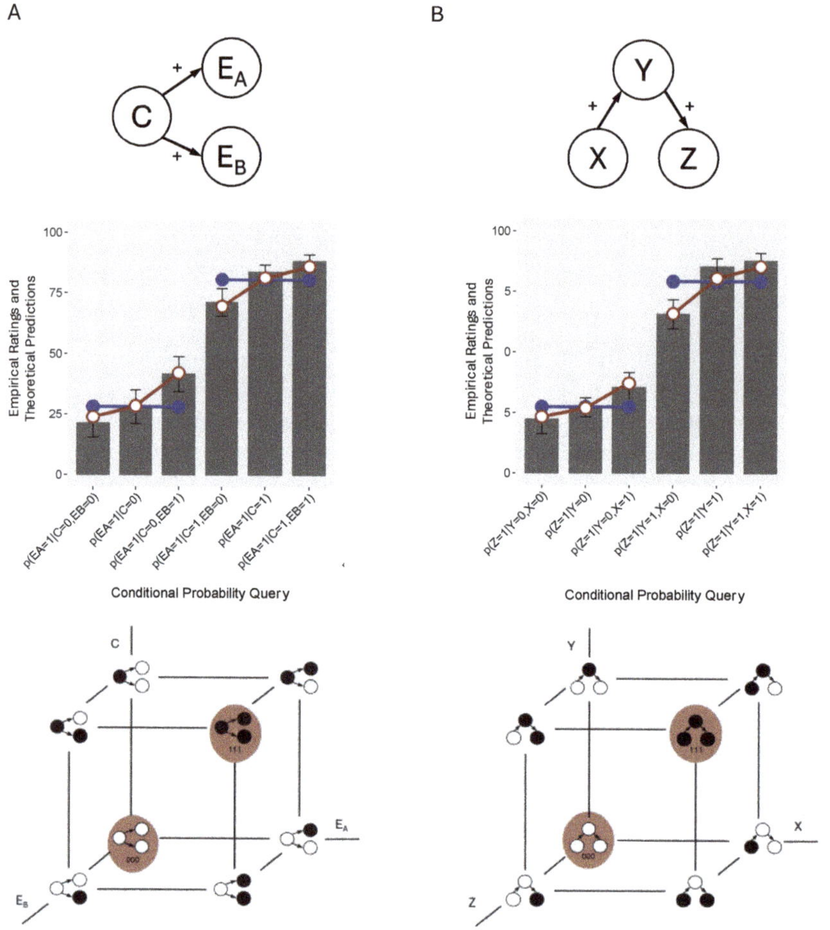


**Figure 1.** Empirical results from two conditions reported in one study of causal reasoning [15] and the associated theoretical model fits. Panel (**A**): The generative–generative condition of Experiment 1 that tested a common cause network. Panel (**B**): The generative–generative condition of Experiment 2 that tested a chain network. In one of three domains (economics, meteorology, or sociology), university undergraduates were taught a new theory consisting of hypothetical causal relations between binary variables and then asked to draw several causal inferences. Subsets of those inferences are shown on the x-axis of each graph, and the subjects' average responses (recorded on a 0–100 scale) are the gray bars. The error bars are standard errors. The blue lines with closed plot points are the fits of the normative model, and the red lines with open plot points are those of the mutation sampler. The highlighted system states in the lattice at the bottom of each panel represent the prototypes at which the mutation sampler will commence sampling.

But what makes the mutation sampler useful as a *psychological* model is that there are simple ways to degrade its performance so that its predictions diverge from the normative ones but potentially begin to mimic those of human reasoners. Two assumptions are needed. The first is that there is a limit on the cognitive resources that are available for sampling, so that only, say, a dozen or so samples are taken rather than the thousands or millions associated with MCMC methods when an accurate representation of a distribution is required. The second assumption is that sampling tends to commence at those causal network states that are perceived to be of high probability, states referred to by Davis and Rehder as *prototype states*. For example, in the case of the common cause network in Figure 1A the claim is that reasoners will carry out a superficial but low-cost analysis of the network and conclude that the states in which all variables are present ($C = 1$, $E_A = 1, E_B = 1$, abbreviated "111") or all are absent ($C = 0, E_A = 0, E_B = 0$, "000") are highly probable and, so, they are good places to start sampling. These states are highlighted in red in the lattice in Figure 1A. Note that the reasoner's derivation of the prototype states is superficial in that it ignores all quantitative information (e.g., the causal strengths $w_{C,E_A}$ and $w_{C,E_B}$) and even the direction of the causal relations.

On the one hand, biasing where sampling begins has some justification. Davis and Rehder showed that, holding the number of samples constant, starting at high probability states leads to causal inferences that are generally more accurate for a wide variety of network parameterizations [7]. Yet it also introduces systematic errors. For example, a key property of causal Bayes nets is the *Markov condition*, which states that a variable is independent of its non-descendants conditioned on the states of its immediate parents [16]. Applied to the common cause network of Figure 1A, this means, for example, that the probability of $E_A$ should be unaffected by the state of $E_B$ when the state of C is known. In other words, C should *screen off* $E_A$ from $E_B$, such that $p(E_A = 1|C, E_B = 0) = p(E_A = 1|C) = p(E_A = 1|C, E_B = 1)$ should hold for any value of C. Yet, conditional probability judgments derived from a distorted joint distribution—such as ones computed by the mutation sampler with a modest chain length and a bias in the starting point—will also be distorted, with the result that they may exhibit violations of the Markov condition.

The human judgments presented in Figure 1A are those that are relevant to assessing whether people honor the Markov condition when reasoning about a common cause scenario. On the left side of the graph are the three judgments regarding the probability of the effect $E_A$, given that the common cause is absent ($C = 0$) as a function of the state of the other effect $E_B$: $p(E_A = 1|C = 0, E_B = 0)$, $p(E_A = 1|C = 0)$, and $p(E_A = 1|C = 0, E_B = 1)$. On the right are analogous judgments when C is present. The gray bars are the subjects' responses to those queries on a 0–100 scale.

The blue lines represent the predictions of the normative causal graphical model (multiplied by 100), where the model's parameters ($w_C$, $w_{C,E_A}$, $w_{C,E_B}$, etc.) are optimized to fit each subject's complete set of judgments. That the blue lines are horizontal reflects the Markov condition: the probability of $E_A$ varies with C but not with the state of the other effect $E_B$. In contrast, the empirical results show that the human judgments violated the Markov violation: the probability of $E_A$ was generally lower when $E_B$ was absent (i.e., $p(E_A = 1|C, E_B = 0) < p(E_A = 1|C)$) and generally higher when it was present ($p(E_A = 1|C) < p(E_A = 1|C, E_B = 1)$ both when $C = 0$ and $C = 1$.

The fitted predictions of the mutation sampler (red lines) illustrate how that model reproduces these violations. It does so because its assumption that sampling commences at one of the two prototypes combined with a limited number of samples introduces a distortion into the sampled representation of the causal model's joint distribution and, so, the conditional probabilities derived from that joint distribution. This finding of Markov violations in the positive direction—$p(E_A = 1|C, E_B)$ is larger when $E_B$ is present versus absent—when testing common cause networks with generative relations has been observed in a large number of studies [17–27].

Tests of how people reason with other causal structures have corroborated the predictions of the mutation sampler. For example, the same study also tested subjects on a causal chain $X \to Y \to Z$, as shown in Figure 1B [15]. The Markov condition stipulates that a causal chain embodies another instance of conditional independence: it is now $X$ and $Z$

that should be independent, conditioned on $Y$. The graph in Figure 1B presents the subjects' predictions regarding the presence $Z$ given $Y$, varying whether $X$ is absent, unknown, or present. The fits of the normative causal model (again, with parameters optimized to each subject's ratings) shown by the blue horizontal lines illustrate the Markov condition: the state of $X$ should have no effect on the estimated probability of $Z$ when the state of $Y$ is known. In contrast, the subjects committed Markov violations: $Z$ was judged to be more likely when the supposedly screened-off $X$ was present versus absent. Moreover, Figure 1B indicates that the fitted mutation sampler reproduces these judgments quite closely. Because its principles for determining prototypes are insensitive to causal direction, the lattice in Figure 1B shows that the mutation sampler assumes the same prototypes for a chain network as it did for a common cause network; namely, 000 and 111.

The study in [15] also tested a *common effect* network, in which the subjects reasoned with the network in Figure 2A, where $C_A$ and $C_B$ were each independent causes of $E$. Whereas when applied to common cause and chain networks the Markov condition stipulates that two variables become independent conditioned on a third, for a common effect network it stipulates that the two causes are *unconditionally* independent, such that, say, $p(C_A = 1|C_B = 0) = p(C_A = 1|C_B = 1)$ should hold. The predictions of the normative causal model fitted to the empirical data in Figure 2A confirmed that $C_A$ and $C_B$ should be independent (horizontal blue line). In contrast, the subjects instead judged that $p(C_A = 1|C_B = 0) < p(C_A = 1|C_B = 1)$. The fitted predictions of the mutation sampler indicate that it is able to reproduce this effect (assuming, again, prototypes of 000 and 111; see the lattice in Figure 2A).

Note that an important characteristic of common effect networks is *explaining away*, in which, when the effect $E$ is known to be present the presence/absence of, say, $C_A$ results in the lowering/raising of the probability of $C_B$; that is, $p(C_A = 1|E = 1, C_B = 0) > p(C_A = 1|E = 1) > p(C_A = 1|E = 1, C_B = 1)$ should hold. Explaining away is illustrated by the blue line in Figure 2A with the negative slope. The subjects, however, exhibited explaining away that was substantially weaker than predicted by the normative causal model. The mutation sampler's prototypes reproduced this effect as well, as illustrated by the red line with a shallower negative slope. This result illustrates how the mutation sampler's distorted joint probabilities affect the calculation of all conditional probabilities, not just those involved in the Markov condition. These results testing common effect structures—both the violations of independence and weak explaining away—have also been demonstrated in multiple studies [22,23,25,26,28–30].

Although the empirical tests reviewed so far all involved *generative* causal relations in which the cause increases the probability of its effect, ref. [15] also tested causal networks where one or more of the causal relations was described as *inhibitory*. For example, Figure 2B presents the results with a common cause network in which $C \rightarrow E_A$ and $C \rightarrow E_B$ were described as generative and inhibitory, respectively. Remarkably, whereas all previous demonstrations of Markov violations reported violations that were in the positive direction (e.g., $p(E_A = 1|C, E_B)$ is higher when $E_B$ was present versus absent), in this new condition they were *negative* ($p(E_A = 1|C, E_B)$ was lower when $E_B$ was present versus absent). The mutation sampler reproduces this result because, rather than assuming that the prototypes are 000 and 111, it assumes that they are 110 ($C$ and $E_A$ both present, $E_B$ absent) or 001 ($C$ and $E_A$ both absent, $E_B$ present), an assumption that is sensible given that the inhibitory relation between $C$ and $E_B$ means that those variables should have opposite values. In fact, ref. [15] showed that Markov violations were negative for every causal network topology that involved a mixture of generative and inhibitory causal relations (and, intriguingly, they reverted to the positive direction when all causal relations were inhibitory) and that these results were accounted for by the mutation sampler.

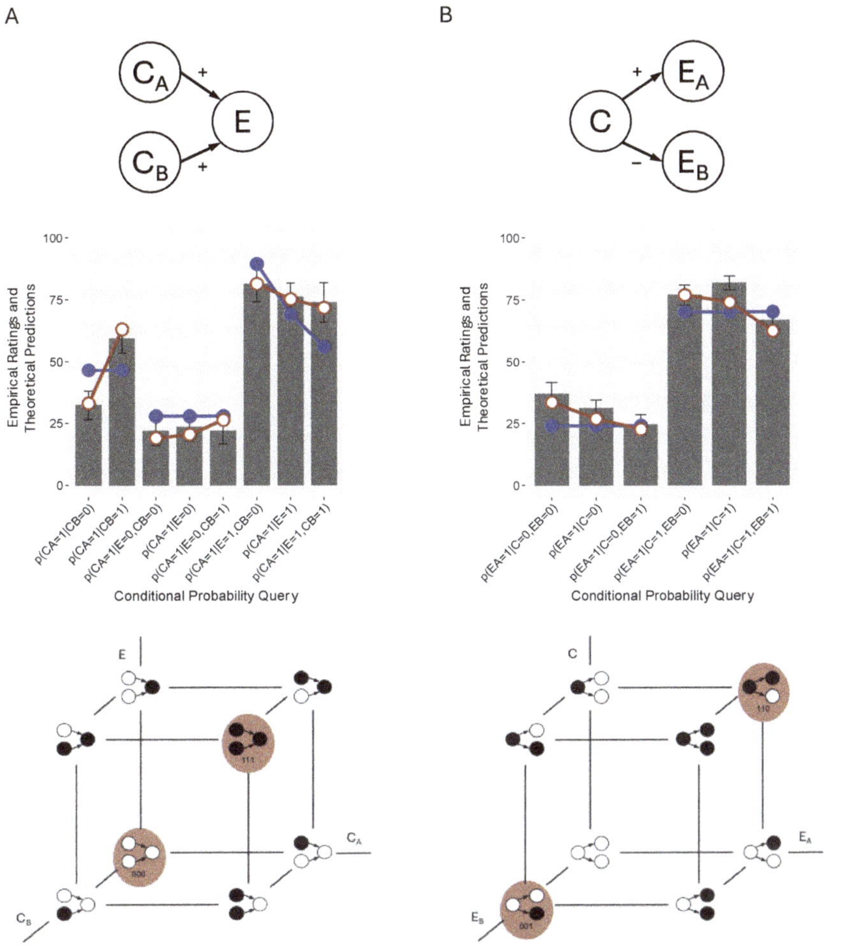


**Figure 2.** Empirical results from two additional conditions reported in [15]. Panel (**A**): The generative–generative condition of Experiment 3 that tested a common effect network. Panel (**B**): The generative–inhibitory condition of Experiment 1 that tested a common cause network with one inhibitory causal relation. The error bars are standard errors. The blue lines with closed plot points are the fits of the normative model, and the red lines with open plot points are those of the mutation sampler.

## 3. The Magic Act: Eliminating Markov Violations

Given the robustness of Markov violations in psychological research—they have been observed in more than a dozen studies—an experimental result with both empirical and theoretical importance would be one where such errors *failed* to occur. The findings reviewed above demonstrated the value of the mutation sampler in being able to identify conditions in which the sign of Markov violations would switch from positive to negative. Here, the mutation sampler is used to identify conditions in which Markov violations should fail to appear altogether.

Consider the causal networks shown in Figure 3. In all three networks a variable $X$ is the cause of both $Y_A$ and $Y_B$, which, in turn, are independent causes of $Z$. In Figure 3A, all four causal relationships are stipulated to be generative; that is, each cause makes its effect more likely. In contrast, in Figure 3B,C one of the four causal relationships is described as inhibitory instead. In Figure 3B the inhibitory relation is $Y_A \rightarrow Z$, whereas in Figure 3C it is $Y_B \rightarrow Z$.

Now, consider the independence properties of these networks. Firstly, there are no instances of unconditional independence. Any pair of variables that are directly causally related will exhibit dependence, and of those pairs that are not directly related, $Y_A$ and $Y_B$ are dependent on their common cause $X$, and $X$ and $Z$ are dependent because of the mediators $Y_A$ and $Y_B$. However, consider the situation where the state of $X$ is known. As we have seen, a key prediction of causal Bayes nets is that in common cause networks (such as the $Y_A \leftarrow X \rightarrow Y_B$ subnetwork that appears in each panel of Figure 3) the two effects $Y_A$ and $Y_B$ are independent when conditioning on the cause $X$. Of course, $Y_A$ and $Y_B$ are also causally related to $Z$. However, we have also seen that a principle of common effect networks (such as the $Y_A \rightarrow Z \leftarrow Y_B$ subnetworks in Figure 3) is that the two causes $Y_A$ and $Y_B$ are independent so long as no information about $Z$ is available. In summary, in all the networks in Figure 3 $Y_A$ and $Y_B$ should exhibit independence when conditioning on $X$.

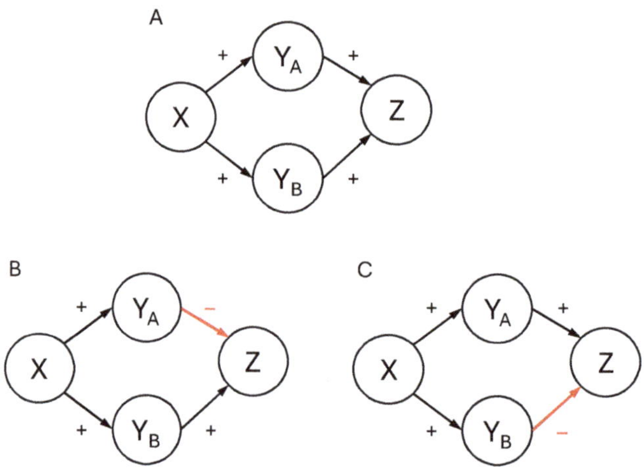


**Figure 3.** Three causal conditions tested in the current study. Panel (**A**): The Generative condition. Panel (**B**): The $Y_A$-Inhibitory condition. Panel (**C**): The $Y_B$-Inhibitory condition.

The mutation sampler makes different predictions. Because it stipulates that sampling will begin at those network states that exhibit qualitative consistency with the causal relations, for the network with all generative relations in Figure 3A the prototypical states are either all four variables present (1111) or all four absent (0000). And the consequence of those prototypes should come as no surprise: subjects should commit positive Markov violations, just as they did for the networks in Figures 1 and 2 with all generative relations. That is, instead of treating $Y_A$ and $Y_B$ as independent when conditioning on $X$, the mutation sampler predicts that they will judge that $p(Y_A = 1|Y_B = 0, X) > p(Y_A = 1|X) > p(Y_A = 1|Y_B = 1, X)$ and $p(Y_B = 1|Y_A = 0, X) > p(Y_B = 1|X) > p(Y_B = 1|Y_A = 1, X)$.

However, the mutation sampler's predictions differ for the networks in Figure 3B,C. For these networks, the key question is: What are the prototypes? On the one hand, nothing in nature precludes real-world causal processes in which some variable $X$ has a positive causal influence on a variable $Z$ through one mediator but a negative influence through another. However, for a human reasoner who is carrying out only a superficial, qualitative analysis, the apparent contradiction that $X$ makes $Z$ both more and less likely means that these networks have no prototypes: that is, there are no settings of the four variables that are qualitatively consistent with all four causal relations. In such a case, Davis and Rehder speculated that there will be no bias in the starting point of the sampling chain, because there are no grounds for favoring one state over another: all are (qualitatively) (in)consistent with the causal relations [7]. And the consequence is that for the networks in Figure 3B,C Markov violations disappear.

These predictions were tested in the following experiment. The subjects were assigned to either a *Generative* condition, in which all causal relations were generative as in Figure 3A, or an *Inhibitory* condition, in which one causal relation was inhibitory. Within the Inhibitory condition, half of the subjects were told that $Y_A \rightarrow Z$ was inhibitory and the other half that $Y_B \rightarrow Z$ was inhibitory. Based on previous research, there was a strong expectation that positive Markov violations would be observed in the Generative condition. The main question asked here is whether the predicted elimination of Markov violations in the Inhibitory conditions was observed.

## 4. Methods

### *4.1. Materials*

Three content domains were tested: economics, meteorology, and sociology. The subjects were first told that the domain they were about to study included four binary variables. In the domain of economics, the variables were interest rates (either low or normal), trade deficits (small or normal), retirement savings (high or normal), and job mobility (low or normal). In the domain of meteorology, the variables were ozone level, air pressure, humidity, and wind drafts. In sociology, they were degree of urbanization, interest in religion, socio-economic mobility, and interest in sports.

The subjects were then presented with a verbal description of the four causal relations that formed the structures in Figure 3. In the Generative condition (Figure 3A), all causal relations were described as generative. For example, one of the generative relationships in the domain of economics was "Low interest rates cause small trade deficits. The low cost of borrowing money leads businesses to invest in the latest manufacturing technologies, and the resulting low-cost products are exported around the world". In contrast, in the $Y_A$-Inhibitory (Figure 3B) and $Y_B$-Inhibitory (Figure 3C) conditions, $Y_A \rightarrow Z$ and $Y_B \rightarrow Z$ were described as inhibitory, respectively. For example, "High retirement savings prevent high job mobility. With their financial future assured, workers are less motivated to look for new, higher-paying jobs".

The subjects were then presented with the inference test. Each trial presented the values of one or two variables and asked the subject to predict the state of another. For example, a subject might be told that an economy had low interest rates and a normal trade deficit and be asked the probability of it having a high level of retirement savings. The subjects entered their response by moving a tick on a rating scale with ends labeled 0% and 100%. To ensure that the subjects did not have to rely on their memory, the causal relationships were repeated on the bottom half of the screen. The subjects were presented with the 32 distinct conditional probability queries, including those required to assess the independence of $Y_A$ and $Y_B$. The order of these queries was randomized for each participant.

### *4.2. Design and Participants*

The experiment consisted of a 3 (content domain: economics, meteorology, or sociology) × 2 (Generative versus Inhibitory) × 2 ($Y_A$-Inhibitory vs. $Y_B$-Inhibitory) between-subject design. The subjects were randomly assigned to these 3 × 2 × 2 = 12 between-subject cells, subject to the constraint that an approximately equal number appeared in each cell. For participating, 112 New York University undergraduates received course credit. This sample size is similar to those in previous tests of causal reasoning using these materials (e.g., Rehder, 2024 [15]).

## 5. Results

The initial analyses revealed no effect of content domain and so the key inference ratings in each condition are presented in Figure 4 collapsed over that factor. Figure 4A presents the results in the Generative condition. Moving from left to right, the first three bars present the probability of $Y_A$ as a function of whether $Y_B$ is absent, unknown, or present, given that $X$ is absent. The next three bars are the same queries with $X$ present. The final six bars are the same queries with the role of $Y_A$ and $Y_B$ reversed.

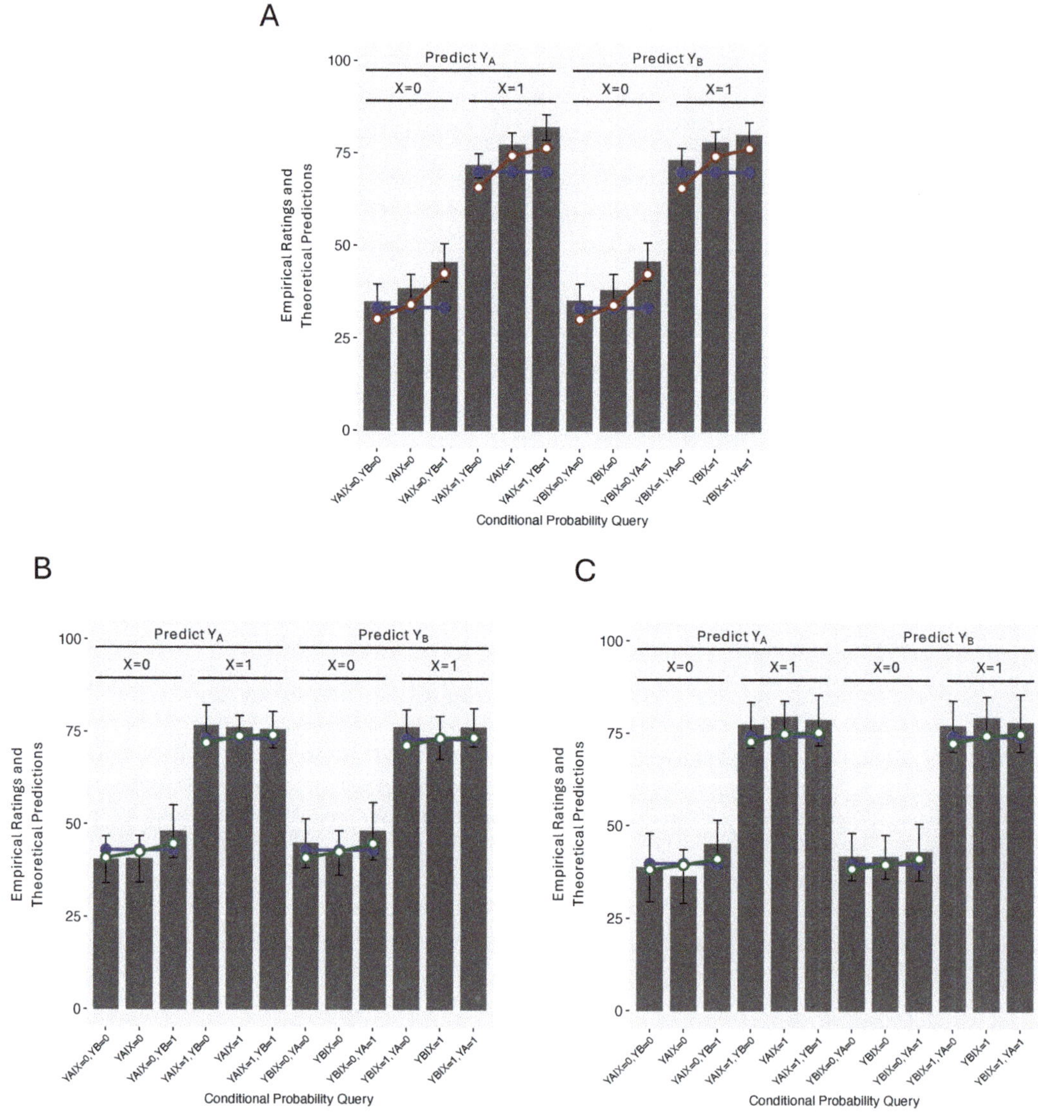


**Figure 4.** Empirical ratings and theoretical model fits. Panel (**A**): Generative condition. Panel (**B**): $Y_A$-Inhibitory condition. Panel (**C**): $Y_B$-Inhibitory. The blue lines with closed plot points are the fits of the normative model, the red lines are those of the mutation sampler with 1111 and 0000 prototypes, and the green lines are those of the mutation sampler assuming no prototypes. The error bars are standard errors.

Starting with the Generative condition, Figure 4A indicates that the subjects in this condition committed positive Markov violations: within each triplet of ratings in the figure, the rated probability of one $Y$ was lower when the other $Y$ was absent and higher when the other $Y$ was present. This is a novel result, insofar as, to my knowledge, there have been no prior demonstrations of Markov violations with the causal structure in Figure 4A. Nevertheless, they are unsurprising in light of the widespread presence of positive Markov violations with causal structures with only generative relations (e.g., in Figures 1A,B and 2A).

The more interesting results appear in Figure 4B,C, which show that the Markov violations that were so prominent in Figure 4A are largely absent in the $Y_A$-Inhibitory and $Y_B$-Inhibitory conditions. Although these results are surprising, in light of the demonstrations of pervasive Markov violations reviewed above, recall that they were predicted on the basis of the mutations sampler's assumption regarding the absence of prototype states in these conditions.

A summary measure of the Markov violation in the three conditions was computed by subtracting $p(Y_i = 1|C, Y_j = 1)$ from $p(Y_i = 1|C, Y_j = 0)$ for each pairing of the Ys and each level of $C$ and averaging the results. These results are presented in Figure 5. The average Markov violation in the Generative condition was 9.6, a result quite comparable to other studies that tested networks with generative relations. In contrast, in the $Y_A$-Inhibitory and $Y_B$-Inhibitory conditions those violations were a much more modest 2.5 and 2.5, respectively. A one-way ANOVA of these results yielded a statistically significant effect of condition, $F(2, 109) = 5.77, p = 0.004$. Individual t-testing of the three conditions yielded a statistically significant Markov violation in the Generative condition, $t(55) = 6.80, p < 10^{-8}, BF > 10^6$, but not in the other two conditions, both $p$s > 0.25. and $BF$s < 0.38 (Bayes factors were computed via the R BayesFactor package, version 0.9.12-4.5.).

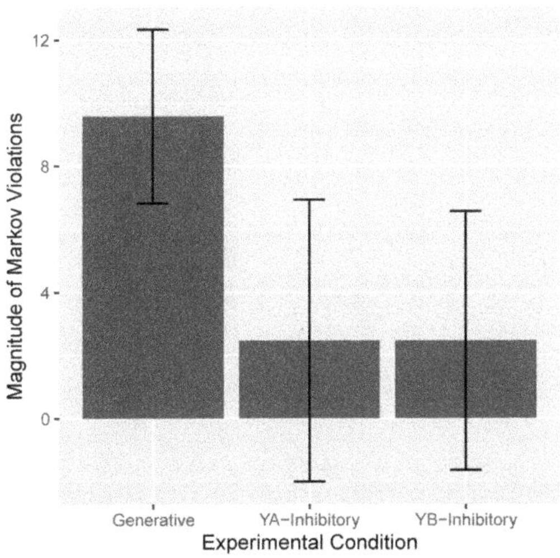


**Figure 5.** The magnitude of the Markov violation in each condition. Generative condition. $Y_A$-Inhibitory condition. $Y_B$-Inhibitory condition. The error bars are 95% confidence intervals.

*Theoretical Modeling*

Two versions of the mutation sampler were fitted to each subject's 32 conditional probability judgments. One version assumed the prototypes that are deemed appropriate for causal networks with all generative relations; namely, ones where the variables are all present (1111) or all absent (0000). The other version assumed the absence of prototypes, which is appropriate for causal networks for which no qualitatively consistent set of variable values exist, such as those in the $Y_A$-Inhibitory and $Y_B$-Inhibitory conditions. For this model, sampling began at a randomly chosen system state. For both models, the fitting procedure involved identifying the best fitting values for $w_X$ (the probability of the root cause X), $w_Z$ (the strength of the exogenous causes of Z), and $\lambda$ (the mutation sampler's chain length parameter). A single parameter $w_{gen}$ estimated the strength of all the generative causal relations. In the $Y_A$-Inhibitory and $Y_B$-Inhibitory conditions, an additional parameter estimated the strength of the single inhibitory relation ($w_{inh}$). Additional details of the model fitting procedure can be found in [15]. Table 1 presents each model's best fitting parameters averaged over the participants in each condition, along with a number of measures of fit, including the correlation between predicted and observed values averaged over participants (*R*) and a measure (*AIC*) that takes into account a model's number of parameters ($AIC = n*log(SSE/n) + 2*(p + 1)$, where *SSE* = sum of squared error, *n* = number of data points fit, and *p* = a model's number of parameters. Thus, lower values of *AIC* reflect a better fit. This measure has been deemed appropriate for comparing models fit by least squares [31]. The last column of Table 1 presents the percentage of participants best fitted by that model in each condition.

**Table 1.** Fits of mutation sampler with and without prototypes 0000 and 1111.

| Model | Average Parameter Estimates | | | | | Measures of Fit | | |
|---|---|---|---|---|---|---|---|---|
| | $w_X$ | $w_{gen}$ | $w_{inh}$ | $w_Z$ | $\lambda$ | *R* | *AIC* | % Subjects |
| **Generative** | | | | | | | | |
| With Prototypes | 0.649 | 0.476 | | 0.454 | 17.5 | 0.815 | 166.0 | 67.9 |
| | (0.028) | (0.033) | | (0.028) | (1.09) | (0.016) | (3.17) | |
| No Prototypes | 0.699 | 0.774 | | 0.344 | 16.9 | 0.804 | 168.0 | 32.1 |
| | (0.045) | (0.032) | | (0.039) | (1.90) | (0.015) | (3.32) | |
| **$Y_A$Z-Inhibitory** | | | | | | | | |
| With Prototypes | 0.612 | 0.456 | −0.338 | 0.479 | 35.6 | 0.708 | 178.6 | 41.3 |
| | (0.026) | (0.037) | (0.032) | (0.027) | (1.10) | (0.029) | (3.71) | |
| No Prototypes | 0.736 | 0.714 | −0.395 | 0.440 | 16.2 | 0.718 | 178.3 | 58.6 |
| | (0.047) | (0.052) | (0.038) | (0.039) | (1.21) | (0.027) | (3.61) | |
| **$Y_B$Z-Inhibitory** | | | | | | | | |
| With Prototypes | 0.619 | 0.519 | −0.396 | 0.483 | 32.3 | 0.714 | 186.6 | 25.9 |
| | (0.040) | (0.052) | (0.038) | (0.039) | (1.13) | (0.038) | (3.13) | |
| No Prototypes | 0.673 | 0.732 | −0.441 | 0.389 | 16.6 | 0.728 | 186.3 | 74.1 |
| | (0.061) | (0.052) | (0.071) | (0.042) | (1.24) | (0.031) | (3.13) | |

*Note*: "% Subjects" are the percentage of subjects best fitted by the mutation sampler. Because they were not normally distributed, the reported average chain length parameter $\lambda$ was computed by exponentiating the average of the logarithm of the subjects' individual chain length parameters. Standard errors are shown in parentheses. AIC = Akaike information criterion.

The results of these fits averaged over subjects are shown in Figure 4 superimposed on the empirical data. As expected, Figure 4A indicates that the mutation sampler with prototypes did a good job reproducing the subjects' positive Markov violations. Table 1 indicates that these effects resulted in it yielding a better fit (*AIC* of 166.0) as compared to a mutation sampler without prototypes (168.0). According to *AIC*, 68% of the subjects were better fitted by a mutation sampler that began sampling at either 1111 or 0000.

In contrast, the mutation sampler without prototypes yielded a better fit in both the $Y_A$-Inhibitory (*AIC* of 178.3 vs. 178.6; number of subject fit best = 59%) and the $Y_B$-Inhibitory (*AIC* of 186.3 vs. 186.6; number of subject fit best = 74%) conditions. Figure 4B,C confirm that this model reproduced the *absence* of substantial Markov violations in these conditions.

It is informative to compare the fitted chain length parameters in the $Y_A$-Inhibitory and $Y_B$-Inhibitory conditions. For the mutation sampler without prototypes, the average chain length parameter in those conditions was 16.2 and 16.6, respectively, values that were very comparable to those estimated in the Generative condition. But the mutation sampler with prototypes estimated much larger chain length parameters (35.6 and 32.3). The reason for this difference was that in these conditions the prototypes led the model to predict Markov violations that the subjects, in fact, did not commit. Larger chain lengths were estimated, in order to minimize the impact of those prototypes and so allow the model's predictions to be more in line with subjects' actual judgments. Rather than assuming that the subjects reasoned with prototypes but then sampled excessively to minimize their influence, the more parsimonious explanation offered here is that the subjects in the $Y_A$-Inhibitory and $Y_B$-Inhibitory conditions did not have a bias in where they started sampling.

Figure 4 also presents the fits of the normative model in each condition. Unsurprisingly, in the Generative condition the mutation sampler with prototypes yielded a better fit than the normative model (*AIC*s of 166.0 vs. 170.0), because the former model reproduced that condition's Markov violations whereas the latter did not. In contrast, but still unsurprisingly, in the conditions with an inhibitory causal relation the mutation sampler without prototypes did *not* yield better fits than the normative model (*AIC*s of 178.3 vs. 176.9 in the $Y_A$-Inhibitory condition and 186.3 vs. 185.1 in the $Y_B$-Inhibitory condition). This is unsurprising, because the mutation sampler without a bias in where sampling starts is simply an approximation of the normative model, which means that it will lose any comparison with the normative model due to its extra chain length parameter $\lambda$.

## 6. Discussion

In psychological research, one sign of understanding a phenomenon is knowing how to make the phenomenon disappear. Positive Markov violations are so ubiquitous in the causal reasoning literature that failing to observe them is of theoretical importance. Using a theoretical model—the mutation sampler—as a guide, this study derived the specific conditions under which Markov violations should fail to materialize. In fact, asking subjects to reason with causal structures in which there was no setting of the variables that were qualitatively consistent with that structure was sufficient to eliminate Markov violations. In contrast, when subjects reasoned with a causal structure that was identical, except that one of the four causal relations was generative rather than inhibitory, Markov violations of about the same magnitude as observed in other studies once again revealed themselves.

The prototype states that the mutation sampler posits as the underlying cause for Markov violations (and other causal reasoning errors, such as weak explaining away) are intended to reflect a reasoner's superficial but cost-effective analysis of a causal network. The mutation sampler makes several claims about that analysis. Firstly, it assumes that the direction of causality is ignored so that, for example, the common cause, chain, and common effect networks with only generative relations shown earlier all have the same prototypes. Secondly, quantitative information, such as the strength of the causal relations, is ignored. Thirdly, there is no consideration of the details of how multiple causal influences combine. However, what the present results suggest is that the analysis that yields prototype states *is* sensitive to whether the causal relations are generative or inhibitory, as indicated by the elimination of Markov violations when just one of four generative causal relations was described as inhibitory. Of course, this conclusion is corroborated by the results described earlier, in which the sign of Markov violations changed from positive to negative when a causal network contained a mix of generative and inhibitory relations (but, unlike in the current study, still allowed the identification of qualitatively consistent prototype states) [15].

It is important to have a balanced perspective on the notion of prototype states. Starting sampling at high probability prototypes states might seem generally unwise, given that they introduce systematic errors into people's causal inferences. But, as mentioned, it has a benefit, as well, which is that it tends to maximize the overall accuracy of a reasoner's causal inferences when the cognitive resources available are limited [7]. Under this view, Markov violations are the price one must pay in order to maximize the overall quality of one's causal inferences.

These current results suggest several new avenues for research. One involves the notion of prototypes themselves. The current formulation of the mutation sampler specifies that prototypes are an "all or none" concept; that is, they are system states that are *completely* (qualitatively) consistent with the causal relations. Because they exhibit no completely consistent states, this definition led to the assumption that the networks in Figure 3B,C have no prototypes and, thus, no bias in where sampling starts. But it would be possible to adopt a more graded notion of prototypes whereby system states are chosen as places to start sampling with a probability that is a function of the *number* of inconsistencies (the number of "broken" causal links) they exhibit. For example, for the $Y_A$-Inhibitory network in Figure 3B one might specify that sampling was more likely to commence at state $X = 1, Y_A = 0, Y_B = 1, Z = 1$, which has one broken causal link (namely, $X \rightarrow Y_A$), than at $X = 1, Y_A = 0, Y_B = 0, Z = 1$, which has three ($X \rightarrow Y_A$, $X \rightarrow Y_B$, and $Y_B \rightarrow Z$). The differences in behavior that this alternative view predicts are likely to be subtle but could be explored in future research (I thank an anonymous reviewer for raising the possibility).

More generally, it is worth noting that as a process model the mutation sampler makes predictions about dependent variables that are often not emphasized in the causal reasoning literature. For example, a recent study by Kolvoort et al. aimed to assess the sources of subjects' response variability; that is, why an individual might give a different answer to logically equivalent causal queries [14]. The mutation sampler predicts this sort of within-subject variability because the outcome of the stochastic sampling process might differ from one invocation to the next. Indeed, Kolvoort et al. found that the mutation sampler provided a better account of that variability than other sources (motor noise in subjects' responses, misreading the causal query, etc.). As a cognitive process model, the mutation sampler is, thus, well positioned to provide potential explanations of data related to not just *what* causal inferences humans draw but also how they draw them [32–36].

**Funding:** This research received no external funding.

**Institutional Review Board Statement:** The study was conducted in accordance with the Declaration of Helsinki, and approved by the Institutional Review Board of New York University (protocol code IRB-FY2024-8851, 18 June 2024).

**Data Availability Statement:** Data and study materials from these experiments are available: https://osf.io/35qke/, 8 December 2024.

**Conflicts of Interest:** The author declares no conflicts of interest.

## References

1. Hagmayer, Y. Causal Bayes nets as psychological theories of causal reasoning: Evidence from psychological research. *Synthes* **2016**, *193*, 1107–1126. [CrossRef]
2. Rehder, B. Concepts as causal models: Classification. In *The Oxford Handbook of Causal Reasoning*; Waldmann, M.R., Ed.; Oxfor University Press: Oxford, UK, 2017; pp. 347–376.
3. Rehder, B. Concepts as causal models: Induction. In *The Oxford Handbook of Causal Reasoning*; Waldmann, M.R., Ed.; Oxfor University Press: Oxford, UK, 2017; pp. 377–414.

. Rottman, B.M.; Hastie, R. Reasoning about causal relationships: Inferences on causal networks. *Psychol. Bull.* **2014**, *140*, 109–139. [CrossRef] [PubMed]

. Sloman, S.A.; Lagnado, D. Causality in thought. *Annu. Rev. Psychol.* **2015**, *66*, 223–247. [CrossRef] [PubMed]

. Waldmann, M.R. *The Oxford Handbook of Causal Reasoning*; Oxford University Press: Oxford, UK, 2017.

. Davis, Z.J.; Rehder, B. A process model of causal reasoning. *Cogn. Sci.* **2020**, *44*, e12839. [CrossRef]

. Dasgupta, I.; Schulz, E.; Gershman, S.J. Where do hypotheses come from? *Cogn. Psychol.* **2017**, *96*, 1–25. [CrossRef]

. Dasgupta, I.; Schulz, E.; Goodman, N.D.; Gershman, S.J. Remembrance of inferences past: Amortization in human hypothesis generation. *Cognition* **2018**, *178*, 67–81. [CrossRef] [PubMed]

0. Johnson, J.G.; Busemeyer, J.R. A computational model of the attention process in risky choice. *Decision* **2016**, *3*, 254–280. [CrossRef]

1. Lieder, F.; Griffiths, T.; Goodman, N. Burn-in, bias, and the rationality of anchoring. In Proceedings of the Advances in Neural Information Processing Systems, Lake Tahoe, NV, USA, 3–6 December 2012; Volume 25, pp. 2690–2798.

2. Vul, E.; Goodman, N.; Griffiths, T.L.; Tenenbaum, J.B. One and done? Optimal decisions from very few samples. *Cogn. Sci.* **2014**, *38*, 599–637. [CrossRef]

3. Kolvoort, I.; Temme, N.; van Maanen, L. The Bayesian Mutation Sampler explains distributions of causal judgments. *Open Mind Discov. Cogn. Sci.* **2023**, *7*, 318–349. [CrossRef]

4. Kolvoort, I.; Davis, Z.J.; Rehder, B.; Van Maanen, L. Models of variability in probabilistic causal judgments. *Comput. Brain Behav.* **2025**, *8*, 162–188. [CrossRef]

5. Rehder, B. Extending a Rational Process Model of Causal Reasoning: Assessing Markov Violations and Explaining Away with Inhibitory Causal Relations. *J. Exp. Psychol. Learn. Mem. Cogn.* **2024**, *50*, 1463–1488. [CrossRef] [PubMed]

6. Pearl, J. *Causality: Models, Reasoning and Inference*; Springer: Berlin/Heidelberg, Germany, 2000; Volume 29.

7. Ali, N.; Chater, N.; Oaksford, M. The mental representation of causal conditional reasoning: Mental models or causal models. *Cognition* **2011**, *119*, 403–418. [CrossRef] [PubMed]

8. Fernbach, P.M.; Rehder, B. Cognitive shortcuts in causal inference. *Argum. Comput.* **2013**, *4*, 64–88. [CrossRef]

9. Lagnado, D.A.; Sloman, S. The advantage of timely intervention. *J. Exp. Psychol. Learn. Mem. Cogn.* **2004**, *30*, 856–876. [CrossRef] [PubMed]

0. Mayrhofer, R.; Waldmann, M.R. Agents and Causes: Dispositional Intuitions As a Guide to Causal Structure. *Cogn. Sci.* **2015**, *39*, 65–95. [CrossRef]

1. Park, J.; Sloman, S.A. Mechanistic beliefs determine adherence to the Markov property in causal reasoning. *Cogn. Psychol.* **2013**, *67*, 186–216. [CrossRef]

2. Rehder, B.; Burnett, R.C. Feature inference and the causal structure of categories. *Cogn. Psychol.* **2005**, *50*, 264–314. [CrossRef]

3. Rehder, B. Independence and dependence in human causal reasoning. *Cogn. Psychol.* **2014**, *72*, 54–107. [CrossRef]

4. Rehder, B. Beyond Markov: Accounting for independence violations in causal reasoning. *Cogn. Psychol.* **2018**, *103*, 42–84. [CrossRef]

5. Rehder, B.; Waldmann, M.R. Failures of explaining away and screening off in described versus experienced causal learning scenarios. *Mem. Cogn.* **2017**, *45*, 245–260. [CrossRef]

6. Rottman, B.M.; Hastie, R. Do people reason rationally about causally related events? Markov violations, weak inferences, and failures of explaining away. *Cogn. Psychol.* **2016**, *87*, 88–134. [CrossRef] [PubMed]

7. Walsh, C.R.; Sloman, S.A. Revising causal beliefs. In Proceedings of the Annual Meeting of the Cognitive Science Society, Chicago, IL, USA, 4–7 August 2004; Volume 26.

8. Cruz, N.; Hahn, U.; Fenton, N.; Lagnado, D. Explaining away, augmentation, and the assumption of independence. *Front. Psychol.* **2020**, *11*, 502751. [CrossRef] [PubMed]

9. Perales, J.C.; Catena, A.; Maldonado, A. Inferring non-observed correlations from causal scenarios: The role of causal knowledge. *Learn. Motiv.* **2004**, *35*, 115–135. [CrossRef]

0. Rehder, B. The role of functional form in causal-based categorization. *J. Exp. Psychol. Learn. Mem. Cogn.* **2015**, *41*, 670–692. [CrossRef]

1. Burnham, K.P.; Anderson, D.R. *Model Selection and Inference: A Practical Information-Theoretical Approach*; Springer: New York, NY, USA, 1998.

2. Bonawitz, E.; Denison, S.; Griffiths, T.L.; Gopnik, A. Probabilistic models, learning algorithms, and response variability: Sampling in cognitive development. *Trends Cogn. Sci.* **2014**, *18*, 497–500. [CrossRef]

3. Denison, S.; Bonawitz, E.; Gopnik, A.; Griffiths, T.L. Rational variability in children's causal inferences: The sampling hypothesis. *Cognition* **2013**, *126*, 285–300. [CrossRef] [PubMed]

4. O'Neill, K.; Henne, P.; Bello, P.; Pearson, J.; De Brigard, F. Confidence and gradation in causal judgment. *Cognition* **2022**, *223*, 1–17. [CrossRef]

35. Zhu, J.Q.; Sanborn, A.N.; Chater, N. The Bayesian sampler: Generic Bayesian inference causes incoherence in human probabilit judgments. *Psychol Rev.* **2020**, *127*, 719–748. [CrossRef]
36. Huang, J.; Busemeyer, J.R.; Ebelt, Z.; Pothos, E.M. Bridging the gap between subjective probability and probability judgment The quantum sequential sampler. *Psychol Rev.* **2024**. [CrossRef]

*entropy*

*Article*

# Higher Algebraic K-Theory of Causality

Sridhar Mahadevan

Adobe Research, 345 Park Avenue, San Jose, CA 95110, USA; smahadev@adobe.com

**Abstract:** Causal discovery involves searching intractably large spaces. Decomposing the search space into classes of observationally equivalent causal models is a well-studied avenue to making discovery tractable. This paper studies the topological structure underlying causal equivalence to develop a categorical formulation of Chickering's transformational characterization of Bayesian networks. A homotopic generalization of the Meek–Chickering theorem on the connectivity structure within causal equivalence classes and a topological representation of Greedy Equivalence Search (GES) that moves from one equivalence class of models to the next are described. Specifically, this work defines causal models as propable symmetric monoidal categories (cPROPs), which define a functor category $\mathcal{C}^P$ from a coalgebraic PROP $P$ to a symmetric monoidal category $\mathcal{C}$. Such functor categories were first studied by Fox, who showed that they define the right adjoint of the inclusion of Cartesian categories in the larger category of all symmetric monoidal categories. cPROPs are an algebraic theory in the sense of Lawvere. cPROPs are related to previous categorical causal models, such as Markov categories and affine CDU categories, which can be viewed as defined by cPROP maps specifying the semantics of comonoidal structures corresponding to the "copy-delete" mechanisms. This work characterizes Pearl's structural causal models (SCMs) in terms of Cartesian cPROPs, where the morphisms that define the endogenous variables are purely deterministic. A higher algebraic K-theory of causality is developed by studying the classifying spaces of observationally equivalent causal cPROP models by constructing their simplicial realization through the nerve functor. It is shown that Meek–Chickering causal DAG equivalence generalizes to induce a homotopic equivalence across observationally equivalent cPROP functors. A homotopic generalization of the Meek–Chickering theorem is presented, where covered edge reversals connecting equivalent DAGs induce natural transformations between homotopically equivalent cPROP functors and correspond to an equivalence structure on the corresponding string diagrams. The Grothendieck group completion of cPROP causal models is defined using the Grayson–Quillen construction and relate the classifying space of cPROP causal equivalence classes to classifying spaces of an induced groupoid. A real-world domain modeling genetic mutations in cancer is used to illustrate the framework in this paper.

**Keywords:** causal inference; structural causal models; Bayesian networks; symmetric monoidal categories; PROPs; higher algebraic K-theory; homotopy; classifying spaces

## 1. Introduction

Causal discovery using methods such as FCI [1] or IC [2], as well as the many variants and extensions of these classic methods developed over the past several decades [3–7], involves searching super-exponential spaces as the number of causal DAGs grows extremely large in the number of variables. To reduce this intractable search space, it is often possible to form equivalence classes of observationally equivalent causal models (see Figure 2). There are approximately $10^{18}$ DAG models on just 11 labeled variables. To make matters worse, DAG models capture only a tiny portion of the space because for $n = 4$, there are 18,300 conditional independence structures, but DAG models capture only roughly 1% of this space! As we illustrate later in Section 2, constructing causal models for pancreatic cancer requires dealing with many thousands of potentially mutated genes that combine in a dozen known pathways, leading to a search space of causal models that can be astronomically large. More powerful models like integer-valued multisets (imsets) [8] that model conditional independences by mapping the powerset of all variables into integers grow even larger still (of the order of $2^{2^n}$). Representing this space efficiently with categorical representations like affine CDU categories [9] or Markov categories [10] will require defining equivalence classes over string diagrams to combat this curse of dimensionality. This challenge motivates the need for a deeper categorical understanding of the equivalence classes of observationally indistinguishable models [11]. While allowing for arbitrary interventions on causal models enables accurate identification [6,7], such interventions are rarely practical in the real world. Insights such as the Meek–Chickering theorem [3,12,13] allow a deeper understanding of connected paths among equivalent causal DAG models, which we propose to study using a homotopy framework in this paper.

To generalize the Meek–Chickering theorem to the categorical setting, some challenges need to be addressed. Figure 1 shows a string diagram representation of a pollution causal model first used in our previous paper on universal causality [14]. Such string diagrams are used in affine CD [9] and Markov categories [10]. As the number of causal models grows exponentially, so does the number of string diagrams, and to develop deeper insight into the underlying topological structure of causal equivalences, we introduce a coalgebraic theory of causal inference based on a categorical structure we call cPROP, which is defined as a functor category from a PROP [15] to a symmetric monoidal category [16].

To help motivate the need for cPROPs, note that in a causal model, variables are "reused" across different local causal mechanisms. A simple example is the DAG $A \leftarrow B \rightarrow C$, whose joint distribution $P(A, B, C) = P(A|B)P(C|B)$ decomposes in a way that reflects the conditional independence structure of the DAG. Here, the variable $B$ is used twice, and to make it accessible across multiple expressions, any such variable must be "copied". Such a copy mechanism has been used in previous work on categorical causal models based on string diagrams [9,10,17], which have been referred to as "copy-delete-uniform" (CDU) categories. Here, "deletion" refers to the requirement that any distribution $P$ can be marginalized to 1 by summing over all its values, which in categorical terms are modeled by a "delete" mechanism $f : X \rightarrow I$ (where $X$ is some object that represents a distribution). cPROPs provide a way to define such an "internal" category over an external category that specifies such "copy" and "delete" mechanisms by modeling them as "comonoid" objects within a category.

Causal discovery poses some unique challenges for categorical modeling. Figure 2 illustrates the structure of causal equivalence classes on causal DAGs for a simple causal model in the pancreatic cancer domain described in Section 2. As first observed in Verma and Pearl [11], two DAGs are equivalent if their underlying skeletons (undirected graph structure ignoring edge directions) and V-structures $X \rightarrow Z \leftarrow Y$ are the same. Our goal here is to build on the ideas in [3] on connected paths between observationally equivalent models, in particular the Meek–Chickering theorem, which we want to generalize to the categorical setting. As Chickering [3] notes, this theorem, which was originally a conjecture by Meek, implies that there exists a sparse search space, where each candidate model is connected to a small fraction of the total space, given a generative distribution that has a perfect map in a DAG defined over the observables. This property leads to the development of a greedy search algorithm that in the limit of training data can identify the correct model.

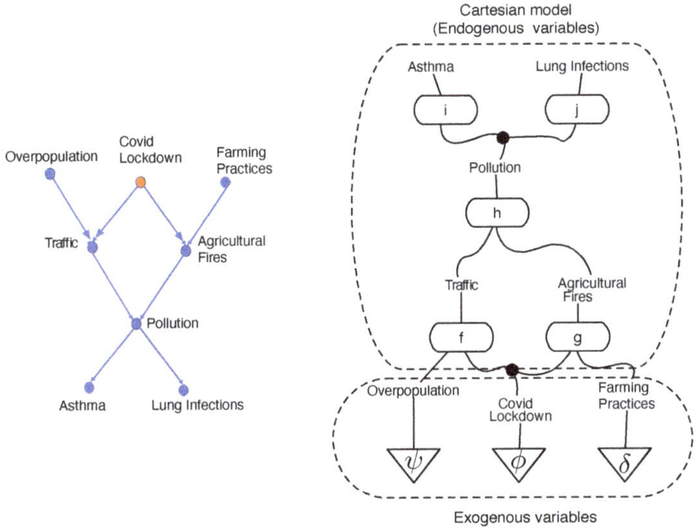


**Figure 1.** A Cartesian cPROP causal model that represents a structural causal model of pollution in New Delhi, India (based on original model defined in [14]). Here, following the usual custom in SCMs [2], the functions defining endogenous variables ($f, g, h, i$, and $j$) are deterministic, whereas the exogenous variables are defined by probability distributions (e.g., $\psi : I \rightarrow$ Overpopulation defines a distribution in a Markov category). In keeping with the usual practice [9,17], information flows from bottom to top in string diagrams, which is the opposite of DAG models. Also, nodes in DAG models represent variables, and the functions are implicitly defined by the edges. In string diagrams, the edges define variables, and the functions are explicitly represented as boxes. To fully specify a cPROP causal model, we have to define a functor that maps such a string diagram into a decomposable stochastic process, which is illustrated later in Figure 12.

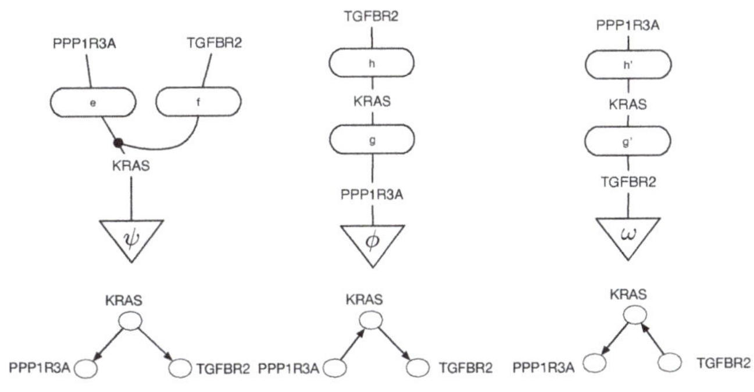


**Figure 2.** Equivalence classes of causal DAGs and cPROP string diagrams on 3 variables from a pancreatic cancer domain described in Section 2 in more detail. KRAS, TGFBR2, and PPP1R3A define three genes which are mutated in many pancreatic cancer tumors, and the challenge in causal modeling is to discover a partial ordering of the gene mutations. For each DAG at the bottom, the corresponding cPROP string diagram is shown above. The three DAGs shown form a single equivalence class, which implies the three string diagrams also are equivalent. The causal discovery method GES [3], described in Section 3, searches in the space of such equivalence classes.

In practice, existing causal discovery algorithms, such as PC [1] or IC [2] or their many extensions and variants, combine both directional and non-directional encoding of causal models. Specifically, a common assumption, such as in PC, is that given an unknown true causal model (shown in Figure 3 by panel (i)), the initial causal model (shown as (ii) in

Figure 3) is an undirected graph connecting all variables to each other, which satisfies no conditional independences, and is progressively refined (panels (ii)–(vi) in Figure 3) based on conditional independence data and using edge orientation and propagation rules, such as the Meek rules [12]. For example, the initial stage is to simply check all marginal independences, and given that $X \perp\!\!\!\perp Y$, that eliminates the undirected edge between $X$ and $Y$. However, each undirected edge between two vertices, say $A$ and $B$, that needs to be eliminated due to conditional independence must be checked for increasingly large subsets $(A \perp\!\!\!\perp B|C)$, and while methods like FCI and later enhancements [6,7] incorporate rather sophisticated methods to prune the space, this process remains computationally expensive, and its practicality remains in question, as in the real world, interventions on arbitrary separating sets [6] may be infeasible. While remarkable progress has been made over the past few decades (see [7] for a state of the art method), it still can be prohibitive and does not always end up with the right model. Edges that remain undirected are interpreted to indicate latent confounders.

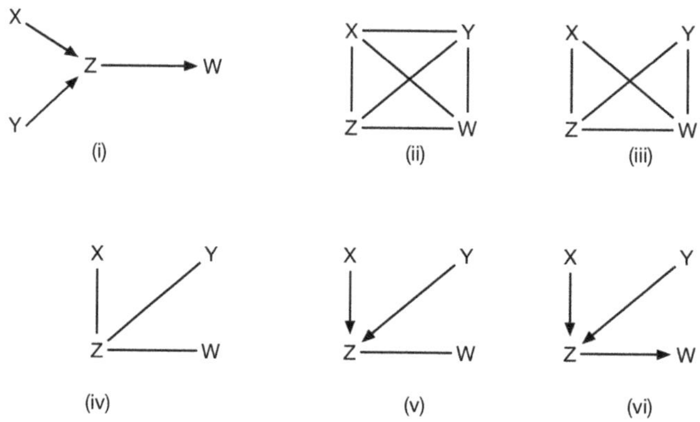


**Figure 3.** Example of causal discovery with the PC algorithm [5]. Panel (i) shows the original causal model, and panels (ii)–(vi) show the sequence of models constructed by PC.

This paper builds on the work of Fox [18], who studied functor categories mapping PROPs to symmetric monoidal categories in his PhD dissertation in 1976. Crucially, Fox [18] studied a particular functor category from a coalgebraic PROP to symmetric monoidal categories that defined a right adjoint from the category **MON** of all symmetric monoidal categories to **CART**, which is the category of all Cartesian categories. We use the term coalgebraic in the universal algebraic sense as used by Fox [18]. It differs from the modern interpretation as in [19]. In this sense, cPROPs are formally an algebraic theory in the sense of Lawvere [20].

Objects in a cPROP are functors mapping a PROP $P$—a symmetric monoidal category over natural numbers—to a symmetric monoidal category $\mathcal{C}$. The structure PROP (for Products and Permutations) was originally introduced by Maclane [15], and it has seen widespread use in many areas such as modeling connectivity in networks [21,22]. A trivial example of a PROP is the free monoidal category $\Gamma$, whose objects can be interpreted as the natural numbers, the unit object is 0, and the tensor product is addition. More generally, a PROP $P$ is a small monoidal category with a strict monoidal functor $\Gamma \rightarrow P$ that is a bijection on objects. A cPROP is a functor category $C^P$, where C is a symmetric monoidal category, where in addition there are usually some constraints placed on the specific PROP $P$.

As a simple example, we consider cPROPs where the PROP $P$ is generated by a *coalgebraic* structure defined by the maps $\delta : 1 \rightarrow 2$ and $\epsilon : 1 \rightarrow 0$ satisfying a set of commutative diagrams. Such cPROPs are closely related to symmetric monoidal category structures used in previous work on categorical models of causality, probability, and statistics [10,14,23–25]. In particular, Markov categories [10,17] and affine CDU ("copy-delete-uniform") categories used to model causal inference include a comonoidal "copy delete" structure corresponding to such a cPROP, which we note is distinctive in that "delete" has a uniform structure but "copy" does not, leading to a semi-Cartesian category.

In my previous work on universal causality [14], I proposed the use of simplicial sets, which provide a way to encode both directional and non-directional edges, as well as form the basis for topological realization for cPROPs and play a central role in higher-order $\infty$-categories [26,27]. We study the classifying spaces [28] of cPROPs in this paper, showing that they provide deeper insight into the connections between different cPROP categories that correspond to Markov categories, such as **FinStoch** [17].

In particular, this work builds on longstanding ideas in abstract homotopy theory on modeling the equivalence classes of objects in a category [29] by mapping a category into a topological space, where (weak) equivalences can be modeled in terms of topological structures, such as homotopies. To make this more concrete, Jacobs et al. [9] modeled a Bayesian network as a CDU functor $\mathcal{F} : \mathcal{C} \to \mathbf{FinStoch}$ between two affine CDU or Markov categories, with one specifying the graph structure of the model and the other modeling its semantics as an object in the category of finite stochastic processes defined as **FinStoch**. A CDU functor is a special type of cPROP functor. Two Bayesian networks modeled as cPROP functors that are observationally equivalent—such as $A \to B \to C$ and $A \to B \leftarrow C$, since the edge $B \leftarrow C$ is a covered edge that can be reversed—induce a natural transformation $\tau : \mathcal{F}_1 \Rightarrow \mathcal{F}_2$. Using the associated classifying spaces $\mathcal{BC}$ and $\mathcal{B}$ **FinStoch**, the natural transformation induces a homotopy between $\mathcal{F}_1$ and $\mathcal{F}_2$.

The idea of associating a topological space with a category goes back to Grothendieck but was popularized by Segal [28]: map a category $\mathcal{C}$ to a sequence of sets (or objects) $X_0, X_1, \ldots$, where the $k$-simplex $X_k$ represents composable morphisms of length $k$. A standard topological realization proposed by Milnor [30] constructs a topological CW complex out of simplicial sets. Segal called such a construction the classifying space $\mathcal{BC}$ of category $\mathcal{C}$. This paper can be seen as an initial step in building a higher algebraic K-theory [31] for causal inference, using as a concrete example the study of classifying spaces of cPROPs. A 0-simplex in a simplicial cPROP would be defined by its objects $X, Y, X \otimes Y, \ldots$, which map to 0-cells in its classifying space. An example 2-simplex in a cPROP, such as $I \to X \otimes Y \to X$, maps to a 2 cell or simplicial triangle.

This paper builds on the insight underlying Fox's dissertation on universal coalgebras [18], which shows that the subcategory of coalgebraic objects in a monoidal category forms its Cartesian closure. The adjoint functor theorems show that cofree algebras—right adjoints to forgetful functors—exist in such cases. In particular, Fox's theorem implies that cPROPs that come with a type of "uniform copy-delete" structure [32] are Cartesian symmetric monoidal categories, where the tensor product $X \otimes Y$ becomes a Cartesian product operation through natural transformations rather than the standard universal property. It is noted that Markov categories are semi-Cartesian because the comonoidal $\mathsf{copy}_X$ structure is not uniform, but only $\mathsf{del}_X$ is. However, they contain a subcategory of deterministic morphisms that induce a Cartesian category using the uniform copy delete structure. It is worth noting here that Pearl [2] has long advocated causality as being being intrinsically deterministic in his structural causal models (SCMs), where the role of probabilities is reflected in the uncertainty associated with exogenous variables that cannot be causally manipulated.

Here is a roadmap to the rest of the paper. To concretize the abstractions presented in the paper, it begins in Section 2 with an application to constructing causal models of pancreatic cancer [33–35]. Section 3 describes a concrete procedure for causal discovery called

Greedy Equivalent Search (GES) [3,12] that uses a specific notion of causal equivalence based on a transformational characterization of Bayesian networks, which are generalized to a homotopical setting. GES is also illustrative of a broad class of similar algorithms. Numerous refinements are possible, including the ability to intervene on arbitrary subsets [6,7], which are overlooked in the interests of simplicity. Section 4 begins with an introduction to algebraic theories of the type proposed by Lawvere [20], a brief review of symmetric monoidal categories, and an introduction to PROPs and cPROPs. Functor categories mapping a PROP to a symmetric monoidal category are defined. The central result of Fox is reviewed, showing that the inclusion of all Cartesian categories CART in the larger category of all symmetric monoidal categories MON has a right adjoint, which is defined by a coalgebraic PROP functor category. This coalgebraic structure relates to the "uniform copy-delete" structure studied by [32]. In Section 5, the relationships between cPROPs with uniform copy and delete natural transformations and previous work on affine CDU categories [25] and Markov categories [17] are explored. Section 6 explores the relationship between Pearl's structural causal models (SCMs) and Cartesian cPROPs defined by deterministic morphisms, exploiting the property that SCMs are defined by purely deterministic mappings from exogenous variables to endogenous variables. In Section 7, simplicial objects in cPROP categories are defined. Section 8 defines the abstract homotopy of cPROPs at a high level. Section 9 drills down into showing the homotopic structure of cPROP functors that represent Bayesian networks, which closely relates to the work on CDU functors [9]. Natural transformations in the functor category of Bayesian networks modeled as cPROPs using Yoneda's coend calculus [16] are characterized, and an equivalence relationship among functors is defined. In particular, categorical generalizations of the definitions of equivalent causal models in [3,12] are presented, and a homotopic generalization of the well-known Meek–Chickering theorem for cPROPs is stated. Each edge reversal of a covered edge corresponds to natural transformation between its corresponding cPROP functor. This work formally characterizes the classifying spaces of cPROPs in terms of associative and commutative $H$-spaces [29]. Finally, the results of the previous section in Section 11 are combined, stating the main result that the Grayson–Quillen procedure applied to cPROP yields a category $\mathcal{C}^{-1}\mathcal{C}$ that represents a Grothendieck group completion of cPROP category $\mathcal{C}$ and whose connected components that define the 0th order homology (loop) space are isomorphic to the Meek–Chickering equivalence classes. In Section 12, a more advanced application of the framework to open games [36] and network economics [37] is defined, wherein both of these fields can be defined using symmetric monoidal categories and are therefore amenable to the approach given here. In Section 13, the paper is summarized, and an outline of a few directions for further work is given.

## 2. Causal Models of Genetic Mutations in Cancer

This section illustrates a real-world application that will serve as a running example to illustrate the causal framework: modeling mutations of genes for understanding the processes that underlie various types of cancer [33,38]. Cancer is an evolutionary disease that is generally characterized by an accumulating series of genetic mutations. The temporal order of these mutations can be viewed as a partially ordered set, or DAG model, which can be further modeled using specific temporal information with respect to when particular mutations occur. A wide range of causal models can be applied to this problem, such as *conjunctive Bayesian Networks* [34], which are a simpler class of Bayesian networks that exploit the property that mutations induce a partial ordering over genes, as they are irreversible.

Table 1 illustrates the general type of data that is available for many types of cancer, including colorectal cancer, pancreatic cancer, primary gliolastoma, etc. The 0, 1 values in the table indicate whether a particular gene was mutated in a specific instance of a tumor. There is generally a partial ordering that defines the allowable sequences of mutations that are observed in many types of cancer. It is not the case that mutations occur in any order, and in most cancers, it is usually the case that the mutations form particular types of sequences. Modeling these posets through a causal model has been extensively studied in the literature [34,38]. We discuss one specific case study of pancreatic cancer, which has been explored in our previous work and will be used to illustrate the causal cPROP framework studied in this paper [35].

**Table 1.** A hallmark of cancerous tumors is their *genotype* of mutations of particular genes.

| Tumor | Gene A | Gene B | Gene C | Gene D | ... |
|---|---|---|---|---|---|
| Tumor 1 | 0 | 1 | 1 | 0 | ... |
| Tumor 2 | 1 | 0 | 1 | 1 | ... |

*Pancreatic Cancer*

Figure 4 shows a small fragment of a dataset for pancreatic cancer of around 19,000 genes that are subject to mutation in around 40 tumors [33]. In any given tumor, only a relatively small number of genes are mutated. Figure 5 shows a causal DAG model learned from this dataset using a causal discovery algorithm described in greater detail in my previous work [35] based on ideas developed in [6,34]. Specifically, a causal model for pancreatic cancer can be viewed as an example of a cPROP category [16]. The pancreatic cancer causal DAG shown in Figure 5 can be straightforwardly mapped into a cPROP model using the illustrations given previously for simpler DAG models.

| Tumor | Gene |
|---|---|
| Pa017C | KRAS |
| Pa017C | TP53 |
| Pa019C | KRAS |
| Pa022C | KRAS |
| Pa022C | SMAD4 |
| Pa022C | TP53 |
| Pa032X | CDKN2A |

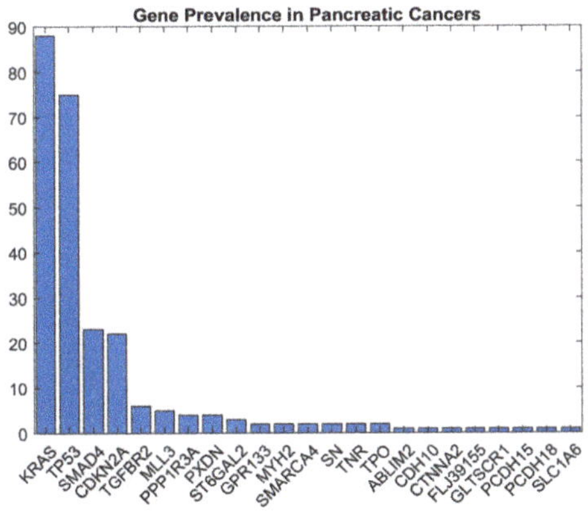


**Figure 4.** A small fragment of a dataset for analyzing pancreatic cancer [33]. Each tumor is characterized by a set of mutations of genes. The histogram plots the prevalence of each gene over all tumors in the dataset, showing that mutations in the genes KRAS and TP53 are highly indicative of pancreatic cancer.

Like many cancers, pancreatic cancer is marked by a particular partial ordering of mutations in some specific genes, such as KRAS, TP53, and so on. In order to understand how to model and treat this deadly disease, it is crucial to understand the inherent partial ordering in the mutations of such genes. Pancreatic cancer remains one of the most prevalent and deadly forms of cancer. Roughly half a million humans contract the disease each year, most of whom succumb to it within a few years. Figure 4 shows the roughly

20 most common genes that undergo mutations during the progression of this disease. The most common gene, the KRAS gene, provides instructions for making a protein called K-Ras that is part of a signaling pathway known as the RAS/MAPK pathway. The protein relays signals from outside the cell to the cell's nucleus. The second most common mutation occurs in the TP53 gene, which makes the p53 protein that normally acts as the supervisor in the cell as the body tries to repair damaged DNA. Like many cancers, pancreatic cancers occur as the normal reproductive machinery of the body is taken over by the cancer.

In the pancreatic cancer problem, the table in Figure 4 shows that each tumor is characterized by significant mutation events that mark the progression of the disease. In particular, the table shows that specific genes are mutated at specific locations by the change of an amino acid, causing the gene to malfunction. We can model a tumor in terms of its *genotype*, namely, the subset of $X$—the gene events that characterize the tumor. For example, the table shows that the tumor Pa022C can be characterized by the genotype KRAS, SMAD4, and TP53. We can build a causal model based on analyzing the elements of the space of genetic events and the subspaces (i.e., the genomes) that underlie the model.

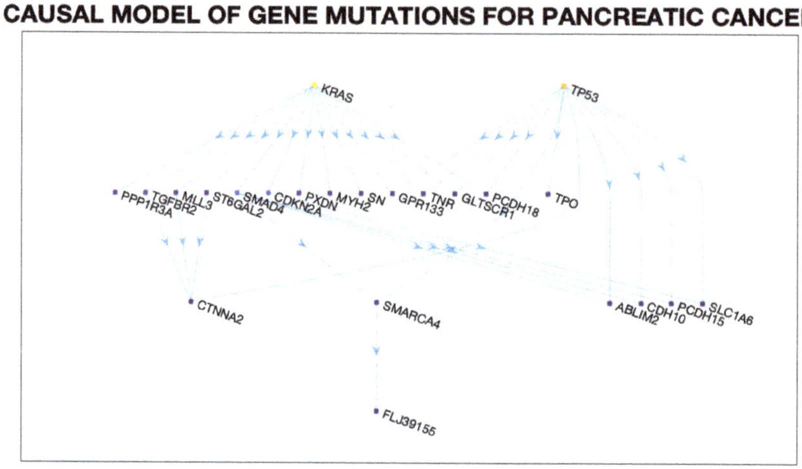


**Figure 5.** A causal DAG model of pathways in pancreatic cancer learned from a real-world dataset of around 19,000 genes and 40 tumors [33], showing genetic mutations occur along distinct pathways. The importance of mutations in the genes `KRAS` and `TP53` is consistent with the histogram profile shown earlier in Figure 4, and the directed edges reveal possible causal pathways. To limit the size of this DAG for illustrative purposes, the model was learned only on a portion of the most widely prevalent genes that are mutated in pancreatic cancer. We are also suppressing quantitative information regarding the frequency of each gene mutation, which serves to define the model parameters (further examples are given in [38]). Such causal models can be learned through a variety of methods explored in the literature [34,38]. This particular DAG was constructed using a topological causal discovery method described in our previous work [35], building on the idea of using separating sets [6].

The progression of many types of cancer is marked by mutations of key genes whose normal reproductive machinery is subverted by the cancer [33]. Often, viruses such as HIV and COVID-19 are constantly mutating to combat the pressure of interventions such as drugs, and successful treatment requires understanding the partial ordering of mutations. A number of past approaches use topological separability constraints on the data, assuming observed genotypes as separate events which, as will be shown, are abstractly a separability constraint on the underlying topological space.

A key computational level in making model discovery tractable in evolutionary processes, such as pancreatic cancer, is that multiple sources of information are available that guide the discovery of the underlying poset model. In particular, for pancreatic cancer [33], in addition to the tumor genotype information show in Figure 4, it is also known that the disease follows certain pathways, as shown in Table 2. This type of information from multiple sources gives the ability to construct multiple posets that reflect different event constraints [39]. In the previous work [35], a generalization of past algorithms that infer conjunctive Bayesian networks (CBNs) from a dataset of events (e.g., tumors or signaling pathways) and their associated genotypes (e.g., sets of genes) was described [34,39]. The causal pathways DAG shown in Figure 6 were learned using the pancreatic cancer dataset published in [33].

**Table 2.** Core signaling pathways and processes genetically altered in most pancreatic cancers [33].

| Regulatory Pathway | % Altered Genes | Tumors | Representative Altered Genes |
|---|---|---|---|
| Apoptosis | 9 | 100% | CASP10, VCP, CAD, HIP1 |
| DNA damage control | 9 | 83% | ERCC4, ERCC6, EP300, TP53 |
| G1/S phase transition | 19 | 100% | CDKN2A, FBXW7, CHD1, APC2 |
| Hedgehog signaling | 19 | 100% | TBX5, SOX3, LRP2, GLI1, GLI3 |
| Homophilic cell adhesion | 30 | 79% | CDH1, CDH10, CDH2, CDH7, FAT |
| Integrin signaling | 24 | 67% | ITGA4, ITGA9, ITGA11, LAMA1 |
| c-Jun N-terminal kinase | 9 | 96% | MAP4K3, TNF, ATF2, NFATC3 |
| KRAS signaling | 5 | 100% | KRAS, MAP2K4, RASGRP3 |
| Regulation of invasion | 46 | 92% | ADAM11, ADAM12, ADAM19 |
| Small GTPase-dependent | 33 | 79% | AGHGEF7, ARHGEF9, CDC42BPA |
| TGF-$\beta$ signaling | 37 | 100% | TGFBR2, BMPR2, SMAD4, SMAD3 |
| Wnt/Notch signaling | 29 | 100% | MYC, PPP2R3A, WNT9A |

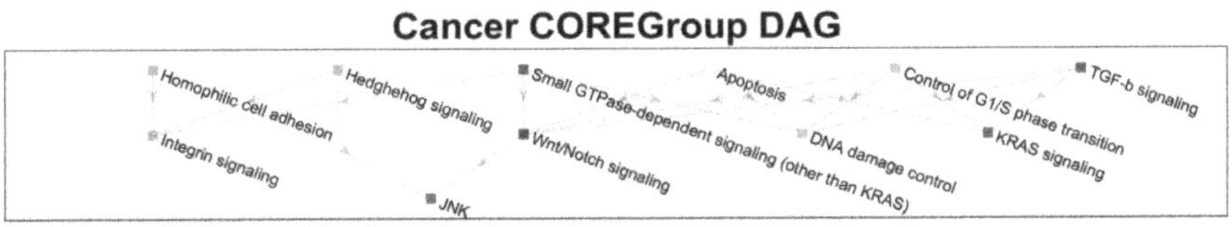


**Figure 6.** Causal DAG model of the possible 12 pathways and processes whose component genes are most likely mutated in most pancreatic cancers [33]. The specific method used to construct this causal model are described in detail in the previous work on causal homotopy [35], and related methods are described in other previous work [6,34].

## 3. Greedy Equivalence Search

To motivate the theoretical development in subsequent sections, we focus our attention in this section to a specific causal discovery algorithm, Greedy Equivalence Search (GES), originally proposed by Meek [12], whose correctness and asymptotic optimality were subsequently shown by Chickering [3], constituting an a algorithmic proof of the Meek–Chickering theorem. This framework is not presented as a state-of-the-art causal discovery algorithm (e.g., Zanga and Stella [4] provide a detailed survey of many causal discovery methods), but rather as an exemplar of the idea of searching in a space of equivalence classes of DAG models. The ultimate goal is to provide a topological and abstract homotopic characterization of the search space in causal discovery, both for DAG and non-DAG models. It would help to concretize the following theoretical abstractions to ground out the ideas in a specific algorithm. The notion of a *covered edge* is fundamental to the work on causal equivalence classes in [3,12].

**Definition 1.** *Let $\mathcal{G} = (V, E)$ be any causal DAG model. An edge $X \rightarrow Y \in E$ is covered if X and Y have identical parents, with the caveat that X is not a parent of itself. In other words, the parents of Y in $\mathcal{G}$ are the parents of X along with X itself.*

For the sake of space, the discussion of GES will be brief, and we shall relegate all missing details to the original paper [3]. Broadly, the idea underlying GES is to search over equivalence classes of DAGs by moving at each step to a *neighbor*—meaning a model outside the current equivalence class by edge addition or deletion—that has the highest Bayesian score on a given IID dataset if it improves the score. GESs in the space of DAGs that result from adding one edge to a given equivalence class in the forward direction (see Figure 7). Similarly, Figure 8 shows the two equivalence classes of DAGs that result from *deleting* a single edge to the DAGs in Figure 2. This describes the second reverse phase of the GES. It is proven in [3] that this two-phase procedure is asymptotically optimal in the limit of large datasets, provided the data were generated from some DAG. The challenge addressed in this paper is how to mathematically model the equivalence classes used in a method like GES by mapping them into equivalence among topological embeddings of string diagrams. Our motivation is to see if these ideas can be generalized to a larger class of causal models than DAGs and ultimately design improved methods, although that goal lies beyond the scope of this paper.

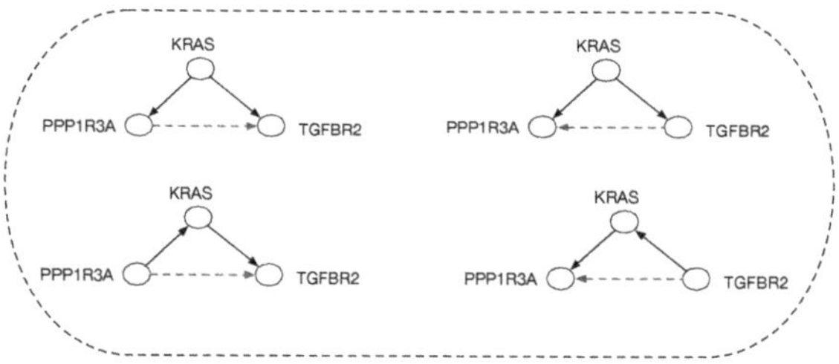


**Figure 7.** The equivalence class of DAGs that results from a single edge addition to the DAGs in Figure 2.

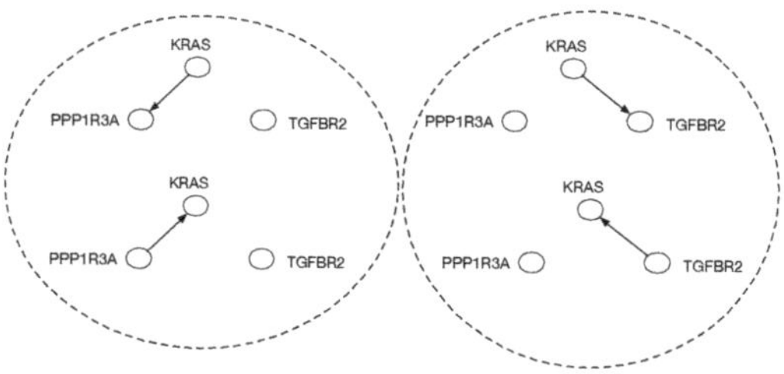


**Figure 8.** A single edge deletion to the DAGs in Figure 2 yields two equivalence classes of DAGs.

Bayesian approaches to learning models from data use a scoring function, such as the Bayesian Information Criterion (BIC), denoted as $S(\mathcal{G}, \mathbf{D})$, where $\mathbf{D}$ is an IID (independent and identically distributed) dataset sampled from the original (unknown) model. It is commonly assumed that such a score is locally decomposable, meaning that

$$S(\mathcal{G}, \mathbf{D}) = \sum_{i=1}^{n} s(X_i, \mathbf{Pa}_i^{\mathcal{G}})$$

The overall score of a candidate DAG G is the sum of local scores for each node $X_i$ that is purely a function of the projected data **D** onto the node and its parents $\mathbf{Pa}_i^{\mathcal{G}}$. Given a DAG G and a probability distribution $p(.)$, G is a *perfect* map of $p$ if (i) every independence constraint in $p$ is implied by the structure of G and (ii) every independence constraint implied by the structure of G holds in $p$. If there exists a DAG G that is a perfect map of distribution $p(.)$, $p$ is called *DAG-perfect*. Under the assumption that the dataset **D** is an IID sample from some DAG-perfect distribution $p(.)$, the GES algorithm consists of two phases that are guaranteed to find the correct DAG G optimally in the limit of large datasets. The precise statement is as follows.

**Theorem 1** ([3]). *Let $\mathcal{E}^*$ denote the equivalence class that is a perfect map of the generative distribution $p(.)$, and let $m$ be the number of samples in a dataset* **D**. *Then in the limit of large $m$, $S_B(\mathcal{E}^*, \mathbf{D}) > S_B(\mathcal{E}, \mathbf{D})$ for any equivalence class $\mathcal{E} \neq \mathcal{E}^*$.*

Here, $S_B$ is a Bayesian scoring method, like the BIC, and it is assumed to score all DAGs in an equivalence class the same. The notion of equivalence classes is obviously fundamental to the GES, and the formal statement of this characterization comes from the following transformational characterization of Bayesian networks. As previously noted, a *covered edge* in a DAG G is an edge $X \rightarrow Y$ with the property that the parents of $Y$ are the same as the parents of X along with X itself.

**Theorem 2 (Meek–Chickering Theorem** [3,12]**).** *Let $\mathcal{G}$ and $\mathcal{H}$ be any pair of DAGs such that $\mathcal{G} \leq \mathcal{H}$, meaning that $\mathcal{H}$ is an independence map of $\mathcal{G}$, that is, every independence property in $\mathcal{H}$ holds in $\mathcal{G}$. Intuitively, $\mathcal{G} \leq \mathcal{H}$ implies that $\mathcal{H}$ contains more edges than $\mathcal{G}$. Let $r$ be the number of edges in $\mathcal{H}$ that have opposite orientations in $\mathcal{G}$, and let $m$ be the number of edges in $\mathcal{H}$ that do not exist in either orientation in G. Then, there is a sequence of $r + 2m$ edge reversals and additions in $\mathcal{G}$ with the following properties:*

- *Each edge reversed is a covered edge.*
- *After each reversal and addition, $\mathcal{G}$ is a DAG, and $\mathcal{G} \leq \mathcal{H}$.*
- *After all reversals and additions, $\mathcal{G} = \mathcal{H}$.*

To relate this result and the ensuing GES algorithm to the original PC algorithm illustrated in Figure 3, unlike the PC, the GES begins at the opposite end of the lattice of DAG models shown in Figure 2, the empty DAG (which can be viewed as the $\mathcal{G}$ DAG in Theorem 2), then progressively adds edges in the first phase, and then deletes edges in the second phase. In Section 9, this theorem will be generalized to construct a topological and abstract homotopical equivalence across functors between cPROP categories. These functors are equivalent to the CDU functors proposed by Jacobs et al. [9] to model Bayesian networks previously. Edge reversals or additions will correspond to natural transformations.

A further characterization of causal equivalence classes emerges from our application of higher algebraic K-theory [28,31]. Informally, we can define the notion of connectedness of a category in terms of the equivalence class of the relation defined over morphisms (two objects are in the same equivalence class if they are connected by a (perhaps zig-zag) morphism). We can treat each equivalence class as a topologically locally connected space, and then the homotopy groups $\pi_n(\mathcal{B}C)$ of the classifying space BC of cPROP category $\mathcal{C}$ gives us an algebraic invariant of causal equivalence classes.

*Exploiting Additional Constraints in Causal Discovery*

The basic idea behind the GES is to search in the space of causal equivalence classes and use a Bayesian scoring function to find the most plausible model. One significant challenge in applying the GES to the cancer domain described in Section 2 is that the datasets available are of limited size ($\sim$100 tumor samples) but feature high-dimensionality ($\sim$19,000 genes). The theoretical result stated in Theorem 1 may be of limited use in such situations. The approach that is generally taken in actual real-world applications of causal inference (e.g., [38]) is to bring in additional structural constraints that are motivated from particular domains. Some of these are briefly described below:

1. *Domain constraints*: In cancer, genes mutate in particular sequences, and once a gene has mutated, then it stays mutated. In other words, rather than search over all possible DAG models, it may suffice to consider restricted subclasses of DAGs, such as *conjunctive Bayesian networks* [34] (these are also referred to as "noisy-AND" models in [40]). It is often necessary to bring in such domain constraints in most real-world applications. This strategy was studied in our previous work [35] and applied to the pancreatic cancer domain.
2. *Topological representations of causal DAG models:* It is possible to convert a DAG model—viewed as a partially ordered set—into a finite space topology [41,42] by using the Alexandroff topology. In simple terms, each variable in the model is associated with its *downset* (all variables that it dominates in the partial ordering) or *upset* (all variables that dominate it in the partial ordering). The intersection of all such open or closed sets defines the Alexandroff topology embedding for each variable. This transformation can be used to determine whether two DAG (poset) models are *homotopic* and used to produce a more scalable way to enumerate posets. The results in [35,41] show several orders of magnitude improvement, at least for relatively small models.
3. *Asymptotic combinatorics:* It is a classic result from extremal combinatorics [43] that almost all partial orders of comprised of just three levels. This result is initially surprising, but the intuition behind this combinatorial result is that by carefully counting the set of all possible partial orders on $N$ variables, it can be shown that as $N \to \infty$, there is a concentration phenomena that occurs where almost all partial orders are of height 3. An intriguing physical explanation is given in [44] based on phase transitions. The ramifications of this concentration phenomena were explored in a previous paper on asymptotic causality [45].

To summarize, while we will focus in the remainder of the paper on characterizing the equivalence classes of causal models using categorical techniques, it is important to point out that real-world applications will invariably require bringing in other sources of knowledge. We will return to discuss this point in Section 13.

## 4. Introduction to cPROPs and Symmetric Monoidal Categories

In this section, we will define cPROPs more formally, building on the work of Fox [18] who studied functor categories mapping PROPs to symmetric monoidal categories in his PhD dissertation in 1976. A cPROP is a functor category whose objects are functors mapping a PROP $P$—a symmetric monoidal category over natural numbers—to a symmetric monoidal category $\mathcal{C}$. In the next Section 5, we will consider cPROPs where the PROP $P$ is generated by a *coalgebraic* structure defined by the maps $\delta : 1 \to 2$ and $\epsilon : 1 \to 0$ satisfying a set of commutative diagrams. Such cPROPs are related to symmetric monoidal category structures used in previous work on categorical models of causality, probability, and statistics [10,14,23–25].

### 4.1. Categories and Functors

The concept of *functor* is central to category theory [16] and to our formalization of causal equivalence classes. Functors map from one category into another (possibly the same category, in which case they are viewed as *endofunctors*). Formally, a *category* $\mathcal{C}$ is a collection of *objects*, usually denoted by lower case letters such as $c \in C$ and, crucially, also consisting of a collection of *morphisms* $\mathcal{C}(c,d)$ mapping object $c$ to object $d$. Categories can be arbitrarily complex: in fact, the category **Cat** of all categories is also a category (!), which is certainly not the case for the set of all sets. In **Cat**, the set of morphisms between two categories $\mathcal{C}$ and $\mathcal{D}$ are *functors*.

Functors in general are much more expressive than functions [16]. A functor $F : \mathcal{C} \to \mathcal{D}$ from a domain category $\mathcal{C}$ to a codomain category $\mathcal{D}$ consists of two components:

1. An *object function* that maps each object in the domain category to an object of the codomain category. Thus, for the given functor $F : \mathcal{C} \to \mathcal{D}$, for any object $c \in \mathcal{C}$, the functor maps $c$ to the codomain object $Fc \in \mathcal{D}$. In this sense, functors resemble functions.
2. A *mapping of morphisms* that maps each morphism $f : c \to c'$ in category $\mathcal{C}$ to a corresponding morphism $Ff : Fc \to Fc'$ in category $\mathcal{D}$.

cPROPs are categories comprising functor objects, as they are intended to serve as a categorical representation of Bayesian networks, structural causal models, and other types of topological causal representations studied in the literature [35,46]. Causal models map from a "syntactic" category of "diagrams" to another suitable "semantic" category. In the canonical setting of Bayesian networks that is extensively studied in our paper, the syntax category is a symmetric monoidal category that represents the structure of a DAG model (or a structural causal model (SCM) [2] or a general directed graph model [47]); the semantic category is the symmetric monoidal category **FinStoch** of stochastic processes, which represents the parameters of a Bayesian network.

### 4.2. Algebraic Theories

In an influential paper, Lawvere [20] defined an *algebraic theory* as a small category A, whose objects are the natural numbers $0, 1, \ldots$, in which each object $n$ is the categorical product (i.e., addition) of the unit object 1 with itself $n$ times. Morphisms in A are defined as maps $n \to m$. Lawvere [20] showed that many common algebraic structures such as groups, monoids, and rings, which are defined using finitary operations, determine an algebraic theory. Homomorphisms between algebraic structures, such as groups or rings, in turn can be used to define a category.

**Definition 2** ([20])**.** *Every map of algebraic theories* $f : \mathcal{A} \to \mathcal{B}$ *determines a contravariant set-valued functor* $\mathbf{Sets}^f : \mathbf{Sets}^B \to \mathbf{Sets}^A$, *where* $\mathbf{Set}^f$ *is defined as an algebraic functor, and* $\mathbf{Sets}^A$ *is defined as an algebraic category.*

**Example 1.** *The category of rings (with a unit element) and that of monoids are algebraic categories, and the functor that assigns to a ring the monoid consisting of the same objects under multiplication only is an algebraic functor.*

A fundamental theorem shown by Lawvere [20] states the following.

**Theorem 3** ([20])**.** *Every algebraic functor has an adjoint.*

In terms of Example 1, the adjoint of the algebraic functor mapping rings to monoids is the free ring constructed from the elements of the monoid.

We show below that cPROPs are exactly (co)algebraic theories in the sense of Lawvere [20], as they are defined as the right adjoint of the inclusion functor from the category **CART** of all Cartesian categories into **MON**, the category of all symmetric monoidal categories. We will review these notions first before introducing cPROPs more formally.

### 4.3. Symmetric Monoidal Categories

It is assumed that the reader understands the basics of symmetric monoidal categories, which are briefly reviewed below (see Figure 9). Good introductions are available in a number of textbooks [16,29]. A brief introduction to some basic category theory suitable for causal inference is found in my previous paper [14]. Detailed overviews of symmetric monoidal categories appear in many books, and the definitions presented here are based on [29].

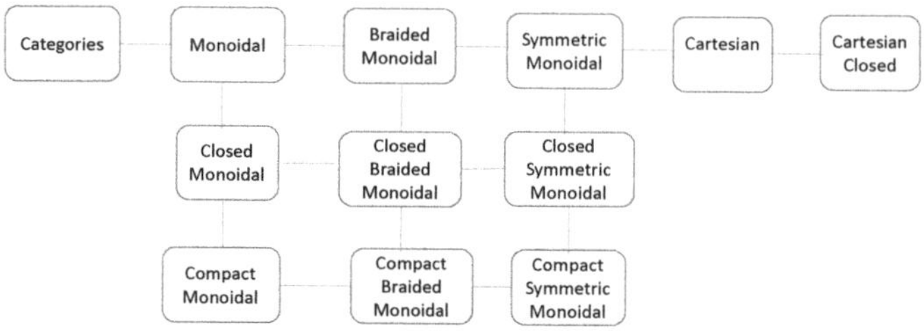


**Figure 9.** Structure of monoidal categories.

**Definition 3.** *A monoidal category is a category C together with a functor* $\otimes : \mathcal{C} \times \mathcal{C} \to \mathcal{C}$, *an identity object e of C, and natural isomorphisms* $\alpha, \lambda, \rho$ *defined as follows:*

$$\begin{aligned} \alpha_{C_1,C_2,C_3} : C_1 \otimes (C_2 \otimes C_3) &\cong (C_1 \otimes C_2) \otimes C_2, \textit{ for all objects } C_1, C_2, C_3 \\ \lambda_C : e \otimes C &\cong C, \textit{ for all objects } C \\ \rho : C \otimes e &\cong C, \textit{ for all objects } C \end{aligned}$$

The natural isomorphisms must satisfy coherence conditions called the "pentagon" and "triangle" diagrams [16]. An important result shown in [16] is that these coherence conditions guarantee that all well-formed diagrams must commute.

There are many natural examples of monoidal categories, with the simplest one being the category of finite sets, termed **FinSet** in [17], where each object $C$ is a set, and the tensor product $\otimes$ is the Cartesian product of sets, with functions acting as arrows. Deterministic causal models can be formulated in the category **FinSet**. Other examples include the category of sets with relations as morphisms and the category of Hilbert spaces [32]. The category **FinSet** has other properties, principally that the $\otimes$ is actually a product (in that it satisfies the universal property of products in categories and is formally a limit). Not all monoidal categories satisfy this property. Sets are also Cartesian closed categories, meaning that there is a right adjoint to the tensor product, which represents exponential objects and is often referred to as the "internal hom" object. Markov categories to be defined in Section 5 are monoidal categories, where the identity element $e$ is also a terminal object, meaning there is a unique "delete" morphism $d_e : X \to e$ associated with each object $X$. This property can be used to show that projections of tensor products $X \otimes Y$ exist, but they do not satisfy the universal property. We will return to this question below in Section 5.1. Markov categories do not satisfy uniform copying.

**Definition 4.** *A symmetric monoidal category is a monoidal category* $(\mathcal{C}, \otimes, e, \alpha, \lambda, \rho)$, *together with a natural isomorphism*

$$\tau_{C_1,C_2} : C_1 \otimes C_2 \cong C_2 \otimes C_1, \textit{ for all objects } C_1, C_2$$

*where* $\tau$ *satisfies the additional conditions: for all objects* $C_1, C_2$ $\tau_{C_2,C_1} \circ \tau_{C_1,C_2} \cong 1_{C_1 \otimes C_2}$ *and for all objects* $C$, $\rho_C = \lambda_C \circ \tau_{C,e} : C \otimes e \cong C$.

An additional hexagon axiom is required to ensure that the $\tau$ natural isomorphism is compatible with $\alpha$. The $\tau$ operator is called a "swap" in Markov categories [17]. These isomorphisms are easier to visualize as string diagrams, as will be illustrated below in Section 5.

### *4.4. PROPs*

The structure PROP (for Products and Permutations) was originally introduced by Maclane [15], and it has seen widespread use in many areas such as modeling connectivity in networks [21,22]. A trivial example of a PROP is the free monoidal category $\Gamma$ over the category $\underline{1}$, whose objects can be interpreted as the natural numbers, the unit object 0, and the tensor product being addition. More generally, a PROP $P$ is a small monoidal category with a strict monoidal functor $\Gamma \rightarrow P$ that is a bijection on objects. A cPROP is a functor category $\mathrm{C}^P$, where C is a symmetric monoidal category, and in addition, there are usually some constraints placed on the specific PROP $P$.

**Definition 5** ([18]). *A PROP $\underline{P}$ is a small symmetric monoidal category with a strict monoidal functor $\Gamma \rightarrow \underline{P}$, which is a bijection on objects. A PROP $\underline{P}$ is algebraic (respectively, coalgebraic) if its set of maps is generated by a set of maps having codomain 1 (respectively, domain 1).*

Given a map $\sigma$ in $\underline{P}$, let $\sigma d$ and $\sigma r$ define its domain and range, respectively (both are natural numbers). Fox [18] defines a *propable* category $C^P$ as one that satisfies the following commutative diagram:

$$\begin{array}{ccc} A^{\sigma d} & \xrightarrow[a^{\sigma d}]{} & B^{\sigma d} \\ \downarrow{\scriptstyle \sigma} & & \downarrow{\scriptstyle \sigma} \\ A^{\sigma r} & \xrightarrow{a^{\sigma r}} & B^{\sigma r} \end{array}$$

For example, given the PROP map $\epsilon : 1 \rightarrow 0$, the commutative diagram states that there is a natural transformation $\epsilon_X : X \rightarrow I$ for each object X in C (where $X^0 = I$ and is the unit element). In Section 5, we will see that this structure defines the $\mathrm{del}_X$ "delete" structure in Markov and affine CDU categories.

### *4.5. cPROPs*

We now define a cPROP as a functor category whose objects are functors from a PROP $\underline{P}$ to a symmetric monoidal category $\mathcal{C}$.

**Definition 6.** *A cPROP is a functor category from a PROP $\underline{P}$ to a symmetric monoidal category C, which comes with the usual forgetful functor mapping a functor in cPROP to a symmetric monoidal category C.*

We are usually interested in cPROPs with a special structure on $\underline{P}$, which captures some of the typical structures used in applications, such as causal inference [1,2]. In such cases, we would like to be able to represent probability distributions, do causal interventions on graphs representing distributions, and marginalize over distributions to compute answers using rules like those of do-calculus [2]. We identify one simple example of such a regularity, which will turn out to be important in terms of its relationship to previous work on categorical causal models discussed in Section 5.

**Definition 7.** *Let $c\underline{P}$ denote a cPROP as a functor category from a coalgebraic PROP $\underline{P}$ generated by the maps $\delta : 1 \rightarrow 2$ and $\epsilon : 1 \rightarrow 0$, satisfying the following commutative diagrams (where $\tau$ is a "twist" morphism also commonly referred to as a braiding [16]).*

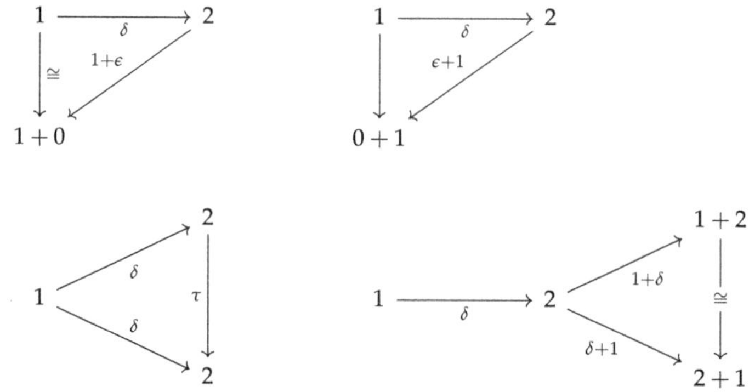


Note that the $\delta$ coalgebraic map in Markov and affine CDU categories defines the $\text{copy}_X$ map, which we discuss in more detail in Section 5. Fox [18] shows that the cPROP category $c\underline{P}$ of coalgebraic structures defined by the above commutative diagrams is Cartesian. This result also is shown by Heunen and Vicary [32], whose work is discussed in Section 5. It is worth emphasizing that in Markov categories, $\text{del}_X$ is assumed to obey its commutative diagram above, but $\text{copy}_X$ does not. We can easily model a Markov category as a cPROP where the commutative diagram for copy is not imposed uniformly over the category C as it is for del.

**Theorem 4** ([18])**.** *The cPROP category $c\underline{P}$ is Cartesian.*

**Proof.** The category $c\underline{P}$ consists of comonoidal objects $(C_i, \delta_i, \epsilon_i)$ over which a tensor product structure can be defined as follows. If $(C_1, \epsilon_1, \delta_1)$ and $(C_2, \delta_2, \epsilon_2)$ are two objects in $c\underline{P}$, their tensor product in $c\underline{P}$ is defined to be object

$$(C_1 \otimes C_2, (1 \otimes \tau \otimes 1) \circ (\delta_1 \otimes \delta_2), \epsilon_1 \otimes \epsilon_2)$$

It may be easier to visualize this as a string diagram (see Equation (4) for the specific example from Markov categories). To show that this particular tensor product is actually the categorical product in $c\underline{P}$, let $(C, \delta, \epsilon)$ be any object in $c\underline{P}$, and let the "projection" arrows in $c\underline{P}$ be defined as $a : C \to C_1$ and $b : C \to C_2$. A diagram chase using the below commutative diagram shows that $1 \otimes \epsilon_2 : C_1 \otimes C_2 \to C_1$ is indeed the product projection.

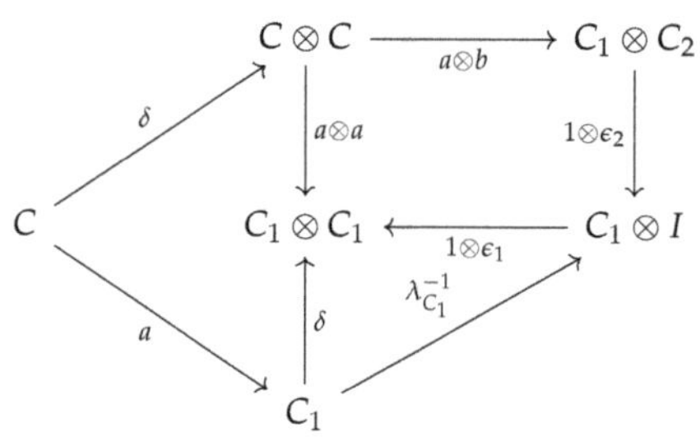


□

Fox [18] additionally proved the following result, showing that the coalgebraic category $c\underline{P}$ forms a Cartesian closure of the category of symmetric monoidal categories **MON**.

**Theorem 5** ([18])**.** *Define* **CART** *to be the category of all Cartesian categories with strictly product-preserving functors and* **MON** *to be the category of symmetric monoidal categories with strict monoidal functors as arrows. Then, the functor F that maps a category in* **MON** *to* **CART** *via its coalgebraic PROP structure is right adjoint to the inclusion functor from* **CART** *to* **MON***.*

**Proof.** Define a functor $F$ that maps a category in **MON** to the CPROP category $c\underline{P}$ using the PROP maps $\delta : 1 \rightarrow 2$ and $\epsilon : 1 \rightarrow 0$. Let $\mathcal{D}$ be any Cartesian category, and let $F : \mathcal{D} \rightarrow \mathcal{C}$ be an arrow in **MON**, i.e., a strictly monoidal functor. For any object X in D, let $\Delta : X \rightarrow X \times X$ be its diagonal map (which exists because D is Cartesian), and define the composed morphism $\epsilon_X : X \xrightarrow{\cong} X \otimes I \xrightarrow{\pi} I$ (where the projection $\pi$ exists because $I$ is terminal). Define the functor $F$ that maps from **MON** to **CART** by mapping an object $X$ to the comonoidal object $c\underline{P}$ as $(F(X), F(\Delta), F(\epsilon))$. $F$ preserves products by the diagram chase shown above. Then, $F$ has a left adjoint defined by the forgetful functor $U$ from the cPROP category $c\underline{P}$ to **MON**. □

*4.6. Closed Locally Presentable cPROPs*

We turn now to discuss the property of closedness and accessibility in cPROP categories. These will be useful in forming exponential objects, as well as in being able to apply the special adjoint functor theorem (SAFT) [16] (Theorem 2, Section V.8).

**Definition 8.** *A cPROP category C is closed Cartesian if it has all finite products and if the symmetric monoidal structure* $(\mathcal{C}, \times, e)$ *is closed. In other words, for all objects C, the functor* $(-) \otimes C$ *possess a right adjoint (which is referred to as an "exponential" object or an "internal hom" object).*

$$\mathcal{C}(X \otimes Y, Z) \cong \mathcal{C}(X, Z^Y)$$

We define subobjects of the objects in cPROP categories.

**Definition 9.** *For any cPROP category C, given two monomorphisms* $f : X \rightarrow Y$ *and* $g : Z \rightarrow Y$ *that share a common co-domain, let* $f \leq g$ *when f factors through g, namely,* $f = g \circ f'$ *for some arrow* $f'$ *(which must also be a monomorphism). If both* $f \leq g$ *and* $g \leq f$*, the induced equivalence classes of monomorphisms* $f \equiv g$ *with codomain Y define the subobjects of Y.*

To construct accessible cPROP categories, they need to be locally presentable through a cogenerating set $\mathcal{M}$ of objects.

**Definition 10.** *A cogenerating set of objects M for a cPROP category C that exists if for every parallel pair of arrows* $h \neq h' : X \rightarrow Y$*, there is an object Q in M and an arrow* $g : Y \rightarrow Q$ *such that* $g \circ h \neq g \circ h'$*.*

This property lets us construct initial objects for cPROP categories.

**Theorem 6** ([16])**.** *Special Initial-Object Theorem: If a cPROP category C is small-complete (implying that it has finite products and a terminal object), and there is a small cogenerating set M, then C has an initial object assuming every set of subobjects of X in C has a finite intersection.*

The proof is simple and involves constructing the product $X_0$ of all objects in the cogenerating set M and then taking the intersection of all the subobjects of $X_0$. Since the set of subobjects is a partial ordering under the relation $\leq$ in Definition 9, and the Cartesianness of the cPROP category gives us pullbacks, we can use this universal construction to find the meet or intersection of any set of subobjects. An important result that depends on this property is the Special Adjoint Functor Theorem [16].

**Theorem 7.** *Special Adjoint Functor Theorem (SAFT): Given a small-complete cPROP category M, with small hom sets and a small cogenerating set M, where every set of subobjects of objects in C has a pullback, then any functor $G : \mathcal{C} \to \mathcal{D}$ has a left adjoint if and only if G preserves all small limits and all pullbacks of families of monomorphisms.*

Fox [18] showed that the cPROP category $c\underline{P}$ has a small cogenerating set of objects and that the functor $F$ from $c\underline{P}$ to **MON** creates colimits. This was used to show that $c\underline{P}$ is locally presentable, and by the SAFT, there exists a right adjoint to the forgetful functor $U : c\underline{P} \to$ **MON**.

## 5. Affine CDU and Markov Categories as cPROPs

In this section, we will relate cPROPs to previous work on affine CDU categories [25] and Markov categories [17]. Markov categories have been studied extensively as a unifying categorical model for causal inference, probability, and statistics. They are symmetric monoidal categories, which we reviewed in Section 4.3, combined with a comonoidal structure on each object. Importantly, Markov categories are semi-Cartesian because they do not use uniform copying but contain a Cartesian subcategory defined by deterministic morphisms. I give a brief review of Markov categories, and significant additional details that are omitted can be found in [10,17,25]. For the sake of clarity, we will follow the definitions in [17], although we will explore some of the subtleties in these definitions in Section 5.1 relating to the Cartesian structure of a Markov category.

**Definition 11.** *A* Markov category $\mathcal{C}$ *[17] is a symmetric monoidal category in which every object $X \in \mathcal{C}$ is equipped with a commutative comonoid structure given by a comultiplication* $\mathsf{copy}_X : X \to X \otimes X$ *and a counit* $\mathsf{del}_X : X \to I$*, depicted in string diagrams as*

(1)

*and satisfying the commutative comonoid equations*

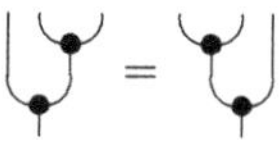
(2)

(3)

*as well as compatibility with the monoidal structure*

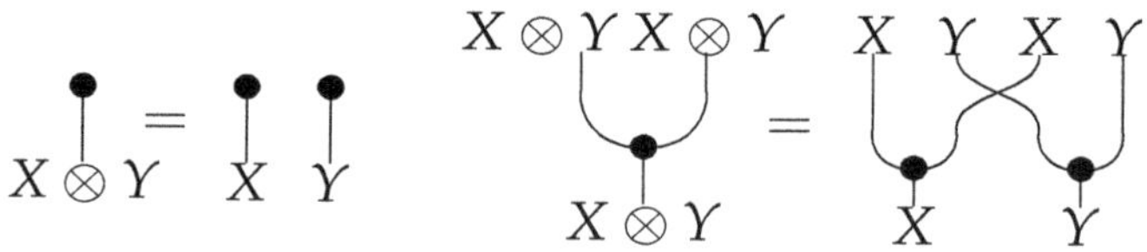

(4)

*and the naturality of* del*, which means that*

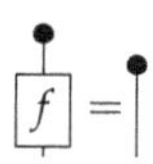

(5)

*for every morphism $f$.*

Note that to adequately represent discovery algorithms like PC, and their many extensions and variants like Greedy Equivalent Search [3], it is necessary to modify string diagrams to represent equivalence class of causal models. The challenge we have to face is that causal discovery requires searching through a super-exponentially large space of such string diagrams. Note that string diagrams defined over Markov categories are essentially induced by the PROP maps that define their (co)algebraic structure. In Sections 7 and 8, it will be shown how such string diagrams can be converted into continuous maps over "nice" topological spaces, in particular CW-complexes using the nerve functor that maps a (symmetric monoidal) category into a simplicial set [28]. Thus, the tensor product bifunctor $\otimes : \mathcal{C} \times \mathcal{C} \rightarrow \mathcal{C}$ leads to an $H$-space, or a topological space with a chosen basepoint (which can be defined as the topological 0-cell associated with the terminal object $I$ in a Markov category), as well as a continuous map $\mathcal{BC} \times \mathcal{BC} \rightarrow \mathcal{BC}$. The comonoid comultiplication $\mathsf{copy}_X : X \rightarrow X \otimes X$ induces a diagonal map $\mathcal{BC} \rightarrow \mathcal{BC} \times \mathcal{BC}$. Since $I$ is a terminal object in a Markov category, its classifying spaces $\mathcal{BC}$ are contractible.

Figure 10 illustrates a cPROP Markov category string diagram showing how the reversal of covered edges induces an equivalence of the associated string diagrams.

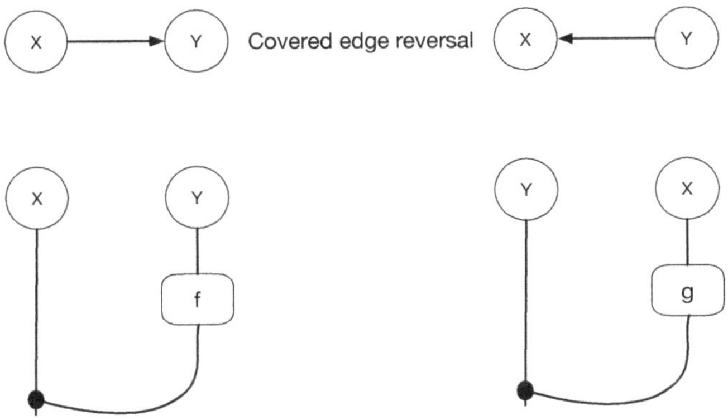


**Figure 10.** Meek–Chickering equivalence by reversal of covered edges induces an equivalence of the associated string diagrams.

### 5.1. Cartesian Structure in Markov Categories

I now discuss a subcategory of Cartesian categories within Markov that involves uniform $\mathsf{copy}_X$ and $\mathsf{del}_X$ morphisms. One fundamental property of Markov categories is that they are *semi-Cartesian*, as the unit object is also a terminal object. But, a subtlety arises in how these copy and delete operators are modeled, as will be discussed below.

**Definition 12.** *A symmetric monoidal category $\mathcal{C}$ is Cartesian if the tensor product $\otimes$ is the categorical product.*

If $\mathcal{C}$ and $\mathcal{D}$ are symmetric monoidal categories, then a functor $F : \mathcal{C} \rightarrow \mathcal{D}$ is monoidal if the tensor product is preserved up to coherent natural isomorphisms. $F$ is strictly monoidal if all the monoidal structures are preserved exactly, including $\otimes$, unit object $I$, symmetry, and associative and unit natural isomorphisms. Denote the category of symmetric monoidal categories with strict functors as arrows as **MON**. Let us review the basic definitions given by Heunen and Vicary [32], which will give some further clarity on the Cartesian structure in affine CDU and Markov categories.

**Definition 13.** *The subcategory of comonoids* **coMON** *in the ambient category* **MON** *of all symmetric monoidal categories is defined for any specific category C as a collection of "coalgebraic"* *objects* $(X, copy_X, del_X)$*, where X is in C, and arrows defined as comonoid homomorphisms from* $(X, copy_X, del_X)$ *to* $(Y, copy_Y, del_Y)$ *act uniformly in the sense that if* $f : X \to Y$ *is any morphism in C, then*

$$(f \otimes f) \circ copy_X = copy_Y \circ f$$
$$del_Y \circ f = del_X$$

Heunen and Vicary [32] defined the process of "uniform copying and deleting" in the category **coMON**, which we will now relate to Markov categories. A subtle difference worth emphasizing with Definition 11 is that in Markov categories, only $\text{del}_X$ is "uniform", but not $\text{copy}_X$ in the sense defined by Heunen and Vicary [32]. This distinction can be modeled in a cPROP category that is semi-Cartesian like Markov categories by suitably modifying the definition of the associated PROP map for copying.

**Definition 14** ([32]). *A symmetric monoidal category C admits uniform deleting if there is a natural transformation* $e_X : X \xrightarrow{e_X} I$ *for all objects in the subcategory* $C_{\textbf{coMON}}$ *of comonoidal objects, where* $e_I = id_I$*, as shown in Equation* (5).

This condition was referred to by Cho and Jacobs [25] as a *causality* condition on the arrow $e_X$. Essentially, it states that if you process some object and then discard it, it is equivalent to discarding it without processing.

**Theorem 8** ([32]). *A symmetric monoidal category C has uniform deleting if and only if I is terminal.*

This property holds for Markov categories, as noted in [17], and a simple diagram chasing proof is given in [32].

**Definition 15** ([32]). *A symmetric monoidal category C has uniform copying if there is a natural transformation* $copy_X : X \to X \otimes X$ *such that* $del_I = \rho_I^{-1}$*, satisfying Equations* (2) *and* (3).

We can now state an important result proved in [32] (Theorem 4.28), which relates to the more general results shown earlier by Fox [18]

**Theorem 9** ([18,32]). *The following conditions are equivalent for a symmetric monoidal category C:*

- *The category C is Cartesian, with tensor products* $\otimes$ *given by the categorical product, and the tensor unit is given by the terminal object.*
- *The symmetric monoidal category C has uniform copying and deleting, and Equation* (2) *holds.*

As noted by Fritz [17], not all Markov categories are Cartesian, because their $\mathbf{copy}_X$ is not uniform, but only $\mathbf{del}_X$ is. For example, consider the category **FinStoch**, where a joint distribution is specified by the morphism $\psi : I \to X \otimes Y$. In this case, the marginal distributions can be formed as the composite morphisms

$$I \xrightarrow{\psi} X \otimes Y \xrightarrow{\text{del}_Y} X$$
$$I \xrightarrow{\psi} X \otimes Y \xrightarrow{\text{del}_X} Y$$

But to require that in this case $\otimes$ is the categorical product implies that the marginal distributions defined as the above composites must be in bijection with the joint distribution.

### 5.2. cPROP Causal Category for Pancreatic Cancer

We can transform the causal DAGs in Figures 5 and 6 into equivalent cPROP string diagram categorical models using the general process of mapping DAGs into string diagram category structures (see [9,17]). For example, for the cPROP category underlying the causal model in Figure 5, we can now construct a morphism for each edge in this DAG model, such as

$$f : \text{KRAS} \to \text{SMAD4}, \quad g : \text{TP53} \to \text{TPO},$$

and so on for the other edges. Analogously, we can construct a cPROP category based on the causal DAG pathway model in Figure 6, whose morphisms would include

$$f : \text{Homophilic cell adhesion} \to \text{Integrin signalling},$$

and similar morphisms corresponding to other edges. An intriguing direction for further exploration of this application is to construct a symmetric monoidal product cPROP category that combines both these cPROP categories into a product cPROP category.

We can also construct equivalence classes of these two causal DAGs using reversals of covered edges (and their corresponding natural transformations mapping each causal DAG in an equivalence class into a cPROP functor object), as described in Section 8. A crucial advantage of our proposed framework in this domain is that by capturing the underlying equivalence classes more compactly using the higher-algebraic k-theory framework, it opens the possibility of constructing more compact models that include a larger percentage of the genes mutated by pancreatic cancer. Since there are potentially tens of thousands of genes, previous work was limited to building models on only the most likely mutated genes, as the number of possible DAG models grows explosively in size, as noted in the introduction. A more detailed analysis of this application using the theoretical framework proposed below will be reported in a subsequent paper and is beyond the scope of this paper.

To summarize this section, we reviewed affine CD categories [25] and Markov categories [17] and showed that they are closely related to cPROPs. Markov categories are semi-Cartesian, as the unit element $I$ is terminal, but they are not Cartesian, as they do not allow uniform copying. They do contain a subcategory defined by their comonoidal objects that is Cartesian. In the remainder of this paper, we will construct simplicial objects over cPROP categories, and then in Section 8, we will define the basic concepts of homotopies in cPROP categories.

## 6. Structural Causal Models as Cartesian cPROPs

In this section, we will briefly discuss how Pearl's structural causal models (SCMs) [2] can be defined as a special type of cPROP involving deterministic morphisms, as defined in [17]. Recall from the previous section that, in general, a Markov category has uniform deletion but not uniform copying. However, as noted in [17], a morphism is defined to be deterministic if it leads to uniform copying. Using the results from Theorem 9 above, we can conclude therefore that the subclass of Markov categories with uniform copying and deleting is Cartesian and hence sufficient to model SCMs in so far as the mapping from exogenous variables to endogenous variables is deterministic. Recall that in an SCM, the mapping from exogenous variables (i.e., variables external to the model) to endogenous variables (i.e., variables internal to the model) is purely *deterministic*. The uncertainty derives purely from the fact that external variables are assumed to be defined with respect to some probability distribution. We will begin with a review of Pearl's SCM framework and then show how it corresponds to a special type of cPROP Markov category using deterministic morphisms.

**Definition 16** ([2]). *A structural causal model (SCM) is defined as the triple* $\langle U, V, F \rangle$ *where* $V = \{V_1, \ldots, V_n\}$ *is a set of* endogenous *variables,* $U$ *is a set of* exogenous *variables, and* $F$ *is a set* $\{f_1, \ldots, f_n\}$ *of purely deterministic "local functions"* $f_i : U \cup (V \setminus V_i) \rightarrow V_i$ *whose composition induces a unique function* $F$ *from* $U$ *to* $V$.

**Definition 17** ([2]). *Let* $M = \langle U, V, F \rangle$ *be a causal model defined as an SCM, let* $X$ *be a subset of variables in* $V$*, and let* $x$ *be a particular realization of* $X$*. A submodel* $M_x = \langle U, V, F_x \rangle$ *of* $M$ *is the causal model* $M_x = \langle U, V, F_x \rangle$*, where* $F_x = \{f_i : V_i \notin X\} \cup \{X = x\}$.

**Definition 18** ([2]). *Let* $M$ *be an SCM,* $X$ *be a set of variables in* $V$*, and* $x$ *be a particular realization of* $X$*. The effect of an action* $do(X = x)$ *on* $M$ *is given by the submodel* $M_x$.

**Definition 19** ([2]). *Let* $Y$ *be a variable in* $V$*, and let* $X$ *be a subset of* $V$*. The potential outcome of* $Y$ *in response to an action* $do(X = x)$*, denoted* $Y_x(u)$*, is the solution of* $Y$ *for the set of equations* $F_x$.

*SCMs as Cartesian cPROPs*

Recall from Theorem 9 that symmetric monoidal categories that are Cartesian admit uniform copying and deleting. We can use this property to define deterministic morphisms in a cPROP (or Markov) category as follows.

**Definition 20** ([17]). *A morphism* $f : X \rightarrow Y$ *in a cPROP category* $\mathcal{C}$ *is deterministic if it admits uniform copying.*

We can now define an SCM as a cPROP category where all the morphisms between exogenous variables and endogenous variables are deterministic.

**Definition 21.** *A structural causal model (SCM) [2] can be defined as a restricted type of cPROP category* $\mathcal{C}_{SC\mathcal{M}}$ *whose collection of objects* $Obj = \{U, V\}$ *is partitioned into a collection of exogenous objects* $U$ *and a collection of endogenous objects* $V$ *such that every morphism* $f : X \rightarrow Y$ *from an exogenous object* $X \in U$ *to an endogenous object* $Y \in V$ *is deterministic.*

Observe that any product of exogenous objects $X_1 \otimes X_2 \ldots X_n$ is exogenous if each object $X_i$ is exogenous, and similarly, any product of endogenous objects is also endogenous if each object in the product is endogenous. Thus, every exogenous variable is defined with respect to some probability distribution $P$.

**Definition 22.** *Given a Cartesian cPROP category* $\mathcal{C}_{SC\mathcal{M}}$ *corresponding to a structural causal model, to every object corresponding to an exogenous variable* $X$*, there exists a morphism* $\psi : I \rightarrow X$ *that defines a distribution over* $X$.

Figure 1 illustrates an example of a structural causal model defining pollution in New Delhi, India (based on the original example in [14]), translated into a string diagram defining a Cartesian cPROP. Note that the exogenous variables here are defined by probability distributions (morphisms) in a Markov category as follows:

$$\psi : I \rightarrow \text{Overpopulation}, \quad \phi : I \rightarrow \text{Covid Lockdown}, \quad \delta : I \rightarrow \text{Farming Practices}$$

The Cartesian model specifying the endogenous variables are defined purely using deterministic morphisms, which includes the following:

$$\begin{aligned} f : \text{Overpopulation} &\otimes \text{Covid Lockdown} \rightarrow \text{Traffic} \\ g : \text{Covid Lockdown} &\otimes \text{Farming Practices} \rightarrow \text{Agricultural practices} \end{aligned}$$

and is similar for the morphisms $h$ and $w$.

## 7. Simplicial Objects in cPROPs

We now turn to the embedding of cPROPs in the category of simplicial sets, which will be a prelude to constructing "nice" topological realizations and the study of their classifying spaces. Figure 11 gives the high level intuition. A simplicial set $X$ is defined as a collection of sets $X_0, X_1, \ldots$, which is combined with face maps (indicated as $d_i$ in the figure) and degeneracy maps (indicated as $s_j$ in the figure). As a simple guide to help build intuition, any directed graph can be viewed as a simplicial set, where $X_0$ is the set $V$ of vertices, $X_1$ is the $E$ of edges, and the two face maps $d_0$ and $d_1$ from $X_1$ to $X_0$ yield the initial and final vertex of the edge. The single degeneracy map $s_0$ between $X_0$ and $X_1$ adds a self loop to each vertex. Simplicial sets generalize graphs when we consider higher-order simplices. For example, between $X_1$ and $X_2$, there are three face maps, mapping a simplicial triangle (a 2-simplex) $\Delta$ to each of its 1-simplicial components, namely, its edges.

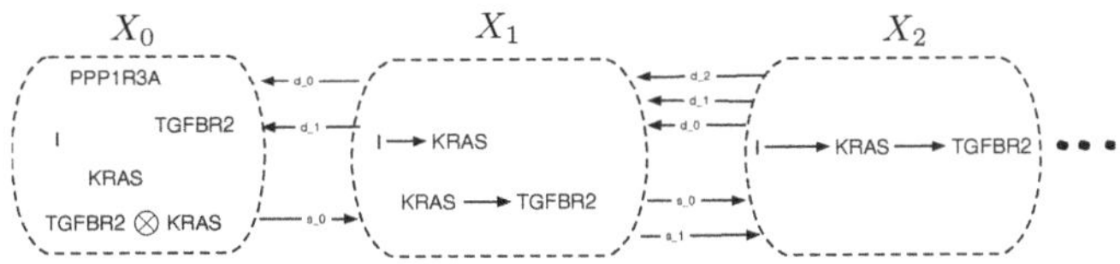


**Figure 11.** A simplicial object in a cPROP category. $X_0$ defines the 0-simplices represented by objects: in the pancreatic cancer domain, these represent individual mutated genes or the initial object $I$ (denoting a marginalized distribution). $X_1$ defines the 1-simplices represented by single morphisms, such as the distribution $I \rightarrow$ **KRAS**. Similarly, 2-simplices represent composable morphisms of length 2, such as $I \rightarrow$ **KRAS** $\rightarrow$ **TGFBR2** and so on.

A brief review of simplicial sets is given, summarizing some points made in my previous paper on simplicial set representations in causal inference [14]. A more detailed review can be found in many references [29,48]. Simplicial sets are higher-dimensional generalizations of directed graphs, partially ordered sets, and regular categories themselves. Importantly, simplicial sets and simplicial objects form a foundation for higher-order category theory [26,27]. Using simplicial sets and objects enables a powerful machinery to reason about both directional and non-directional paths in causal models and to model equivalence classes of causal models.

Simplicial objects have long been a foundation for algebraic topology [48,49] and more recently in higher-order category theory [26,27,50]. The category $\Delta$ has non-empty ordinals $[n] = \{0, 1, \ldots, n\}$ as objects and order-preserving maps $[m] \rightarrow [n]$ as arrows. An important property in $\Delta$ is that any many-to-many mapping is decomposable as a composition of an injective and a surjective mapping, each of which is decomposable into a sequence of elementary injections $\delta_i : [n] \rightarrow [n+1]$ called *coface* mappings, which omit $i \in [n]$, and a sequence of elementary surjections $\sigma_i : [n] \rightarrow [n-1]$, called *co-degeneracy* mappings, which repeat $i \in [n]$. The fundamental simplex $\Delta([n])$ is the presheaf of all morphisms into $[n]$, that is, the representable functor $\Delta(-, [n])$. The Yoneda Lemma [16] assures us that an $n$-simplex $x \in X_n$ can be identified with the corresponding map $\Delta[n] \rightarrow X$. Every morphism $f : [n] \rightarrow [m]$ in $\Delta$ is functorially mapped to the map $\Delta[m] \rightarrow \Delta[n]$ in $\mathcal{S}$.

Any morphism in the category $\Delta$ can be defined as a sequence of *codegeneracy* and *coface* operators, where the coface operator $\delta_i : [n-1] \rightarrow [n], 0 \leq i \leq n$ is defined as

$$\delta_i(j) = \begin{cases} j, & \text{for } 0 \leq j \leq i-1 \\ j+1 & \text{for } i \leq j \leq n-1 \end{cases}$$

Analogously, the codegeneracy operator $\sigma_j : [n+1] \to [n]$ is defined as

$$\sigma_j(k) = \begin{cases} j, & \text{for } 0 \le k \le j \\ k-1 & \text{for } j < k \le n+1 \end{cases}$$

Note that under the contravariant mappings, coface mappings turn into face mappings, and codegeneracy mappings turn into degeneracy mappings. That is, for any simplicial object (or set) $X_n$, we have $X(\delta_i) := d_i : X_n \to X_{n-1}$, and likewise, $X(\sigma_j) := s_j : X_{n-1} \to X_n$.

The compositions of these arrows define certain well-known properties [29,48]:

$$\begin{aligned} \delta_j \circ \delta_i &= \delta_i \circ \delta_{j-1}, \; i < j \\ \sigma_j \circ \sigma_i &= \sigma_i \circ \sigma_{j+1}, \; i \le j \\ \sigma_j \circ \delta_i(j) &= \begin{cases} \sigma_i \circ \sigma_{j+1}, & \text{for } i < j \\ 1_{[n]} & \text{for } i = j, j+1 \\ \sigma_{i-1} \circ \sigma_j, \text{for } i > j+1 \end{cases} \end{aligned}$$

**Example 2.** *The "vertices" of a simplicial object $X$ in a cPROP category $\mathcal{C}$ are the objects $X_0$ in $\mathcal{C}$, and the "edges" $X_1$ are its arrows $f : C_i \to C_j$, where $C_i$ and $C_j$ are objects in $\mathcal{C}$. Note that $X_0$ is a contravariant functor $X : [0] \to \mathcal{C}$, and since $[0]$ has only one object, the effect of this functor is to pick out objects in $\mathcal{C}$. The simplicial object is $X_1 : [1] \to \mathcal{C}$. Given any such arrow, the face operators $d_0 f = C_j$ and $d_1 f = C_i$ recover the source and target of each arrow. Also, given an object $X$ of category $\mathcal{C}$, we can regard the degeneracy operator $s_0 X$ as its identity morphism $\mathbf{1}_X : X \to X$.*

**Example 3.** *Given a cPROP category $\mathcal{C}$, we can identify an n-simplex $X_n$ of a simplicial object in a cPROP category $s\mathcal{C}_n$ with the following sequence:*

$$X_n = C_o \xrightarrow{f_1} C_1 \xrightarrow{f_2} \ldots \xrightarrow{f_n} C_n$$

*and the face operator $d_0$ applied to $X_n$ yields the sequence*

$$d_0 X_n = C_1 \xrightarrow{f_2} C_2 \xrightarrow{f_3} \ldots \xrightarrow{f_n} C_n$$

*where the object $C_0$ is "deleted" along with the morphism $f_0$ leaving it.*

**Example 4.** *Given a cPROP category $\mathcal{C}$ and an n-simplex $X_n$ of the simplicial object in a cPROP category $X_n$, the face operator $d_n$ applied to $X_n$ yields the sequence*

$$d_n X_n = C_0 \xrightarrow{f_1} C_1 \xrightarrow{f_2} \ldots \xrightarrow{f_{n-1}} C_{n-1}$$

*where the object $C_n$ is "deleted" along with the morphism $f_n$ entering it.*

**Example 5.** *Given a cPROP category $\mathcal{C}$ and an n-simplex $X_n$ of the simplicial object, the face operator $d_i, 0 < i < n$ applied to $X_n$ yields the sequence*

$$d_i X_n = C_0 \xrightarrow{f_1} C_1 \xrightarrow{f_2} \ldots C_{i-1} \xrightarrow{f_{i+1} \circ f_i} C_{i+1} \ldots \xrightarrow{f_n} C_n$$

*where the object $C_i$ is "deleted", and the morphisms $f_i$ are composed with morphism $f_{i+1}$.*

**Example 6.** *Given a cPROP category $\mathcal{C}$ and an n-simplex $X_n$ of the simplicial object defined over the cPROP category, the degeneracy operator $s_i, 0 \leq i \leq n$ applied to $X_n$ yields the sequence*

$$s_i X_n = C_0 \xrightarrow{f_1} C_1 \xrightarrow{f_2} \ldots C_i \xrightarrow{\mathbf{1}_{C_i}} C_i \xrightarrow{f_{i+1}} C_{i+1} \ldots \xrightarrow{f_n} C_n$$

*where the object $C_i$ is "repeated" by inserting its identity morphism $\mathbf{1}_{C_i}$.*

**Definition 23.** *Given a cPROP category $\mathcal{C}$ and an n-simplex $X_n$ of the simplicial object associated with the category, $X_n$ is a degenerate simplex if some $f_i$ values in $X_n$ are an identity morphism, in which case $C_i$ and $C_{i+1}$ are equal.*

### 7.1. Nerve of a Category

There is a general way to construct a simplicial set representation of any category by constructing its *nerve* functor [28]. This construction formalizes what was illustrated in the above examples.

**Definition 24.** *The nerve of a category $\mathcal{C}$ is the set of composable morphisms of length n for $n \geq 1$. Let $N_n(\mathcal{C})$ denote the set of sequences of composable morphisms of length n.*

$$\{C_o \xrightarrow{f_1} C_1 \xrightarrow{f_2} \ldots \xrightarrow{f_n} C_n \mid C_i \text{ is an object in } \mathcal{C}, f_i \text{ is a morphism in } \mathcal{C}\}$$

The set of $n$-tuples of composable arrows in C, denoted by $N_n(\mathcal{C})$, can be viewed as a functor from the simplicial object $[n]$ to $\mathcal{C}$. Note that any non-decreasing map $\alpha : [m] \rightarrow [n]$ determines a map of sets $N_m(\mathcal{C}) \rightarrow N_n(\mathcal{C})$. The nerve of a category C is the simplicial set $N_\bullet : \Delta \rightarrow N_n(\mathcal{C})$, which maps the ordinal number object $[n]$ to the set $N_n(\mathcal{C})$.

The importance of the nerve of a category comes from a key result [29,51], showing that it defines a full and faithful embedding of a category.

**Theorem 10.** *The nerve functor $N_\bullet$ : **Cat** $\rightarrow$ **Set** is fully faithful. More specifically, there is a bijection $\theta$ defined as*

$$\theta : \mathbf{Cat}(\mathcal{C}, \mathcal{C}') \rightarrow \mathbf{Set}_\Delta(N_\bullet(\mathcal{C}), N_\bullet(\mathcal{C}')$$

Unfortunately, the left adjoint to the nerve functor is not a full and faithful encoding of a simplicial set back into a suitable category. Note that a functor $G$ from a simplicial object $X$ to a category $\mathcal{C}$ can be lossy. For example, we can define the objects of $\mathcal{C}$ to be the elements of $X_0$ and the morphisms of $\mathcal{C}$ as the elements $f \in X_1$, where $f : a \rightarrow b$, $d_0 f = a$, $d_1 f = b$, and $s_0 a, a \in X$ define the identity morphisms $\mathbf{1}_a$. Composition in this case can be defined as the free algebra defined over elements of $X_1$, which is subject to the constraints given by elements of $X_2$. For example, if $x \in X_2$, we can impose the requirement that $d_1 x = d_0 x \circ d_2 x$. Such a definition of the left adjoint would be quite lossy because it only preserves the structure of the simplicial object $X$ up to the 2-simplices. The right adjoint from a category to its associated simplicial object, in contrast, constructs a full and faithful embedding of a category into a simplicial set. In particular, the nerve of a category is such a right adjoint.

### 7.2. Topological Embedding of cPROP Categories

Simplicial objects in cPROP categories can be embedded in a topological space using a construction originally proposed by Milnor [30].

**Definition 25.** *The geometric realization $|X|$ of a simplicial object $X$ in the cPROP category $\mathcal{C}$ is defined as the topological space*

$$|X| = \bigsqcup_{n \geq 0} X_n \times \Delta^n / \sim$$

*where the n-simplex $X_n$ is assumed to have a* discrete *topology (i.e., all subsets of $X_n$ are open sets), and $\Delta^n$ denotes the* topological *n-simplex*

$$\Delta^n = \{(p_0, \dots, p_n) \in \mathbb{R}^{n+1} \mid 0 \leq p_i \leq 1, \sum_i p_i = 1$$

*The spaces $\Delta^n, n \geq 0$ can be viewed as* cosimplicial *topological spaces with the following degeneracy and face maps:*

$$\delta_i(t_0, \dots, t_n) = (t_0, \dots, t_{i-1}, 0, t_i, \dots, t_n) \text{ for } 0 \leq i \leq n$$

$$\sigma_j(t_0, \dots, t_n) = (t_0, \dots, t_j + t_{j+1}, \dots, t_n) \text{ for } 0 \leq i \leq n$$

*Note that $\delta_i : \mathbb{R}^n \rightarrow \mathbb{R}^{n+1}$, whereas $\sigma_j : \mathbb{R}^n \rightarrow \mathbb{R}^{n-1}$.*

*The equivalence relation $\sim$ above that defines the quotient space is given as*

$$(d_i(x), (t_0, \dots, t_n)) \sim (x, \delta_i(t_0, \dots, t_n))$$

$$(s_j(x), (t_0, \dots, t_n)) \sim (x, \sigma_j(t_0, \dots, t_n))$$

### 7.3. *Topological Embeddings as Coends*

We will now bring in the perspective that topological embeddings of simplicial objects in cPROP categories can be interpreted as a coend [16] as well. Consider the functor

$$F : \Delta^o \times \Delta \rightarrow \text{Top}$$

where

$$F([n], [m]) = X_n \times \Delta^m$$

where $F$ acts *contravariantly* as a functor from $\Delta$ to **Sets** mapping $[n] \mapsto X_n$, and *covariantly* mapping $[m] \mapsto \Delta^m$ acts as a functor from $\Delta$ to the category Top of topological spaces.

The coend defines a topological embedding of a simplicial object $X$ in a cPROP category, where $X_n$ represents composable morphisms of length $n$. Given this simplicial object, we can now construct a topological realization of it as a coend object

$$\int^n (X_n) \cdot \Delta n$$

where $X : \Delta^{op} \rightarrow \mathcal{C}$ is the simplicial object defined by the contravariant functor from the simplicial category $\Delta$ into the category of simplicial objects in cPROP categories, and $\Delta : |\Delta| \rightarrow$ **Top** is a functor from the topological $n$-simplex realization of the simplicial category $\Delta$ into topological spaces **Top**. As MacLane [16] explains it picturesquely, the "coend formula describes the geometric realization in one gulp". The formula says essentially to take the disjoint union of affine $n$-simplices, one for each $n \in X_n$, and glue them together using the face and degeneracy operations defined as arrows of the simplicial category $\Delta$.

## 8. Homotopy in cPROP Categories

We define homotopy in cPROP categories somewhat abstractly in this section, but we will illustrate these definitions more concretely for Bayesian networks defined as functors between cPROP categories, which are analogous to the CDU functors [9] defined later in Section 9.

To motivate the need for considering homotopy in categorical models of causal inference, and in particular for cPROP categories, note that causal models can only be determined up to some equivalence class from data, and while many causal discovery algorithms assume that arbitrary interventions can be carried out, for example, on separating sets [6] and other types of subsets [7], to discover the unique structure, such interventions are generally impossible to do in practical applications. The concept of essential graph [52] and chain graph [53] are attempts to formulate the notion of a "quotient space" of graphs, but similar issues arise more generally for non-graph-based models as well. Thus, it is useful to understand how to formulate the notion of equivalent classes of causal models in an arbitrary category. For example, given the conditional independence structure $A \perp\!\!\!\perp B|C$, there are at least three different symmetric monoidal categorical representations that all satisfy this conditional independence [9,10,23], and we need to define the quotient space over all such equivalent categories.

### 8.1. Homotopy in cPROP Categories

We will discuss homotopy in cPROP categories more generally now. This abstract notion of homotopy generalizes the notion of homotopy in topology, which defines why an object like a coffee cup is topologically homotopic to a doughnut (they have the same number of "holes").

**Definition 26.** *Let $C$ and $C'$ be a pair of objects in a cPROP category $\mathcal{C}$. We say $C$ is a retract of $C'$ if there exists maps $i : C \to C'$ and $r : C' \to C$ such that $r \circ i = id_C$.*

**Definition 27.** *Let $\mathcal{C}$ be a cPROP category. We say that a morphism $f : C \to D$ is a retract of another morphism $f' : C \to D$ if it is a retract of $f'$ when viewed as an object of the functor category $\mathbf{Hom}([1], \mathcal{C})$. A collection of morphisms $T$ of $\mathcal{C}$ is closed under retracts if for every pair of morphisms $f, f'$ of $\mathcal{C}$, if $f$ is a retract of $f'$, and $f'$ is in $T$; then, $f$ is also in $T$.*

**Definition 28.** *Let $X$ and $Y$ be simplicial cPROP categories represented as simplicial sets, and suppose we are given a pair of morphisms $f_0, f_1 : X \to Y$. A homotopy from $f_0$ to $f_1$ is a morphism $h : \Delta^1 \times X \to Y$ satisfying $f_0 = h|_{0 \times X}$ and $f_1 = h_{1 \times X}$.*

### 8.2. Classifying Spaces of cPROP Categories

I now introduce a formal way to define causal effects in our cPROP framework, which relies on the construction of a topological space associated with the nerve of a cPROP category. As shown in [28], the nerve of a category is a full and faithful embedding of a category as a simplicial object.

**Definition 29.** *The classifying space $\mathcal{BC}$ of a cPROP category $\mathcal{C}$ is the topological space associated with the nerve of the category $\mathcal{C}$.*

To understand the classifying space $\mathcal{BC}$ of a cPROP category $\mathcal{C}$, let us go over some simple examples to gain some insight.

**Example 7.** *Consider a discrete cPROP category $\mathcal{C}_X$ as a subcategory over **FinSet** defined as discrete finite sets $X$ with no non-trivial morphisms, where the classifying space $B\mathcal{C}_X$ is just the discrete topology over $X$ (where the open sets are all possible subsets of $X$).*

**Example 8.** *Consider a cPROP category $C$ defined as a partially ordered set $[n]$, with its usual order-preserving morphisms; then, the nerve of $[n]$ is isomorphic to the representable functor $\Delta(-,[n])$, as shown by the Yoneda Lemma, and in that case, the classifying space is just the topological space associated with $\Delta_n$ (the topological n-simplex). For the pancreatic cancer domain described in Section 2, if we view causal models as posets, then their classifying space is given by the topological n-simplex.*

### 8.3. Homotopy Colimits of cPROP Categories

**Definition 30.** *The homotopy colimit of a cPROP category model is defined as a nerve of the category of elements associated with the set-valued functor $\delta : C \to$ **Set** mapping the cPROP category $C$ to a dataset, namely, $B(\int \delta)$.*

In general, we may want to evaluate the homotopy colimit of a cPROP category not only with respect to the data used in a causal experiment but also with respect to some underlying topological space or some measurable space. We can extend the above definition straightforwardly to these cases using an appropriate functor $\mathcal{T}$: **Set** $\to$ **Top** or, alternatively $\mathcal{M}$: **Set** $\to$ **Meas**. These augmented constructions can then be defined with respect to a more general notion called the *homotopy colimit* [29] of a causal model.

**Definition 31.** *The topological homotopy colimit $hocolim_{\mathcal{T}\circ\delta}$ of a cPROP category $C$, along with its associated category of elements associated with a set-valued functor $\delta : C \to$ **Set** and a topological functor $\mathcal{T}$: **Set** $\to$ **Top**, is isomorphic to topological space associated with the nerve of the category of elements that is $hocolim_{\mathcal{T}\circ\delta} \simeq \mathcal{B}(\int \delta)$.*

**Example 9.** *The classifying space $\mathcal{B}C_{CDU}$ associated with CDU symmetric monoidal category encoding of a causal Bayesian DAG [9] is defined using the monoidal category (**C**, $\otimes$, $I$), where each object $A$ has a copy map $C_A : A \to A \otimes A$, discarding map $D_A : A \to I$, and a uniform state map $U_A : I \to A$, which is defined as the topological realization of its nerve. As before, the nerve $B(C)$ of the CDU (or Markov) category is defined as the set of sequences of composable morphisms of length $n$.*

$$\{C_o \xrightarrow{f_1} C_1 \xrightarrow{f_2} \dots \xrightarrow{f_n} C_n \mid C_i \text{ is an object in } C, f_i \text{ is a morphism in } C\}$$

*Note that the CDU category was associated with a CDU functor $F$ : **Syn**$_G \to$ **Stoch** to the category of stochastic matrices. We can now define the homotopy colimit $hocolim_{\mathcal{F}}$ of the CDU causal model associated with the CDU category $C$, along with its associated category of elements associated with a set-valued functor $\delta : C \to$ **Set**, and a topological functor $\mathcal{F}$: **Set** $\to$ **Stoch** is isomorphic to the topological space associated with the nerve of the category of elements over the composed functor, that is, $hocolim_{\mathcal{F}\circ\delta}$.*

### 8.4. Defining Causal Effect in cPROP Categories Using Homotopy

Finally, we turn to defining causal effect using the notion of classifying space and homotopy colimits, as defined above. Space does not permit a complete discussion of this topic, but the basic idea is that once a causal model is defined as a topological space, there are a large number of ways of comparing two topological spaces from analyzing their chain complexes, or we can use a topological data analysis method such as UMAP [54].

**Definition 32.** *Let the classifying space under "treatment" be defined as the topological space $BC_1|$ associated with the nerve of a cPROP category $C_1$ under some intervention, which may result in a topological deformation of the model (e.g., deletion of an edge). Similarly, the classifying space under "no treatment" be defined as the $BC_0$ under a no-treatment setting, with no intervention. A causally* *non-isomorphic effect exists between cPROP categories $\mathcal{C}_1$ and $\mathcal{C}_0$ or $\mathcal{C}_1 \not\cong \mathcal{C}_0$ if and only if there is no invertible morphism $f : \mathcal{B}\mathcal{C}_1 \rightarrow \mathcal{B}\mathcal{C}_0$ between the "treatment" and "no-treatment" topological spaces, namely, $f$ must be both* left invertible *and* right invertible.

There is an equivalent notion of causal effect using the homotopy colimit definition proposed above, which defines the nerve functor using the category of elements. This version is particularly useful in the context of evaluating a causal model over a dataset.

**Definition 33.** *Let the homotopy colimit $hocolim_1 = \mathcal{B} \int \delta_1$ be the topological space associated with a cPROP category $\mathcal{C}_1$ under the "treatment' condition defined with respect to an associated category of elements defined by a set-valued functor $\delta_1 : \mathcal{C} \rightarrow$ **Set** over a dataset of "treated" variables, and let "no-treatment" $hocolim_0 = \mathcal{B} \int \delta_0$ be the topological space of a causal model associated with a cPROP category $\mathcal{C}_0$ defined over an associated category of elements defined by a set-valued functor $\delta_0 : \mathcal{C} \rightarrow$ **Set** over a dataset of "placebo" variables. A causally non-isomorphic effect exists between cPROP categories $\mathcal{C}_1$ and $\mathcal{C}_0$ or $\mathcal{C}_1 \not\cong \mathcal{C}_0$ if and only if there is no invertible morphism $f : \mathcal{B} \int \delta_1 \rightarrow \mathcal{B}\delta_0$ between the "treatment" and "no-treatment" homotopy colimit topological spaces, namely, $f$ must be both left invertible and right invertible.*

## 9. Classifying Spaces of Bayesian Networks

In this section, we will drill down from the abstractions above to prove a set of more concrete results regarding the classifying spaces of cPROP functors that correspond to Bayesian networks [40] and that can be seen as analogous to CDU functors in affine CD categories [9]. In this section, we will restrict our attention to the cPROP category $c\underline{P}$ defined by the coalgebraic PROP $\underline{P}$ defined by the PROP maps $\delta : 1 \rightarrow 2$ and $\epsilon : 1 \rightarrow 0$, as discussed earlier in Section 4. We will also build on the results of the previous sections to state a categorical generalization of the Meek–Chickering (MC) theorem for cPROP categories [3,12]. This theorem, originally stated as a conjecture in Meek's dissertation [12], was formally proved by Chickering [3]. The MC theorem states that, given any two causal DAG models $\mathcal{G}$ and $\mathcal{H}$, $\mathcal{H}$ is an *independence map* of $\mathcal{G}$ that is any conditional independence implied by the structure of $\mathcal{H}$ that is also implied by the structure of $\mathcal{G}$. Furthermore, there exists a finite sequence of edge additions and *covered* edge reversals such that after each edge change, $\mathcal{G}$ remains a DAG, $\mathcal{H}$ remains an independence map of $\mathcal{G}$, and, finally, $\mathcal{G} = \mathcal{H}$ after the sequence is completed.

To begin with, we build on the characterization of a causal DAGs $\mathcal{G}$, or Bayesian networks [2,40], as functors from the cPROP (or equivalently CDU) category $\mathbf{Syn}_G$ to **FinStoch** (see [9] for more details). It is assumed that the reader is familiar with the terminology of DAG models in this section, and the reader is referred to [3] for additional details that have been omitted in the interests of space. A brief overview of the Markov category **FinStoch** is given (which was called **Stoch** in [9]), whose objects are finite sets and morphisms $f : A \rightarrow B$. States are stochastic matrices from a trivial input $I := \{*\}$, which are essentially column vectors representing marginal distributions. The counit is a stochastic matrix with a row vector consisting only of 1's. The composition of morphisms is defined by matrix multiplication. The monoidal product $\otimes$ in **FinStoch** is the Cartesian product on the objects and Kronecker product of matrices $(f \otimes g)^{(k,l)}_{(i,j)} := f^k_i g^l_j$. The Kronecker product corresponds to taking product distributions. **FinStoch** realizes the "swap" operation defined by the string diagram in Definition 11 as $\sigma : A \otimes B \rightarrow B \otimes A$ given by $\sigma^{kl}_{ij} := \delta^l_i \delta^k_j$, making it into a symmetric monoidal category. Figure 12 gives an example of such a functorial representation of Bayesian networks from the pancreatic cancer domain described in Section 2. The probability values shown in the figure are estimated frequencies from actual data in [38].

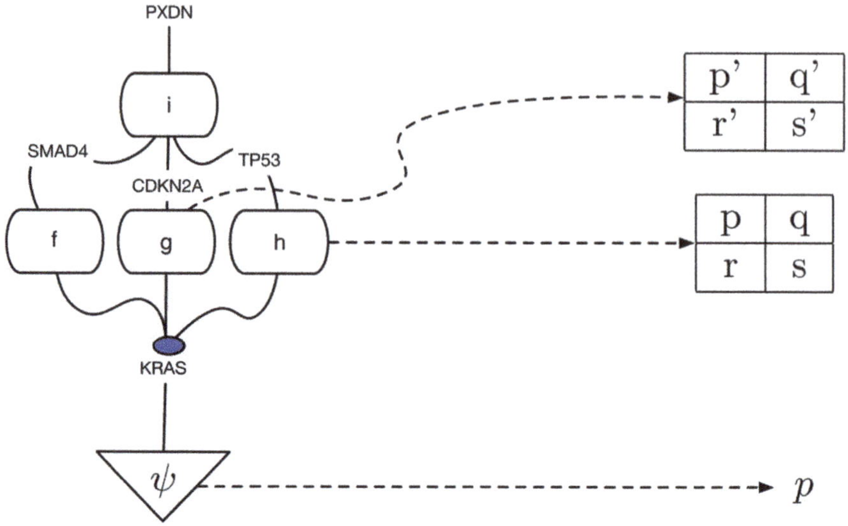


**Figure 12.** Example showing a cPROP functor modeling a causal model from the pancreatic cancer domain. The domain category is a string diagram represented as a Markov category [17]. The codomain category is **FinStoch**, the category of finite stochastic processes. The dashed arrows show how each morphism in the domain category is mapped to a corresponding conditional probability table, in the usual manner for Bayesian network models (each $(i, j)$ entry defines the conditional probability of whether a gene has mutated or not, depending on the mutation status of the gene that precedes it in the partial ordering). Not all object or morphism mappings are shown: to fully specific a functor, each object and morphism in the domain category must be mapped into a suitable object and morphism in the codomain category.

**Theorem 11** (Proposition 3.1, [9]). *There is a 1–1 correspondence between Bayesian networks based on a DAG $\mathcal{G}$ and cPROP functors of the type $F : \mathbf{Syn}_{\mathcal{G}} \rightarrow \mathbf{FinStoch}$.*

This theorem is essentially the same as that in [9], since functors between the CDU categories $\mathbf{Syn}_{\mathcal{G}}$ and **FinStoch** are special types of functors between cPROP categories. We can model the category of all Bayesian networks as a functor category $\mathbf{FinStoch}^{\mathrm{Syn}_{\mathcal{G}}}$ on cPROP categories. In this section, we will explore the homotopic structure of this functor category, whose objects are Bayesian networks represented as functors and whose arrows are natural transformations.

Let us now build on the homotopic structures defined earlier in Section 8 in terms of viewing each cPROP category $\mathcal{C}$ in terms of its classifying space $\mathcal{BC}$. The following theorem is straightforward to prove.

**Theorem 12.** *Each Bayesian network encoded as a cPROP functor $F : \mathbf{Syn}_{G} \rightarrow \mathbf{FinStoch}$ induces a continuous and cellular map of CW complexes (i.e., compactly generated spaces with a weak Hausdorff topology [55]).*

$$\mathcal{BF} : \mathcal{B}\mathbf{Syn}_{G} \rightarrow \mathcal{B}\mathbf{FinStoch}$$

**Proof.** Recall that $\mathcal{B}$ is a functor from the category `Cat` to the category Top of topological spaces defined as the classifying space of a category, which is constructed by forming the simplicial set using the nerve of the category (where each $n$-simplex represents composable morphisms in a category of length $n$) and using its topological realization as defined by Milnor [30]. □

We can define an equivalence structure on cPROP functors representing DAG models, generalizing the classical definitions in Pearl [2] and using Theorem 11 above.

**Theorem 13.** *Two cPROP functors* $F_1 : \mathbf{Syn}_{\mathcal{G}_1} \rightarrow \mathbf{FinStoch}$ *and* $F_2 : \mathbf{Syn}_{\mathcal{G}_2} \rightarrow \mathbf{FinStoch}$ *are* **equivalent** *and denoted as* $F_1 \approx F_2$*, where we use the same symbol* $\approx$ *used in [3] for DAG equivalence if they are constructed from DAG models* $\mathcal{G}_1$ *and* $\mathcal{G}_2$*, respectively, that have the same skeletons and the same V-structures.*

**Proof.** Two DAGs are known to be equivalent, meaning they are *distributionally equivalent* and *independence equivalent* if their *skeletons*, namely, the underlying undirected graph ignoring edge orientations, are isomorphic and have the same *V-structures*, meaning an ordered triple of nodes $(X, Y, Z)$ where $\mathcal{G}$ contains the edges $X \rightarrow Y$ and $Z \rightarrow Y$, and $X$ and $Z$ are not adjacent in $\mathcal{G}$. Given that Theorem 11 gives us a 1–1 correspondence between the DAG models and cPROP functors, the theorem follows straightforwardly. □

### 9.1. Natural Transformations Between Causal Models

I now introduce another significant concept from category theory—*natural transformations*—and use it to define the relationships between two causal models, such as Bayesian networks. In a range of situations in causal inference, from representing the effect of an intervention [2,9] to searching the space of DAG models in the GES algorithm [3], it is necessary to relate two causal models with each other. In the previous section, it has been shown how each causal model, such as a Bayesian network, can be viewed as a functor from a "syntactic" category to a "semantic" category. Here, the section will introduce how natural transformations between two functors capture the relationships between two Bayesian networks or other causal models.

**Definition 34.** *Given any two functors* $F : C \rightarrow D$ *and* $G : C \rightarrow D$ *between the same pair of categories, a natural transformation from* $F$ *to* $G$ *is defined through a collection of mappings: one for each object* $c$ *of* $C$*, thereby defining a morphism in* $D$ *for each object in* $C$*. They are defined as follows:*

- *An arrow* $\alpha_c : Fc \rightarrow Gc$ *in* $D$ *for each object* $c \in C$*, which together define the components of the natural transformation.*
- *For each morphism* $f : c \rightarrow c'$*, the following commutative diagram holds true:*

$$
\begin{array}{ccc}
Fc & \xrightarrow{\alpha_c} & Gc \\
{\scriptstyle Ff}\downarrow & & \downarrow{\scriptstyle Gf} \\
Fc' & \xrightarrow[\alpha_{c'}]{} & Gc'
\end{array}
$$

*A natural isomorphism is a natural transformation* $\alpha : F \Rightarrow G$ *in which every component* $\alpha_c$ *is an isomorphism.*

To concretize this abstract notion of a natural transformation, let us define as the functor $F$ the causal model shown in Figure 12, and let the functor $G$ be defined by the causal model in Figure 13, which deletes the morphism from **KRAS** to **SMAD4**. In terms of the natural transformation, note that each path in the above commutative diagram defines a morphism in the codomain "semantic" category. For the specific deleted morphism $f$, note that $Ff$ will continue to denote the original mapping from **KRAS** to **SMAD4**, but $Gf$ will now be mapped into the empty mapping, as there is now no causal pathway in the intervened model.

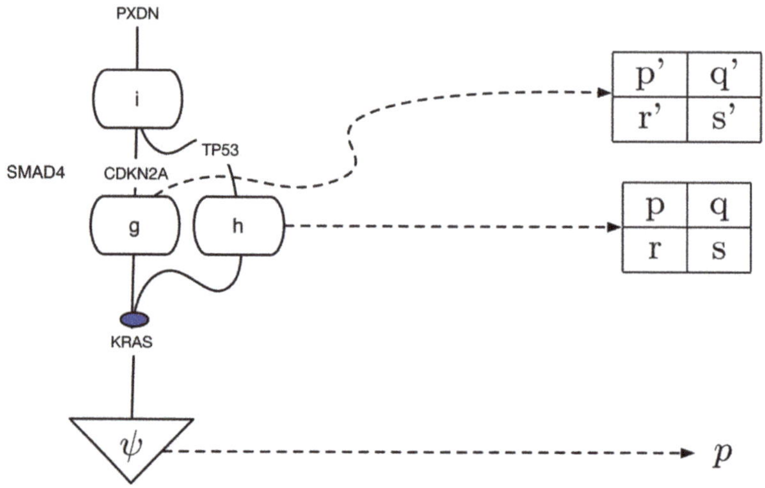


**Figure 13.** The functor $G$ that defines a causal model resulting from modifying the original functor $F$ in Figure 12 by an intervention that deletes the influence of the gene **SMAD4** on the mutation of gene **PXDN**.

To generalize from the example just given, if we want to define the set of all possible natural transformations between two causal models represented as functors, we can use an elegant framework introduced by Yoneda called (co)end calculus [16]. Specifically, we can characterize the interaction between two Bayesian networks represented as cPROP functors through Yoneda's (co)end calculus, where for simplicity we use the same cPROP category $\mathbf{Syn}_\mathcal{G}$ to denote that these DAGs have the same skeleton and V-structures.

**Theorem 14.** *Given two cPROP functors $F_1 : \mathbf{Syn}_G \to \mathbf{FinStoch}$ and $F_2 : \mathbf{Syn}_G \to \mathbf{FinStoch}$ representing two DAG models, the set of natural transformations between them can be defined as an end*

$$\mathbf{FinStoch}^{Syn_G}(F_1, F_2) = \int_c \mathbf{FinStoch}(F_1(c), F_2(c))$$

**Proof.** The proof of this result follows readily from the standard result that the set of natural transformations between two functors is an end (see page 223 in [16]). □

We can this use this result to construct a homotopic structure on the topological space of all continuous and cellular maps of CW complexes defined in Theorem 12 above.

**Theorem 15.** *The topological space of all continuous and cellular maps of CW complexes, where each map is defined as*

$$\mathcal{BF} : \mathcal{B}\mathbf{Syn}_\mathcal{G} \to \mathcal{B}\mathbf{FinStoch}$$

*is decomposed into equivalence classes by the equivalence relation $\approx$ defined in Theorem 13.*

**Proof.** The equivalence relation $\approx$ on cPROP functors is reflexive, symmetric, and transitive, because as Theorem 11 showed, there is a 1–1 correspondence between causal DAG models and cPROP functors. Each equivalence class of DAG models maps precisely into an equivalence class of cPROP functors. □

**Theorem 16.** *We can now bring to bear some properties of the classifying space developed by Segal [28] to construct a homotopy on cPROP categories and functors:*

- *For any two cPROP functors $F_1 : \mathbf{Syn}_{\mathcal{G}} \to \mathbf{FinStoch}$ and $F_2 : \mathbf{Syn}_{\mathcal{G}} \to \mathbf{FinStoch}$, a natural transformation $\tau : F_1 \Rightarrow F_2$ induces a homotopy between $\mathcal{B}F_1$ and $\mathcal{B}F_2$.*
- *If $F : \mathbf{Syn}_{\mathcal{G}} \to \mathbf{FinStoch}_{\mathcal{G}}$ and $G : \mathbf{FinStoch}_{\mathcal{G}} \to \mathbf{Syn}_{\mathcal{G}}$ is an adjoint pair of functors, then $\mathcal{B}\mathbf{FinStoch}_{G}$ is homotopy equivalent to $\mathcal{B}\mathbf{Syn}_{G}$ (here, $\mathbf{FinStoch}_{\mathcal{G}}$ is a subcategory of $\mathbf{FinStoch}$ that is defined by the mapping of each object and morphism in $\mathbf{Syn}_{\mathcal{G}}$).*

**Proof.**

- We can think of the natural transformation $\tau$ as a functor $T_{\mathcal{G}}$ from $\mathbf{Syn}_{\mathcal{G}} \times [1]$ to $\mathbf{FinStoch}_{\mathcal{G}}$. We define the action of $T_{\mathcal{G}}$ on objects as $T_{\mathcal{G}}(C,0) = F_1(C)$ and $T_{\mathcal{G}}(C,1) = F_2(C)$. On morphisms $f \in \mathbf{Syn}_{\mathcal{G}}(C_1, C_2)$, we can set $T_{\mathcal{G}}(f, 1_0) = F_1(f)$ and $T_{\mathcal{G}(}f, 1_1) = F_2(f)$. For the only non-trivial morphism $0 < 1$ in $[1]$, we define $T_{\mathcal{G}}(1_C, 0 < 1) = \tau_C$. The composite structure

$$\mathcal{B}\mathbf{Syn}_{\mathcal{G}} \times [0,1] \equiv \mathcal{B}(\mathbf{Syn}_{\mathcal{G}} \times [1]) \xrightarrow{\mathcal{B}(T_{\mathcal{G}})} \mathcal{B}\mathbf{Stoch}_{\mathcal{G}}$$

  yields the desired homotopy.
- Given any adjoint pair of functors $F : \mathbf{Syn}_{\mathcal{G}} \to \mathbf{FinStoch}_{\mathcal{G}}$ and $G : \mathbf{FinStoch}_{\mathcal{G}} \to \mathbf{Syn}_{\mathcal{G}}$, we can define the induced natural transformations $\eta : \mathrm{Id} \Rightarrow GF$ and $\epsilon : FG \Rightarrow \mathrm{Id}$. From the just established results on the natural transformation $\tau$, the desired homotopy follows.

□

*9.2. Generalizing the Meek–Chickering Theorem to cPROP Categories*

Since cPROP functors are in 1–1 correspondence with DAG models from Theorem 11, we can associate with any covered edge in a DAG model $\mathcal{G}$ an equivalent covered morphism in the Markov category $\mathbf{Syn}_{\mathcal{G}}$ associated with the DAG model $\mathcal{G}$.

**Theorem 17.** *Let $\mathcal{G}$ be any DAG model, with associated cPROP functor $F_{\mathcal{G}}$, let $\mathcal{G}'$ be the result of reversing the edge $X \to Y$, and let $F_{\mathcal{G}'} : \mathbf{Syn}_{\mathcal{G}'} \to \mathbf{Stoch}_{\mathcal{G}'}$ be the corresponding modified cPROP functor. Then, there is an induced natural transformation corresponding to reversing an edge and $F_{\mathcal{G}} \approx F_{\mathcal{G}'}$ using the definition of cPROP functor equivalence in Theorem 13 if and only if the edge $X \to Y$ is a covered edge in $\mathcal{G}$.*

**Proof.** The proof of this theorem follows readily from Lemma 2 in [3], showing that $\mathcal{G}'$ is a DAG model that is equivalent to $\mathcal{G}$ if and only if the edge that is reversed, namely, $X \to Y$ is covered in $\mathcal{G}$. □

**Theorem 18** ([3]). *Let $F_{\mathcal{G}}$ and $F_{\mathcal{G}'}$ be a pair of equivalent cPROP functors corresponding to two equivalent DAG models $\mathcal{G}$ and $\mathcal{G}'$, for which there $\delta$ edges in $\mathcal{G}$ that have the opposite orientation in $\mathcal{G}'$. Then, there exists a sequence of $\delta$ corresponding natural transformations transforming the functor $F_{\mathcal{G}}$ into the functor $F_{\mathcal{G}'}$, where natural transformation can be implemented by constructing the cPROP functor for each intervening DAG model that is based on reversing a single additional edge, satisfying the following properties:*

- *Each natural transformation in $F_{\mathcal{G}}$ must correspond to a covered edge in $\mathcal{G}$.*
- *After each natural transformation, the functors $F_{\mathcal{G}} \approx F_{\mathcal{G}'}$.*
- *After all natural transformations are composed, the two functors $F_{G} \approx F_{G'}$.*

**Proof.** Once again, the proof follows readily from the equivalent Theorem 3 in [3] exploiting the isomorphism between causal DAG models and cPROP functors from Theorem 11. □

To state the homotopic generalization of the Meek–Chickering theorem for functors between cPROP categories, we need to define the partial ordering on cPROP functors.

**Definition 35.** *Define the partial ordering* $\mathbf{Syn}_{\mathcal{G}} \leq \mathbf{Syn}_{\mathcal{H}}$ *to indicate that the corresponding causal DAG* $\mathcal{H}$ *is an independence map of* $\mathcal{G}$*. Here,* $\leq$ *implies that if* $\mathcal{G} \leq \mathcal{H}$*, then by necessity* $\mathcal{H}$ *contains more edges than* $\mathcal{G}$*.*

Once again, it follows from the 1–1 correspondence between Bayesian networks and cPROP functors that the corresponding cPROP category $\mathbf{Syn}_{\mathcal{H}}$ must contain more morphisms than $\mathbf{Syn}_{\mathcal{G}}$. We can now state the generalized Meek–Chickering theorem for functors between cPROP categories.

**Theorem 19.** *Let* $\mathbf{Syn}_{\mathcal{G}}$ *and* $\mathbf{Syn}_{\mathcal{H}}$ *be cPROP categories corresponding to any pair of DAGs* $\mathcal{G}$ *and* $\mathcal{H}$ *such that* $\mathcal{G} \leq \mathcal{H}$*. Let* $r$ *be the number of edges in* $\mathcal{H}$ *that have the opposite orientation in* $\mathcal{G}$*, and let* $m$ *be the number of edges in* $\mathcal{H}$ *that do not exist in either orientation in* $\mathcal{G}$*. These edges translate correspondingly to the differences in morphisms in* $\mathbf{Syn}_{\mathcal{G}}$ *and* $\mathbf{Syn}_{\mathcal{H}}$*. Then, there exists a sequence of at most* $r + 2m$ *natural transformations that map the cPROP functor* $F_{\mathcal{G}}$ *into the cPROP functor* $F_{\mathcal{H}}$ *satisfying the following properties:*

- *Each edge reversal and corresponding natural transformation corresponds to a covered edge.*
- *After each natural transformation corresponding to an edge reversal and edge addition,* $\mathbf{Syn}_{\mathcal{G}} \leq \mathbf{Syn}_{\mathcal{H}}$*.*
- *After all* $r + 2m$ *natural transformations are composed,* $Syn_{\mathcal{G}} \approx Syn_{\mathcal{H}}$ *is a natural isomorphism.*

**Proof.** The proof generalizes in a straightforward way from Theorem 4 in [3], since we are exploiting the 1–1 correspondences between causal DAG models and cPROP functors. The proof of this theorem in [3] is constructive, since it involves an algorithm, and it would take more space than we have to sketch out the entire process of categorifying it. But, each step in the Algorithm `APPLY-EDGE-ORIENTATION` in [3] can be equivalently implemented for cPROP categories using the correspondences between causal DAGs and cPROP functors. □

*9.3. Homotopy Groups of Meek–Chickering Causal Equivalences*

We can now define the equivalence classes under the Meek–Chickering formulation in a more abstract manner using abstract homotopy. First, we define the notion of an equivalence class of objects in any category $\mathcal{C}$ simply as that defined by the connectedness relation defined by the morphisms. Two objects $C$ and $C'$ are in the same equivalence class $\mathcal{E}$ in a category $\mathcal{C}$ if the following structure holds true:

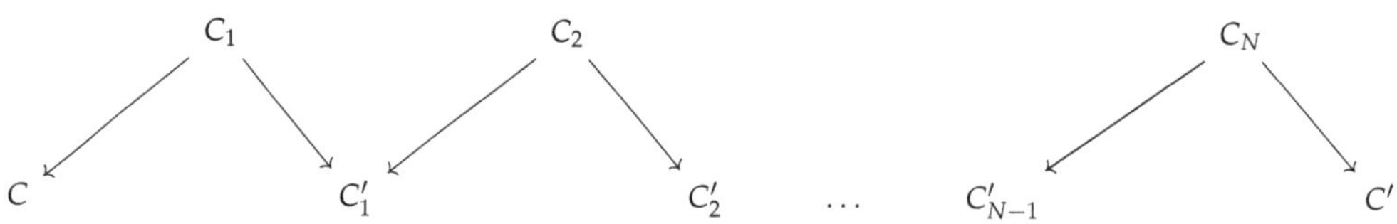


**Definition 36.** *Define the set of path components of a category* $\mathcal{C}$ *as the set of equivalence classes of the morphism relation on the objects by* $\pi_0\mathcal{C}$*.*

**Theorem 20** ([29])**.** *The set of path components of the topological space* $B\mathcal{C}$*, namely,* $\pi_0 B\mathcal{C}$*, is in bijection with the set of path components of* $\mathcal{C}$*.*

This relationship between the original category $\mathcal{C}$ and its topological realization $\mathcal{BC}$ now gives us a homotopic characterization of the GES algorithm described in Section 3. More formally, the GES proceeds by moving from one equivalence class of causal models to the next by addition or removal of (non-covered) edges. These steps can be characterized in terms of the natural transformations between equivalence classes of the cPROP (or CDU [9]) functors that define the causal DAGs. We treat the equivalence class of DAGs within each connected component as a locally connected topological space. Thus, the set $\pi_0\mathcal{C}$ is exactly the number of equivalence classes, which is again the same as the number of connected components in $\pi_0\mathcal{BC}$, defining the $0^{th}$ homotopy group in the topological realization of the category $\mathcal{C}$.

**Theorem 21.** *The GES procedure can be formally characterized topologically as moving from one equivalence class of connected topological spaces in $\mathcal{BC}$ to another, where an equivalence class of connected objects in $\mathcal{BC}$ is defined by the connectedness relation of natural transformations that correspond to reversals of covered edges within an equivalence class.*

**Proof.** The proof of this theorem follows directly from Theorems 2 and 20 and its homotopic version stated as Theorem 19. □

To summarize the results of this section, it has been described how to construct the classifying spaces corresponding to Bayesian network causal models, which lets us construct a homotopic equivalence across causal models represented as functors on cPROP categories. Categorical generalizations of the definitions in [3] have been introduced, and the categorical generalization of the Meek–Chickering theorem for Markov categories has been stated.

## 10. Classifying Spaces of cPROP Categories

We now return to a more abstract discussion of the classifying spaces $\mathcal{BC}$ of a general cPROP category $\mathcal{C}$. As a cPROP category, $\mathcal{C}$ is a symmetric monoidal category, and there is a wealth of known results that can be brought to bear on its homotopic structure; a full discussion of this topic is beyond the scope of this introductory paper. I want to give the reader a taste of the many approaches that can be brought to bear on the structure of equivalence classes in causal models. First, I want to discuss the connection between the multiplicative structure of symmetric monoidal categories, like Markov categories, and the commutative $H$-space structure on $\mathcal{BC}$, which is its classifying space.

**Definition 37** ([29]). *An H-space is a topological space X with a chosen base point $x_0$ (which in cPROP categories can be associated with the topological realization of the terminal object) and a continuous map $\mu : X \times X \to X$ such that the maps $\mu(x_0, .)$ and $\mu(., x_0)$ are homotopic to the identity map on X with respect to homotopies that preserve the basepoint $x_0$. An H-space is associative if $\mu$ is associative up to homotopy, and it is commutative if $\mu$ is commutative up to homotopy.*

**Definition 38** ([29]). *An H-space X is group-like if there is a continuous map $\chi : X \to X$ such that $\mu \circ (1_{id} \times \chi) \circ \Delta$ is homotopic to the identity, where $\Delta$ is the the diagonal map on X.*

It is worth mentioning that the comonoidal structure of a cPROP category $\mathcal{C}$ induces a diagonal map $\Delta : \mathcal{BC} \to \mathcal{BC} \times \mathcal{BC}$ on its topological realization through the nerve through the (uniform) copy map $\text{copy}_X : X \to X \otimes X$.

**Theorem 22.** *Let $\mathcal{C}$ be a cPROP category. Then, its classifying space $\mathcal{BC}$ is an associative and commutative H-space.*

**Proof.** The proof of this theorem is based on a simple diagram chase, building on the standard result for (small) symmetric monoidal categories.

$$\begin{array}{ccc} \mathcal{B}\mathcal{C} \times \mathcal{B}\mathcal{C} & \xrightarrow{\cong} & \mathcal{B}(C \times C) \\ & \searrow^{\mu} & \downarrow{\scriptstyle \mathcal{B}(\otimes)} \\ & & \mathcal{B}\mathcal{C} \end{array}$$

The complete proof can be seen in [29] (Theorem 13.1.4). □

**Theorem 23.** *The classifying space $\mathcal{B}\mathcal{C}$ of a small cPROP category $\mathcal{C}$ is contractible.*

**Proof.** This result follows from the fact that the tensor unit element $I$ in a cPROP category is a terminal element, implying that there is a unique morphism $\text{del}_X : X \to I$, as discussed previously. Using the result from Theorem 16, we exploit the fact that there is an adjoint pair of functors from $\mathcal{C}$ to $[0]$ and the topological realization $\mathcal{B}[0]$ is a point. □

We can define the higher homotopy groups of a cPROP category C as follows.

**Definition 39.** *Given a cPROP category $\mathcal{C}$ and an arbitrary object $X$ in $\mathcal{C}$, for $n \geq 0$, the $n^{th}$ homotopy group of $\mathcal{C}$ with respect to the basepoint $X$ is defined as*

$$\pi_n(X, \mathcal{C}) = \pi_n(\mathcal{B}\mathcal{C}, [X])$$

*where $[X]$ is the 0-simplex associated with the basepoint $X$.*

## 11. A Higher Algebraic K-Theory of cPROP Categories

Finally, we build on the above results to give a formal higher algebraic K-theory of causal inference in terms of the causal equivalence classes. To make the construction concrete, we begin with the notion of Grothendieck group completion defined by the Grayson–Quillen construction. Here, the intuition is to begin with an Abelian monoid and make it into a universal group by adding "inverse" elements to each monoid element. The result is a characterization of the K-theory structure.

### 11.1. Grayson-Quillen Group Completion

The basic idea for a "K-theory" arose from the notion of a Grothendieck "K" group that came out from his proof of the Riemann–Roch theorem, which involved the analysis of isomorphism classes of objects of an Abelian category with a tensor product (direct sum). This specific construction was later generalized in the following way. Consider a commutative monoid $M$ for which the most general Abelian group $K$ needs to be constructed by building "inverse" elements to all the elements of $M$. Such a "group completion" always exists and is characterized by a universal property

$$i : M \to K,$$

where $i$ is a monoid homomorphism mapping $M$ to the group $K$ that satisfies the universal property that for any other monoid homomorphism

$$f : M \to A,$$

there is a unique group homomorphism

$$g : K \to A$$

such that $f = g \circ i$. To show the relevance of this construction to causal inference, we briefly outline the Grayson–Quillen K-theory for symmetric monoidal categories Grayson [56] that we can use to associate with any cPROP category $\mathcal{C}$ an augmented category $\mathcal{C}^{-1}\mathcal{C}$ using a particular group completion method.

**Definition 40.** *Let $(\mathcal{C}, \otimes, e, \tau)$ be a small symmetric monoidal category. Denote by $\mathcal{C}^{-1}\mathcal{C}$ the category whose objects are pairs of objects of $\mathcal{C}$. Morphisms in $\mathcal{C}^{-1}\mathcal{C}$ from $(C_1, D_1)$ to $(C_2, D_2)$ are equivalence classes of pairs of morphisms*

$$(f : C_1 \otimes E \to C_2, g : D_1 \otimes E \to D_2)$$

*where E is an object of C. Such pairs of morphisms are equivalent to*

$$(f' : C_1' \otimes E' \to C_2, g' : D_1 \otimes E' \to D_2)$$

*if there is an isomorphism $h \in \mathcal{C}(E, E')$ such that the following diagram commutes:*

$$\begin{array}{ccc} (C_1 \otimes E, D_1 \otimes E) & \xrightarrow{(1_{C_1} \otimes h, 1_{D_1} \times h)} & (C_1 \otimes E', D_1 \otimes E') \\ & {\scriptstyle (f,g)} \searrow \quad \swarrow {\scriptstyle (f',g')} & \\ & (C_2, D_2) & \end{array}$$

*The category $\mathcal{C}^{-1}\mathcal{C}$ is called the Grayson–Quillen construction of C.*

Note that this construction depends on the choice of object $E$. If $E$ is selected to be the unit element $I$ of a cPROP (or Markov category), then every pair of morphisms in $\mathcal{C}$ gives rise to a morphism in $\mathcal{C}^{-1}\mathcal{C}$.

**Theorem 24** ([29], Lemma 13.3.2). *The category $\mathcal{C}^{-1}\mathcal{C}$ is symmetric monoidal as well, and there is a lax monoidal functor $j : \mathcal{C} \to \mathcal{C}^{-1}\mathcal{C}$, and $\pi_0(\mathcal{B}\mathcal{C}^{-1}\mathcal{C})$ is an Abelian group.*

**Definition 41.** *The K-Theory space associated with a cPROP category $\mathcal{C}$ is the classifying space $\mathcal{K}\mathcal{C} = \mathcal{B}\mathcal{C}^{-1}\mathcal{C}$, where the $n^{th}$ K-group of $\mathcal{C}$ is its $n^{th}$ homotopy group $\pi_n \mathcal{B}\mathcal{C}^{-1}\mathcal{C}$. Specifically, the fundamental group $\pi_0(\mathcal{B}\mathcal{C}^{-1}\mathcal{C})$ is the Grothendieck group completion of the Abelian monoid induced by the path components $\pi_0(\mathcal{C})$.*

Let us now connect this procedure with the $0^{th}$ homotopy group of the Meek–Chickering equivalence class.

**Theorem 25.** *Let the cPROP category $\mathcal{C}$ correspond to causal DAG models, that is, each object is a functor representing a Bayesian network, and the arrows are natural transformations representing the corresponding covered edge reversals within a class. These connected components represent Meek–Chickering equivalence classes. Then,*

$$K_0(\mathcal{C}) = \pi_0(\mathcal{K}\mathcal{C}) =\simeq G_0(\pi_0(\mathcal{C}))$$

**Proof.** This theorem states that the $0^{th}$ order homotopy group corresponding to the Meek–Chickering equivalence classes is isomorphic to the Grothendieck group completion of the Abelian monoid $\pi_0(\mathcal{C})$. The proof follows readily from the more general result that holds in any symmetric monoidal category (see Lema 13.3.4 in [29]). □

*11.2. cPROP Groupoids and Their Classifying Spaces*

A groupoid is a category whose every morphism is invertible. We can characterize the Meek–Chickering causal equivalences in terms of the classifying spaces of their induced groupoids.

**Definition 42.** *Define the Moore–Chickering groupoid as the cPROP category $\mathcal{G}_{MC}$ whose objects are defined as the equivalence classes defined by the Moore–Chickering theorem and whose invertible morphisms correspond to covered edge reversals that map from an object back to itself.*

We can now give a simple characterization of the Moore–Chickering equivalence classes in terms of the classifying space of their induced groupoids.

**Theorem 26.** *The classifying space of the Moore–Chickering groupoid category $\mathcal{BG}_{MC}$ is defined as*

$$\mathcal{BG}_{MC} = \bigsqcup_i \mathcal{BG}^i_{MC}$$

*where the disjoint sum index i ranges over equivalence classes.*

## 12. Causal Inference in Open Games and Network Economics

This section will briefly describe more advanced applications of the causal framework to open games [36], using a categorical compositional model that extends traditional Nash non-cooperative game theory [57], as well as network economics [37]. Both open games and network economics can be modeled using string diagrams in symmetric monoidal (Abelian) categories, which makes these applications amenable to analysis using the theoretical framework. A full discussion is beyond the scope of this paper, but I will provide sufficient detail here to explain how these applications can be modeled. Game theory has been used for many decades to model interactions among economic players. Billions of dollars of products, such as auctions of radio frequency bands by governments worldwide, have been sold using the principles of game theory. However, traditional game theory is non-compositional: a simple Prisoners Dilemma game between two players cannot be combined with another instance of such a game to create a larger game. In fact, it is not obvious that such a compositional approach is even possible.

A remarkable outcome of applying category theory to game theory is the compositional framework of *open games* [36]. The basic idea underlying compositional game theory is to model a game as a symmetric monoidal category. This formulation requires one crucial idea called *lenses* that has been previously used in categorical models of databases and deep learning [58]. Essentially, in addition to modeling each player's move, as in traditional game theory, compositional game theory also adds the novel idea of a *coplay*, which is an extra mechanism that is used to transmit information backwards from one game theory module to its antecedent game module.

Network economics [37] has been extensively used to model games involving the trade of some electronic, monetary, or physical goods across a network. The underlying mathematics used to solve network economics games uses variational inequalities (VIs) [59]. We will briefly examine how to model a network economy as an open game and then describe how our cPROP causal framework applies to model causal interventions in network economics. An earlier paper of mine [60] explored causal inference in variational inequalities, without using the symmetric monoidal categorical framework described in this paper. Here, I introduce briefly the idea of a categorical framework for network economies.

### 12.1. Open Games

Ghani et al. [36] introduced the definition of an open game:

**Definition 43.** *Let $X$, $S$, $Y$, and $R$ denote sets of a game $\mathcal{G}$. An open game $\mathcal{G} : (X,S) \to (Y,R)$ is defined as a 4-tuple $\mathcal{G} : (\Sigma_{\mathcal{G}}, \mathbf{P}_{\mathcal{G}}, \mathbf{C}_{\mathcal{G}}, \mathbf{B}_{\mathcal{G}})$ such that the following are determined:*

- *$\Sigma_{\mathcal{G}}$ is the set of strategy profiles of $\mathcal{G}$.*
- *$\mathbf{P}_{\mathcal{G}} : \Sigma_{\mathcal{G}} \times X \to Y$ is the play function of game $\mathcal{G}$.*
- *$\mathbf{C}_{\mathcal{G}} : \Sigma_{\mathcal{G}} \times X \times R \to S$ is called the coplay function of $\mathcal{G}$.*
- *$\mathbf{B}_{\mathcal{G}} : X(Y \to R) \to Rel(\Sigma_{\mathcal{G}})$ is defined as the best response function of $\mathcal{G}$, where $Rel(\Sigma_{\mathcal{G}})$ is a meet-semilattice of all endo-relations $R \subseteq \Sigma_{\mathcal{G}} \times \Sigma_{\mathcal{G}}$.*

What is crucial about this definition is that it is composable, meaning that we can form the sequential and parallel composition of open games to form larger open games, which is a crucial advantage that is not possible in traditional Nash games. I relegate the details to [36] but give the basic gist of the idea here before proceeding to outline how it can be used to define network economies as a symmetric monoidal category.

**Definition 44.** *Given a pair of open games $\mathcal{G} : (X,S) \to (Y,R)$ and $\mathcal{H} : (Y,R) \to (Z,Q)$, the sequential composition $\mathcal{H} \circ \mathcal{G} : (X,S) \to (Z,Q)$ is defined as follows:*

- *The set of strategy profiles is the Cartesian product $\Sigma_{\mathcal{H}\circ\mathcal{G}} = \Sigma_{\mathcal{G}} \times \Sigma_{\mathcal{H}}$.*
- *The play function for the composite game $\mathcal{H} \circ \mathcal{H}$ is simply the composition of the individual play functions:*
$$\mathbf{P}_{\mathcal{H}\circ\mathcal{G}}((\sigma,\tau),x) = \mathbf{P}_{\mathcal{H}}(\tau, \mathbf{P}_{\mathcal{G}}(\sigma,x))$$
- *The coplay function for the composite game is defined as*
$$\mathbf{C}_{\mathcal{H}\circ\mathcal{G}}((\sigma,\tau),x,q) = \mathbf{C}_{\mathcal{G}}(\sigma,x,\mathbf{C}_{\mathcal{H}}(\tau,\mathbf{P}_{\mathcal{G}}(\sigma,x),q))$$
- *Finally, the best response relation of the composite game is defined as $((\sigma,\tau),(\sigma',\tau')) \in \mathbf{B}_{\mathcal{H}\circ\mathcal{G}}(x,k)$ that holds iff $(\sigma,\sigma') \in \mathbf{B}_{\mathcal{G}}(x,k')$ and $(tau, tau') \in \mathbf{B}_{\mathcal{H}}(\mathbf{P}_{\mathcal{G}}(\sigma,x),k)$, where $k' : Y \to R$ is defined as*
$$k'(y) - \mathbf{C}_{\mathcal{H}}(\tau,y,k(\mathbf{P}_{\mathcal{H}}(\tau,y)))$$

One can similarly define the parallel composition of open games, wherein I will refer the reader to [36] for the requisite details. Figure 14 illustrates a string diagram representation of a symmetric monoidal category of a simultaneous move open game. The causal framework can now be applied to analyze equivalence classes in such open games, since these are now essentially string diagrams of the type we have illustrated previously in the paper. For example, a causal intervention in an open game might involve changing the payoff structure, which will involve a change in the game's Nash equilibrium. I will discuss a more complex example below involving a multistage economic game on a network. We can apply our analysis of the classifying spaces of open games under causal interventions, which is a problem for future work.

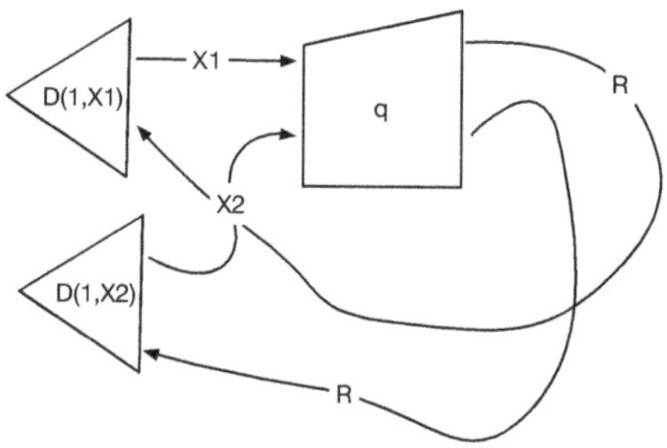


**Figure 14.** A string diagram of a symmetric monoidal category of a simultaneous move game [36].

### 12.2. Causal Inference in Variational Inequalities

I now give a brief introduction to variational inequalities (VIs) [59], which represent a mathematical framework used to solve problems in network economics [37]. VIs were originally developed in physics in the mid-1960s for modeling equilibrium problems in continuum mechanics, which generalizes= (convex) optimization, non-cooperative games, fixed point equation solving, and complementarity problems. VIs have been applied to a wide range of problems in network economics [37]. A VI is usually defined as a set of deterministic multidimensional vector field mappings $F_i : K_i \rightarrow \mathbb{R}^n$, where $K_i$ is a convex set defined over a set of exogenous non-manipulable variables $U$ and a set of endogenous modifiable variables $V$. The ensemble of vector field mappings jointly defines a global vector field mapping $F : K \rightarrow \mathbb{R}^n$. Solving a variational inequality means finding an element $x \in K$ where the set of inequalities holds:

$$\langle F(x^*), (x - x^*) \rangle \geq 0, \ \forall x \in K \tag{6}$$

where $\langle ., . \rangle$ denotes the inner product in $\mathbb{R}^n$. Variational inequalities were originally developed for infinite-dimensional Hilbert spaces. We consider only $n$-dimensional Euclidean spaces in this paper. Either setting can be modeled in terms of an enriched symmetric monoidal Abelian category [16]. To see the connection with optimization, note that if $F(x) = \nabla f(x)$, the gradient of a (convex) multidimensional function, then the above condition is precisely the requirement for $x^*$ to be the (global) minimum.

Broadly speaking, we will interpret causal intervention as inducing a submodel mapping $F_w$, which usually may be due to the manipulation of some endogenous variable $w$. However, our framework is agnostic on the particular manipulation mechanisms and extends to other possibilities, such as modifying a pricing function or a change in demand. As a simple example to build intuition, consider a network economy consisting of $m$ producers of personal protective equipment (PPE) and $n$ demand markets (see Figure 15). For trade to occur between the producer $i$ and the demand market $j$, the following equilibrium condition must be satisfied:

$$\pi_i(Q) + c_{ij}(Q) \;=\; \rho_j \text{ if } Q^*_{ij} > 0 \tag{7}$$

$$\pi_i(Q) + c_{ij}(Q) \;\geq\; \rho_j \text{ if } Q^*_{ij} = 0 \tag{8}$$

This condition asserts that trade, measured by $Q_{ij}$ between the producer $i$ and demand market $j$, will occur precisely when the supply price $\pi_i$ plus the transportation cost $c_{ij}$ is equal to the demand price $\rho_j$; otherwise, $Q^*_{ij} = 0$. Note that the supply price and transportation costs are a function of trade volume $Q$ over the whole network. We can write this equilibrium condition in the form of a variational inequality as follows:

$$(\pi_i(Q) + c_{ij}(Q) - \rho_j)(Q_{ij} - Q^*_{ij}) \geq 0$$

Note that if $Q^*_{ij} > 0$, then according to Equation (7), the first term above must equal 0. Alternatively, if $Q^*_{ij} = 0$, then the reason is that the combined cost of manufacturing $\pi_i$ and transportation $c_{ij}$ exceeds the demand price $\rho_j$; hence, the inequality is again satisfied. We can view each equilibrium condition above as a submodel $F_{ij}(Q)$, and there will be one such submodel for each producer and consumer. The number of submodels is equal to the number of trade paths, which collectively define the overall vector field mapping $F$. We can now model causal interventions in this system, such as raising or lowering prices, as inducing a modified model $F_w$, and analyze the effect of these causal interventions on the equilibrium trade between producers and suppliers. If we view the imposition of tariffs as a causal intervention, then the previous equilibrium solution of the network economy reflected in the amount of goods sold from producers to consumers and shipped via transporters will change, as recent events have shown. The causal intervention now requires recomputing a new solution to the multiplayer game represented by the network economy.

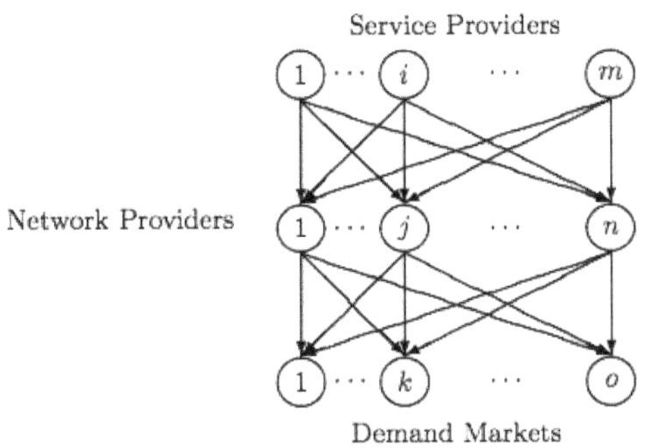


**Figure 15.** A generic network economic model based on [37]. Demand markets consisting of individual users or groups of users who choose combinations of service providers and transport providers, both of whom compete with each other for demand markets.

*12.3. Example of a Network Economy*

We will now describe a concrete example of a network economics problem. Network economics games can be considerably more complex than the single-layer games discussed in the previous section (see Figure 15) [37]. This network economics model comprises three tiers of agents: producer agents who want to sell their goods, transport agents who ship merchandise from producers, and demand market agents interested in purchasing the products or services. The model applies both to electronic goods, such as video streaming, token streaming for vendors of large language models (LLMs), and physical goods, such as smartphones or cars. This approach has also been used to model tariffs [61].

The model assumes $m$ service providers, $n$ network providers, and $o$ demand markets. Each firm's utility function is defined in terms of the non-negative service quantity (Q), quality (q), and price ($\pi$) delivered from service provider $i$ by network provider $j$ to consumer $k$. The production costs, demand functions, delivery costs, and delivery opportunity costs are designated by $f$, $\rho$, $c$, and $oc$, respectively. Service provider $i$ attempts to maximize its utility function $U^1_i(Q, q^*, \pi^*)$ by adjusting $Q_{ijk}$ (Equation (9a)). Likewise, network provider $j$ attempts to maximize its utility function $U^2_j(Q^*, q, \pi)$ by adjusting $q_{ijk}$ and $\pi_{ijk}$ (Equation (9b)).

$$U_i^1(Q, q^*, \pi^*) = \sum_{j=1}^{n} \sum_{k=1}^{o} \hat{\rho}_{ijk}(Q, q^*) Q_{ijk} - \hat{f}_i(Q) - \sum_{j=1}^{n} \sum_{k=1}^{o} \pi_{ijk}^* Q_{ijk}, \quad Q_{ijk} \geq 0 \tag{9a}$$

$$U_j^2(Q^*, q, \pi) = \sum_{i=1}^{m} \sum_{k=1}^{o} \pi_{ijk} Q_{ijk}^* - \sum_{i=1}^{m} \sum_{k=1}^{o} (c_{ijk}(Q^*, q) + oc_{ijk}(\pi_{ijk})), \quad q_{ijk}, \pi_{ijk} \geq 0 \tag{9b}$$

We assume the governing equilibrium is Cournot–Bertrand–Nash and the utility functions are all concave and fully differentiable. This establishes the equivalence between the equilibrium state we are searching for and the variational inequality to be solved, where the $F$ mapping is a vector consisting of the negative gradients of the utility functions for each firm. Since $F$ is essentially a concatenation of gradients arising from multiple independent, conflicting objective functions, it does not correspond to the gradient of any single objective function.

$$\langle F(X^*), X - X^* \rangle \geq 0, \forall X \in \mathcal{K}, \tag{10a}$$

$$\text{where} \quad X = (Q, q, \pi) \in \mathbb{R}^{3mno+}$$

$$\text{and} \quad F(X) = (F_{ijk}^1(X), F_{ijk}^2(X), F_{ijk}^3(X))$$

$$F_{ijk}^1(X) = \frac{\partial f_i(Q)}{\partial Q_{ijk}} + \pi_{ijk} - \rho_{ijk} - \sum_{h=1}^{n} \sum_{l=1}^{o} \frac{\partial \rho_{ihl}(Q, q)}{\partial Q_{ijk}} \times Q_{ihl} \tag{10b}$$

$$F_{ijk}^2(X) = \sum_{h=1}^{m} \sum_{l=1}^{o} \frac{\partial c_{hjl}(Q, q)}{\partial q_{ijk}} \tag{10c}$$

$$F_{ijk}^3(X) = -Q_{ijk} + \frac{\partial oc_{ijk}(\pi_{ijk})}{\partial \pi_{ijk}} \tag{10d}$$

The variational inequality in Equation (10a) represents the result of combining the utility functions of each firm into standard form. $F_{ijk}^1$ is derived by taking the negative gradient of $U_i^1$ with respect to $Q_{ijk}$. $F_{ijk}^2$ is derived by taking the negative gradient of $U_j^2$ with respect to $q_{ijk}$. And $F_{ijk}^3$ is derived by taking the negative gradient of $U_j^2$ with respect to $\pi_{ijk}$.

Note that a causal intervention, such as an imposition of tariffs, will require that Equation (10a) be resolved to reflect the new costs incurred in the production or shipment of goods, and that, in turn, will be reflected in the change in demand.

### 12.4. Causal Inference in Network Economics

We can apply our cPROP framework to network economics by converting the network economy in Figure 15 into an open game symmetric monoidal category with an associated string diagram, where causal inferences will now be reflected as "string diagram surgery" [9]. The new solution of the resulting VI will quantitatively measure the impact of the causal intervention. We can apply the framework of open games described above to the network economics framework as illustrated in Figure 15, where each node in the network (producer, transporter, or consumer) is viewed as a player in a network game. Each player is then modeled as shown in Figure 14, where the sequential and parallel composition of players in the network game is modeled in terms of the sequential and parallel composition in a symmetric monoidal category. To apply our higher-algebraic K-theory causal framework, we must note that there may be many equivalent string diagrams that are all causally equivalent to each other, and our theoretical results will help determine a more compact representation of this exponentially large space. A full analysis of this complex real-world domain is beyond the scope of this paper and is a topic for a future paper.

## 13. Summary and Future Work

In this paper, I analyzed the homotopic structure of observationally equivalent causal models using a categorical structure called cPROPs, which is a functor category from a coalgebraic PROP $P$ to a symmetric monoidal category $\mathcal{C}$. Such functor categories define the right adjoint of the inclusion of Cartesian categories in the larger category of all symmetric monoidal categories. cPROPs are an algebraic theory in the sense of Lawvere [20]. cPROPs relate closely to previous categorical models, such as Markov categories [17] and affine CDU categories [9,25], which can be viewed as a special type of cPROP defined by the PROP maps $\delta : 1 \to 2$ and $\epsilon : 1 \to 0$ that satisfies a set of commutative diagrams. To obtain topological insight into observationally equivalent classes of causal models, I characterized the classifying spaces of cPROPs by constructing their simplicial realization through the nerve functor. As a concrete application to causal inference, I showed that causal DAG equivalence generalizes to induce a homotopic equivalence across observationally equivalent cPROP functors. I presented a homotopic generalization of the Meek–Chickering theorem on causal equivalence in DAG models, where I viewed covered edge reversals connecting causally equivalent DAGs in terms of natural transformations between homotopically equivalent cPROPs. These results are a small sampling of the wide range of tools available in abstract homotopy theory, which I briefly describe next.

### 13.1. Operads and Iterated Loop Spaces

There is a rich set of theoretical results that connect the K-theory classifying spaces of symmetric monoidal categories and cPROP and Markov categories, with the geometry of iterated loop spaces and operads [62]. In particular, it is known that all connective spectra are based on some symmetric monoidal category and that special types of monoidal categories called permutative categories that yield Barrat–Eccles operads as their classifying spaces, which are a type of $E_\infty$ operad. A full discussion of these connections is a topic for future papers.

### 13.2. Model Categories on cPROP Categories

A standard approach to performing abstract homotopy on a category is to define its associated model structure. One way to do that implicit in our work is through its simplicial object structure. The category of simplicial sets is well known to have a rich model structure, which has been extensively studied [63]. This construction requires partitioning the space of morphisms into *fibrations*, *cofibrations*, and *weak equivalences* to construct a model category structure for causal inference [64]. I plan to devote a separate paper on this topic.

### 13.3. cPROPs for Non-Graphical Causal Models

I have restricted our attention in this paper to defining cPROPs for causal directed acyclic graph (DAG) models, as these are the most popular representation studied in previous work on categorical causality [9,10,14,23]. But, the general framework of cPROPs can be easily extended to non-graphical representations, such as integer-valued multisets (or imsets) [8]. For the specific case of a DAG model $\mathcal{G} = (V, E)$, an imset in standard form [8] is defined as

$$u_{\mathcal{G}} = \delta_V - \delta_{\emptyset} + \sum_{i \in V} (\delta_{\mathbf{Pa}_i} - \delta_{i \cup \mathbf{Pa}_i})$$

where each $\delta_V$ term is the characteristic function associated with a set of variables $V$. Finally, a separoid [65] is an algebraic framework for characterizing conditional independence as an abstract property, which is defined by a join semi-lattice equipped with a partial ordering $\leq$ and a ternary property $\perp\!\!\!\perp$ over triples of elements such that $X \perp\!\!\!\perp Y | Z$ defines the property that $X$ is conditionally independent of $Y$ given $Z$. One can define cPROPs for separoids as well.

**Funding:** This research was supported by Adobe Corporation.

**Data Availability Statement:** Data used in this article are available from cited references as noted in the paper.

**Conflicts of Interest:** Sridhar Mahadevan was employed by the company Adobe Research.

## References


1. Spirtes, P.; Glymour, C.; Scheines, R. *Causation, Prediction, and Search*, 2nd ed.; Adaptive Computation and Machine Learning MIT Press: Cambridge, MA, USA, 2000.
2. Pearl, J. *Causality: Models, Reasoning and Inference* , 2nd ed.; Cambridge University Press: New York, NY, USA, 2009.
3. Chickering, D.M. Optimal Structure Identification with Greedy Equivalence Search. *J. Mach. Learn. Res.* **2002**, *3*, 507–554.
4. Zanga, A.; Stella, F. A Survey on Causal Discovery: Theory and Practice. arXiv **2023**, arXiv:2305.10032. [CrossRef]
5. Glymour, C.; Zhang, K.; Spirtes, P. Review of Causal Discovery Methods Based on Graphical Models. *Front. Genet.* **2019**, *10* [CrossRef] [PubMed]
6. Kocaoglu, M.; Shanmugam, K.; Bareinboim, E. Experimental Design for Learning Causal Graphs with Latent Variables. In *Advances in Neural Information Processing Systems 30, Proceedings of the Annual Conference on Neural Information Processing Systems 2017, Long Beach, CA, USA, 4–9 December 2017*; Guyon, I., von Luxburg, U., Bengio, S., Wallach, H.M., Fergus, R., Vishwanathan S.V.N., Garnett, R., Eds.; Curran Associates: Red Hook, NY, USA, 2017; pp. 7018–7028.
7. Choo, D.; Shiragur, K. Subset verification and search algorithms for causal DAGs. *arXiv* **2024**, arXiv:2301.03180.
8. Studeny, M. *Probabilistic Conditional Independence Structures*; Information Science and Statistics; Springer: London, UK, 2010.
9. Jacobs, B.; Kissinger, A.; Zanasi, F. Causal Inference by String Diagram Surgery. *arXiv* **2018**. [CrossRef]
10. Fritz, T.; Klingler, A. The d-Separation Criterion in Categorical Probability. *J. Mach. Learn. Res.* **2023**, *24*, 1–49.
11. Verma, T.; Pearl, J. Equivalence and synthesis of causal models. In Proceedings of the Sixth Annual Conference on Uncertainty in Artificial Intelligence, UAI '90, New York, NY, USA, 27–29 July 1990 ; pp. 255–270.
12. Meek, C. Graphical Models: Selecting Causal and Statistical Models. Ph.D. Thesis, Carnegie Mellon University, Pittsburgh, PA USA, 1997.
13. Castelo, R.; Kocka, T. On inclusion-driven learning of bayesian networks. *J. Mach. Learn. Res.* **2003**, *4*, 527–574. [CrossRef]
14. Mahadevan, S. Universal Causality. *Entropy* **2023**, *25*, 574. [CrossRef]
15. Maclane, S. Categorical Algebra. *Bull. Amer. Math. Soc.* **1965**, *71*, 40–106. [CrossRef]
16. MacLane, S. *Categories for the Working Mathematician*; Graduate Texts in Mathematics; Springer: New York, NY, USA, 1971 Volume 5, pp. ix+262.
17. Fritz, T. A synthetic approach to Markov kernels, conditional independence and theorems on sufficient statistics. *Adv. Math* **2020**, *370*, 107239. [CrossRef]
18. Fox, J. Universal Coalgebras. Ph.D. Thesis , McGill University, Montreal, QC, Canada, 1976.
19. Jacobs, B. *Introduction to Coalgebra: Towards Mathematics of States and Observation*; Cambridge Tracts in Theoretical Computer Science, Cambridge University Press: Cambridge, UK, 2016; Volume 59. [CrossRef]
20. Lawvere, W. Functorial Semantics of Algebraic Theories. *Proc. Natl. Acad. Sci. USA* **1963**, *50*, 869–872. [CrossRef] [PubMed]
21. Baez, J.C.; Coya, B.; Rebro, F. PROPS in Network Theory. *Theory Appl. Categ.* **2018**, *33*, 727–783.
22. Fong, B.; Spivak, D.I. *Seven Sketches in Compositionality: An Invitation to Applied Category Theory*; Cambridge University Press Cambridge, UK, 2018.
23. Fong, B. Causal Theories: A Categorical Perspective on Bayesian Networks. Master's Thesis, Oxford University, Oxford UK, 2012.

Golubtsov, P.V.; Moskaliuk, S.S. Method of Additional Structures on the Objects of a Monoidal Kleisli Category as a Background for Information Transformers Theory. *arXiv* **2002**, arXiv:math-ph/0211067.

Cho, K.; Jacobs, B. Disintegration and Bayesian inversion via string diagrams. *Math. Struct. Comput. Sci.* **2019**, *29*, 938–971. [CrossRef]

Joyal, A. Quasi-categories and Kan complexes. *J. Pure Appl. Algebra* **2002**, *175*, 207–222. . [CrossRef]

Lurie, J. *Higher Topos Theory*; Annals of Mathematics Studies; Princeton University Press: Princeton, NJ, USA, 2009.

Segal, G. Classifying Spaces and Spectral Sequences. *Mathématiques L'institut Hautes Sci.* **1968**, *34*, 92–100. [CrossRef]

Richter, B. *From Categories to Homotopy Theory*; Cambridge Studies in Advanced Mathematics; Cambridge University Press: Cambridge, UK, 2020.

Milnor, J. The Geometric Realization of a Semi-Simplicial Complex. *Ann. Math.* **1957**, *65*, 357–362. [CrossRef]

Quillen, D. Higher algebraic K-theory: I. In *Higher K-Theories*; Bass, H., Ed.; Springer: Berlin/Heidelberg, Germany, 1973; pp. 85–147.

Heunen, C.; Vicary, J. *Categories for Quantum Theory: An Introduction*; Oxford University Press: Oxford, UK, 2019. [CrossRef]

Jones, S.; Zhang, X.; Parsons, D.W.; Lin, J.C.H.; Leary, R.J.; Angenendt, P.; Mankoo, P.; Carter, H.; Kamiyama, H.; Jimeno, A.; et al. Core Signaling Pathways in Human Pancreatic Cancers Revealed by Global Genomic Analyses. *Science* **2008**, *321*, 1801–1806.

Beerenwinkel, N.; Eriksson, N.; Sturmfels, B. Conjunctive Bayesian networks. *Bernoulli* **2007**, *13*, 893–909. [CrossRef]

Mahadevan, S. Causal Homotopy. *arXiv* **2021**. [CrossRef]

Ghani, N.; Hedges, J.; Winschel, V.; Zahn, P. Compositional game theory. *arXiv* **2018**, arXiv:1603.04641.

Nagurney, A. *Network Economics: A Variational Inequality Approach*; Kluwer Academic Press: Dordrecht, The Netherlands, 1999.

Gerstung, M.; Eriksson, N.; Lin, J.; Vogelstein, B.; Beerenwinkel, N. The Temporal Order of Genetic and Pathway Alterations in Tumorigenesis. *PLoS ONE* **2011**, *6*, e27136. [CrossRef] [PubMed]

Beerenwinkel, N.; Eriksson, N.; Sturmfels, B. Evolution on distributive lattices. *J. Theor. Biol.* **2006**, *242*, 409–420. [CrossRef] [PubMed]

Pearl, J. *Probabilistic Reasoning in Intelligent Systems—Networks of Plausible Inference*; Morgan Kaufmann Series in Representation and Reasoning; Morgan Kaufmann: San Francisco, CA, USA, 1989.

May, J.P. Finite Spaces and Larger Contexts. Available online: https://math.uchicago.edu/~may/FINITE/FINITEBOOK/FINITEBOOKCollatedDraft.pdf (accessed on 9 May 2025).

Barmak, J.A. *Algebraic Topology of Finite Topological Spaces and Applications*; Lecture Notes in Mathematics; Springer: Berlin/Heidelberg, Germany, 2011.

Kleitman, D.J.; Rothschild, B. Asymptotic Enumeration of Partial Orders on a Finite Set. *Trans. Am. Math. Soc.* **2001**, *205*, 213–233. [CrossRef]

Dhar, D. Entropy and phase transitions in partially ordered sets. *J. Math. Phys.* **1978**, *19*, 1711–1713. [CrossRef]

Mahadevan, S. Asymptotic Causal Inference. *arXiv* **2021**. [CrossRef]

Heymann, B.; de Lara, M.; Chancelier, J.P. Causal Information with Information Fields. In Proceedings of the Neural Information Processing Systems Workshop on Causal Discovery and Causality-inspired Machine Learning, Virtual, 11–12 December 2020.

Forré, P.; Mooij, J.M. Markov Properties for Graphical Models with Cycles and Latent Variables. *arXiv* **2017**, arXiv:1710.08775.

May, J. *Simplicial Objects in Algebraic Topology*; University of Chicago Press: Chicago, IL, USA, 1992.

May, J. *A Concise Course in Algebraic Topology*; Chicago Lectures in Mathematics; University of Chicago Press: Chicago, IL, USA, 1999.

Boardman, M.; Vogt, R. *Homotopy Invariant Algebraic Structures on Topological Spaces*; Springer: Berlin/Heidelberg, Germany, 1973.

Lurie, J. Kerodon. 2022. Available online: https://kerodon.net (accessed on 9 May 2025).

Andersson, S.A.; Madigan, D.; Perlman, M.D. A characterization of Markov equivalence classes for acyclic digraphs. *Ann. Stat.* **1997**, *25*, 505–541. [CrossRef]

Lauritzen, S.L.; Richardson, T.S. Chain graph models and their causal interpretations. *J. R. Stat. Soc. Ser. B Stat. Methodol.* **2002**, *64*, 321–348.

McInnes, L.; Healy, J.; Melville, J. UMAP: Uniform Manifold Approximation and Projection for Dimension Reduction. *arXiv* **2018**. [CrossRef]

Munkres, J.R. *Elements of Algebraic Topology*; Addison-Wesley: Boston, MA, USA, 1984.

Grayson, D. Higher algebraic K-theory: II. In *Algebraic K-Theory*; Stein, M.R., Ed.; Springer: Berlin/Heidelberg, Germany, 1976; pp. 217–240.

Osborne, M. *An Introduction to Game Theory*; Oxford University Press: New York, NY, USA, 2004.

Fong, B.; Johnson, M. Lenses and Learners. *arXiv* **2019**, arXiv:1903.03671.

Facchinei, F.; Pang, J. *Finite-Dimensional Variational Inequalities and Complementarity Problems*; Springer: Berlin/Heidelberg, Germany, 2003.

Mahadevan, S. Causal Inference in Network Economics. *arXiv* **2021**, arXiv:2109.11344.

61. Nagurney, A.; Besik, D.; Dong, J. Tariffs and Quotas in World Trade: A Unified Variational Inequality Framework. *Eur. J. Op. Res.* **2019**, *275*, 347–360. [CrossRef]
62. May, J.P. *The Geometry of Iterated Loop Spaces*; Lecture Notes in Mathematics; Springer: Berlin/Heidelberg, Germany, 197 Volume 271.
63. Riehl, E.; Verity, D. Infinity category theory from scratch. *arXiv* **2019**, arXiv:1608.05314.
64. Quillen, D.G. *Homotopical Algebra*; Springer: Berlin/Heidelberg, Germany, 1967.
65. Dawid, A.P. Separoids: A Mathematical Framework for Conditional Independence and Irrelevance. *Ann. Math. Artif. Intell.* **200** *32*, 335–372. [CrossRef]

*entropy*

MDPI

*Article*

# A Novel Hyper-Heuristic Algorithm with Soft and Hard Constraints for Causal Discovery Using a Linear Structural Equation Model

**Yinglong Dang, Xiaoguang Gao * and Zidong Wang**

School of Electronic and Information, Northwestern Polytechnical University, Xi'an 710129, China; dangyinglong@mail.nwpu.edu.cn (Y.D.); nwpu_wzd@mail.nwpu.edu.cn (Z.W.)
* Correspondence: cxg2012@nwpu.edu.cn

**Abstract:** Artificial intelligence plays an indispensable role in improving productivity and promoting social development, and causal discovery is one of the extremely important research directions in this field. Acyclic directed graphs (DAGs) are the most commonly used tool in causal modeling because of their excellent interpretability and structural properties. However, in the face of insufficient data, the accuracy and efficiency of DAGs learning are greatly reduced, resulting in a false perception of causality. As intuitive expert knowledge, structural constraints control DAG learning by limiting the causal relationship between variables, which is expected to solve the above-mentioned problem. However, it is often impossible to build a DAG by relying on expert knowledge alone. To solve this problem, we propose the use of expert knowledge as a hard constraint and the structural prior gained via data learning as a soft constraint. In this paper, we propose a fitness-rate-rank-based multiarmed bandit (FRRMAB) hyper-heuristic that integrates soft and hard constraints into the DAG learning process. For a linear structural equation model (SEM), soft constraints are obtained via partial correlation analysis. The experimental results on different networks show that the proposed method has higher scalability and accuracy.

**Keywords:** causal discovery; structural constraint; structural equation model; hyper-heuristics

## 1. Introduction

The representation of causality relies on interpretable graph structures, and causal discovery learns these graph structures from data. One of the most classic and widely used examples is the DAG, which is widely used in various fields [1–4]. There are two common ways to build a DAG: building with expert knowledge and building with data learning. DAG construction with expert knowledge determines whether there is a causal link between nodes by consulting experts in related fields, using scoring and voting combined with the actual situation, to build the most consistent DAG. However, this approach to building DAGs on the basis of expert knowledge is time-consuming and expensive. Therefore, for large-scale DAGs, building suitable structures using only expert knowledge is unrealistic. Compared with expert knowledge methods, data learning methods are less resource-intensive and more efficient. However, because the size of the structure space of the DAG increases super-exponentially with the number of nodes and the number of states of the nodes, DAG learning becomes an NP-hard problem. To reduce the complexity of the computation and search in DAG learning, data learning and expert knowledge can be combined. Integrating expert knowledge into data learning and deleting unreasonable and unrealistic directed edges can ensure that the structure learned in the process of data learning is reasonable and legal. On the one hand, it can remove some variables that are not closely related to the model to be constructed in data processing, thus reducing the complexity of learning. On the other hand, when the amount of training data is insufficient or there is considerable noise, the learned DAG structure may differ greatly from the actual structure, and the expert can correct the learned structure to ensure that the constructed Bayesian network structure is in line with practical applications. In this paper, expert knowledge is used as a hard constraint in the DAG learning process.

Currently, the methods for learning DAGs from data fall into three main categories: constraint-based methods, score-based methods, and hybrid methods. The constraint-based method is divided into two steps: the first step is to conduct an exhaustive set of CI tests, and the second step is to infer a class of DAGs on the basis of the CI test. However, the DAG learning algorithms based on constraint satisfaction have two assumptions: causal faithfulness and causal sufficiency. The score-based method is also divided into two steps: score calculation, which involves the selection and score calculation of the candidate parent set of each node, and structure optimization, which uses a certain search strategy to find the optimal solution in the specified search space. The research on the first stage is mature, and scholars have made more improvements in the second stage. These algorithms can be divided into two categories: approximate methods and exact methods. The exact approach cannot solve the large-scale network learning problems, and the approximate learning algorithm focuses on improving the learning efficiency of the DAG and the maximum network size that can be learned, so it cannot guarantee that the learned result is the global optimal solution theoretically. Hill climbing (HC) [5], the most widely used approximate method, is prone to falling into local optima. To escape local optima, many bionic algorithms inspired by biological systems, such as the genetic algorithm (GA) [6], ant colony optimization (ACO) [7], particle swarm optimization (PSO) [8,9], artificial bee colony algorithm (ABC) [10], cuckoo optimization (CO) [11], firefly algorithm (FA) [12], bacterial foraging optimization (BFO) [13], and water cycle optimization (WCO) [14], have emerged in recent years. Although these optimization algorithms have demonstrated their accuracy and efficiency in DAG learning through experiments, the following challenges remain:

- The scalability of a single meta-heuristic algorithm needs to be improved.
- For a large DAG, a single meta-heuristic algorithm easily falls into local optima with low convergence accuracy.

Recently, hyper-heuristic algorithms have replaced meta-heuristic algorithms as the research hotspot in the field of combinatorial optimization and have been applied to many practical engineering problems, such as the knapsack problem (KP) [15], traveling salesperson problem (TSP) [16], and vehicle routing problem (VRP) [17]. While hyper-heuristic algorithms can be used to solve practical problems, many high-quality heuristic selection strategies are produced: choice function, FRRMAB, and several meta-heuristic strategies, such as simulating annealing (SA), tabu search, and swarm intelligent selection. In this paper, we employ FRRMAB as a hyper-heuristic high-level selection strategy.

In addition, some scholars have proposed hybrid methods, which use a method based on constraint satisfaction to limit the search space and then use a method based on score search to perform local optimization. The max–min hill climbing algorithm (MMHC) [18] is a classical hybrid algorithm for solving large-scale DAG learning problems. Limiting the search space can be considered a soft constraint, and the hybrid method is actually a learning method based on knowledge fusion [19]. In this paper, we use partial correlation analysis to identify the partial V-structure and limit the search space. These structure priors obtained through data mining are used as soft constraints to guide the search direction of the algorithm. In summary, in our algorithm, there are two kinds of structural constraints: soft constraints, which are applied by intervening in the learning process, and hard constraints, which force the learned network to meet certain conditions.

The main contributions of the paper are summarized as follows:

1. We use both soft and hard constraints to guide or limit the whole process of the hyper-heuristic algorithm.
2. We construct a low-level operator library of hyper-heuristic algorithms in the DAG learning field.
3. We propose a multi-population FRRMAB hyper-heuristic (M-FRRMAB-HH). Multi-population strategies can provide sufficient search space coverage and communicate with each other through migration operators through different groups.

This paper is organized as follows: Section 2 presents related works. Section 3 introduces the preliminaries. Section 4 describes our proposed algorithm. Section 5 discusses our experimental results. Section 6 concludes this paper.

## 2. Related Works

At present, the DAG learning problem is solved mainly as a combinatorial optimization problem or continuous optimization problem. For the combinatorial optimization problem, the core goal is to design a scoring function to evaluate the generated network and then find the network with the highest score. There are two main solutions: constraint satisfaction and score search. The methods based on constraint satisfaction can be divided into global structure learning or local structure learning.

Global structure learning attempts to discover the graph structure of all variables on the basis of the CI test. One of the classic algorithms is the SGS algorithm, which first removes the edges between the independent variables starting with the fully connected graph and then discovers the V structure and the orientation of the remaining undirected edges. The PC algorithm is an improvement over the SGS algorithm, reducing the time cost. However, the classical PC algorithm is related to the node order, so it can easily incorrectly remove the directed edge. A method called the PC-Stable [20] algorithm, which is independent of the node order, was subsequently proposed. Aiming at hidden variables and confounding factors, the FCI algorithm and its improved RFCI [21] method were proposed. Local structure learning focuses on identifying parent—child node sets or Markov blankets (MBs) in the DAG. The GS was the first algorithm used to discover the MB structure and consists of two steps: growth and reduction. The IAMB [22] algorithm and its improved versions, such as Inter-IAMB and Fast-IAMB, were subsequently proposed together. The MMPC, HITON-PC, and SI-HITON-PC [19] algorithms were also proposed for the discovery of parent—child node sets.

The methods based on score search can be divided into exact learning and approximate learning. Exact learning, which focuses on finding globally optimal structures for scoring, was first mentioned in node-ordered spaces because of its low complexity and ease of global searching. The idea of dynamic programming was first applied to DAG learning [23]. Yuan and Malone found that dynamic programming searches are very inefficient, so they used the A* [24] algorithm to search the order graph. The branch and bound (B&B) [25] algorithm was the first algorithm used to solve the global optimal structure in the DAG space. Since the superexponential number of states severely restricts the development of accurate learning in the DAG space, scholars have carried out a series of studies on how to prune the space without affecting global optimality. Integer linear programming (ILP) [26] is the best of these algorithms. It uses convex constraints and clival constraints to limit the search space. The structure learning problem is solved as an integer programming problem.

Unlike exact learning, approximate learning can be generalized to large DAGs. Approximate learning is the most widely used method. The search space can be divided into a DAG space, an equivalent class (EC) space and an ordering space. In the DAG space, various heuristic algorithms have been proposed to solve local optimum problems. In the EC space, greedy equivalence search (GES) [27] is the classic score search method; it includes two processes, forward search and reverse search; uses insertion and deletion operators, respectively, to achieve the neighborhood search of the DAG; and learns the final structure by constantly updating the optimal valence class. Ramsey et al. [28] developed a parallel version of GES, FGES, and Bernaola et al. [29] proposed the FGES-merge algorithm for hyperscale networks. The ordering space has the least complexity and is more efficient than the DAG space and the EC space. The K2 [30] algorithm was the first to explore how to obtain the optimal DAG corresponding to a given node order.

The continuous optimization problem is a new research direction that has emerged in recent years, but, once it was proposed, it was recognized by the majority of scholars. Its purpose is to construct the corresponding DAG for some multimodal data, such as parametric/nonparametric, linear/nonlinear, and Gaussian/nonGaussian data, and solve it using a continuous optimization algorithm. To characterize causality, such algorithms make assumptions about the distribution of the data in advance, such as the linear non-Gaussian cyclic model (LiNGAM) [31,32], postlinearity (PNL) [33], additive noise model (ANM) [34], and generalized linear model (GLM). On the premise that causal adequacy is satisfied, Shimizu [32] proved that the structure that best fits these hypotheses can be solved by independent component analysis. Zheng et al. [35] proposed a classical algorithm, NOTEARS, which represents a directed acyclic constraint with the use of a weight matrix and regards finding the optimal network as a process of loss minimization. In addition, many works based on NOTEARS, such as NOFEARS [36] and NOBEARS [37], have emerged in recent years. Yu et al. [38] proposed the use of a GNN to reconstruct the loss function. Then, autoencoders [39] and reinforcement learning [40] were also introduced to perform as solvers.

To date, approximate learning has been the most widely used method in practice. However, their optimization strategies have obvious randomness, and the complexity of their search space increases exponentially when the scale of the variables increases, so the search accuracy of random strategies is difficult to guarantee, and expert knowledge should be introduced to guide the direction of greedy search to rescue. However, the current approximate algorithms [6–12] cannot glean knowledge from data without given constraints nor do they investigate how greedy optimization can be performed heuristically under given structural constraints. Therefore, integrating expert knowledge and structural priors into the heuristic search process is a topic worth studying.

## 3. Background

### 3.1. DAG Model

$G$ represents a DAG, which can be represented as a binary group $G = (V, E)$, where $V = \{X_1, \cdots, X_n\}$ represents the set of variables (or the set of nodes), and $E$ represents the set of directed edges between variables.

### 3.2. SEMs

SEM is usually used to represent the DAG structure under continuous variables:

$$x_i = f_{X_i}(pa(X_i), u_{X_i}) \quad (1)$$

where the functions $f_{X_i}$ are the decision function, $pa(X_i)$ represents the parent node set, and $u_{X_i}$ represents the noise distribution. In particular, the decision function can be defined as either linear or nonlinear. When it is defined as linear, we can define a linear SEM:

$$x_i = w_{X_i}^T pa(X_i) + u_{X_i} \quad (2)$$

### 3.3. Scoring Function

For linear SEM, we use the BIC score, which is defined as follows:

$$Score_{BIC} = \sum_{j=1}^{n} \left( NLL\left(X_j, pa(X_j), \hat{\theta}_j^{mle}\right) + \frac{\left|\hat{\theta}_j^{mle}\right|}{2} \log m \right) \quad (3)$$

where $NLL\left(X_j, pa(X_j), \hat{\theta}^{mle}\right)$ represents the negative log-likelihood, and the calculation formula is as follows:

$$NLL\left(X_j, pa(X_j), \hat{\theta}_j^{mle}\right) = \sum_{j=1}^{m} \left( x_{ij} - \left(\hat{\theta}_j^{mle}\right)^T pa(x_{ij}) \right)^2 \quad (4)$$

$$\hat{\theta}_j^{mle} = (x'x)^{-1} x' x_j \quad (5)$$

where $x_i$ denotes the $m \times 1$ vector of observations on $X_i$, in which the $j$th element of $x_i$ is $x_{ji}$.

## 4. Methodology

In our algorithm, structural constraints consist of two parts: soft constraints and hard constraints. For soft constraints, we first mine conditional independent information according to the SPPC [41] algorithm, identify the partial V-structure, obtain three restricted search spaces (GSS, CSS, and LSS), and integrate these structural priors into the search process of the hyper-heuristic algorithm as soft constraints. For hard constraints, we randomly select a certain percentage of correct edges and a certain percentage of forbidden edges as expert knowledge to enforce in the final generated structure. In addition, the three search spaces described above, CSS, GSS, and LSS, are also forced to remove those edges that were determined from expert knowledge to exist or not exist, forming three new, narrower search spaces.

### 4.1. Proposed M-FRRMAB-HH Algorithm

Figure 1 shows the framework of the proposed hyper-heuristic solver, which consists of two levels: the low-level heuristics (LLHs) and the high-level strategy. In the low-level problem domain, we define a set of scheduling heuristic operators with the corresponding expertise, while, in the high-level control domain, we design appropriate selection strategies and acceptance criteria to select high-quality heuristic operators and maintain the diversity of choices.

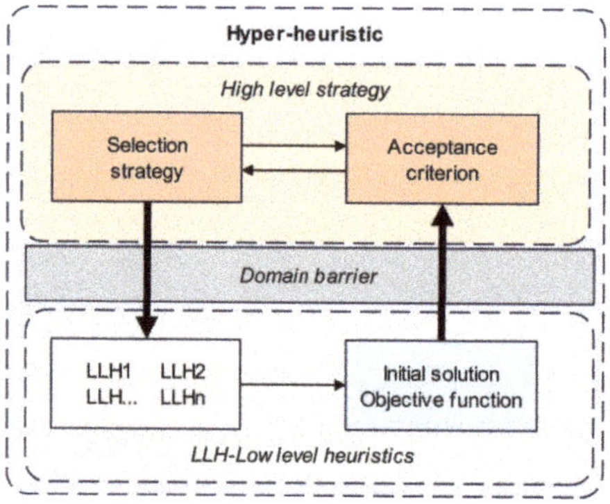


**Figure 1.** Proposed framework of the hyper-heuristic.

### 4.2. The High-Level Strategy

In this paper, FRRMAB is used as a high-level selection strategy, and Accept All Moves is used as an acceptance criterion. It has the following three main features:

1. A sliding window is used to store the performance information of the recent operator.
2. A decay mechanism is used to increase the selection frequency of the operator with good performance.
3. Each subgroup executes its own independent high-level policy and communicates when the interaction conditions are met.

Our high-level selection strategy has two main parts: credit assignment and operator selection. The most critical part of credit assignment is the metric that measures the performance of the operator. In DAG learning, the most commonly used index for measuring the performance of an operator is the improved value of the BIC score. However, improvements in BIC scores are much larger and easier in the early stages than in the later stages, so we used fitness improvement rates (FIRs) as an assessment measure [42] and converted them linearly into intervals $(0.1, 0.5)$.

$$FIR_{i,t} = \frac{pf_{i,t} - cf_{i,t}}{-1 \times pf_{i,t}} \tag{6}$$

where $pf_{i,t}$ represents the score of the parent; $cf_{i,t}$ represents the score of the child.

The sliding window, whose length is W, is divided into two lines: the first line records the serial number of each selected operator, and the second line records the FIR after the operator is executed. When the algorithm is running, the most recently selected operator index number and corresponding FIR are added to the end of the sliding window, while the first record is deleted to keep the window size unchanged. To increase the likelihood of choosing the best-performing operators, we use a decay mechanism for credit assignment. This process is as follows:

1. We calculate the sum of the FIRs for each operator in the second row, denoted as $Reward_i$.
2. $Reward_i$ is sorted in descending order and assigned a ranking. The first place has a rank of 1, and so on.
3. $Reward_i$ is converted to $Decay_i$ according to the following formula:

$$Decay_i = D^{Rank_i} \times Reward_i \tag{7}$$

   where D represents the decaying factor, and its value is $(0, 1)$.
4. The credit assignment value for each operator is calculated as follows:

$$FRR_{i,t} = \frac{Decay_i}{\sum_{j=1}^{K}\left(Decay_j\right)} \tag{8}$$

The pseudocode of credit assignment is given in Algorithm 1. After the credit assignment is complete, we use a bandit-based operator selection scheme to select the operator, which uses the upper confidence bound (UCB) algorithm. The UCB algorithm assigns a value to each operator via the following formula:

$$FRR_{i,t} + \sqrt{\frac{2 \times \ln \sum_{j=1}^{K} n_{j,t}}{n_{i,t}}} \tag{9}$$

where $n_i$ represents the number of times that the underlying operator i is selected by the high-level strategy. At the beginning of the search, we randomly select operators until no operator has been applied at least once and then use FRRMAB to select the operator with the largest value.

**Algorithm 1:** Procedure for the Credit Assignment.

```
Initialize Reward_i = 0, n_i = 0;
for i ← 1 to SlidingWindow.length do
    op = SlidingWindow.GetIndexOp(i);
    FIR = SlidingWindow.GetFIR(i);
    Reward_op = Reward_op + FIR;
    n_op + +;
end
Rank Reward_i in descending order and set Rank_i to be the rank value of operator i;
for op ← 1 to K do
    Decay_op = D^(Rank_op) × Reward_op;
end
DecaySum = Σ_{op=1}^{K} Decay_op;
for op ← 1 to K do
    FRR_op = Decay_op / DecaySum;
end
```

### 4.3. *Low-Level Heuristics*

The LLH pool is an important part of the hyper-heuristic algorithm, which is as important to the whole algorithm as the foundation of a tall building. Experimental studies have shown that the design of LLHs has a great effect on the final efficiency of the hyper-heuristic algorithm [43]. The design principle of LLHs is simple and rich. Operators require simple design: because LLHs are too complex, the final algorithm generated by the high-level heuristic strategy is too complex and consumes too much unnecessary operation time. Operators require a rich design, because only diversified operators can make the search of various problem domains richer, better, and faster to find the optimal solution. Various optimization algorithms and their improvements can be put into LLHs. For the DAG learning domain, 13 operators are extracted to construct the underlying operation base by analyzing various heuristic algorithms. Below, we introduce the source and working principle of each operator in detail.

#### 4.3.1. Mutation Operator and Neighborhood Perturbation Operator

The mutation operator is derived from the BNC-PSO algorithm, and the modification we made is to limit the search space to the GSS. The neighborhood perturbation operator randomly selects an edge to add, remove, or reverse to ensure that these edges are within our limited search space (LSS).

4.3.2. Cognitive Personal Operator

The cognitive personal operator is derived from the BNC-PSO algorithm. In this operator, if the generated random number is less than the learning probability $p$, each individual learns from its historically optimal structure; otherwise, the individual remains unchanged. The learning probability $p$ varies linearly from 0.82 to 0.32 with the number of iterations.

4.3.3. Cooperative Global Operator

The cooperative global operator is also derived from the BNC-PSO algorithm. In this operator, if the generated random number is less than the learning probability $p$, each individual learns from the globally optimal structure; otherwise, the individual remains unchanged. The learning probability $p$ varies linearly from 0.1 to 0.5 with the number of iterations.

4.3.4. Chemotactic Operator

The chemotactic operator is derived from the BFO algorithm. To improve the efficiency of large-scale DAG learning, only one node is operated on at a time. That is, the addition action is greedy to add the parent node if the score increases, the delete action is greedy to remove the existing parent nodes if the score increases, and the reverse action is greedy to reverse the parent node if the score increases. These actions work only in the GSS.

4.3.5. Elimination and Dispersal Operator

The elimination and dispersal operator is derived from the BFO algorithm, which restarts the parent set of only one node of the globally optimal structure. The procedure is as follows:

1. Select a node $X$ in a preset order and delete all the parent nodes of this node.
2. Parent nodes are added to $X$ if the score increases, and the resulting set of parent nodes is then sorted by partial correlation values as the potential parent importance of X. Then, all the parent nodes of X are deleted.
3. Add nodes from the potential parent to $X$ one by one. If the score increases, both the node and its parent are added as the parent of $X$, while the new structure is used as the new starting point.
4. Greedily remove the nodes that are currently least able to increase the score and use the new structure as a new starting point until the score cannot be increased by removing the parent node.
5. Greedily invert the parent of X if the score can be increased.

The elimination and dispersal operator starts when the generated random number is less than the parameter, and the parameter is dynamically adjusted according to the following formula:

$$c_3 = 0.1 + 0.9(L/L_{\max}) \tag{10}$$

where $L$ represents the number of iterations in which the highest score does not increase, and $L_{\max}$ represents the maximum number of allowed iterations in which the highest score does not increase.

#### 4.3.6. Employed Bees and Onlooker Bees

Both the employed bees and onlooker bees are derived from the ABC algorithm. The employed bees perform a local mountain climbing operation on the individual itself. The onlooker bees use roulette to select a good individual for climbing operations. Both of these are local optimization operators that operate within a restricted search space, GSS.

#### 4.3.7. Employed Bees and Onlooker Bees

The scout bees are derived from the ABC algorithm. To improve the learning efficiency of large DAGs, we consider restarting the parent set of only one node of the globally optimal structure. The procedure is as follows:

1. Select a node $X$ in a preset order and record its parent set as $P$.
2. Pick one node in $P$ and invert the edge.
3. Execute the addition, deletion, and reverse chemotaxis operators in sequence. If the score increases, the new DAG replaces the original DAG. Continue with Step 2 until $P$ is empty.

When the iteration where the highest score is not increased is greater than $l_m$, the scout bee can perform; otherwise, it remains unchanged.

#### 4.3.8. Moth–Flame Optimization

Moth–flame optimization is based on a moth–flame optimization algorithm that randomly arranges the historically optimal structures of individuals as flames. The moth flying around the flame refers to the moth learning from its flame, and its learning method is similar to that of the BNC-PSO algorithm.

#### 4.3.9. Teaching-Learning-Based Optimization

In the teaching-learning-based optimization operator, each student is randomly assigned a collaborator and learns from the collaborator if the score is higher than their own, and its learning method is similar to that of the BNC-PSO algorithm.

#### 4.3.10. Expert Knowledge Operator

The expert knowledge operator selects a certain proportion of individuals to accept structural constraints, that is, to include all hard constraints and V structures.

#### 4.3.11. Pruning Operator

The pruning operator is designed to avoid overfitting by setting a threshold $\mu$ and then removing all edges that cause the score to increase less than $\mu$.

### *4.4. Framework of Our Algorithm*

The pseudocode of the M-FRRMAB-HH algorithm we propose is shown in Algorithm 2. First, the initial population contains the edges determined by the hard and soft constraints, and it is evenly divided into several subgroups, each of which performs the high-level selection strategy independently. When the migration condition is satisfied, information is exchanged between subgroups. In addition, when the score cannot be improved in the GSS, the search space switching operator is executed to convert the GSS to a CSS. Finally, the algorithm stops when any termination condition is satisfied.

#### 4.4.1. Migration Operator

The migration operation records the highest score structure of each subgroup, swaps the highest and lowest score structures, and is controlled by two indicators: the minimum number of interval iterations and the inbreeding rate. In this paper, the minimum number of interval iterations is set to a smaller value of both 100 and $N$. The inbreeding rate, which prevents premature population maturation, is designed as the number of close relatives of the highest score structure of each subgroup and the global optimal structure divided by the number of subgroups and was limited to no more than 0.6 in this study. In this study, if the Hamming distance between the highest score structure in the subgroup and the global optimal structure was less than 4, we considered them to be close relatives.

**Algorithm 2:** M-FRRMAB-HH.

```
Input: MaxIt,N,Lmax,μ
Output: Gbest,SBest
Generate initial population G
Divide the population and record:Gbest,Sbest
L ← 1, j ← 1, sign ← 0
while L < L_max ∨ j < MaxIt do
    j++
    Each subswarm individually chooses an LLH
    Update: Gbest,Sbest
    %  Migration operator
    if mod(j, min(100, N)) = 0 then
        Calculate inbreeding rate Ir
        if Ir <0.6 then
            Perform migration
        end
    end
    if Sbest(j) − Sbest(j − 1) <μ then
        L++
    else
        L = 0
    end
    %  Search space switching operator
    if L = L_max ∧ sign = 0 then
        Switch the search space of global search operators
        sign = 1
        L = 0
    end
end
Prune(Gbest)
Return Gbest,Sbest
```

4.4.2. Search Space Switching Operator

When the DAG is large or complex, the use of the GSS as the search space is prone to the incorrect deletion of some correct edges. Therefore, we considered introducing a search space switching operator to further improve accuracy, which is executed to correct possible errors due to an incomplete search space in the GSS when the number of iterations without increasing the global maximum score reaches $L_{\max}$. After the search space is switched, the scout bees as well as elimination and dispersal operators work within the CSS. Obviously, working on the GSS can improve the efficiency of our algorithm early on, and switching to the CSS can further improve the accuracy of our algorithm later on.

## 5. Experiments

Several algorithms and benchmark networks were selected to evaluate the performance of our proposed M-FRRMAB-HH algorithm. All the experiments were performed on an AMD 1.7 GHz CPU with 16 GB of RAM.

### 5.1. Networks and Datasets

In our experiment, all datasets were generated through six benchmark networks from the BNLEARN repository (https://www.bnlearn.com/bnrepository/, accessed on 9 October 2024), which are summarized in Table 1. Of the six networks, Alarm [44] belongs to the medium network. Hepar2 [45] and Win95pts are large networks. Andes [46], Munin [47], and Pigs are very large networks.

For linear SEM, we designed three SEMs to generate data, including Gaussian and non-Gaussian data. For each combination of network and SEM, we randomly generated a dataset of 1000 samples.

$$\begin{aligned} (1)x_i &= w_{1X_i}^T pa(X_i) + N(0,1) \\ (2)x_i &= w_{2X_i}^T pa(X_i) + N(0,1) \\ (3)x_i &= w_{1X_i}^T pa(X_i) + \text{rand}(-1,1) \end{aligned} \tag{11}$$

where $w_{1X_i} = \pm 1 + N(0,1)/4$, and $w_{2X_i} = \text{rand}(0.2,1)$. SEM (1) and SEM (2), since their noise follows a Gaussian distribution, belong to the Gaussian model. For SEM (3), the noise is uniformly distributed and is a non-Gaussian model.

We used different metrics to evaluate the effectiveness and efficiency of the algorithm, which are as follows:

- BIC: BIC score of the learned network (higher is better).
- SBS: BIC score of the original network.
- AE: The number of edges not present in the original network but added.
- DE: The number of edges present in the original network but undetected.
- RE: The number of edges correctly detected but in the opposite direction.
- RT: Running time of the algorithm.
- F1: F1 score of the learned network (higher is better).

**Table 1.** Summary of networks.

| Network | Nodes | Edges | Max.indeg | Max.outdeg | Avg.deg |
|---|---|---|---|---|---|
| Alarm | 37 | 46 | 4 | 5 | 2.49 |
| Hepar2 | 70 | 123 | 6 | 17 | 3.51 |
| Win95pts | 76 | 112 | 7 | 10 | 2.95 |
| Munin | 189 | 282 | 3 | 15 | 2.98 |
| Andes | 223 | 338 | 6 | 12 | 3.03 |
| Pigs | 441 | 592 | 2 | 39 | 2.68 |

### 5.2. Comparison Algorithms and Parameter Settings

We compared the M-FRRMAB-HH algorithm with five common algorithms, including the PC-stable, LiNGAM, PCS [48], BNC-PSO, and NOTEARS algorithms (https://github.com/xunzheng/notears, accessed on 9 October 2024). NOTEARS was tested in its Python implementations, and the other algorithms were run in MATLAB R2020a.

The main parameters of M-FRRMAB-HH are listed in Table 2. Since the causal relationship between variables is easier to negate than to establish, we set the constraint rate $p$ for an edge that was determined to exist to 0.1 and the constraint rate $q$ for an edge that was determined to not exist to 0.5. The parameters of the other algorithms were set according to the original literature, but soft constraints were introduced in the BNC-PSO algorithm to enable a fair comparison with our proposed algorithm in terms of global search performance.

**Table 2.** Parameters of the M-FRRMAB-HH.

| Param. | Value | Description |
|---|---|---|
| $p$ | 0.1 | The constraint rate of the edge that is sure to exist |
| $q$ | 0.5 | The constraint rate of the nonexistent edge |
| $W$ | 10 | the length of sliding window |
| $C$ | 10 | Equilibrium coefficient |
| $D$ | 0.5 | Decay coefficient |
| $nPop$ | 50 | The population size |
| $L_{max}$ | $2 \times n$ | The maximum number of unpromoted iterations allowed |
| $MaxIt$ | 5000 | The maximum number of iterations allowed |
| $sn$ | 5 | The number of subgroups |
| $\mu$ | $\ln m$ | The threshold of pruning |
| $l_m$ | 20 | Control parameters of the elimination and dispersal operator |
| $zj$ | 0.5 | Percentage receiving expert guidance |

### 5.3. Performance Evaluation of M-FRRMAB-HH

To evaluate the performance of M-FRRMAB-HH, we list the means and standard deviations of 10 runs of the algorithm on each dataset in Table 3.

First, for all the datasets on the three SEMs, the BIC scores of the learned network meet or exceed the BIC scores of the original network, and the standard deviation of both the BIC scores and F1 scores is 0. This shows that for different SEMs, our algorithm can learn a high-score network with stable F1 scores, which means that our proposed algorithm can work stably for both Gaussian and non-Gaussian models. For structural errors on the Alarm and Hepar2 networks, the AE, DE, and RE on all datasets are zero, indicating that our algorithm can stably learn a DAG that is consistent with the original network on the two networks. For the Win95pts and Andes networks, only on SEM2 is an edge incorrectly identified. For the Munin and Pigs networks, the networks learned on all datasets are missing 53 or 324 edges, with a small number of added edges and misdirected edges on some datasets. Notably, for all the datasets with structural errors, the BIC scores are higher than the SBS scores. After analysis, these false edges occurred because the dataset does not support them. By looking at all of these structural errors and BIC scores, we believe that our proposed algorithm can stably learn a high-scoring structure with a score no lower than that of the original network. On the basis of the above observations and analysis, we can conclude that our proposed algorithm is an effective and reliable method for learning the DAG on a linear SEM.

To illustrate the effect of expert knowledge on the performance of our proposed algorithm, we report the algorithm's performance without hard constraints (p = 0, q = 0). As shown in Table 4, all datasets in the four networks Alarm, Hepar2, Win95pts, and Andes, regardless of expert knowledge, output a structure with the same BIC score and F1 score. For the Munin and Pigs networks, after removing the constraint of expert knowledge, the output network has a higher BIC score, but the number of DEs also increases. This is because expert knowledge contains some of the real edges that can cause the BIC scores to decrease. For run time, after removing the constraint of expert knowledge, the run time increases on all datasets, and the increase is particularly significant on the large Andes and Pigs networks. In summary, the constraint of expert knowledge can reduce the time cost of the algorithm and can correct the structural errors in the output structure.

LLHs contain several operators, among which the restart operator (elimination and dispersal operator, scout bees) is the core operator that hops out of the local optimum and the operator with the highest time cost. Therefore, in our algorithm, these two operators are likely the operators that have the greatest impact on the efficiency of the algorithm. To explore the working mechanism and function of the restart operator in the algorithm, we generated three new LLHs by eliminating the restart operator: LLH1 (remove elimination and dispersal operator from LLH), LLH2 (remove scout bees from LLH), and LLH3 (remove two restart operators from LLH). Table 5 shows the performance of our algorithm under the three new LLH pools.

Comparing Tables 3 and 5, we can see that for the Alarm and Pigs networks, all three derived algorithms can output the same structure of BIC scores and F1 scores as the original algorithm. For the other four networks, the graph accuracy of the structure output by the algorithm under LLH3 decreases and the output structure is no longer stable. This shows the necessity of the restart operator. For the running time, the running time on LLH3 is significantly shorter than that on the other LLHs, which indicates that the addition of restart operators increases the time cost of the algorithm. Comparing LLH1 and LLH2, we find that for both the Hepar2 and Win95pts networks, neither of the derived algorithms can output a stable structure. This shows that the two cannot replace each other and can work better if they are used together. On the basis of the above analysis, we can conclude that both restart operators play important roles in running the algorithm and that removing either operator reduces the performance of the algorithm.

**Table 3.** Performance of M-FRRMAB-HH algorithm on different datasets. Bold denotes that BIC is greater than SBS.

| Network | SEM | BIC | SBS | AD | DD | RD | SET(s) | F1 |
|---|---|---|---|---|---|---|---|---|
| alarm | 1 | $-1.8710 \times 10^4 \pm 0$ | $-1.8710 \times 10^4$ | $0 \pm 0$ | $0 \pm 0$ | $0 \pm 0$ | 1.58 | $1 \pm 0$ |
| | 2 | $-1.8638 \times 10^4 \pm 0$ | $-1.8638 \times 10^4$ | $0 \pm 0$ | $0 \pm 0$ | $0 \pm 0$ | 1.27 | $1 \pm 0$ |
| | 3 | $-6.3849 \times 10^3 \pm 0$ | $-6.3849 \times 10^3$ | $0 \pm 0$ | $0 \pm 0$ | $0 \pm 0$ | 1.17 | $1 \pm 0$ |
| hepar2 | 1 | $-3.5372 \times 10^4 \pm 0$ | $-3.5372 \times 10^4$ | $0 \pm 0$ | $0 \pm 0$ | $0 \pm 0$ | 20.40 | $1 \pm 0$ |
| | 2 | $-3.5318 \times 10^4 \pm 0$ | $-3.5318 \times 10^4$ | $0 \pm 0$ | $0 \pm 0$ | $0 \pm 0$ | 20.57 | $1 \pm 0$ |
| | 3 | $-1.2133 \times 10^4 \pm 0$ | $-1.2133 \times 10^4$ | $0 \pm 0$ | $0 \pm 0$ | $0 \pm 0$ | 15.31 | $1 \pm 0$ |
| win95pts | 1 | $-3.8374 \times 10^4 \pm 0$ | $-3.8374 \times 10^4$ | $0 \pm 0$ | $0 \pm 0$ | $0 \pm 0$ | 13.28 | $1 \pm 0$ |
| | 2 | $\mathbf{-3.8309} \times 10^4 \pm 0$ | $-3.8310 \times 10^4$ | $0 \pm 0$ | $0 \pm 0$ | $1 \pm 0$ | 10.42 | $0.9911 \pm 0$ |
| | 3 | $-1.3083 \times 10^4 \pm 0$ | $-1.3083 \times 10^4$ | $0 \pm 0$ | $0 \pm 0$ | $0 \pm 0$ | 12.91 | $1 \pm 0$ |
| munin | 1 | $\mathbf{-9.5504} \times 10^4 \pm 0$ | $-9.5663 \times 10^4$ | $0 \pm 0$ | $53 \pm 0$ | $0 \pm 0$ | 106.15 | $0.8963 \pm 0$ |
| | 2 | $\mathbf{-9.5399} \times 10^4 \pm 0$ | $-9.5561 \times 10^4$ | $0 \pm 0$ | $53 \pm 0$ | $1 \pm 0$ | 116.39 | $0.8924 \pm 0$ |
| | 3 | $\mathbf{-3.2219} \times 10^4 \pm 0$ | $-3.2393 \times 10^4$ | $0 \pm 0$ | $53 \pm 0$ | $0 \pm 0$ | 83.29 | $0.8963 \pm 0$ |
| andes | 1 | $-1.1296 \times 10^5 \pm 0$ | $-1.1296 \times 10^5$ | $0 \pm 0$ | $0 \pm 0$ | $0 \pm 0$ | 345.71 | $1 \pm 0$ |
| | 2 | $\mathbf{-1.1280} \times 10^5 \pm 0$ | $-1.1281 \times 10^5$ | $1 \pm 0$ | $0 \pm 0$ | $0 \pm 0$ | 396.59 | $0.9985 \pm 0$ |
| | 3 | $-3.8190 \times 10^4 \pm 0$ | $-3.8190 \times 10^4$ | $0 \pm 0$ | $0 \pm 0$ | $0 \pm 0$ | 402.05 | $1 \pm 0$ |
| pigs | 1 | $\mathbf{-2.2207} \times 10^5 \pm 0$ | $-2.2301 \times 10^5$ | $0 \pm 0$ | $324 \pm 0$ | $0 \pm 0$ | 1208.06 | $0.6233 \pm 0$ |
| | 2 | $\mathbf{-2.2219} \times 10^5 \pm 0$ | $-2.2316 \times 10^5$ | $1 \pm 0$ | $324 \pm 0$ | $0 \pm 0$ | 1484.07 | $0.6225 \pm 0$ |
| | 3 | $\mathbf{-7.4305} \times 10^4 \pm 0$ | $-7.5375 \times 10^4$ | $0 \pm 0$ | $324 \pm 0$ | $0 \pm 0$ | 1428.41 | $0.6233 \pm 0$ |

**Table 4.** Performance of M-FRRMAB-HH algorithm without hard constraints. Bold denotes that BIC is greater than SBS.

| Network | SEM | BIC | SBS | AD | DD | RD | SET(s) | F1 |
|---|---|---|---|---|---|---|---|---|
| alarm | 1 | $-1.8710 \times 10^4 \pm 0$ | $-1.8710 \times 10^4$ | $0 \pm 0$ | $0 \pm 0$ | $0 \pm 0$ | 2.29 | $1 \pm 0$ |
| | 2 | $-1.8638 \times 10^4 \pm 0$ | $-1.8638 \times 10^4$ | $0 \pm 0$ | $0 \pm 0$ | $0 \pm 0$ | 2.14 | $1 \pm 0$ |
| | 3 | $-6.3849 \times 10^3 \pm 0$ | $-6.3849 \times 10^3$ | $0 \pm 0$ | $0 \pm 0$ | $0 \pm 0$ | 1.95 | $1 \pm 0$ |
| hepar2 | 1 | $-3.5372 \times 10^4 \pm 0$ | $-3.5372 \times 10^4$ | $0 \pm 0$ | $0 \pm 0$ | $0 \pm 0$ | 28.07 | $1 \pm 0$ |
| | 2 | $-3.5318 \times 10^4 \pm 0$ | $-3.5318 \times 10^4$ | $0 \pm 0$ | $0 \pm 0$ | $0 \pm 0$ | 24.57 | $1 \pm 0$ |
| | 3 | $-1.2133 \times 10^4 \pm 0$ | $-1.2133 \times 10^4$ | $0 \pm 0$ | $0 \pm 0$ | $0 \pm 0$ | 23.25 | $1 \pm 0$ |
| win95pts | 1 | $-3.8374 \times 10^4 \pm 0$ | $-3.8374 \times 10^4$ | $0 \pm 0$ | $0 \pm 0$ | $0 \pm 0$ | 19.16 | $1 \pm 0$ |
| | 2 | $\mathbf{-3.8309} \times 10^4 \pm 0$ | $-3.8310 \times 10^4$ | $0 \pm 0$ | $0 \pm 0$ | $1 \pm 0$ | 14.12 | $0.9911 \pm 0$ |
| | 3 | $-1.3083 \times 10^4 \pm 0$ | $-1.3083 \times 10^4$ | $0 \pm 0$ | $0 \pm 0$ | $0 \pm 0$ | 18.61 | $1 \pm 0$ |
| munin | 1 | $\mathbf{-9.5488} \times 10^4 \pm 0$ | $-9.5663 \times 10^4$ | $0 \pm 0$ | $59 \pm 0$ | $0 \pm 0$ | 160.46 | $0.8832 \pm 0$ |
| | 2 | $\mathbf{-9.5380} \times 10^4 \pm 0$ | $-9.5561 \times 10^4$ | $0 \pm 0$ | $59 \pm 0$ | $1 \pm 0$ | 179.94 | $0.8792 \pm 0$ |
| | 3 | $\mathbf{-3.2199} \times 10^4 \pm 0$ | $-3.2393 \times 10^4$ | $0 \pm 0$ | $59 \pm 0$ | $0 \pm 0$ | 177.87 | $0.8832 \pm 0$ |
| andes | 1 | $-1.1296 \times 10^5 \pm 0$ | $-1.1296 \times 10^5$ | $0 \pm 0$ | $0 \pm 0$ | $0 \pm 0$ | 660.71 | $1 \pm 0$ |
| | 2 | $\mathbf{-1.1280} \times 10^5 \pm 0$ | $-1.1281 \times 10^5$ | $1 \pm 0$ | $0 \pm 0$ | $0 \pm 0$ | 559.27 | $0.9985 \pm 0$ |
| | 3 | $-3.8190 \times 10^4 \pm 0$ | $-3.8190 \times 10^4$ | $0 \pm 0$ | $0 \pm 0$ | $0 \pm 0$ | 676.99 | $1 \pm 0$ |
| pigs | 1 | $\mathbf{-2.2197} \times 10^5 \pm 0$ | $-2.2301 \times 10^5$ | $0 \pm 0$ | $357 \pm 0$ | $0 \pm 0$ | 2850.50 | $0.5683 \pm 0$ |
| | 2 | $\mathbf{-2.2209} \times 10^5 \pm 0$ | $-2.2316 \times 10^5$ | $1 \pm 0$ | $357 \pm 0$ | $0 \pm 0$ | 3184.71 | $0.5676 \pm 0$ |
| | 3 | $\mathbf{-7.4199} \times 10^4 \pm 0$ | $-7.5375 \times 10^4$ | $0 \pm 0$ | $357 \pm 0$ | $0 \pm 0$ | 2984.92 | $0.5683 \pm 0$ |

**Table 5.** Performance of M-FRRMAB-HH algorithm under different LLHs.

| Network | LLH | BIC | AD | DD | RD | SET(s) | F1 |
|---|---|---|---|---|---|---|---|
| alarm | 1 | $-1.8710 \times 10^4 \pm 0$ | $0 \pm 0$ | $0 \pm 0$ | $0 \pm 0$ | 1.78 | $1 \pm 0$ |
| | 2 | $-1.8710 \times 10^4 \pm 0$ | $0 \pm 0$ | $0 \pm 0$ | $0 \pm 0$ | 1.53 | $1 \pm 0$ |
| | 3 | $-1.8710 \times 10^4 \pm 0$ | $0 \pm 0$ | $0 \pm 0$ | $0 \pm 0$ | 1.45 | $1 \pm 0$ |
| hepar2 | 1 | $-3.5733 \times 10^4 \pm 311.46$ | $0 \pm 0$ | $2 \pm 0.71$ | $0 \pm 0$ | 22.62 | $0.9918 \pm 0.0029$ |
| | 2 | $-3.7564 \times 10^4 \pm 1225.67$ | $0 \pm 0$ | $1.60 \pm 0.89$ | $0 \pm 0$ | 13.30 | $0.9934 \pm 0.0037$ |
| | 3 | $-4.9708 \times 10^4 \pm 0$ | $0 \pm 0$ | $12 \pm 0$ | $0 \pm 0$ | 7.31 | $0.9487 \pm 0$ |
| win95pts | 1 | $-3.8496 \times 10^4 \pm 35.49$ | $0.80 \pm 1.10$ | $1 \pm 0$ | $0 \pm 0$ | 15.70 | $0.9920 \pm 0.0048$ |
| | 2 | $-3.8440 \times 10^4 \pm 146.06$ | $0 \pm 0$ | $0.20 \pm 0.45$ | $0 \pm 0$ | 12.21 | $0.9991 \pm 0.0020$ |
| | 3 | $-4.0845 \times 10^4 \pm 35.49$ | $0.80 \pm 1.10$ | $3 \pm 0$ | $0 \pm 0$ | 7.40 | $0.9829 \pm 0.0048$ |
| munin | 1 | $-9.5504 \times 10^4 \pm 0$ | $0 \pm 0$ | $53 \pm 0$ | $0 \pm 0$ | 502.06 | $0.8963 \pm 0$ |
| | 2 | $-9.5504 \times 10^4 \pm 0$ | $0 \pm 0$ | $53 \pm 0$ | $0 \pm 0$ | 71.03 | $0.8963 \pm 0$ |
| | 3 | $-9.7568 \times 10^4 \pm 0$ | $0 \pm 0$ | $57 \pm 0$ | $0 \pm 0$ | 44.17 | $0.8876 \pm 0$ |
| andes | 1 | $-1.1296 \times 10^5 \pm 0$ | $0 \pm 0$ | $0 \pm 0$ | $0 \pm 0$ | 785.12 | $1 \pm 0$ |
| | 2 | $-1.3746 \times 10^5 \pm 3.3554 \times 10^4$ | $1.60 \pm 2.19$ | $2 \pm 2.74$ | $0 \pm 0$ | 574.69 | $0.9947 \pm 0.0073$ |
| | 3 | $-3.2952 \times 10^6 \pm 4.2327 \times 10^6$ | $8.80 \pm 0.45$ | $13.40 \pm 0.55$ | $2.40 \pm 0.55$ | 303.37 | $0.9598 \pm 0.0021$ |
| pigs | 1 | $-2.2207 \times 10^5 \pm 0$ | $0 \pm 0$ | $324 \pm 0$ | $0 \pm 0$ | 785.58 | $0.6233 \pm 0$ |
| | 2 | $-2.2207 \times 10^5 \pm 0$ | $0 \pm 0$ | $324 \pm 0$ | $0 \pm 0$ | 779.83 | $0.6233 \pm 0$ |
| | 3 | $-2.2207 \times 10^5 \pm 0$ | $0 \pm 0$ | $324 \pm 0$ | $0 \pm 0$ | 194.52 | $0.6233 \pm 0$ |

### *5.4. Comparison with Some Other Algorithms*

To compare the graph accuracy between the networks learned by different algorithms, we report the F1 scores and BIC scores on different SEMs and networks in Tables 6 and 7, with a sample size of 1000 and the best results on each dataset highlighted in black. To make a fair comparison, our algorithm did not take into account expert knowledge.

The M-FRRMAB-HH algorithm achieved the highest BIC score on 15/18 datasets and the highest F1 score on all datasets. These high F1 scores and low BIC scores occurred because the data were not faithful to the original structure. The comparisons of the BIC scores supported the conclusion that M-FRRMAB-HH > NOTEARS > BNC-PSO > PCS > LiNGAM > PC, and the ranking of the F1 scores was M-FRRMAB-HH > BNC-PSO > NOTEARS > PCS > PC > LiNGAM. Therefore, we believe that compared with the other five algorithms, our proposed algorithm has higher accuracy.

For NOTEARS, there were 11 outputs on the 18 datasets, and no outputs were found seven times. Comparing NOTEARS and M-FRRMAB-HH on these 11 datasets, NOTEARS won three times in terms of the BIC score and only once in terms of the F1 score. This shows that the network learned by NOTEARS had a higher BIC score, and our algorithm was more likely to acquire a structure with lower structural error because of the addition of structural constraints. In our experiments, both BNC-PSO and the PCS adopted structural soft constraints and heuristic searches. However, for large-scale networks such as Munin, Andes and Pigs, the BIC scores and F1 scores both decreased significantly, which indicated that the heuristic methods they employ have poor search performance on large-scale networks, whereas our algorithm has greater global search capability and is suitable for structural learning on large-scale networks. The performance of PC-Stable and LiNGAM was significantly lower than that of the other score-based algorithms, and the performance varied dramatically on different datasets, especially on the Andes network, where the BIC score was three orders of magnitude different from that of the other algorithms.

On the basis of the above results and analysis, we can conclude that structural constraints improve the search efficiency and learning accuracy of our algorithm. Compared with the single heuristic algorithm, the multi-population hyper-heuristic algorithm has a greater global search ability and is a suitable solution for large DAG learning problems.

**Table 6.** F1 scores of the algorithms for different SEMs. Bold denotes the F1 score that was the best amongst all methods. "-" indicates that no result was displayed.

| SEM | Network | PC-Stable | LiNGAM | PCS | NOTEARS | BNC-PSO | M-FRRMAB-HH |
|---|---|---|---|---|---|---|---|
| SEM1 | alarm | 0.8539 | 0.6387 | 0.9787 | 0.9892 | 0.9892 | **1** |
| | hepar2 | 0.5871 | 0.7103 | 0.8593 | - | 0.9049 | **1** |
| | win95pts | 0.7882 | 0.4683 | 0.8631 | 0.9912 | 0.9715 | **1** |
| | munin | 0.7546 | 0.3350 | 0.6314 | - | 0.8611 | **0.8832** |
| | andes | 0.5497 | 0.2823 | 0.6826 | - | 0.8768 | **1** |
| | pigs | 0.4766 | 0.1650 | 0.3612 | 0.5683 | 0.5272 | **0.5683** |
| SEM2 | alarm | 0.8605 | 0.6116 | 0.9787 | 0.9451 | 0.9778 | **1** |
| | hepar2 | 0.6346 | 0.7117 | 0.8651 | 0.7603 | 0.9048 | **1** |
| | win95pts | 0.8491 | 0.6154 | 0.9136 | 0.9646 | 0.9695 | **0.9911** |
| | munin | 0.7976 | 0.3724 | 0.6216 | 0.8151 | 0.8607 | **0.8792** |
| | andes | 0.8394 | 0.4008 | 0.6000 | - | 0.9327 | **0.9985** |
| | pigs | 0.4174 | 0.1499 | 0.3265 | 0.5600 | 0.5141 | **0.5676** |
| SEM3 | alarm | 0.8276 | 0.9388 | 0.9892 | 0.9053 | **1** | **1** |
| | hepar2 | 0.5545 | 0.7413 | 0.8696 | - | 0.9392 | **1** |
| | win95pts | 0.8020 | 0.5542 | 0.9912 | 0.9442 | 0.9713 | **1** |
| | munin | 0.7670 | 0.3627 | 0.7876 | - | 0.8739 | **0.8832** |
| | andes | 0.5209 | 0.2649 | 0.7862 | - | 0.9200 | **1** |
| | pigs | 0.4687 | 0.1783 | 0.5098 | 0.5642 | 0.5631 | **0.5683** |

**Table 7.** BIC scores of the algorithms for different SEMs. Bold denotes the BIC score that was the best amongst all methods. "-" indicates that no result was displayed.

| SEM | Network | PC-Stable | LiNGAM | PCS | NOTEARS | BNC-PSO | M-FRRMAB-HH |
|---|---|---|---|---|---|---|---|
| SEM1 | alarm | $-2.23 \times 10^4$ | $-2.15 \times 10^4$ | $-1.87 \times 10^4$ | $-1.87 \times 10^4$ | $-1.87 \times 10^4$ | $\mathbf{-1.87} \times 10^4$ |
| | hepar2 | $-1.48 \times 10^5$ | $-4.26 \times 10^4$ | $-3.97 \times 10^4$ | - | $-4.73 \times 10^4$ | $\mathbf{-3.54} \times 10^4$ |
| | win95pts | $-7.70 \times 10^4$ | $-4.94 \times 10^4$ | $-4.09 \times 10^4$ | $-3.84 \times 10^4$ | $-4.08 \times 10^4$ | $\mathbf{-3.84} \times 10^4$ |
| | munin | $-1.29 \times 10^5$ | $-1.51 \times 10^5$ | $-1.22 \times 10^5$ | - | $-9.86 \times 10^4$ | $\mathbf{-9.55} \times 10^4$ |
| | andes | $-3.97 \times 10^8$ | $-5.77 \times 10^8$ | $-4.39 \times 10^5$ | - | $-6.49 \times 10^6$ | $\mathbf{-1.13} \times 10^5$ |
| | pigs | $-2.28 \times 10^5$ | $-2.46 \times 10^5$ | $-2.26 \times 10^5$ | $\mathbf{-2.22} \times 10^5$ | $-2.23 \times 10^5$ | $-2.22 \times 10^5$ |
| SEM2 | alarm | $-2.04 \times 10^4$ | $-1.95 \times 10^4$ | $-1.86 \times 10^4$ | $-1.88 \times 10^4$ | $-1.90 \times 10^4$ | $\mathbf{-1.86} \times 10^4$ |
| | hepar2 | $-4.48 \times 10^4$ | $-3.79 \times 10^4$ | $-3.63 \times 10^4$ | $-3.68 \times 10^4$ | $-3.69 \times 10^4$ | $\mathbf{-3.53} \times 10^4$ |
| | win95pts | $-4.63 \times 10^4$ | $-4.03 \times 10^4$ | $-3.83 \times 10^4$ | $-3.84 \times 10^4$ | $-3.85 \times 10^4$ | $\mathbf{-3.83} \times 10^4$ |
| | munin | $-9.70 \times 10^4$ | $-1.06 \times 10^5$ | $-9.85 \times 10^4$ | $-9.59 \times 10^4$ | $-9.57 \times 10^4$ | $\mathbf{-9.54} \times 10^4$ |
| | andes | $-1.52 \times 10^5$ | $-1.47 \times 10^5$ | $-1.24 \times 10^5$ | - | $-1.18 \times 10^5$ | $\mathbf{-1.13} \times 10^5$ |
| | pigs | $-2.25 \times 10^5$ | $-2.32 \times 10^5$ | $-2.23 \times 10^5$ | $\mathbf{-2.22} \times 10^5$ | $-2.22 \times 10^5$ | $-2.22 \times 10^5$ |
| SEM3 | alarm | $-7.87 \times 10^3$ | $-6.40 \times 10^3$ | $-6.39 \times 10^3$ | $-6.50 \times 10^3$ | $\mathbf{-6.38} \times 10^3$ | $\mathbf{-6.38} \times 10^3$ |
| | hepar2 | $-3.90 \times 10^4$ | $-1.57 \times 10^4$ | $-1.38 \times 10^4$ | - | $-1.69 \times 10^4$ | $\mathbf{-1.21} \times 10^4$ |
| | win95pts | $-2.07 \times 10^4$ | $-1.61 \times 10^4$ | $-1.31 \times 10^4$ | $-1.32 \times 10^4$ | $-1.39 \times 10^4$ | $\mathbf{-1.31} \times 10^4$ |
| | munin | $-4.68 \times 10^4$ | $-4.28 \times 10^4$ | $-3.37 \times 10^4$ | - | $-3.25 \times 10^4$ | $\mathbf{-3.22} \times 10^4$ |
| | andes | $-1.88 \times 10^8$ | $-6.22 \times 10^7$ | $-1.04 \times 10^5$ | - | $-2.35 \times 10^6$ | $\mathbf{-3.82} \times 10^4$ |
| | pigs | $-7.60 \times 10^4$ | $-8.31 \times 10^4$ | $-7.55 \times 10^4$ | $\mathbf{-7.42} \times 10^4$ | $-7.44 \times 10^4$ | $-7.43 \times 10^4$ |

## 6. Conclusions and Future Research

In this work, soft constraints were obtained via partial correlation analysis, and the hard constraints were determined via expert knowledge. Both serve as structural constraints to guide our proposed hyper-heuristic algorithm to improve the search efficiency and accuracy of our algorithm. The effect of expert knowledge and LLH pool on the efficiency of our algorithm was discussed. The experimental results showed that M-FRRMAB-HH is an effective and accurate causal discovery method under linear SEMs. Compared to other state-of-the-art methods, it output structures that are closer to real causality. We still need to make more efforts to improve our method. In the LLH pool, the restart operator we designed has a high time cost, so we need to develop a better heuristic operator library.

**Author Contributions:** Conceptualization, Y.D.; methodology, Y.D.; software, Y.D.; validation, Y.D.; formal analysis, Y.D. and Z.W.; investigation, Y.D.; resources, Y.D.; data curation, Y.D. and Z.W.; writing—original draft preparation, Y.D.; writing—review and editing, Y.D.; visualization, Y.D.; supervision, X.G.; project administration, Y.D. and Z.W.; funding acquisition, X.G. All authors have read and agreed to the published version of the manuscript.

**Funding:** This work was supported by the National Natural Science Foundation of China (61573285), the Fundamental Research Funds for the Central Universities, China (No. G2022KY0602), and the key core technology research plan of Xi'an, China (No. 21RGZN0016).

**Institutional Review Board Statement:** Not applicable.

**Data Availability Statement:** The true networks of all eight datasets are known, and they are publicly available (http://www.bnlearn.com/bnrepository, accessed on 30 October 2024).

**Acknowledgments:** I have benefited from the presence of my supervisor and classmates. I am very grateful to my supervisor Xiaoguang Gao who gave me encouragement, careful guidance, and helpful advice throughout the writing of this thesis.

**Conflicts of Interest:** The authors declare no conflicts of interest.

## Abbreviations

The following abbreviations are used in this manuscript:

| | |
|---|---|
| ABC | Artificial bee colony |
| BFO | Bacterial foraging optimization |
| BIC | Bayesian information criterion |
| CI | Conditional independence |
| CSS | Complete search space |
| DAG | Directed acyclic graph |
| FIR | fitness improvement rate |
| FRRMAB | Fitness-rate-rank-based multiarmed bandit |
| GSS | Global search space |
| LLH | Low-level heuristic |
| LSS | Local search space |
| MB | Markov blanket |
| NLL | Negative log-likelihood |
| PSO | Particle swarm optimization |
| SEM | Structural equation model |
| SPPC | Structural priors by partial correlation |

## References


1. Yang, J.; Jiang, L.F.; Xie, K.; Chen, Q.Q.; Wang, A.G. Lung nodule detection algorithm based on rank correlation causal structure learning. *Expert Syst. Appl.* **2023**, *216*, 119381. [CrossRef]
2. McLachlan, S.; Dube, K.; Hitman, G.A.; Fenton, N.E.; Kyrimi, E. Bayesian networks in healthcare: Distribution by medical condition. *Artif. Intell. Med.* **2020**, *107*, 101912. [CrossRef] [PubMed]
3. Wang, Z.W.; Wang, Z.W.; He, S.W.; Gu, X.W.; Yan, Z.F. Fault detection and diagnosis of chillers using Bayesian network merged distance rejection and multi-source non-sensor information. *Appl. Energy* **2017**, *188*, 200–214. [CrossRef]
4. Tien, I.; Kiureghian, A.D. Algorithms for Bayesian network modeling and reliability assessment of infrastructure systems. *Reliab. Eng. Syst. Saf.* **2016**, *156*, 134–147. [CrossRef]
5. Koller, D.; Friedman, N. *Probabilistic Graphical Models: Principles and Techniques*; MIT Press: Cambridge, MA, USA, 2009.
6. Lee, J.; Chung, W.Y.; Kim, E. Structure learning of Bayesian networks using dual genetic algorithm. *IEICE Trans. Inf. Syst.* **2008**, *91*, 32–43. [CrossRef]
7. Gámez, J.A.; Puerta, J.M. Searching for the best elimination sequence in Bayesian networks by using ant colony optimization. *Pattern Recognit. Lett.* **2002**, *23*, 261–277. [CrossRef]
8. Sun, B.D.; Zhou, Y.; Wang, J.J.; Zhang, W.M. A new PC-PSO algorithm for Bayesian network structure learning with structure priors. *Expert Syst. Appl.* **2021**, *184*, 11. [CrossRef]
9. Gheisari, S.; Meybodi, M.R. BNC-PSO: Structure learning of Bayesian networks by Particle Swarm Optimization. *Inf. Sci.* **2016**, *348*, 272–289. [CrossRef]
10. Ji, J.Z.; Wei, H.K.; Liu, C.N. An artificial bee colony algorithm for learning Bayesian networks. *Soft Comput.* **2013**, *17*, 983–994. [CrossRef]
11. Askari, M.B.A.; Ahsaee, M.G. *Bayesian Network Structure Learning Based on Cuckoo Search Algorithm*; IEEE: Piscataway, NJ, USA, 2018; pp. 127–130.
12. Wang, X.C.; Ren, H.J.; Guo, X.X. A novel discrete firefly algorithm for Bayesian network structure learning. *Knowl.-Based Syst.* **2022**, *242*, 10. [CrossRef]
13. Yang, C.C.; Ji, J.Z.; Liu, J.M.; Liu, J.D.; Yin, B.C. Structural learning of Bayesian networks by bacterial foraging optimization. *Int. J. Approx. Reason.* **2016**, *69*, 147–167. [CrossRef]
14. Wang, J.Y.; Liu, S.Y. Novel binary encoding water cycle algorithm for solving Bayesian network structures learning problem. *Knowl.-Based Syst.* **2018**, *150*, 95–110. [CrossRef]
15. Drake, J.H.; Özcan, E.; Burke, E.K. A Case Study of Controlling Crossover in a Selection Hyper-heuristic Framework Using the Multidimensional Knapsack Problem. *Evol. Comput.* **2016**, *24*, 113–141. [CrossRef] [PubMed]
16. Pandiri, V.; Singh, A. A hyper-heuristic based artificial bee colony algorithm for k-Interconnected multi-depot multi-traveling salesman problem. *Inf. Sci.* **2018**, *463*, 261–281. [CrossRef]
17. Wang, Z.; Liu, J.L.; Zhang, J.L. Hyper-heuristic algorithm for traffic flow-based vehicle routing problem with simultaneous delivery and pickup. *J. Comput. Des. Eng.* **2023**, *10*, 2271–2287. [CrossRef]

18. Tsamardinos, I.; Brown, L.E.; Aliferis, C.F. The max-min hill-climbing Bayesian network structure learning algorithm. *Mac Learn.* **2006**, *65*, 31–78. [CrossRef]
19. Kitson, N.K.; Constantinou, A.C.; Guo, Z.G.; Liu, Y.; Chobtham, K. A survey of Bayesian Network structure learning. *Artif. Inte Rev.* **2023**, *56*, 8721–8814. [CrossRef]
20. Colombo, D.; Maathuis, M.H. Order-Independent Constraint-Based Causal Structure Learning. *J. Mach. Learn. Res.* **2014**, *1* 3741–3782.
21. Ogarrio, J.M.; Spirtes, P.; Ramsey, J. A Hybrid Causal Search Algorithm for Latent Variable Models. *JMLR Workshop Conf. Pro* **2016**, *52*, 368–379.
22. Tsamardinos, I.; Aliferis, C.F.; Statnikov, A. Time and sample efficient discovery of Markov blankets and direct causal relations. I Proceedings of the ACM SIGKDD International Conference on Knowledge Discovery and Data Mining, Washington, DC, US 24–27 August 2003; pp. 673–678.
23. Koivisto, M.; Sood, K. Exact Bayesian structure discovery in Bayesian networks. *J. Mach. Learn. Res.* **2004**, *5*, 549–573.
24. Yuan, C.; Malone, B. Learning Optimal Bayesian Networks: A Shortest Path Perspective. *J. Artif. Intell. Res.* **2013**, *48*, 23–6 [CrossRef]
25. de Campos, C.P.; Ji, Q. Efficient Structure Learning of Bayesian Networks using Constraints. *J. Mach. Learn. Res.* **2011**, *12*, 663–68
26. Cussens, J.; Järvisalo, M.; Korhonen, J.H.; Bartlett, M. Bayesian Network Structure Learning with Integer Programming: Polytope Facets and Complexity. *J. Artif. Intell. Res.* **2017**, *58*, 185–229. [CrossRef]
27. Chickering, D.M. Optimal structure identification with greedy search. *J. Mach. Learn. Res.* **2003**, *3*, 507–554.
28. Ramsey, J.; Glymour, M.; Sanchez-Romero, R.; Glymour, C. A million variables and more: The Fast Greedy Equivalence Searc algorithm for learning high-dimensional graphical causal models, with an application to functional magnetic resonance image *Int. J. Data Sci. Anal.* **2017**, *3*, 121–129. [CrossRef]
29. Bernaola, N.; Michiels, M.; Larrañaga, P.; Bielza, C. Learning massive interpretable gene regulatory networks of the human brai by merging Bayesian networks. *PLoS Comput. Biol.* **2023**, *19*, e1011443. [CrossRef]
30. Cooper, G.F.; Herskovits, E. A Bayesian method for the induction of probabilistic networks from data. *Mach. Learn.* **1992**, 309–347. [CrossRef]
31. Shimizu, S.; Hoyer, P.O.; Hyvärinen, A.; Kerminen, A. A linear non-Gaussian acyclic model for causal discovery. *J. Mach. Learn Res.* **2006**, *7*, 2003–2030.
32. Shimizu, S.; Inazumi, T.; Sogawa, Y.; Hyvärinen, A.; Kawahara, Y.; Washio, T.; Hoyer, P.O.; Bollen, K. DirectLiNGAM: A Direc Method for Learning a Linear Non-Gaussian Structural Equation Model. *J. Mach. Learn. Res.* **2011**, *12*, 1225–1248.
33. Zhang, K.; Wang, Z.K.; Zhang, J.J.; Schölkopf, B. On Estimation of Functional Causal Models: General Results and Application t the Post-Nonlinear Causal Model. *ACM Trans. Intell. Syst. Technol.* **2016**, *7*, 22. [CrossRef]
34. Hoyer, P.O.; Janzing, D.; Mooij, J.M.; Peters, J.; Schölkopf, B. Nonlinear causal discovery with additive noise models. I Proceedings of the Advances in Neural Information Processing Systems 21—Proceedings of the 2008 Conference, Vancouver, BC Canada, 8–11 December 2008; pp. 689–696.
35. Zheng, X.; Aragam, B.; Ravikumar, P.; Xing, E.P. DAGs with NO TEARS: Continuous Optimization for Structure Learning. I Proceedings of the 32nd Conference on Neural Information Processing Systems (NIPS), Montreal, QC, Canada, 2–8 December 201
36. Wei, D.; Gao, T.; Yu, Y. DAGs with no fears: A closer look at continuous optimization for learning Bayesian networks. I Proceedings of the Advances in Neural Information Processing Systems, Virtual, 6–12 December 2020.
37. Lee, H.C.; Danieletto, M.; Miotto, R.; Cherng, S.T.; Dudley, J.T. Scaling structural learning with NO-BEARS to infer causa transcriptome networks. In Proceedings of the Pacific Symposium on Biocomputing, Fairmont Orchid, HI, USA, 3–7 Januar 2020; pp. 391–402.
38. Yu, Y.; Chen, J.; Gao, T.; Yu, M. DAG-GNN: DAG Structure Learning with Graph Neural Networks. In Proceedings of the 36t International Conference on Machine Learning (ICML), Long Beach, CA, USA, 9–15 June 2019.
39. Zhang, M.H.; Jiang, S.L.; Cui, Z.C.; Garnett, R.; Chen, Y.X. D-VAE: A Variational Autoencoder for Directed Acyclic Graphs. I Proceedings of the 33rd Conference on Neural Information Processing Systems (NeurIPS), Vancouver, BC, Canada, 8–14 December 201
40. Wang, X.; Du, Y.; Zhu, S.; Ke, L.; Chen, Z.; Hao, J.; Wang, J. Ordering-Based Causal Discovery with Reinforcement Learning. I Proceedings of the IJCAI International Joint Conference on Artificial Intelligence, Montreal, QC, Canada, 19–27 August 2021 pp. 3566–3573.
41. Dang, Y.L.; Gao, X.G.; Wang, Z.D. Choice Function-Based Hyper-Heuristics for Causal Discovery under Linear Structura Equation Models. *Biomimetics* **2024**, *9*, 9060350. [CrossRef] [PubMed]
42. Li, K.; Fialho, A.; Kwong, S.; Zhang, Q.F. Adaptive Operator Selection With Bandits for a Multiobjective Evolutionary Algorithm Based on Decomposition. *IEEE Trans. Evol. Comput.* **2014**, *18*, 114–130. [CrossRef]
43. Mısır, M.; Verbeeck, K.; De Causmaecker, P.; Berghe, G.V. An investigation on the generality level of selection hyper-heuristics under different empirical conditions. *Appl. Soft Comput.* **2013**, *13*, 3335–3353. [CrossRef]

Beinlich, I.A.; Suermondt, H.J.; Chavez, R.M.; Cooper, G.F. The ALARM Monitoring System: A Case Study with Two Probabilistic Inference Techniques for Belief Networks. In Proceedings of the 2nd European Conference on Artificial Intelligence in Medicine, London, UK, 29–31 August 1989; Springer: Berlin/Heidelberg, Germany, 1989; pp. 247–256.

Onisko, A. Probabilistic Causal Models in Medicine: Application to Diagnosis of Liver Disorders. Ph.D. Dissertation, Institute of Biocybernetics and Biomedical Engineering, Polish Academy of Science, Warsaw, Poland, 2003.

Conati, C.; Gertner, A.S.; VanLehn, K.; Druzdzel, M.J. On-line Student Modeling for Coached Problem Solving Using Bayesian Networks. In Proceedings of the 6th International Conference on User Modeling, Sardinia, Italy, 2–5 June 1997; Springer: Berlin/Heidelberg, Germany, 1997; pp. 231–242.

Andreassen, S.; Jensen, F.V.; Andersen, S.K.; Falck, B.; Kjærulff, U.; Woldbye, M.; Sørensen, A.R.; Rosenfalck, A.; Jensen, F. MUNIN—An Expert EMG Assistant. In *Computer-Aided Electromyography and Expert Systems*; Elsevier: Amsterdam, The Netherlands, 1989; Chapter 21.

Yang, J.; Li, L.; Wang, A.G. A partial correlation-based Bayesian network structure learning algorithm under linear SEM. *Knowl.-Based Syst.* **2011**, *24*, 963–976. [CrossRef]

entropy

MDPI

*Article*

# Identifying Causal Effects Under Functional Dependencies †

**Yizuo Chen * and Adnan Darwiche**

Computer Science Department, University of California, Los Angeles, CA 90095, USA; darwiche@cs.ucla.edu
* Correspondence: yizuo.chen@ucla.edu

† This article is a revised and expanded version of a paper entitled "Identifying Causal Effects Under Functional Dependencies", which was accepted by the Thirty-Eighth Annual Conference on Neural Information Processing Systems (NeurIPS) held at the Vancouver Convention Center.

**Abstract:** We study the identification of causal effects, motivated by two improvements to identifiability that can be attained if one knows that some variables in a causal graph are functionally determined by their parents (without needing to know the specific functions). First, an unidentifiable causal effect may become identifiable when certain variables are functional. Secondly, certain functional variables can be excluded from being observed without affecting the identifiability of a causal effect, which may significantly reduce the number of needed variables in observational data. Our results are largely based on an elimination procedure that removes functional variables from a causal graph while preserving key properties in the resulting causal graph, including the identifiability of causal effects. Our treatment of functional dependencies in this context mandates a formal, systematic, and general treatment of positivity assumptions, which are prevalent in the literature on causal effect identifiability and which interact with functional dependencies, leading to another contribution of the presented work.

**Keywords:** causal effects; identifiability; functional dependencies

## 1. Introduction

A causal effect measures the impact of an intervention on some events of interest and is exemplified by the question, "What is the probability that a patient would recover had they taken a drug?". This type of question, also known as an interventional query, belongs to the second rung of Pearl's causal hierarchy [1], so it ultimately requires experimental studies if it is to be estimated from data. However, it is well known that such interventional queries can sometimes be answered based on observational queries (first rung of the causal hierarchy), which can be estimated from observational data. This becomes very significant when experimental studies are either not available, expensive to conduct, or would entail ethical concerns. Hence, a key question in causal inference asks when and how a causal effect can be estimated from available observational data, assuming a causal graph is provided [2].

More precisely, given a set of *treatment* variables ($\mathbf{X}$) and a set of *outcome* variables ($\mathbf{Y}$), the causal effect of $\mathbf{x}$ on $\mathbf{Y}$, denoted as $\Pr(\mathbf{Y}|do(\mathbf{x}))$ or $\Pr_{\mathbf{x}}(\mathbf{Y})$, is the marginal probability on $\mathbf{Y}$ when an intervention sets the states of variables ($\mathbf{X}$) to $\mathbf{x}$. The problem of identifying a causal effect studies whether $\Pr_{\mathbf{x}}(\mathbf{Y})$ can be *uniquely* determined from a causal graph and a distribution ($\Pr(\mathbf{V})$) over some variables ($\mathbf{V}$) in the causal graph [2], where $\Pr(\mathbf{V})$ is typically estimated from observational data. The casual effect is guaranteed to be identifiable if $\mathbf{V}$ corresponds to all variables in the causal graph (with some positivity assumptions), that is, if all variables in the causal graph are observed. When some variables are hidden (unobserved), it is possible that different parameterizations of the causal graph will induce the same distribution ($\Pr(\mathbf{V})$) but different values for the causal effect ($\Pr_{\mathbf{x}}(\mathbf{Y})$), which leads to unidentifiablility. In the past few decades, a significant amount of effort has been devoted to studying the identifiability of causal effects (see, e.g., [2–7]). Some early works include the *back-door criterion* [2,8] and the *front-door criterion* [2,3]. These criteria are sound but incomplete, as they may fail to identify certain causal effects that are, indeed, identifiable. Complete identification methods include the do-calculus method [2], the identification algorithm presented in [9], and the ID algorithm proposed in [10]. These methods require some positivity assumptions (constraints) on the observational distribution ($\Pr(\mathbf{V})$) and can derive an identifying formula that computes the causal effect based on $\Pr(\mathbf{V})$ when the causal effect is identifiable. Some recent works take a different approach by first estimating the parameters of a causal graph to obtain a fully specified causal model, which is then used to estimate causal effects through inference [11–14]. Further works focus on the efficiency of estimating causal effects from finite data, e.g., [15–18].

One main challenge of these algorithms is that they try to identify causal effects from limited information in the form of a causal graph and data on observed variables ($\mathbf{V}$). This becomes a problem when only a small number of variables ($\mathbf{V}$) is observed, since $\Pr(\mathbf{V})$ alone may not provide enough information for deciding the values of causal effects. Such scenarios happen when the collection of data on some variables is infeasible, e.g., if these variables (such as gender and age) involve confidential information. A recent line of work mitigates this problem by studying the impact of additional information on identifiability beyond causal graphs and observational data. For example, Tikka et al. [19] showed that certain unidentifiable causal effects can become identifiable given information about context-specific independence. Our work in this paper follows the same direction, as we consider the problem of causal effect identification in the presence of a particular type of qualitative knowledge called *functional dependencies* [20]. We say there is a functional dependency between a variable ($X$) and its parents ($\mathbf{P}$) in the causal graph if the distribution ($\Pr(X|\mathbf{P})$) is deterministic but we do not know the distribution itself (i.e., the specific values of $\Pr(x|\mathbf{p})$). In this case, we also say that variable $X$ is *functional*. Previous works have shown that functional dependencies can be exploited to improve the efficiency of Bayesian network inference [13,21–24]. We complement these works by showing that functional dependencies can also be exploited to improve the identifiability of causal effects, especially in the presence of hidden variables. In particular, we show that some unidentifiable causal effects may become identifiable, given such functional dependencies; propose techniques for testing identifiability in this context; and highlight other implications of such dependencies on the practice of identifiability.

Consider the following motivational example where we are interested in how the enforcement of speed limits may affect car accidents. The driving age ($A$) is functionally determined by country ($C$), driving age and country are causes of speed ($X$), and speed and driving age are causes of accidents ($Y$). The DAG on the right captures the causal relations among these variables, where variable $A$ is circled to indicate it is functional. Furthermore, suppose that variables $C, X, Y$ are observed. According to classical cause–effect identification methods (e.g., do-calculus and ID algorithm), the causal effect of $X$ on $Y$ is unidentifiable in this case. However, if we take into account that variable $A$ is a function of $C$, which restricts the class of distributions under consideration, then the causal effect of $X$ on $Y$ becomes identifiable. This exemplifies the improvements to identifiability pursued in this paper.

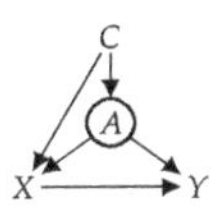


Consider a causal graph ($G$) and a distribution ($\Pr(\mathbf{V})$) over the observed variables ($\mathbf{V}$) in $G$. To check the identifiability of a causal effect, it is standard to first apply the *projection* operation proposed in [25,26], which constructs another causal graph ($G'$) with $\mathbf{V}$ as its non-root variables, followed by the application of an identification algorithm to $G'$, like the ID algorithm [10]. We call this two-stage procedure *project-ID*. One restriction of project-ID is that it is applicable only under some positivity constraints (assumptions), such as strict positivity ($\Pr(\mathbf{V}) > 0$), which preclude some events from having a zero probability.

Nevertheless, these positivity constraints are not always satisfiable in practice and may contradict functional dependencies. For example, if $Y$ is a function of $X$, then the positivity constraint ($\Pr(X,Y) > 0$) never holds. To systematically treat this interaction between positivity constraints and functional dependencies, we formulate the notion of *constrained identifiability*, which takes positivity constraints as an input (in addition to the causal graph ($G$) and distribution ($\Pr(\mathbf{V})$)). We also formulate the notion of *functional identifiability*, which further takes functional dependencies as an input. This allows us to explicitly treat the interactions between positivity constraints and functional dependencies, which is needed for the combination of classical methods like project-ID with the results we present in this paper.

The paper is structured as follows. We start with some technical preliminaries in Section 2. We formally define positivity constraints and functional dependencies in Section 3, where we also introduce the problems of constrained and functional identifiability. Section 4 introduces two primitive operations, *functional elimination* and *functional projection*, which are needed for later treatments. Section 5 presents our core results on functional identifiability and how they can be combined with existing identifiability algorithms. We conduct experiments to evaluate the effectiveness of functional dependencies on cause–effect identifiability in Section 6. Finally, we close with concluding remarks in Section 7. Proofs of all results are included in Appendix C. This paper is an extended version of [27].

## 2. Technical Preliminaries

We consider discrete variables in this work. Single variables are denoted by uppercase letters (e.g., $X$), and their states are denoted by lowercase letters (e.g., $x$). Sets of variables are denoted by bold uppercase letters (e.g., $\mathbf{X}$), and their instantiations (sets of values) are denoted by bold lowercase letters (e.g., $\mathbf{x}$).

### 2.1. Causal Bayesian Networks and Interventions

A Causal Bayesian Network (CBN) is a pair $\langle G, \mathcal{F} \rangle$, where $G$ is a *causal graph* in the form of a directed acyclic graph (DAG) and $\mathcal{F}$ is a set of conditional probability tables (CPTs). We have one CPT for each variable ($X$) with parents $\mathbf{P}$ in $G$, denoted as $f_X(X, \mathbf{P})$, which specifies the conditional probability distributions ($\Pr(X|\mathbf{P})$). It follows that every CPT ($f_X(X, \mathbf{P})$) satisfies the following properties: $f_X(x, \mathbf{p}) \in [0,1]$ for all instantiations $(x, \mathbf{p})$ and $\sum_x f_X(x, \mathbf{p}) = 1$ for each instantiation ($\mathbf{p}$). For simplicity, we also denote $f_X(X, \mathbf{P})$ as $f_X$.

A CBN induces a joint distribution over its variables ($\mathbf{V}$), which is exactly the product of its CPTs, i.e., $\Pr(\mathbf{V}) = \prod_{V \in \mathbf{V}} f_V$. In the CBN shown in Figure 1a, for example, $\Pr(A, B, X_1, C, D, E, X_2, Y) = f_A(A) f_B(B, A) f_{X_1}(X_1, B) f_C(B, C) f_D(D, X_1, C)\, f_E(E, D)\, f_{X_2}(X_2, D) f_Y(Y, E, X_2)$. Applying a treatment ($do(\mathbf{x})$) to the joint distribution yields a new distribution called the *interventional distribution*, denoted as $\Pr_{\mathbf{x}}(\mathbf{V})$. One way to compute the interventional distribution is to consider the *mutilated CBN* $\langle G', \mathcal{F}' \rangle$ that is constructed from the original CBN $\langle G, \mathcal{F} \rangle$ as follows: Remove from $G$ all edges that point to variables in $\mathbf{X}$; then, replace the CPT in $\mathcal{F}$ for each $X \in \mathbf{X}$ with a CPT ($f_X(X)$ where $f_X(x) = 1$ if $x$ is consistent with $\mathbf{x}$ and $f_X(x) = 0$ otherwise). Figure 1a depicts a causal graph ($G$), and Figure 1b depicts the mutilated causal graph ($G'$) under a treatment ($do(x_1, x_2)$). The interventional distribution ($\Pr_{\mathbf{x}}$) is the distribution induced by the mutilated CBN $\langle G', \mathcal{F}' \rangle$, where $\Pr_{\mathbf{x}}(\mathbf{Y})$ corresponds to the causal effect ($\Pr(\mathbf{Y}|do(\mathbf{x}))$, also notated by $\Pr(\mathbf{Y}_{\mathbf{x}})$). In this example, the causal effect of $do(x_1, x_2)$ on $Y$ can be computed by $\Pr_{x_1,x_2}(y) = \sum_{a,b,c,d,e} f_A(a) f_B(b,a) f_C(b,c) f_D(d, x_1, c) f_E(e,d) f_Y(y, e, x_2)$.

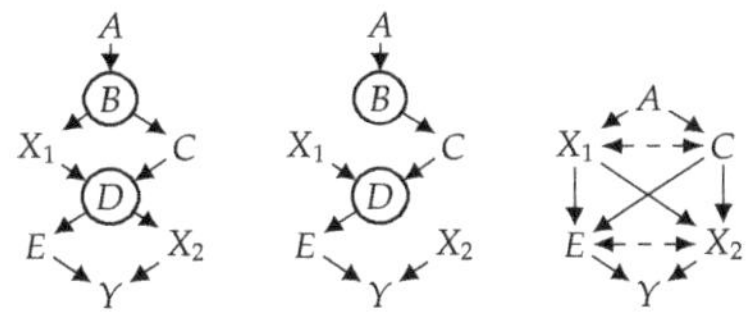


**Figure 1.** Mutilated and projected graphs of a causal graph. Hidden variables are circled. A bidirected edge ($V_1 \leftarrow\!\!-\!\!-\!\!\rightarrow V_2$) is aa compact notation for $V_1 \leftarrow H \rightarrow V_2$, where $H$ is an auxiliary hidden variable. (**a**) Causal graph; (**b**) mutilated graph; (**c**) projected graph.

### 2.2. Identifying Causal Effects

A key question in causal inference is to check whether a causal effect can be (uniquely) computed given the causal graph ($G$) and a distribution ($\Pr(\mathbf{V})$) over a subset ($\mathbf{V}$) of its variables. If the answer is yes, we say that the causal effect is *identifiable*, given $G$ and $\Pr(\mathbf{V})$. Otherwise, the causal effect is *unidentifiable*. Variables ($\mathbf{V}$) are said to be *observed*, and the remaining variables are said to be *hidden*, where $\Pr(\mathbf{V})$ is usually estimated from observational data. We start with the general definition of identifiability (not necessarily for causal effects) from [2] (Ch. 3.2.4), with a slight rephrasing.

**Definition 1** (Identifiability [2]). *Let $Q(M)$ be any computable quantity of a model ($M$). We say that $Q$ is identifiable in a class of models if, for any pair of models ($M_1$ and $M_2$) from this class, $Q(M_1) = Q(M_2)$ whenever $\Pr_{M_1}(\mathbf{V}) = \Pr_{M_2}(\mathbf{V})$, where $\mathbf{V}$ represents the observed variables.*

In the context of causal effects, the problem of identifiability is to check whether every pair of fully specified CBNs ($M_1$ and $M_2$ in Definition 1) that induces the same distribution ($\Pr(\mathbf{V})$) also produces the same value for the causal effect. Equivalently, to show that a causal effect is *unidentifiable*, it suffices to find two CBNs that induce the same distribution ($\Pr(\mathbf{V})$) yet different causal effects. Note that Definition 1 does not restrict the considered models ($M_1$ and $M_2$) based on the properties of the distributions ($\Pr_{M_1}(\mathbf{V})$ and $\Pr_{M_2}(\mathbf{V})$). However, in the literature on identifying causal effects, it is quite common to only consider CBNs (models) that induce distributions that satisfy some positivity constraints, such as $\Pr(\mathbf{V}) > 0$. We examine such constraints more carefully in Section 3, as they may contradict functional dependencies, which we introduce later.

It is well known that under some positivity constraints (e.g., $\Pr(\mathbf{V}) > 0$), the identifiability of causal effects can be efficiently tested using what we call the *project-ID* algorithm. Given a causal graph ($G$), project-ID first applies the projection operation proposed in [25,26,28] to yield a new causal graph ($G'$) whose hidden variables are all roots, each with exactly two children. These properties are needed by the ID algorithm [10], which is then applied to $G'$ to yield an identifying formula if the causal effect is identifiable and resulting in an outcome of FAIL otherwise. Consider the causal effect ($\Pr_{x_1 x_2}(y)$) in Figure 1a, where hidden variables are the non-root variables ($B, D$). We first project the causal graph ($G$) in Figure 1a onto its observed variables to yield the causal graph ($G'$) in Figure 1c (all hidden variables in $G'$ are auxiliary and roots). We then run the ID algorithm on $G'$, which returns the following (simplified) identifying formula: $\Pr_{x_1 x_2}(y) = \sum_c \Pr(c) \sum_e \Pr(y|e, x_2) \Pr(e|x_1, c)$. Hence, the causal effect ($\Pr_{x_1 x_2}(y)$) is identifiable and can be computed using the above formula. Moreover, all quantities in the formula can be obtained from the distribution ($\Pr(A, C, E, X_1, X_2, Y)$) over observed variables, which can be estimated from observational data. More details on the projection operation and the ID algorithm can be found in Appendix A.

## 3. Constrained and Functional Identifiability

As mentioned earlier, Definition 1 of identifiability [2] (Ch. 3.2.4) does not restrict the pair of considered models ($M_1$ and $M_2$). However, it is common in the literature on cause–effect identifiability to only consider CBNs with distributions ($\Pr(\mathbf{V})$ )that satisfy some positivity constraints. Strict positivity ($\Pr(\mathbf{V}) > 0$) is, perhaps, the mostly widely used constraint [2,9,28], that is, in Definition 1, we only consider CBNs $M_1$ and $M_2$, which induce distributions $\Pr_{M_1}$ and $\Pr_{M_2}$ that satisfy $\Pr_{M_1}(\mathbf{V}) > 0$ and $\Pr_{M_2}(\mathbf{V}) > 0$, respectively. Weaker and somewhat intricate positivity constraints were employed by the ID algorithm in [10] as discussed in Appendix A, but we apply this algorithm only under strict positivity to keep things simple (see [29,30] for a recent discussion of positivity constraints).

Positivity constraints are motivated by two considerations: technical convenience and the fact that most causal effects would be unidentifiable without some positivity constraints (more on this later). Given the multiplicity of positivity constraints considered in the literature and the subtle interaction between positivity constraints and functional dependencies (which are the main focus of this work), we next provide a systematic treatment of identifiability under positivity constraints.

### 3.1. Positivity Constraints

We first formalize the notion of a *positivity constraint*, then define the notion of *constrained identifiability*, which takes a set of positivity constraints as input (in addition to the causal graph ($G$) and distribution ($\Pr(\mathbf{V})$)).

**Definition 2.** *A positivity constraint on* $\Pr(\mathbf{V})$ *is an inequality of the form* $\Pr(\mathbf{S}|\mathbf{Z}) > 0$*, where* $\mathbf{S} \subseteq \mathbf{V}, \mathbf{Z} \subseteq \mathbf{V}$ *and* $\mathbf{S} \cap \mathbf{Z} = \emptyset$*, that is, for all instantiations* $(\mathbf{s}, \mathbf{z})$*, if* $\Pr(\mathbf{z}) > 0$*, then* $\Pr(\mathbf{s}, \mathbf{z}) > 0$*.*

When $\mathbf{Z} = \emptyset$, the positivity constraint is defined on a marginal distribution ($\Pr(\mathbf{S}) > 0$). To illustrate, the positivity constraint, $\Pr(X_2|X_1, C) > 0$ in Figure 1a specifies the constraint whereby $\Pr(x_2, x_1, c) > 0$ if $\Pr(x_1, c) > 0$ for every instantiation $(x_2, x_1, c)$. We may impose multiple positivity constraints on a set of variables ($\mathbf{V}$). We use $\mathcal{C}_\mathbf{V}$ to denote the set of positivity constraints imposed on $\Pr(\mathbf{V})$ and $\texttt{vars}(\mathcal{C}_\mathbf{V})$ to denote all the variables mentioned by $\mathcal{C}_\mathbf{V}$. Consider the constraints expressed as $\mathcal{C}_\mathbf{V} = \{\Pr(X_1, X_2|B, C) > 0, \Pr(Y|C, D) > 0\}$; then, $\texttt{vars}(\mathcal{C}_\mathbf{V}) = \{X_1, X_2, B, C, D, Y\}$. The weakest set of positivity constraints is $\mathcal{C}_\mathbf{V} = \{\}$ (no positivity constraints, as in Definition 1), and the strongest positivity constraint is $\mathcal{C}_\mathbf{V} = \{\Pr(\mathbf{V}) > 0\}$ (strict positivity).

We next provide a definition of identifiability for the causal effect of treatments ($\mathbf{X}$) on outcomes ($\mathbf{Y}$) in which positivity constraints are an input to the identifiability problem. We call it *constrained identifiability*, in contrast to the (unconstrained) identifiability of Definition 1.

**Definition 3.** *We call* $\langle G, \mathbf{V}, \mathcal{C}_\mathbf{V} \rangle$ *an identifiability tuple, where* $G$ *is a causal graph (DAG),* $\mathbf{V}$ *is its set of observed variables, and* $\mathcal{C}_\mathbf{V}$ *is a set of positivity constraints.*

**Definition 4** (Constrained Identifiability). *Let* $\langle G, \mathbf{V}, \mathcal{C}_\mathbf{V} \rangle$ *be an identifiability tuple. The causal effect of* $\mathbf{X}$ *on* $\mathbf{Y}$ *is said to be identifiable with respect to* $\langle G, \mathbf{V}, \mathcal{C}_\mathbf{V} \rangle$ *if* $\Pr^1_\mathbf{x}(\mathbf{y}) = \Pr^2_\mathbf{x}(\mathbf{y})$ *for any pair of distributions* ($\Pr^1$ *and* $\Pr^2$) *that are induced by* $G$ *and that satisfy* $\Pr^1(\mathbf{V}) = \Pr^2(\mathbf{V})$*, as well as the positivity constraints* ($\mathcal{C}_\mathbf{V}$)*.*

For simplicity, we say "identifiability" to mean "constrained identifiability" in the rest of this paper. We next show that without some positivity constraints, most causal effects would not be identifiable. We first define a notion called *first ancestor* on a causal graph as follows. We say that a treatment ($X \in \mathbf{X}$) is a *first ancestor* of some outcome ($Y \in \mathbf{Y}$) if $X$ is an ancestor of $Y$ in causal graph $G$ and that there exists a directed path from $X$ to $Y$ that is not intercepted by $\mathbf{X} \setminus \{X\}$. Consider the causal graph in Figure 2a with hidden variable $U$; treatment $X_2$ is a first ancestor of outcome $Y_2$, and outcome $Y_1$ does not have any first ancestor. A first ancestor must exist if some treatment variable is an ancestor of some outcome variable. The following result states a criterion under which a causal effect is never identifiable.

**Proposition 1.** *The casual effect of* $\mathbf{X}$ *on* $\mathbf{Y}$ *is not identifiable with respect to an identifiability tuple* $\langle G, \mathbf{V}, \mathcal{C}_{\mathbf{V}} \rangle$ *if some* $X \in \mathbf{X}$ *is a first ancestor of some* $Y \in \mathbf{Y}$ *and* $\mathcal{C}_{\mathbf{V}}$ *does not imply* $\Pr(X) > 0$.

Hence, identifiability is not possible without some positivity constraints if at least one treatment variable is an ancestor of some outcome variable (which is common). According to Proposition 1, the causal effect of $\{X_1, X_2\}$ on $\{Y_1, Y_2\}$ is not identifiable in Figure 2a if the considered distributions do not satisfy $\Pr(X_2) > 0$, as $X_2$ is a first ancestor of $Y_2$.

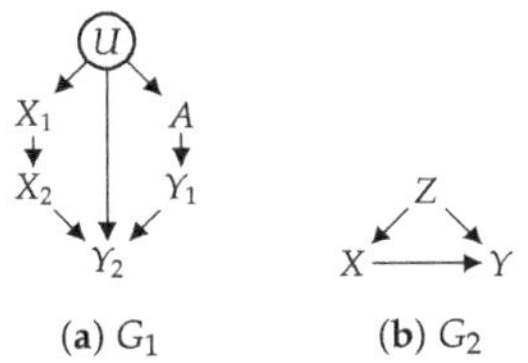


(**a**) $G_1$ (**b**) $G_2$

**Figure 2.** Examples for positivity.

As positivity constraints become stronger, more causal effects become more likely to be identifiable, since the set of considered models becomes smaller, that is, an unidentifiable causal effect under positivity constraint $\mathcal{C}^1_{\mathbf{V}}$ may become identifiable under positivity constraint $\mathcal{C}^2_{\mathbf{V}}$ if $\mathcal{C}^2_{\mathbf{V}}$ implies $\mathcal{C}^1_{\mathbf{V}}$. Consider the causal graph in Figure 2b, in which all variables are observed ($\mathbf{V} = \{X, Y, Z\}$). Without positivity constraints ($\mathcal{C}_{\mathbf{V}} = \emptyset$), the causal effect of $X$ on $Y$ is not identifiable. However, it becomes identifiable given strict positivity ($\mathcal{C}_{\mathbf{V}} = \{\Pr(X, Y, Z) > 0\}$), leading to an identifying formula expressed as $\Pr_x(y) = \sum_z \Pr(y|x, z) \Pr(z)$. This causal effect is also identifiable under the weaker positivity constraint, i.e., $\mathcal{C}_{\mathbf{V}} = \{\Pr(X|Z) > 0\}$. In this example, the positivity assumption ($\mathcal{C}_{\mathbf{V}} = \{\Pr(X, Y, Z) > 0\}$) is sufficient to make the identifying formula well defined because $\Pr(y|x, z) \Pr(z)$ in the formula is equal to zero when $\Pr(z) = 0$ and is computable when $\Pr(z) > 0$ (the conditional probability $\Pr(y|x, z)$ is well defined if $\Pr(x|z) > 0$). This is an example where strict positivity may be assumed for technical convenience only, as it may facilitate the application of some identifiability techniques like do-calculus [2].

### 3.2. Functional Dependencies

A variable ($X$) in a causal graph is said to *functionally depend* on its parents ($\mathbf{P}$) if its distribution is deterministic ($\Pr(x|\mathbf{p}) \in \{0, 1\}$) for every instantiation ($x, \mathbf{p}$). Variable $X$ is also said to be *functional* in this case. In this work, we assume *qualitative* functional dependencies. *We do not know the distribution* ($\Pr(X|\mathbf{P})$)*; we only know that it is deterministic.* We assume that root variables cannot be functional, as such variables can be removed from the causal graph.

The table on the right shows two variables ($B$ and $C$) that both have $A$ as their parent. Variable $C$ is functional, but variable $B$ is not. The CPT for variable $C$ is called a *functional CPT* in this case. Functional CPTs are also known as (causal) mechanisms and are expressed using structural equations in structural causal models (SCMs) [31–33]. By definition, in an SCM, every non-root variable is assumed to be functional (when noise variables are represented explicitly in the causal graph).

| $A$ | $B$ | $C$ | $\Pr(B\|A)$ | $\Pr(C\|A)$ |
|---|---|---|---|---|
| 0 | 0 | 0 | 0.2 | 0 |
| 0 | 1 | 1 | 0.8 | 1 |
| 1 | 0 | 0 | 0.6 | 1 |
| 1 | 1 | 1 | 0.4 | 0 |

Qualitative functional dependencies are a longstanding concept. For example, they are common in relational databases (see, e.g., [34,35]), and their relevance to probabilistic reasoning was previously brought up in [20] (Ch. 3). One example of a (qualitative) functional dependency is that different countries have different driving ages, so we know that "driving age" functionally depends on "country", even though we may not know the specific driving age for each country. Another example is that a "Letter grade" for a class is functionally dependent on the student's "weighted average", even though we may not know the scheme for converting a weighted average to a letter grade.

In this work, we assume that we are given a causal graph ($G$) in which some variables ($\mathbf{W}$) have been designated as functional. The presence of functional variables further restricts the set of distributions (Pr) that we consider when checking identifiability. This leads to a more refined problem that we call *functional identifiability (F-identifiability)*, which depends on four elements.

**Definition 5.** *We call $\langle G, \mathbf{V}, \mathcal{C}_\mathbf{V}, \mathbf{W}\rangle$ an F-identifiability tuple when $G$ is a DAG, $\mathbf{V}$ is its set of observed variables, $\mathcal{C}_\mathbf{V}$ is a set of positivity constraints, and $\mathbf{W}$ is a set of functional variables in $G$.*

**Definition 6** (F-Identifiability). *Let $\langle G, \mathbf{V}, \mathcal{C}_\mathbf{V}, \mathbf{W}\rangle$ be an F-identifiability tuple. The causal effect of $\mathbf{X}$ on $\mathbf{Y}$ is F-identifiable with respect to $\langle G, \mathbf{V}, \mathcal{C}_\mathbf{V}, \mathbf{W}\rangle$ if $\mathrm{Pr}^1_\mathbf{x}(\mathbf{y}) = \mathrm{Pr}^2_\mathbf{x}(\mathbf{y})$ for any pair of distributions ($\mathrm{Pr}^1$ and $\mathrm{Pr}^2$) that are induced by $G$, that satisfy $\mathrm{Pr}^1(\mathbf{V}) = \mathrm{Pr}^2(\mathbf{V})$ and the positivity constraints ($\mathcal{C}_\mathbf{V}$), and in which variables ($\mathbf{W}$) functionally depend on their parents.*

Both $\mathcal{C}_\mathbf{V}$ and $\mathbf{W}$ represent constraints on the models (CBNs) we consider when checking identifiability, and these two types of constraints may contradict each other. We next define two notions that characterize some important interactions between positivity constraints and functional variables.

**Definition 7.** *Let $\langle G, \mathbf{V}, \mathcal{C}_\mathbf{V}, \mathbf{W}\rangle$ be an F-identifiability tuple. Then, $\mathcal{C}_\mathbf{V}$ and $\mathbf{W}$ are consistent if there exists a parameterization for $G$ that induces a distribution satisfying $\mathcal{C}_\mathbf{V}$ and in which variables ($\mathbf{W}$) functionally depend on their parents. Moreover, $\mathcal{C}_\mathbf{V}$ and $\mathbf{W}$ are separable if $\mathbf{W} \cap \mathtt{vars}(\mathcal{C}_\mathbf{V}) = \emptyset$.*

If $\mathcal{C}_\mathbf{V}$ is inconsistent with $\mathbf{W}$, then the set of distributions (Pr) considered in Definition 6 is empty; hence, the causal effect is not well defined (and trivially identifiable according to Definition 6). As such, one would usually want to ensure such consistency. Here are some examples of positivity constraints that are always consistent with a set of functional variables ($\mathbf{W}$): positivity foreach treatment variable, i.e., $\{\mathrm{Pr}(X) > 0, X \in \mathbf{X}\}$; positivity for the set of non-functional treatments, i.e., $\{\mathrm{Pr}(\mathbf{X} \setminus \mathbf{W}) > 0\}$; and positivity for all non-functional variables, i.e., $\{\mathrm{Pr}(\mathbf{V} \setminus \mathbf{W}) > 0\}$. It turns out that all these examples are special cases of the following condition. For a functional variable ($W \in \mathbf{W}$), let $\mathbf{H}_W$ be variables that intercept all directed paths from non-functional variables to $W$ (such a $\mathbf{H}_W$ may not be unique). If none of the positivity constraints in $\mathcal{C}_\mathbf{V}$ mentions both $W$ and $\mathbf{H}_W$, then $\mathcal{C}_\mathbf{V}$ and $\mathbf{W}$ are guaranteed to be consistent (see Proposition A4 in Appendix C).

Separability is a stronger condition, and it intuitively implies that the positivity constraints do not rule out any possible functions for the variables in $\mathbf{W}$. We need such a condition for one of the results we present later. Some examples of positivity constraints that are separable from $\mathbf{W}$ are $\{\mathrm{Pr}(\mathbf{X} \setminus \mathbf{W}) > 0\}$ and $\{\mathrm{Pr}(\mathbf{V} \setminus \mathbf{W}) > 0\}$. Studying the interactions between positivity constraints and functional variables, as we do in this section, will prove helpful later when utilizing existing identifiability algorithms (which require positivity constraints) for the testing of functional identifiability.

## 4. Functional Elimination and Projection

Our approach for testing identifiability under functional dependencies is based the elimination of functional variables from the causal graph, followed by the invocation of the project-ID algorithm on the resulting graph. This can be subtle, though, since the described process does not work for every functional variable, as we discuss in the next section. Moreover, one needs to handle the interaction between positivity constraints and functional variables carefully. However, the first step is to formalize the process of eliminating a functional variable and to study the associated guarantees.

Eliminating variables from a probabilistic model is a well studied operation also known as marginalization (see, e.g., [36–38]). When eliminating variable $X$ from a model that represents distribution $\Pr(\mathbf{Z})$, the goal is to obtain a model that represents the marginal distribution ($\Pr(\mathbf{Y}) = \sum_x \Pr(x, \mathbf{Y})$, where $\mathbf{Y} = \mathbf{Z} \setminus \{X\}$). Elimination can also be applied to a DAG ($G$) that represents conditional independencies ($\mathcal{I}$), leading to a new DAG ($G'$) that represents independencies ($\mathcal{I}'$) that are implied by $\mathcal{I}$. In fact, the projection operation we discussed earlier [25,26] can be understood in these terms. We next propose an operation that eliminates functional variables from a DAG and that comes with stronger guarantees compared to earlier elimination operations as far as preserving independencies.

**Definition 8.** *The functional elimination of a variable (X) from a DAG (G) yields a new DAG attained by adding an edge from each parent of X to each child of X, then removing X from G.*

Appendix B extends this definition to causal Bayesian networks (i.e., updating both CPTs and the causal graph). For convenience, we sometimes say "elimination" to mean "functional elimination" when the context is clear. From the viewpoint of independence relations, functional elimination is not sound if the eliminated variable is not functional. In particular, the DAG ($G'$) that results from this elimination process may satisfy independencies (identified by d-separation) that do not hold in the original DAG ($G$). As we show later, however, every independence implied by $G'$ must be implied by $G$ if the eliminated variable is functional. In the context of SCMs, functional elimination may be interpreted as replacing the eliminated variable ($X$) with its function in all structural equations that contain $X$. Functional elimination applies in broader contexts than SCMs, though. Eliminating multiple functional variables in any order yields the same DAG (see Proposition A3 in Appendix B). For example, eliminating variables $\{C, D\}$ from the DAG in Figure 3a yields the DAG in Figure 3c whether we use the order of $\pi_1 = C, D$ or the order of $\pi_2 = D, C$.

Functional elimination preserves independencies that hold in the original DAG and that are not preserved by other elimination methods, including projection, as defined in [25,26]. These independencies are captured using the notion of D-separation [39,40], which is more refined than the classical notion of d-separation [41,42] (uppercase D versus lowercase d). The original definition of D-separation can be found in [40]. We provide a simpler definition next, stated as Proposition 2, as the equivalence between the two definitions is not immediate.

**Proposition 2.** *Let $\mathbf{X}, \mathbf{Y}, \mathbf{Z}$ be disjoint variable sets and $\mathbf{W}$ be a set of functional variables in DAG G. Then, $\mathbf{X}$ and $\mathbf{Y}$ are D-separated by $\mathbf{Z}$ in $\langle G, \mathbf{W}\rangle$ iff $\mathbf{X}$ and $\mathbf{Y}$ are d-separated by $\mathbf{Z}'$ in G, where $\mathbf{Z}'$ is obtained as follows. Initially, $\mathbf{Z}' = \mathbf{Z}$. The next step is repeated until $\mathbf{Z}'$ stops changing. Then, every variable in $\mathbf{W}$ whose parents are in $\mathbf{Z}'$ is added to $\mathbf{Z}'$.*

To illustrate the difference between d-separation and D-separation, consider, again, the DAG in Figure 3a and assume that variables $C$ and $D$ are functional. Variables $G$ and $I$ are not d-separated by $A$, but they are D-separated by $A$, that is, there are distributions that are induced by the DAG in Figure 3a and in which $G$ and $I$ are not independent given $A$. However, $G$ and $I$ are independent given $A$ in every induced distribution in which variables $C$ and $D$ are functionally determined by their parents. Functional elimination preserves D-separation in the following sense.

**Theorem 1.** *Consider a DAG (G) with functional variables ($\mathbf{W}$). Let $G'$ be the result of functionally eliminating variables $\mathbf{W}' \subseteq \mathbf{W}$ from G. For any disjoint sets ($\mathbf{X}$, $\mathbf{Y}$, and $\mathbf{Z}$) in $G'$, $\mathbf{X}$ and $\mathbf{Y}$ are D-separated by $\mathbf{Z}$ in $\langle G, \mathbf{W}\rangle$ iff $\mathbf{X}$ and $\mathbf{Y}$ are D-separated by $\mathbf{Z}$ in $\langle G', \mathbf{W} \setminus \mathbf{W}'\rangle$.*

The above result is stated with respect to eliminating a subset of the functional variables. If we eliminate all functional variables, then D-separation is reduced to d-separation.

For example, variables $G$ and $I$ are D-separated by $A$ in Figure 3c and in Figure 3a as suggested by Theorem 1. In fact, $G$ and $I$ are also d-separated by $A$ in Figure 3c, since we eliminated all functional variables. We now have the following stronger result.

**Corollary 1.** *Consider a DAG ($G$) with functional variables ($\mathbf{W}$). Let $G'$ be the result of functionally eliminating all variables ($\mathbf{W}$) from $G$. For any disjoint sets ($\mathbf{X}$, $\mathbf{Y}$, and $\mathbf{Z}$) in $G'$, $\mathbf{X}$ and $\mathbf{Y}$ are d-separated by $\mathbf{Z}$ in $G'$ iff $\mathbf{X}$ and $\mathbf{Y}$ are D-separated by $\mathbf{Z}$ in $\langle G, \mathbf{W} \rangle$.*

We now define the operation of functional projection, which augments the original projection operation proposed in [25,26] in the presence of functional dependencies.

**Definition 9.** *Let $G$ be a DAG, $\mathbf{V}$ be its observed variables, and $\mathbf{W}$ be its hidden functional variables ($\mathbf{W} \cap \mathbf{V} = \emptyset$). The functional projection of $G$ on $\mathbf{V}$ is a DAG obtained by functionally eliminating variables ($\mathbf{W}$) from $G$, then projecting the resulting DAG on variables ($\mathbf{V}$).*

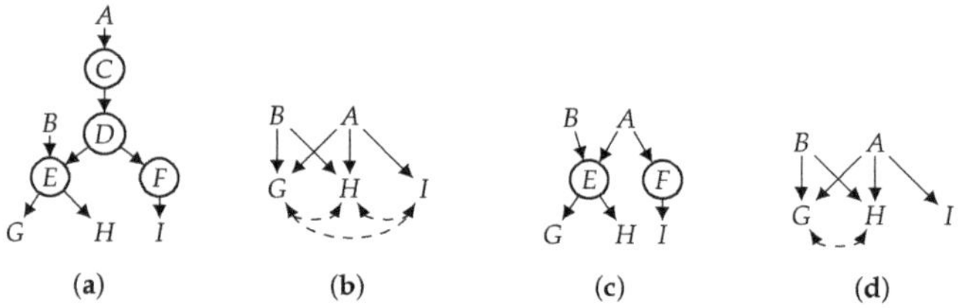


**Figure 3.** Contrasting projection with functional projection. $C$ and $D$ are functional. Hidden variables are circled. (**a**) DAG; (**b**) proj. (**a**) on $A, B, G, H, I$; (**c**) eliminate $C, D$ from (**a**); (**d**) proj. (**c**) on $A$, $B$, $G$, $H$, $I$.

We now contrast functional projection and classical projection using the causal graph in Figure 3a, assuming that the observed variables are $\mathbf{V} = \{A, B, G, H, I\}$ and the functional variables are $\mathbf{W} = \{C, D\}$. Applying classical projection to this causal graph yields the causal graph in Figure 3b. To apply functional projection, we first functionally eliminate $C$ and $D$ from Figure 3a, which yields Figure 3c; then, we project Figure 3c on variables ($\mathbf{V}$), which yields the causal graph in Figure 3d. So we now need to contrast Figure 3b (classical projection) with Figure 3d (functional projection). The latter is a strict subset of the former, as it is missing two bidirected edges. One implication of this is that variables $G$ and $I$ are not d-separated by $A$ in Figure 3b because they are not d-separated in Figure 3a. However, they are D-separated in Figure 3a; hence, they are d-separated in Figure 3d. So functional projection yields a DAG that exhibits more independencies. Again, this is because $G$ and $I$ are D-separated by $A$ in the original DAG, a fact that is not visible to the projection but is visible to (and exploitable by) the functional projection.

An important corollary of functional projection is the following.

**Corollary 2.** *Let $G$ be a DAG; $\mathbf{V}$ be its observed variables; $\mathbf{W}$ be its functional variables, which are all hidden; and $G'$ be the result of functionally projecting $G$ on $\mathbf{V}$. For any disjoint sets ($\mathbf{X}$, $\mathbf{Y}$, and $\mathbf{Z}$) in $G'$, $\mathbf{X}$ and $\mathbf{Y}$ are d-separated by $\mathbf{Z}$ in $G'$ iff $\mathbf{X}$ and $\mathbf{Y}$ are D-separated by $\mathbf{Z}$ in $\langle G, \mathbf{W} \rangle$.*

In other words, classical projection preserves d-separation, but functional projection preserves D-separation, which subsumes d-separation. Corollary 2 is a bit more subtle and powerful than it may first seem. First, it concerns D-separations based on hidden functional variables, not all functional variables. Secondly, it shows that such D-separations in $G$ appear as classical d-separations in $G'$ which allows us to feed $G'$ into existing identifiability algorithms, as we show later. This is a key enabler of some results we present next on the testing of functional identifiability.

## 5. Causal Identification with Functional Dependencies

Consider the causal graph ($G$) in Figure 4a and let $\mathbf{V} = \{A, X, Y\}$ be its observed variables. According to Definition 4 of identifiability, the causal effect of $X$ on $Y$ is not identifiable with respect to $\langle G, \mathbf{V}, \mathcal{C}_{\mathbf{V}} \rangle$, where $\mathcal{C}_{\mathbf{V}} = \{\Pr(A, X, Y) > 0\}$. We can show this by projecting the causal graph ($G$) on the observed variables ($\mathbf{V}$), which yields the causal graph ($G'$) in Figure 4b, then applying the ID algorithm to $G'$, which returns FAIL. Suppose now that the hidden variable ($B$) is known to be functional. According to Definition 6 of F-identifiability, this additional knowledge reduces the number of considered models, so it actually renders the causal effect identifiable—the identifying formula is $\Pr_x(y) = \sum_a \Pr(a) \Pr(y|a, x)$, as we show later. Hence, an unidentifiable causal effect becomes identifiable in light of knowledge that some variable is functional, even without knowing the structural equations for this variable.

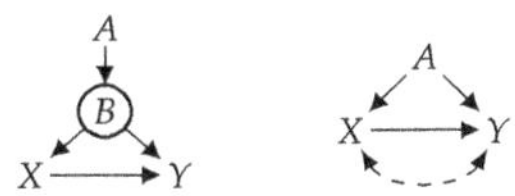


(**a**) (**b**)

**Figure 4.** $B$ is functional. (**a**) DAG; (**b**) projection.

The question now is how to algorithmically test F-identifiability. We propose two techniques for this purpose, the first of which is geared towards exploiting existing algorithms for classical identifiability. This technique is based on the elimination of functional variables from the causal graph while preserving F-identifiability, with the goal of getting to a point where F-identifiability becomes equivalent to classical identifiability. If we reach this point, we can use existing algorithms for classical identifiability, like the ID algorithm, to test F-identifiability. This can be subtle, though, since hidden functional variables behave differently from observed ones. We start with the following result.

**Theorem 2.** *Let $\langle G, \mathbf{V}, \mathcal{C}_{\mathbf{V}}, \mathbf{W} \rangle$ be an F-identifiability tuple. If $G'$ is the result of functionally eliminating the hidden functional variables ($\mathbf{W} \setminus \mathbf{V}$) from $G$, then the causal effect of $\mathbf{X}$ on $\mathbf{Y}$ is F-identifiable with respect to $\langle G, \mathbf{V}, \mathcal{C}_{\mathbf{V}}, \mathbf{W} \rangle$ iff it is F-identifiable with respect to $\langle G', \mathbf{V}, \mathcal{C}_{\mathbf{V}}, \mathbf{V} \cap \mathbf{W} \rangle$.*

An immediate corollary of this theorem is that if all functional variables are hidden, then we can reduce the question of F-identifiability to identifiability, since $\mathbf{V} \cap \mathbf{W} = \emptyset$, so F-identifiability with respect to $\langle G', \mathbf{V}, \mathcal{C}_{\mathbf{V}}, \mathbf{V} \cap \mathbf{W} = \emptyset \rangle$ collapses into identifiability with respect to $\langle G', \mathbf{V}, \mathcal{C}_{\mathbf{V}} \rangle$.

**Corollary 3.** *Let $\langle G, \mathbf{V}, \mathcal{C}_{\mathbf{V}}, \mathbf{W} \rangle$ be an F-identifiability tuple, where $\mathcal{C}_{\mathbf{V}} = \{\Pr(\mathbf{V}) > 0\}$ and $\mathbf{W}$ are all hidden. If $G'$ is the result of functionally projecting $G$ on variables ($\mathbf{V}$), then the causal effect of $\mathbf{X}$ on $\mathbf{Y}$ is F-identifiable with respect to $\langle G, \mathbf{V}, \mathcal{C}_{\mathbf{V}}, \mathbf{W} \rangle$ iff it is identifiable with respect to $\langle G, \mathbf{V}, \mathcal{C}_{\mathbf{V}} \rangle$ (We require the positivity constraint $\Pr(\mathbf{V}) > 0$, as we suspect the projection operation in [26] requires it even though that was not made explicit in the paper; if not, then $\mathcal{C}_{\mathbf{V}}$ can be empty in Corollary 3).*

This corollary suggests a method for using the ID algorithm, which is popular for testing identifiability, to establish F-identifiability by coupling ID with functional projection instead of classical projection. Consider the causal graph ($G$) in Figure 5a with observed variables of $\mathbf{V} = \{A, B, C, F, X, Y\}$. The causal effect of $X$ on $Y$ is not identifiable under $\Pr(\mathbf{V}) > 0$; projecting $G$ on observed variables ($\mathbf{V}$) yields the causal graph ($G'$) in Figure 5b, and the ID algorithm produces FAIL on $G'$. Suppose now that the hidden variables ($\{D, E\}$) are functional. To test whether the causal effect is F-identifiable using Corollary 3, we functionally project $G$ on the observed variables ($\mathbf{V}$), which yields the causal graph ($G''$) in Figure 5c. Applying the ID algorithm to $G''$ produces the following identifying formula: $\Pr_x(y) = \sum_{bf} \Pr(f|b,x) \sum_{acx'} \Pr(y|a,b,c,f,x') \Pr(a,b,c,x')$; therefore, $\Pr_x(y)$ is F-identifiable.

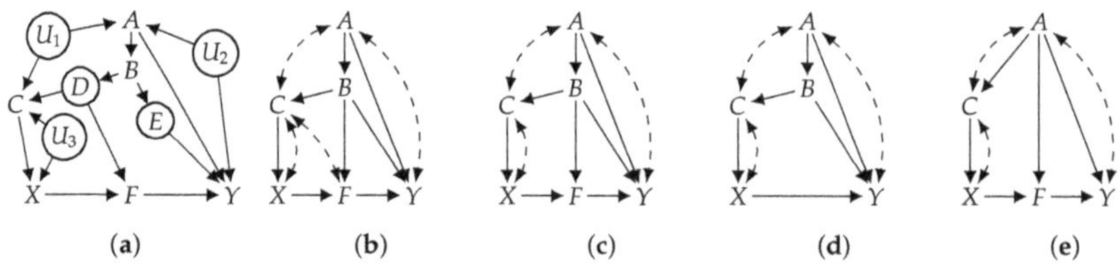

**Figure 5.** Variables $A, B, C, F, X$, and $Y$ are observed. Variables $D$ and $E$ are functional (and hidden). (**a**) Causal graph; (**b**) proj. of (**a**); (**c**) F-proj. of (**a**); (**d**) F-elim. $F$; (**e**) F-elim. $B$.

We stress, again, that Corollary 3 and the corresponding F-identifiability algorithm apply only when all functional variables are hidden. We now treat the case when some of the functional variables are observed. The subtlety here is that, unlike hidden functional variables, eliminating an observed functional variable does not always preserve F-identifiability. However, the following result identifies conditions that guarantee the preservation of F-identifiability based on the notion of separability in Definition 7. If all observed functional variables satisfy these conditions, we can, again, reduce F-identifiability into identifiability, so we can exploit existing methods for identifiability like the ID algorithm and do-calculus.

**Theorem 3.** *Let $\langle G, \mathbf{V}, \mathcal{C}_\mathbf{V}, \mathbf{W} \rangle$ be an F-identifiability tuple. Let $\mathbf{Z}$ be a set of observed functional variables that are neither treatments nor outcomes, are separable from $\mathcal{C}_\mathbf{V}$, and have observed parents. If $G'$ is the result of functionally eliminating variables ($\mathbf{Z}$) from $G$, then the causal effect of $\mathbf{X}$ on $\mathbf{Y}$ is F-identifiable with respect to $\langle G, \mathbf{V}, \mathcal{C}_\mathbf{V}, \mathbf{W} \rangle$ iff it is F-identifiable with respect to $\langle G', \mathbf{V} \setminus \mathbf{Z}, \mathcal{C}_\mathbf{V}, \mathbf{W} \setminus \mathbf{Z} \rangle$.*

Intuitively, the theorem allows us to remove observed functional variables from a causal graph if they satisfy the given conditions. We now have the following important corollary of Theorems 2 and 3, which subsumes Corollary 3.

**Corollary 4.** *Let $\langle G, \mathbf{V}, \mathcal{C}_\mathbf{V}, \mathbf{W} \rangle$ be an F-identifiability tuple, where $\mathcal{C}_\mathbf{V} = \{\Pr(\mathbf{V} \setminus \mathbf{W}) > 0\}$ and every variable in $\mathbf{W} \cap \mathbf{V}$ satisfies the conditions of Theorem 3. If $G'$ is the result of functionally projecting $G$ on $\mathbf{V} \setminus \mathbf{W}$, then the causal effect of $\mathbf{X}$ on $\mathbf{Y}$ is F-identifiable with respect to $\langle G, \mathbf{V}, \mathcal{C}_\mathbf{V}, \mathbf{W} \rangle$ iff it is identifiable with respect to $\langle G', \mathbf{V} \setminus \mathbf{W}, \mathcal{C}_\mathbf{V} \rangle$.*

Consider, again, the causal effect of $X$ on $Y$ in graph $G$ of Figure 5a with observed variables of $\mathbf{V} = \{A, B, C, F, X, Y\}$. Suppose now that the observed variable ($F$) is also functional (in addition to hidden functional variables $D$ and $E$) and assume $\Pr(A, B, C, X, Y) > 0$. Using Corollary 4, we can functionally project $G$ on $A$, $B$, $C$, $X$, and $Y$ to yield the causal graph ($G'$) in Figure 5d, which reduces F-identifiability on $G$ to classical identifiability on $G'$. Since strict positivity holds in $G'$, we can apply any existing identifiability algorithm and conclude that the causal effect is not identifiable. For another scenario, suppose that the observed variable ($B$) (instead of $F$) is functional and we have $\Pr(A, C, F, X, Y) > 0$. Again, using Corollary 4, we functionally project $G$ onto $A$, $C$, $F$, $X$, and $Y$ to yield the causal graph ($G''$) in Figure 5e, which reduces F-identifiability on $G$ to classical identifiability on $G''$. If we apply the ID algorithm to $G''$, we obtain the following identifying formula (which we denote as Equation (A1)): $\Pr_x(y) = \sum_{af} \Pr(f|a,x) \sum_{cx'} \Pr(y|a,c,f,x') \Pr(a,c,x')$. In both scenarios presented above, we were able to test F-identifiability using an existing algorithm for identifiability.

Corollary 4 (and Theorem 3) has yet another key application: it can help us pinpoint observations that are not essential for identifiability. To illustrate, consider the second scenario presented above, where the observed variable ($B$) is functional in the causal graph ($G$) of Figure 5a. The fact that Corollary 4 allowed us to eliminate variable $B$ from $G$ implies that observation of this variable is not needed to render the causal effect F-identifiable and, hence, is not needed to compute the causal effect. This can be seen by examining the identifying formula (Equation (A1)), which does not contain variable $B$. This can be further generalized to the causal graph on the right with functional variables $(B_1, \ldots, B_n)$, where we assume $\Pr(A, C, X, D, Y) > 0$. According to Corollary 4, we can functionally project the graph onto $\mathbf{V}' = \{A, C, X, D, Y\}$ while preserving F-identifiability. Moreover, applying the ID algorithm (or do-calculus) to $G$ yields an identifying formula for $\Pr_x(Y)$ over only $\mathbf{V}'$, that is, in this example, we only need to observe a constant number (five) of variables to render the causal effect F-identifiable, even though the number of observed variables in the original graph is unbounded. This application of Corollary 4 can be quite significant in practice, especially when some variables are expensive to measure (observe) or when they may raise privacy concerns see (e.g., [43,44]).

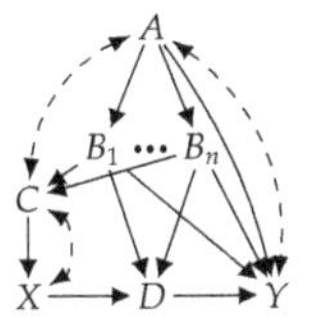


Theorems 2 and 3 are more far-reaching than what the above discussion may suggest. In particular, even if we cannot eliminate every (observed) functional variable using these theorems, we may still be able to reduce F-identifiability to identifiability due to the following result.

**Theorem 4.** *Let $\langle G, \mathbf{V}, \mathcal{C}_{\mathbf{V}}, \mathbf{W}\rangle$ be an F-identifiability tuple. If every functional variable has at least one hidden parent, then a causal effect of $\mathbf{X}$ on $\mathbf{Y}$ is F-identifiable with respect to $\langle G, \mathbf{V}, \mathcal{C}_{\mathbf{V}}, \mathbf{W}\rangle$ iff it is identifiable with respect to $\langle G, \mathbf{V}, \mathcal{C}_{\mathbf{V}}\rangle$.*

That is, if we still have functional variables in the causal graph after applying Theorems 2 and 3 and if each such variable has at least one hidden parent, then F-identifiability is equivalent to identifiability. Consider, again, the causal effect of $X$ on $Y$ in $G$ of Figure 5a with observed variables of $\mathbf{V} = \{A, B, C, F, X, Y\}$. Now, suppose that the observed variables ($A$, $B$, $C$, $X$, and $Y$ are also functional (in addition to hidden functional variables $D$ and $E$) and assume $\Pr(A, C, F, X, Y) > 0$. We can reduce F-identifiability to classical identifiability by combining Theorems 3 and 4. In particular, according to Theorem 3, we first reduce F-identifiability on $G$ to F-identifiability on $G'$ in Figure 5e by functionally eliminating $D$, $E$, and $B$. Since all the remaining functional variables ($A$, $C$, $X$, and $Y$) have a hidden parent, we can further reduce F-identifiability to identifiability on $G'$ according to Theorem 4, then apply existing algorithms (e.g., ID and do-calculus) to conclude that the causal effect is identifiable.

The method we have presented thus far for the testing of F-identifiability is based on the elimination of functional variables from the causal graph, followed by the application of existing tools for causal effect identification, such as the project-ID algorithm and do-calculus. This F-identifiability method is complete if every observed functional variable either satisfies the conditions of Theorem 3 or has at least one hidden parent that is not functional.

We next present another technique for reducing F-identifiability to identifiability. This method is more general and much more direct than the previous one, but it does not allow us to fully exploit some existing tools, like the ID algorithm, due to the positivity assumptions they make. The new method involves pretending that some of the hidden functional variables are actually observed, inspired by Proposition 2, which reduces D-separation to d-separation using a similar technique.

**Theorem 5.** *Let $\langle G, \mathbf{V}, \mathcal{C}_{\mathbf{V}}, \mathbf{W}\rangle$ be an F-identifiability tuple, where $\mathcal{C}_{\mathbf{V}} = \{\Pr(X) > 0, X \in \mathbf{X}\}$. A causal effect of $\mathbf{X}$ on $\mathbf{Y}$ is F-identifiable with respect to $\langle G, \mathbf{V}, \mathcal{C}_{\mathbf{V}}, \mathbf{W}\rangle$ iff it is identifiable with respect to $\langle G, \mathcal{C}_{\mathbf{V}}, \mathbf{V}'\rangle$, where $\mathbf{V}'$ is obtained as follows. Initially, $\mathbf{V}' = \mathbf{V}$. This is repeated until $\mathbf{V}'$ stops changing. Then, a functional variable from $\mathbf{W}$ is added to $\mathbf{V}'$ if its parents are in $\mathbf{V}'$.*

Consider the causal effect of $X$ on $Y$ in graph $G$ of Figure 5a and suppose the observed variables are $\mathbf{V} = \{A, B, C, X, Y\}$; the functional variables are $D$, $E$, and $F$; and we have $\Pr(X) > 0$. According to Theorem 5, the causal effect of $X$ on $Y$ is F-identifiable iff it is identifiable in $G$ while pretending that variables $\mathbf{V}' = \{A, B, C, D, E, F, X, Y\}$ are all observed. In this case, the casual effect is not identifiable, but we cannot obtain this answer by applying an identifiability algorithm that requires positivity constraints that are stronger than $\Pr(X) > 0$. If we have stronger positivity constraints that imply $\Pr(X) > 0, X \in \mathbf{X}$, then only the if part of Theorem 5 holds, assuming $\mathcal{C}_{\mathbf{V}}$ and $\mathbf{W}$ are consistent, that is, confirming identifiability with respect to $\langle G, \mathcal{C}_{\mathbf{V}}, \mathbf{V}'\rangle$ confirms F-identifiability with respect to $\langle G, \mathbf{V}, \mathcal{C}_{\mathbf{V}}, \mathbf{W}\rangle$, but if identifiability is not confirmed, then F-identifiability may still hold. This suggests that to fully exploit the power of Theorem 5, one would need a new class of identifiability algorithms that can operate under the weakest possible positivity constraints.

## 6. Experiments

We next report on a simple experiment to empirically demonstrate how knowledge of functional dependencies can aid the identifiability of causal effects. We randomly generated 50 causal graphs (DAGs) with $N \in \{50, 100, 150\}$ variables using the Erdős–Rényi method [45], where every edge in the causal graphs appears with a probability of 0.1 and every variable has, at most, 6 parents. We then randomly picked $0.8N$ observed variables, $0.2N$ treatment variables, $0.2N$ outcome variables, and $W \in \{0.25N, 0.5N, 0.75N\}$ functional variables from the causal graphs.

For each combination of $N$ and $W$, Table 1 records the number of causal effects (out of 50) that are (1) unidentifiable (UID); and (2) unidentifiable but F-identifiable (UID-FID). The table also records the average number of observed variables after applying Theorems 2–4 (#OBS); these are the observed variables passed to the project-ID algorithm (We assume that strict positivity holds for the remaining observed variables after applying Theorems 2–4).

The following patterns are clear. First, more unidentifiable causal effects become F-identifiable when more variables exhibit functional dependencies. This observation demonstrates that knowledge of functional dependencies can greatly improve the identifiability of causal effects. Secondly, the number of observed variables required by the project-ID algorithm becomes smaller when there are more functional variables, implying that we only need to collect data on a smaller set of variables to estimate the (identifiable) causal effects. Again, this is because more observed functional variables can be functionally eliminated from the causal graphs by Theorem 3.

**Table 1.** Numbers of causal effects that are unidentifiable (UID) and that are unidentifiable but F-identifiable (UID-FID) and average number of observed variables passed to project-ID (#OBS) for causal graphs with various numbers of variables ($N$) and functional ones ($W$).

| $N$ | $W$ | UID | UID-FID | #OBS |
|---|---|---|---|---|
| 50 | $0.25N$ | 15 | 3 | 36.5 |
| | $0.5N$ | 15 | 10 | 32.6 |
| | $0.75N$ | 15 | 11 | 27.3 |
| 100 | $0.25N$ | 50 | 0 | 74.7 |
| | $0.5N$ | 50 | 6 | 68.1 |
| | $0.75N$ | 50 | 18 | 57.3 |
| 150 | $0.25N$ | 50 | 0 | 113.2 |
| | $0.5N$ | 50 | 2 | 103.6 |
| | $0.75N$ | 50 | 5 | 89.7 |

## 7. Conclusions

We studied the identification of causal effects in the presence of a particular type of knowledge called functional dependencies. This augments earlier works that considered other types of knowledge, such as context-specific independence. Our contributions include the formalization of the notion of functional identifiability; the introduction of an operation for eliminating functional variables from a causal graph that comes with stronger guarantees compared to earlier elimination methods; and the employment (under some conditions) of existing algorithms, such as the ID algorithm, for the testing of functional identifiability and to obtain identifying formulas. We further provided a complete reduction of functional identifiability to classical identifiability under very weak positivity constraints and showed how our results can be used to reduce the number of variables needed in observational data. Last but not least, we proposed a more general definition of identifiability based on a broader class of positivity assumptions, which opens the door to uncover causal identification algorithms under weaker positivity assumptions.

**Author Contributions:** Conceptualization, Y.C. and A.D.; Formal analysis, Y.C. and A.D.; Funding acquisition, A.D.; Investigation, Y.C. and A.D.; Methodology, Y.C. and A.D.; Project administration, A.D.; Resources, Y.C. and A.D.; Supervision, A.D.; Validation, Y.C. and A.D.; Visualization, Y.C. and A.D.; Writing—original draft, Y.C. and A.D.; Writing—review and editing, Y.C. and A.D. All authors have read and agreed to the published version of the manuscript.

**Funding:** This work was partially supported by ONR grant N000142212501.

**Institutional Review Board Statement:** Not applicable.

**Data Availability Statement:** Data are contained within the article.

**Conflicts of Interest:** The authors declare no conflicts of interest.

## Appendix A. More On Projection and the ID Algorithm

As mentioned in the main paper, the project-ID algorithm involves two steps: the projection operation and the ID algorithm. We review more technical details of each step in this section.

### *Appendix A.1. Projection*

The projection [25,26,28] of $G$ onto $\mathbf{V}$ constructs a new DAG ($G'$) over variables ($\mathbf{V}$) as follows. Initially, DAG $G'$ contains variables ($\mathbf{V}$) but no edges. Then, for every pair of variables ($X, Y \in \mathbf{V}$), an edge is added from $X$ to $Y$ to $G'$ if $X$ is a parent of $Y$ in $G$ or if there exists a directed path from $X$ to $Y$ in $G$ such that none of the internal nodes on the path is in $\mathbf{V}$. Furthermore, a bidirected edge ($X \dashleftarrow\dashrightarrow Y$) is added between every pair of variables ($X$ and $Y$) in $G'$ if there exists a divergent path (A divergent path between $X$ and $Y$ is a path in the form of $X \leftarrow \cdots \leftarrow U \rightarrow \cdots \rightarrow Y$) between $X$ and $Y$ in $G$ such that none of the internal nodes on the path is in $\mathbf{V}$. For example, the projection of the DAG in Figure 1a onto $A, C, E, X_1, X_2, Y$ yields Figure 1c. A bidirected edge ($X \dashleftarrow\dashrightarrow Y$) is a compact notation for $X \leftarrow H \rightarrow Y$, where $H$ is an auxiliary hidden variable. Hence, the projected DAG in Figure 1c can be interpreted as a classical DAG but with additional, hidden root variables.

The projection operation is guaranteed to produce a DAG ($G'$) in which hidden variables are all roots and each has exactly two children. Graphs that satisfy this property are called *semi-Markovian* and can be fed as inputs to the ID algorithm for testing of identifiability [10]. Moreover, projection preserves some properties of $G$, such as d-separation [25] among $\mathbf{V}$, which guarantees that identifiability is preserved when working with $G'$ instead of $G$ [26].

### *Appendix A.2. ID Algorithm*

After obtaining a projected causal graph, we can apply the ID algorithm for identification of causal effects [10,46]. The algorithm returns either an identifying formula if the causal effect is identifiable or FAIL otherwise. The algorithm is sound, since each line of the algorithm can be proven with basic probability rules and do-calculus. The algorithm is also complete, since a causal graph must contain a *hedge*, a graphical structure that induces the unidentifiability, if the algorithm returns FAIL. However, the algorithm is only sound and complete under certain positivity constraints, which are weaker but more subtle than strict positivity ($\Pr(\mathbf{V}) > 0$).

The positivity constraints required by ID can be summarized as follows ($\mathbf{X}$ represents the treatment variables): (1) $\Pr(\mathbf{X}|\mathbf{P}) > 0$, where $\mathbf{P} = \text{Parents}(\mathbf{X}) \setminus \mathbf{X}$, and (2) $\Pr(\mathbf{Z}) > 0$ for all quantities $\Pr(\mathbf{S}|\mathbf{Z})$ considered by the ID algorithm. The second constraint depends on a particular run of the ID algorithm and can be interpreted as follows. First, if the ID algorithm returns FAIL, then the causal effect is not identifiable, even under the strict positivity constraint of $\Pr(\mathbf{V}) > 0$. However, if the ID algorithm returns "identifiable", then the causal effect is identifiable under the above constraints, which are now well defined given a particular run of the ID algorithm. We illustrate with an example next.

Consider the causal graph on the right, which contains observed variables $\{A, B, C, X, Y\}$. Suppose we are interested in the causal effect of $X$ on $Y$. Applying the ID algorithm returns the following identifying formula: $\Pr_x(y) = \sum_{abc} \Pr(c|a,b,x) \sum_{x'} \Pr(y|a,b,c,x') \Pr(a,b,x')$. The positivity constraint extracted from this run of the algorithm is $\Pr(a,b,c,x) > 0$ for all of $a$, $b$, $c$, and $x$, that is, we can only safely declare the causal effect identifiable based on the ID algorithm if this positivity constraint is satisfied.

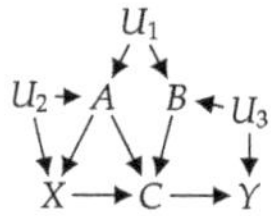


**Appendix B. Functional Elimination for CBNs**

The functional elimination in Definition 8 removes functional variables from a DAG ($G$) and yields another DAG ($G'$) for the remaining variables. We showed in the main paper that the functional elimination preserves the D-separations. Here, we extend the notion of functional elimination to causal Bayesian networks (CBNs), which contain not only a causal graph (DAG) but also CPTs. We show that (extended) functional elimination preserves the marginal distribution of the remaining variables, that is, given any CBN with causal graph $G$, we can construct another CBN with causal graph $G'$ such that the two CBNs induce the same distribution of the variables in $G'$, where $G'$ is the result of eliminating functional variables from $G$. Moreover, we show that the functional elimination operation further preserves the causal effects, which makes it applicable to causal identification. This extended version of functional elimination and the corresponding results are used as proofs in Appendix C.

Recall that a CBN $\langle G, \mathcal{F} \rangle$ contains a causal graph ($G$) and a set of CPTs ($\mathcal{F}$). We first extend the definition of functional elimination (Definition 8) from DAGs to CBNs.

**Definition A1.** *The functional elimination of a functional variable ($X$) from a CBN $\langle G, \mathcal{F} \rangle$ yields another CBN $\langle G', \mathcal{F}' \rangle$ obtained as follows. The DAG ($G'$) is obtained from $G$ according to Definition 8. For each child ($C$) of $X$, its CPT in $\mathcal{F}'$ is ($\sum_X f_X f_C$), where $f_X$ and $f_C$ are the corresponding CPTs in $\mathcal{F}$.*

We first show that the new CPTs produced by Definition A1 are well defined.

**Proposition A1.** *Let $f_X$ and $f_Y$ be the CPTs for variables $X$ and $Y$ in a CBN; then, ($\sum_X f_X f_Y$) is a valid CPT for $Y$.*

The next proposition shows that functional elimination preserves the functional dependencies.

**Proposition A2.** *Let $\mathcal{M}'$ be the CBN resulting from functionally eliminating a functional variable from a CBN ($\mathcal{M}$). Then, each variable (from $\mathcal{M}'$) is functional in $\mathcal{M}'$ if it is functional in $\mathcal{M}$.*

The next theorem shows that the order of functional elimination does not matter.

**Proposition A3.** *Let $\mathcal{M}$ be a CBN and $\pi_1$ and $\pi_2$ be two variable orders over a set of functional variables ($\mathbf{W}$). Then, functionally eliminating $\mathbf{W}$ from $\mathcal{M}$ according to $\pi_1$ and $\pi_2$ yields the same CBN.*

The next result shows that eliminating functional variables preserves the marginal distribution.

**Theorem A1.** *Consider a CBN ($\mathcal{M}$) that induces* $\Pr$. *Let $\mathcal{M}'$ be the result of functionally eliminating a set of functional variables ($\mathbf{W}$) from $\mathcal{M}$, which induces* $\Pr'$. *Then,* $\Pr' = \sum_{\mathbf{W}} \Pr$.

One key property of functional elimination is that it preserves the interventional distribution over the remaining variables. This property allows us to eliminate functional variables from a causal graph and estimate the causal effects in the resulting graph.

**Theorem A2.** *Let $\mathcal{M}'$ be the CBN over variables ($\mathbf{V}$) resulting from functionally eliminating a set of functional variables ($\mathbf{W}$) from a CBN ($\mathcal{M}$). Then, $\mathcal{M}'$ and $\mathcal{M}$ attain the same* $\Pr_{\mathbf{x}}(\mathbf{V})$ *for any* $\mathbf{X} \subseteq \mathbf{V}$.

## Appendix C. Proofs

The proofs of the results are ordered slightly differently from the order in which they appear in the main body of the paper.

**Proof of Proposition 1.** Our goal is to construct two different parameterizations ($\mathcal{F}^1$ and $\mathcal{F}^2$) that induce the same $\Pr(\mathbf{V})$ but different $\Pr_{\mathbf{x}}(\mathbf{y})$. This is done by first creating a parameterization ($\mathcal{F}$) that contains strictly positive CPTs for all variables, then constructing $\mathcal{F}^1$ and $\mathcal{F}^2$ based on $\mathcal{F}$.

Let $\mathcal{P}$ be the directed path from $X = X_i$ to $Y$, denoted as $X \to Z \to \cdots \to Y$, which does not contain any treatment variables other than $X$. Let $\mathbf{P}_X$ be the parents of $X$ in $G$. For each node $M$ on the path, let $\mathbf{P}_M$ be the parents of $M$, except for the parent that lies on $\mathcal{P}$. Moreover, for each variable ($M$) on $\mathcal{P}$, we only modify the conditional probability for a single state ($m^*$) of $M$, where $x^* \in \mathbf{x}$ is the treated state of $X$. Let $\epsilon$ be an arbitrarily small constant (close to 0). Next, we show the modifications for the CPTs in $\mathcal{F}^1$.

$$f^1(x|\mathbf{p}_X) = \begin{cases} 0 & \text{if } x = x^* \\ 1/(|X|-1), & \text{otherwise} \end{cases}$$

$$f^1(z|x,\mathbf{p}_Z) = \begin{cases} 1-\epsilon, & \text{if } x = x^*, z = z^* \\ \epsilon/(|Z|-1), & \text{if } x = x^*, z \neq z^* \\ \epsilon, & \text{if } x \neq x^*, z = z^* \\ (1-\epsilon)/(|Z|-1), & \text{if } x \neq x^*, z \neq z^* \end{cases}$$

For every variable ($T \notin \{X, Z\}$) that has parent $Q$ on the path $\mathcal{P}$, we assign

$$f^1(t|q,\mathbf{p}_T) = \begin{cases} 1-\epsilon, & \text{if } q = q^*, t = t^* \\ \epsilon/(|T|-1), & \text{if } q = q^*, t \neq t^* \\ \epsilon, & \text{if } q \neq q^*, t = t^* \\ (1-\epsilon)/(|T|-1), & \text{if } q \neq q^*, t \neq t^* \end{cases}$$

We assign the same CPTs for $X$ and all variables ($T \notin \{X, Z\}$) but a different CPT for $Z$ in $\mathcal{F}^2$.

$$f^2(z|x, \mathbf{p}_Z) = \begin{cases} \epsilon, & \text{if } x = x^*, z = z^* \\ (1-\epsilon)/(|Z|-1), & \text{if } x = x^*, z \neq z^* \\ \epsilon, & \text{if } x \neq x^*, z = z^* \\ (1-\epsilon)/(|Z|-1), & \text{if } x \neq x^*, z \neq z^* \end{cases}$$

The two parameterizations ($\mathcal{F}^1$ and $\mathcal{F}^2$) induce the same $\Pr(\mathbf{V})$, where $\Pr(\mathbf{v}) = 0$ if $x^* \in \mathbf{v}$ and $\Pr(\mathbf{v}) > 0$ otherwise. Next, we show that the parameterization satisfies each positivity constraint ($\Pr(\mathbf{S}|\mathbf{Z})$) as long as it does not imply $\Pr(X) > 0$. We first show that $X \in \mathbf{S}$ implies $\Pr(X) > 0$. This is because $\Pr(\mathbf{S}) = \sum_{\mathbf{z}} \Pr(\mathbf{S}|\mathbf{z}) \Pr(\mathbf{z})$ and there must exist some instantiation ($\mathbf{z}$) where $\Pr(\mathbf{z}) > 0$ and $\Pr(\mathbf{S}|\mathbf{z}) > 0$ by constraint. This implies $\Pr(\mathbf{S}) > 0$ and, therefore, $\Pr(X) > 0$. Hence, $\mathcal{C}_{\mathbf{V}}$ does not contain such a constraint ($\Pr(\mathbf{S}|\mathbf{Z})$) where $X \in \mathbf{S}$. Suppose $X \in \mathbf{Z}$; then, $\Pr(\mathbf{z}) > 0$ if and only if $x^* \notin \mathbf{z}$. Moreover, since $\Pr(\mathbf{v}) > 0$, whenever $x^* \notin \mathbf{v}$, it is guaranteed that $\Pr(\mathbf{S}, \mathbf{z}) > 0$ when $\Pr(\mathbf{z}) > 0$, which implies $\Pr(\mathbf{S}|\mathbf{Z}) > 0$. Finally, suppose $X \notin (\mathbf{S} \cup \mathbf{Z})$; then, $\Pr(\mathbf{S}, \mathbf{Z}) = \sum_x \Pr(\mathbf{S}, \mathbf{Z}, x) > 0$. Hence, the positivity constraint is satisfied by both parameterizations. By construction, $\Pr^1$ and $\Pr^2$ induce different values for the causal effect ($\Pr_{\mathbf{x}}(\mathbf{y})$), since the probability of $Y = y^*$ under treatment $do(X = x^*)$ differs under the two parameterizations. □

**Proposition A4.** *Let $G$ be a causal graph and $\mathbf{V}$ be its observed variables. A set of functional variables ($\mathbf{W}$) is consistent with positivity constraints ($\mathcal{C}_{\mathbf{V}}$) if no single constraint in $\mathcal{C}_{\mathbf{V}}$ mentions both $W \in \mathbf{W}$ and a set ($\mathbf{H}_W$) that intercepts all directed paths from non-functional variables to $W$.*

**Proof of Proposition A4.** We construct a parameterization ($\mathcal{F}$) and show that the distribution (Pr) induced by $\mathcal{F}$ satisfies $\mathcal{C}_{\mathbf{V}}$, which ensures consistency. The states of each variable ($V$) are represented in the form of $(s_V, p_1, \ldots, p_m)$, where $s_V$ and $p_i$ ($i \in \{1, \ldots, m\}$) are both binary indicators (0 or 1). Specifically, each $p_i$ corresponds to a "functional descendant path" of $V$ defined as follows: A functional descendant path of $V$ is a directed path that starts with $V$, and all variables on the path (excluding $V$) are functional. Suppose $V$ does not have any functional descendant path; then, the states of $V$ are simply represented as $(s_V)$.

Next, we show how to assign CPTs for each variable in the causal graph ($G$) based on whether the variable is functional. For each non-functional variable, we assign a uniform distribution. For each functional variable ($W$) whose parents are $T_1, \ldots, T_n$ and whose functional descendant paths are $\mathcal{P}_1, \ldots, \mathcal{P}_m$, we assign the CPT ($f_W$) as follows:

$$\begin{aligned} s_W &\leftarrow p^{T_1}_{Ind(T_1,W)} \oplus \cdots \oplus p^{T_n}_{Ind(T_n,W)} \\ p_1 &\leftarrow p^{T_1}_{1,1} \oplus \cdots \oplus p^{T_n}_{n,1} \\ &\cdots \\ p_m &\leftarrow p^{T_1}_{1,m} \oplus \cdots \oplus p^{T_n}_{n,m} \end{aligned} \tag{A1}$$

where $Ind(T_i, W)$ denotes the index assigned to the path $\{(T_i, W)\}$ (which contains a single edge) in the state of $T^i$ and $p^{T_i}_{i,j}$ denotes the indicator in the state of $T_i$ for functional descendant path $\mathcal{P}'$ that contains functional descendant path $\mathcal{P}_j$, i.e., $\mathcal{P}' = \{(T_i, W)\} \cup \mathcal{P}_j$.

For simplicity, we call the set of variables ($\mathbf{H}_W$) that satisfies the condition in the proposition a "functional ancestor set" of $W$. We show that $\Pr(\mathbf{S}, \mathbf{Z}) > 0$ for each positivity constraint in the form of $\Pr(\mathbf{S}|\mathbf{Z}) > 0$. Let $\mathbf{W} \subseteq \mathbf{S} \cup \mathbf{Z}$ be a subset of functional variables. Since $\mathbf{S} \cup \mathbf{Z}$ does not contain any functional ancestor set of $W$ for each $W \in \mathbf{W}$, it follows that there exist directed paths from a set of non-functional variables ($\mathcal{A}'_W$ to $W$) that are unblocked by $\mathbf{M} = \mathbf{S} \cup \mathbf{Z} \setminus \{W\}$ and contain only functional variables (excluding $\mathcal{A}'_W$). We can further assume that $\mathcal{A}'_W$ is chosen such that the set $\mathcal{A}_W = \mathbf{M} \cup \mathcal{A}'_W$ forms a valid functional ancestor set for $W$. Next, we show that for any state $(w)$ of $W$ and instantiation $(\mathbf{m})$ of $\mathbf{M}$, there exists at least one instantiation $(\mathbf{a})$ of $\mathcal{A}'_W$ such that $\Pr(w, \mathbf{m}, \mathbf{a}) > 0$.

Let $\mathbf{P}^W$ denote the set of all directed paths from $\mathcal{A}_W$ to $W$ that do not contain $\mathcal{A}_W$ (except for the first node on the path). Let $\mathbf{P}_1^W \subseteq \mathbf{P}^W$ be the paths that start with a variable in $\mathbf{M}$ and $\mathbf{P}_2^W \subseteq \mathbf{P}^W$ be other paths that start with a variable in $\mathcal{A}'_W$. Moreover, for any path $(\mathcal{P})$, let $\texttt{pathval}(\mathcal{P})$ be the binary indicator (e.g., $p_1$) for $\mathcal{P}$ in the state of $\mathcal{P}(0)$ (first variable in $\mathcal{P}$). Since the value assignments for $\texttt{pathval}(\mathcal{P})$ are independent for different $\mathcal{P}$s, we can always find some instantiation $(\mathbf{a} \in \mathcal{A}'_W)$ such that the following equality holds given $w$ and $\mathbf{m}$:

$$\bigoplus_{\mathcal{P}_2 \in \mathbf{P}_2^W} \texttt{pathval}(\mathcal{P}_2) = s_W \oplus \bigoplus_{\mathcal{P}_1 \in \mathbf{P}_1^W} \texttt{pathval}(\mathcal{P}_1)$$

We next assign values for other path indicators of $\mathbf{a}$ such that the indicators for the functional descendant paths in state $w$ are set correctly. In particular, for each functional descendant path $(\mathcal{P})$ of $W$, let $\mathbf{P}$ be the set of functional descendant paths of $\mathcal{A}_W$ that do not contain $\mathcal{A}_W$ (except for the first node on the path) and that contain $\mathcal{P}$ as a sub-path. Let $\mathbf{P}_1 \subseteq \mathbf{P}$ be the paths that start with a variable in $\mathbf{M}$ and $\mathbf{P}_2 \subseteq \mathbf{P}$ be other paths that start with a variable in $\mathcal{A}'_W$. Again, since all the indicators for paths in $\mathcal{P}$ are independent, we can assign the indicators for $\mathbf{a} \in \mathcal{A}'_W$ such that

$$\bigoplus_{\mathcal{P}_2 \in \mathbf{P}_2} \texttt{pathval}(\mathcal{P}_2) = \texttt{pathval}(\mathcal{P}) \oplus \bigoplus_{\mathcal{P}_1 \in \mathbf{P}_1} \texttt{pathval}(\mathcal{P}_1).$$

Finally, we combine the cases for each individual $W \in \mathbf{W}$ by creating the following set: $\mathcal{A}_\mathbf{W} = \bigcup_{W \in \mathbf{W}} \mathcal{A}_W$. Since all the functional descendant paths we considered for different $W$s are disjoint, we can always find an assignment $(\mathbf{a})$ for $\mathcal{A}_\mathbf{W}$ that is consistent with the functional dependencies (does not produce any zero probabilities). Consequently, there must exist some full instantiation $((\mathbf{u}, \mathbf{v}))$ compatible with $\mathbf{s}$, $\mathbf{z}$, and $\mathbf{a}$ such that $\Pr(\mathbf{u}, \mathbf{v}) > 0$, which implies $\Pr(\mathbf{s}, \mathbf{z}) > 0$. □

**Proof of Proposition A1.** Suppose $Y$ is not a child of $X$ in the CBN; then, $\sum_X f_X f_Y = f_Y(\sum_X f_X)$, which is guaranteed to be a CPT for $Y$. Suppose $Y$ is a child of $X$. Let $\mathbf{P}_X$ denote the parents of $X$ and $\mathbf{P}_Y$ denote the parents of $Y$, excluding $X$. The new factor $(g = \sum_X f_X f_Y)$ is defined over $\mathbf{P}_X \cup \mathbf{P}_Y \cup \{Y\}$. Consider each instantiation ($\mathbf{p}_X$ and $\mathbf{p}_Y$); then, $\sum_y g(\mathbf{p}_X, \mathbf{p}_Y, y) = \sum_y \sum_x f_X(x|\mathbf{p}_x) f_Y(y|\mathbf{p}_Y, x) = \sum_x f_X(x|\mathbf{p}_X) \sum_y f_Y(y|\mathbf{p}_Y, x) = 1$. Hence, $g$ is a CPT for $Y$. □

**Proof of Proposition A2.** Let $X$ be the functional variablethat is functionally eliminated. By definition, the elimination only affects the CPTs for the children of $X$. Hence, any functional variable that is not a child of $X$ remains functional. For each child $(C)$ of $X$ that is functional, the new CPT $(\sum_X f_X f_C)$ only contains values that are either 0 or 1, since both $f_X$ and $f_C$ are functional. □

**Proof of Proposition A3.** First, note that $\pi_2$ can always be obtained from $\pi_1$ by a sequence of "transpositions", where each transposition swaps two adjacent variables in the first sequence. Let $\pi$ be an elimination order, and let $\pi'$ be the elimination order resulting from swapping $\pi_i = X$ and $\pi_{i+1} = Y$ from the $\pi$, i.e.,

$$\pi = (\ldots, X, Y, \ldots) \qquad \pi' = (\ldots, Y, X, \ldots)$$

We show that functional elimination according to $\pi$ and $\pi'$ yields the same CBN, which can be applied inductively to conclude that elimination according to $\pi_1$ and $\pi_2$ yields the same CBN. Since $\pi$ and $\pi'$ agree on the elimination order up to $X$, they yield the same CBN before eliminating variables $X, Y$. It suffices to show the CBNs resulting from eliminating $(X, Y)$ those resulting from the and elimination of $(Y, X)$ are the same. Let $\langle G, \Pr \rangle$ be the CBN before eliminating variables $X, Y$. Suppose $X$ and $Y$ do not belong to the same family (which contains a variable and its parents), the eliminations of $X$ and $Y$ are independent, and the order of elimination does not matter. Suppose $X$ and $Y$ belong to the same family; then, they are either parent and child or co-parents ($X$ and $Y$ are co-parents if they have a same child).

Without loss of generality, suppose $X$ is a parent of $Y$. Eliminating $(X,Y)$ and eliminating $(Y,X)$ yield the same causal graph that is defined as follows. Each child ($C$) of $Y$ has parents $\mathbf{P}_X \cup \mathbf{P}_Y \cup \mathbf{P}_C \setminus \{X,Y\}$, and any other child $C$ of $X$ has parents $\mathbf{P}_X \cup \mathbf{P}_C \setminus \{X\}$. We next consider the CPTs. For each common child ($C$) of $X$ and $Y$, its CPT resulting from eliminating $(X,Y)$ is $f_C^1 = \sum_Y(\sum_X f_C f_X)(\sum_X f_Y f_X)$, and the CPT resulting from eliminating $(Y,X)$ is $f_C^2 = \sum_X f_X(\sum_Y f_C f_Y)$. Since $X$ is a parent of $Y$, we have $Y \notin f_X$ and

$$\begin{aligned} f_C^2 &= \sum_X\sum_Y f_X f_C f_Y = \sum_Y\sum_X f_X f_C f_Y \\ &= \sum_Y(\sum_X f_X f_C)(\sum_X f_X f_Y) = f_C^1 \end{aligned}$$

Next, we consider the case when $C$ is a child of $Y$ but not a child of $X$. The CPT for $C$ resulting from eliminating $(X,Y)$ is $f_C^1 = \sum_Y f_C(\sum_X f_Y f_X)$, and the CPT resulting from eliminating $(Y,X)$ is $f_C^2 = \sum_X f_X(\sum_Y f_C f_Y)$. Again, since $X$ is a parent of $Y$, we have $Y \notin f_X$ and

$$\begin{aligned} f_C^2 &= \sum_X\sum_Y f_X f_C f_Y = \sum_Y\sum_X f_X f_C f_Y \\ &= \sum_Y f_C(\sum_X f_X f_Y) = f_C^1 \end{aligned}$$

Finally, we consider the case when $C$ is a child of $X$ but not a child of $Y$. Regardless of the order of $X$ and $Y$, the CPT for $C$ resulting from eliminating $X$ and $Y$ is $(\sum_X f_X f_C)$.

Next, we consider the case when $X$ and $Y$ are co-parents. Regardless of the order of $X$ and $Y$, the causal graph resulting from the elimination satisfies the following properties: (1) for each common child ($C$) of $X$ and $Y$, the parents for $C$ are $\mathbf{P}_X \cup \mathbf{P}_Y \cup \mathbf{P}_C \setminus \{X,Y\}$; (2) the parents of each $C$ that is a child of $X$ but not a child of $Y$ are $\mathbf{P}_X \cup \mathbf{P}_C \setminus \{X\}$; and (3) the parents of each $C$ that is a child of $Y$ but not a child of $X$ are $\mathbf{P}_Y \cup \mathbf{P}_C \setminus \{Y\}$. Next, we consider the CPTs. The CPT for each common child $C$ of $X$ and $Y$ resulting from eliminating $(X,Y)$ is $f_C^1 = \sum_Y f_Y(\sum_X f_X f_C)$, and the CPT resulting from eliminating $(Y,X)$ is $f_C^2 = \sum_X f_X(\sum_Y f_Y f_C)$. Since $X$ and $Y$ are not parent and child, we have $X \notin f_Y$, $Y \notin f_X$, and

$$f_C^1 = \sum_Y\sum_X f_Y f_X f_C = \sum_X\sum_Y f_Y f_X f_C = f_C^2$$

For each $C$ that is a child of $X$ but not a child of $Y$, regardless of the order of $X$ and $Y$, the CPT for $C$ resulting from eliminating variables $X$ and $Y$ is $(\sum_X f_X f_C)$. A similar result holds for each $C$ that is a child of $Y$ but not a child of $X$. □

**Proof of Theorem A1.** It suffices to show that $\mathrm{Pr}' = \sum_X \mathrm{Pr}$ when we eliminate a single variable ($X$). Let $\mathcal{F}$ denote the set of CPTs for $\mathcal{M}$. Since $f_X$ is a functional CPT for $X$, we can replicate $f_X$ in $\mathcal{F}$, which yields a new CPT set (replication) ($\mathcal{F}'$) that induces the same distribution as $\mathcal{F}$ (see details in ([21], Theorem 4)). Specifically, we pair the CPT for each child ($C$) of $X$ with an extra copy of $f_X$, denoted as $(f_X, f_C)$, which yields a list of pairs $((f_X, f_{C_1}), \ldots, (f_X, f_{C_k})$, where $C_1, \ldots, C_k$ are the children of $X$). Functionally eliminating $X$ from $\mathcal{F}'$ yields ([21], Corollary 1)

$$\begin{aligned} \sum_X \mathrm{Pr} = \sum_X \mathcal{F}' &= \mathcal{H} \cdot (\sum_X f_X f_{C_1}) \cdots (\sum_X f_X f_{C_k}) \\ &= \mathcal{H} \cdot f'_{C_1} \cdots f'_{C_k} = \mathrm{Pr}' \end{aligned} \tag{A2}$$

where $\mathcal{H}$ represent the CPTs in $\mathcal{F}$ that do not contain $X$ and each $f'_{C_i}$ is the CPT for child $C_i$ in $\mathcal{M}'$. □

*Proof of Theorem A2*

**Lemma A1.** *Consider a CBN $\langle G, \mathcal{F}\rangle$ and its mutilated CBN $\langle G_{\mathbf{x}}, \mathcal{F}_{\mathbf{x}}\rangle$ under $do(\mathbf{x})$. Let $W$ be a functional variable not in $\mathbf{X}$ and let $\langle G', \mathcal{F}'\rangle$ and $\langle G'_{\mathbf{x}}, \mathcal{F}'_{\mathbf{x}}\rangle$ be the results of functionally eliminating $W$ from $\langle G, \mathcal{F}\rangle$ and $\langle G_{\mathbf{x}}, \mathcal{F}_{\mathbf{x}}\rangle$, respectively. Then, $\langle G'_{\mathbf{x}}, \mathcal{F}'_{\mathbf{x}}\rangle$ is the mutilated CBN for $\langle G', \mathcal{F}'\rangle$.*

**Proof.** First, observe that the children of $W$ in $G$ and $G_{\mathbf{x}}$ can only differ by the variables in $\mathbf{X}$. Let $\mathbf{C}_1$ be the children of $W$ in both $G$ and $G_{\mathbf{x}}$, and let $\mathbf{C}_2$ be the children of $W$ in $G$ but not in $G_{\mathbf{x}}$. According to the definition of mutilated CBN, $W$ has the same set of parents and CPT in $\langle G, \mathcal{F}\rangle$ and $\langle G_{\mathbf{x}}, \mathcal{F}_{\mathbf{x}}\rangle$. Similarly, each child ($C \in \mathbf{C}_1$) has the same set of parents and CPT in $\langle G, \mathcal{F}\rangle$ and $\langle G_{\mathbf{x}}, \mathcal{F}_{\mathbf{x}}\rangle$. Hence, eliminating $W$ yields the same set of parents and CPT for each $C \in \mathbf{C}$ in $\langle G', \mathcal{F}'\rangle$ and $\langle G'_{\mathbf{x}}, \mathcal{F}'_{\mathbf{x}}\rangle$. Next, we consider the set of parents and CPT for each child ($C \in \mathbf{C}_2$). Since $W$ is not a parent of $C$ in $\langle G_{\mathbf{x}}, \mathcal{F}_{\mathbf{x}}\rangle$, variable $C$ has the same set of parents and CPT in $\langle G'_{\mathbf{x}}, \mathcal{F}'_{\mathbf{x}}\rangle$. Exactly same set of parents (empty) and CPT are assigned to $C$ in the mutilated CBN for $\langle G', \mathcal{F}'\rangle$. □

**Proof of Theorem A2.** Consider a CBN $\langle G, \mathcal{F}\rangle$ and its mutilated CBN $\langle G_{\mathbf{x}}, \mathcal{F}_{\mathbf{x}}\rangle$. Let Pr and $\text{Pr}_{\mathbf{x}}$ be the distributions induced by $\mathcal{F}$ and $\mathcal{F}_{\mathbf{x}}$ over variables $\mathbf{V}$, respectively. According to Lemma A1, we can eliminate each $W \in \mathbf{W}$ inductively from $\langle G, \mathcal{F}\rangle$ and $\langle G_{\mathbf{x}}, \mathcal{F}_{\mathbf{x}}\rangle$ and obtain $\langle G', \mathcal{F}'\rangle$ and its mutilated CBN $\langle G'_{\mathbf{x}}, \mathcal{F}'_{\mathbf{x}}\rangle$. According to Theorem A1, the distribution induced by $\mathcal{F}'_{\mathbf{x}}$ is exactly $\sum_{\mathbf{W}} \text{Pr}_{\mathbf{x}}(\mathbf{V})$. □

**Proof of Proposition 2.** First, note that the extended set ($\mathbf{Z}'$) contains $\mathbf{Z}$ and all variables that are functionally determined by $\mathbf{Z}$. Consider any path ($\mathcal{P}$) between some $X \in \mathbf{X}$ and $Y \in \mathbf{Y}$. We show that $\mathcal{P}$ is blocked by $\mathbf{Z}'$ iff it is blocked by $\mathbf{Z}$ according to the definition presented in [40]. We first show the if part. Suppose there is a convergent valve (see [38] (Ch. 4) for more details on convergent, divergent, and sequential valves) for a variable $W$ that is closed when conditioned on $\mathbf{Z}$; then, the valve is still closed when conditioned on $\mathbf{Z}'$ unless the parents of $W$ are in $Z'$. However, the path ($\mathcal{P}$) is blocked in the latter case, since the parents of $W$ must have sequential/divergent valves. Suppose there is a sequential/divergent valve that is closed when conditioned on $\mathbf{Z}$ according to [40]; then, $W$ must be in $\mathbf{Z}'$, since it is functionally determined by $\mathbf{Z}$. Hence, the valve is also closed when conditioned on $\mathbf{Z}'$.

Next, we show the only–if part. Suppose a convergent valve for variable $W$ is closed when conditioned on $\mathbf{Z}'$; then, none of $\mathbf{Z}$ is a descendant of $W$, since $\mathbf{Z}'$ is a superset of $\mathbf{Z}$. Suppose a sequential/divergent valve for variable $W$ is closed when conditioned on $\mathbf{Z}'$; then, $W$ is functionally determined by $\mathbf{Z}$ by the construction of $\mathbf{Z}'$. Thus, the valve is closed as described in [40]. □

**Proof of Theorem 1.** By induction, it suffices to show that $\mathbf{X}$ and $\mathbf{Y}$ are D-separated by $\mathbf{Z}$ in $\langle G, \mathbf{W}\rangle$ iff they are D-separated by $\mathbf{Z}$ in $\langle G', \mathbf{W}'\rangle$, where $G'$ is the result of functionally eliminating a single variable ($T \in \mathbf{W}$) from $G'$ and $\mathbf{W}' = \mathbf{W} \setminus \{T\}$. We first show the contrapositive of the if part. Suppose $\mathbf{X}$ and $\mathbf{Y}$ are not D-separated by $\mathbf{Z}$ in $\langle G, \mathbf{W}\rangle$; owing to the completeness of D-separation, there exists a parameterization ($\mathcal{F}$) on $G$ such that $(\mathbf{X} \not\perp\!\!\!\perp \mathbf{Y} | \mathbf{Z})_{\mathcal{F}}$. If we eliminate $T$ from the CBN $\langle G, \mathcal{F}\rangle$, we obtain another CBN $\langle G', \mathcal{F}'\rangle$, where $\mathcal{F}'$ is the parameterization for $G'$. According to Theorem A1, the marginal probabilities are preserved for the variables in $G'$, which include $\mathbf{X}, \mathbf{Y}, \mathbf{Z}$. Hence, $(\mathbf{X} \not\perp\!\!\!\perp \mathbf{Y} | \mathbf{Z})_{\mathcal{F}'}$ and $\mathbf{X}$ and $\mathbf{Y}$ are not D-separated by $\mathbf{Z}$ in $\langle G', \mathbf{W}'\rangle$.

Next consider the contrapositive of the only–if part. Suppose $\mathbf{X}$ and $\mathbf{Y}$ are not D-separated by $\mathbf{Z}$ in $\langle G', \mathbf{W}'\rangle$; then, there exists a parameterization ($\mathcal{F}'$) of $G'$ such that $(\mathbf{X} \not\perp\!\!\!\perp \mathbf{Y} | \mathbf{Z})_{\mathcal{F}'}$ owing to the completeness of D-separation. We construct a parameterization ($\mathcal{F}$) for $G$ such that $\mathcal{F}'$ is the parameterization of $G'$, which results from eliminating $T$ from the CBN $\langle G, \mathcal{F}\rangle$. This is sufficient to show that $\mathbf{X}$ and $\mathbf{Y}$ are not D-separated by $\mathbf{Z}$ in $\langle G, \mathbf{W}\rangle$, since the marginals are preserved by Theorem A1.

**Construction Method** Let $\mathbf{P}_T$ and $\mathbf{C}_T$ denote the parents and children of $T$ in $G$, respectively. Our construction assumes that the cardinality of $T$ is the number of instantiations for its parents ($\mathbf{P}_T$), that is, there is a one-to-one correspondence between the states of $T$ and the instantiations of $\mathbf{P}_T$, and we use $\alpha(t)$ to denote the instantiation ($\mathbf{p}_T$) corresponding to state $t$. The functional CPT for $T$ is assigned as $f_T(t|\mathbf{p}_T) = 1$ if $\alpha(t) = \mathbf{p}_T$ and $f_T(t|\mathbf{p}_T) = 0$ otherwise for each instantiation ($\mathbf{p}_T$) of $\mathbf{P}_T$. Now, consider each child ($C \in \mathbf{C}_T$) that has parents $\mathbf{P}_C$ (excluding $T$) and $T$ in $G$. It immediately follows from Definition 8 that $C$ has parents $\mathbf{P}_T \cup \mathbf{P}_C$ in $G'$. Next, we construct the CPT ($f_C$) in $\mathcal{F}$ based on its CPT ($f'_C$) in $\mathcal{F}'$. Consider each parent instantiation $(t, \mathbf{p}_C)$, where $t$ is a state of $T$ and $\mathbf{p}_C$ is an instantiation of $\mathbf{P}_C$. If $\alpha(t)$ is consistent with $\mathbf{p}_C$, $f_C(c|t, \mathbf{p}_C) = f'_C(c|\alpha(t), \mathbf{p}_C)$ is assigned for each state ($c$) (For clarity, we use the notation $|$ to separate a variable and its parents in a CPT). Otherwise, any functional distribution is assigned for $f_C(C|t, \mathbf{p}_C)$. This construction ensures that the constructed CPT ($f_T$) for $T$ is functional and that the functional dependencies among other variables are preserved. In particular, for each child ($C$) of $T$, the constructed CPT ($f_C$) is functional iff $f'_C$ is functional. This construction method is reused later in other proofs.

Now, we just need to show that CBN $\langle G', \mathcal{F}' \rangle$ is the result of eliminating $T$ from the (constructed) CBN $\langle G, \mathcal{F} \rangle$. In particular, we need to check that the CPT for each child ($C \in \mathbf{C}_T$) in $\mathcal{F}'$ is correctly computed from the constructed CPTs in $\mathcal{F}$. For each instantiation $(\mathbf{p}_T, \mathbf{p}_C)$ and state ($c$) of $C$,

$$\begin{aligned} f'_C(c|\mathbf{p}_T, \mathbf{p}_C) &= f_C(c|t^*, \mathbf{p}_C) = f_T(t^*|\mathbf{p}_T) f_C(c|t^*, \mathbf{p}_C) \\ &= \sum_t f_T(t|\mathbf{p}_T) f_C(c|t, \mathbf{p}_C) \end{aligned}$$

where $t^*$ is the state of $T$ such that $\alpha(t^*) = \mathbf{p}_T$. □

**Proof of Theorem 2.** We prove the theorem by induction. It suffices to show the following statement: For each causal graph ($G$) with observed variables ($\mathbf{V}$) and functional variables ($\mathbf{W}$), the causal effect ($\Pr_{\mathbf{x}}(\mathbf{Y})$) is F-identifiable with respect to $\langle G, \mathbf{V}, \mathcal{C}_{\mathbf{V}}, \mathbf{W} \rangle$ iff it is F-identifiable with respect to $\langle G', \mathbf{V}, \mathcal{C}_{\mathbf{V}}, \mathbf{W}' \rangle$, where $G'$ is the result of functionally eliminating some hidden functional variable ($T \in \mathbf{W}$) and $\mathbf{W}' = \mathbf{W} \setminus \{T\}$.

We first show the contrapositive of the if part. Suppose $\Pr_{\mathbf{x}}(\mathbf{Y})$ is not F-identifiable with respect to $\langle G, \mathbf{V}, \mathcal{C}_{\mathbf{V}}, \mathbf{W} \rangle$; then, there exist two CBNs ($\langle G, \mathcal{F}_1 \rangle$ and $\langle G, \mathcal{F}_2 \rangle$) that induce distributions ($\Pr_1, \Pr_2$) such that $\Pr_1(\mathbf{V}) = \Pr_2(\mathbf{V})$ but $\Pr_{1\mathbf{x}}(\mathbf{Y}) \neq \Pr_{2\mathbf{x}}(\mathbf{Y})$. Let $\langle G', \mathcal{F}'_1 \rangle$ and $\langle G', \mathcal{F}'_2 \rangle$ be the results of eliminating $T \notin \mathbf{V}$ from $\langle G, \mathcal{F}_1 \rangle$ and $\langle G, \mathcal{F}_2 \rangle$, respectively; the two CBNs attain the same marginal distribution on $\mathbf{V}$ but different causal effects according to Theorems A1 and A2. Hence, $\Pr_{\mathbf{x}}(\mathbf{Y})$ is not F-identifiable with respect to $\langle G', \mathbf{V}, \mathcal{C}_{\mathbf{V}}, \mathbf{W}' \rangle$ either.

Next, we show the contrapositive of the only–if part. Suppose $\Pr_{\mathbf{x}}(\mathbf{Y})$ is not F-identifiable with respect to $\langle G', \mathbf{V}, \mathcal{C}_{\mathbf{V}}, \mathbf{W}' \rangle$; then, there exist two CBNs ($\langle G', \mathcal{F}'_1 \rangle$ and $\langle G', \mathcal{F}'_2 \rangle$) that induce distributions ($\Pr'_1, \Pr'_2$) such that $\Pr'_1(\mathbf{V}) = \Pr'_2(\mathbf{V})$ but $\Pr'_{1\mathbf{x}}(\mathbf{Y}) \neq \Pr'_{2\mathbf{x}}(\mathbf{Y})$. We can obtain $\langle G, \mathcal{F}_1 \rangle$ and $\langle G, \mathcal{F}_2 \rangle$ by, agains, considering the construction method outlined in Theorem 1, where we assign a one-to-one mapping for $T$ and adopt the CPTs from $\mathcal{F}'_1$ and $\mathcal{F}'_2$ for the children of $T$. This way, $\langle G', \mathcal{F}'_1 \rangle$ and $\langle G', \mathcal{F}'_2 \rangle$ become the results of eliminating $T$ from the constructed $\langle G, \mathcal{F}_1 \rangle$ and $\langle G, \mathcal{F}_2 \rangle$, respectively. Since $T \notin \mathbf{V}$, $\Pr_1(\mathbf{V}) = \Pr'_1(\mathbf{V}) = \Pr'_2(\mathbf{V}) = \Pr_2(\mathbf{V})$ according to Theorem A1 and $\Pr_{1\mathbf{x}}(\mathbf{Y}) = \Pr'_{1\mathbf{x}}(\mathbf{Y}) \neq \Pr'_{2\mathbf{x}}(\mathbf{Y}) = \Pr_{2\mathbf{x}}(\mathbf{Y})$ according to Theorem A2. Hence, $\Pr_{\mathbf{x}}(\mathbf{Y})$ is not F-identifiable with respect to $\langle G, \mathbf{V}, \mathcal{C}_{\mathbf{V}}, \mathbf{W} \rangle$ either. □

**Proof of Theorem 3.** Since we only functionally eliminate variables that have observed parents, it is guaranteed that each $Z \in \mathbf{Z}$ has observed parents when it is eliminated. By induction, it suffices to show that $\Pr_{\mathbf{x}}(\mathbf{Y})$ is F-identifiable with respect to $\langle G, \mathbf{V}, \mathcal{C}_{\mathbf{V}}, \mathbf{W} \rangle$ iff it is F-identifiable with respect to $\langle G', \mathbf{V}', \mathcal{C}_{\mathbf{V}}, \mathbf{W}' \rangle$, where $G'$ is the result of eliminating a single functional variable ($Z \in \mathbf{W}$) with observed parents from $G$, $\mathbf{V}' = \mathbf{V} \setminus \{Z\}$, and $\mathbf{W}' = \mathbf{W} \setminus \{Z\}$.

We first show the contrapositive of the if part. Suppose $\Pr_{\mathbf{x}}(\mathbf{Y})$ is not F-identifiable with respect to $\langle G, \mathbf{V}, \mathcal{C}_{\mathbf{V}}, \mathbf{W}\rangle$; then, there exist two CBNs ($\langle G, \mathcal{F}_1\rangle$ and $\langle G, \mathcal{F}_2\rangle$) that induce distributions $\Pr_1, \Pr_2$, where $\Pr_1(\mathbf{V}) = \Pr_2(\mathbf{V})$ but $\Pr_{1\mathbf{x}}(\mathbf{Y}) \neq \Pr_{2\mathbf{x}}(\mathbf{Y})$. Let $\langle G', \mathcal{F}_1'\rangle$ and $\langle G', \mathcal{F}_2'\rangle$ be the results of eliminating $Z$ from $\langle G, \mathcal{F}_1\rangle$ and $\langle G, \mathcal{F}_2\rangle$, respectively; the two CBNs induce the same marginal distribution ($\Pr_1'(\mathbf{V}') = \Pr_2'(\mathbf{V}')$) according to Theorem A1 but different causal effects ($\Pr_{1\mathbf{x}}'(\mathbf{Y}) \neq \Pr_{2\mathbf{x}}'(\mathbf{Y})$) according to Theorem A2. Hence, $\Pr_{\mathbf{x}}(\mathbf{Y})$ is not F-identifiable with respect to $\langle G', \mathbf{V}', \mathcal{C}_{\mathbf{V}}, \mathbf{W}'\rangle$.

We now consider the contrapositive of the only–if part. Suppose $\Pr_{\mathbf{x}}(\mathbf{Y})$ is not F-identifiable with respect to $\langle G', \mathbf{V}', \mathcal{C}_{\mathbf{V}}, \mathbf{W}'\rangle$; then, there exist two CBNs ($\langle G', \mathcal{F}_1'\rangle$ and $\langle G', \mathcal{F}_2'\rangle$) that induce distributions ($\Pr_1', \Pr_2'$) such that $\Pr_1'(\mathbf{V}') = \Pr_2'(\mathbf{V}')$ but $\Pr_{1\mathbf{x}}'(\mathbf{Y}) \neq \Pr_{2\mathbf{x}}'(\mathbf{Y})$. We, again, consider the construction method from the proof of Theorem 1, which produces two CBNs ($\langle G, \mathcal{F}_1\rangle$ and $\langle G, \mathcal{F}_2\rangle$). Moreover, $\langle G', \mathcal{F}_1'\rangle$ and $\langle G', \mathcal{F}_2'\rangle$ are the results of eliminating $Z$ from $\langle G, \mathcal{F}_1\rangle$ and $\langle G, \mathcal{F}_2\rangle$, respectively. It is guaranteed that the two constructed CBNs produce different causal effects ($\Pr_{1\mathbf{x}}(\mathbf{Y}) = \Pr_{1\mathbf{x}}'(\mathbf{Y}) \neq \Pr_{2\mathbf{x}}'(\mathbf{Y}) = \Pr_{2\mathbf{x}}(\mathbf{Y})$) according to Theorem A2. We need to show that $\langle G, \mathcal{F}_1\rangle$ and $\langle G, \mathcal{F}_2\rangle$ induce the same distribution over variables of $\mathbf{V} = \mathbf{V}' \cup \{Z\}$. Consider any instantiation $(\mathbf{v}', z)$ of $\mathbf{V}$. Since $\mathcal{F}_1$ and $\mathcal{F}_2$ assign the same one-to-one mapping ($\alpha$) between $Z$ and its parents in $G$, it is guaranteed that the probabilities are $\Pr_1(\mathbf{v}', z) = \Pr_2(\mathbf{v}', z) = 0$, except for the single state ($z^*$) where $\alpha(z^*) = \mathbf{p}$, where $\mathbf{p}$ is the parent instantiation of $Z$, consistent with $\mathbf{v}'$. By construction, $\Pr_1(\mathbf{v}', z^*, \mathbf{u}) = \Pr_1'(\mathbf{v}', \mathbf{u})$ for every instantiation $(\mathbf{u})$ of hidden variables $(\mathbf{U})$. Similarly, $\Pr_2(\mathbf{v}', z^*, \mathbf{u}) = \Pr_2'(\mathbf{v}', \mathbf{u})$ for every instantiation $(\mathbf{v}', z, \mathbf{u})$. It then follows that $\Pr_1(\mathbf{v}', z^*) = \sum_{\mathbf{u}} \Pr_1(\mathbf{v}', z^*, \mathbf{u}) = \sum_{\mathbf{u}} \Pr_1'(\mathbf{v}', \mathbf{u}) = \Pr_1'(\mathbf{v}')$ $= \Pr_2'(\mathbf{v}') = \sum_{\mathbf{u}} \Pr_2'(\mathbf{v}', \mathbf{u}) = \sum_{\mathbf{u}} \Pr_2(\mathbf{v}', z^*, \mathbf{u}) = \Pr_2(\mathbf{v}', z^*)$. This means $\Pr_{\mathbf{x}}(\mathbf{Y})$ is not F-identifiable with respect to $\langle G, \mathbf{V}, \mathcal{C}_{\mathbf{V}}, \mathbf{W}\rangle$ either. □

*Proof of Theorem 4*

**Lemma A2.** *Let $G$ be a causal graph, $\mathbf{V}$ be its observed variables, and $\mathbf{W}$ be its functional variables. Let $Z$ be a non-descendant of $\mathbf{W}$ that has at least one hidden parent; then, a causal effect is F-identifiable with respect to $\langle G, \mathbf{V}, \mathcal{C}_{\mathbf{V}}, \mathbf{W}\rangle$ iff it is F-identifiable with respect to $\langle G, \mathbf{V}, \mathcal{C}_{\mathbf{V}}, \mathbf{W} \cup \{Z\}\rangle$.*

**Proof.** Let $\mathbf{W}'$ denote the set expressed as $\mathbf{W} \cup \{Z\}$. The only–if part holds immediately due to the fact that every distribution that can possibly be induced from $\langle G, \mathbf{W}'\rangle$ can also be induced from $\langle G, \mathbf{W}\rangle$. Next, we consider the contrapositive of the if part. Suppose a causal effect is not F-identifiable with respect to $\langle G, \mathbf{V}, \mathcal{C}_{\mathbf{V}}, \mathbf{W}\rangle$; then, there exist two CBNs ($\langle G, \mathcal{F}_1\rangle$ and $\langle G, \mathcal{F}_2\rangle$) that induce distributions ($\Pr_1, \Pr_2$) such that $\Pr_1(\mathbf{V}) = \Pr_2(\mathbf{V})$ but $\Pr_{1\mathbf{x}}(\mathbf{Y}) \neq \Pr_{2\mathbf{x}}(\mathbf{Y})$. Next, we construct $\langle G, \mathcal{F}_1''\rangle$ and $\langle G, \mathcal{F}_2''\rangle$, which constitute an example of unidentifiability with respect to $\langle G, \mathbf{V}, \mathcal{C}_{\mathbf{V}}, \mathbf{W}'\rangle$. In particular, the CPTs for $Z$ need to be functional in the constructed CBNs.

Without losing generality, we show the construction of $\langle G, \mathcal{F}_1''\rangle$ from $\langle G, \mathcal{F}_1\rangle$, which involves two steps (the construction of $\langle G, \mathcal{F}_2''\rangle$ from $\langle G, \mathcal{F}_2\rangle$ follows the same procedure). Let $\mathbf{P}$ be the parents of $Z$. The first step constructs a CBN $\langle G', \mathcal{F}_1'\rangle$ based on the known method that transforms any (non-functional) CPT into a functional CPT. This is done by adding an auxiliary hidden root parent ($U$) for $Z$ whose states correspond to the possible functions between $\mathbf{P}$ and $Z$. The CPTs for $U$ and $Z$ are assigned accordingly such that $f_Z = \sum_U f_U' f_Z'$, where $f_U'$ and $f_Z'$ are the constructed CPTs in $\mathcal{F}_1'$ (Each state ($u$) of $U$ corresponds to a function ($\gamma_u$), where $\gamma_u(\mathbf{p})$ is mapped to some state of $Z$ for each instantiation ($\mathbf{p}$). Thus, variable $U$ has $|Z|^{|\mathbf{P}|}$ states, since there is a total of $|Z|^{|\mathbf{P}|}$ possible functions from $\mathbf{P}$ to $Z$. For each instantiation $(z, u, \mathbf{p})$, the functional CPT for $Z$ is defined as $f_Z'(z|u, \mathbf{p}) = 1$ if $z = \gamma_u(\mathbf{p})$ and $f_Z'(z|u, \mathbf{p}) = 0$ otherwise. The CPT for $U$ is assigned as $f_U'(u) = \prod_{\mathbf{p} \in \mathbf{P}} f_Z(\gamma_u(\mathbf{p})|\mathbf{p})$). It follows that $\mathcal{F}_1$ and $\mathcal{F}_1'$ induce the same distribution over $\mathbf{V}$, since $\mathcal{F}_1 = \sum_U \mathcal{F}_1'$. The causal effect is also preserved, since the summing out of $U$ is independent of other CPTs in the mutilated CBN for $\langle G', \mathcal{F}_1'\rangle$.

Our second step involves converting the CBN $\langle G', \mathcal{F}_1'\rangle$ (constructed in the first step) into the CBN $\langle G, \mathcal{F}_1''\rangle$ over the original graph ($G$). Let $T \in \mathbf{P}$ be the hidden parent of $W$ in

$G$. We merge the auxiliary parents ($U$ and $T$) into a new variable ($T'$) and substitute it for $T$ in $G$, i.e., $T'$ has the same parents and children as $T$. $T'$ is constructed as the Cartesian product of $U$ and $T$. Each state of $T'$ is represented as a pair $(u, t)$, where $u$ is a state of $U$ and $t$ is a state of $T$. We are ready to assign new CPTs for $T'$ and its children. For each parent instantiation ($\mathbf{p}$) of $\mathbf{P}$ and each state ($(u, t)$) of $T'$, we assign the CPT for $T'$ in $\mathcal{F}''$ as $f''_{T'}((u,t)|\mathbf{p}) = f'_U(u) f'_T(t|\mathbf{p})$. Next, consider each child ($C$) of $T'$ that has parents ($\mathbf{P}_C$) (excluding $T'$). For each instantiation ($\mathbf{p}_C$) of $\mathbf{P}_C$ and each state $(u, t)$ of $T'$, we assign the CPT for $C$ in $\mathcal{F}''$ as $f''_C(c|\mathbf{p}_C, (u,t)) = f'_C(c|\mathbf{p}_C)$ for each state ($c$). Note that $f''_C$ is functional iff $f'_C$ is functional. Hence, the CPTs for $\mathbf{W}$ are all functional in $\mathcal{F}''$.

We need to show that $\langle G, \mathcal{F}''_1 \rangle$ preserves the distribution on $\mathbf{V}$ and the causal effect from $\langle G', \mathcal{F}'_1 \rangle$. Let $\mathbf{U}''$ be the hidden variables in $\langle G, \mathcal{F}''_1 \rangle$ and $\mathbf{U}'$ be the hidden variables in $\langle G', \mathcal{F}'_1 \rangle$. The distribution on $\mathbf{V}$ is preserved, since there is a one-to-one correspondence between each instantiation $(\mathbf{v}, \mathbf{u}'')$ in $\langle G, \mathcal{F}''_1 \rangle$ and each instantiation $(\mathbf{v}, \mathbf{u}')$ in $\langle G', \mathcal{F}'_1 \rangle$, where the two instantiations agree on $\mathbf{v}$ and are assigned with the same probability, i.e., $\Pr''_1(\mathbf{v}, \mathbf{u}'') = \Pr'_1(\mathbf{v}, \mathbf{u}')$. Hence, $\Pr''_1(\mathbf{v}) = \sum_{\mathbf{u}''} \Pr''_1(\mathbf{v}, \mathbf{u}'') = \sum_{\mathbf{u}'} \Pr'_1(\mathbf{v}, \mathbf{u}') = \Pr'_1(\mathbf{v})$ for every instantiation ($\mathbf{v}$). The preservation of the causal effect can be shown similarly but on the mutilated CBNs. Thus, $\langle G, \mathcal{F}''_1 \rangle$ preserves both the distribution on $\mathbf{V}$ and the causal effect from $\langle G, \mathcal{F}_1 \rangle$. Similarly, we can construct $\langle G, \mathcal{F}''_2 \rangle$, which preserves the distribution on $\mathbf{V}$ and the causal effect from $\langle G, \mathcal{F}_2 \rangle$. The two CBNs ($\langle G, \mathcal{F}''_1 \rangle$ and $\langle G, \mathcal{F}''_2 \rangle$) constitute an example of unidentifiability with respect to $\langle G, \mathbf{V}, \mathcal{C}_\mathbf{V}, \mathbf{W}' \rangle$. □

**Proof of Theorem 4.** We prove the theorem by induction. We first order all the functional variables in a bottom-up order. Let $W^i$ denote the $i$th functional variable in the order and $\mathbf{W}^{(i)}$ denote the functional variables that are ordered before $W^i$ (including $W^i$). It follows that we can go over each $W^i$ in the order and show that a causal effect is F-identifiable with respect to $\langle G, \mathbf{V}, \mathcal{C}_\mathbf{V}, \mathbf{W}^{(i-1)} \rangle$ iff it is F-identifiable with respect to $\langle G, \mathbf{V}, \mathcal{C}_\mathbf{V}, \mathbf{W}^{(i)} \rangle$ according to Lemma A2. Since F-identifiability with respect to $\langle G, \mathbf{V}, \mathcal{C}_\mathbf{V}, \mathbf{W}^{(0)} \rangle$ is equivalent to identifiability with respect to $\langle G, \mathbf{V}, \mathcal{C}_\mathbf{V} \rangle$, we conclude that the causal effect is F-identifiable with respect to $\langle G, \mathbf{V}, \mathcal{C}_\mathbf{V}, \mathbf{W} \rangle$ iff it is identifiable with respect to $\langle G, \mathbf{V}, \mathcal{C}_\mathbf{V} \rangle$. □

*Proof of Theorem 5*

The proof of the theorem is organized as follows. We start with a lemma (Lemma A3) that allows us to modify the CPT of a variable when the marginal probability over its parents contains zero entries. We then show a main lemma (Lemma A4) that allows us to reduce F-identifiability to identifiability when all functional variables are observed or have a hidden parent. Finally, we prove the theorem based on the main lemma and previous theorems.

**Lemma A3.** *Consider two CBNs that have the same causal graph and induce distributions* $\Pr_1$ *and* $\Pr_2$. *Suppose the CPTs of the two CBNs only differ by* $f_X(X, \mathbf{P})$. *Then,* $\Pr_1(\mathbf{p}) = 0$ *iff* $\Pr_2(\mathbf{p}) = 0$ *for all instantiations* ($\mathbf{p}$) *of* $\mathbf{P}$.

**Proof.** Let $f_Y$ and $g_Y$ denote the CPTs for $Y$ in the first and second CBN, respectively. Let $\mathcal{A}n(\mathbf{P})$ be the ancestors of variables in $\mathbf{P}$ (including $\mathbf{P}$). If we eliminate all variables other than $\mathcal{A}n(\mathbf{P})$, then we obtain the factor set expressed as $\mathcal{F}_1 = \prod_{Y \in \mathcal{A}n(\mathbf{P})} f_Y$ for the first CBN and that expressed as $\mathcal{F}_2 = \prod_{Y \in \mathcal{A}n(\mathbf{P})} g_Y$ for the second CBN. Since all CPTs are the same for variables in $\mathcal{A}n(\mathbf{P})$, it is guaranteed that $\mathcal{F}_1 = \mathcal{F}_2$. If we further eliminate variables other than $\mathbf{P}$ from $\mathcal{F}_1$ and $\mathcal{F}_2$, we obtain marginal distributions of $\Pr_1(\mathbf{P}) = \overset{=}{\sum}_\mathbf{P} \mathcal{F}_1$ and $\Pr_2(\mathbf{P}) = \overset{=}{\sum}_\mathbf{P} \mathcal{F}_2$, where $\overset{=}{\sum}_\mathbf{P}$ denotes the projection operation that sums out variables other than $\mathbf{P}$ from a factor. Hence, $\Pr_1(\mathbf{P}) = \Pr_2(\mathbf{P})$, which concludes the proof. □

**Lemma A4.** *If a causal effect is F-identifiable with respect to* $\langle G, \mathbf{V}, \mathcal{C}_\mathbf{V}, \mathbf{W} \rangle$ *but is not identifiable with respect to* $\langle G, \mathbf{V}, \mathcal{C}_\mathbf{V} \rangle$, *then there must exist at least one functional variable that is hidden and whose parents are all observed.*

**Proof.** The lemma is the same as saying that if every functional variable is observed or has a hidden parent, then F-identifiability is equivalent to identifiability. We go over each functional variable ($W_i \in \mathbf{W}$) in a bottom-up order ($\Pi$) and prove the following inductive statement: A causal effect ($\Pr_x(\mathbf{Y})$) is F-identifiable with respect to $\langle G, \mathbf{V}, \mathcal{C}_{\mathbf{V}}, \mathbf{W}^{(i)} \rangle$ iff it is F-identifiable with respect to $\langle G, \mathbf{V}, \mathcal{C}_{\mathbf{V}}, \mathbf{W}^{(i-1)} \rangle$, where $\mathbf{W}^{(i)}$ is a subset of variables in $\mathbf{W}$ that are ordered before $W_i$ (and including $W_i$) in $\Pi$. Note that $\mathbf{W}^{(0)} = \emptyset$ and F-identifiability with respect to $\langle G, \mathbf{V}, \mathcal{C}_{\mathbf{V}}, \mathbf{W}^{(0)} \rangle$ collapses into identifiability with respect to $\langle G, \mathbf{V}, \mathcal{C}_{\mathbf{V}} \rangle$.

The if part follows from the definitions of identifiability and F-identifiability. Next, we consider the contrapositive of the only–if part. Let $Z$ be the functional variable in $\mathbf{W}$ that is considered in the current inductive step. Let $\langle G, \mathcal{F}_1 \rangle$ and $\langle G, \mathcal{F}_2 \rangle$ be the two CBNs inducing distributions $\Pr_1$ and $\Pr_2$, which constitute the unidentifiability, i.e., $\Pr_1(\mathbf{V}) = \Pr_2(\mathbf{V})$ and $\Pr_{1x}(\mathbf{Y}) \neq \Pr_{2x}(\mathbf{Y})$. Our goal is to construct two CBNs ($\langle G, \mathcal{F}_1''' \rangle$ and $\langle G, \mathcal{F}_2''' \rangle$) that induce distributions $\Pr_1'''$ and $\Pr_2'''$ and contain functional CPTs for $Z$ such that $\Pr_1'''(\mathbf{V}) = \Pr_2'''(\mathbf{V})$ and $\Pr_{1x}'''(\mathbf{Y}) \neq \Pr_{2x}'''(\mathbf{Y})$. Suppose $Z$ has a hidden parent; we directly employ Lemma A2 to construct the two CBNs. Next, we consider the case when $Z$ is observed and has observed parents. By default, we use $f_Z$ to $g_Z$ to denote the CPTs for $Z$ in $\mathcal{F}_1$ and $\mathcal{F}_2$.

The following three steps are considered to construct an instance of unidentifiability.

**First Step:** We construct $\langle G, \mathcal{F}_1' \rangle$ and $\langle G, \mathcal{F}_2' \rangle$ by modifying the CPTs for $Z$. Let $\mathbf{P}$ be the parents of $Z$ in $G$. For each instantiation ($\mathbf{p}$) of $\mathbf{P}$ where $\Pr_1(\mathbf{p}) = \Pr_2(\mathbf{p}) = 0$, we modify entries $f_Z'(Z|\mathbf{p})$ and $g_Z'(Z|\mathbf{p})$ for CPTs $f_Z'$ and $g_Z'$ in $\mathcal{F}_1'$ and $\mathcal{F}_2'$ as follows. Since $\Pr_{1x}(\mathbf{Y}) \neq \Pr_{2x}(\mathbf{Y})$, there exists an instantiation ($\mathbf{y}$) such that $\Pr_{1x}(\mathbf{y}) \neq \Pr_{2x}(\mathbf{y})$. Without losing generality, assume $\Pr_{1x}(\mathbf{y}) > \Pr_{2x}(\mathbf{y})$. Since $\Pr_{1x}(\mathbf{y})$ is computed as the marginal probability of $\mathbf{y}$ in the mutilated CBN for $\langle G, \mathcal{F}_1 \rangle$, it can be expressed in the form of a *network polynomial* as shown in [38,47]. If we treat the CPT entries of $f_Z(Z|\mathbf{p})$ as unknown, then we can write $\Pr_{1x}(\mathbf{y})$ as follows:

$$\Pr_{1x}(\mathbf{y}) = \alpha_0 + \alpha_1 f_Z(z_1|\mathbf{p}) + \cdots + \alpha_k f_Z(z_k|\mathbf{p})$$

where $\alpha_0, \alpha_1, \ldots, \alpha_k$ are constants and $z_1, \ldots, z_k$ are the states of variable $Z$. Similarly, we can write $\Pr_{2x}(\mathbf{y})$ as follows:

$$\Pr_{2x}(\mathbf{y}) = \beta_0 + \beta_1 g_Z(z_1|\mathbf{p}) + \cdots + \beta_k g_Z(z_k|\mathbf{p})$$

Let $\alpha_i$ be the *maximum* value among $\alpha_1, \ldots, \alpha_k$ and $\beta_j$ be the *minimum* value among $\beta_1, \ldots, \beta_k$; our construction method assigns $f_Z'(z_i|\mathbf{p}) = 1$ and $g_Z'(z_j|\mathbf{p}) = 1$. By construction, it is guaranteed that $\Pr_{1x}'(\mathbf{y}) - \Pr_{2x}'(\mathbf{y}) \geq \Pr_{1x}(\mathbf{y}) - \Pr_{2x}(\mathbf{y}) > 0$, where $\Pr_{1x}'(\mathbf{y})$ and $\Pr_{2x}'(\mathbf{y})$ denote the causal effects under the updated CPTs $f_Z'(Z|\mathbf{p})$ and $g_Z'(Z|\mathbf{p})$, respectively. We repeat the above procedure for all $\mathbf{p}$, where $\Pr_1(\mathbf{p}) = 0$, which yields the new CBNs ($\langle G, \mathcal{F}_1' \rangle$ and $\langle G, \mathcal{F}_2' \rangle$) in which $f_Z'(Z|\mathbf{p})$ and $g_Z'(Z|\mathbf{p})$ are functional whenever $\Pr_1(\mathbf{p}) = 0$. Next, we show that $\mathcal{F}_1'$ and $\mathcal{F}_2'$ (with the updated $f_Z'$ and $g_Z'$) constitute an example of unidentifiability. $\Pr_{1x}'(\mathbf{Y}) \neq \Pr_{2x}'(\mathbf{Y})$, since $\Pr_{1x}'(\mathbf{y}) > \Pr_{2x}'(\mathbf{y})$ for the particular instantiation ($\mathbf{y}$). We are left to show that the distributions of $\Pr_1'$ and $\Pr_2'$ induced by $\langle G, \mathcal{F}_1' \rangle$ and $\langle G, \mathcal{F}_2' \rangle$ are the same over the observed variables ($\mathbf{V}$). Consider each instantiation ($\mathbf{v}$) of $\mathbf{V}$ and $\mathbf{p}$ of $\mathbf{P}$, where $\mathbf{p}$ is consistent with $\mathbf{v}$. If $\Pr_1(\mathbf{p}) = 0$, then $\Pr_1'(\mathbf{p}) = \Pr_2'(\mathbf{p}) = 0$ according to Lemma A3; thus, $\Pr_1'(\mathbf{v}) = \Pr_2'(\mathbf{v}) = 0$. Otherwise, $\Pr_1'(\mathbf{v}) = \Pr_1(\mathbf{v}) = \Pr_2(\mathbf{v}) = \Pr_2'(\mathbf{v})$, since none of the CPT entries consistent with $\mathbf{v}$ was modified.

**Second Step:** We construct $\langle G'', \mathcal{F}_1'' \rangle$ and $\langle G'', \mathcal{F}_2'' \rangle$ from $\langle G, \mathcal{F}_1' \rangle$ and $\langle G, \mathcal{F}_2' \rangle$, respectively, by introducing an auxiliary root parent for $Z$ and assigning a functional CPT for $Z$. We add a root variable, denoted as $R$, to be an auxiliary parent of $W$, which specifies all possible functions from $\mathbf{P}^*$ to $Z$, where $\mathbf{P}^*$ contains all instantiations of $\mathbf{p}^*$, where $\Pr_1'(\mathbf{p}^*) = \Pr_2'(\mathbf{p}^*) > 0$. Each state ($r$) of $R$ corresponds to a function ($\varphi_r$), where $\varphi_r(\mathbf{p}^*)$ is mapped to some state of $Z$ for each instantiation ($\mathbf{p}^*$). Thus, the $R$ variable has $|Z|^{|\mathbf{P}^*|}$ states, since there is total of $|Z|^{|\mathbf{P}^*|}$ possible functions from $\mathbf{P}^*$ to $Z$. For each instantiation ($z, r, \mathbf{p}$), if $\mathbf{p} \in \mathbf{P}^*$, we define $f_Z''(z|r, \mathbf{p}) = 1$ if $z = \varphi_r(\mathbf{p})$ and $f_Z''(z|r, \mathbf{p}) = 0$ otherwise. If $\mathbf{p} \notin \mathbf{P}^*$, we define $f_Z''(z|r, \mathbf{p}) = f_Z'(z|\mathbf{p})$. The CPT for $R$ is assigned as $f_R''(r) = \prod_{\mathbf{p} \in \mathbf{P}^*} f_Z'(\varphi_r(\mathbf{p})|\mathbf{p})$.

Moreover, we remove all the states $(r)$ of $R$, where $f''_R(r) = 0$, which ensures $f''_R(r) > 0$ for all remaining $r$. We assign CPT $g''_Z$ in $\mathcal{F}''_2$ in a similar way. Note that $f''_R = g''_R$, since $f'_Z(\varphi_r(\mathbf{p})|\mathbf{p}) = \Pr'_1(\varphi_r(\mathbf{p})|\mathbf{p}) = \Pr'_2(\varphi_r(\mathbf{p})|\mathbf{p}) = g'_Z(\varphi_r(\mathbf{p})|\mathbf{p})$ for each $\mathbf{p} \in \mathbf{P}^*$ (where $\Pr'_1(\mathbf{p}) = \Pr'_2(\mathbf{p}) > 0$).

Next, we show that $\langle G'', \mathcal{F}''_1 \rangle$ and $\langle G'', \mathcal{F}''_2 \rangle$ constitute unidentifiability. One key observation is that $f'_T(t|\mathbf{p}) = \sum_r f''_R(r) f''_T(t|\mathbf{p}, r)$ and $g'_T(t|\mathbf{p}) = \sum_r g''_R(r) g''_T(t|\mathbf{p}, r)$. Consider each instantiation $(\mathbf{v}, r)$ that contains an instantiation $(\mathbf{p})$ of $\mathbf{P}$ and the state $(z)$ of $Z$. Suppose $\Pr'_1(\mathbf{p}) = 0$; then, $\Pr''_1(\mathbf{p}) = 0$, since the marginal distribution over $\mathbf{V}$ is preserved in $\Pr''_1$. Hence, $\Pr''_1(\mathbf{v}, r) = \Pr''_2(\mathbf{v}, r) = 0$. Suppose $\Pr'_1(\mathbf{p}) \neq 0$; then, $\Pr''_1(\mathbf{v}, r) = (\prod_{V \in \mathbf{V} \setminus \{Z\}} f'_V) \cdot f''_R(r)$ when $z = \varphi_r(\mathbf{p})$ and $\Pr''_1(\mathbf{v}, r) = 0$ otherwise. Similarly, $\Pr''_2(\mathbf{v}, r) = (\prod_{V \in \mathbf{V} \setminus \{Z\}} g'_V) \cdot g''_R(r)$ when $z = \varphi_r(\mathbf{p})$ and $\Pr''_2(\mathbf{v}, r) = 0$ otherwise. In both cases, $\Pr''_1(\mathbf{v}, r) = \Pr''_2(\mathbf{v}, r)$, since $\mathcal{F}''_1$ and $\mathcal{F}''_2$ assign the same function $(\varphi_r)$ for each state $(r)$ of $R$ and $f'_V = g'_V$ for all $V \in \mathbf{V} \setminus \{Z\}$. With respect to $\Pr''_{1x}(\mathbf{Y}) = \Pr'_{1x}(\mathbf{Y})$ and $\Pr''_{2x}(\mathbf{Y}) = \Pr'_{2x}(\mathbf{Y})$, note that summing out $R$ from $\Pr''_{1x}(\mathbf{V}, R)$ and $\Pr''_{2x}(\mathbf{V}, R)$ yields $\Pr'_{1x}(\mathbf{V})$ and $\Pr'_{2x}(\mathbf{V})$, respectively.

**Third Step:** We construct $\langle G, \mathcal{F}'''_1 \rangle$ and $\langle G, \mathcal{F}'''_2 \rangle$ from $\langle G'', \mathcal{F}''_1 \rangle$ and $\langle G'', \mathcal{F}''_2 \rangle$, respectively, by merging the auxiliary root variable $(R)$ with an observed parent $(T)$ of $Z$. We merge $R$ and $T$ into a new node $(T')$ and substitute it for $T$ in $G$, i.e., $T'$ has the same parents and children as $T$ in $G$. Specifically, $T'$ is constructed as the Cartesian product of $R$ and $T$. Each state of $T'$ can be represented as $(r, t)$, where $r$ is a state of $R$ and $t$ is a state of $T$. We then assign the CPT $(f'''_{T'}(T'|\mathbf{P}_T))$ in $\mathcal{F}'''_1$ as follows. For each parent instantiation $(\mathbf{p}_{T'})$ and each state $(r, t)$ of $T'$, $f'''_{T'}((r, t)|\mathbf{p}_{T'}) = f''_R(r) f''_T(t|\mathbf{p}_{T'})$. For each child $(C)$ of $T'$ that has parents $(\mathbf{P}_C)$ (excluding $T'$), the CPT for $C$ in $\mathcal{F}'''_1$ is assigned as $f'''_C(c|\mathbf{p}_C, (r, t)) = f''_C(c|\mathbf{p}_C, t)$. Similarly, we assign the CPTs ($g'''_{T'}$ and $g'''_C$) in $\mathcal{F}'''_2$. The distributions over observed variables are preserved, since there is a one-to-one correspondence between the instantiations over $\mathbf{V} \cup \{R\}$ in $\langle G'', \mathcal{F}''_1 \rangle$ and the instantiations over $\mathbf{V}$ in $\langle G, \mathcal{F}'''_1 \rangle$. Next, we consider the causal effect. Suppose $T$ is neither a treatment nor an outcome variable; then, merging does not affect the causal effect in a one-to-one correspondence between instantiations and $\Pr'''_{1x}(\mathbf{Y}) = \Pr''_{1x}(\mathbf{Y}) \neq \Pr''_{2x}(\mathbf{Y}) = \Pr'''_{2x}(\mathbf{Y})$. Suppose $T$ is an outcome variable; since $\Pr''_{1x}(\mathbf{Y}) \neq \Pr''_{2x}(\mathbf{Y})$, there exists an instantiation $(\mathbf{y}', r, t)$ where $\mathbf{Y}' = \mathbf{Y} \setminus \{T\}$ such that $\Pr''_{1x}(\mathbf{y}', r, t) \neq \Pr''_{2x}(\mathbf{y}', r, t)$. This implies $\Pr'''_{1x}(\mathbf{y}', (r, t)) \neq \Pr'''_{2x}(\mathbf{y}', (r, t))$ for the particular instantiation $(\mathbf{y}')$ and the state $(r, t)$ of $T'$. Suppose $T$ is the treatment variable $(X)$; since $\Pr''_{1x}(\mathbf{Y}) \neq \Pr''_{2x}(\mathbf{Y})$, there exists an instantiation $(\mathbf{y}, r)$ such that $\Pr''_{1x}(\mathbf{y}, r) \neq \Pr''_{2x}(\mathbf{y}, r)$. Moreover, $\Pr''_{1x}(r) = \Pr''_1(r) = \Pr''_2(r) = \Pr''_{2x}(r) > 0$ (otherwise, $\Pr''_{1x}(\mathbf{y}, r) = \Pr''_{2x}(\mathbf{y}, r) = 0$). This implies $\Pr''_{1x}(\mathbf{y}|r) \neq \Pr''_{2x}(\mathbf{y}|r)$. Since $R$ is a root in the mutilated CBN, $\Pr''_{1(xr)}(\mathbf{y}) = \Pr''_{1x}(\mathbf{y}|r) \neq \Pr''_{2x}(\mathbf{y}|r) = \Pr''_{2(xr)}(\mathbf{y})$. We now consider treatment $do(T' = (r, x))$ on $G$ instead of treatment $do(R = r, X = x)$ on $G''$. We have $\Pr'''_{1((r,x))}(\mathbf{y}) = \Pr''_{1(r,x)}(\mathbf{y}) \neq \Pr''_{2(r,x)}(\mathbf{y}) = \Pr'''_{2((r,x))}(\mathbf{y})$ for the particular state $(r, x)$ of $T'$. Moreover, $\Pr'''_1((r, x)) = \Pr''_1(r, x) = \Pr''_1(r) \Pr''_1(x) > 0$ according to the positivity assumption of $\Pr''_1(x)$. Thus, the positivity still holds for $\Pr'''_1$ and, similarly, for $\Pr'''_2$. □

**Proof of Theorem 5.** Let $\mathbf{H} = \mathbf{V}' \setminus \mathbf{V}$ be a set of hidden functional variables that are functionally determined by $\mathbf{V}$. According to Theorem 2, the set is F-identifiable with respect to $\langle G, \mathbf{V}, \mathcal{C}_{\mathbf{V}}, \mathbf{W} \rangle$ iff it isF-identifiable with respect to $\langle G', \mathbf{V}, \mathcal{C}_{\mathbf{V}}, \mathbf{W} \setminus \mathbf{H} \rangle$, where $G'$ is the result of functionally eliminating $\mathbf{H}$ from $G$. By construction, every variable in $\mathbf{H}$ has parents in $\mathbf{V}'$. Hence, according to Theorem 3, a variable is F-identifiable with respec t to $\langle G', \mathbf{V}, \mathcal{C}_{\mathbf{V}}, \mathbf{W} \setminus \mathbf{H} \rangle$ iff it is F-identifiable with respect to $\langle G, \mathbf{V}', \mathcal{C}_{\mathbf{V}}, \mathbf{W} \rangle$. If we consider each functional variable $(W \in \mathbf{W})$, it is either in $\mathbf{V}'$ or has a parent that is not in $\mathbf{V}'$ (otherwise, $W$ would have been added to $\mathbf{V}'$). According to Lemma A4, a functional variable is F-identifiable with respect to $\langle G, \mathbf{V}', \mathcal{C}_{\mathbf{V}}, \mathbf{W} \rangle$ iff it is identifiable with respect to $\langle G, \mathbf{V}', \mathcal{C}_{\mathbf{V}} \rangle$. □

## References

1. Pearl, J.; Mackenzie, D. *The Book of Why: The New Science of Cause and Effect*; Basic Books: New York, NY, USA, 2018.
2. Pearl, J. *Causality: Models, Reasoning, and Inference*, 2nd ed.; Cambridge University Press: Cambridge, UK, 2009.
3. Pearl, J. Causal Diagrams for Empirical Research. *Biometrika* **1995**, *82*, 669–688. [CrossRef]
4. Spirtes, P.; Glymour, C.; Scheines, R. *Causation, Prediction, and Search*, 2nd ed.; Adaptive Computation and Machine Learning; MIT Press: Cambridge, MA, USA, 2000.
5. Imbens, G.W.; Rubin, D.B. *Causal Inference for Statistics, Social, and Biomedical Sciences: An Introduction*; Cambridge University Press: Cambridge, UK, 2015.
6. Peters, J.; Janzing, D.; Schölkopf, B. *Elements of Causal Inference: Foundations and Learning Algorithms*; MIT Press: Cambridge, MA, USA, 2017.
7. Hernán, M.A.; Robins, J.M. *Causal Inference: What If*; Chapman & Hall/CRC: Boca Raton, FL, USA, 2020.
8. Pearl, J. [Bayesian Analysis in Expert Systems]: Comment: Graphical Models, Causality and Intervention. *Stat. Sci.* **1993**, *8*, 266–269. [CrossRef]
9. Huang, Y.; Valtorta, M. Identifiability in Causal Bayesian Networks: A Sound and Complete Algorithm. In Proceedings of the AAAI; AAAI Press: Menlo Park, CA, USA, 2006; pp. 1149–1154.
10. Shpitser, I.; Pearl, J. Identification of Joint Interventional Distributions in Recursive Semi-Markovian Causal Models. In Proceedings of the AAAI; AAAI Press: Menlo Park, CA, USA, 2006; pp. 1219–1226.
11. Zaffalon, M.; Antonucci, A.; Cabañas, R. Causal Expectation-Maximisation. *arXiv* **2020**, arXiv:2011.02912.
12. Zaffalon, M.; Antonucci, A.; Cabañas, R.; Huber, D. Approximating counterfactual bounds while fusing observational, biased and randomised data sources. *Int. J. Approx. Reason.* **2023**, *162*, 109023. [CrossRef]
13. Darwiche, A. Causal Inference with Tractable Circuits. *arXiv* **2021**, arXiv:2202.02891.
14. Huber, D.; Chen, Y.; Antonucci, A.; Darwiche, A.; Zaffalon, M. Tractable Bounding of Counterfactual Queries by Knowledge Compilation. In Proceedings of the Sixth Workshop on Tractable Probabilistic Modeling @ UAI 2023, Pittsburgh, PA, USA, 4 August 2023.
15. Jung, Y.; Tian, J.; Bareinboim, E. Estimating Causal Effects Using Weighting-Based Estimators. In Proceedings of the AAAI; AAAI Press: Menlo Park, CA, USA, 2020; pp. 10186–10193.
16. Jung, Y.; Tian, J.; Bareinboim, E. Learning Causal Effects via Weighted Empirical Risk Minimization. *Adv. Neural Inf. Process. Syst.* **2020**, *33*, 12697–12709.
17. Jung, Y.; Tian, J.; Bareinboim, E. Estimating Identifiable Causal Effects through Double Machine Learning. In Proceedings of the AAAI; AAAI Press: Menlo Park, CA, USA, 2021; pp. 12113–12122.
18. Jung, Y.; Tian, J.; Bareinboim, E. Estimating Identifiable Causal Effects on Markov Equivalence Class through Double Machine Learning. In Proceedings of the Machine Learning Research, Online, 18–24 July 2021; Volume 139, pp. 5168–5179.
19. Tikka, S.; Hyttinen, A.; Karvanen, J. Identifying Causal Effects via Context-specific Independence Relations. In Proceedings of the NeurIPS, Vancouver, BC, Canada, 8–14 December 2019; pp. 2800–2810.
20. Pearl, J. *Probabilistic Reasoning in Intelligent Systems: Networks of Plausible Inference*; Morgan Kaufmann: San Mateo, CA, USA, 1988.
21. Darwiche, A. An Advance on Variable Elimination with Applications to Tensor-Based Computation. In Proceedings of the 24th European Conference on Artificial Intelligence, Santiago de Compostela, Spain, 29 August–8 September 2020; Frontiers in Artificial Intelligence and Applications; IOS Press: Amsterdam, The Netherlands, 2020; Volume 325, pp. 2559–2568.
22. Chen, Y.; Choi, A.; Darwiche, A. Supervised Learning with Background Knowledge. In Proceedings of the 10th International Conference on Probabilistic Graphical Models (PGM), Skørping, Denmark, 23–25 September 2020.
23. Chen, Y.; Darwiche, A. On the Definition and Computation of Causal Treewidth. In Proceedings of the UAI, 38th Conference on Uncertainty in Artificial Intelligence, Eindhoven, The Netherlands, 1–5 August 2022.
24. Han, Y.; Chen, Y.; Darwiche, A. On the Complexity of Counterfactual Reasoning. *arXiv* **2022**, arXiv:2211.13447.
25. Verma, T.S. *Graphical Aspects of Causal Models*; Technical Report; UCLA: Los Angeles, CA, USA, 1993; Volume R-191.
26. Tian, J.; Pearl, J. On the Testable Implications of Causal Models with Hidden Variables. In Proceedings of the UAI, Edmonton, AB, Canada, 1–4 August 2002; Morgan Kaufmann: San Francisco, CA, USA, 2002; pp. 519–527.
27. Chen, Y.; Darwiche, A. Identifying Causal Effects Under Functional Dependencies. In Proceedings of the NeurIPS, Vancouver, BC, Canada, 10–15 December 2024.
28. Tian, J.; Pearl, J. *On the Identification of Causal Effects*; Technical Report; UCLA: Los Angeles, CA, USA, 2003; Volume R-290-L.
29. Kivva, Y.; Mokhtarian, E.; Etesami, J.; Kiyavash, N. Revisiting the general identifiability problem. In Proceedings of the UAI, Eindhoven, The Netherlands, 1–5 August 2022; Proceedings of Machine Learning Research; Volume 180, pp. 1022–1030.
30. Hwang, I.; Choe, Y.; Kwon, Y.; Lee, S. On Positivity Condition for Causal Inference. In Proceedings of the ICML, Vienna, Austria, 21–27 July 2024.
31. Balke, A.; Pearl, J. Counterfactuals and Policy Analysis in Structural Models. In Proceedings of the UAI, San Francisco, CA, USA, 18–20 August 1995; Morgan Kaufmann: San Mateo, CA, USA, 1995; pp. 11–18.
32. Galles, D.; Pearl, J. An axiomatic characterization of causal counterfactuals. *Found. Sci.* **1998**, *3*, 151–182. [CrossRef]
33. Halpern, J.Y. Axiomatizing causal reasoning. *J. Artif. Intell. Res.* **2000**, *12*, 317–337. [CrossRef]
34. Halpin, T.A.; Morgan, T. *Information Modeling and Relational Databases*, 2nd ed.; Morgan Kaufmann: San Mateo, CA, USA, 2008.
35. Date, C.J. *Database Design and Relational Theory—Normal Forms and All That Jazz*; O'Reilly: Sebastopol, CA, USA, 2012.

36. Zhang, N.L.; Poole, D.L. Exploiting Causal Independence in Bayesian Network Inference. *J. Artif. Intell. Res.* **1996**, *5*, 301–32 [CrossRef]
37. Dechter, R. Bucket Elimination: A unifying framework for probabilistic inference. In Proceedings of the Twelfth Annua Conference on Uncertainty in Artificial Intelligence (UAI), Portland, OR, USA, 1–4 August 1996; pp. 211–219.
38. Darwiche, A. *Modeling and Reasoning with Bayesian Networks*; Cambridge University Press: Cambridge, UK, 2009.
39. Geiger, D.; Pearl, J. On the logic of causal models. In Proceedings of the UAI, Minneapolis, MN, USA, 10–12 July 198 North-Holland: Amsterdam, The Netherlands, 1988; pp. 3–14.
40. Geiger, D.; Verma, T.; Pearl, J. Identifying independence in bayesian networks. *Networks* **1990**, *20*, 507–534. [CrossRef]
41. Pearl, J. Fusion, Propagation, and Structuring in Belief Networks. *Artif. Intell.* **1986**, *29*, 241–288. [CrossRef]
42. Verma, T.; Pearl, J. Causal networks: Semantics and expressiveness. In Proceedings of the UAI, Minneapolis, MN, USA, 10–1 July 1988; North-Holland: Amsterdam, The Netherlands, 1988; pp. 69–78.
43. Tikka, S.; Karvanen, J. Enhancing Identification of Causal Effects by Pruning. *J. Mach. Learn. Res.* **2017**, *18*, 194:1–194:23.
44. van der Zander, B.; Liskiewicz, M.; Textor, J. Separators and adjustment sets in causal graphs: Complete criteria and an algorithmi framework. *Artif. Intell.* **2019**, *270*, 1–40. [CrossRef]
45. Erdős, P.; Rényi, A. On Random Graphs. *Publ. Math. Debr.* **1959**, *6*, 290–297. [CrossRef]
46. Shpitser, I.; Pearl, J. Complete Identification Methods for the Causal Hierarchy. *J. Mach. Learn. Res.* **2008**, *9*, 1941–1979.
47. Darwiche, A. A differential approach to inference in Bayesian networks. *J. ACM* **2003**, *50*, 280–305. [CrossRef]

entropy

MDPI

rticle

# ausal Learning: Monitoring Business Processes Based on ausal Structures

ernando Montoya [1,2,3,*], Hernán Astudillo [4,*], Daniela Díaz [5] and Esteban Berríos [3]

1 Nexus Payment Systems SpA, Santiago 8320123, Chile
2 Campus Casa Central, Universidad Técnica Federico Santa María, Valparaíso 2390123, Chile
3 Fundación Instituto Profesional Duoc UC, Santiago 8240000, Chile; es.berriosp@duocuc.cl
4 Instituto de Tecnología para la Innovación en Salud y Bienestar, Universidad Andres Bello, Viña del Mar 2530958, Chile
5 IT Solution SpA, Santiago 8320000, Chile; ddiazb4@correo.uss.cl
* Correspondence: fernando.montoya@usm.cl (F.M.); hernan@acm.org (H.A.)

**Abstract:** Conventional methods for process monitoring often fail to capture the causal relationships that drive outcomes, making hard to distinguish causal anomalies from mere correlations in activity flows. Hence, there is a need for approaches that allow causal interpretation of atypical scenarios (anomalies), allowing to identify the influence of operational variables on these anomalies. This article introduces (*CaProM*), an innovative technique based on causality techniques, applied during the planning phase in business process environments. The technique combines two causal perspectives: *anomaly attribution* and *distribution change attribution*. It has three stages: (1) process events are collected and recorded, identifying flow instances; (2) causal learning of process activities, building a directed acyclic graphs (DAGs) represent dependencies among variables; and (3) use of DAGs to monitor the process, detecting anomalies and critical nodes. The technique was validated with a industry dataset from the banking sector, comprising 562 activity flow plans. The study monitored causal structures during the planning and execution stages, and allowed to identify the main factor behind a major deviation from planned values. This work contributes to business process monitoring by introducing a causal approach that enhances both the *interpretability* and *explainability of anomalies*. The technique allows to understand which specific variables have caused an atypical scenario, providing a clear view of the causal relationships within processes and ensuring greater accuracy in decision-making. This causal analysis employs cross-sectional data, avoiding the need to average multiple time instances and reducing potential biases, and unlike time series methods, it preserves the relationships among variables.

**Keywords:** causal graph; causal attribution of anomalies; causal attribution of distributional change; business process monitoring; business process mining

## 1. Introduction

The monitoring of business processes has become a critical challenge in modern management due to the dynamic environment, increasing complexity, and interconnection of activity flows [1]. These factors demand methods that go beyond simple metric evaluations. Traditionally, such oversight has relied on static models, predefined metrics, and comparisons of established execution patterns, which limit the ability to identify and understand the true underlying causal relationships in business processes. In this context, there is a need for an approach that facilitates not only the observation but also the interpretation and explanation of business process behavior from a causal perspective.

Despite advances in predictive [2–4], as well as prescriptive [5,6], analysis techniques for process monitoring, such techniques are still primarily based on patterns of correlation or association, without delving into causal reasoning. This limits the ability to identify the true underlying structures that govern operations. While correlation can indicate relationships between variables, it does not necessarily establish a cause–effect relationship. Without a methodology that explains the implications of causal effects, the understanding of operational dynamics remains incomplete, which can lead to biased decisions and hinder effective problem solving. This underscores the need for a causal approach that identifies causes and interprets their implications, improving decision making in complex business environments. Throughout a business process flow, multiple distinct instances may arise due to the diversity of operational objectives. This results in varied and often complex causal relationships. Therefore, it is essential to implement advanced approaches that go beyond traditional monitoring. These approaches must be capable of interpreting and thoroughly explaining the variations in business processes, grounded in a solid causal structure.

The remainder of this paper is structured as follows: Section 2 formalizes the problem; Section 3 surveys related work; Section 4 explains the proposed technique; Section 5 presents the case study; Section 6 discusses the results; and Section 7 summarizes and concludes.

## 2. Context and Problem

This section formalizes the description of the research problem as one of causal reasoning on business processes.

### 2.1. Problem Description

Figure 1 illustrates a business process flow in which execution instances are represented as tokens corresponding to specific tasks defined in the planning of various projects. In this context, organizational areas continuously monitor a series of key performance indicators (KPIs) to manage and optimize the processes. These KPIs include compliance with service-level agreements (SLAs); resource utilization; and other critical factors, such as hours allocated to specific tasks, personnel assigned to essential roles, and the achievement of departmental objectives [7]. This systematic approach enables the measurement of anomalies in the process flow, based on the defined metrics, which manifest in critical scenarios such as those described in *A* and *B*.

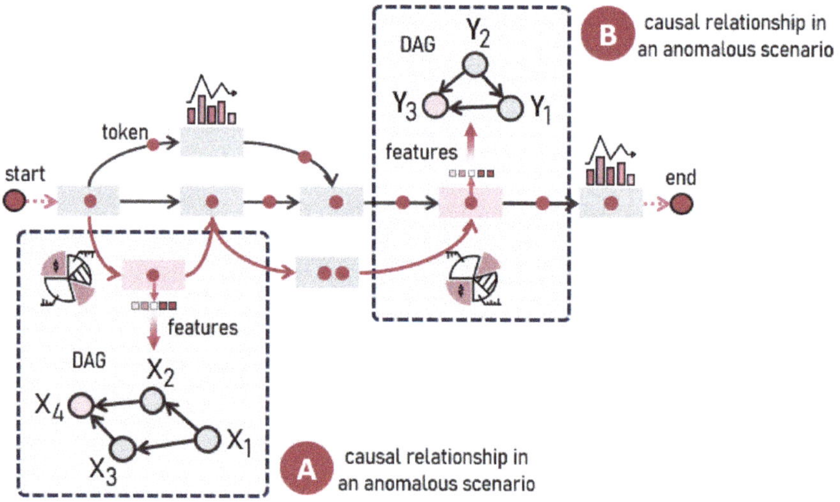


**Figure 1.** Characterization of causal variables in business process activities during anomalous scenarios with respect to the effect variables exhibiting anomalies.

Interpreting and explaining the causal relationships in these scenarios presents a considerable challenge, as it involves uncovering the underlying causal relationships connecting the various events and metrics involved. Moreover, understanding the causal direction of the variables that trigger these events is crucial to ensuring more precise and proactive process management, allowing for timely adjustments in resource allocation and task planning.

Approaching this analysis from a causal perspective establishes the directed acyclic graph (DAG) as a key tool for understanding the connections between variables [8,9], as DAGs not only aid in identifying the causes of anomalous events but also provide a more comprehensive understanding of the operational interactions within the process. Nevertheless, their implementation demands a deep understanding of causal topology. In Figure 1, the DAGs from scenarios $A$ and $B$ reveal different levels of complexity, where, within the same process, the operational aspects of two distinct activities are represented by the variables $X_i$ and $Y_i$, respectively. Both significantly influence the overall flow, as their interactions can determine both the stability and performance of the process, potentially leading to anomalous scenarios in the business process flow.

### 2.2. Causal Reasoning in the Business Process Context

Business process monitoring not only entails supervising key indicators but also examining how the relationships between variables influence overall performance. Understanding these relationships from a causal perspective is crucial for improving decision making and optimizing operational performance. Through causal learning, it is possible to identify how variables interact and impact the process flow, enabling early detection and correction of anomalies. Scenarios $A$ and $B$ (see Figure 1) illustrate how this causal approach can influence different activities within the same business process, given the distinct causal topologies between variables $X_i$ and $Y_i$.

In Scenario $A$, variables $X_1$, $X_2$, $X_3$, and $X_4$ are part of a specific activity within the process, where $X_1$ directly influences $X_2$ and $X_3$ and these two, in turn, affect $X_4$. Applying causal learning shows that $X_2$ and $X_3$ are independent of each other when conditioned on $X_1$, which is expressed as $X_2 \perp\!\!\!\perp X_3 \mid X_1$; however, when conditioned on $X_4$, which acts as a collider, $X_2$ and $X_3$ become dependent. This understanding introduces important considerations for business process decision making because if an anomaly occurs in $X_4$, causal learning identifies that the potential causes lie in $X_2$ and $X_3$. Due to the conditional independence between these variables given $X_1$, it is possible to analyze each one separately to determine which is contributing to the anomaly, facilitating more effective mitigation by allowing interventions to be specifically directed at the problematic variable without unnecessarily affecting other parts of the process.

On the other hand, in scenario $B$, corresponding to a different activity within the same process flow, the variables $Y_1$, $Y_2$, and $Y_3$ interact differently. $Y_2$ directly influences both $Y_1$ and $Y_3$, and $Y_1$ also influences $Y_3$. This creates a causal chain where $Y_2$ affects $Y_3$ both directly and indirectly through $Y_1$, indicating that all influences must be considered when analyzing $Y_3$. Causal learning indicates that an anomaly in $Y_3$ could be the result of multiple inter-related factors, requiring decision makers to account for both the direct and indirect influences of $Y_2$ and $Y_1$. Mitigating the anomaly, therefore, requires a comprehensive approach addressing all the variables involved to identify and resolve the root cause of the problem.

These scenarios highlight the importance of having previous causal insights and mechanisms for interpreting anomalies using DAGs. Without a thorough understanding of the causal relationships and dependency topology in business processes, decision making can become inefficient. Implementing causal learning and developing tools that interpret anomalies according to the causal structure allow for the identification of underlying causes and the design of effective interventions. This approach not only facilitates the resolution of current anomalies but also helps to prevent future incidents, ultimately improving the overall performance of the business.

### 2.3. Research Questions

This work proposes a monitoring methodology based on two causal perspectives, anomaly attribution and distributional change attribution [10,11]. This approach allows for identifying the contributions of each node to the observed anomalies and changes in the system's causal mechanisms, facilitating a deep understanding of the variations and their underlying causes.

#### 2.3.1. Anomaly Attribution

The purpose of these questions is to evaluate how the causal connections between variables explain the severity of observed anomalies [10].

- ***RQ*1**: *What is the causal contribution of a specific variable (e.g., $X_1$ or $Y_2$) to the anomaly observed in a target variable (e.g., $X_4$ or $Y_3$), taking into account the entire causal graph?* The influence of variables like $X_1$ or $Y_2$ is key to understanding the origin of anomalous deviations in the system, allowing for the identification of critical points that generate these unexpected behaviors.
- ***RQ*2**: *How do causal paths, such as $X_1 \rightarrow X_2 \rightarrow X_4$ or $Y_2 \rightarrow Y_1 \rightarrow Y_3$, affect the severity of the anomalies observed in $X_4$ and $Y_3$?* Causal paths, such as $X_1 \rightarrow X_2 \rightarrow X_4$ or $Y_2 \rightarrow Y_1 \rightarrow Y_3$, break down the internal dynamics of the system, revealing how intermediate interactions contribute to the final magnitude of the observed anomaly.

#### 2.3.2. Distributional Change Attribution

The focus of these questions is to analyze how changes in causal mechanisms and interactions between nodes affect the observed distributions in different scenarios [11,12].

- ***RQ*3**: When comparing two different contexts, *how can we identify and quantify the changes in the distributions of target variables (e.g., $X_4$ or $Y_3$), and what evidence suggests that these differences are due to alterations in the causal mechanisms of specific variables (e.g., $X_1$ or $Y_2$)?* This question aims to identify which nodes experience changes in their mechanisms and how they impact the distribution of the target variables under different conditions.
- ***RQ*4**: *How do changes in causal interactions within paths $X_1 \rightarrow X_2 \rightarrow X_4$ and $Y_2 \rightarrow Y_1 \rightarrow Y_3$ impact the distributional properties of $X_4$ and $Y_3$?* This question examines how modifications in the causal relationships within specific paths alter the distributions of variables $X_4$ and $Y_3$.

## 3. Related Work

Recent literature on business process monitoring has explored causal approaches to improving efficiency and effectiveness in management. Traditionally, causal inference for estimation of effects has largely depended on expert knowledge, which may introduce potential limitations and biases in the analysis. However, there is a growing need to apply causal learning techniques to enable the autonomous discovery of causal relationships.

For example, Shoush et al. [13] used algorithms such as orthogonal random forests (**ORF**) to optimize resource allocation and intervention policies, leveraging historical data to predict needs in credit origination. This approach is complemented by the work described by Bozorgi et al. [14], which combines causal inference with reinforcement learning to enhance treatment policies, maximizing net benefits in business processes. Both studies emphasize the importance of accurately evaluating the effects of interventions, although they depend on expert knowledge to define initial causal relationships.

In a similar context, Mehdiyev et al. [15] addressed uncertainty in predictive process monitoring by integrating information systems, machine learnig, and operations research techniques. By using quantile regression forests (**QRF**) and Shapley Additive Explanations (**SHAPs**), they provided a deeper understanding of model uncertainties. This methodology resonates with the findings of Wang et al. [16], who applied deep learning techniques such as **CNN** and **BigRu** to capture dependencies in business processes, improving the prediction of future activities. Both approaches underscore the importance of managing uncertainty and dependencies in data to enhance intervention decisions.

Furthermore, Kotsias et al. [17] integrated deep learning techniques into Business Process Management (**BPM**) through process mining. Their innovative approach combined predictive and prescriptive monitoring using Reinforcement Learning (**RL**) in the banking sector. Methods such as LSTM and Q-learning were employed to predict future states and optimize decisions, highlighting the Inductive Miner, a process discovery algorithm, for its flexibility and scalability. Results showed that the RL model outperformed traditional methods, suggesting future research in RL algorithms and deep learning for complex business environments.

Zahra et al. [18] introduced a prescriptive approach that applies causal inference to estimate the effects of interventions in real time, particularly in the execution of approval request processes. This method adjusts intervention decisions based on user-defined policies and is related to work aiming to improve accuracy in measuring causal effects, as detailed by Pavlos Delias et al. [19]. In this context, doubly robust estimation techniques were employed to mitigate biases and enhance the precision of effect estimates, using simulated process execution data.

Building on the theme of improving predictive accuracy in business processes, Jens Brunk et al. [20] focused on predicting future events by considering context, using dynamic Bayesian networks to model cause–effect relationships. This approach, which combines predictive analytics and machine learning, aligns with the efforts of the previously mentioned articles in seeking to improve the accuracy of predictive process monitoring (**PPM**). However, as in other studies, causality is often assumed based on expert knowledge, which can limit the generalization of the models.

Focusing on the analysis of time series in business processes, Hompes et al. [21] present a technique for identifying causal factors that influence process performance. Their approach, based on Granger causality and combining domain knowledge with advanced clustering and filtering techniques, enables the systematic analysis of event logs to generate causal graphs that reveal underlying relationships between different process variables. The proposed technique includes the creation of a decomposition graph and an inclusion graph, facilitating the discovery of complex interactions between process features and performance metrics.

In summary, there is a need to apply independent and objective causal discovery techniques for anomaly detection in business process monitoring. This approach aims to reduce reliance on expert knowledge and enable a comprehensive interpretation of anomalous event causality, facilitating effective and targeted interventions.

## 4. Proposed Technique

This article presents *CaProM*, an innovative technique for business process monitoring, focused on managing anomalies caused by noise in variables and shifts in the distribution of causal graphs. Unlike previous approaches that rely on expert knowledge [13,14], *CaProM* employs automated causal discovery [22,23], setting itself apart from time series based approaches [21]. It involves independently monitoring causal graphs within each activity of the process flow, providing a deeper understanding that goes beyond effect estimation by identifying the variables that significantly contribute to anomalous events. *CaProM* facilitates the determination of specific actions to address concrete events within the process.

*CaProM* has three stages. First, process events are collected and recorded from project plans, reflecting flow instances that will be executed in the business process. Second, causal learning is carried out by constructing independent directed acyclic graphs (**DAGs**) for each process activity, which represent the dependencies between variables. Third and finally, these DAGs are used to monitor the process, detecting anomalies and critical nodes, based on techniques [10,11].

### 4.1. Project Event Log

*CaProM*'s first stage (Figure 2A) applies process mining techniques to event logs from several projects, to capture the complete model that will be executed. This provides a more accurate representation of operational reality, overcoming the limitations of documented process flows that are often not strictly followed. Event logs for the projects can be sourced from Gantt schedules, and estimates of operational variable usage can be provided by several process roles. Analyzing aggregated traces from the projects allows to identify critical activities and process variants.

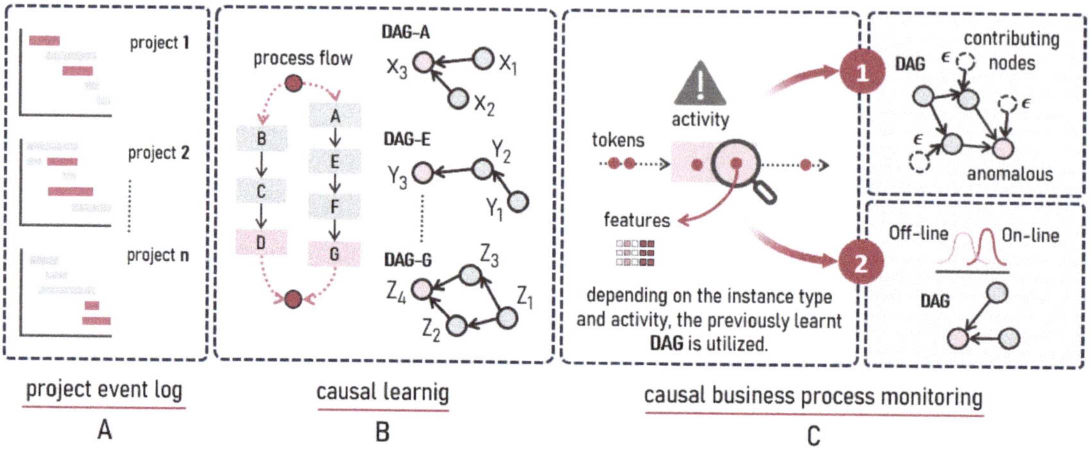


**Figure 2.** Stages of the proposed *CaProM* technique: event logging, causal learning, and monitoring of anomalies.

For example, software development projects have critical activities proper to software development (e.g. integration and testing), and changes in their requirements impact their execution effort. This first stage is essential to understand the actual execution of processes and uncover patterns and deviations that are not reflected in the official documentation.

In addition, the event log in project planning, as shown in Table 1, includes elements such as the event identifier linked to the project, the planned activity, the timestamp showing the allocated time for completing the activity, the responsible person, and the associated operational variables. These logs detail each stage of the project, allowing for precise tracking of the actual planning for its execution.

**Table 1.** Project event log.

| Project ID | Activity | Time Span | $Role_1$ | $Feature_1$ | $Feature_2$ | ... | $Feature_n$ |
|---|---|---|---|---|---|---|---|
| $proj._1$ | A | 350.2 ms | $role._1$ | - | $feat._2$ | ... | $feat._n$ |
| $proj._1$ | B | 270.2 ms | $role._2$ | $feat._1$ | $feat._2$ | ... | - |
| $proj._1$ | C | 450.5 ms | $role._4$ | - | $feat._2$ | ... | $feat._n$ |
| $proj._2$ | A | 510.4 ms | $role._5$ | $feat._1$ | - | ... | $feat._n$ |
| $proj._2$ | B | 350.8 ms | $role._1$ | $feat._1$ | $feat._2$ | ... | - |
| ... | ... | ... | ... | ... | ... | ... | ... |
| $proj._n$ | A | 230.4 ms | $role._5$ | - | $feat._2$ | ... | $feat._n$ |
| $proj._n$ | B | 130.6 ms | $role._2$ | $feat._1$ | - | ... | $feat._n$ |
| $proj._n$ | C | 310.2 ms | - | $feat._1$ | $feat._2$ | ... | - |

### 4.2. Causal Learning

*CaProM*'s second stage (Figure 2B), focuses on the causal analysis of the activities in the process model, obtained from the event logs of multiple projects. Each activity considers a set of operational variables $V^a = \{X_1^a, \ldots, X_n^a, Y_1^a, \ldots, Y_m^a\}$. Using causal discovery algorithms specifically designed for cross-sectional data, DAGs are constructed to represent the causal relationships between these variables, based on simultaneous observations of multiple instances of the activity.

The main goal of this technique is identifying the causal graph that correctly describes the interactions among operational variables, to allowing understanding the causal topology and the specific interrelationships within each process activity. To this end, it employs an algorithm based on the Linear Non-Gaussian Acyclic Model (LiNGAM) that assumes linear relationships and non-Gaussian error terms, thus enabling identification of causal direction even in complex situations with cross-sectional data [24].

$$Y_i^a = f_a(\theta_a, X_i^a) + \epsilon_{Y_i}^a \tag{1}$$

where $Y_i^a$ represents the effect variable of activity $a_i$ for process instance $i$; $X_i^a$ is the specific causal variable; $\theta_a$ denotes the global parameters; and $\epsilon_{Y_i}^a$ is the non-Gaussian error term. In addition to LiNGAM, other causal discovery algorithms from the following two main families are employed: *constraint-based* and *score-based methods*.

Constraint-based algorithms, such as the Peter–Clark algorithm (PC), determine the causal structure by conducting conditional independence tests, systematically evaluating whether $X_1^a \perp\!\!\!\perp Y_1^a \mid Z$ for variables $X_1^a$, $Y_1^a$, and sets of variables $Z$, thereby determining the existence or absence of edges in the dependency graph ($G_{PC}$). PC starts with a fully connected graph and removes edges based on detected conditional independencies, resulting in a Partially Directed Acyclic Graph (CPDAG).

Score-based algorithms, such as Greedy Equivalence Search (GES), search for the structure that maximizes a scoring function ($S(G)$). GES operates by performing a greedy search in the space of causal structures, finding $G^* = \arg\max_G S(G)$, where $G^*$ is the optimal graph according to the scoring function.

Figure 3 illustrates the generalized causal model derived from the causal discovery algorithms [22,23]. This representation explicitly captures the global parameters ($\theta_a$) associated with the effect variables ($Y_i^a$), as well as the error terms ($\epsilon_{X_i}^a$ and $\epsilon_{Y_i}^a$), allowing LiNGAM to exploit non-Gaussianity to infer causal direction. In the same graph, the PC and GES algorithms integrate $\theta_a$ into their methodologies; PC implicitly utilizes $\theta_a$ in the conditional independence tests to determine the dependency relationships between the effect variables ($Y_i^a$), while GES optimizes a scoring function that incorporates $\theta_a$ to evaluate and select the most suitable causal structure from the space of possible graphs.

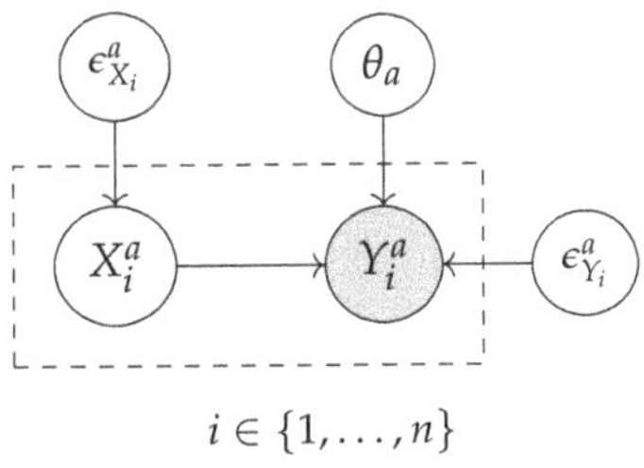


**Figure 3.** Generalized causal graph illustrating the causal relationships between operational variables, where $X_1^a$ has a causal effect on $Y_1^a$, situated in activity $a$ of the business process.

The causal model for the variables involved in each business process activity can be expressed in terms of their joint probability as follows:

$$P(V^a, \theta_a) = P(\theta_a) \prod_{i=1}^{n} P(Y_i^a | X_i^a, \theta_a) \tag{2}$$

where this probabilistic framework facilitates the integration of various causal discovery algorithms to infer the causal structure and estimate the functional relationships between the operational variables. The factorization of the joint probability reflects the structure of the DAG obtained by the algorithms, with each variable ($Y_i^a$) depending on its direct causes

($X_i^a$) and the parameters ($\theta_a$). Variables ($X_i^a$) can be considered exogenous or dependent on other variables within the causal model.

### 4.3. Causal Monitoring

In *CaProM*'s third stage, process flow monitoring is based on the previously established DAG, to identify and examine anomalous events in the operational variables. Figure 2C illustrates the process of comparing the variables of interest with a predetermined threshold. When a variable exceeds the established operational limits, the analysis focuses on the causal variables that contributed to the anomaly. To address this causal analysis, two specific techniques are proposed, as described in the following subsections.

#### 4.3.1. Causal Analysis of Anomalous Attributes

A causal analysis of anomalous attributes is conducted by identifying and understanding causal relationships among sources of atypical behavior, by evaluating the data captured during process planning [10], as documented in project event logs (Section 4.1). Additionally, this technique analyzes how noise present in key variables impacts the metrics of interest, to detect unusual patterns and attribute them to specific causes.

Based on the causal graph topology shown in Figure 4, the perturbations in the error terms ($\epsilon_{B_i}^a$, $\epsilon_{C_i}^a$, and $\epsilon_{Y_i}^a$) are evaluated, and their effects on $Y_i^a$ are analyzed. Initially, an outlier score for $Y_i^a$ is established using anomaly detection models such as the difference of means. Subsequently, the contributions of $B_i^a$, $C_i^a$, and other causal nodes are quantified, determining how variations in $\epsilon_{B_i}^a$, $\epsilon_{C_i}^a$, and $\epsilon_{Y_i}^a$ influence the probability of $Y_i^a$ exhibiting anomalous values. This impact is calculated as the probability that $Y_i^a$ exceeds a threshold ($g(Y_i^a)$) when the values of $\epsilon_{B_i}^a$, $\epsilon_{C_i}^a$, and $\epsilon_{Y_i}^a$ are replaced with random values. it is measured as $-\log P(Y_i^a \geq g(Y_i^a) \mid \text{replace } \epsilon_i^a \text{ with random value}$, where the threshold $g(Y_i^a)$ (e.g. difference between means) determines whether $Y_i^a$ is anomalous. This logarithmic measure provides a clear assessment of the direct impact of the perturbations.

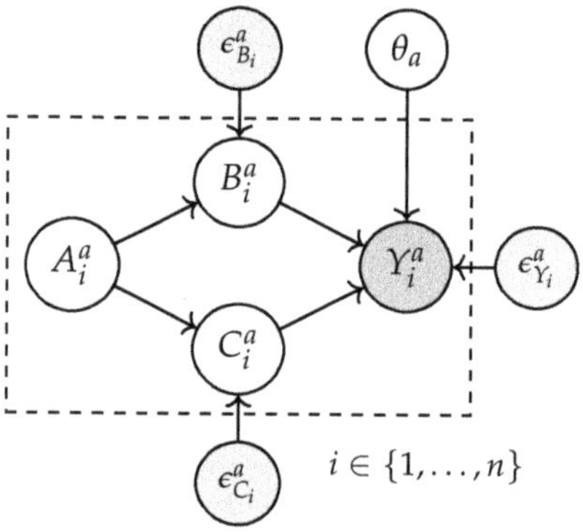


**Figure 4.** Characterization of the impact of noise on the variables of $Y_i^a$.

#### 4.3.2. Causal Attribution of Distributional Changes

The causal attribution of distributional changes aims to identify how changes in variables, such as $X_i^a = \{A_i^a, B_i^a, C_i^a\}$ affect the distribution of the variable of interest ($Y_i^a$) [11,12]. In Figure 5, the nodes on the left represent the prior data ($P(Y_i^a \mid X_i^a)$) obtained from the project event logs, while the nodes on the right show the current data ($\hat{P}(Y_i^{a'} \mid X_i^{a'})$) collected during the current process execution of the process (see Equation (2)). This is crucial for business process monitoring, as it allows for an understanding of how changes in operational conditions affect key outcomes.

Unlike previous proposals [13,14,18,20], which focused on estimating causal effects and specific interventions, *CaProM* analyzes variations in the variables distribution. It thus provides a more comprehensive view of how operational environment changes influence the process, capturing not only direct causes but also noise and influences from previous activities. Moreover, the approach is independent of the intervention training, allowing a wider evaluation of operational conditions that could trigger anomalous events.

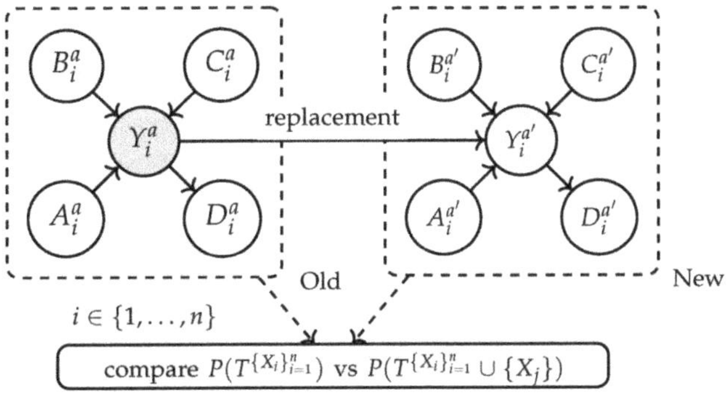


**Figure 5.** Characterization of distribution change attribution in a DAG for activity $a_i$.

The process begins with estimation of the conditional distributions of the variables using $P(Y_i^a \mid X_i^a)$, where $X_i^a$ represents the set of direct causal variables that influence $Y_i^a$; These distributions reflect the planning and expectations based on previous events (project). Next, the previous causal mechanisms ($P(Y_i^a \mid X_i^a)$) are systematically replaced with the mechanisms based on the new data ($\hat{P}(Y_i^{a'} \mid X_i^{a'})$), which reflect the current reality of process execution. This replacement generates new marginal distributions for $Y_i^{a'}$, denoted as $\hat{P}(T^{X_n})$, allowing to observe how these changes affect the variable of interest.

The next step involves comparing the marginal distributions before and after the replacement, specifically $P(T^{\{X_i\}_{i=1}^n})$ versus $P(T^{\{X_i\}_{i=1}^n} \cup \{X_j\})$. Here, $T$ represents the set of nodes considered in the analysis, and $\{X_i\}_{i=1}^n$ represents the variables of interest whose distributions are being measured. The notation $\cup\{X_j\}$ indicates the inclusion of the distribution of $X_j$ with a set of distributions of $X_i$, where $X_j$ is a new variable or a modification of an existing variable, being evaluated to see how its inclusion or change affects the distribution of the variables of interest.

This analysis helps to identify which node changes (e.g. $A_i^a$, $B_i^a$ or $C_i^a$) are responsible for the observed variations. Understanding the changes in the conditional distributions ($\hat{P}(Y_i^{a'} \mid X_i^{a'})$) affect $Y_i^{a'}$ allows to identify the underlying causes of variations in the performance of process activities. In turn, this enables precise adjustments in operational variables to mitigate issues and optimize system performance.

## 5. Results

This section presents the results obtained by applying the *CaProM* technique described in Section 4, which adapts causal discovery techniques to enable causal learning in the planning and execution stages of a business process. The findings show the efficacy of *CaProM* in detecting and causally interpreting anomalies and distributional shifts during the monitoring of the execution stage. *CaProM* provides insights that go beyond traditional correlations in the analysis of business processes.

### 5.1. Dataset

The validation dataset includes information from 562 projects, each with specific technological and regulatory requirements for a group of banking entities. This dataset provides a comprehensive view of the business process, allowing for the monitoring of planned activities throughout the workflow, observing them in both the planning and execution phases (see Table 2). The stages share the same activities, although they are given different names depending on the phase. For example, an activity labeled *Preliminary Evaluation* during the planning phase may correspond to *Requirement Implementation* during the execution phase, both with the same objective of specifying and fulfilling project requirements.

**Table 2.** Process flow activities.

| No. | Planning Activities | Execution Activities |
|---|---|---|
| 1 | Requirements Analysis | Integrity Review |
| 2 | Preliminary Evaluation | Requirements Validation |
| 3 | Functional Specification | Functional Implementation |
| 4 | Technical Design | Development and Integration |
| 5 | Test Design | Test Execution |
| 6 | Architecture Design | Architecture Validation |
| 7 | Project Approval | Deliverables Approval |
| 8 | Implementation Planning | Production Deployment |
| 9 | Request Closure | Project Closure |

Additionally, the data follow the structure described in Section 4.1 based on event logging. Key elements include the *Instance ID* to identify each project, the *Activity Name* specifying the actions, the *Execution Times* capturing the duration, the *Roles* assigning responsibilities, and several operational variables.

## 5.2. From Project Plans to Process Map

The application of *CaProM* (see Figure 2B) allowed to discover the process model from the dataset derived from project planning (Section 4.1). The flow was generated using Apromore, a cloud-based process mining tool that employs an advanced discovery algorithm based on Split Miner [25]. The analysis identified the activities and their interactions, which are represented in Figure 6.

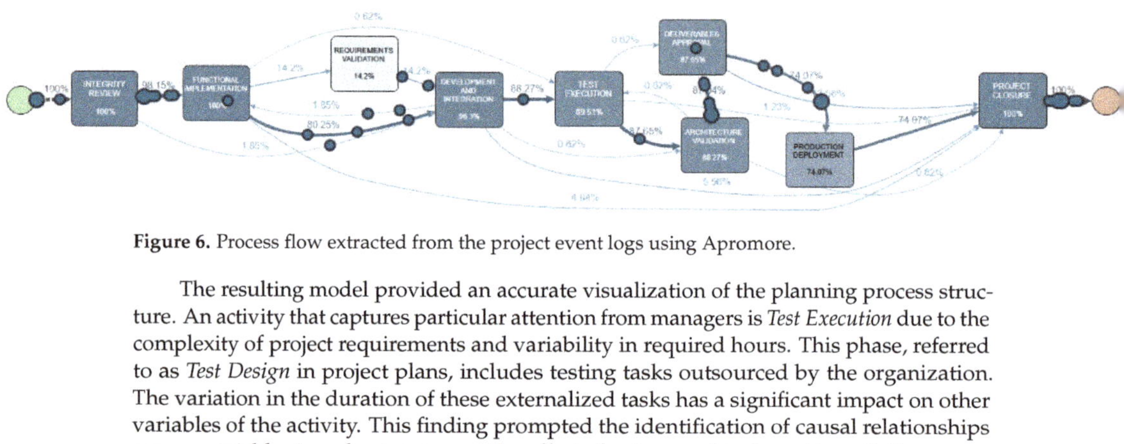


**Figure 6.** Process flow extracted from the project event logs using Apromore.

The resulting model provided an accurate visualization of the planning process structure. An activity that captures particular attention from managers is *Test Execution* due to the complexity of project requirements and variability in required hours. This phase, referred to as *Test Design* in project plans, includes testing tasks outsourced by the organization. The variation in the duration of these externalized tasks has a significant impact on other variables of the activity. This finding prompted the identification of causal relationships among variables in order to interpret the effect of outsourced tasks on the activity.

## 5.3. Operational Variables Extracted from Test Design for Causal Monitoring in Test Execution

Table 3 presents the key operational variables monitored during the *Test Execution* activity. These variables encompass various aspects of the process, such as code coverage, number of meetings, people involved, and test cases. Note that hour-related variables, such as *testing_hours* and *regression_time*, represent estimates of required quantities, not actual measurements over time. These estimates are made by those responsible during the planning phase, and are monitored throughout the test execution.

**Table 3.** Variables in the *Test Execution* activity.

| No. | Variable | Description |
|---|---|---|
| 1 | test_coverage | Percentage of code or requirements covered by tests |
| 2 | num_meetings | Hours dedicated to meetings for coordination, clarification, and scope changes |
| 3 | testing_hours | Hours dedicated to testing |
| 4 | num_testers | Number of people involved in testing |
| 5 | regression_time | Time spent on regression testing after changes |
| 6 | complexity_level | Complexity level of the requirement |
| 7 | num_test_cases | Number of cases in the test plan |
| 8 | defects_found | Number of defects identified during testing |
| 9 | automation_level | Percentage of test cases that are automated |
| 10 | num_requirements | Number of associated functional requirements |

The analysis confirmed the cross-sectional nature of the data, where each observation represents a unique instance of the process. Although the variables are recorded with a *Time Span* interval based on the project log (see Table 1), multiple execution instances exist at the same temporal point. Addressing temporality under these conditions would require the averaging of data from different simultaneously executed instances, i.e., calculation of an average value ($\bar{X}_t^a = \frac{1}{n_t}\sum_{i=1}^{n_t} X_{it}^a$) for each instant ($t$), where $n_t$ is the number of instances at time $t$ in activity $a$. However, this procedure can introduce biases and the loss of crucial information, affecting the estimation of the causal effect ($P(Y_i \mid do(X_i))$). Here, the notation $do(X_i)$ represents an intervention on the variable $X_i$, that is, evaluation an improvement action. Averaging could mask individual variations and temporal dynamics essential for causal discovery, hindering the identification of reliable structures.

Additionally, there is a risk of incurring in Simpson's paradox, where trends present in subgroups disappear or reverse when data are combined. Consequently, the cross-sectional approach was maintained to preserve the integrity of the relationships between variables and ensure the reliability of the results in the causal discovery methods.

### 5.4. Interpretability with Causal Graphs

The causal learning process shown in Figure 2B was implemented using three algorithms: LiNGAM, PC, and GES (Section 4.2). The application of these diverse methods enabled an exhaustive search for possible causal structures in the dataset, exploring different aspects of the relationships between variables.

To assess the consistency and significance of the causal relationships identified by the algorithms, a measure based on the entropy associated with each arc ($X_i^a \rightarrow Y_i^a$) was used. After applying the algorithms to each bootstrap sample ($S^{(1)}, S^{(2)}, \ldots, S^{(m)}$) yield causal graphs ($G^{(1)}, G^{(2)}, \ldots, G^{(m)}$). For each identified arc ($X_i^a \rightarrow Y_i^a$), its probability was calculated as ($p_{X_i^a \rightarrow Y_i^a} = \frac{1}{m}\sum_{b=1}^{m} \delta_{X_i^a \rightarrow Y_i^a}^{(b)}$), where $\delta_{X_i^a \rightarrow Y_i^a}^{(b)} = 1$ if the arc $X_i^a \rightarrow Y_i^a$ is present in the graph $G^{(b)}$, and $= 0$ otherwise.

The entropy $H(X_i^a \rightarrow Y_i^a)$ associated with each arc ($X_i^a \rightarrow Y_i^a$) was calculated as $-\left[p_{X_i^a \rightarrow Y_i^a} \log p_{X_i^a \rightarrow Y_i^a} + (1 - p_{X_i^a \rightarrow Y_i^a}) \log(1 - p_{X_i^a \rightarrow Y_i^a})\right]$, where $p_{X_i^a \rightarrow Y_i^a}$ is a Bernoulli random variable. A low value of $H$ indicates that the presence or absence of the arc is consistent across the bootstrap samples, suggesting greater reliability and significance in the inference of that causal relationship. This approach allows to quantify the uncertainty associated with each arc, providing a solid foundation for the interpretation of the dependencies among the operational variables identified by the algorithms.

Analyzing the extracted DAG (see Figure 7) allows to identify several significant causal relationships among the operational variables. The complexity level influences the number of requirements, which affects the number of test cases which in turn determines the necessary testing hours. Furthermore, the number of testers directly impacts the testing hours which in turn influence the number of required meetings. These connections allow to understand how the monitored variables interact in the test execution process, reflecting the underlying causal structure identified through the applied algorithms.

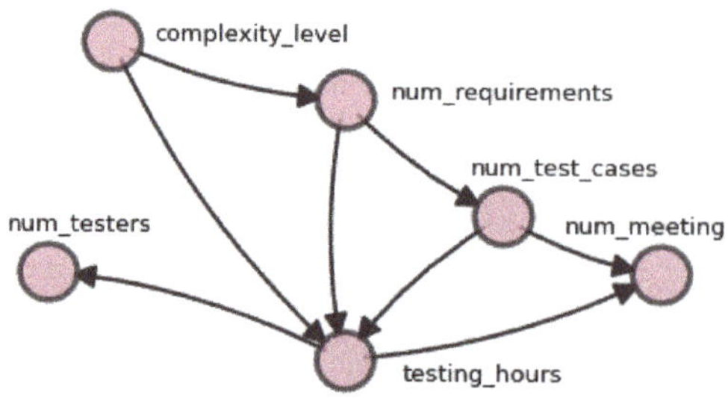


**Figure 7. DAG** extracted in the *Test Design* activity and monitored in the *Test Execution* activity.

According to the correlation heat map presented in Figure 8, which uses Spearman's correlation due to the nonlinearity present in some data relationships, it is observed that not all variables in Table 3 exhibit significant correlations, although some demonstrate direct causal relationships. For instance, between *num_requirements* and *num_test_cases*, a moderate correlation of 0.28 is observed, despite there being a direct causal relationship between them. Similarly, variables such as *testing_hours* and *num_testers* show a positive correlation of 0.53, supporting their causal relationship. However, in the case of *complexity_level*, a causal influence is identified on the number of requirements, but the correlation is low (0.15), illustrating that a low correlation does not imply the absence of causality.

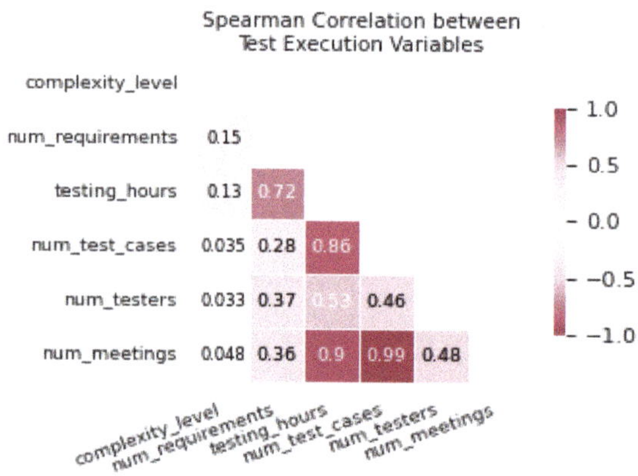


**Figure 8.** Correlations of the **DAG** variables in the *Test Execution* activity.

### *5.5. Explainability of Anomaly Attribution through Causal Graph*

At this stage, as described in Section 4.3.1, the causal graph obtained during the planning phase (see Figure 7) was monitored throughout the execution. A threshold of $3\sigma$ (*three standard deviations*) was applied to detect potential anomalies in key variables, allowing for the identification of values that significantly deviated from expected outcomes. Variables exceeding this threshold were flagged as anomalous events, aiding in the identification of specific deviations during project execution. Among the cases identified using this approach are the deviations listed in Table 4. The values recorded during execution, when compared to the distribution estimated from the planning phase (see Figure 9), revealed significant deviations in several variables. Specifically, *num_requirements* (37), *testing_hours* (290.9), *num_test_cases* (132), and *num_meetings* (29.52) exceeded the threshold of three standard deviations. These anomalies, detected through the monitoring of the causal graph, indicate that project execution deviated considerably from the original plan, likely due to unforeseen complexities or changes in scope.

The violin plots presented in Figure 9 clearly show that these anomalous values were situated outside the estimated distributions.

**Table 4.** Anomalous values of a *Test Execution* requirement versus its *Test Design* planned value.

| Variable | Anomalous Values |
|---|---|
| complexity_level | 2.0 |
| num_requirements | 37.0 |
| testing_hours | 290.90 |
| num_test_cases | 132.0 |
| num_testers | 6.0 |
| num_meetings | 29.52 |

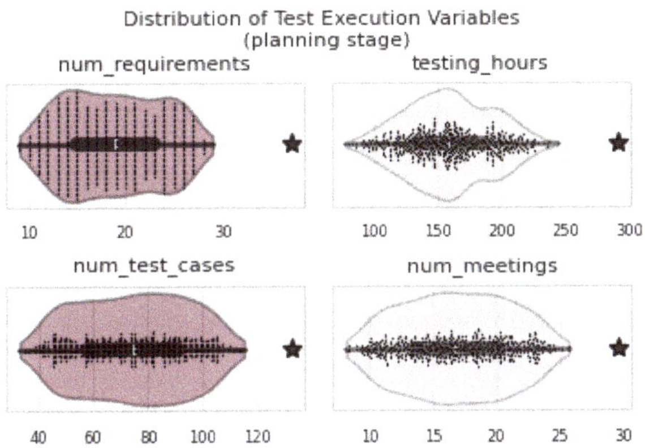


**Figure 9.** The stars (★) represent outlier values in *Test Execution* variables that exceeded ($3\sigma$).

At this analysis stage, the anomaly attribution DAG-based algorithm (see Figure 7) identified the causal topology for the observed value of *num_meetings* ($Y_i^a$). This enabled monitoring of the relationships among variables during the DAG execution, evaluating perturbations in the error terms ($\epsilon_i$) for each variable, and quantifying the perturbations impact on the anomalous behavior of $Y_i^a$.

Decomposing the system to understand how interactions among upstream nodes impact to the final outcome is crucial to calculate the probability that $Y_i^a$ exceeded the $3\sigma$ reference threshold.

The score attribution graph Figure 10 show how variables *num_requirements* (37) and *num_test_cases* (132) had a causal impact on the observed anomaly in *num_meetings* (29.52), exceeding the deviation thresholds. The direct impact of perturbations in these key variables showed that *num_requirements* achieved an attribution score close to 4.5, reflecting its predominant influence. *num_test_cases* had a score close to 4, also a significant impact albeit somewhat lower. In contrast, *complexity_level* (2) and *num_meetings* presented low scores of around 0 and 0.5, respectively, indicating that their influence was marginal and mediated by other variables.

The anomaly attribution analysis focused on the observed behavior of *num_meetings* ($Y_i = 29.52$). By applying attribution techniques, perturbations in the error terms ($\epsilon_{H_i}$, $\epsilon_{C_i}$, and $\epsilon_{Y_i}$) were evaluated to examine how these variations affected the probability of $Y_i$ exhibiting an anomalous value. In the context of the causal graph, upstream variables such as *testing_hours* ($H_i = 290.90$) and *complexity_level* ($C_i = 2$) were considered. However, their contributions to the anomaly were significantly smaller than those of *num_requirements* ($R_i = 37.0$) and *num_test_cases* ($N_i = 132$). This analysis allowed to quantify the contribution of variations in $\epsilon_i$ to the anomalous behavior of *num_meetings*, by calculating $-\log P(Y_i \geq g(Y_i) \mid \text{replacement of } \epsilon_i \text{with random values})$, where $g(Y_i)$ represents the reference threshold to determine whether $Y_i$ is anomalous.

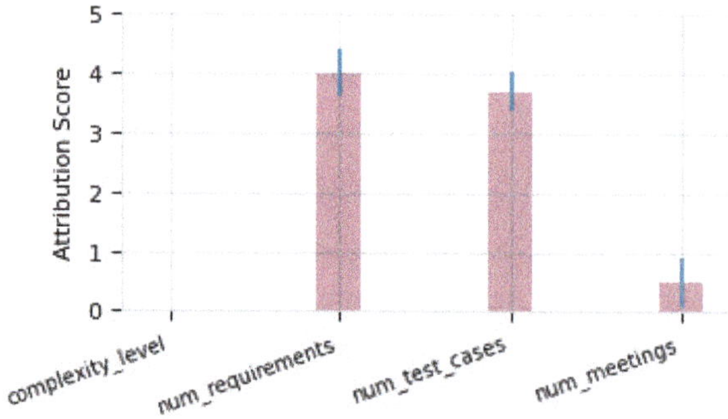


**Figure 10.** Attribution score of the anomalous values.

The results confirmed that *num_requirements* ($R_i$ = 37.0) was the primary trigger, generating a cascade effect that significantly impacted other variables connected to its downstream nodes in the *Test Execution* activity during project execution.

### 5.6. Explainability of Distributional Changes through Causal Graph

An analysis of distribution changes in a representative subset of the data showed a significant discrepancy in *testing_hours* between the planned and observed values (see Figure 11). The planned distribution had a mean close to 150 h but the observed distribution (*execution*) had a central concentration around 250 h. This shift was confirmed with a *t*-statistic of (−11.60), evidencing a statistically significant difference in the analyzed sample. Further analysis showed that the testing times executed in this subset considerably exceeded the planned estimates, indicating a potential impact on system performance. The technique (Section 4.3.2) quantified this deviation, highlighting the need to identify the underlying causes in the DAG [11].

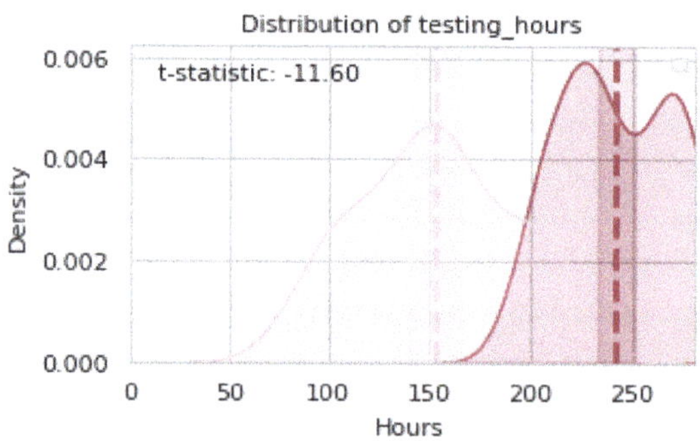


**Figure 11.** Distribution of *testing_hours* between the 37 Specific and Planned Cases.

The application of the distributional causal analysis technique to *testing_hours* involved comparing the conditional distributions of $P(Y_i^a \mid X_i^a)$ (*planning*) and $\hat{P}(Y_i^a \mid X_i^a)$ (*execution*). *testing_hours* ($Y_i^a$) was identified as the variable of interest, with parent nodes ($X_i^a$) including *num_test_cases*, *complexity_level*, *num_requirements*, and *num_meetings*. $P(Y_i^a \mid X_i^a)$ was estimated from the planning data and replaced by $\hat{P}(Y_i^a \mid X_i^a)$ using the data observed during execution. This produced a new distribution ($\hat{P}(T^{X_n})$), which allowed for observation of how variations in the parent nodes affected the total testing time. The KL divergence ($D_{KL}(P(Y_i^a \mid X_i^a) \parallel \hat{P}(Y_i^a \mid X_i^a))$) quantified the impact of these changes, allowing for the identification of the main causes of the discrepancy in *testing_hours*.

The analysis results show that *num_test_cases* was the primary cause of the distribution shift of *testing_hours*, with an observed difference of 250 h during execution. The Comparison of distributions confirmed a significant alteration, highlighting discrepancies between the planning and execution of the projects.

The bar chart reflects the contribution of each variable to the change in the distribution of *testing_hours* (Figure 12). *num_test_cases* has an attribution score close to 10, indicating a causal responsibility with respect to the observed change. In contrast, other variables *complexity_level*, *num_requirements*, and *num_testers* present attribution scores near zero, confirming that their effects on the distributional shift were minimal. These results highlight that the most significant change occurred in *testing_hours*, driven primarily by the causal factors represented in *num_test_cases*, while the other variables had a marginal influence.

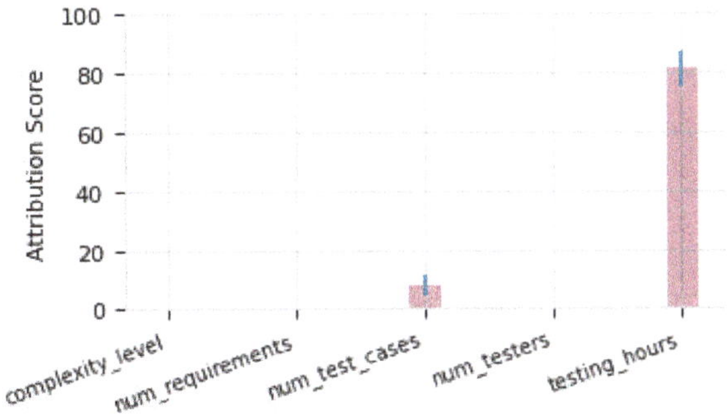


**Figure 12.** Attribution Score for the Distribution Change of *testing_hours*.

## 6. Discussion

The study of the process flow (see Figure 6) demonstrated the way in which activities recorded in the projects can be modeled as a business process flow using process mining algorithms. This representation enabled the precise identification of activities and their interactions, emphasizing the importance of the *Test Execution* activity for managers due to the outsourcing of tasks. The combined application of causal discovery algorithms, with connections evaluated through entropy (Section 5.4), facilitated the creation of a reliable causal graph, represented as a DAG (see Figure 7), which showed the causal relationships between operational variables (Section 5.3).

The anomalous values (Table 4) identified in key process variables were linked to the proposed research questions (see Section 2.3). The resulting causal graph enabled the examination of these questions through the analysis of causal pathways. The path of *num_requirements* → *testing_hours* → *num_meetings* showed the propagation of anomalies in the system (RQ.2). The graph facilitated the assessment of how specific variables influenced the observed anomalies (RQ.1), for example, the effect of *num_requirements* on *testing_hours*. This approach also allowed for the analysis of changes in the distribution of *testing_hours* (RQ.3 and RQ.4) in a subset of 37 projects, revealing how changes in causal relationships impacted the *Test Execution* activity during process execution.

Unlike previous studies [13,14,19,20], *CaProM* incorporated causal discovery into process planning. It not only identified causal relationships but also determined the influence of operational variables on anomalies and distributional changes in process activities. The integration of causality into project planning allowed addressing the dynamic nature of the environment, facilitating adjustments based on causal evidence. The causal analysis employed cross-sectional data, avoiding the need to average multiple time instances and reducing potential biases. Unlike time-series methods (e.g., [21]), this approach better preserves the relationships among variables. By avoiding issues with simultaneous data (Sections 5.3 and 5.4), the causal discovery is beneficial to process managers, minimizing spurious relationships and providing actionable information for decision making.

The results in (Sections 5.5 and 5.6) show that causal anomalies were identified in the *Test Execution* activity during the execution phase, which was monitored because of the outsourced tasks. The attribute anomalies in *num_requirements* (37) and *num_test_cases* (132) exceeded the $3\sigma$ threshold, affecting execution and contributing to the anomaly in *num_meetings* (29.52). In terms of distributional anomalies, *testing_hours* exhibited a significant shift (planned average: 150 h; observed: 250 h). Causal analysis attributed this change primarily to *num_test_cases*, with a score close to 10, while *complexity_level*, *num_requirements*, and *num_testers* made minimal contributions.

This work still has some limitations. The primary limitation (and requirement) is the fundamental need for detailed records of process planning, which are crucial for causal learning; this restricts its applicability in contexts where planning data are unavailable or incomplete. Also, the omission of organizational external factors may affect the accuracy of the causal relationships. Finally, the use of large data volumes (i.e. event logs) introduces computational challenges of its own.

## 7. Conclusions

This article has presented applied research aimed at improving the monitoring and interpretation of anomalous events in business process management through the early integration of causal discovery techniques. It introduced *CaProM*, an approach that uses knowledge of causal structures from initial project stages to enable monitoring and greater explainability during process execution. The key findings of this study are:

- Successful adaptation of causal discovery algorithms (LiNGAM, PC, and GES) to identify causal structures in 562 activity flow plans during the planning phase (see Section 5.1), revealing relationships not evident with traditional methods;
- Practical application of causal attribution techniques for anomalies and distributional changes, using the causal knowledge obtained during planning to more accurately interpret anomalous events during the execution of business process; and
- Demonstration of how integrating causal learning from the planning phase can significantly enhance the interpretability and explainability of anomalies during process execution, enabling a more informed and effective response.

*CaProM* advances the adaptation of causal learning techniques for monitoring business processes, promoting a shared understanding of project managers and process managers. It enhances analysis during execution, drawing on causal knowledge obtained during planning, and providing a solid foundation for the causal detection and explanation of anomalies and for making informed decisions. *CaProM* introduces a new way to anticipate causal scenarios in complex processes, enabling organizations to monitor them more effectively and make informed decisions during their execution. By integrating a causal view from the planning phase, managers can detect anomalies and understand their root causes using existing causal knowledge. Additionally, *CaProM* can interpret distributional changes to enable dynamic process adaptation, providing a competitive advantage in dynamic business environments that demand rapid detection, explanation, and response to changes in process patterns [26].

Future research will address unobserved confounding variables and explore the grouping of variables by process instance type, which could generate multiple **DAGs** per activity. This approach would offer a more detailed view of operational dynamics in numerous business contexts.

**Author Contributions:** Conceptualization, F.M. and H.A.; Methodology, F.M. and H.A.; Software, E.B.; Validation, F.M., H.A., D.D. and E.B.; Formal analysis, F.M. and H.A.; Investigation, F.M. and H.A.; Resources, H.A. and D.D.; Data curation, F.M., D.D. and E.B.; Writing—review & editing, F.M., H.A., D.D. and E.B.; Visualization, F.M., D.D. and E.B.; Supervision, H.A.; Project administration, H.A. All authors have read and agreed to the published version of the manuscript.

**Funding:** This research received no external funding.

**Institutional Review Board Statement:** Not applicable.

**Data Availability Statement:** The data used in this study are not publicly available due to confidentiality agreements and legal restrictions with the company that provided the information.

**Conflicts of Interest:** Author Fernando Montoya was employed by the company Nexus Payment Systems SpA. Author Daniela Díaz was employed by the company IT Solution SpA. The remaining authors declare that the research was conducted in the absence of any commercial or financial relationships that could be construed as a potential conflict of interest.

## eferences


Pérez-Álvarez, J.M.; Maté, A.; Gómez-López, M.T.; Trujillo, J. Tactical Business-Process-Decision Support based on KPIs Monitoring and Validation. *Comput. Ind.* **2018**, *102*, 23–39. [CrossRef]

Márquez-Chamorro, A.E.; Resinas, M.; Ruiz-Cortés, A. Predictive monitoring of business processes: A survey. *IEEE Trans. Serv. Comput.* **2017**, *11*, 962–977. [CrossRef]

Jalayer, A.; Kahani, M.; Pourmasoumi, A.; Beheshti, A. HAM-Net: Predictive Business Process Monitoring with a hierarchical attention mechanism. *Knowl.-Based Syst.* **2022**, *236*, 107722. [CrossRef]

Cuzzocrea, A.; Folino, F.; Guarascio, M.; Pontieri, L. Predictive monitoring of temporally-aggregated performance indicators of business processes against low-level streaming events. *Inf. Syst.* **2019**, *81*, 236–266. [CrossRef]

Kubrak, K.; Milani, F.; Nolte, A.; Dumas, M. Prescriptive process monitoring: Quo vadis? *PeerJ Comput. Sci.* **2022**, *8*, e1097. [CrossRef] [PubMed]

Weinzierl, S.; Dunzer, S.; Zilker, S.; Matzner, M. Prescriptive business process monitoring for recommending next best actions. In Proceedings of the International Conference on Business Process Management, Online, 13–18 September 2020; Springer: Cham, Switzerland, 2020.

van de Ven, M.; Lara, Machado, P.; Athanasopoulou, A.; Aysolmaz, B.; Turetken, O. Key performance indicators for business models: A systematic review and catalog. *Inf. Syst. E-Bus. Manage.* **2023**, *21*, 753–794. [CrossRef]

Dawid, P. What Is a Causal Graph? *Algorithms* **2024**, *17*, 93. [CrossRef]

Vowels, M.J.; Camgoz, N.C.; Bowden, R. D'ya Like DAGs? A Survey on Structure Learning and Causal Discovery. *ACM Comput.* **2022**, *55*, 1–36. [CrossRef]

Budhathoki, K.; Minorics, L.; Blöbaum, P.; Janzing, D. Causal structure-based root cause analysis of outliers. In International Conference on Machine Learning, Baltimore, MD, USA, 17–23 July 2022.

Budhathoki, K.; Janzing, D.; Bloebaum, P.; Ng, H. Why did the distribution change? In Proceedings of the 24th International Conference on Artificial Intelligence and Statistics, Virtual, 13–15 April 2021.

Tian, J.; Pearl, J. Causal discovery from changes. In *Proceedings of the 17th Conference in Uncertainty in Artificial Intelligence.* Morgan Kaufmann Publishers Inc.: San Francisco, CA, USA, 2001; pp. 512–521.

Shoush, M., Dumas, M. Prescriptive process monitoring under resource constraints: A causal inference approach. In Proceedings of the International Conference on Process Mining, Eindhoven, The Netherlands, 31 October–4 November 2021; Springer International Publishing: Cham, Switzerland, 2021; pp. 180–193.

Bozorgi, Z.D.; Dumas, M.; Rosa, M.L.; Polyvyanyy, A.; Shoush, M.; Teinemaa, I. Learning When to Treat Business Processes: Prescriptive Process Monitoring with Causal Inference and Reinforcement Learning. In *Advanced Information Systems Engineering*; Indulska, M., Reinhartz-Berger, I., Cetina, C., Pastor, O., Eds.; In Proceedings of the CAiSE 2023, Zaragoza, Spain, 12–16 June 2023; Springer: Cham, Switzerland, 2023.

Mehdiyev, N.; Majlatow, MFettke, P. Quantifying and explaining machine learning uncertainty in predictive process monitoring: An operations research perspective. *Ann. Oper. Res.* **2024**, 1–40.. [CrossRef]

Wang, J.; Chang, V.; Yu, D.; Liu, C.; Ma, X.; Yu, D. Conformance-oriented Predictive Process Monitoring in BPaaS Based on Combination of Neural Networks. *J. Grid Comput.* **2022**, *20*, 25. [CrossRef]

Kotsias, S.; Kerasiotis, A.; Bousdekis, A.; Theodoropoulou, G.; Miaoulis, G. Predictive and Prescriptive Business Process Monitoring with Reinforcement Learning. In Proceedings of the Novel Intelligent Digital Systems, 2nd International Conference (NiDS 2022), Athens, Greece, 29–30 September 2022; Krouska, A., Troussas, C., Caro, J., Eds.; Springer: Cham, Switzerland, 2022.

Bozorgi, Z.D.; Teinema, I.; Dumasa, M.; Rosa, M.L.; Polyvyanyy, A. Prescriptive process monitoring based on causal effect estimation. *Inf. Syst.* **2003**, *116*, 102198. [CrossRef]

Delias, P.; Mittas, N.; Florou, G. A doubly robust approach for impact evaluation of interventions for business process improvement based on event logs. *Decis. Anal. J.* **2023**, *8*, 100291. [CrossRef]

Brunk, J.; Stierle, M.; Papke, L.; Revoredo, K.; Matzner, M.; Becker, J. Cause vs. effect in context-sensitive prediction of business process instances. *Inf. Syst.* **2021**, *95*, 101635. [CrossRef]

Hompes, B.F.A.; Maaradji, A.; La Rosa, M.; Dumas, M.; Buijs, J.C.A.M.; van der Aalst, W.M.P. Discovering Causal Factors Explaining Business Process Performance Variation. In *Lecture Notes in Computer Science, Proceedings of the Advanced Information Systems Engineering, CAiSE 2017, Essen, Germany, 12–16 June 2017;* Dubois, E., Pohl, K., Eds.; Springer: Cham, Switzerland, 2017.

Zanga, A.; Ozkirimli, E.; Stella, F. A Survey on Causal Discovery: Theory and Practice. *Int. J. Approx. Reason.* **2022**, *151*, 101–129. [CrossRef]

Zhou, W.; Chen, Q. A Survey on Causal Discovery. In *Knowledge Graph and Semantic Computing: Knowledge Graph Empowers the Digital Economy*; Sun, M., Qi, G., Liu, K., Ren, J., Xu, B., Feng, Y., Liu, Y., Chen, Y., Eds.; Springer Nature: Singapore, 2022.

24. Wang, L.; Huang, S.; Wang, S.; Liao, J.; Li, T.; Liu, L. A survey of causal discovery based on functional causal model. *Eng. Ap Artif. Intell.* **2024**, *133*, 108258. [CrossRef]
25. Augusto, A.; Conforti, R.; Dumas, M.; La Rosa, M. Split miner: Discovering accurate and simple business process models fro event logs. In Proceedings of the IEEE International Conference on Data Mining, New Orleans, LA, USA, 18-21 November 20
26. Zyphur, M.J.; Bonner, C.V.; Tay, L. Structural equation modeling in organizational research: The state of our science and son proposals for its future. *Annu. Rev. Organ. Psychol. Organ. Behav.* **2023**, *10*, 495–517. [CrossRef]

entropy

MDPI

Systematic Review

# Causal Artificial Intelligence in Legal Language Processing: A Systematic Review

Philippe Prince Tritto [1,*] and Hiram Ponce [2]

1 Facultad de Derecho, Universidad Panamericana, Augusto Rodin 498, Mexico City 03920, Mexico
2 Facultad de Ingeniería, Universidad Panamericana, Augusto Rodin 498, Mexico City 03920, Mexico; hponce@up.edu.mx
* Correspondence: pprince@up.edu.mx

**Abstract:** Recent advances in legal language processing have highlighted limitations in correlation-based artificial intelligence approaches, prompting exploration of Causal Artificial Intelligence (AI) techniques for improved legal reasoning. This systematic review examines the challenges, limitations, and potential impact of Causal AI in legal language processing compared to traditional correlation-based methods. Following the Joanna Briggs Institute methodology, we analyzed 47 papers from 2017 to 2024 across academic databases, private sector publications, and policy documents, evaluating their contributions through a rigorous scoring framework assessing Causal AI implementation, legal relevance, interpretation capabilities, and methodological quality. Our findings reveal that while Causal AI frameworks demonstrate superior capability in capturing legal reasoning compared to correlation-based methods, significant challenges remain in handling legal uncertainty, computational scalability, and potential algorithmic bias. The scarcity of comprehensive real-world implementations and overemphasis on transformer architectures without causal reasoning capabilities represent critical gaps in current research. Future development requires balanced integration of AI innovation with law's narrative functions, particularly focusing on scalable architectures for maintaining causal coherence while preserving interpretability in legal analysis.

**Keywords:** causal artificial intelligence; causal machine learning; legal language processing; legal AI; natural language processing; legal reasoning; systematic review; causal inference; machine learning; legal text analysis

## 1. Introduction

Legal language processing is an application of artificial intelligence (AI) techniques for natural language processing (NLP) to legal language. NLP is a major area of research and development in the field of information technology, attempting to replicate human abilities to process text. The ultimate purpose of NLP is natural language understanding (NLU). According to Elizabeth Liddy [1], a full NLU system would be able to paraphrase text, translate it, answer questions about its contents, and draw inferences from it.

It is now accepted that the goal of NLP is the true understanding that can be expected from a machine. Answering specific questions according to input text is one of the objectives that particularly interests us in our research, since legal problems may arise when deciding. Decisions in NLP may have subtle legal overtones, and the decisions that the machine must make when dealing automatically with natural language may face legal dilemmas, such as ensuring that the inferences generated from a text do not present a racist bias despite allowing a more efficient delivery of justice.

### 1.1. NLP and the Open Texture of Legal Language

In the field of NLP, technical language is easier to interpret than ordinary language, due to the low polyvalence of the meaning of its words. However, law represents a unique challenge, as illustrated by Hart's analysis of a simple rule "prohibiting the use of vehicles in the park" [2]. While this rule clearly applies to cars, Hart demonstrates how edge cases like bicycles, roller skates, or toy cars create interpretative challenges. This exemplifies what Hart calls the *open texture* of law: "uncertainty at the borderline is the price to be paid for the use of general classifying terms in any form of communication concerning matters of fact" [2].

The interpretation of legal language is thus central to legal praxis, since causal relationships between verbal elements and human experience condition the understanding of the text and the adoption of solutions.

### 1.2. Causality in Theoretical Computer Science and Its Use in NLP

In computer science, causality provides a fundamental framework for understanding and modeling how systems produce their effects. While traditional AI approaches focus on identifying statistical patterns in data, Causal AI (while some literature distinguishes between Causal Machine Learning (focusing specifically on machine learning techniques) and Causal AI (encompassing broader artificial intelligence approaches), we use Causal AI as an umbrella term that includes machine learning applications, consistent with our systematic search methodology detailed in Section 2) represents a paradigm shift toward systems that can reason about cause-and-effect relationships. This shift is particularly significant in natural language processing, where moving beyond statistical correlations (we use the word "association" to refer to any general relationship between two variables, indicating that certain values of one variable tend to co-occur with certain values of another. This term is broad and encompasses all types of relationships, whether they are linear or non-linear, and applies to various data types, including nominal, ordinal, interval, and ratio scales [3]. We use the word "correlation" as a specific statistical measure, a type of association that quantifies the strength and direction of a linear relationship between two quantitative variables [3])to causal understanding is crucial for improving the robustness, fairness, and interpretability of language models [4]. These systems combine computational methods with formal theories of causation to model not just what happens, but why and how it happens.

The foundations of modern causal inference trace back to the Neyman–Rubin causal model, which formalizes causation through the concept of potential outcomes [5]. This framework defines causal effects as the difference between potential outcomes under treatment and control conditions, though only one outcome can ever be observed for any unit [6]. While originally developed for experimental settings, this model has profound implications for observational studies in law, where researchers must carefully consider counterfactuals and selection bias [7]. The framework's emphasis on explicit counterfactual reasoning aligns naturally with legal analysis, where courts frequently engage in counterfactual inquiry—considering what would have happened "but for" a defendant's actions [8]. Modern Causal AI approaches in legal language processing build upon these foundations while addressing the unique challenges of extracting causal relationships from unstructured text [4].

Causal AI systems are distinguished by three key capabilities [4,9,10]: first, they can answer "what if" questions through interventional reasoning, allowing them to predict the effects of actions even in previously unseen scenarios. Second, they can evaluate counterfactuals, determining what would have happened under different circumstances. Third, they explicitly model the mechanisms that generate data, rather than merely capturing statistical correlations. In the context of language processing, these capabilities extend to understanding how textual interventions affect outcomes, evaluating counterfactual text variations, and modeling the underlying generative processes of language [4].

The field encompasses a vast array of methodologies, from classical approaches like Regression Discontinuity Designs and Difference-in-Differences to modern techniques like Dynamic Treatment Regimes and Synthetic Controls, though not all have yet been applied to legal NLP.

Structural Causal Models (SCMs) provide a mathematical foundation for representing causal relationships [11]. Causal diagrams model the world based on prior knowledge, making explicit the assumptions about how variables influence each other [10]. In the context of natural language processing, unique challenges emerge when applying these frameworks to text data [4], including the high dimensionality of language representations, the need for sophisticated modeling to measure semantically meaningful factors, and careful consideration of what constitutes a valid intervention in text. As Judea Pearl points out in *The Book of Why*, "Causal analysis is emphatically not just about data; in causal analysis we must incorporate some understanding of the process that produces the data" [12].

Early implementations combined Bayes' rule with computing power to draw causal links between concepts using a priori knowledge. Modern approaches extend this foundation through do-calculus—a mathematical framework for determining when causal effects can be inferred from observational data—and sophisticated graphical models that can represent complex causal relationships [9].

The central challenge in developing these systems lies in what philosophers call *the problem of induction* —how to reliably infer general causal principles from specific instances [13]. Induction represents the process of deriving generalizations from particular cases, while deduction applies these generalizations to new instances. This challenge is particularly acute in language processing, where the high dimensionality of text and the complexity of semantic relationships make it difficult to distinguish genuine causal effects from spurious correlations [4].

A promising framework for addressing this challenge comes from Harriman's analysis of inductive reasoning in physics [13]. Harriman argues that human causal understanding develops hierarchically—beginning with direct perception of simple causal connections and gradually building to more abstract causal reasoning through the development of appropriate concepts. This framework suggests that attempts to implement causal reasoning in AI systems may be hampered by trying to begin at too high a level of abstraction, without first establishing foundations analogous to humans' basic causal perception. As we examine the current state of Causal AI in legal reasoning, this developmental perspective provides valuable context for understanding both the challenges and potential solutions.

These fundamental challenges in causal inference for language processing become even more pronounced in legal contexts, where interpretation requires not only understanding statistical patterns but also complex legal reasoning and domain expertise. As we will explore, the application of causal frameworks to legal language processing must address both the general challenges [4] and the specific requirements of legal interpretation discussed in the following sections.

### *1.3. The Lack of Empirical Context in Legal Texts*

Legal concepts require particularly acute expertise to be understood. Terms evolve over time and through interpretations that may require extensive knowledge. For example, a single article of a country's Constitution can generate volumes of analysis when examined word by word.

This illustrates that the immediate context of a legal text is insufficient. Legal formulations come with their history and intent beyond natural language. As a modification of Firth's famous punchline: You shall *not* know a legal word by the company it keeps [14] (p. 11).

The international element further complicates this, as the rule of law differs between countries. Therefore, NLP techniques for normative natural languages cannot be the same as those for non-normative natural languages.

### *1.4. Relation Between Causality and Legal Language*

Traditional AI systems for automatic language processing are correlation machines. Marcos [15] summarizes Marcus (2020b) [16], explaining that Large Language Models (LLMs) tend to rely on superficial statistical patterns rather than the adaptable reasoning characteristic of human cognition. However, correlations can indicate confounding relationships between concepts. This is particularly relevant in legal language processing, where semantic causality helps distinguish misleading correlations from valid ones [17].

A striking example is the COMPAS system used in U.S. courts to assess recidivism risk. While the system showed correlations between demographic factors and recidivism rates, these correlations masked underlying discriminatory biases:

> "... blacks are almost twice as likely as whites to be labeled a higher risk but not actually re-offend, [whereas COMPAS] makes the opposite mistake among whites: They are much more likely than blacks to be labeled lower-risk but go on to commit other crimes." [18]

This exemplifies Simpson's paradox [19], where a correlation valid from a mathematical perspective becomes discriminatory from a legal standpoint. Causal AI techniques could potentially address this by examining *what if* scenarios to establish genuine causal links rather than relying on correlations.

### *1.5. Legal Assessment in Causal Models for Legal Language Processing*

Recent research has explored various approaches to causal linkage in legal texts. Liu et al. [17] propose a Graph-based Causal Inference (GCI) framework that recognizes word groups from key elements in legal texts. Their work, along with others in the field, points to both the potential and challenges of implementing causal analysis in legal language processing.

Similarly, in a study of U.S. states from 1965 to 2012, a novel shift-share design was applied to text-based legislative flows, showing that states enacting more comprehensive and carefully worded statutes experienced higher growth rates [20]. This result was robust to a range of specifications and controls, suggesting that an expanded legislative contract—particularly one embedding contingent clauses—can meaningfully lower uncertainty and encourage business investments requiring relationship-specific assets. The authors' findings align with the broader hold-up perspective, in which greater legal clarity reduces the risk of opportunistic behavior and thereby stimulates economic activity. Moreover, the text-based natural language processing methods in that analysis, using text as the instrument, provide an illustrative example of how advanced empirical strategies can substantiate the causal role of legislative outputs, echoing the broader need for data-driven causal inference frameworks in legal language contexts.

The integration of classical causal inference principles with legal language processing demands careful consideration of identification strategies and assumptions. The potential outcomes framework highlights fundamental challenges in establishing causation from observational data [21], which become particularly acute when working with legal texts, where controlled experiments are rarely possible. This theoretical foundation underscores the importance of developing Causal AI approaches that can explicitly model counterfactuals while accounting for the complex, context-dependent nature of legal reasoning [7]. Understanding these limitations helps explain both the promise and constraints of current Causal AI applications in legal contexts, setting realistic expectations for what automated systems can achieve.

Since the context of our research leads us to evaluate the possibility of mathematizing legal rules through causal links, while considering the requirements of energy efficiency and computational scalability, this requires mindful reflection on the explainability, algorithmic transparency, and trustworthiness of NLP models [22] while working with reliably extracted legal information [23,24].

### 1.6. *Objective*

The intersection of Causal AI and legal language processing demands methodological rigor that transcends traditional narrative reviews. While individual studies have illuminated specific aspects of this relationship, the field's evolution and inherent interdisciplinarity create an epistemic challenge that only systematic investigation can adequately address. A systematic review methodology offers a structured framework for critically examining how causal inference mechanisms interact with legal reasoning's distinctive characteristics—its narrative functions, its requirement for interpretability, and its fundamental role in maintaining the rule of law.

Through a comprehensive analysis of the literature guided by the Preferred Reporting Items for Systematic Reviews and Meta-Analyses (PRISMA) methodology [25,26], we examine both the technical feasibility of Causal AI in legal contexts and its epistemological foundations as well as its normative implications. This methodological choice enables us to move beyond mere technological assessment toward a deeper understanding of how causal frameworks might preserve—or potentially transform—law's essential functions while addressing its computational challenges. Moreover, the systematic approach allows us to identify critical gaps in current understanding and potential methodological blindspots that might otherwise remain obscured in more conventional reviews.

Our rigorous examination of existing research provides an essential foundation for future investigations while maintaining careful skepticism about both the promises and limitations of causal approaches in legal language processing.

## 2. Materials and Methods

We used PRISMA's eight-step process [26] and the PICOC method [27] (p. 41) to frame our research question: What is the current state of research on the challenges, limitations, and potential impact of using Causal AI techniques for automatic legal language processing and its application in legal decision-making compared to non-Causal AI models relying on correlations?

Specifically, our review addresses three questions:

1. What challenges do AI models face in interpreting legal language accurately?
2. How can causal inference improve AI's understanding of legal language compared to correlation-based methods?
3. How can we address the lack of empirical data in causal analysis of legal texts?

### 2.1. *Drafting the Protocol*

#### 2.1.1. Inclusion Criteria

We conducted a literature search across academic databases (Google Scholar, SpringerLink, vLex, Tirant Online), private sector publications (AI Now Institute, The Future Society, OpenAI), and public policy documents (from the European Commission, US Department of Justice, UN, UNESCO, and the Council of Europe). Figure 1 illustrates our systematic selection process. We supplemented database searches with citation tracking to identify relevant papers using different terminology.

We included materials in English, French, and Spanish published between January 2017 and December 2024, focusing on peer-reviewed journals and published theses. Our search employed boolean combinations of terms across three domains: (1) causal analysis terms (e.g., "Causal AI", "Causal Discovery", "Causal Inference"); (2) legal applications (e.g., "Legal decision-making"); and (3) NLP terms (e.g., "Legal NLP").

After removing 43 duplicates from our initial 433 search results, we obtained 390 unique documents for our preliminary analysis.

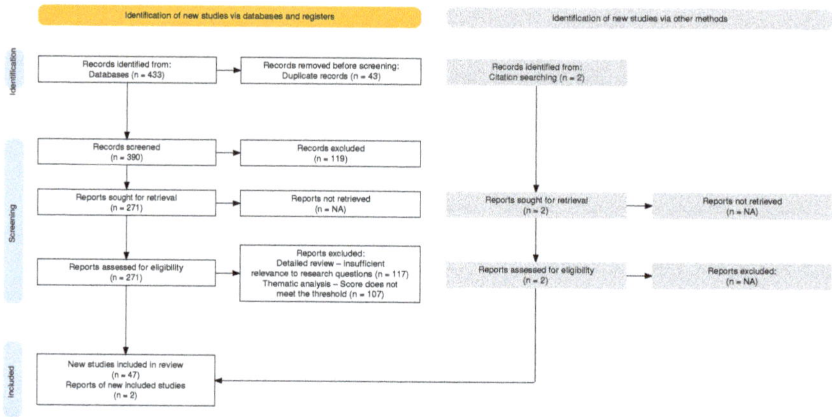


**Figure 1.** PRISMA flow diagram of the study selection process. Created using the PRISMA Flow Diagram tool [28].

### 2.1.2. Exclusion Criteria

We implemented a multi-stage exclusion process: (1) title review excluded 69 documents not directly addressing our research questions; (2) abstract review excluded 50 documents lacking abstracts or that were self-authored; (3) skim-reading excluded 117 additional materials irrelevant to our focus. This process yielded 154 documents that met our preliminary eligibility criteria.

We then scored each article across four dimensions: Causal AI implementation (40 points), legal domain relevance (30 points), NLP applications (20 points), and methodological quality (10 points). Articles scoring 40 points or more (47 articles) formed our final corpus.

### 2.1.3. Data Extraction

We used a data extraction form adapted from the CASP critical appraisal checklist [29]. We considered declarations of conflicts of interest (financial, ideological, professional, political) and assessed potential publication bias, though neither led to document exclusion.

### 2.1.4. Data Analysis

We employed thematic analysis principles [30] to analyze our final corpus of 47 articles, beginning with comprehensive reading to identify patterns and categorize findings according to our research questions.

We conducted citation network analysis to identify relevant papers that might have been missed by our keyword-based search. Two thematically relevant cited papers were reviewed against our inclusion criteria.

Our analysis incorporated advanced techniques including LLM-as-a-judge, extraction of practical applications and Causal AI methods, keyword frequency analysis, and cosine similarity checks between abstracts and research questions. We analyzed citation networks to compute disruption measures above 0.5 as defined by [31] and identify key research clusters, providing insight into the evolution and dynamics of this research field. We used various visualization tools including Mermaid diagrams and tables to organize findings, which we synthesized in our Results section.

## 3. Results

The results section of this study aims to provide a detailed examination of the current research on Causal AI techniques in legal language processing, focusing on the main research question: "What is the current state of research on the challenges, limitations, and potential impact of using Causal AI techniques for automatic legal language processing and its application in legal decision-making compared to non-Causal AI models relying on correlations?" This section is structured into four subsections. The first one presents influential trends in the literature and research clusters while showing real-world implementations and potential applications in legal practice encountered in literature. The three subsequent ones correspond to the research questions formulated in the methodology, aiming to build a comprehensive understanding of how Causal AI could reshape legal NLP applications.

### *3.1. Trends Analysis*

#### 3.1.1. Disruption Measures

Figure 2 presents the subset of articles in the corpus with a disruption measure [31] exceeding 0.5. These works stand out as potentially influential in reshaping their respective domains, as their citation patterns indicate a break from prior literature. The visual representation contextualizes the temporal distribution of these disruptive articles, allowing for an appreciation of whether such shifts occur steadily or cluster within specific timeframes.

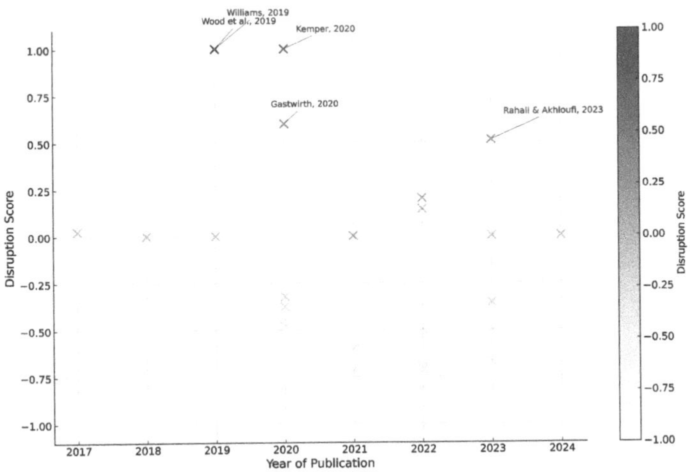


**Figure 2.** Disruptive articles in the corpus (Disruption Score > 0.5) [32–36]. This scatter plot displays articles with a disruption measure [31] above 0.5, indicating a significant departure from the prior literature. Each point represents an article, positioned according to its year of publication and disruption score. Higher values suggest that subsequent works primarily cite the article itself rather than its references, signaling a shift in research direction. Annotations highlight selected articles with notable disruption scores.

The disruption analysis presented in Figure 2 identifies five papers that significantly departed from previous research trajectories. The introduction of predictive contracting [32] and the framework for ethical AI implementation in legal decision-making [33] represent fundamental shifts in how the field conceptualizes the integration of AI into legal practice. The systematic examination of statistical evidence in civil litigation [34] established new methodological foundations for quantitative legal analysis. However, some papers scoring high on the disruption measure, such as the genomic sequence alignment approach to causality extraction [35] and the analysis of transformer architectures [36], while technically innovative, have had less direct impact on legal applications. This variance between disruption scores and practical influence in the legal domain suggests that methodological innovation alone may not translate into transformative impact in legal AI applications.

The temporal distribution of these disruptive papers reveals an important pattern in the field's development. Early disruptive works focused on fundamental frameworks for integrating AI into legal practice, while more recent contributions have emphasized technical methodologies. This shift reflects a broader tension in legal AI development between technical sophistication and practical legal application. The high disruption scores of papers focusing purely on technical innovation [35,36] may indicate the field's increasing emphasis on transformer architectures and sophisticated NLP techniques, potentially at the expense of deeper engagement with legal reasoning challenges.

This pattern informs our subsequent analysis in two crucial ways. First, it suggests that while technical innovations may score highly on quantitative measures of disruption, their impact on legal practice often requires mediation through frameworks that explicitly address law's unique requirements. Second, it highlights a potential gap in current research: while sophisticated technical approaches proliferate, frameworks for meaningfully integrating these advances into legal practice remain relatively scarce. These insights guide our treatment of various contributions throughout this review, particularly in assessing how technical innovations translate into practical legal applications.

Technical innovation versus practical application directly foreshadows three key challenges that will be explored in subsequent sections: (1) the fundamental difficulty of interpreting legal language with AI models, as evidenced by the high disruption scores of papers focusing on technical methodologies rather than legal understanding; (2) the need for improved causal inference approaches, demonstrated by the emergence of papers bridging technical and legal domains; and (3) the persistent challenge of empirical context in legal texts, reflected in the relatively few highly disruptive papers addressing this specific issue.

#### 3.1.2. Causal AI Applications Trends in Legal Practice

The present analysis revealed several clusters of Causal AI methods emerging in legal NLP research. While the broader field of causal inference encompasses numerous other established methodologies—such as Principal Stratification, Regression Discontinuity Designs, and Time-Series-Based Causal Analysis—Table 1 synthesizes the methods that have been specifically documented in legal NLP applications, organizing each into nine overarching clusters alongside their real-world legal tasks.

Reviewing the citation trends alongside the clusters in Table 1 clarifies why certain methodological innovations (e.g., Causal Representation Learning [37] or Graph-Based Causal Inference [38]) may gain traction in legal NLP. Works that achieve high citation counts often introduce tools or corpora (e.g., large pretraining datasets, specialized benchmarks) that subsequent research employs to tackle causal questions in contract analysis, criminal justice, and policy simulation. In other words, while the table enumerates distinct causal techniques for legal text analysis, their real-world uptake is frequently accelerated when grounded in widely embraced, high-performance language models—facilitating an intersection of advanced representation learning and causal methods. The synergy between large-scale pretrained models [39–41] and targeted causal inference practices underscores the growing maturity and sophistication of the field, suggesting that future high-impact publications will likely continue to integrate domain-specific language modeling with rigorous causal frameworks.

**Table 1.** Clustering of causal methods in legal NLP research.

| Cluster | Method | Practical Applications | References |
| --- | --- | --- | --- |
| 1. Causal Reasoning Paradigms | Actual Causation Theory | Automated text analysis; Legal reasoning support systems | [42] |
| 2. Structural & Graphical Approaches | Bayesian Networks | Policy simulation; Legislative impact analysis; Legal argument construction; Judicial reasoning modeling; Societal value change simulation | [8] |
| | Directed Acyclic Graphs (DAG) | Drug law enforcement | [43] |
| | Structural Causal Models (SCM) | Policy simulation; Legislative impact analysis; Legal argument construction; Judicial reasoning modeling; Societal value change simulation | [8] |
| | Structural Equations Model (SEM) | Drug law enforcement | [43] |
| | Structural Equations | Automated text analysis; Legal reasoning support systems | [42] |
| | Path Coefficients Analysis | Policy simulation; Legislative impact analysis; Legal argument construction; Judicial reasoning modeling; Societal value change simulation | [8] |
| | Path-Specific Effects | Drug law enforcement | [43] |
| | Causal Structural Modeling | Policy research; Legal text analysis | [44] |
| 3. Causal Inference & Identification | Propensity Scoring/Matching | Privacy protection; Criminal justice; Policy research; Legal text analysis | [44,45] |
| | Inverse Probability Weighting | Privacy protection; Criminal justice | [45] |
| | Instrumental Variable Regression | Similar charge disambiguation; Automated contract analysis; Bias detection | [37] |
| | Do-Calculus | Policy simulation; Legislative impact analysis; Legal argument construction; Judicial reasoning modeling; Societal value change simulation | [8] |
| | Intervention-Based Causal Inference | Policy simulation; Legislative impact analysis; Legal argument construction; Judicial reasoning modeling; Societal value change simulation | [8] |

**Table 1.** *Cont.*

| Cluster | Method | Practical Applications | References |
| --- | --- | --- | --- |
| | Causal Inference Network | Electronic court records management; Online legal consulting; Digital case filing; Legal document digitization | [46] |
| | Graph-Based Causal Inference (GCI) | Automated judicial assistance; Legal advisory services; Criminal case analysis | [38] |
| | Greedy Fast Causal Inference (GFCI) | Automated judicial assistance; Legal advisory services; Criminal case analysis | [38] |
| 4. Effect Estimation & Assessment | Average Treatment Effect (ATE) | Automated judicial assistance; Legal advisory services; Criminal case analysis | [38] |
| | Causal Effect Estimation | Contract analysis; Bias detection | [47] |
| | Long-Term Causal Effect Estimation | Privacy protection; Criminal justice | [45] |
| | Causal Strength Assessment | Automated judicial assistance; Legal advisory services; Criminal case analysis | [38] |
| 5. Mediation & Indirect Effects | Causal Mediation Analysis | Contract analysis; Bias detection; Privacy protection; Criminal justice; Policy research; Legal text analysis; Similar charge disambiguation; Automated contract analysis | [37,44,45,47] |
| 6. Counterfactual Approaches | Counterfactual Reasoning | Contract analysis; Bias detection; Privacy protection; Criminal justice; Drug law enforcement | [43,45,47,48] |
| | Attentional & Counterfactual-Based NLG (AC-NLG) | Court's view generation; Debiasing judgment narratives; Enhanced interpretability of supportive vs. non-supportive cases | [49] |
| 7. Adversarial & Deconfounding | Adversarial Deconfounding | Litigation strategy decisions; Case outcome inference; Legal decision support systems | [50] |
| | Gradient Reversal Layer | Litigation strategy decisions; Case outcome inference; Legal decision support systems | [50] |
| 8. RL & Decision-Making | Causal Bandits | Civil litigation document review; Anti-corruption audits; Social welfare benefits adjudication | [51] |
| | Causal Decision-Making Policies | Civil litigation document review; Anti-corruption audits; Social welfare benefits adjudication | [51] |
| | Constrained Reinforcement Learning | Civil litigation document review; Anti-corruption audits; Social welfare benefits adjudication | [51] |

**Table 1.** *Cont.*

| Cluster | Method | Practical Applications | References |
|---|---|---|---|
| 9. Representation Learning (Text/NLP) | Causal Representation Learning | Similar charge disambiguation; Automated contract analysis; Bias detection | [37] |
| | BERT-Based Embeddings | General use in legal texts analysis | [52] |
| | Word2vec Adaptation | General use in legal texts analysis | [52] |
| | Deep Similarity Search | General use in legal texts analysis | [52] |
| | BERT | Personal injury cases; Patent infringement; Small claims tribunals; Legal document generation; Discovery process | [53] |
| | GIDBERT | Personal injury cases; Patent infringement; Small claims tribunals; Legal document generation; Discovery process | [53] |

The clustering described in the present section offers a nuanced view of how, for example, causality-focused techniques like Instrumental Variable Regression [37] or Adversarial Deconfounding [50] are being used to address particular challenges in contract analysis, bias detection, litigation strategy, and policy simulation. By mapping each Causal AI methodology to specific applications documented in the literature, Table 1 underscores the variety of causal-driven legal tools already in use or under active development, reflecting the field's growing emphasis on inferring and leveraging causal structures rather than mere correlations.

Trends in these causal methods collectively point to a future where AI can assist legal practitioners in tasks ranging from policy simulation to automated contract review. However, as we detail in the following sections, the trajectory of Causal AI in legal applications is far from straightforward.

- First, we explore the fundamental challenges in interpreting legal language with AI models—challenges that continue to persist despite the sophisticated nature of these emerging causal and correlation-based methods (Section 3.2).
- Next, we examine how causal inference, specifically, addresses these challenges by offering a deeper structural understanding and a more law-aligned approach to reasoning, as opposed to correlation-based methods (Section 3.3).
- Finally, we discuss the scarcity of empirical data and contextual cues in legal domains and show how this gap hampers robust causal analysis (Section 3.4). In doing so, we provide an overview of existing dataset resources and highlight the methodological innovations tackling data limitations.

In short, the trends highlighted here form the backbone of a rapidly evolving landscape, but the subsequent sections underscore the remaining hurdles and the immense potential for future research.

### *3.2. Challenges in Interpreting Legal Language with AI Models*

Legal language processing presents formidable challenges for AI models due to the inherent complexity, ambiguity, and context-dependence of legal texts. The specialized terminology, intricate syntactic structures, and nuanced meanings embedded within legal documents demand extensive domain knowledge for accurate analysis. These linguistic intricacies pose substantial obstacles for AI attempting to analyze and make decisions based on legal documents.

### 3.2.1. Complexity and Ambiguity of Legal Language

As demonstrated by Mamakas et al., even state-of-the-art language models struggle with the length and complexity of legal texts, often truncating important information [54]. Cemri et al. highlighted the need for legal text simplification, underscoring the necessity for sophisticated AI approaches capable of handling the nuances of legal discourse [55]. Hassani et al. draw parallels between legal texts and big data environments, both characterized by vast scale and intricate relationships that complicate the identification of causal links [56]. Barale further emphasizes the difficulty in breaking down human decision-making processes into logical steps and identifying inference and causal links, which are not always apparent in human thought [57].

### 3.2.2. Limitations of Current AI Techniques

General-purpose NLP techniques often fall short in the legal domain. Lam et al. revealed that semantic similarity between cases does not necessarily translate to legal similarity, highlighting the limitations of standard text analysis metrics in capturing the nuanced legal concepts specific to different cases [58]. This is not a mere detail. It tells us that the metrics that are usually used in computer science for text analysis, for instance to make Retrieval Augmented Generation (RAG), are not suited to the practice of law. In other words, the similarity check between texts has a different meaning in computer science and in law.

This limitation becomes particularly acute when considering causation in legal analysis. According to Pearl, cited by Mik [59], it is impossible for systems to learn causal inference solely from observational data. This presents a critical challenge for legal AI, as understanding causation requires pre-existing world knowledge that cannot be derived purely from pattern recognition. LLMs, confined to learning from text alone, cannot bridge this fundamental gap between correlation and causation that is essential for legal reasoning [59].

As Meneceur & Barbaro emphasize, current AI models face significant challenges due to their reliance on mathematical formalism, which is fundamentally ill-suited for the open, nuanced nature of legal reasoning [60]. This limitation becomes particularly acute when considering law's fundamental narrative function. Szilagyi states, "law and culture are inseparable; therefore, law and stories are inseparable" [61]. The application of purely correlative methods to legal reasoning risks severing this essential connection between law and cultural narrative, potentially alienating law from the human collective whose movements give its existence meaning.

Current AI approaches in law rely heavily on correlation, pattern matching, and probability distributions derived from historical case data [50,62]. While these methods have achieved some success in tasks like document classification and precedent retrieval, they fundamentally fail to capture the nuanced causal reasoning and narrative understanding essential to legal analysis. Zhang et al.'s analysis of machine reasoning challenges show this limitation, highlighting how traditional neural networks excel at perceptual tasks but struggle with the cognitive reasoning demanded by legal applications [48].

These limitations are exemplified by recent work on transformer architectures like Lawformer [41], which despite sophisticated attention mechanisms and domain-specific training, still fundamentally relies on statistical pattern matching rather than causal understanding. While Lawformer successfully addresses the challenge of processing longer legal documents, it highlights how even state-of-the-art language models remain constrained by their correlational nature.

The limitations of correlation-based methods are also exemplified by research on European Court of Human Rights decisions. While researchers claimed 79% accuracy in categorizing Court decisions, this merely revealed document formatting patterns rather than true legal reasoning, noting that such models would "struggle with a raw account from a future applicant before the Court in Strasbourg" [60] (p. 5).

This challenge is amplified by the increasing complexity and scale of legal data, where identifying genuine causal relationships becomes significantly more complex as data volume and dimensionality increase [56].

Work by Cheng highlights how this poses particular challenges for legal AI systems that must fulfill social responsibilities and ethical principles while maintaining fairness and interpretability [45]. Szilagyi warns that such "machine-ations", if left unchecked, threaten to destabilize our core institutions and lead to an unintended reordering of our normative framework for the Rule of Law [61].

#### 3.2.3. Need for Domain-Specific Approaches and Causal Reasoning

The necessity for domain-specific AI approaches is evident. Papaloukas et al. demonstrate that legal text classification becomes increasingly difficult as the number of possible classes grows, with performance dropping significantly when moving from broad to specific categories [63]. Their experiments show that domain-specific BERT (Bidirectional Encoder Representations from Transformers; a machine learning model for natural language processing, developed by Google in 2018 [39]. It is designed to understand the context of words in text by looking at the words that come both before and after them)models outperform generic language models and traditional approaches, particularly when classifying detailed legal categories.

A comprehensive survey by Cui et al. identified three primary challenges in legal judgment prediction: inadequate information from facts, the need for complex legal logical reasoning, and the requirement for interpretability [64]. These challenges align with areas where Causal AI could offer significant benefits. Causal models might help in reasoning with incomplete information, capturing complex logical relationships, and providing more interpretable decision-making processes.

This analysis is extended by connecting these challenges to emerging regulatory frameworks like the European General Data Protection Regulation of 2016 (GDPR) and the California Consumer Privacy Act of 2018 (CCPA), which require AI systems to demonstrate trustworthiness, robustness, and transparency—attributes that correlation-based approaches struggle to deliver [48].

The importance of causal reasoning in legal AI is further emphasized by Zhao et al., who highlighted the potential of causal inference approaches to improve AI's understanding of legal texts [38].

Kemper argues that causal logic in algorithmic legal systems serves verification rather than decision-making [33]. He emphasizes that counterfactual explanations are necessary in the legal field but are primarily found in the explicability of algorithmic decision-making systems evaluating supporting systems.

We will further explore these solutions in Section 3.3 on causal inference.

#### 3.2.4. Explainability and Interpretability

Explainability is a significant challenge in legal AI systems. Kirat et al. proposed a hierarchical framework for algorithmic explanation, highlighting the need for AI models to not only achieve accurate interpretation but also generate contextually appropriate explanations that satisfy diverse stakeholder requirements within specific regulatory boundaries [65]. Rubicondo et al. emphasized the importance of transparency in high-stakes domains [66]. Their findings on AI performance degradation under distributional shifts underscore the potential value of causal approaches in legal AI, where robust and interpretable decision-making is crucial [66].

#### 3.2.5. Ethical and Legal Implications

The narrative and cultural aspects of law present significant challenges for AI systems attempting to interpret and apply legal language [61]. An unduly data-driven approach threatens to strand us in the past, unable to engage in the visioning exercise proposed by law's narrative arc. Delegating legal decision-making to AI risks transforming the "Rule of Law" into a "Rule by Law", potentially compromising the integrity of democratic institutions [61].

The COMPAS algorithm case that we mentioned in Section 1.4 provides a stark illustration of these limitations. Despite not explicitly including ethnic origin in its calculations, the algorithm's correlation-based approach led to biased outcomes through indirect data relationships. Indeed, "cross-referencing of data (including place of residence) indirectly gave too much weighting to this aspect to the detriment of other individual social factors" [60] (p. 8).

Henderson et al. illuminated broader challenges in applying AI to law and public policy. They highlight the "advertisement fallacy", referring to the naive application of algorithms from one domain to legal and policy contexts without considering their unique challenges [51]. They emphasize the need for AI systems that can provide clear, causal explanations for their interpretations and decisions, crucial in legal contexts where the rationale behind a decision is as important as the decision itself.

The challenges of relying solely on correlational approaches are further highlighted by recent research demonstrating how technical choices in supervised learning can have significant social implications, even when decision rules appear neutral [65]. The analysis reveals that seemingly unbiased algorithmic decisions can generate disproportionate impacts across social groups due to the inability of correlation-based methods to capture underlying causal mechanisms.

#### 3.2.6. Potential Solutions and Future Directions

Addressing these challenges requires a multifaceted approach. Developing more sophisticated language models tailored to legal discourse is essential. The integration of domain-faithful machine learning techniques, as proposed by Balashankar, offers a promising avenue for enhancing the robustness and reliability of AI systems in interpreting and applying legal language [67].

Combining sentence context with event context, as suggested by Khethan et al., could improve causality detection in legal texts [68]. This approach could enhance AI's ability to capture the subtle implications and context-dependent meanings crucial in legal interpretation. The need for careful adaptation of data mining techniques to the specific demands of legal analysis is underscored [56], suggesting that clustering algorithms must align with legally meaningful categories rather than superficial textual similarities.

Collaboration between AI researchers, legal experts, linguists, and ethicists is vital. Developing robust methodologies to assess the technical feasibility of legally mandated explainability requirements is emphasized in our analyzed literature [65], proposing investigating explainability as a potential mechanism for achieving algorithmic fairness and calling for structured collaboration to ensure technical capabilities align with legal requirements while maintaining interpretability and fairness.

In the following section, we will be exploring advanced methodologies that can capture the nuanced causal reasoning inherent in legal analysis.

### 3.3. *How Causal Inference Improves AI's Understanding of Legal Language Compared to Correlation-Based Methods*

After having emphasized the challenges in Section 3.2, the present Section examines how causal inference frameworks can enhance legal AI systems by addressing the limitations of purely correlative approaches. We begin by exploring causal inference as a solution, showing how it better captures the nuanced reasoning essential to legal analysis. The empirical evidence supporting these approaches demonstrates their superior performance across multiple legal tasks. We then delve into the mathematical and theoretical foundations that enable such advances, followed by an examination of key implementation challenges and their solutions. Recent innovations in causal relationship extraction showcase promising new directions, while our final discussion of domain knowledge integration highlights the importance of combining technical capabilities with legal expertise. Through these sections, we demonstrate both the significant potential and current limitations of causal approaches in legal AI.

#### 3.3.1. Causal Inference as a Solution

We begin with Chen et al's work on logically dependent multi-task learning (MTL) that provides insights into how causal inference can address the limitations we highlighted in Section 3.2 [47]. Their research demonstrates that conventional multi-task learning models make problematic assumptions about conditional independence between tasks, failing to capture the inherent logical dependencies in legal judgement prediction. They advocate for a framework for logically dependent MTL using causal inference: causal multi-task learning (CMTL). Unlike traditional approaches that treat tasks as independent, CMTL mimics human reasoning in teamwork. If you think of each legal task as a team and their interactions as dependencies, CMTL is like a smart coordinator that ensures smooth communication and logical consistency. This way, CMTL explicitly captures how the outcome of one legal task influences another, both directly and indirectly. We will explore the mathematical formalization of CMTL in Section 3.3.3.

It is worth considering Xiao et al.'s work on legal event extraction and event-based knowledge representation, which essentially approaches the problem of mapping textual evidence to underlying causal structures. Recognizing events and the causal relations among them is foundational for legal case analysis [46] (p. 412). These events—often composed of a trigger and its associated arguments—mirror the building blocks that causal inference frameworks employ to model legal scenarios. By integrating insights from large-scale event detection benchmarks like LEVEN (Legal Event benchmark; a Chinese dataset designed for event extraction in legal documents, containing annotated legal events and their relationships [69]), researchers can more effectively identify the causal threads that tie together legal facts, thus bridging the gap between descriptive textual representations and the underlying causal mechanisms that guide judicial reasoning [46]. Such efforts complement the broader endeavor to use causal inference for formalizing legal logic, underlining that legal event knowledge extraction and causal inference techniques are not distinct pursuits but interconnected strategies for deeper understanding of legal language.

So's comprehensive examination of causality modeling in law demonstrates how formal causal frameworks can transcend the limitations of purely correlative approaches while preserving law's essential narrative function [8]. This aligns with the observation that law's normative force adheres in language, meaning, and interpretation [61]. Causal frameworks provide a mechanism for preserving these essential elements of legal reasoning that correlation-based approaches cannot capture.

Consider a case where multiple parties may have contributed to harm. While correlation can highlight associations between actions and outcomes, causal modeling can help determine whether each party's actions were necessary and/or sufficient causes through counterfactual analysis [8]. From an argumentative standpoint, Pryzant's framework for analyzing reader responses provides additional tools for understanding how different linguistic presentations of evidence might influence behavior, and thus legal decision-making, helping to disentangle the causal effects of language from confounding contextual factors [70].

Sun et al. demonstrated how this principle can be applied in practice through their Law-Match framework [37]. Legal case matching helps identify how similar two cases are, an important task in legal research. Traditional methods rely heavily on comparing the words and sentences in case documents. However, these methods often miss the legal essence, because they do not consider the relevant laws cited in each case. Law-Match uses a two-step method. First, it separates the information in a legal case into two parts: law-related details (the aspects directly influenced by the cited laws, like key legal points) and other details (the unique facts and circumstances of the case). Then, it combines these parts to make a more informed comparison between cases. This framework achieved superior performance in legal case-matching tasks by explicitly modeling the causal relationship between law articles and case similarities [37].

Overall, research reveals how causal modeling can formalize traditional legal tests like the "but-for" test in tort law [8], while preserving the essential narrative and interpretative functions of law [61]. Through the application of do-calculus and counterfactual reasoning, causal models can represent sophisticated legal concepts such as necessity, sufficiency, and remoteness that correlation-based methods cannot capture. For example, the *reasonable care* concept has different standards across situations [8] which require narrative understanding to interpret properly [61].

Causal inference offers a promising path forward for legal AI. By providing a formal framework for representing legal reasoning about causation, it seems to enable more transparent and accountable decision-making processes. Indeed, the ability to explicitly model interventions and counterfactuals aligns closely with legal practitioners' actual reasoning processes, potentially leading to AI systems that better support legal analysis and decision-making. Keith's contributions to measuring and adjusting for confounding variables in text data provide concrete steps toward realizing these benefits in practice [44]. These findings build on the Socially Responsible AI Framework, which emphasizes the need for legal AI systems that fulfill both functional and ethical responsibilities while maintaining interpretability and fairness [45]. It demonstrates that causal learning approaches are essential for developing AI systems that can understand and reason about legal relationships in ways that align with human values and societal expectations.

The analysis of emerging reasoning approaches highlights a crucial transition from traditional symbolic reasoning to hybrid approaches that combine neural networks with explicit reasoning capabilities [48].

#### 3.3.2. Empirical Evidence Supporting Causal Approaches

The previous observations have been empirically validated by recent work on the European Court of Human Rights, where Ichim and Grabmair demonstrated that models explicitly incorporating relationships between legal texts and case facts consistently outperform those relying solely on statistical patterns [71]. Their findings align with Williams' research on predictive contracting, which demonstrates that purely correlative approaches cannot identify the underlying mechanisms connecting contract terms to outcomes—a crucial capability for effective legal AI systems [32]. The analysis of legal judgment prediction systems further validates this concern, demonstrating that models trained purely on observational data often learn spurious correlations that fail to generalize to novel legal scenarios [64]. As we briefly mentioned in Section 3.2, their findings reveal that inadequate information from facts and complex legal logical reasoning remain fundamental challenges that correlation-based approaches struggle to address effectively.

Wang et al.'s comprehensive analysis of Law School Admission Test (LSAT) reasoning tasks provides empirical validation for hybrid systems that combine pre-trained models with task-specific reasoning modules [72]. Their findings highlight the importance of integrating symbolic knowledge with interpretable reasoning steps, which are crucial for addressing the analytical and logical inference challenges characteristic of complex legal reasoning tasks. For example, the use of explicit symbolic modules to process constraints or logical relations enhances the interpretability and accuracy of these systems, particularly in tasks requiring nuanced legal analysis.

Empirical validation of these benefits is provided in the literature, showing how causal learning approaches significantly outperformed traditional correlation-based methods across multiple datasets and evaluation metrics [37], while others demonstrated even stronger results through the integration of causal inference with neural architectures, achieving significant improvements in prediction accuracy across multiple legal tasks [38]. Together, these studies provide robust empirical evidence supporting the conclusion that hybrid systems, leveraging both symbolic reasoning and neural representations, excel in tackling complex legal reasoning challenges [72].

Successful legal reasoning systems must integrate symbolic and neural components to achieve robust performance [72]. While pre-trained language models offer a strong foundation for understanding legal language, their effectiveness is significantly enhanced by task-specific architectural choices and explicit reasoning modules. These modules enable systems to interpret constraints, deduce logical implications, and address the nuanced analytical reasoning required in legal applications, such as LSAT tasks. However, challenges like data sparsity and the scalability of symbolic methods remain areas for future research and refinement.

The empirical success of frameworks like Law-Match [37], Keith's probabilistic modeling approaches [44], and GCI [17,38], which have demonstrated significant improvements over correlation-based approaches across multiple legal tasks, provides concrete evidence for the practical value of causal approaches in legal AI applications. Through continued development of hybrid approaches that combine causal inference with advanced NLP techniques, the field moves closer to AI systems that can truly understand and reason about legal causation while maintaining compliance with established legal principles and constraints.

Cohen et al.'s research on deep learning applications in legal contexts provides additional validation for these approaches [53]. Their work with BERT models demonstrates how advanced language models can help overcome the limitations of traditional AI in legal applications. Their findings suggest that deep learning models trained on both legal and negotiation texts can achieve superior performance in understanding legal concepts and relationships, particularly when dealing with unstructured data and implicit causal relationships.

#### 3.3.3. Mathematical and Theoretical Foundations

The development of causal frameworks in legal AI has followed a clear evolutionary path (Figure 3). Research employs Judea Pearl's Structural Causal Models (SCM) and the Halpern-Pearl (HP) definitions of actual causality to model legal decisions, providing a mathematical foundation for representing causal relationships in legal reasoning [8]. This approach directly addresses what Pearl terms the "first law of causal inference"—that no causal conclusion can be drawn from purely statistical correlations without additional assumptions about the underlying mechanisms [8].

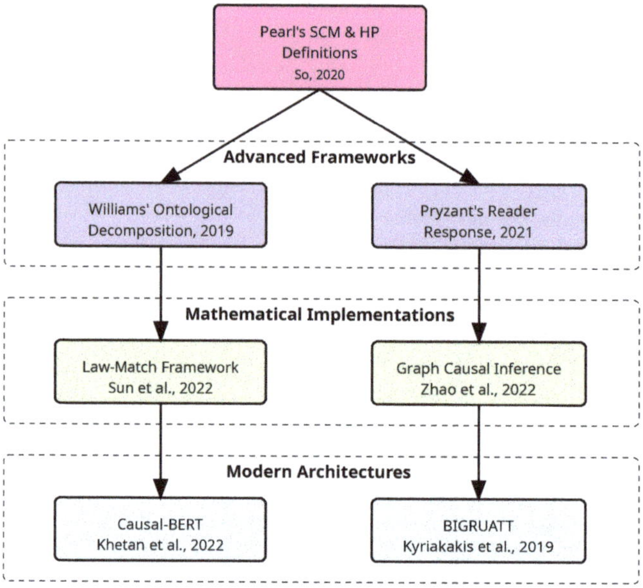


**Figure 3.** Evolution of causal frameworks in legal AI (2017–2022) [8,32,37,38,68,70,73]. The diagram illustrates the progression from Pearl's foundational Structural Causal Models (SCM) and Halpern-Pearl (HP) definitions [8] to modern architectures. Color coding represents different developmental stages: foundational theory (pink), advanced frameworks (blue), mathematical implementations (green), and modern architectures (cyan). Arrows indicate direct theoretical or methodological influence between approaches.

Other findings complement this theoretical framework by showing how AI systems can decompose legal language into constituent ontological parts to better understand causal mechanisms, rather than just identifying surface-level correlations [32]. Research on reader response algorithms provides additional methodological insights, demonstrating how strategic architectural choices like residualization and adversarial learning can help disentangle confounding factors—a fundamental task in legal contexts where multiple variables may influence outcomes [70]. Building upon these theoretical foundations, the aforementioned Law-Match framework, which operationalizes causal principles by leveraging law articles as instrumental variables to decompose legal case representations into law-related and law-unrelated components [37].

This direction benefits from further advances through a graph-based causal inference (GCI) framework [17] that constructs causal graphs from fact descriptions without extensive manual intervention, enabling more accurate modeling of legal relationships and presenting a method for predicting court decisions by analyzing case details using advanced techniques [38]. The system acts as a decision-support tool for legal professionals. By analyzing the details of a case, it predicts likely legal outcomes in a way that mimics the reasoning process of judges. Its predictions are informed by patterns learned from a large dataset of previous cases, trying to ensure that outputs are both relevant and interpretable within the legal framework.

It combines causal inference, which identifies cause-and-effect relationships in case facts, with a specialized language model, *Lawformer* [41], to process legal texts accurately.

By learning from a large database of past judgments, the system predicts applicable laws, charges, and sentences, simulating the combined expertise of multiple legal professionals. This multi-task approach improves accuracy and efficiency, offering lawyers insights into potential outcomes and helping non-experts better understand legal scenarios. The approach balances automation with interpretability, making it a valuable tool for legal decision-making.

The GCI framework constructs a causal graph to model relationships between key factors extracted from case descriptions. The framework processes unstructured legal text as follows:

1. Keyword extraction: Key legal terms, denoted as $\{\mathbf{x}_1, \mathbf{x}_2, \ldots, \mathbf{x}_p\}$, are extracted using the modified YAKE algorithm. This algorithm prioritizes terms based on their frequency, position, and contextual relevance within the text.
2. Clustering: Keywords are grouped into $q$ clusters, $\{\mathbf{C}_1, \mathbf{C}_2, \ldots, \mathbf{C}_q\}$, using the $k$-means clustering algorithm. Each cluster represents a set of semantically related legal concepts.
3. Causal graph construction: Clusters are treated as nodes in the graph, and edges are established using the Greedy Fast Causal Inference (GFCI) algorithm. Edges are classified into four types:
    - $\mathbf{A} \rightarrow \mathbf{B}$: **A** causally influences **B**.
    - $\mathbf{A} \leftrightarrow \mathbf{B}$: **A** and **B** share an unobserved confounding factor.
    - $\mathbf{A} \leftrightarrow \mathbf{B}$: Ambiguous causation or shared confounding factor.
    - $\mathbf{A} \leftrightarrow \mathbf{B}$: Reciprocal causation or ambiguity.
4. Prediction integration: The causal graph informs the prediction model by integrating causal strength metrics, enabling the identification of applicable laws, charges, and sentences.

This framework is formalized mathematically as a directed graph:

$$\mathbf{G} = (\mathbf{V}, \mathbf{E}), \tag{1}$$

where $\mathbf{V} = \{\mathbf{C}_1, \mathbf{C}_2, \ldots, \mathbf{C}_q\}$ are the nodes (clusters of key terms), and **E** represents the edges with causality types. The causal relationships are weighted by a scoring function $S(e)$, which evaluates the strength and direction of the causal link, ensuring legal consistency in downstream predictions.

This aligns with other findings showing that causally-aware methods can significantly improve the robustness and generalizability of AI systems by capturing underlying data generation processes rather than superficial correlations [45]. Causal-BERT architecture provides a practical mechanism for implementing these theoretical insights, demonstrating how masked event context and pre-training on diverse datasets can help models learn the implicit structural representations needed for robust causal inference [68]. These findings—that models pre-trained on out-of-domain data can perform well on low-resource tasks—are particularly relevant for legal applications, where annotated causal datasets are often scarce.

The mathematical foundations for causal understanding in legal language have been significantly enhanced by both Chen et al.'s introduction of label transfer mechanisms in CMTL [47] and Ritov et al.'s development of conditional parity [43].

On the one hand, the CMTL approach is formalized through a novel mediation assumption that explicitly models the causal relationships between tasks:

$$P(\mathbf{Y}^m, \mathbf{Y}^n \mid \mathbf{X}) = P(\mathbf{Y}^m \mid \mathbf{X}) P(\mathbf{Y}^n \mid \mathbf{X}, \mathbf{Y}^m), \tag{2}$$

where $\mathbf{Y}^m$ and $\mathbf{Y}^n$ represent different legal tasks, and $\mathbf{X}$ represents the input text [47]. This formalization captures the crucial insight that legal tasks are not conditionally independent, but exhibit causal relationships that must be explicitly modeled. This implementation through label transfer (LT) and Gumbel sampling (GS) provides a practical mechanism for capturing these dependencies while mitigating cascading errors. LT enables the model to reuse label embeddings from lower-level tasks to inform predictions for higher-level tasks. Specifically, the transferred hidden states for task $k$, denoted as $\mathbf{th}_i^k$, are computed as follows:

$$\mathbf{th}_i^k = \overrightarrow{\text{LSTM}}^{(\text{LT})}\left(\mathbf{le}_i^{k-1}, \mathbf{th}_i^{k-1}\right), \quad (3)$$

The arrow on Long Short-Term Memory ($\overrightarrow{\text{LSTM}}$) denotes a forward-directional LSTM, which processes sequences from left to right. This LSTM layer takes label embeddings ($\mathbf{le}_i^{k-1}$) from the previous task and the hidden states ($\mathbf{th}_i^{k-1}$) from the previous task's transfer process as inputs, producing new hidden states ($\mathbf{th}_i^k$) that incorporate information from both sources for the label transfer mechanism.

This mechanism allows the model to propagate information across tasks in a logically consistent manner, aligning with the mediation assumption. GS is then used during training to sample from predicted probability distributions, ensuring smoother gradients and avoiding train-test discrepancies by approximating counterfactual reasoning [47].

On the other hand, while traditional fairness metrics often focus on statistical parity, *conditional parity* (CP) frameworks emerge directly from causal reasoning principles [43]. CP extends beyond surface-level statistical relationships by explicitly modeling how protected attributes causally influence outcomes through various pathways. This causal grounding makes CP particularly valuable for legal applications, where establishing genuine discriminatory mechanisms rather than mere correlations is essential. By examining how outcomes vary across protected groups while conditioning on relevant variables, CP enables the identification of genuine causal mechanisms underlying discriminatory effects. Formally, conditional parity is defined as:

$$L(\mathbf{x} \mid \mathbf{a} = a, \mathbf{z} = z) = L(\mathbf{x} \mid \mathbf{a} = a', \mathbf{z} = z) \quad \forall a, a' \in \mathbf{A}, \quad (4)$$

where $\mathbf{x}$ is the outcome, $\mathbf{a}$ the protected attribute, and $\mathbf{z}$ the conditioning variable. This ensures outcome distributions are identical across protected groups when conditioned on $\mathbf{z}$.

This formalization allows for rigorous causal investigation of whether disparate impacts arise from legitimate differences in conditioning variables versus discriminatory mechanisms [43]. The framework's integration with kernel-based conditional independence tests provides robust validation of causal relationships in legal texts, particularly valuable when empirical data is limited.

For example, *equalized odds*, an instance of CP, requires:

$$L(\hat{\mathbf{y}} \mid \mathbf{a} = a, \mathbf{y} = y) = L(\hat{\mathbf{y}} \mid \mathbf{a} = a', \mathbf{y} = y) \quad \forall y \in \mathbf{Y}, \quad (5)$$

where $\hat{\mathbf{y}}$ is the predicted outcome, and $\mathbf{y}$ the actual outcome.

CP also supports post-processing, ensuring that any function $f(\mathbf{x})$ inherits fairness if $\mathbf{x}$ satisfies CP. This framework provides a robust mathematical foundation for fairness.

The authors demonstrate the framework's utility through practical applications [43], such as addressing disparities in insurance premiums charged to minority neighborhoods, emphasizing the importance of fairness in automated systems (using the conditional cross-covariance operator). Therefore, they address challenges in large-scale causal extraction, as highlighted by Hassanzadeh et al. [52]. The kernel-based approach offers several advantages over traditional correlation-based methods:

1. It captures non-linear relationships commonly found in legal language.
2. It provides a principled test for conditional independence.
3. It scales effectively to high-dimensional feature spaces, typical in legal applications.

This causal interpretation of fairness metrics enhances the broader project of applying causal inference to legal texts and in contexts related to legal situations, such as avoiding de facto discrimination by automated systems. Where traditional correlation-based approaches may identify surface-level disparities, conditional parity frameworks help isolate genuine causal mechanisms of discrimination [43]. This capability proves especially valuable for legal applications where distinguishing correlation from causation is essential for establishing discriminatory impact.

Dymitruk et al.'s research further extends this mathematical foundation through their investigation of the NESS (Necessary Element of a Sufficient Set) approach, which presents a more restricted version of existing counterfactual approaches in law [42]. Their formalization describes a causally relevant condition as a necessary element of a set of conditions jointly sufficient for the outcome, providing a robust framework for distinguishing genuine causation from mere correlation in legal contexts. This approach aligns with Hart and Honoré's emphasis on the conditionality of necessary and sufficient conditions, offering a precise mechanism for evaluating complex causal chains in legal scenarios. They announce preliminary results in developing a semi-formal framework based on language to model and evaluate degrees of causation in law, validating it in a vaccine injury case [42].

On this subject, Santosh explored deconfounding methods for legal judgment prediction, aiming to identify genuine causal relationships between legal factors [50]. This approach has the potential to reduce AI's reliance on spurious correlations and improve its ability to reason with legal concepts in a manner more aligned with human experts.

By leveraging these methods, researchers can more accurately test and validate causality in legal data, ensuring precision in downstream tasks.

The evaluation of causal relationships in legal texts requires frameworks that can handle both local and global dependencies [47].

The DocScript model introduces a novel approach to predicting the logical sequence of events in long-form documents, such as contracts or Wikipedia articles, by leveraging advanced NLP techniques [74]. Unlike prior methods that focus on sentence-level event relationships, DocScript addresses the complexities of document-level analysis, where events are often dispersed across multiple paragraphs and require an understanding of both temporal (time-based) and causal (cause-effect) relationships. The system constructs an Event Logic Graph to represent the interactions between events and employs innovative training tasks that enable it to recognize correct event sequences, reorder scrambled events, and identify connections among events within the document. By incorporating optimal transport techniques, implemented through the Sinkhorn algorithm to align event representations, DocScript provides a more nuanced evaluation of causal understanding compared to traditional classification metrics. The alignment process is mathematically defined as:

$$L_{\text{causal}} = \text{Sinkhorn}(\mathbf{E}, \hat{\mathbf{E}}'), \tag{6}$$

where $\mathbf{E}$ represents the true causal relationships and $\hat{\mathbf{E}}'$ the model's predictions. This framework provides a more nuanced evaluation of causal understanding than traditional classification metrics, though it still faces limitations in capturing the full complexity of legal reasoning [74].

The DocScript architecture's evaluation approach aligns with recent advances in transformer-based models, particularly in handling the bidirectional context essential for legal reasoning [36]. This includes edge-based attention mechanisms and optimal transport-based alignments that build upon sequence-to-sequence architectures' capabilities while addressing their inherent limitations in processing long-form legal documents.

An analysis of Canadian legal cases demonstrates how SCMs can explicitly represent the direction of influence in legal relationships, capturing the crucial distinction between post hoc ergo propter hoc fallacies and legitimate causal chains [8]. This aligns precisely with methods to measure and adjust for confounding variables encoded in text data, thereby offering a framework for more accurate causal estimates in legal contexts [44]. This capability proves particularly valuable in complex cases involving multiple potential causes, intervening acts, and questions of legal responsibility.

Teney et al. propose *gradient supervision* , a technique that uses counterfactual examples to guide neural network training by aligning model gradients with causal mechanisms [75]. Counterfactual examples are pairs of scenarios with minimal differences that lead to different outcomes, to help the AI identify what truly matters. For instance, in a legal context, comparing a case where a contract breach caused harm with one where it did not helps the AI understand the importance of causality. By aligning its decision-making process with these examples, the system learns to generalize better, handle unfamiliar situations, and make fairer, more reliable decisions based on the core principles of a task rather than irrelevant or biased data patterns. This alignment is achieved through a gradient supervision loss function, which ensures the AI's decision-making boundaries are shaped to follow the logic indicated by these counterfactual examples. By constraining the AI's decision gradient—the way it changes predictions in response to input changes—this loss function helps the model focus on meaningful causal relationships, leading to more robust and principled generalization. The gradient supervision loss is defined as:

$$\mathcal{L}_{\text{GS}}(\mathbf{g}_i, \hat{\mathbf{g}}_i) = 1 - \frac{\mathbf{g}_i \cdot \hat{\mathbf{g}}_i}{\|\mathbf{g}_i\|\|\hat{\mathbf{g}}_i\|} \tag{7}$$

where $\mathbf{g}_i = \nabla_{\mathbf{x}} f(\mathbf{x}_i)$ is the model's gradient at input $\mathbf{x}_i$, and $\hat{\mathbf{g}}_i = \mathbf{x}_j - \mathbf{x}_i$ represents the desired gradient direction derived from counterfactual pairs $(\mathbf{x}_i, \mathbf{y}_i)$ and $(\mathbf{x}_j, \mathbf{y}_j)$ with $\mathbf{y}_i \neq \mathbf{y}_j$.

In other words, having two cases that are very similar but lead to opposite outcomes—for example, one where a breach of contract caused harm and another where it did not—the difference between these cases highlights what truly matters for the decision. This loss function ensures the system pays attention to such meaningful changes. It works by comparing how the system's *reasoning* shifts when moving from one case to another, ensuring its *logic* aligns with the core differences in the examples. In simple terms, it is similar to giving the system feedback on how to connect the dots between similar cases with different results, helping it focus on the principles that matter most [75].

This approach enhances generalization by encouraging models to learn causal rather than correlational patterns, making it particularly relevant for applications requiring counterfactual reasoning, such as legal causation analysis. This complements SCM by offering a practical training objective that encourages models to learn causal rather than merely correlational patterns [8]. The approach is particularly relevant for legal applications where counterfactual reasoning ("but-for" causation) plays a central role.

Finally, it is worthwhile to mention Kyriakakis et al.'s study on transfer learning for causal sentence detection, which offers significant findings on the scalability and effectiveness of different architectural approaches [73]. The study evaluates several architectures, including bidirectional GRU with self-attention (BIGRUATT), ELMO, and BERT, emphasizing the pronounced benefits of transfer learning in small datasets containing hundreds of instances. These findings are especially relevant for specialized legal domains where annotated data is scarce, exploring how AI can detect sentences describing cause-and-effect relationships. They showed that advanced AI techniques, like using pre-trained models (which learn from general data before focusing on specific tasks), work well even with small datasets, a common issue in specialized fields like law. By testing and improving methods, they demonstrated that AI could effectively identify causality in complex texts, making it a valuable tool for legal professionals to analyze cases, find key arguments, and predict outcomes more efficiently.

The research demonstrates that model performance plateaus with just a few thousand training instances, indicating that increasing dataset size alone does not yield further improvements in causal detection. This aligns with observations on the constraints imposed by limited annotation budgets in legal domains [44] and reinforces the emphasis on the importance of efficient learning strategies in low-data scenarios [51].

The mathematical representation provided for the BIGRUATT architecture is as follows [73]:

$$\mathbf{H}^f = \langle \mathbf{h}_1^f, \ldots, \mathbf{h}_n^f \rangle = \mathrm{GRU}^f(\mathbf{e}_1, \ldots, \mathbf{e}_n), \tag{8}$$
$$\mathbf{H}^b = \langle \mathbf{h}_1^b, \ldots, \mathbf{h}_n^b \rangle = \mathrm{GRU}^b(\mathbf{e}_1, \ldots, \mathbf{e}_n), \tag{9}$$
$$\mathbf{H} = \langle [\mathbf{h}_1^f; \mathbf{h}_1^b], \ldots, [\mathbf{h}_n^f; \mathbf{h}_n^b] \rangle \tag{10}$$

where $\mathbf{H}$ represents the bidirectional encoding of the sentence, $^f$ and $^b$ the forward and backward directions, and $[;]$ denotes concatenation.

A linear attention mechanism computes attention scores for each hidden state:

$$\tilde{a}_i = \mathbf{u}_{\mathrm{att}} \cdot \mathbf{h}_i, \tag{11}$$
$$a_i = \mathrm{softmax}(\tilde{a}_i, \tilde{a}_1, \ldots, \tilde{a}_n) \tag{12}$$

where $\mathbf{u}_{\mathrm{att}}$ is the attention weight vector. The sentence embedding $\mathbf{s}$ is then computed as a weighted sum of the hidden states:

$$\mathbf{s} = \sum_{i=1}^{n} a_i \mathbf{h}_i. \tag{13}$$

Finally, the probability of a sentence being causal is calculated using a logistic regression layer:

$$p = \sigma(\mathbf{u}_p \cdot \mathbf{s} + b_p), \tag{14}$$

where $\sigma$ denotes the sigmoid function, and $\mathbf{u}_p$ and $b_p$ are the parameters of the logistic regression layer.

The BIGRUATT architecture achieved area under the curve (AUC) scores exceeding 0.95 on certain datasets, demonstrating its capability to capture complex linguistic patterns, including implicit causal relationships prevalent in legal texts [73]. Furthermore, their experiments revealed that BERT combined with BIGRUATT consistently outperformed simpler architectures such as BERT+LR in AUC measurements. This suggests the necessity of deeper, task-specific models for robust causal detection in legal applications.

### 3.3.4. Implementation Challenges and Solutions

The implementation of causal inference in legal AI faces several fundamental challenges. Recent work by [74] demonstrates that extracting causal relationships across long documents requires handling complex dependencies between events that may be paragraphs apart, necessitating sophisticated multi-hop reasoning capabilities. Their findings show that contemporary LLMs struggle with document-level causal reasoning, particularly when temporal sequences span multiple pages, highlighting a key limitation of current approaches.

Causal understanding becomes particularly critical in sequential decision-making (SDM) contexts. Off-the-shelf deployment of existing SDM models to the public sector is insufficient due to the unique challenges posed by legal and policy constraints [51]. SDM algorithms must adapt to handle batched and delayed feedback in legal contexts, where the consequences of decisions may not be immediately observable and may arrive in groups rather than individually [51].

Zhao et al. [38] and Keith [44] extend this capability. In the first case with the aforementioned GCI framework, by automatically extracting and clustering key legal concepts from case descriptions, causal relationships were established between these elements through a combination of sliding window attention mechanisms and global attention patterns [38]. In the second case, by developing methods for identifying causal relationships from text data even with minimal supervision, it was shown how latent disjunction models can aggregate evidence across multiple textual mentions to make entity-level predictions, thus validating these benefits by showing how proper measurement of textual variables combined with causal modeling can significantly improve the robustness of legal predictions, particularly when dealing with distribution shifts common in legal applications [44]. Such legal applications require consideration of multiple objectives simultaneously—for instance, balancing the need to identify causally relevant precedents while ensuring fair and consistent application across different demographic groups [51].

An illustrative approach for addressing severe confounding in legal text generation is the Attentional and Counterfactual based Natural Language Generation (AC-NLG) model, which leverages *backdoor adjustment* to mitigate data imbalance issues [49]. This method involves a claim-aware encoder for highlighting critical aspects of plaintiff claims alongside fact descriptions, coupled with a pair of specialized decoders that generate two distinct views (supportive vs. non-supportive) by counterfactually intervening on the judgment variable. In practice, the system de-biases the data-driven relationship between fact patterns and legal decisions by treating the potential overrepresentation of supportive outcomes as a confounder. By explicitly modeling judgment plausibility and learning separate pathways for supported and non-supported cases, the AC-NLG framework has demonstrated strong performance gains in both accuracy and fairness. The underlying principle relies on intervening on the input representations so that the dominant proportion of supported cases no longer overshadows the minority class, thus yielding a more balanced, confounder-free perspective. This strategy aligns with our broader emphasis on causal inference for improving legal text modeling, especially where label skew or spurious correlations compromise model generalizability and reliability.

However, these challenges are further complicated by the need to handle both explicit and implicit causal relationships in legal texts. Even state-of-the-art language models exhibit significant limitations in zero-shot temporal relation extraction, suggesting fundamental constraints in their causal reasoning capabilities [74]. Indeed, supervised models often outperform larger language models in capturing complex causal dependencies in legal documents [74]. The same applies for Lawformer's sliding window attention mechanism that, while improving performance on standard NLP tasks, does not address the fundamental limitation of correlation-based approaches in capturing legal reasoning [41].

Causal models can incorporate contextual variables and their relationships explicitly, while correlation-based methods struggle with such context-dependent meaning [8]. The HP definitions' evolution, particularly in handling pre-emption and overdetermination scenarios, mirrors the legal system's own development of causation frameworks [8]. The Law-Match framework demonstrates this principle in practice by using law articles as instrumental variables to identify and separate the contextual legal knowledge from case-specific circumstances [37], while the multi-expert FTOPJUDGE mechanism further refines this approach by explicitly modeling the interdependencies between different legal tasks [38]. Such frameworks must also account for distribution shifts in the small data regime typical of legal applications, where the relationships between variables may change over time due to evolving legal interpretations or societal changes [51]. Furthermore, careful measurement of these contextual variables from text data is essential for valid causal inference, and methods have been proposed to handle linguistic complexity while maintaining interpretable relationships between variables [44].

A critical limitation in current approaches is the lack of robust evaluation frameworks for assessing causal understanding in legal AI systems. While traditional metrics like accuracy can measure basic performance, they fail to capture the nuanced understanding required for legal reasoning. The DocScript architecture [74] introduces novel evaluation approaches, including edge-based attention mechanisms and optimal transport-based alignment, providing potential frameworks for assessing causal understanding. However, these metrics still struggle to fully capture the complex interplay between temporal and causal relationships characteristic of legal texts.

Additionally, the construction of accurate causal models requires domain expertise and careful consideration of contextual factors. Different causal models can lead to different legal interpretations, reflecting the inherent complexity of legal reasoning [8]. This complexity is further emphasized by findings regarding the challenges of bridging formal theories with practical legal reasoning [42]. While formal approaches like NESS and actual causation provide valuable theoretical frameworks, their practical application requires careful adaptation to handle the nuanced and context-dependent nature of legal reasoning. The need for semi-formal frameworks that can accommodate both strict and defeasible rules has been emphasized by the literature, allowing for more flexible and realistic modeling of legal arguments [42].

Table 2 summarizes the key implementation challenges identified across the literature in legal AI causal inference.

**Table 2.** Summary of implementation challenges in legal AI causal inference. Challenges are categorized by type and mapped to key literature sources.

| Challenge Category | Key Challenges | Sources |
|---|---|---|
| Technical & Computational | Long-range dependency handling, Document-level temporal reasoning, Bidirectional context processing limitations, Computational complexity in counterfactuals, Integration with correlational systems, Implicit causal relationship handling, Cross-domain performance consistency | Mathur et al. [74]; Rahali and Akhloufi [36]; So [8]; Khetan et al. [68] |
| Data-Related | Limited labeled data availability, Small annotation budgets, Settlement data integration, Intervention data scarcity | Keith [44]; Cohen et al. [53] |
| Implementation | Batched/delayed feedback handling, Distribution shift adaptation, Model interpretability, Unstructured data complexity | Henderson et al. [51]; Cohen et al. [53] |
| Legal Domain-Specific | Context-dependent meaning, Multiple objective optimization, Predictability-flexibility balance, Legal expertise requirements | So [8]; Henderson et al. [51] |

Recent research has highlighted additional technical constraints in implementing causal inference for legal AI. The DocScript study [74] reveals that learning longer-range dependencies between events remains a key challenge, with performance degrading significantly as document length increases. This limitation is particularly relevant for legal applications, where causal chains may span entire documents and require maintaining coherent reasoning across multiple sections.

These limitations stem partly from fundamental architectural constraints in current language models. Rahali and Akhloufi indicate that Causal Language Models (CLMs), which form the backbone of many legal analysis systems, are inherently limited by their unidirectional nature [36]. While they can process text either left-to-right or right-to-left, they cannot effectively utilize bidirectional context—a crucial capability for understanding complex legal relationships that may span multiple sections of a document [36]. Even advanced transformer architectures like T5 and BART, while offering improvements through sequence-to-sequence processing, still face challenges in maintaining coherent reasoning across lengthy legal texts [36].

The challenges of ensuring accuracy in causal extraction at scale has also been investigated, particularly when dealing with the nuanced and context-dependent nature of legal language [52]. While large-scale text mining can effectively identify potential causal relationships, the precision of these extractions remains a critical challenge, especially in legal applications where accuracy is paramount [52]. Additionally, the integration of normality orderings and blame attribution into causal models remains an active area of development. Several key challenges have been identified in this space [44]:

1. Measurement challenges: Extracting relevant variables from legal text requires handling linguistic complexity, ambiguity, and diversity while maintaining accurate measurement.
2. Legal expertise is required for annotation, making it costly to obtain large labeled datasets.
3. Distribution shifts: Legal interpretations evolve over time, requiring models that are robust to changes in variable relationships.
4. Legal applications demand transparent and interpretable models that can be validated by domain experts.

Cohen et al. expanded on these challenges [53], emphasizing that:

1. Most disputes are resolved through negotiation rather than court decisions, necessitating the incorporation of settlement data for accurate modeling.
2. Legal and negotiation texts vary considerably, making it difficult to structure data properly for machine learning algorithms.
3. A judicial system that is too predictable may be problematic, especially if the status quo is unfair or if decision-making is heavily influenced by extraneous factors.

These theoretical challenges are reflected in practical implementations. For instance, the effectiveness of the Law-Match framework depends critically on the quality and relevance of the law articles used as instrumental variables [37]. Causal-BERT also reveals additional technical challenges specific to language-based causal detection [68]: the need to handle implicit causal relationships that lack explicit linguistic markers, the challenge of maintaining consistent performance across different writing styles and legal domains, and the difficulty of transferring causal knowledge between different areas of law. These findings reinforce the importance of robust pre-training strategies and careful consideration of model architecture when implementing causal inference systems for legal applications.

In sum, the challenges can be classified as follows [8]:

1. Model construction: Building accurate causal models requires significant domain expertise and careful consideration of variables and relationships. The flexibility in model construction means different valid interpretations may exist.

2. Data requirements: Causal inference often requires intervention data that may not be available in legal contexts. While do-calculus can help, some causal relationships may remain difficult to verify empirically.
3. Computational complexity: Causal inference, especially counterfactual analysis, can be computationally intensive for complex legal scenarios with many interacting factors.
4. Integration with existing systems: Most current legal AI systems are built around correlational approaches. Integrating causal reasoning capabilities requires significant architectural changes.

Additionally, by carefully addressing the unique challenges of sequential decision-making in legal contexts—including multi-objective optimization, batched feedback, and distribution shifts—the field moves closer to AI systems that can truly understand and reason about legal causation while maintaining compliance with policy requirements and legal constraints [51].

#### 3.3.5. Innovations in Causal Relationship Extraction

Recent years have witnessed significant advances in causal relationship extraction methods for legal applications, each offering distinct advantages and addressing specific challenges in the field. Table 3 provides a comprehensive comparison of these methods, highlighting their respective strengths, limitations, and optimal use cases.

**Table 3.** Comparative analysis of causal extraction methods. Each method presents distinct trade-offs between computational requirements, data needs, and capability scope.

| Method | Key Strengths | Limitations | Best Use Case |
|---|---|---|---|
| Causal-BERT [68] | Handles explicit/implicit causality; Strong contextual understanding; Minimal feature engineering | High computational requirements; Large training data needed; Complex model architecture | Complex legal texts with subtle causal relationships |
| Evolutionary Algorithms [76] | Sophisticated counterfactual generation; Preserves structural relationships; Outperforms baseline methods | Computationally intensive; Requires significant training data; Complex parameter tuning | Generating counterfactual scenarios in legal reasoning |
| Two-Side Scoring [77] | Clear directional causality assessment; Probabilistic framework; Simple implementation | May oversimplify relationships; Requires domain-specific training; Limited to binary relationships | Determining causal direction in legal arguments |
| OpBerg [35] | Works with limited training data; Efficient POS-based matching; $\mathcal{O}(n^2)$ complexity | Limited to pattern-based causality; May miss complex relationships; Requires POS accuracy | Quick causal analysis with limited training data |
| Thrill-K [78] | Structured knowledge organization; Multiple knowledge tiers; Strong domain integration | Complex architecture; Resource intensive; Requires knowledge engineering | Complex legal reasoning with multiple knowledge sources |

Building on this comparative framework, we can examine each method in greater detail.

Causal-BERT represents a breakthrough in handling both explicit and implicit causal relationships without relying on traditional pattern-matching rules [68]. This approach demonstrates particular strength in legal applications where causal relationships often require sophisticated contextual understanding.

The development of Causal-BERT represents a significant advance in addressing these challenges, demonstrating that language models can effectively detect both explicit and implicit causal relationships in text without relying on brittle pattern-matching rules or extensive feature engineering [68]. This approach is particularly relevant to legal applications, where causal relationships are often expressed implicitly and require sophisticated contextual understanding to identify.

Recent methodological innovations have further expanded the toolkit for extracting causal relationships from legal texts.

Building on work with evolutionary algorithms for counterfactual sequence generation, recent methodological innovations have further expanded the toolkit for extracting causal relationships from legal texts [76]. Indeed, evolutionary optimization has shown to generate viable counterfactual sequences while preserving essential structural relationships [76]—this is particularly necessary given that, in legal applications, the ordering and dependencies between events carry significant meaning. Evolutionary approaches consistently outperform both random and case-based baselines in generating high-quality counterfactuals, which provides important validation for more sophisticated generative approaches in legal contexts [76].

Arsenyan and Shahnazaryan explore causal relationship extraction in biomedical contexts using methods such as semantic role labeling (SRL) and open-book question answering (QA) [77]. A notable contribution is their two-sided scoring method, which compares the probabilities of directional relationships between entities to infer causality. This approach is particularly relevant for fields like law, where determining causal direction is critical. Their method involves the following formalization:

$$\text{Given entities } \mathbf{a} \text{ and } \mathbf{b}, \text{ and a context } \mathbf{C}: \tag{15}$$

$$P(\mathbf{a} \mid \mathbf{b}, \mathbf{C}) \quad \text{vs} \quad P(\mathbf{b} \mid \mathbf{a}, \mathbf{C}), \tag{16}$$

where the higher probability determines the causal direction. For instance, if $P(\mathbf{a} \mid \mathbf{b}, \mathbf{C}) > P(\mathbf{b} \mid \mathbf{a}, \mathbf{C})$, then $\mathbf{b} \to \mathbf{a}$ (i.e., $\mathbf{b}$ causes $\mathbf{a}$). This scoring provides a framework for assessing causal relationships by leveraging language models trained with domain-specific data.

The application of this framework could be extended to legal texts, enabling the extraction and evaluation of causal relationships critical for legal reasoning. By adapting this method to legal language models, it could be possible to address nuances in legal discourse and improve the interpretability of causal inferences.

A framework for mining causal knowledge from extensive text corpora has also been proposed, addressing significant challenges in domains like legal applications [52]. The proposed system employs a combination of unsupervised and weakly supervised methods, effectively navigating the diverse representations of causality inherent in legal language. The framework is designed to identify and retrieve causal relationships while providing a quantitative measure of causality through a scoring mechanism.

The system integrates neural embeddings and advanced language models, such as Word2Vec and BERT, to handle the vast variety of causal expressions in natural language. These embeddings enhance the framework's ability to analyze and retrieve causally related sentences, enabling robust evidence retrieval. Specifically, the causality scoring mechanism calculates the likelihood of a causal relationship between two entities, $(\mathbf{X}, \mathbf{Y})$, using multiple methods, including [52]:

- Directional ratio scoring: The score is computed as:

$$\text{Causality score} = \frac{\text{Hits}(\mathbf{X} \rightarrow \mathbf{Y})}{\text{Hits}(\mathbf{Y} \rightarrow \mathbf{X})} \tag{17}$$

  where $\text{Hits}(\mathbf{X} \rightarrow \mathbf{Y})$ and $\text{Hits}(\mathbf{Y} \rightarrow \mathbf{X})$ represent the frequency of observed directional causal relations.
- Sentence embedding similarity: Using neural sentence embeddings, the framework calculates the average similarity between the input sentence (e.g., "**X** may cause **Y**") and top-$k$ causal sentences from the corpus.
- Combined scoring: A hybrid approach that blends directional ratio scoring and embedding-based similarity for enhanced reliability.

Moreover, their framework's evidence retrieval capability aligns with the legal need for substantiated causal claims. The retrieved evidence includes metadata, such as source documents, to ensure transparency and traceability [52].

In addition, this approach complements methodologies such as Keith's text measurement framework [44], enabling scalable identification and validation of causal relationships in legal contexts. By integrating domain-specific adaptations, the system underscores the necessity of legal-contextual fine-tuning [77].

This system's ability to construct *mind maps* of causal relationships also represents a key innovation. Starting from a small set of seed phrases, it generates visualizable graphs of high-scoring cause–effect pairs, significantly reducing the labor involved in manual causal analysis [52].

On the other hand, Wood et al. introduced *OpBerg*, an algorithm that adapts genomic sequence alignment techniques to identify causal relationships in text through optimal alignments of part-of-speech (POS) representations [35].

OpBerg efficiently identifies cause-and-effect sentences in scientific texts by comparing their grammatical structures. Unlike other methods that rely on word lists or extensive training data, OpBerg focuses on patterns in sentence roles (e.g., verbs, nouns). It uses a recursive mathematical approach inspired by DNA sequence alignment, breaking sentences into parts and finding the best matches based on similarity [35]. The process balances accuracy and simplicity by penalizing unnecessary complexity (like too many splits) while maximizing meaningful alignments.

The recursive framework behind OpBerg can be explained intuitively: each sentence can be conceptualized as a chain of linked parts (its grammatical structure). The algorithm evaluates each part against a reference, asking two main questions: *Should this part continue the alignment, or should we start a new one?* and *Does adding this alignment improve the overall score?* Mathematically, this is represented by equations that balance these decisions [35]:

$$\mathbf{X}(i,j) = \max \begin{cases} \mathbf{X}(i-1,j) + Q, & \text{continue alignment} \\ \mathbf{X}(i-1,j-1) + S(a_i,b_j), & \text{match parts} \\ \mathbf{X}(i,j-1) + Q, & \text{start a new alignment} \\ 0, & \text{start fresh at this point} \end{cases} \tag{18}$$

where:

- $\mathbf{X}(i,j)$: The alignment score at position $(i,j)$, which represents the comparison of the $i$-th element of one sequence (or sentence structure) with the $j$-th element of another.
- $\mathbf{X}(i-1,j)$: The score if we continue alignment without matching the current element of the second sequence.
- $\mathbf{X}(i-1,j-1)$: The score if the $i$-th and $j$-th elements are matched.

- $\mathbf{X}(i, j-1)$: The score if a new alignment starts, skipping the current element in the first sequence.
- $Q$: The penalty for introducing a gap (i.e., skipping elements rather than aligning them).
- $S(a_i, b_j)$: The score for matching the $i$-th element of one sequence ($a_i$) with the $j$-th element of the other sequence ($b_j$). Higher scores indicate stronger alignment.
- 0: The decision to start fresh, ignoring previous alignments.

The algorithm recursively evaluates all possibilities, keeping the optimal alignments without requiring pre-specified parameters. This ensures it can efficiently pinpoint meaningful cause-and-effect patterns while avoiding over-complication. For non-mathematicians, think of it as a clever scoring game: the algorithm moves through the structure of a sentence, choosing the path that maximizes coherence while penalizing unnecessary detours.

OpBerg enhances the traditional Alignment with Gap Excision (AGE) algorithm, a method originally designed for genomic sequence alignment, by introducing improvements, such as avoiding the need for pre-specified parameters (e.g., the number of local alignments) or generalizing alignment strategies to allow efficient processing of linguistic data.

Eventhough OpBerg was not developed nor applied in legal contexts, these innovations make it particularly suitable for applications in Legal NLP, where labeled training data is often scarce. By focusing on the POS representations of sentences rather than words, OpBerg reliably identifies patterns that characterize causal relationships.

The algorithm operates with a complexity of $\mathcal{O}(n^2)$ in time, where $n$ is the length of the input POS sequence [35]. This is a significant improvement compared to the naive approaches, which can have much higher complexity for similar tasks (e.g., $\mathcal{O}(n^3)$). However, for massive corpora, or datasets with millions of sentences, this complexity can lead to significant delays and is harder to parallelize than linear operations.

A promising architectural direction for addressing the challenges we highlighted in Legal AI emerges from Singer et al.'s Thrill-K framework, which proposes a three-tiered approach to knowledge organization that could significantly enhance causal understanding in legal contexts [78]. Their architecture distinguishes between instantaneous knowledge (for rapid response), standby knowledge (requiring deeper processing), and retrieved external knowledge (accessing additional sources)—a partition that aligns well with the different types of causal reasoning required in legal analysis. This framework complements existing approaches by providing a structured way to integrate different forms of causal knowledge while maintaining computational efficiency.

The Thrill-K architecture's emphasis on deeply structured knowledge, particularly its incorporation of dynamic models and causal relationships, offers several advantages for legal applications [78]:

1. Enhanced ability to represent complex legal relationships through multiple knowledge dimensions;
2. Improved handling of context and source attribution—crucial for legal reasoning;
3. Better integration of values and priorities, essential for ethical legal decision-making; and
4. More efficient resource allocation through strategic partitioning of knowledge.

#### 3.3.6. Integration of Domain Knowledge and Constraints

AI models often diverge from established domain knowledge when deployed in real-world legal scenarios, leading to spurious correlations and low accuracy in data-sparse or counterfactual scenarios [44,67].

Evidence suggests that AI models often diverge from established domain knowledge when deployed in real-world scenarios, leading to spurious correlations and low accuracy in data-sparse or counterfactual scenarios [67]. Incorporating domain-specific constraints at all stages of the machine learning pipeline is crucial for building robust predictive models that align with legal principles and reasoning. Careful measurement of text data through an empirical pipeline that combines NLP with causal inference has shown to help reduce these spurious correlations [44]. Other research complements these observations, with an emphasis on addressing the challenges of unsupervised symbolic knowledge extraction and enhancing interpretability in legal reasoning systems [72], further highlighting the necessity of hybrid approaches for legal analytics.

It has been shown that deep learning models must incorporate domain-specific constraints to achieve robust performance in legal applications for several reasons [67]:

1. Models trained purely on observational data often learn spurious correlations that fail to generalize to novel legal scenarios;
2. Incorporating domain knowledge through explicit constraints improves model robustness;
3. The effectiveness of constraints depends critically on proper formalization of legal concepts and relationships; and
4. Continuous refinement and validation of constraints is essential as legal interpretations evolve.

Causal inference in legal contexts is further supported by the analysis of model performance across multiple legal tasks [64], which demonstrate that incorporating domain-specific constraints and structure at all stages of the machine learning pipeline is crucial for building robust predictive models that align with legal principles and reasoning.

These insights complement the existing work on causal frameworks, especially work on measurement and causal inference with text data [44], by providing practical mechanisms for incorporating domain expertise into legal AI systems. The combination of careful text measurement, causal modeling, and domain-faithful learning provides a promising path forward for developing AI systems that can truly understand and reason about legal causation while maintaining compliance with established legal principles and constraints.

We will now explore the last aspect of our research question, examining how the lack of empirical context, a precondition for causal inference, is addressed in the existing literature.

### 3.4. *Addressing the Lack of Empirical Context for Causal AI in Legal Texts*

This section addresses the lack of empirical context for Causal AI in legal texts. We begin by examining foundational challenges and data limitations that hinder causal analysis in legal domains. We then explore methodological advances and implementation strategies that have emerged to address these constraints. After discussing NLP applications and current limitations, we present theoretical frameworks and available dataset resources. The section concludes with future directions and research priorities for improving empirical foundations in legal Causal AI.

#### 3.4.1. Foundational Challenges and Data Limitations

The challenge of empirical data scarcity in legal causal analysis stems from both structural and methodological constraints. Legal data exist in heterogeneous formats spanning textual documents, metadata, and contextual factors, creating significant barriers to systematic causal inference. The fragmentation of data across jurisdictions and non-interoperable systems further compounds these challenges. Indeed, law and public policy pose unique methodological problems, with challenges in multi-objective decision making, batched and delayed feedback, and the requirement for rational, causal decision-making policies that the machine learning community has not yet fully addressed [51].

As discussed in Section 3.2, the narrative nature of law complicates empirical quantification [61]. A comprehensive review of causality analysis in big data demonstrates how the volume and heterogeneity of modern legal datasets pose fundamental challenges for identifying causal relationships [56], revealing that data mining techniques serve as essential tools for managing this complexity, with entity extraction, clustering, association rule mining, and classification emerging as primary approaches for processing large-scale causal information.

The unstructured nature of legal texts poses significant hurdles for AI models. While most judgments follow a structured template, they vary considerably, making it difficult for machine learning algorithms to yield accurate results without proper data structuring [53]. This aligns with findings regarding the limitations of purely correlative approaches in predictive contracting [32]. Transforming unstructured legal data into structured data is a research-intensive endeavor requiring significant computing power and a skilled interdisciplinary team [53].

Data scarcity in legal AI is also a recurrent challenge mentioned in literature. Legal texts are, by nature, high-dimensional and linguistically complex [44]. The distribution of legal concepts and arguments may vary significantly between different areas of law or over time, complicating AI training. Indeed, models struggle particularly with few-shot learning scenarios, especially in specialized areas of law where training data may be limited [63].

### 3.4.2. Core Methodological Advances

Recent methodological advances demonstrate promising approaches to address these limitations while preserving law's narrative integrity. Building upon the GCI framework discussed in Section 3.3, recent methodological advances address data limitations by proposing a sliding window attention mechanism to process long-form legal documents efficiently and dilated sliding window attention to capture relationships between distant elements in legal texts [38]. This integration provides two key advantages: it enables the model to learn from both explicit causal relationships documented in legal texts and implicit patterns identified through statistical learning, and by incorporating multiple expert networks focused on different aspects of legal analysis, the framework can effectively leverage limited training data across related legal tasks.

In response to data scarcity, transfer learning and pre-training on out-of-domain data have been explored to address this challenge. While pre-training can improve performance in low-resource causality detection tasks, it may not be a panacea for all challenges [68]. As previously noted in Section 3.3, transfer learning offers solutions to data scarcity; using as a baseline a bidirectional model with self-attention and transfer learning techniques like ELMO and BERT has been shown to significantly improve performance in causal sentence detection [73]. However, for larger datasets (thousands of instances), performance reached a plateau, and transfer learning provided minimal additional benefits. This pattern may well apply to legal language processing tasks, suggesting that while transfer learning can be beneficial for specialized legal tasks with limited data, it may not be a panacea for all challenges in legal AI. This approach aligns with findings regarding the challenges of limited labeled data in specialized domains, demonstrating how carefully designed architectures can help overcome the constraints of small annotation budgets [70]. This is particularly valuable for legal applications where manual annotation is costly but important relationships must be extracted from large document collections.

Gastwirth emphasizes that to produce accurate results, data-driven models must be trained using both legal and non-legal data [34]. He argues that making predictions based solely on legal precedent can yield inaccurate results, as most disputes are resolved via negotiation and hence are unobserved in the data. This aligns with findings regarding the limitations of purely data-driven approaches in legal contexts [53]. While AI can help predict broad outcomes, achieving precise predictions remains challenging due to the inherent flexibility required in legal decision-making. Some level of inconsistency is inevitable and perhaps desirable in judicial processes, as it allows for adaptation to specific circumstances while maintaining sufficient predictability to ensure legal certainty [53]. Thus, effective legal AI systems must incorporate both court decisions and negotiation outcomes to provide accurate predictions and recommendations [53].

Building upon the Law-Match framework discussed in Section 3.3, which leverages law articles as instrumental variables, we note its particular effectiveness in addressing data scarcity [37]. By employing IV regression to decompose legal case embeddings, Law-Match allows for nuanced analysis of legal texts even in scenarios with limited empirical data. This capability is critical for improving Causal AI applications where empirical context is sparse.

Extending the theoretical foundations discussed in Section 3.3, the introduction of conditional parity offers a robust framework for ensuring non-discrimination in AI systems [43]. Particularly, its mathematically rigorous kernel-based conditional independence tests are invaluable for validating causal relationships in legal texts when empirical data is limited. This approach proves essential for managing the complexity of large-scale legal data while upholding statistical rigor.

#### 3.4.3. Implementation Strategies and Practical Applications

Expanding on Williams' approach discussed in Section 3.3 [32], data collection strategies include structured data collection through integrated contract management systems, transfer learning and few-shot learning techniques for handling limited training data, NLP for extracting structured variables from unstructured legal texts, and standardized frameworks for collecting and analyzing outcome data. While technical constraints around data sufficiency and representativeness remain, these structured approaches to data collection and analysis can help generate the empirical context needed for robust causal analysis of legal texts.

Building on these foundations, Mathis demonstrated sophisticated techniques for extracting structured empirical data from legal texts, achieving an overall quality score of 87.5% for information extraction [79]. His two-step training process combines Conditional Random Fields (CRF) and Flair algorithms, achieving 90% accuracy for legal reference extraction. The demonstrated success in handling different jurisdictional levels and types of litigation suggests these methods could be adaptable across various legal domains. The integration of Mathis's information extraction techniques with the graph-based causal inference framework presents a particularly promising direction for populating causal graphs with empirical variables.

These practical applications were further advanced by introducing the generative probabilistic modeling approach for prevalence estimation and a latent disjunction model for entity-event measurement [44], as outlined in Section 3.3. Corpus-level evaluation could be efficient for legal causal analysis, as it allows for the assessment of methods at scale, mirroring the vast body of legal texts that often need to be analyzed in practice [44]. The proposed methods are designed to handle linguistic complexity and ambiguity, which are particularly pertinent in legal texts.

#### 3.4.4. Advanced NLP and Deep Learning Applications

As explored in Section 3.3, advanced NLP models like BERT can be fine-tuned for legal applications [53]. This research demonstrates how fine-tuning BERT for legal and negotiation text can create what they term a "Generalized Intelligence in Dispute Resolution" (GIDBERT). This approach addresses the challenge of limited empirical data by learning from massive volumes of legal and negotiation text, including "the entire corpus of European and American case law, academic papers, textbooks, legislation, and even Talmudic law" [53] (p. 6).

#### 3.4.5. Current Limitations and Implementation Challenges

Despite these advances, significant challenges remain. Chalkidis et al. have revealed persistent difficulties in achieving consistent performance across different jurisdictions, languages, and legal areas through their FairLex multilingual benchmark [62]. Their analysis demonstrates that even state-of-the-art fine-tuning techniques cannot reliably guarantee fairness or effectively mitigate group disparities in legal NLP applications.

Specific vulnerabilities in Legal Judgment Prediction (LJP) systems are also highlighted as shallow, distracting surface signals arising from corpus construction, case distribution, and confounding factors [50]. The expert-informed deconfounding method strategically identifies statistically predictive but legally irrelevant information, demonstrating better alignment with expert rationales compared to baseline models. This work emphasizes the vulnerability of LJP models to irrelevant data and the need for more robust approaches that align with expert legal reasoning.

As mentioned in Section 3.4.1, transforming unstructured legal data requires significant resources [53]. This highlights how relying solely on legal precedent data can yield inaccurate results, as most disputes are resolved through negotiation rather than court decisions.

#### 3.4.6. Theoretical Frameworks and Integration Approaches

Extending the theoretical frameworks discussed in Section 3.3, recent developments point toward promising integrative approaches [8]. The application of formal causal models to describe legal decisions provides a crucial link between theoretical frameworks and practical legal reasoning while promoting accountability and minimizing biases [8]. A significant insight is that causal frameworks can promote accountability and minimize biases in legal decision-making, aligning with ongoing efforts in the AI community to develop fair, accountable, and transparent (FAccT) systems [8].

A semi-formal framework has been proposed, employing defeasible logic to bridge theoretical and practical approaches to causation in law, integrating linguistic analysis with evidential reasoning approaches [42]. This integration of multiple analytical techniques could helps address the empirical limitations by leveraging both explicit causal relationships documented in legal texts and implicit patterns identified through linguistic and logical analysis.

Data mining approaches complement these methodological frameworks—for instance, the graph-based causal inference framework can leverage these techniques to more effectively process large volumes of legal documents [56]. As with the Law-Match framework discussed earlier, data mining approaches can enhance scalability when scaling to large legal corpora [37].

#### 3.4.7. Available Dataset Resources

Recent developments in legal document analysis have produced structured datasets that create new opportunities for Causal AI research, while simultaneously exposing methodological challenges in causation detection. Building upon earlier discussions of causal frameworks, emerging datasets specifically address the complexities of long-form legal documents. A comprehensive survey reveals the existence of 43 legal judgment prediction datasets spanning nine different languages, encompassing civil law, common law, and hybrid legal systems [64]. These datasets represent a significant empirical foundation for developing causal models, offering diverse contexts for studying legal reasoning patterns and decision-making processes.

A promising development in this direction is the emergence of LEXTREME, a multilingual and multi-task legal benchmark that incorporates 11 datasets covering 24 languages and multiple jurisdictions [80]. LEXTREME provides standardized evaluation protocols for classification and named entity recognition tasks, highlighting how domain-specific benchmarks can illuminate causal relationships in settings where text length, jurisdictional diversity, and specialized legal terminology pose considerable challenges. By offering a curated set of linguistically diverse datasets, LEXTREME could serve as an empirical backbone for assessing whether causal inference techniques generalize across legal systems and languages, thus reducing the field's heavy reliance on English-centric or single-jurisdiction corpora.

The temporal nature of legal proceedings manifests prominently in contemporary datasets. Collections like CAIL-Long contain longitudinal data enabling the study of causal effects over time, while datasets such as QAjudge provide annotated rationales and intermediate reasoning steps, offering insights into the causal mechanisms underlying judicial decision-making [64]. These resources prove particularly valuable for understanding how temporal dependencies influence legal outcomes, aligning with earlier discussions of the Law-Match framework's use of law articles as instrumental variables [37]. Expanding this foundation, LegalBench introduces a specialized dataset focusing on legal reasoning causality, distinguishing between statistical and direct-probative evidence in establishing causal links [81]. This dataset addresses a critical gap in the evaluation of causal reasoning capabilities, particularly in discrimination cases where statistical evidence often serves as the primary mechanism for establishing causation.

A significant methodological challenge emerges from the hierarchical nature of legal documentation. Datasets like TOPJUDGE-CJO, TOPJUDGE-PKU, and TOPJUDGE-CAIL capture complex relationships between legal articles, charges, and prison terms [64], requiring sophisticated causal modeling approaches. The presence of these hierarchical relationships necessitates theoretical frameworks that can account for both direct and indirect causal influences, echoing the conditional parity approaches discussed in relation to AI systems fairness [43]. LegalBench's approach to dataset construction, involving manual extraction and coding of causality-focused passages, demonstrates the intricate nature of identifying causal reasoning patterns in legal texts [81].

The DocSEP corpus introduces specialized datasets derived from legal contracts and Wikipedia articles [74], presenting unique challenges for causal analysis with documents averaging 2479 words for contracts. The significant word distance between related events (averaging 212 words) necessitates models capable of maintaining coherence across extended textual spans. This characteristic aligns with LegalBench's emphasis on understanding complex causal chains in legal reasoning, where statistical evidence must be evaluated within broader contextual frameworks [81].

Recent work by Mathur et al. demonstrates how emerging datasets enable more sophisticated analysis of legal texts. Their two-step training process combines Conditional Random Fields (CRF) and Flair algorithms, achieving 90% accuracy for legal reference extraction across different jurisdictional levels [74]. This success in handling jurisdictional variations suggests potential approaches for developing generalizable causal frameworks.

The integration of these diverse datasets creates new possibilities for Causal AI research in legal domains. Building upon the GCI framework discussed previously, researchers can now validate causal models across different legal systems and jurisdictions. The multi-task nature of many datasets, combining charge prediction, article recommendation, and prison term determination, provides natural experimental settings for studying causal relationships in legal reasoning. However, the successful extraction of causal relationships requires careful consideration of document-level context and the ability to maintain coherence across extended textual spans [74].

Particularly promising is the presence of datasets with explicit reasoning chains, such as those found in Court-View-Gen and AC-NLG collections [64]. These datasets enable researchers to study not just correlations between case facts and outcomes, but the causal mechanisms through which legal professionals arrive at their decisions. LegalBench extends this capability by providing annotated examples distinguishing between statistical and direct evidence in causal reasoning, offering a valuable resource for developing and evaluating automated approaches to legal causation analysis [81]. This development aligns with the approach on combining legal and non-legal data for accurate predictions [34], while highlighting the challenges of maintaining causal consistency across extended document spans.

## 4. General Discussion and Synthesis

### 4.1. Practical Implementation Guidelines

Causal AI research has increasingly focused on legal applications through structured models and counterfactual approaches. Actual Causation Theory [42] serves as a foundation for automated text analysis and legal reasoning systems, identifying direct causal links to clarify arguments in legal corpora.

Structural approaches including Bayesian Networks and Structural Causal Models [8] support graphical representation of legal cause-effect relationships, helping evaluate downstream impacts of regulations and judicial decisions. Similarly, Directed Acyclic Graphs and Structural Equations Models [43] clarify causal structures in specialized legal contexts.

For causal effect identification, Propensity Scoring and Inverse Probability Weighting [44,45] help control confounding variables in privacy protection and criminal justice analyses. Instrumental Variable Regression [37] proves valuable for estimating causal relationships from observational data with potential unobserved confounding, offering courts and policymakers rigorous methods for inferring legal causality.

Adversarial Deconfounding techniques and the Gradient Reversal Layer [50] concept address bias and spurious correlations in litigation strategy and legal decision support systems. For regulatory applications, Causal Bandits and Constrained Reinforcement Learning [51] improve resource allocation in civil litigation document review and benefits adjudication.

In judicial narrative generation, the AC-NLG model de-biases the court's view generation using a backdoor-inspired approach to mitigate confounding from imbalanced training data [49]. By modeling support probability as a potential confounder, it improves both rationale generation and judgment accuracy, demonstrating how counterfactual reasoning creates more interpretable legal texts.

Representation Learning approaches, including Causal Representation Learning [37] and BERT-Based Embeddings [52,53], accelerate legal document analysis by capturing nuanced textual features correlated with specific outcomes. These implementations demonstrate that Causal AI provides practical mechanisms for ensuring fairness, transparency, and efficiency across legal practice, while also revealing patterns and challenges that span multiple dimensions of the field.

### 4.2. Synthesis of Findings

Our systematic analysis of Causal AI in legal language processing reveals both significant promise and substantial challenges across multiple dimensions of legal practice. Our findings highlight the interplay between technological capabilities and legal requirements, manifested in three key areas: interpretative challenges, causal reasoning capabilities, and empirical foundations.

The interpretation of legal language through AI models presents interconnected challenges spanning technical, operational, and ethical dimensions, as illustrated in Figure 4. These challenges emerge from the inherent complexity of legal language, technical limitations of current AI approaches, strict legal requirements, operational constraints, and ethical considerations.

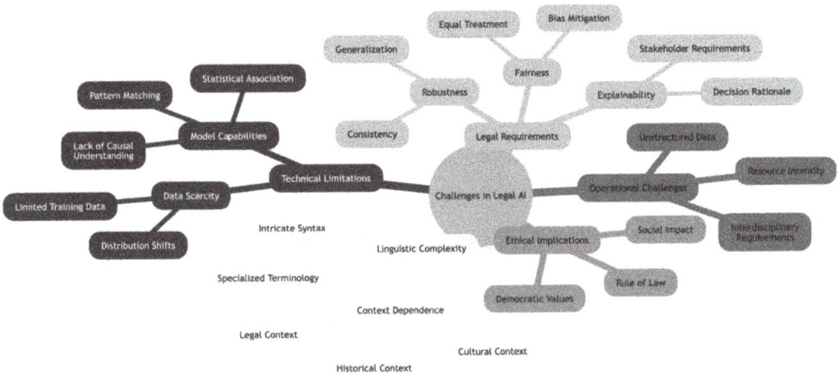


**Figure 4.** Hierarchical mapping of challenges in legal AI interpretation across five major categories: Linguistic Complexity, Technical Limitations, Legal Requirements, Operational Challenges, and Ethical Implications.

A fundamental tension exists between current correlation-based approaches and the causal reasoning requirements of legal analysis, as depicted in Figure 5. While correlation-based methods excel at pattern recognition, they fail to capture the nuanced causal reasoning essential to legal analysis [48].

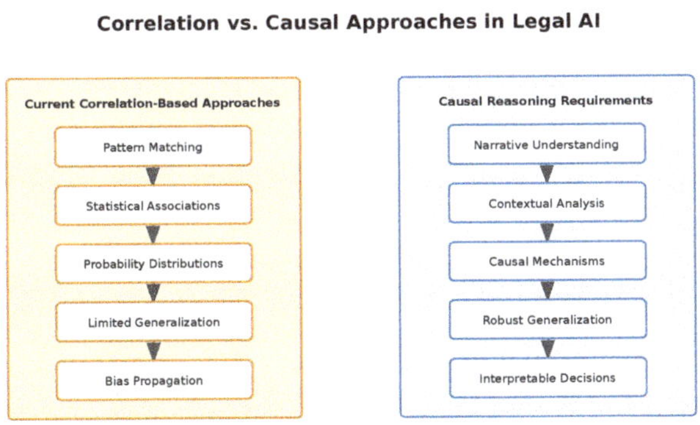


**Figure 5.** Comparative analysis of correlation-based versus causal reasoning approaches in legal AI, contrasting pattern matching and opaque decision-making with narrative understanding and interpretable decisions.

Our investigation reveals how causal modeling can address these limitations by formalizing traditional legal tests while preserving essential narrative and interpretative functions. Through mechanisms like Label Transfer and Gumbel sampling, these models can represent sophisticated legal concepts such as necessity, sufficiency, and remoteness that correlation-based methods cannot capture [47].

The empirical evidence supporting causal approaches demonstrates their superiority across multiple legal tasks. Through frameworks like Law-Match and probabilistic modeling [44], causal methods achieve significant improvements in predictive accuracy while maintaining interpretability. However, these advances face substantial challenges in empirical grounding. The emergence of datasets like LegalBench [81] creates new imperatives for developing architectural solutions that maintain causal coherence across substantial document lengths while preserving legal reasoning's narrative integrity.

### 4.3. Future Directions and Critical Perspective

Our systematic review reveals both significant promise and substantial challenges in applying Causal AI to legal language processing. While correlation-based approaches demonstrate utility in basic legal tasks, they fundamentally fail to capture the nuanced reasoning essential to legal analysis [61]. Causal frameworks offer a more sophisticated approach, potentially bridging the gap between statistical pattern matching and genuine legal reasoning [8].

Despite promising implementations across diverse areas—policy simulation using Bayesian Networks, automated judicial assistance through GCI, and legal decision support systems leveraging adversarial deconfounding—most represent specialized use cases rather than comprehensive systems deployed at scale [51]. Our analysis revealed two notable patterns: first, many advances in Causal AI techniques that could benefit legal applications originate from other domains; second, current implementations typically adapt general causal approaches to legal contexts rather than developing techniques specifically engineered for legal reasoning's unique challenges.

Several critical limitations demand attention. First, there is a notable scarcity of real-world case studies demonstrating successful implementations of causal approaches in legal practice. Second, the current literature inadequately addresses how causal models handle legal uncertainty and ambiguity, particularly in scenarios where causation itself is disputed [42]. Third, the computational requirements and scalability challenges of causal approaches remain poorly understood, raising questions about practical deployment in large-scale legal systems [56].

Our analysis of excluded documents revealed a troubling trend: many were excluded because they discussed AI in legal contexts only through transformer architectures, without reflecting on their limitations. This suggests the current fascination with large language models is overshadowing more foundational work on causal reasoning in legal AI, potentially delaying progress on developing robust causal understanding.

The core challenge facing Causal AI in legal domains aligns with Harriman's developmental pattern of human causal reasoning [13]. Current architectures typically attempt to implement high-level causal reasoning directly through statistical patterns, bypassing the foundational level of causal understanding that Harriman identified as crucial. This helps explain why correlation-based methods continue to dominate despite their known limitations—they sidestep rather than solve the fundamental problem of causal understanding.

Our review also highlights significant gaps in addressing "legal black swan events"—unprecedented cases that defy historical causal patterns [82]. Furthermore, the construction of reliable causal models faces challenges rarely acknowledged: legal datasets often lack clear ground truth for causal relationships, with interpretations varying across jurisdictions and time periods [44]. While the literature extensively critiques bias in correlation-based systems [60], insufficient attention has been paid to potential biases in causal approaches themselves [65].

Nevertheless, recent methodological advances offer promising directions. The emergence of hybrid architectures combining symbolic reasoning with neural representations, exemplified by frameworks like GCI [38] and Law-Match [37], demonstrates potential for systems that can both process legal text efficiently and reason about its implications. The development of sophisticated causal extraction techniques [68] and specialized legal datasets like LegalBench [81] and DocSEP [74] provide essential building blocks for advancement.

Future research directions should prioritize: (1) developing robust evaluation frameworks for assessing causal understanding in legal contexts [74]; (2) creating architectures capable of maintaining causal coherence across lengthy legal documents while remaining computationally feasible [36]; (3) advancing theoretical frameworks that better integrate statistical and direct-probative evidence while preserving law's narrative functions [61]; and (4) investigating the transferability of these approaches across different legal systems to enhance their generalizability in addressing empirical data scarcity.

A key research priority is bridging the methodological gap between statistical and direct-probative evidence in establishing causation, as highlighted by LegalBench's annotations. This requires developing models that can distinguish and appropriately weigh different forms of causal evidence while handling substantial document lengths characteristic of legal datasets.

For practitioners, these findings suggest a measured approach to implementing Causal AI. While the technology shows promise for enhancing legal analysis [44], it should be deployed strategically, beginning with well-defined tasks where causal reasoning requirements are clear and consequences of errors are manageable [67]. Success will require close collaboration between legal experts and AI researchers to ensure systems remain aligned with legal principles while leveraging technological advances [45].

The field stands at a crucial juncture where theoretical advances meet practical demands. Future progress depends on balancing technological innovation with preservation of law's fundamental role in society, while addressing identified limitations—namely, maintaining a realistic perspective on what Causal AI can achieve in legal contexts. Most importantly, it requires recognition that while Causal AI may enhance legal analysis, it cannot replace the fundamental human elements of legal reasoning—the moral judgment, cultural understanding, and narrative interpretation that give law its meaning and legitimacy.

## 5. Conclusions

Our systematic review revealed three concrete findings that directly address our research question about the current state, challenges, limitations, and potential impact of Causal AI in legal language processing:

First, regarding the current state, Causal AI implementations in legal contexts currently exist primarily as specialized solutions rather than comprehensive systems. The most successful current applications focus on narrow tasks: policy simulation using Bayesian Networks [8], which enable explicit modeling of conditional dependencies between legal variables and outcomes, legal case matching through Law-Match [37], which leverages instrumental variables to decompose case representations into law-related and case-specific components, and bias mitigation through adversarial deconfounding [50], which employs gradient reversal layers to identify and remove spurious correlations.

Second, concerning limitations and challenges, our analysis identified three critical constraints in current implementations: (1) the inability to maintain causal coherence across long legal documents, with performance degrading significantly beyond average distances of 212 words between related events [74]; (2) computational scalability issues when processing long documents, which represents the majority of legal texts [81]; and (3) inadequate handling of legal uncertainty, particularly in novel situations or when causation itself is disputed [42]. These limitations suggest that current Causal AI systems, while promising, remain insufficient for general legal reasoning tasks.

Third, regarding potential impact, our findings indicate that Causal AI offers three specific advantages over correlation-based methods: (1) superior performance in legal case matching, with Law-Match demonstrating improvement in accuracy over correlation-based baselines [37]; (2) enhanced interpretability through explicit modeling of legal reasoning steps, as demonstrated by the Graph-based Causal Inference framework [38]; and (3) better handling of bias and fairness concerns through techniques like conditional parity [43]. However, these benefits currently manifest only in narrow, well-defined tasks rather than general legal analysis.

These findings lead to three concrete recommendations for advancing the field: (1) prioritize the development of scalable architectures specifically designed for maintaining causal coherence in long legal documents; (2) focus research on handling legal uncertainty and novel situations through hybrid approaches combining causal inference with symbolic reasoning; and (3) establish standardized evaluation frameworks for assessing causal understanding in legal contexts, particularly focusing on document-level coherence and reasoning transparency.

**Author Contributions:** Conceptualization, P.P.T.; methodology, P.P.T.; software, P.P.T.; validation, P.P.T. and H.P.; formal analysis, P.P.T.; investigation, P.P.T.; resources, P.P.T.; data curation, P.P.T.; writing—original draft preparation, P.P.T.; writing—review and editing, P.P.T. and H.P.; visualization, P.P.T.; supervision, H.P.; project administration, P.P.T.; funding acquisition, P.P.T. All authors have read and agreed to the published version of the manuscript.

**Funding:** This research was funded by Universidad Panamericana.

**Data Availability Statement:** No new data were created or analyzed in this study. Data sharing is not applicable to this article.

**Acknowledgments:** During the preparation of this study, the authors utilized AI language models (*OpenAI's ChatGPT 4, 4o and o1-preview* and *Anthropic's Claude 3.5 Sonnet*) and APIs to enhance research efficiency and quality. These tools assisted with document processing (organizing files, formatting citations in BibTeX, extracting relevant information), analysis support (LLM-as-a-judge techniques, generating summaries), technical documentation (crafting Mermaid diagrams, designing LaTeX tables and equations), and editorial tasks (rephrasing, proofreading). Automatic analysis were used to enhance the quality of our work, merely as a help in prioritizing the reviews, but did not replace human judgment. We always checked the soundness of generated text and manually validated classifications. The integration of LLMs into our methodology was driven by their demonstrated capabilities in facilitating large-scale text analysis, clustering, and visualization tasks. Outputs were cross-verified by human reviewers to ensure accuracy, relevance, and consistency with the study's objectives. Outputs that did not meet validation criteria were either refined or excluded from the final analysis. This approach aligns with emerging trends in using AI-assisted tools to enhance the efficiency and scalability of systematic reviews in interdisciplinary fields.

**Conflicts of Interest:** The authors declare no conflicts of interest.

## References

1. Liddy, E.D. Natural Language Processing. In *Encyclopedia of Library and Information Science*, 2nd ed.; Marcel Decker, Inc.: New Yo NY, USA, 2001.
2. Hart, H.L.A.; Raz, J.; Bulloch, P. *The Concept of Law (Clarendon Law Series)*, 2nd ed.; Oxford University Press: Oxford, UK, 199
3. Sapra, R.L.; Saluja, S. Understanding statistical association and correlation. *Curr. Med. Res. Pract.* **2021**, *11*, 31–38. [CrossRef]

Feder, A.; Keith, K.A.; Manzoor, E.; Pryzant, R.; Sridhar, D.; Wood-Doughty, Z.; Eisenstein, J.; Grimmer, J.; Reichart, R.; Roberts, M.E.; et al. Causal inference in natural language processing: Estimation, prediction, interpretation and beyond. *Trans. Assoc. Comput. Linguist.* **2022**, *10*, 1138–1158. [CrossRef]

Rubin, D.B. Estimating causal effects of treatments in randomized and nonrandomized studies. *J. Educ. Psychol.* **1974**, *66*, 688. [CrossRef]

Sekhon, J. 271 The Neyman— Rubin Model of Causal Inference and Estimation Via Matching Methods. In *The Oxford Handbook of Political Methodology*; Oxford University Press: Oxford, UK, 2008. [CrossRef]

Pearl, J. *Models, Reasoning and Inference*; Cambridge University Press: Cambridge, UK, 2000; Volume 19, p. 3.

So, F. Modelling Causality in Law = Modélisation de la Causalité en Droit. Ph.D. Thesis, University of Montreal, Montreal, QC, Canada, 2020.

Ness, R. *Causal AI*; Manning Early Access Program (MEAP); Manning Publications: Boston, MA, USA, 2024.

Kaddour, J.; Lynch, A.; Liu, Q.; Kusner, M.J.; Silva, R. Causal machine learning: A survey and open problems. *arXiv* **2022**, arXiv:2206.15475.

Pearl, J. Causal diagrams for empirical research. *Biometrika* **1995**, *82*, 669–688. [CrossRef]

Powell, S. The Book of Why: The New Science of Cause and Effect. Pearl, Judea, and Dana Mackenzie. 2018. Hachette UK. *J. MultiDiscip. Eval.* **2018**, *14*, 47–54. [CrossRef]

Harriman, D. *The Logical Leap: Induction in Physics*; Penguin: New York, NY, USA, 2010.

Firth, J. *Papers in Linguistics 1934–1951*; Oxford University Press: London, UK, 1957.

Marcos, H. Can large language models apply the law? *AI Soc.* **2024**, 1–10. [CrossRef]

Marcus, G. The Next Decade in AI: Four Steps Towards Robust Artificial Intelligence. *arXiv* **2020**, arXiv:2002.06177.

Liu, X.; Yin, D.; Feng, Y.; Wu, Y.; Zhao, D. Everything has a cause: Leveraging causal inference in legal text analysis. *arXiv* **2021**, arXiv:2104.09420.

Larson, J.; Kirchner, L.; Mattu, S.; Angwin, J. *Machine Bias*; CRC Press: Boca Raton, FL, USA, 2022.

Simpson, E.H. The Interpretation of Interaction in Contingency Tables. *J. R. Stat. Soc. Ser. B* **1951**, *13*, 238–241. [CrossRef]

Ash, E.; Morelli, M.; Vannoni, M. *More Laws, More Growth? Evidence from US States*; Evidence from US States (April 25, 2022); BAFFI CAREFIN Centre Research Paper; The University of Chicago Press: Chicago, IL, USA, 2022.

Imbens, G.W.; Rubin, D.B. *Causal Inference in Statistics, Social, and Biomedical Sciences*; Cambridge University Press: Cambridge, UK, 2015.

Leins, K.; Lau, J.H.; Baldwin, T. Give me convenience and give her death: Who should decide what uses of NLP are appropriate, and on what basis? In Proceedings of the 58th Annual Meeting of the Association for Computational Linguistics, Online, 5–10 July 2020; pp. 2908–2913.

Bommarito, M.J., II; Katz, D.M.; Detterman, E.M. LexNLP: Natural language processing and information extraction for legal and regulatory texts. In *Research Handbook on Big Data Law*; Edward Elgar Publishing: Cheltenham, UK, 2021.

Sleimi, A.; Sannier, N.; Sabetzadeh, M.; Briand, L.; Dann, J. Automated extraction of semantic legal metadata using natural language processing. In Proceedings of the 2018 IEEE 26th International Requirements Engineering Conference (RE), Banff, AB, Canada, 20–24 August 2018; IEEE: New York, NY, USA, 2018; pp. 124–135.

Page, M.J.; McKenzie, J.E.; Bossuyt, P.M.; Boutron, I.; Hoffmann, T.C.; Mulrow, C.D.; Shamseer, L.; Tetzlaff, J.M.; Akl, E.A.; Brennan, S.E.; et al. The PRISMA 2020 statement: An updated guideline for reporting systematic reviews. *BMJ* **2021**, *372*, n71. [PubMed]

Peters, M.D.; Godfrey, C.M.; McInerney, P.; Soares, C.B.; Khalil, H.; Parker, D. *The Joanna Briggs Institute Reviewers' Manual 2015: Methodology for JBI Scoping Reviews*; The Joanna Briggs Institute: Adelaide, Australia, 2015.

Petticrew, M.; Roberts, H. *Systematic Reviews in the Social Sciences: A Practical Guide*; Blackwell Publishers: Malden, MA, USA, 2006.

Haddaway, N.R.; Page, M.J.; Pritchard, C.C.; McGuinness, L.A. PRISMA2020: An R package and Shiny app for producing PRISMA 2020-compliant flow diagrams, with interactivity for optimised digital transparency and Open Synthesis. *Campbell Syst. Rev.* **2022**, *18*, e1230. [CrossRef] [PubMed]

Critical Appraisal Skills Programme (CASP). *CASP Systematic Review Checklist*; Critical Appraisal Skills Programme: Oxford, UK, 2018.

Braun, V.; Clarke, V. Using thematic analysis in psychology. *Qual. Res. Psychol.* **2006**, *3*, 77–101.

Wu, L.; Wang, D.; Evans, J.A. Large teams develop and small teams disrupt science and technology. *Nature* **2019**, *566*, 378–382.

Williams, S. Predictive Contracting. *Columbia Bus. Law Rev.* **2019**, *2019*, 621. [CrossRef]

Kemper, C. Kafkaesque AI? Legal Decision-Making in the Era of Machine Learning. *Intellect. Prop. Technol. Law J.* **2019**, *24*, 251.

Gastwirth, J.L. The role of statistical evidence in civil cases. *Annu. Rev. Stat. Its Appl.* **2020**, *7*, 39–60.

35. Wood, J.; Matiasz, N.; Silva, A.; Hsu, W.; Abyzov, A.; Wang, W. OpBerg: Discovering causal sentences using optimal alignmen In Proceedings of the Big Data Analytics and Knowledge Discovery: 24th International Conference, DaWaK 2022, Vienna, Austr 22–24 August 2022; Proceedings; Springer International Publishing: Berlin/Heidelberg, Germany, 2022; pp. 17–30.
36. Rahali, A.; Akhloufi, M. End-to-end transformer-based models in textual-based NLP. *AI* **2023**, *4*, 54–110. [CrossRef]
37. Sun, Z.; Xu, J.; Zhang, X.; Dong, Z.; Wen, J.R. Law Article-Enhanced Legal Case Matching: A Model-Agnostic Causal Learnir Approach. *arXiv* **2022**, arXiv:2210.11012.
38. Zhao, Q.; Guo, R.; Feng, X.; Hu, W.; Zhao, S.; Wang, Z.; Cao, Y. Research on a Decision Prediction Method Based on Caus Inference and a Multi-Expert FTOPJUDGE Mechanism. *Mathematics* **2022**, *10*, 2281. [CrossRef]
39. Kenton, J.D.M.W.C.; Toutanova, L.K. Bert: Pre-training of deep bidirectional transformers for language understanding. I Proceedings of the naacL-HLT, Minneapolis, MN, USA, 2–7 June 2019; Volume 1.
40. Liu, Y. Roberta: A robustly optimized bert pretraining approach. *arXiv* **2019**, arXiv:1907.11692.
41. Xiao, C.; Hu, X.; Liu, Z.; Tu, C.; Sun, M. Lawformer: A pre-trained language model for chinese legal long documents. *AI Op* **2021**, *2*, 79–84. [CrossRef]
42. Dymitruk, M.; Markovich, R.; Liepiña, R.; El Ghosh, M.; van Doesburg, R.; Governatori, G.; Verheij, B. Research in progre Report on the ICAIL 2017 doctoral consortium. *Artif. Intell. Law* **2018**, *26*, 69–76. [CrossRef]
43. Ritov, Y.A.; Sun, Y.; Zhao, R. On conditional parity as a notion of non-discrimination in machine learning. *arXiv* **201** arXiv:1706.08519.
44. Keith, K.A. Social Measurement and Causal Inference with Text. Ph.D. Thesis, University of Massachusetts Amherst, Amher MA, USA, 2021.
45. Cheng, L. Algorithmic Solutions for Socially Responsible AI. Ph.D. Thesis, Arizona State University, Tempe, AZ, USA, 2022.
46. Xiao, C.; Liu, Z.; Lin, Y.; Sun, M. Legal knowledge representation learning. In *Representation Learning for Natural Langua Processing*; Springer Nature: Singapore, 2023; pp. 401–432.
47. Chen, W.; Tian, J.; Xiao, L.; He, H.; Jin, Y. Exploring logically dependent multi-task learning with causal inference. In Proceedin of the 2020 Conference on Empirical Methods in Natural Language Processing (EMNLP), Bangkok, Thailand, 16–20 Novemb 2020; pp. 2213–2225.
48. Zhang, Y.; Zhang, M.; Chen, H.; Chen, X.; Chen, X.; Gan, C.; Dong, X.L. The 1st International Workshop on Machine Reasonin International Machine Reasoning Conference (MRC 2021). In Proceedings of the 14th ACM International Conference on We Search and Data Mining, Hong Kong, China, 8–12 March 2021; pp. 1161–1162.
49. Wu, Y.; Kuang, K.; Zhang, Y.; Liu, X.; Sun, C.; Xiao, J.; Zhuang, Y.; Si, L.; Wu, F. De-biased court's view generation with causali In Proceedings of the 2020 Conference on Empirical Methods in Natural Language Processing (EMNLP), Bangkok, Thailan 16–20 November 2020; pp. 763–780.
50. Santosh, T.Y.S.; Xu, S.; Ichim, O.; Grabmair, M. Deconfounding Legal Judgment Prediction for European Court of Human Righ Cases Towards Better Alignment with Experts. *arXiv* **2022**, arXiv:2210.13836.
51. Henderson, P.; Chugg, B.; Anderson, B.; Ho, D.E. Beyond Ads: Sequential Decision-Making Algorithms in Law and Public Poli In Proceedings of the 2022 Symposium on Computer Science and Law, Berkeley, CA, USA, 3–4 November 2022; pp. 87–100.
52. Hassanzadeh, O.; Bhattacharjya, D.; Feblowitz, M.; Srinivas, K.; Perrone, M.; Sohrabi, S.; Katz, M. Causal knowledge extractic through large-scale text mining. In Proceedings of the AAAI Conference on Artificial Intelligence, New York, NY, USA, 7–1 February 2020; Volume 34, pp. 13610–13611.
53. Cohen, M.C.; Dahan, S.; Rule, C. Conflict Analytics: When Data Science Meets Dispute Resolution. *Manag. Bus. Rev.* **202** 2, 86–92. [CrossRef]
54. Mamakas, D.; Tsotsi, P.; Androutsopoulos, I.; Chalkidis, I. Processing Long Legal Documents with Pre-trained Transforme Modding LegalBERT and Longformer. *arXiv* **2022**, arXiv:2211.00974.
55. Cemri, M.; Çukur, T.; Koç, A. Unsupervised Simplification of Legal Texts. *arXiv* **2022**, arXiv:2209.00557.
56. Hassani, H.; Huang, X.; Ghodsi, M. Big data and causality. *Ann. Data Sci.* **2018**, *5*, 133–156. [CrossRef]
57. Barale, C. Human-centered computing in legal NLP-An application to refugee status determination. In Proceedings of the Secor Workshop on Bridging Human–Computer Interaction and Natural Language Processing, Dublin, Ireland, 11 July 2022; pp. 28–
58. Lam, J.; Chen, Y.; Zulkernine, F.; Dahan, S. Detection of Similar Legal Cases on Personal Injury. In Proceedings of the 20 International Conference on Data Mining Workshops (ICDMW), Virtual, 6–9 December 2021; IEEE: New York, NY, USA, 202 pp. 639–646.
59. Mik, E. Caveat Lector: Large Language Models in Legal Practice. *Rutgers Bus. Law Rev.* **2023**, *19*, 70.
60. Meneceur, Y.; Barbaro, C. Artificial intelligence and the judicial memory: The great misunderstanding. *Cah. Justice* **201** 2, 277–289.
61. Szilagyi, K. Artificial Intelligence & the Machine-Ation of the Rule of Law. Ph.D. Thesis, Université d'Ottawa/University Ottawa, Ottawa, ON, Canada, 2022.

Chalkidis, I.; Pasini, T.; Zhang, S.; Tomada, L.; Schwemer, S.F.; Søgaard, A. Fairlex: A multilingual benchmark for evaluating fairness in legal text processing. *arXiv* **2022**, arXiv:2203.07228.

Papaloukas, C.; Chalkidis, I.; Athinaios, K.; Pantazi, D.A.; Koubarakis, M. Multi-granular legal topic classification on greek legislation. *arXiv* **2021**, arXiv:2109.15298.

Cui, J.; Shen, X.; Nie, F.; Wang, Z.; Wang, J.; Chen, Y. A Survey on Legal Judgment Prediction: Datasets, Metrics, Models and Challenges. *arXiv* **2022**, arXiv:2204.04859.

Kirat, T.; Tambou, O.; Do, V.; Tsoukiàs, A. Fairness and Explainability in Automatic Decision-Making Systems. A challenge for computer science and law. *arXiv* **2022**, arXiv:2206.03226. [CrossRef]

Rubicondo, D.; Rosato, L. *AI Fairness Addressing Ethical and Reliability Concerns in AI Adoption*; Iason Consulting Ltd.: Milan, Italy, 2022.

Balashankar, A. Enhancing Robustness Through Domain Faithful Machine Learning. Ph.D. Thesis, New York University, New York, NY, USA, 2022.

Khetan, V.; Ramnani, R.; Anand, M.; Sengupta, S.; Fano, A.E. Causal bert: Language models for causality detection between events expressed in text. In *Intelligent Computing: Proceedings of the 2021 Computing Conference*; Springer International Publishing: Berlin/Heidelberg, Germany, 2022; Volume 1, pp. 965–980.

Yao, F.; Xiao, C.; Wang, X.; Liu, Z.; Hou, L.; Tu, C.; Li, J.; Liu, Y.; Shen, W.; Sun, M. LEVEN: A large-scale Chinese legal event detection dataset. *arXiv* **2022**, arXiv:2203.08556.

Pryzant, R. Natural Language Processing for Computing the Influence of Language on Perception and Behavior. Ph.D. Thesis, Stanford University, Stanford, CA, USA, 2021.

Ichim, O.; Grabmair, M. Zero Shot Transfer of Legal Judgement Prediction as Article-aware Entailment for the European Court of Human Rights. *arXiv* **2023**, arXiv:2302.00609.

Wang, S.; Liu, Z.; Zhong, W.; Zhou, M.; Wei, Z.; Chen, Z.; Duan, N. From lsat: The progress and challenges of complex reasoning. *IEEE/ACM Trans. Audio Speech Lang. Process.* **2022**, *30*, 2201–2216.

Kyriakakis, M.; Androutsopoulos, I.; Saudabayev, A. Transfer learning for causal sentence detection. *arXiv* **2019**, arXiv:1906.07544.

Mathur, P.; Morariu, V.I.; Garimella, A.; Dernoncourt, F.; Gu, J.; Sawhney, R.; Nakov, P.; Manocha, D.; Jain, R. DocScript: Document-level Script Event Prediction. In Proceedings of the 2024 Joint International Conference on Computational Linguistics, Language Resources and Evaluation (LREC-COLING 2024), Turin, Italy, 20–25 May 2024; pp. 5140–5155.

Teney, D.; Abbasnedjad, E.; van den Hengel, A. Learning what makes a difference from counterfactual examples and gradient supervision. In Proceedings of the Computer Vision–ECCV 2020: 16th European Conference, Glasgow, UK, 23–28 August 2020; Proceedings, Part X 16; Springer International Publishing: Berlin/Heidelberg, Germany, 2020; pp. 580–599.

Hundogan, O. CREATED: The Generation of viable Counterfactual Sequences using an Evolutionary Algorithm for Event Data of Complex Processes. Master's Thesis, Utrecht University, Utrecht, The Netherlands, 2022.

Arsenyan, V.; Shahnazaryan, D. Large Language Models for Biomedical Causal Graph Construction. *arXiv* **2023**, arXiv:2301.12473.

Singer, G.; Bach, J.; Grinberg, T.; Hakim, N.; Howard, P.R.; Lal, V.; Rivlin, Z. Thrill-K Architecture: Towards a Solution to the Problem of Knowledge Based Understanding. In Proceedings of the Artificial General Intelligence: 15th International Conference, AGI 2022, Seattle, WA, USA, 19–22 August 2022; Proceedings; Springer International Publishing: Berlin/Heidelberg, Germany, 2023; pp. 404–412.

Mathis, B. Extracting proceedings information and legal references from court decisions with machine-learning. *SSRN Electron. J.* **2021**. [CrossRef]

Niklaus, J.; Matoshi, V.; Rani, P.; Galassi, A.; Stürmer, M.; Chalkidis, I. Lextreme: A multi-lingual and multi-task benchmark for the legal domain. *arXiv* **2023**, arXiv:2301.13126.

Guha, N.; Nyarko, J.; Ho, D.; Ré, C.; Chilton, A.; Chohlas-Wood, A.; Peters, A.; Waldon, B.; Rockmore, D.; Zambrano, D.; et al. Legalbench: A collaboratively built benchmark for measuring legal reasoning in large language models. *Adv. Neural Inf. Process. Syst.* **2024**, *36*, 44123–44279. [CrossRef]

Nicholas, N. The black swan: The impact of the highly improbable. *J. Manag. Train. Inst.* **2008**, *36*, 56.

MDPI AG
Grosspeteranlage 5
4052 Basel
Switzerland
Tel.: +41 61 683 77 34

*Entropy* Editorial Office
E-mail: entropy@mdpi.com
www.mdpi.com/journal/entropy

www.ingramcontent.com/pod-product-compliance
Lightning Source LLC
Chambersburg PA
CBHW061826210926
51850CB00006B/823
* 9 7 8 3 7 2 5 8 7 9 2 9 8 *